D0934060

OUTDOOR RECREATION

OUTDOOR RECREATION

Hilmi Ibrahim
Whittier College

Kathleen A. Cordes
Miramar College

Madison, Wisconsin • Dubuque, Iowa • Indianapolis, Indiana
Melbourne, Australia • Oxford, England

Book Team

Editor *Chris Rogers*
Developmental Editor *Scott Spoolman*
Production Editor *Scott Sullivan*
Publishing Services Coordinator–Design *Barbara J. Hodgson*
Visuals/Design Developmental Consultant *Marilyn A. Phelps*
Marketing Manager *Pamela S. Cooper*
Advertising Manager *Jodi Rymer*

WCB Brown & Benchmark
A Division of Wm. C. Brown Communications, Inc.

Vice President and General Manager *Thomas E. Doran*
Editor in Chief *Edgar J. Laube*
Executive Editor *Ed Bartell*
Executive Editor *Stan Stoga*
National Sales Manager *Eric Ziegler*
Director of CourseResource *Kathy Law Laube*
Director of CourseSystems *Chris Rogers*
Director of Marketing *Sue Simon*
Director of Production *Vickie Putman Caughron*
Imaging Group Manager *Chuck Carpenter*
Manager of Visuals and Design *Faye M. Schilling*
Design Manager *Jac Tilton*
Art Manager *Janice Roerig*
Permissions/Records Manager *Connie Allendorf*

Wm. C. Brown Communications, Inc.

Chairman Emeritus *Wm. C. Brown*
Chairman and Chief Executive Officer *Mark C. Falb*
President and Chief Operating Officer *G. Franklin Lewis*
Corporate Vice President, President of WCB Manufacturing *Roger Meyer*

Cover photo by Marc Romanelli/The Image Bank

Copyedited by Nikki Herbst

Consulting Editor A. Lockhart

Interior and cover design by Fulton Design

Chapter opener illustrations by Patti Green

The credits section for this book begins on page 407
and is considered an extension of the copyright page.

Library of Congress Catalog Card Number: 92–081355

ISBN 0-697-13152-1

Printed in the United States of America by Wm. C. Brown Communications, Inc.,
2460 Kerper Boulevard, Dubuque, IA 52001

10 9 8 7 6 5 4 3 2

Dedicated to
My Wife Cynthia Ibrahim
and
To My Parents Ed and Rita Cordes

Contents

Introduction

This book is written with a number of objectives in mind. Most important, it tries to avoid duplicating what other books on outdoor recreation do. It not only addresses those whose interest lies in the management of outdoor resources, but it addresses the aficionado as well. This book attempts to look at outdoor pursuits first as a subphenomenon of the larger recreation and leisure phenomenon, but with an added touch, that of the natural element, with its psychological influence and social significance. These two points will be elaborated on in Part One.

Part One begins with two views of nature. The first is based on the experiences and values of the original inhabitants of the New World. The second is derived from the values of members of Western civilization who were transplanted into the New World after its discovery and colonization. These two views are not necessarily incompatible. For despite the exploitation of nature that began with the early European settlers, there were, and still are, those whose love of nature is evident in their writings, advocacy, and leadership. The early transcendentalists, naturalists, and practitioners were ahead of their time. Today the science of psychology shows us why nature is so appealing and soothing to human beings. Since we need nature for our well-being, effective management of our natural resources is a must. Psychology aside, effective managers should be equipped not only with managerial skills but also with a thorough understanding of the socioeconomic factors that have a direct bearing on outdoor recreational pursuits.

Part Two provides the reader with a description of the resources available to the outdoor adventurer. There are four categories of resources: federal, state, local, and private. While these categories prevail in the United States, Canada has a very similar arrangement. Other countries are included in this volume to give an idea of how pervasive the quest for outdoor adventures is globally. Also this information will acquaint the reader with the problems facing the managers and the users of recreation resources abroad.

Part Three is devoted to examining the management of outdoor resources as well as outdoor education. Both future managers and recreation participants would definitely benefit from knowing the policies, procedures, and even the problems of management of outdoor recreation.

Chapter 14 is devoted to outdoor education, which represents the attempt to mitigate these problems through formal and informal educational settings. The reader will be introduced to some of the activities available in nature, and since environmental problems are in the fore, a chapter is devoted to examining them.

An epilogue is provided that expresses our hopes for a bright and prosperous future for outdoor recreation. Finally, the appendices include pertinent information such as a listing of federal and state agencies dealing with outdoor recreation as well as professional and voluntary associations concerned with outdoor pursuits.

ACKNOWLEDGMENTS

We are grateful to Jane Lammers for her assistance, encouragement, and patience. Besides her diligent work on the manuscript, she contributed the majority of the photographs used in this volume. Thank you, Jane.

In the course of the preparation of the manuscript many friends, colleagues, and others have helped us. We wish to express gratitude to the following: Heather Nabours, John Strey, Jim Palmer, Dave Sanderlin, Rick Matthews, Mary Ellen Vick, Ray Young, Barbara Himes, and the many organizations that provided us with data and material.

Our many thanks to Scott Spoolman, Project Editor, for his encouragement and guidance throughout the process, and to Nikki Herbst, copy editor, for her patience and diligence in editing the manuscript. Finally, we are grateful to Chris Rogers, Senior Acquisition Editor, Brown-Benchmark Publishing Company, for his faith and trust in this project.

We also would like to acknowledge and thank our reviewers, whose comments helped improve the manuscript. They are:

Professor Brenda K. Blessing, *Missouri Western State University*
Dr. Craig Kelsey, *University of New Mexico*
Professor Phyllis Ford, *Greenbough Programs*
Professor Wayne Allison, *Lock Haven University*
Professor O. J. Helvey, *Cumberland College*
Professor Jack B. Frost, *California Polytechnic University-Pomona*

H. I.
K. C.
July 8, 1992

OUTDOOR RECREATION

PART

one

The Fundamentals of Outdoor Recreation

The first part of this book is devoted to examining the foundations of outdoor recreation, which include the historical, spiritual, social, psychological, and economic factors that led to its rise in the Western world, particularly in the United States and Canada. Chapter 1 gives an overview of these foundations. Chapter 2 focuses on the spiritual attitudes of Americans toward the outdoors, one aspect of which is the Native American relationship to nature. How outdoor recreation emerged is the result of the change in values and the teaching and leadership of a few people. Some of these teachers and leaders are presented in Chapter 3. Chapter 4 discusses the psychology of the natural environment, and Chapter 5 concentrates on the social aspects of outdoor experiences. The economics of outdoor recreation are discussed in Chapter 6.

1 Foundations of Outdoor Recreation

In this book we use the term *outdoor recreation* to encompass the organized free-time activities that are participated in for their own sake and where there is an interaction between the participant and an element of nature. Surfing is an outdoor recreational activity where there is interaction between the participant and water, an element of nature. Football is not an outdoor recreational activity under our definition, for although it is an organized recreational activity, nature plays a minimal role in it. Nature plays a more important role in mountain climbing or cross-country skiing than it does in football.

Although predicated on play and part of the growing sphere of leisure activities, recreation differs from both play and leisure in that it is basically organized and takes place, mainly, in groups. At the core of recreation is play, and at the core of outdoor recreation is involvement with the natural environment. On the other hand, leisure is defined as the state of mind which allows an individual to participate in certain activities, and availability of leisure time is an important contributor to both recreation and outdoor recreation.

Recent studies have shown that ritual among humans played, and still plays, an important role, not only in establishing social order but also as a vehicle of creativity and expression. Ritual seems to have added to the importance and significance of both leisure and recreation. Elaboration on play, ritual, and outdoor recreation follows.

HUMANS, PLAY, AND RITUAL

Hardly anyone disagrees that humans tend to play. Some may argue that play is witnessed among the young of the human race only, but empirical evidence negates such a claim: some adult activities that may not be considered as play by everyone are in fact play activity, albeit somewhat sophisticated play. Such sophistication results from both the maturation of the individual and the complexity of modern societies. Studies show that the activities of the adults in some primal societies were very similar to children's play (Wood 1871, Roth 1902, Blanchard and Cheska 1985).

Outdoor recreation, the activities that are the main focus of this volume, is practiced by most members of complex modern urbanized and industrial societies. Most Americans and Canadians camp, ski, or go on organized picnics. In previous societies, only the well-to-do could afford to do so. They were the ones whose value system not only allowed but also encouraged enjoyment of picnics and going camping and skiing. While the reasons for the shift that allowed everyone to recreate are societal, be they economic or political, the reason for participation, by wealthy or commoner alike, is based on the tendency to play and, to a great extent, to ritualize.

Play

Some researchers claim that the tendency to play may have a deeper niche in human behavior than was once believed. Humans share this propensity with the upper mammals (deVore 1965 and Lancaster 1975), and there may be a genetic imprint, or a chemical code, that propels us in this direction (Eisen 1988). In order to understand this tendency, an explanation of the structure of the human brain and its evolution is a must.

The simple elementary brain, which is labeled the reptilian brain, is surrounded by a more complicated brain known as the limbic system or the old mammalian brain. While the elementary brain handles basic functions of self preservation and preservation of the species through hunting, homing, mating, fighting, and territoriality, the old mammalian brain is identified with mothering, audiovocal communication, and *play.* Experiments have shown that when the limbic system was severed in some small animals, they reverted to reptilian behavior which is void of play (Ibrahim 1991:1).

The third brain, called the new mammalian brain or the neocortex, surrounds the old mammalian brain and is divided into two hemispheres, each responsible for the opposite side of the body. According to Ornestein and Thompson (1984:34), hemispheric specialization took place at the time when humans were becoming bipedal and using their front limbs in tool making. With the enlarged brain, more complicated processes took place, including the construction and storage of symbols. Mental processes utilizing the two hemispheres can be roughly divided into two groups: processes that help in maintaining order in everyday activities such as language, and others that pertain to insight, imagination, and artistic expression. Sagan (1977) asserts that while the left hemisphere is responsible for the first group, the right hemisphere is responsible for the second.

In the early 1940s brain research led to the assumption that a drive for arousal in both humans and animals helps to avoid boredom (Berlyne 1960). Others today are advocating that a "hormonal code" or "genetic programming" initiates, propels, and, to a lesser degree, regulates play (Eisen 1988). The evidence comes from observation of animals and humans. In the case of animals, it is evident that the higher the animal on the evolutionary scale, the greater the time devoted to play, at least among the young.

Although play varies from species to species among primates, Lancaster indicated that field observers were impressed with the amount of time and energy spent in play by their juveniles (1975:49). For instance, young chimpanzees spend over 50 percent of their waking hours in play. Play behavior is the first seen in the early mornings and the last seen before young baboons retire. The same is observed among young howlers and bonnet macaques (de Vore 1965).

Evidence of a biological base for the tendency to play among young humans comes from the sequence of children's play forms regardless of their social or cultural background. The sequence of manipulative, repetitive, relational, make-believe, and rule-governed play is remarkably stable across diverse populations, which points toward a possible universal blueprint for play (Wolf 1984).

But play is not the only element in the rise of organized recreational activities among the members of a given society. Rituals play an important role as well. The first scholar to bring to our attention the link between play and ritual is Johan Huizinga. He believed that play is the basis of culture and that ritual assisted in the process of bringing about civilized life.

> Now in myth and ritual the great instinctive forces of civilized life have their origin: Law and order, commerce and profit, craft and art, poetry, wisdom, and science. All are rooted in the primeval soil of play (1950:5).

At the time of Huizinga's writing the concept of instinctive play was not quite palatable to many scholars of play. The idea that ritual might also be instinctive was equally unacceptable. In the last few decades, however, research on the brain has lent some credence to Huizinga's advocation that there seems to be some biological basis for both play and ritual.

Ritual

Scholars are just now beginning to understand the role of ritual in human life. Ritual refers to a set or series of acts, with a sequence established by tradition and stemming from the life of a people. Thanksgiving dinner in America, for example, is a tradition with an original purpose which some may have forgotten, yet it is celebrated year after year (with a new element added, a football game to be watched on television). And although the original meaning of the activity may be forgotten, humans ritualistically repeat the activity with great passion. Some scholars believe that it is the repetitiveness that matters and not the activity itself, on the assumption that ritualization has a biological basis in humans and animals.

Ritualization refers to the stylized, repeated gestures and posturing of humans or animals. Ritualization is based on rhythmicity and formation, two biological principles that are essential for survival. Rhythmicity is observed in the alteration of systole and diastole (higher reading and lower reading of blood pressure, respectively) and in the cycle of wakefulness and sleep. Formalization is the tendency to stabilize inner compulsions as well as output by putting things in order—a tendency that paves the way for the act we call ritualization. Rhythmic, formalized, and ritualistic activity give life stability not only for the young, but for the adult as well.

Simple ritualization evolved into complex rituals which, in turn, expanded to five modes as proposed by Grimmes (1982). While decorum, magic, and liturgy are not usually connected with outdoor activities, ceremony and celebration can be. A *ceremony* is a ritual which requires that one surrender to the demands of authority. Examples of nature ceremonies in many societies will be provided in Chapter 2. *Celebration* is the ritual most related to play. Here one participates for the sake of participation and not for an external end. Celebration has permeated human life since early times, including the celebration of nature, as will be seen in the examples given in Chapter 2.

Deegan (1989:5) states that participatory ritual is deeply rooted in social interaction in America. Participatory rituals exhibit three common characteristics. They are social activities

1. requiring participation and face-to-face contact.
2. with a matrix of roles, statuses, and culture.
3. organized by a set of rules for ritual action.

For our purposes, we want to know, for instance, what propels a person to go fishing or hunting year after year during the long weekend designed to celebrate the birth of a president? Is it the tendency to play? Or is it the tendency to ritualize? If the tendencies to play and to ritualize are biologically based, why is it that not all Americans of the same age and sex go fishing on that occasion? Another person may spend the long weekend alone watching nature programs on television, and a third may spend it hiking in the woods. A presentation of two more concepts that affect our outdoor experience is important at this point: leisure and recreation.

LEISURE OR RECREATION

When it comes to adult behavior during free time, analyzing the situation becomes rather complicated. For instance, when camping, is the individual playing, recreating, or at leisure? One does not hear or see terms such as outdoor leisure, or therapeutic play, yet the American lifestyle is full of outdoor recreation, community recreation, and therapeutic recreation. What is the difference? Conceptual differentiation among the definitions for play, recreation, and leisure is necessary at this point. In this work, play refers to activities of the young partaken by choice. On the other hand, recreation refers to organized activity in which an adult participates during free time. The emphasis in leisure is on the state of mind that allows the adult to participate in an activity of his or her choice during the time freed from work or civil or familial obligations.

The state of mind, by itself and in itself, is not easily discernible to the casual observer, but the engagement in a recreational activity is. Recreation gained greater attention at the beginning of this century in the United States because it revolves around the most easily observed feature of the leisure phenomenon, the activity. The other two elements, the state of mind and freed time, were not essential in recreational programs. The activity became central to the thinking of social reformers such as Jane Addams, who advocated that the lack of these activities led to social ills such as delinquency and truancy.

The philosopher Aristotle, who paid serious attention to the leisure phenomenon *qua* a phenomenon and not as a method to combat social ills, may help us understand the nature of leisure. Aristotle believed that leisure encompasses three subsets of activities: contemplative, recreative, and amusive activities. Leisure can be equated with a pyramid, the bottom third of which encompasses amusive activities, on top of which are recreative activities, which is topped by contemplative activities (see Figure 1.1).

THE EMERGENCE OF OUTDOOR RECREATION

Contemplation is only one form of leisure which Americans came to enjoy, the other forms being recreation and amusement. Although free time was being gained by the new settlers of North America, that free time did not transform into leisure easily. Leisure, as a state of being, was fought vigorously by the strict Calvinists of colonial America. Puritan requirements led the colonists to live without the "mispence of time," adhering strictly to the observance of the Sabbath. They tolerated no pagan festivities, no licentious plays and spectacles, no violations of the Sabbath.

Whatever open space there was then in the early settlement of North America was used as Commons, pasture land, or training grounds in hunting. The term Commons describes a piece of land to be shared and enjoyed by all members of the community. By the mid 1700s, the open space was used for recreational pursuits and other amusements. The Dutch settlers in New York, who were less restrained in their religious beliefs, organized a few recreational activities

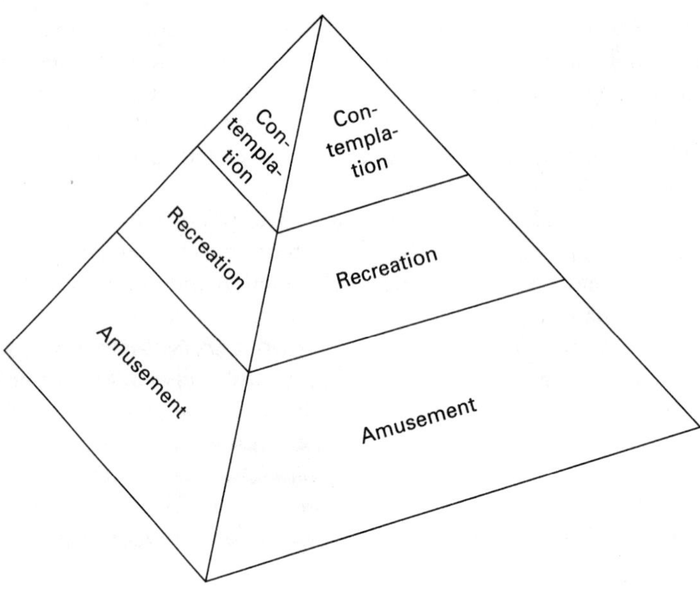

FIGURE 1.1 Hierarchy of leisure

after the Sunday service over the objection of church leaders. Also wealthy Southerners began to socialize and to recreate on the Lord's Day. By the end of the 1600s the colonist's life-style included many recreational activities, among which were pursuits in natural settings such as hunting, fishing, skating, sleighing, and tobogganing. By the mid 1700s, resorts became fashionable among the wealthy.

Despite the proposal to the Continental Congress of 1774 to prohibit extravagance and dissipation such as horse racing, gaming, and cockfighting, outdoor recreation increased steadily after the Revolutionary War, particularly on the frontiers. With America's westward expansion, the frontier people found in hunting, horse racing, rail tossing, and tomahawk hurling the needed release from a life of hard work and isolation. These were also occasions for get-togethers where ritualistic activities such as husking and quilting bees took place.

In the meantime American cities were growing, and the need for open space was being felt. Chicago preserved a site for outdoor recreation near Fort Dearborn in 1839, but it was New York that built the first city park in 1853. Central Park was designed by Frederick Law Olmsted and Calvert Vaux. Olmsted later planned San Francisco's Golden Gate Park, Philadelphia's Fairmount Park, Boston's Franklin Park, and the District of Columbia's Rock Creek Park. More on the father of America's city parks later.

The second half of the nineteenth century witnessed a surge in organized sport such as baseball, basketball, and football, and in outdoor recreational pursuits such as hunting and fishing. Depletion of wildlife became a concern, and in 1887 two prominent sportsmen, Theodore Roosevelt and George Bird Grinnell, editor of *Forest and Stream Magazine,* formed the Boone and Crockett Club to deal with conservation issues on the national level.

Conquering the wilderness during the western expansion meant the destruction of many of America's forests, to which Franklin B. Hough, head of the 1870 Census, sounded the alarm. In 1876 the U.S. Congress authorized him to study the issue, and his reports led to the creation of the Division of Forestry in the U.S. Department of Agriculture in 1881—the forerunner of today's U.S. Forest Service, U.S. Department of Agriculture.

Meanwhile many of the states on the eastern seaboard began to establish game preserves. Deer parks were established to preserve this popular game animal. The concept of preservation reached its pinnacle in 1872 with the establishment of America's first national park.

Although there were two earlier precedents for national preserves, at Hot Springs, Arkansas, in 1832 and Yosemite Valley, California, in 1864, the concept of a national park was born with Yellowstone in 1872. The significance of this event was in the change in public policy from allowing private exploitation of America's natural resources to the setting aside of public land for protection and public enjoyment. In 1890, a bill was passed in the U.S. Congress creating Yosemite National Park. Two years later naturalist John Muir formed the Sierra Club to explore, preserve, and enjoy the mountains of the West Coast of the United States.

The concept of preservation spilled over into America's forests when President Harrison created a 13-million-acre forest preserve in 1891 to which President Cleveland added 20 million acres in 1897. Gifford Pinchot enhanced our knowledge of forests as the first American to study forest management in Europe. In 1896, the Division of Biological Survey was created in the U.S. Department of Agriculture to administer wildlife refuges. It became the forerunner of the U.S. Fish and Wildlife Service, Department of the Interior, when it was combined with the Bureau of Fisheries, U.S. Department of Commerce, in 1940.

President Theodore Roosevelt appointed a National Conservation Commission in 1908 which put together an inventory of America's natural resources. He also took executive actions to preserve vast federal lands as forest preserves, wildlife refuges, and national monuments. Eight years later, in 1916, the National Park Service was established, and in 1924 the first Wilderness Area was designated in the Gila National Forest. The same year witnessed the first National Conference on Outdoor Recreation. Three years earlier, opening of the Appalachian Trail ushered in a new concept in outdoor recreation. Illinois became the first state to establish a state park system in 1909, followed by Indiana in 1919. The first national conference on state parks took place in 1921, and five years later the Federal Recreation Act made some public domain lands available to states for parks.

During the Depression years, and despite the economic conditions, Americans saw the opening of their first scenic parkway, the Blue Ridge Parkway. The Tennessee Valley Authority was created to provide the needed energy to vitalize the region and to control floods, but it also created many opportunities for outdoor recreational pursuits.

In the 1940s, the Bureau of Land Management was formed to control most federal real estate. The Flood Control Act of 1944 charged the U.S. Army Corps of Engineers with providing recreation on many of the reservoirs it built. A 1948 amendment to the 1944 Surplus Property Act provided for the transfer of surplus federal lands at 50 percent of fair market value for use as state and local parks and recreational areas.

The Outdoor Recreation Resources Review Commission and the resultant Bureau of Outdoor Recreation were created in the 1950s. In 1962, the National Park Service began a ten-year mission renovation program. The U.S. Forest Service began Operation Outdoors for the purpose of revitalizing its offerings.

The 1960s witnessed the passage of many federal acts, the impact of which is felt today on outdoor recreation. Among these is the Multiple Use-Sustained Yield Act, which formalized multiple use in national forests and added outdoor recreation to the statutory list of activities provided on these lands. Other federal legislation passed in the 1960s included the Land and Water Conservation Act, the National

Wilderness Preservation System Act, and the Federal Water Project Recreation Act, all of which provided significant funds for federal grants to be matched by equal state and local funds for outdoor recreation areas. The National Trails System Act and the National Wild and Scenic Rivers Act embodied new and significant concepts for outdoor recreation in America.

Significant acts for outdoor recreation were passed in the 1970s, too. The Volunteers in the Park Act authorized the National Park Service to utilize volunteers in its system. Also of significance was the Youth Conservation Corps Act, which employed youth in both the National Park Service and the U.S. Forest Service. A new approach was tested at that time, which was the addition of urban recreation areas to the National Park Service, for example, the Gateway National Recreation Area in New York City and the Golden Gate National Recreation Area in San Francisco. Revenue-sharing programs of the 1970s helped in the establishment of many state and local parks.

According to Clawson (1985:79), a major development at that time was the great expansion of privately owned, privately financed, and privately operated outdoor facilities. These include ski areas, water sport areas, amusement parks, campgrounds, and resorts in outdoor settings. Another important development was the application of new technologies to outdoor settings, the results of which were the modern activities of scuba diving, snowmobiling, and recreational vehicle camping.

By the 1900s outdoor recreation was gaining ground in America. Thanks to the insight of a few persons and to the foresight of America's legislators, today's Americans are enjoying a life-style that includes many opportunities for active and contemplative recreation in outdoor settings.

A parallel movement for the provision of outdoor recreation areas was taking place in Canada (see Chapter 11). Canada and the United States and, to some extent, Australia led the world in this movement. It took the rest of the world almost another one hundred years to try to catch up with these three societies. Leisure and recreation (including outdoor pursuits) are becoming an important part in the life-styles of many of today's world citizens. The following factors have led to this development:

Leisure and Recreation: A Human Right

In 1948 the General Assembly of the United Nations adopted the Universal Declaration of Human Rights. The member nations at that time agreed to the following principle:

> Every citizen has the right to rest and leisure, including reasonable limitation of working hours, and periodic holidays with pay . . . and . . . the right to freely participate in the cultural life of the community, to enjoy the arts. . . .
>
> (U.N. 1978)

This statement by the U.N. represents the culmination of many human endeavors to achieve such a right. It may have begun with the Sixth Right which evolved among the Ancient Israelites. The first five rights were the Right to Live, the Right of Possession, the Right to Work, the Right to Clothing, and the Right to Shelter. The Sixth Right included a provision for a Sabbath. Although the Sabbath was originally for rest and worship, it provided the opportunity for recreation activities which took place at later dates among the Israelites (Ibrahim and Shivers 1979:55).

The ancient Greeks were also interested in the idea of leisure. The free men among them took it seriously and sent their offspring to *schole,* the institution where the young would learn the arts of graceful living, music, philosophy, art, and gymnastics. As mentioned earlier, it was their philosopher Aristotle who underscored leisure as an important ingredient of the good life.

Ibn Khaldun, the Arab philosopher of the fourteenth century, went as far as claiming the desire for leisure as the fifth layer of a five-layer schema of human desires, the first of which is bodily appetites, followed by the desire for safety and calm, the desire for companionship, and the desire for superiority (Ibrahim 1988). The fifth and last of these desires would be satisfied with the United Nations resolution quoted previously. Many nations are working to provide the same right. But the resolution alone did not contribute to the rise of leisure pursuits in today's world.

Increased Free Time

Although time freed from civic and familial obligations began with the rise of the leisure class, as suggested by Veblen (1953), leisure in its "pure" form, as a state of being, did not materialize until very recently. The Sabbath was observed as a day of rest from labor among the Israelites and early Christians, albeit as a day devoted to worship. Labor time was measured by the day which started at sunrise and ended at sundown, leaving little or no free time to speak of. Conditions became worse with the coming of the Industrial Revolution, which initially emphasized production over human happiness.

The movement to reduce work hours among labor began in the United States when, in the early 1800s, Boston machinist Ira Stewart formed the Grand Eight-Hour League of Massachusetts (Viau 1939:25). Much later, the World Labor Organization passed a bill for 40-hour workweeks and a 12-day annual vacation in 1966. Both France and Great Britain had adopted a 40-hour workweek in 1919, which became the standard for many of the industrialized nations.

The standard for paid annual vacation adopted in most of the industrialized nations was two weeks initially, and it has reached four weeks in some of these nations today (Samuel 1986). Adding to free time is the sometimes compulsory retirement from work. Paid retirees are now a fact of life in most countries, not only among those who served in industry but also in services and trade. Productivity in industry, services, and trade continues at a very high level, thanks to the increased use of machines in the twentieth century, which has made even greater free time available to people.

Industrialization and Automation

Initially the Industrial Revolution created unpleasant conditions for those who became pegs in its machinery. Emigration to industrial centers led to crowded conditions in the cities of western Europe and North America. These slum dwellers included many children who worked long hours. Even when the conditions improved, industrialization revolved around tedious repetitive small tasks for the individual worker, and the need for outlets became very apparent. A need for outlets that "would exercise the workers' creative energy and provide a sense of achievement and accomplishment became pressing for people . . ." (MacLean et al. 1985:44). Recreation, including outdoor pursuits, provided the required outlets. Many social reformers worked on providing facilities and programs of recreation. The Playground Association of America was organized in 1906. It was renamed the Playground and Recreation Association of America in 1911, became the National Recreation Association in 1930, and merged with other associations in 1965 to become the National Recreation and Park Association. The association published *Playground Magazine,* now *Parks and Recreation.* The need for such an organization grew as the world's population shifted from the countryside to large cities.

Urbanization

In the mid 1800s there were eighty-five cities in the United States. Most people lived in the country. By 1910 the number of American cities with populations over 100,000 increased to fifty. In Canada there were twenty communities with populations over 5,000 by the mid 1800s; by the turn of the century there were sixty-two. The trend is not limited to North America or western Europe. Today there are eighty-three cities in the world with populations over one million. Only eighteen are in Europe, and nine are in North America. There are thirty-nine in Asia, seven in what used to be the Soviet Union, seven in South America, and three in Africa.

Urban life itself may have increased the need for recreational outlets, including outdoor ones. More important is the role that urbanization plays in modernizing, meaning not only economic growth but cultural and social changes as well. Services such as education, both formal and informal, are easier to provide in urban centers. Improved literacy rates lead to more sophisticated demands, one of which is the demand for recreation outlets. As will be shown in Chapter 5, The Social Aspects of Outdoor Experiences, the higher the education acquired, the more the demand for recreation and for outdoor pursuits in particular. But since most outdoor facilities are located away from urban centers, those who are interested in partaking of an outdoor pursuit must find not only the time but also the means to get there. Mechanized transportation is a fact in modern life.

Transportation

The steam engine was mounted on two vehicles which had tremendous impact on recreation in North America and abroad: the train and the steamboat. Among the first transportation systems that encouraged outdoor recreation on a large scale is the railroad. The Train Excursion, which was organized on Easter Day of 1844, provides a good example of the role of mass transportation in outdoor pursuits. The Excursion, from London to the seaside resort of Brighton, created popular excitement (Lowerson and Myerscough 1977:32). In the United States the steamboat carried people and horses to racing centers along the Mississippi River in the antebellum era. The railroad helped transport people to the growing athletic events, both on the intercollegiate and professional levels, after the Civil War. The same was taking place in Canada.

But it was the invention of the internal combustion engine that helped in the explosion of outdoor recreation. In the last decade of the nineteenth century the automobile was introduced, and Henry Ford converted it into a means of popular transportation. While auto racing became the leisure activity revolving around this new tool initially, outdoor facilities, being large, were built outside urban centers, and the masses used their automobiles to get to golf courses, ski resorts, campgrounds, fishing spots, and hunting lodges wherever they were.

It was not until World War I that the airplane became commercialized. Today it has become the carrier for millions of people seeking rest and recreation in sports that in times past only the privileged few participated in. Tourism has become an important international business. Within the United States and Canada another important means of recreational travel has evolved: the RV (recreational vehicle). Its sales peaked in 1972, at 540,000 a year in the United States, then leveled off and saw a drastic drop until 1985, when sales began to pick up again (Barker 1986:15). Also, pleasure boats have seen a surge in popularity. They may represent a status in life which indicates some form of prestige. This is a function of social mobility.

Mobility

The mere provision of a vehicle such as an RV or a boat does not automatically mean that its owner will visit a park or engage in an outdoor pursuit. Mobility has a psychological dimension as well as a social dimension. The social dimension refers to the movement of an individual from one status to another. Upward mobility leads to improvement in status, downward mobility moves a person to a lower status, and horizontal mobility leads to a new and different status that is similar to the old one. Mobility is a phenomenon that is seen in open societies, the ones that allow for changes in one's status. This creates a psychological dimension which not only allows but also prompts the individual to go after the benefits to be accrued from the new, upward status, such as the type of recreation and the life-style enjoyed by the members of the desired "class." People seek higher pay, longer vacations, and the ability to afford an RV and/or a pleasure boat for both psychological and social reasons.

SUMMARY

In this work outdoor recreation is defined as the organized free time activities that are participated in for their own sake and where there is an interaction between the participant and an element of nature. Such activities are predicated on the tendencies to play and to ritualize. Both of these tendencies have biological roots as well as evolutionary dimensions. Observation of play among animals, particularly the higher forms, along with the studies of the human brain show how profound the tendency to play is. Meanwhile, the tendency to ritualize is seen in ceremonies and celebration of many human societies. Also, outdoor recreational pursuits are affected by a recent phenomenon, leisure, which describes the state of mind that allows a person to participate in an activity solely for the sake of that activity during the time freed from civic and familial obligations.

The need for recreational outlets overcame the objection of those who considered such pursuits as wasteful, if not sinful, among the early European settlers of the New World. Open spaces that were allocated for meeting, grazing, and training of hunters evolved into parks. Fear of wanton destruction of the vast, yet limited, natural resources on this continent led to the rise of a preservation movement which led to the establishment, for the first time in human history, of natural areas allocated for the enjoyment of extant and future generations. A concept of federally designated national parks, born in the United States with the establishment of Yellowstone National Park, is adopted by many nations today.

Expansion of outdoor recreational opportunities required the establishment of many agencies at the federal, state, and local levels. This was in response to demands which were accelerated by 1) the adoption of the Universal Declaration of Human Rights by the General Assembly of the United Nations in 1948, which includes the right to leisure and recreation; 2) an increase in free time for almost every citizen in many countries regardless of social class and lifestyle; 3) the advent of industrialization and automation which allowed for greater free time; 4) an increase in urbanization with the resultant increase in the need for outdoor recreational outlets; 5) the provision of adequate means of transportation which takes the desiring person to the spot of his or her choice; and 6) mobility with its social as well as psychological dimensions that, in the case of upward mobility, drives one to seek recreational pursuits that correspond to the newly acquired status.

REFERENCES

Barker, R. (1986) "On the Road to Recovery: RV Makers Rev up for a Strong Year." *Barons* (24 February): 15, 28–30.

Berlyne, D. E. (1960) *Conflict, Arousal and Curiosity.* New York: McGraw-Hill.

Blanchard, K., and A. Cheska. (1985) *The Anthropology of Sport: An Introduction.* South Hadley, MA: Bergin and Garvey.

Clawson, M. (1985) "Outdoor Recreation: Twenty-five Years of History, Twenty-Five Years of Projection." *Leisure Sciences* 7(1):73–99.

Deegan, M. J. (1989) *American Ritual Dramas: Social Rules and Culture Meanings.* Westport, CT: Greenwood Press.

deVore, I. (1965) *Primate Behavior.* New York: Holt, Reinhart and Winston.

Eisen, G. (1988) "Theories of Play." In *Understanding Leisure* by G. Gerson et al. Dubuque, IA: Kendall-Hunt.

Grimmes, R. (1982) *Beginnings in Ritual Studies.* Landham, MD: University Press of America.

Huizinga, J. (1950) *Homo Ludens.* New York: The Beacon.

Ibrahim, H. (1991) *Leisure and Society: A Comparative Approach.* Dubuque, IA: Wm. C. Brown.

Ibrahim, H. (1988) "Leisure, Idleness and Ibn Khaldun." *Leisure Studies* 7:51-58.

Ibrahim, H., and J. Shivers. (1979) *Leisure: Emergence and Expansion.* Los Alamitos, CA: Hwong Publishing.

Lancaster, J. B. (1975) *Primate Behavior and the Emergence of Human Culture.* New York: Holt, Rinehart and Winston.

Lowerson, J., and J. C. Meyerscough. (1977) *Time to Spare in Victorian England.* Hassocks, Sussex: Harvester Press.

McLean, J., J. Peterson, and W. D. Martin. (1985) *Recreation and Leisure: The Changing Scene.* New York: Macmillan.

Ornestein, R., and R. Thompson. (1984) *The Amazing Brain.* New York: Houghton-Mifflin.

Roth, W. C. (1902) *Games, Sports and Amusements.* Brisbane, Australia: G. A. Vaughan, Government Printer.

Sagan, C. (1977) *The Dragons of Eden.* New York: Random House.

Samuel, N. "Free Time in France: A Historical and Sociological Survey." *International Social Science Journal* 38:49-63.

United Nations (1978) *Human Rights: A Compilation of International Instruments.* New York: United Nations.

Veblen, T. (1953) *The Theory of Leisure Class.* New York: New American Library.

Viau, J. (1939) *Hours and Wages in American Organized Labor.* New York: George Putnam and Sons.

Wolf, D. D. (1984) "Repertoire, Style, and Format: Notions Worth Borrowing from Children's Play." In *Play in Animals and Humans,* edited by P. Smith. Oxford, England: Basil Blackwell.

Wood, J. (1871) *The Uncivilized Races of Man.* Hartford, CT: J. B. Burr.

2 Nature and the Spiritual Life

One aspect of American outdoor recreation is people's respect and even, for some, reverence for nature. This reverence is characteristic of some of the early leaders that laid the foundation for preservation of federal lands. It is also part of our Native American heritage and summer camp experiences that refresh and renew the spirit. In this chapter we will first explore the Native American reverence for nature and then address Western attitudes toward nature. Historically, respect for nature was challenged by American cultural values as seen in the Industrial Revolution during the latter half of the nineteenth century and on into the twentieth century. In recent years there has been movement towards a renewed reverence for nature due to the influence of the ecology and health movements, and a spiritual reawakening. The roots of a modern reverence for nature are traced to the philosopher Rousseau, who popularized the notion that the world in its natural state is closer to the truth (Clark 1969). Today writers such as Thomas Berry in *The Dream of the Earth* (1990) are advocating a new spirituality that includes a fresh respect for the universe and a more harmonious relationship with nature.

A SPIRITUAL RELATIONSHIP TO NATURE

When we look at American history as it relates to nature, the spiritual emphasis plays an interesting role. The first stage was a primal relationship with nature. The Native Americans celebrated and ritualized nature, making efforts to achieve harmony with its many forces and its animal and plant life. The second stage occurred with the arrival of the pioneers. Eager to begin a new life in a new country, the pioneers felt compelled to conquer nature. The third stage was a time of dualities. The wilderness was less threatening, and with more leisure time available, transcendentalists began a philosophical movement back to nature. But during this stage industrialization resulted in the exploitation of American lands. Fortunately, foresighted citizens sought the protection of significant public lands which today provide the setting for a reawakening of the process of spiritual refreshment that can occur in a natural setting.

According to Drovdahl (1991:25), American society has a renewed interest in the spiritual side of life. Bunting (1989:35) writes that our bodies and souls have suffered during our pursuit for maximum information. In response, physical wellness has been emphasized during the past fifteen years, and now we are in the beginning stages of the realization that individuals have spiritual needs and that people are searching for inner peace. Drovdahl (1991:25) believes the *spirit* has come to signify a person's soul, or the nonmaterial, inner-spring of a person's life. Spiritual resources help to provide a route-finding system which enables people to navigate through life's journey. The spiritual, according to Kraus (1984), reflects humankind's "higher nature—a sense of moral values, compassion, and respect for other humans and for the earth itself. It is linked to the development of one's inner feelings, a sense of order and purpose in life, and a commitment to care for others and to behave responsibly in all aspects of one's existence."

According to Kaplan (1979:190), the spiritual aspect of life "opens us to the interdisciplinary, fusionary, holistic prospect of leisure that invites emotional, unforced, free adventuresome levels of experience." Leisure offers time for contemplation and meditation in which human values can be established and enriched. Jay B. Nash considered the highest form of recreational participation to be those activities in which the participant was most fully involved emotionally, physically, and creatively. Kraus (1984:335–36) finds that "leisure provides the arena in which personal values are shaped and in which the individual may reach the highest potential of which he or she is capable. Beyond the purely practical and purposeful goals which characterize work, it [leisure] offers a vision of life carried on for its own sake, in celebration of all that is vital and generous in people." William R. H. Stevens, a writer on leisure and religion, found that the "essential spirit of leisure is that of celebration . . . Real joy is a condition of the spirit deeper than the mere fleeting experience of pleasurable sensation" (Kaplan 1979:187). Leisure may become a spiritual experience, and spiritual forms or aspects of leisure are not limited to special philosophies or church programs.

Mitchell and Meier point out that one of the most significant outcomes of the camp experience is the development of spiritual feelings and values. In this sense they define *spiritual* as connoting "a keen appreciation of nature as well as a kinship with one's fellow beings and an orderly universe" (1983:146). Religious groups have used camps for spiritual settings for years. But spiritual experiences do not always occur at formally arranged times or in specifically designated places. Such experiences may occur when the senses are unusually heightened. The wilderness gives one the opportunity to experience beauty, complexity, and life's mysteries and mystique.

There are two sides to the spiritual or sacred life: the personal, ecstatic side that individuals find hard to describe, and the communal part which may be celebrated year after year through oral histories, rituals, ceremonies, and customs (Beck and Walters 1988:6). The camp experience could nurture both sides of this spiritual life. For instance, one can have an individual peak experience in which the wholeness of life is experienced in a mystical fashion while ascending a mountain or observing a waterfall. Group members can have a communal experience around the campfire in which a unity of spirit is achieved that serves to elevate the group to a more intense spiritual experience. In each case something of the mystery of life is revealed, albeit for a brief moment. The Native Americans experienced a rich spiritual life both individually and communally. Their experience is germane to outdoor recreationists in that they lived close to nature and spent much of their lives in the out-of-doors. Their spiritual life celebrated nature in its diverse aspects. They too sensed the mystical in nature which we will later see many hikers and backpackers refer to in profound ways.

Nature and the Native American Experience

Native Americans view themselves as part of a delicate and balanced universe, not as its masters. All life forms and natural elements interrelate and interplay: no part of nature is considered more important than another. They further believe, generally, that only humans can upset this balance. Everything is naturally alive, and ceremonies retain harmony with the pervasive powers of nature, stressing the relationship of people with the cosmos. Chief Luther Standing Bear of the Oglala Sioux found that "only to the white man was nature a wilderness and only to him was the land 'infested' with 'wild' animals and 'savage' people. To us it was tame. Earth was bountiful and we were surrounded with the blessings of the Great Mystery" (Stegner 1990:35).

Most Native Americans have two common beliefs that play significant roles in their sacred practices: first, a belief in a knowledge of unseen powers, and second, a belief in the knowledge that all things in the universe are dependent on each other. Unseen powers might be worshipped in elaborate ceremonial dance. The mysterious powers of nature, such as the way the seasons change, are often marked by collective rituals and ceremonials that recognize the spirits of the seasons and share the good they bring. The rituals provide order and systematize the way in which the society, the natural environment, and the unseen worlds meet and come together. The rituals provide a physical expression of a mystical experience. In this manner the participants come closer to understanding the mysteries of life. Historically the Native American ritual cycle has contained many celebrations and liturgies that focus on harmony with nature.

Harmony with Nature

By living in harmony with nature Native Americans seek unity with a fundamental *life force* inherent in everything. Ceremonies, rites, and songs serve as aids. Rituals transform the mysterious into something more tangible. It is glorified and celebrated rather than explained. Rituals are not simple, crude, or barbaric; they are complex, pervasive, remarkable human processes. They provide human beings with ways of dealing with forces that seem beyond comprehension and control.

For example, puberty ceremonies were closely linked to nature. A young male Sioux would travel to a hilltop, forest, or remote shore in order to participate in his initiation ceremony or vision quest. Alone, he would contemplate and seek the aid of a spirit guide who would assist him in dealing with nature's spiritual life force. Fasting and thirsting for several days, he would suffer hardships while waiting for a vision or hallucination to appear. An honored animal with superior powers might appear, teaching a song or providing special instructions to aid the young initiate's personal power for the rest of his life. If visions were particularly intense, the young man might be called upon as a shaman (Farb 1968:128–130; Lame Deer and Richard 1972:1–6).

Earth's creation, the creation of humankind, and the relationship of earth and humans are symbolically recreated in the Apache girl's puberty ceremony. This momentous ritual lasts four days and four nights and honors the youth's entry into womanhood as she ritualistically represents Mother Earth or White Painted Woman (Collier 1972:163, 165).

NATURE, DANCE, AND CEREMONY

Human motion has served as a powerful medium in the Native American celebration of nature. Through ritualized dance the spiritual body transcends itself into a prayer for rain, a cure for one who has lost touch with the forces of nature, or a means to celebrate creation or to express gratitude for nature's gifts. Ceremonial dance may shape the circumstances of nature if focused appropriately on the receptive powers of animals. Through the interaction of forces something more arises. Ritual dancers outwardly appear to imitate entities of the natural world, but inwardly endeavor to transform themselves into these entities.

For example the Yaqui deer dancer does not simply represent the image of a deer in the Deer Dance but seeks to transform himself into the deer itself. By doing so he honors his brother the deer while requesting that it willingly allow itself to be sacrificed by the hunter so that humankind might live. Since the Native American does not try to dominate nature, his relationship to the deer is one of intimacy and courtesy (Cordes 1990:4). Similarly when a buffalo was killed, Lame Deer and Richard tell us, "We apologized to his spirit, tried to make him understand why we did it, honoring with a prayer the bones of those who gave their flesh to keep us alive, praying for their return, praying for the life of our brothers, the buffalo nation, as well as our own people" (1972:111).

To encourage animals to return and regenerate as game, the Alaskan Eskimos of Nunivak Island held a dance and feast in honor of the souls of game animals. Throughout the year hunters saved the bladders of the animals to be symbolically buried at the conclusion of the ceremony so that they could return to earth as game (Gill 1982:124).

Some Native Americans utilized animal fetishes, which are objects of any material worn or cherished to ward off evil or attract good fortune. Their use dates from pre-Columbian times.

Small wooden dolls carved from the root of cottonwood trees represent in stylized fashion the Katchina dancers of the Hopi people. These dolls are carved by men prior to the powerful Katchina ceremonies which are believed to bring rain for the crops and help and comfort to all people.

To the Zunis of the Southwest, among the most skillful carvers of fetishes, the objects represent the "Breath of Life." Mother Earth, rain, and all of the life-giving forces upon which humans depend are represented by various fetishes. The living power believed to exist in the fetish provides support.

Cushing (1988:9) explained that any phenomenon of nature can be associated with an animal analogous to that phenomenon. Lightning, for example, is personified by the snake. Both strike instantly, may cause disastrous results, and are easily illustrated by a zigzag design. Since the

Serpent Mound State Park in southern Ohio. This is the largest known serpent-effigy mound in the world and exemplifies American Indian ritual artifacts that express veneration of wild creatures.

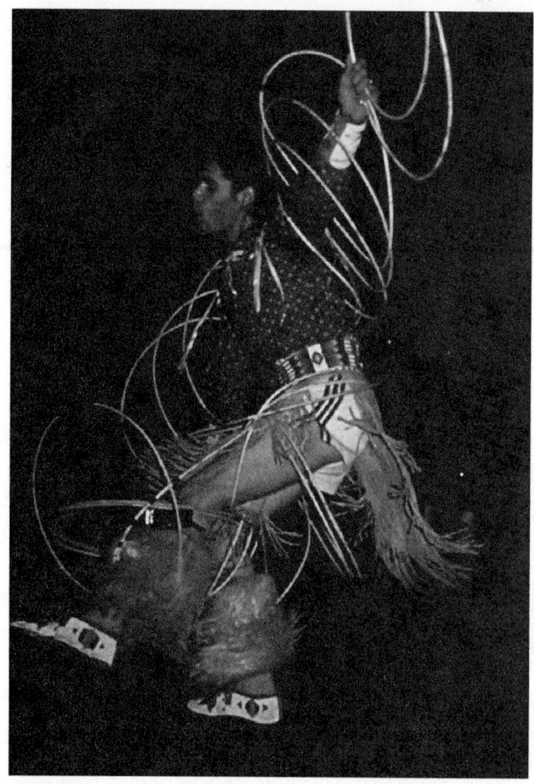

To many tribes the hoop symbolizes the world or the universe. Time and even the seasons move in a circle.

snake is more closely aligned to lightning than is a human, but more closely related to humans than is lightning, the worship and ritualized activity is directed to the more mysterious and remote powers of nature which are transmitted through animals. The animal fetishes are regarded as living forces, provided they are ceremoniously nurtured. An animal of prey worn over the heart during the hunt magically provides aid to the hunter with its instinctiveness. Its heart will overcome the heart of the animal it preys upon ultimately causing it to weaken by charming its senses. Without such recourse, it was considered useless to attempt the chase (Cushing 1988:15, 39). Evidence of snake worship is found in all quarters of the earth. The serpent has been regarded as a "symbol of intelligence, of immortality, of protection against the power of evil spirits, and of a renewal of life and the healing powers of nature" (Bourke 1984:212).

The Hopi Snake Dance is one of the most ancient snake ceremonies still performed. According to Harold Courtlander (1971:82–95), the Hopi snake legend begins with a journey of a chief's son to find out where a certain river ends. During his travels he meets Spider Grandmother, who transforms herself into a small spider and enters his ear so that she is able to offer him advice without anyone knowing. At the river's end he encounters the Snake People, who have the power to transform themselves into snakes. After various trials the son is accepted as a person of good heart, is taught the ceremonies of the Snake People, and is allowed to select a wife. Upon his return to his own people he shares the snake ceremonies which bring rain to the arid Southwest for the corn.

During the August ceremony on the Hopi mesas in Arizona, members of the Hopi snake clan collect snakes from the four cardinal directions: North, South, East, and West. After several days of private rituals, they dance in the plaza wearing short kilts painted with zigzag lines of lightning, each carrying a snake "elder brother" in his mouth. After the snakes are properly blessed they are returned to the four sacred directions of the earth accompanied by the Hopi prayer for rain. Rain-laden August clouds often miss the semiarid Hopi mesas, but after the ceremony, reports generally follow that the skies pour down rain, filling dry washes with wild muddy water (Fergusson 1988:150, 162–67; Fewkes 1986:294–95).

This five-story, twenty-room castle built by the Salado Indians around 1100 A.D. in northern Arizona is protected by Montezuma Castle National Monument. It is 90 percent intact and one of the best preserved cliff dwellings in the United States.

Nature, Architecture and the Cosmos

A culture's relationship with nature may be evident in its sense of space. The Anasazi, the ancient ancestors of the Pueblo people, who lived in Arizona, Colorado, Utah, and New Mexico, ritualized their relationship to the land, which represented the divine. This outlook is evident in their architecture, which manifests balance and harmony with the landscape. The *kiva* or ceremonial center of the Pueblo represents the sacred center of the world. A symbol of the supernatural order of the universe, the kiva was described by an Acoma account as a sacred model of the world. Trees were represented by the four pillars which supported the roof, each pillar pointed in one of the sacred directions, the sky was represented by the walls, and the Milky Way was represented by the beams of the roof. The kivas were originally circular to take on the appearance of the sky. Correspondingly in the Navajo hogan, the door faces east to the rising sun with the fireplace centrally located, symbolizing the cosmic center. Smoke rises through the hole in the ceiling so that the incense will rise to the gods (Hadingham, 1984:150; Highwater 1982:122–124).

Observatories were built by ancient peoples to record the movement of the solar system. Some of the observatories can be visited today in Hovenweep National Monument in Utah, Casa

Structures such as this Anasazi one in Chaco Culture National Historical Park provide evidence of the celestial observations of these early people.

Grande National Monument in Arizona, and Chichen Itza in Mexico. Winter and summer solstices and fall and spring equinoxes were observed by sungazers through alignments with geological features such as mountain peaks, caves, and rock formations. Rock art such as that of the Chumash Indians of California appears to represent studies of the sun, moon, stars, eclipses, and comets. Chumash priests held daily rituals to interpret the behavior of the sky. The event causing the greatest apprehension was the winter solstice. Fearing that the sun might not choose to return, the entire community would emerge for midwinter ceremonies. The high priest, personifying the "Image of the Sun," would impersonate the sun's rays. Ceremoniously he would anchor a wooden shaft into the ground as an emblem of the axis of the world. Capped with a stone disc symbolizing the sun, it was positioned so that only the shadow of the stone would appear on the ground during both solstices. At the appropriate time he would strike it with a magic stone and recite an incantation designed to pull the sun back toward the earth.

THE WESTERN VIEW OF NATURE

The Western view of nature, in contrast, has generally revolved around the belief that humans are superior to all other life forms and that the universe exists to serve their needs. Westerners, in general, place value on those life forms which demonstrate usefulness to humans.

Ritual was relegated to an inferior position and was not incorporated into the technological process by the Westerner. Even basic ritualistic symbols were considered too simple for the language-bound mentality of Western people. European America was cut off from rhythmic-natural expressiveness and most of the population tended to neutralize, rather than ritualize, nature (Highwater 1982:144–48). Granted there are many positives in the advancements of human society, nonetheless, many believe that the loss of the link between people and nature is a negative outcome (Garvey 1990:48).

Moving Away from Ritual and Nature

The movement away from ritual and nature started long ago in both East and West. By the time the cultures of Egypt and the Far East arose, ritual had become highly structured and formalized visually, to influence an observer, not the participant. Priesthood was developed in Egypt, Greece, and Rome, and the concern was with the organization of a sociopolitical structure, no longer with the power in nature but with the hierarchy (Highwater 1985:40). The original impulse which had given rise to the ritual was gone; ritual came to express literal ideas. For instance, during the Hellenic age dance expressed the humanistic value system, and in the Middle Ages it became a source of entertainment. During the Renaissance, ballet emerged as an art. Early Western architecture also turned away from nature. For example, the Greek temple was a place to worship human-conceived divinity rather than nature's divinity (Highwater 1982:124). Although balanced artistically, the temple was not part of nature.

In the new culture of America, pioneers generally had an antagonistic attitude toward the wilderness. The wilderness posed dangers for them, and the major benefit of the forest was in providing wood for shelters and warmth. Contrasting with the Native American outlook, the pioneers believed that civilization, not nature, conveyed the sacred life-style.

The romantic period dissolved some of these antagonistic attitudes toward nature by recognizing nature's seductive splendor, mystery, and spiritual potential. Life was more comfortable and nature less intimidating. Philosopher Jean-Jacques Rousseau (1712–1778) is credited with leading the return to the notion that primal peoples were rational in seeking harmony with nature. He was not at all convinced that the technological advancements of Western society were an improvement in the social condition. This transitional period opened the door to the romantic movement and later to transcendentalism, which established nature as the vehicle to lift consciousness to greater spiritual wisdom.

According to Clark (1969), in the eighteenth century only a few Europeans began to recognize the charm of the lakes and mountains of Switzerland. Mountains were previously seen as a nuisance, inhibiting travel and communication; their recreational potential was not developed. In fact there are only a few early European contacts with the mountains that were recorded. In 1340 the poet Petrarch climbed a mountain to see the view from the top, and Leonardo da Vinci wandered around the Alps to study botany and geology. The backgrounds in some of his paintings show that he was moved by what he saw. The artist Peter Brueghel painted the Alps in an inspired fashion ahead of his time. Recorded, too, was Saint Francis' special relationship with nature, but few other instances are noted. English gardens began to change from rigid walkways to more natural mazelike paths. Walking in the countryside became fashionable, in part inspired by the poet Wordsworth, who walked frequently. Intellectuals, poets, and philosophers followed this trend.

Rousseau was moved by the lakes and alpine valleys of Switzerland. His total absorption in nature was a mystical experience that ultimately had a profound effect on the Western mind, because it moved Rousseau to set forth a new philosophy. Rousseau's original thinking caused him to be persecuted, and eventually he sought refuge on an island in Lake Bien around 1765. Listening and watching the rhythmic waves he surrendered himself completely to nature; he became at one with the experience. He lost all consciousness of an independent self and later realized that existence is nothing more than a succession of moments perceived through the senses. He said, "I feel therefore I am." He believed the qualities of beauty and innocence he observed in nature were also present in human beings. He believed that "natural man" was virtuous, and he is credited with leading the return to the notion that primal peoples were rational in seeking harmony with nature. Rousseau's theories are propounded in his treatise, "A Discourse In The Origins Of Inequality Among Men" (Clark 1969).

Twenty years after Rousseau wrote his treatise, the islands of Tahiti were explored, which seemed to confirm that the simple, natural existence of the natives was superior to the squalor that existed among the eighteenth century European communities. This attractive goodness of natural living, and the ability of a human being to completely surrender to nature in a mystical experience as Rousseau had, was a precursor of a reappearance of nature as a divinity. The early proponents of this belief, Rousseau, Wordsworth, Goethe, and Coleridge, sought to approximate nature with Truth. During the romantic era these concepts were embraced by a larger group of philosophers and artists.

Other significant breakthroughs in the nature movement occurred. The impressionist painters, in their efforts to depict the natural reflections in ripples of water, strove to paint an impression of light. This attempt at pure depiction of the impression, first captured by Monet and Renoir, was an innovation in painting. To capture the natural, the artists were totally absorbed in the subject matter of their paintings. Also, the American Transcendentalist movement viewed nature as a means to transcend everyday life to encounter the divine (see Chapter 3).

Transcendentalism, the movement founded by Ralph Waldo Emerson (1803–1882) and Henry David Thoreau (1817–1862), acknowledged nature's facility to assist one in going beyond or transcending everyday existence. This philosophy influenced future naturalists to attempt to preserve the American wilderness. However, people caught up in the economic expansion in America persisted in utilizing all that nature provided in an effort to achieve a better life on earth. Humanity continued to view nature as a means to an end with little thought of potential repercussions.

According to Clark (1969), however, several elements of this reverence for nature, called "nature religion," took root in the eighteenth and nineteenth century. These elements were as follows:

1. Value exists in the simple life, which is antihierarchical.
2. Walking is both a spiritual and physical exercise.
3. Mountains are viewed as sacred places, and clouds are sources of divine inspiration.
4. There is a healing power in nature.

Outdoor recreation occurs at rendezvous held across North America which celebrate, in anachronistic fashion, the early trappers and explorers.

5. Natural man is virtuous and in general sympathizes with the humble and downtrodden.
6. Nature equals truth.
7. As a result of total absorption in nature, one can lose one's sense of identity and become enraptured.

Modern authors such as Catherine Albanese, author of *Nature Religion in America,* Thomas Berry, author of *The Dream of the Earth,* Charles Cummings, author of *Eco-Spirituality,* Jamake Highwater, author of *The Primal Mind,* and Joseph Campbell, author of *Historical Atlas of World Mythology,* describe the Western separation of humans from nature and draw upon

Meditating by a giant redwood.

Native American rituals which celebrate harmony with nature. Berry believes that in the development of the rational process the West lost touch with its intuitive nature and that Westerners can relearn from Native Americans. He suggests that a renewed reverence for the earth is basic to survival (1990:180–93). The Native American was immersed in nature, in contrast to modern society's experiences in nature, which are usually brief and sandwiched between urban experiences.

The movement back to nature can be observed among contemporary choreographers who added natural movement and ritualization to dance for inspiration. Finding ballet too standardized, Isadora Duncan, the leader of freedom in movement, envisioned dance as a personal ritual capable of supporting ideas and feelings. The new *modern dance* revived the oldest form of dance as a means to provide expression for that which cannot be externalized by rational means. Like the Yaqui deer dancer, performers did not simply imitate but became the dance by transforming themselves into the idea, the feeling, or the motion.

Campbell (1988b:95–96) believes that one can understand what is exalted by a society by discovering its tallest building. In medieval towns it was the cathedral; in an eighteenth century town, the political palace; and in a modern

Hogans, *or Navajo houses, such as this one in Canyon de Chelly National Monument, dot the arid Southwest, where recreation and everyday living of the Navajo come together on reservation lands.*

city, the office buildings. True to Campbell's theory, mainstream American society is still oriented around the economy. Perhaps it is an adverse reaction to this glorification of the economy that has resulted in the burgeoning of outdoor recreation in the late twentieth century. With the towering monuments to the work ethic out of view, the outdoor adventurer is free to escape to nature for a renewal of the spirit.

The trend is not a return to a pioneer state of wilderness or to reenact the Native American rituals but to recognize that modern technological knowledge has neglected the natural and that humans yearn for it. Albanese asserts that concern regarding the environment among many late twentieth century Americans is a call to the natural (1990:197–98). The increase in visitations to national parks and wilderness areas may be attributed in part to this search. Albanese finds that Americans are celebrating nature, and that a twentieth century "nature religion" is growing daily. Cummings refers to a similar phenomenon as "eco-spirituality," or the reverence for life in all its diversity and nonliving things by those with or without religious affiliation.

Citizens of the United States are again participating more intimately with nature. In some cases outdoor recreational activities provide more than the recreational and physical values of the activity—they provide a forum in which activities may become ritualized events allowing attainment of a spiritual level of oneness with nature. These outdoor activities may become our own vision quest in nature. John Monczunski (1990:39) described his experience as follows: "I was there under the blue sky. And I could only be there by being related to everything else that was there. Not only related, but really part of it, an extension of everything else. So I was not so significant, not so separate, not so egotistical, not so important, not so self-derived. I surrendered into it and was part of it."

Inspired and with insights deepened, one is at peace. As one hiker expressed it, "You walk, eat, sit, sleep. And when you've covered some miles, you realize you've learned as much about yourself as about the land you've crossed—and that what you've explored has been the geography of the soul. You may learn that Walt Whitman was right when he said, 'Now I see the secret of making the best persons. It is to grow in the open air and to eat and sleep with the earth!'" (Temple 1990:42).

Today's outdoor rituals may be anachronistic: relating hunting to Native Americans, survival skills to mountain men, or horseback riding to cowboys. Or a participant in the midst of nature's beauty may notice its sights, sounds, and smells. A surfer may admire the power of the ocean, a climber may prepare for a gathering storm, and a birder may recognize a bird vanishing into extinction. An intimacy with nature and even history can be achieved.

According to Rolston (1986:103), the outdoors brings us back to a natural order. We return to basics. We are in contact with *creation,* which is at the root of the word *recreation.* While testing our prowess in the outdoors, we may be participating in our own individual nature ritual. As activities in nature become

The outdoor experience can be more spiritual than physical as the beauty of nature inspires awe in the recreationist's soul and, at times, a sense of the deeper truths in life.

A spontaneous celebration of nature.

ritualized, the meaning of the activity becomes more important than the activity itself. The great outdoors becomes a cathedral to the sacredness of nature. Kerry Temple writes of his backpacking experience, "I try to memorize the view, to lock this feeling inside my head. Whatever God I have is in these mountains, in the forests and fields I've walked, the rivers, woods and deserts I've known" (1990:44–45). Nature is a philosophical, scientific, economic, aesthetic, and recreational resource, but the great outdoors also works on the recreationist's soul. The ego is lost in nature's magnificence as recreation merges with creation. "The happiest man," wrote Emerson, "is he who learns from Nature the lesson of worship" (Temple 1990:42).

Clearly more than amusement is found in outdoor activities. Family backpack trips and campouts held every year at the same time are referred to as a yearly ritual and create deep family bonds. Through outdoor experiences, a common reality is shared. Various roles are assumed by the participants. Moreover many organized camps include daily activities which highlight the spiritual experience. According to Mitchell and Meier (1983:147) these supplementary activities include the following:

1. grace before meals
2. outdoor vespers
3. sunrise services
4. cabin devotions or meditations before taps

5. attendance at religious services
6. group discussions
7. singing of hymns

Mitchell and Meier (1983:148) suggest that the "wilderness cathedral" or "woodland chapel" might be located on a hilltop with a view of a valley, in a natural amphitheater, or at a clearing surrounded by trees.

The ceremonial campfire can be a significant spiritual event to campers. Typically these events start off with a light mood, progress to a more serious tone, and focus on beauty and serenity of the group's experience in nature. Some camps ceremonially mix partially burned wood and ashes from last year's campfire with the first fire of the year. Today there are alternatives to the traditional fire if the law or one's ethics prohibit building one. The alternatives include candles, indirect light from flashlights, artificially colored lights, and slide presentations (Mitchell and Meier 1983:152).

According to Drovdahl (1991:26) the very nature of camp draws campers out of themselves and encourages spiritual growth. Stepping out of his or her routine, a camper at a campfire or on a quiet hike has opportunities to reflect. The camper is surrounded by trees, mountains, sky, and creatures, all elements in life not created by humans. This environment is a natural theater for spiritual reflection.

SUMMARY

In the past, Western civilization believed it had progressed beyond nature by outgrowing the experiences of primal peoples, leaving them behind and making their "primitive" experience less valuable than the focus and priorities of civilized society. The Native American appears to symbolize harmony with nature. Authentic ceremonials on the reservations are religious observations, performed in the same spirit as religious ceremonies held anywhere in the world, and pervading all these ceremonies is the principle of living in harmony with nature. Today, the Westerner is seeking a more harmonious relationship with nature. The outdoor experience of the hiker or camper is often far more than that of an adventure; it is spiritual and even profound for some.

References

Albanese, C. (1981) *America: Religions and Religion.* Belmont, CA: Wadsworth Publishing.

Albanese, C. (1990) *Nature Religion in America.* Chicago and London: The University of Chicago Press.

Beck, P., and A. Walters. (1988) *The Sacred.* Tsaile, AZ: Navajo Community College Press.

Berry, T. (1990) *The Dream of the Earth.* San Francisco, CA: Sierra Club Books.

Bourke, J. (1984) *Snake Dance of the Moquis.* Tucson, AZ: The University of Arizona Press.

Bunting, C. (1989) "The Compatibility of Physical Education and Outdoor Education." *Journal of Health, Physical Education, Recreation and Dance* 60, no. 2 (February).

Campbell, J. (1988a) *Historical Atlas of World Mythology Vol. I. Part II.* New York: Harper and Row.

Campbell, J. (1988b) *The Power of Myth with Bill Moyers.* New York: Doubleday.

Clark, K. (1969) *The Worship of Nature (Civilization, Episode II).* BBC Television Distributors.

Collier, J. (1972) *American Indian Ceremonial Dances.* New York: Crown Publishers.

Cordes, K. (1990) "Values of Another Culture Through Dance and Ceremonials." *International Conference on the Global Village.* Miami, FL: Barry University.

Courtlander, H. (1971) *The Fourth World of the Hopis.* Albuquerque, NM: University of New Mexico Press.

Cummings, C. (1991) *Eco-Spirituality.* Mahwah, NJ: Paulist Press.

Cushing, F. (1988) *Zuni Fetishes.* Las Vegas, NV: K. C. Publications.

Drovdahl, R. (1991) "Touching the Spirit." *Camping Magazine* 63, no. 7 (May). Martinsville, IN: American Camping Association.

Farb, P. (1968) *Man's Rise to Civilization.* New York: E. P. Dutton and Co.

Fergusson, E. (1988) *Dancing Gods: Indian Ceremonials of New Mexico and Arizona.* Albuquerque, NM: University of New Mexico Press.

Fewkes, J. (1986) *Hopi Snake Ceremonies.* Albuquerque, NM: Avanyu Publishing.

Garvey, J. (1990) "The Stories We Live." *Spiritual Journeys* (Spring):48. University of Notre Dame.

Gill, S. (1982) *Native American Religions: An Introduction.* Belmont, CA: Wadsworth.

Hadingham, E. (1984) *Early Man and the Cosmos.* Norman, OK: University of Oklahoma Press.

Highwater, J. (1985) *Dance Rituals of Experience.* New York: Alfred van der Marck Editions.

Highwater, J. (1982) *The Primal Mind.* New York: Penguin.

Kaplan, M. (1979) *Leisure: Lifestyle and Lifespan.* Philadelphia, PA: W. B. Saunders.

Kraus, R. (1984) *Recreation and Modern Society.* Glenview, IL: Scott, Foresman and Co.

Lame Deer, J., and E. Richard. (1972) *Lame Deer Seeker of Visions.* New York: Washington Square Press.

Mitchell, V., and J. Meier. (1983) *Camp Counseling: Leadership and Programming for Organized Camp.* Philadelphia, PA: CBS College Pub.

Moncjunski, J. (1990) "What the Hermits Know." *Spiritual Journeys* (Spring):33–39. University of Notre Dame.

Rolston, H. (1986) "Beyond Recreational Value: The Greater Outdoors Preservation-Related and Environmental Benefits." President's Commission on Americans Outdoors, *Literature Review.* Washington D.C.: U.S. Government Printing Office.

Stegner, W. (1990) "It All Began With Conservation." *Smithsonian Associates.* Washington, D.C. (April).

Temple, K. (1990) "Over the Rise." *Spiritual Journeys* (Spring):40–45. University of Notre Dame.

3 Visionaries and Pioneers

The early Americans, including the Puritans and pioneers, ordinarily had an antagonistic attitude toward nature and wilderness. The wilderness posed dangers, Indians, and fear. The major value of the forest was to cut it down to provide wood for homes and shelters. In contrast to the American Indian philosophy, the Puritans believed that civilization meant that God's kingdom was to be tamed and conquered. These early attitudes toward nature and wilderness began to change through the efforts of a few people who recognized nature's mystery and spiritual potential. The romantics moved toward greater harmony with nature. Also, life in the mid-nineteenth century became more comfortable and nature less intimidating. Romanticism paved the way for transcendentalism, a philosophy that viewed nature as the vehicle to inspire intuitive thought that lifted the consciousness to greater spiritual wisdom. This mode of thought influenced future naturalists toward the preservation of the American wilderness. Two of the leading transcendentalists will be presented here, Emerson and Thoreau.

THE TRANSCENDENTALISTS

As a mode of perception, transcendentalism became an indefinable movement of abstract American intellectual thought. It intrigued New Englanders during the mid-nineteenth century, some of whom were turning to an inner world and exploring oneness with the universe, the supreme being, and nature. To them natural objects commandeered significance and if used properly they reflected universal spiritual truths. Humans have the potential to transcend materialism. Emerson defined transcendentalism simply as "belief in the Higher Law of God" (Wolf

1974:125). Henry David Thoreau expounded on Emerson's idea that when one is close to nature something happens to his or her perceptions. Inspired by Emerson, Thoreau lived close to nature in order to experience and to express his own heightened senses. His writings focused on nature, describing what he beheld and, then, generalized about overlying implications. Emerson on the other hand focused his perceptions on the human being, using deductive logic and philosophical abstractions (Ronald 1987:2). Many characteristics of Emerson's and Thoreau's transcendentalism, such as the trust in organic form, the correspondences between elements of the natural world, the concern with people's relationship to the environment, and the institution of being solitary, are echoed by naturalists today and continue to exert great influence on today's naturalism and wilderness preservation.

Ralph Waldo Emerson (1803–1882)

Born in Boston, Ralph Waldo Emerson became one of the most famous, original nineteenth century thinkers, and one of the most quoted American writers. He endured the loss of his father and sister at an early age, which undoubtedly affected his writing:

> Nature always wears the colors of the spirit. To a man laboring under calamity, the heat of his own fire hath sadness in it. Then there is a kind of contempt of the landscape felt by him who has just lost by death a dear friend. The sky is less grand as it shuts down over less worth in the population (Emerson as found in Atkinson 1950:7).

Drawn to nature, Emerson began to feel a profound affection for it and for the solitude it could provide him, which sustained him for the rest of his life. He proclaimed, "Nature is loved by what is best in us" (Atkinson 1950:411). At fourteen he received a grant from his father's church and entered Harvard College. Appointed "President's freshman," he was provided free board. Here he began writing his journals, which became his constant companion for some 50 years. These gave rise to literary material in lectures, essays, and books. Upon graduation, Emerson joined his brother William in teaching and operating a finishing school in his mother's home. It was an unhappy time for him; his journals were filled with discouragement and self-doubt. He wrote to a friend who was also teaching: "How my heart bleeds for you! Better tug at the oar, dig the mine, or saw wood; better sow hemp, or hang with it, than sow the seeds of instruction" (Gilbert 1914:124).

Descended from eight generations of ministers, Emerson enrolled in the Divinity School at Harvard, and once licensed, his teaching stopped forever. He married Ellen Tucker, whose health was delicate, and after only seventeen months of marriage she died of tuberculosis. Afterwards Emerson resolved that he was not in sympathy with some of the doctrines of his church, and as a result he resigned his post and sailed for Europe. The trip revived him, and upon his return he met and married his second wife, Lydia. Soon he suffered the death of two of his beloved brothers.

After his return from Europe, Emerson spent an allotted portion of each day walking in the woods and along the rivers, with his eyes open to the natural surroundings. Occasionally he preached and lectured to enthusiastic audiences on the moral and psychological interaction between nature and humans. In Concord he became involved in local affairs and was a respected and valued member of the community. He had two daughters and two sons. His eldest son died of scarlet fever at age five.

Emerson helped to organize a discussion group whose members called themselves "transcendentalists." Serving as their first literary proponent, Emerson wrote that he envisioned a unity of nature, humans, and God; he believed that through the use of intuition, a heightened awareness could be reached which would transcend one's thoughts to a grander level of ultimate (transcendental) understanding. Through natural phenomena he believed one could intuitively understand human relationships to the universe, its components, and to God (Ronald 1987). In his first book, *Nature* (1836), he enumerated the values of nature:

> If a man would be alone, let him look at the stars. The rays that come from those heavenly worlds will separate between him and what he touches. One might think the atmosphere was made transparent with this design, to give man, in the heavenly bodies, the perpetual presence of the sublime. Seen in the streets of cities, how great they are! If the stars should appear one night in a thousand years, how would men believe and adore; and preserve for many generations the remembrance of the City of God which had been shown! But every night come out these envoys of beauty, and light the universe with their admonishing smile (Atkinson 1950:5).

Emerson's *Essays* were published in two volumes, and his reputation grew. Many of his ideas came to him on his long afternoon walks in the Concord hills. An observer of nature, he was not generally an active participant. On some occasions he hunted, but his friends implied that he never shot a living thing. Emerson enjoyed his excursions to the mountains with members of the Adirondack Club. Later in life he took a trip to California where he met John Muir (described later in this chapter), and the two men drew close. Muir believed that Emerson was by then only a ghost of what he had once been (M.V-D. 1931:140).

In "Nature," from *Essays: Second Series* (Atkinson 1950:408) Emerson wrote:

> It seems as if the day was not wholly profane in which we have given heed to some natural object. The fall of snowflakes in a still air, preserving to each crystal its perfect form; the blowing of sleet over a wide sheet of water, and over plains; the waving rye-field; the mimic waving of acres of houstonia, whose innumerable florets whiten and ripple before the eye; the reflections of trees and flowers in glassy lakes; the musical, steaming, odorous south wind, which converts all trees to windharps; the crackling and spurting of hemlock in the flames, or of pine logs, which yield glory to the walls and faces in the sitting-room—these are the music and pictures of the most ancient religion.

Henry David Thoreau (1817–1862)

Thoreau was introduced to the Transcendental Club by his longtime friend Ralph Waldo Emerson. Considered to be one of the finest nature writers, he oscillated between a transcendental and scientific examination of nature. This alliance of contemplative thoughtfulness and close observation and speculation was the pattern for his prose and essays, which were neither notably sentimental nor as romantic as Audubon's or Muir's writing (to be discussed later in this chapter).

The third of four children, Henry David Thoreau was raised in a beautiful setting in Concord, Massachusetts. During his early years he shared his mother's love of the out-of-doors and developed an affinity for hunting, fishing, and solitude in nature. He especially admired the pond called Walden. Originally christened "David Henry," he reversed his names at age twenty, demonstrating an early act of independence. His family contributed to his education at Harvard, where he also received aid from a beneficiary fund for needy students. While in college he was granted a leave in order to teach and to assist his father, a pencil manufacturer. After graduation he was unsure of his goals, and teaching appeared to be a means to support himself. He soon resigned after he was coerced into flogging students who lacked discipline. Thoreau returned to pencil-making, which gave him leisure for his reading, studying, and walking. In 1837, after reading Emerson's *Nature,* he began to write about nature in his journal, which he kept throughout his life (Benet 1966:84–90). He lived simply, finding wealth in enjoyment rather than in possession. In later, more successful years he wrote in his journal, "Ah, how I have thriven on solitude and poverty! I cannot overstate this advantage. I do not see how I could have enjoyed it, if the public had been expecting as much of me as there is danger now that they will. If I go abroad lecturing, how shall I ever recover the lost Winter?'' (Teale 1962:73)

Thoreau opened a school with his brother John, and they introduced field trips for nature study, an innovation in American education. In 1839 the two brothers took a 13-day vacation voyage on the Concord and Merrimack rivers, a trip Thoreau later immortalized in his writings. By 1841 the school had closed due to his brother's ill health. Thoreau met Emerson at one of Emerson's lectures, and Emerson invited him to his home and introduced him to other transcendentalists, who also appreciated his freedom of thought. An acquaintance, Nathaniel Hawthorne, believed that Thoreau retained a wild and original nature and observed that he led a life similar to that of the Indians. Thoreau did study the wisdom of the Indians, and he later described in *The Maine Woods* his camping trip with an Indian friend and how he learned from him (Harding 1954:2,6).

As he read widely, from the explorations of Audubon to Hindu philosophy, Thoreau's appreciation of solitude, meditation, and contemplation deepened. The Emerson-Thoreau friendship grew closer with the sorrow they shared in the loss of Emerson's son and Thoreau's brother. Emerson and others encouraged Thoreau to lecture and to write, which he did. He built a cabin on Emerson's land on the northwest shore of Walden Pond, where he began residing in 1845. Here he observed and wrote about nature. During his stay he was arrested for his 1843 nonpayment of a poll tax in protest against slavery. After only one night in jail a disgusted Thoreau was released after his aunt paid the tax. He retold the story in his essay ''Resistance to Civil Government'' (later called ''Civil Disobedience'' and ''On the Duty of Civil Disobedience'') which appeared in 1849.

After living in the cabin for two years, Thoreau returned to his father's house in 1847 with the first draft of his first book, *A Week on the Concord and Merrimack Rivers.* The book, about his trip into the wilderness with his now deceased brother, was released in 1849 at his own risk. It received an unfavorable review, probably due to his unorthodoxy in religion. The reviewer criticized Thoreau's assertion that the Sacred Books of the Brahmins were not inferior to the Bible. In his second book, *Walden,* Thoreau wished to describe nature and to demonstrate that civilized people could escape the evils of competition. *Walden or Life in the Woods* (1854) sold slowly but steadily and became a classic in later years. After spending time at Emerson's home while he was in Europe, Thoreau returned to his father's home and the family atmosphere which he enjoyed for the rest of his life (R.W.A. 1936:491–97; Bolton 1954:126–32; Harding 1954:2,6).

During the 5 years after returning from Walden Pond, Thoreau delighted in his daily walks, toured Cape Cod on foot, spent a week in Canada, and took a second journey to Maine. At this point he became more of a scientific observer and less of a nature poet. Four books, published after his death, derive in part from these expeditions: *Excursions* (1863), *The Maine Woods* (1864), *Cape Cod* (1865), and *A Yankee in Canada* (1866). Dying of tuberculosis at age forty-five, his final words were about his beloved wilderness, ''moose'' and ''Indian'' (R.W.A. 1936:494–95). Emerson delivered a long eulogy and described Thoreau as someone who knew the country like a fox, who was physically fit, a good swimmer, runner, skater, and boatman, and who was a pleasure to walk with. According to Emerson, Thoreau's study of nature inspired his friends, who appreciated seeing the world through his eyes and hearing of his adventures. Reading, writing, and the study of wildlife were the only occupations that suited him. Thoreau's statement in *Walking,* ''In wildness is the preservation of the world,'' became the motto of the Wilderness Society years later (Teale 1962:59).

Thoreau's writings spiritualized his experiences with wilderness and nature and influenced future naturalists who helped to shape the destiny of North America. Living at a time when trees were appraised in terms of board feet, and not as shelters for birds or animals, he feared that human naturalness and oneness with the ecosystems were vanishing. Thoreau was an innovator in concluding that there was a need to preserve parcels of wilderness for the people, and he helped to lead the intellectual revolution that found nature and wilderness attractive as opposed to threatening and disagreeable (Bolton 1954:126–32; Vickery 1989:45). The following selection is taken from *The Maine Woods* (1965:87–88):

> It is difficult to conceive of a region uninhabited by man. We habitually presume his presence and influence everywhere. And yet we have not seen pure Nature, unless we have seen her thus vast and drear and inhuman, though in the midst of cities. Nature was here something savage and awful, though beautiful. I looked with awe at the ground I trod on, to see what the Powers had made there, the form and fashion and material of their work. This was the Earth of which we have heard, made out of Chaos and Old Night. Here was no man's garden, but the unhandseled globe. It was not lawn, nor pasture, nor mead, nor woodland, nor lea, nor arable, nor waste land. It was fresh and natural surface of the planet Earth, as it was made forever and ever. . . .

In the same book, his essay "The Moose Hunt" describes his feelings after observing a moose hunt:

> Strange that so few ever came to the woods to see how the pine lives and grows and spires, lifting its evergreen arms to the light,—to see its perfect success; but most are content to behold it in the shape of many broad boards brought to market, and deem that its true success! But the pine is no more lumber than man is, and to be made into boards and houses is no more its true and highest use than the truest use of a man is to be cut down and made into manure. There is a higher law affecting our relation to pines as well as to men. . . . I saw the tops of the pines waving and reflecting the light at a distance high over all the rest of the forest, I realized that the former were not the highest uses of the pine.

THE NATURALISTS

Although naturalism began with the French philosopher Jean-Jacques Rousseau, on this continent two great men led the natural movement, John James Audubon and John Muir. Rachel Carson, a great woman of the twentieth century, was the first to alert the nation to the damage suffered by the environment as a result of our chemical technology of the 1900s. The devotion of these three people to understanding, depicting, preserving, and writing about nature led to a more intimate understanding of nature.

John James Audubon (1785–1851)

Early conservationist, artist, ornithologist, and perhaps the most popular naturalist of North America, John James Audubon explored the Ohio and Mississippi rivers, the wilderness of Kentucky, the dunes and lagoons of the Texas coast, the palmetto groves of Florida, and the wild coast of Labrador. Writing in his journals, he personalized and revolutionized the study, illustration, and description of birds and mammals.

Born the illegitimate son of a French naval officer, merchant, and slave trader, John James Audubon and his younger (also illegitimate) half-sister were taken to France after his Creole mother died on their plantation in Santa Domingo. There, his father and stepmother adopted and raised them. His stepmother encouraged his early attraction to nature. He also learned to fence and dance, and to play the violin and flute. Later in life, with his flute, he was capable of imitating the songs of birds he observed, and he soon began to sketch them. He always remembered his father's admonition that "all things possessing life and animation were difficult to imitate" (Fisher 1949:15). Not showing much interest in scholarly work, he was sent to Paris to study drawing. He developed a desire to draw birds as they had appeared in the forest, not in profile as they appeared in books, which eluded him (Audubon 1960:14–15; Elman 1977:80–84).

Believing that his son could learn English and enter a profitable trade in the United States, Audubon's father suggested that he tend the family's farm in Mill Grove, Pennsylvania. At this time the boy changed his name to the anglicized John James instead of Jean Jacques, and he considered himself the master of the farm at age eighteen despite his father's hired agent.

Using a vivid personal narrative rather than dry impersonal experimental reports, Audubon explained his methods of observation of wildlife in its natural surroundings. He began to conduct scientific investigations with the birds he sketched and skillfully mastered how to closely examine birds and mammals without alarming them. He handled nestlings without causing the adult birds to abandon them, developing a method used by twentieth century field biologists. In one of his experiments he tied threads as leg bands to phoebes for identification. In this manner he discovered that many of them returned in the spring to their fledgling region after winter migration. Little did he know that 100 years later a Bird Banding Society would be formed to repeat his test in order to gather exact data on migratory species in every part of the American continent (Elman 1977:85-86). Later, in his *Ornithological Biography,* Audubon described one of his experiences in observing nature:

> . . . rambling along the rocky banks . . . observing the watchful King-fisher perched on some projecting stone over the clear water of the stream. Nay, now and then, the Fish Hawk itself, followed by a White-headed Eagle, would make his appearance, and by his graceful aerial motion, raise my thought far above them into the heavens . . . I studied the habits of the Pewee; and there I was taught most forcibly, that to destroy the nest of a bird or to deprive it of its eggs or young, is an act of great cruelty (Elman 1977;85-86).

After quarreling with his father's hired agent on the farm, Audubon borrowed money from his fiancée's uncle and set sail for France, where he remained for a year hunting and drawing, and he may have served in the French navy. After returning to the United States, he formed a partnership with Fernand Rozier and invested in a lead mine which proved a bust. Audubon went to New York to work as an apprentice in business, where he met Samuel L. Mitchell, future founder of the Lyceum of Natural History, now the New York Academy of Sciences. Together they went on excursions to prepare bird and mammal specimens.

Audubon and Rozier opened a retail store in Louisville, Kentucky. Audubon married and soon struck up a friendship with Daniel Boone. Later he met ornithologist Alexander Wilson, who was known for his drawings of birds. Samuel Mitchell believed that Audubon's art was superior to Wilson's and urged him to consider his own professional potential, but Audubon continued to try his luck in business. He left Kentucky and moved to Missouri in the pursuit of business success. The weather during the Missouri move proved to be bitterly cold, with ice forming on the Mississippi River. On the trip Audubon taught his dispirited partner how to winter camp. He expressed his exhilaration in observing the great snow-white birds lying on the ice. This proved to be a turning point in his career. Audubon sold out to his partner and journeyed back to Kentucky on foot, writing of his adventures, which were published later in his *Ornithological Biography.* In his journal he wrote, "Winter was just bursting into spring when I left the land of lead mines. Nature leaped with joy, as it were, at her own new-born marvels, the prairies began to be dotted with beauteous flowers, abounded with deer, and my own heart was filled with happiness at the sights before me" (Audubon 1960:23-31).

Returning to Kentucky, Audubon attempted several different enterprises, his last being a steam grist and lumber mill which were too elaborate for the needs of Henderson. Jailed for debt, he was released on the plea of bankruptcy. He found work as a taxidermist in Cincinnati in the new Western Museum. His wife convinced him that he should devote himself to his artistic talents, and, thereafter, his life took a definite aim. In 1820 he explored the Ohio and Mississippi rivers for birds. To support his undertaking, he painted portraits. Settling in New Orleans, he taught fencing, dancing, and music. His wife, now with three children, joined him and found work as a governess.

Audubon continued to travel in swamps and forests to draw his portraits of birds and animals. Determined to have his work published, he went to Philadelphia, where he found the cost of publication prohibitive. He planned to travel to Europe, where costs of engraving were far less. On his way he stopped in New York and visited his friend Mitchell, now president of the Lyceum of Natural History. Mitchell introduced Audubon to this society. His drawings were shown and were highly praised. He was elected to the Lyceum membership, and his credibility grew with his reading of two papers to the prestigious society. Later his fellow Americans nominated him a fellow of the American Academy of Arts and Sciences.

On Audubon's voyage to Europe, the ship's crew would sometimes lower him to the water in a small boat so that he could collect specimens. He was favorably received at Liverpool, where he obtained the first subscriptions for his book, *Birds in America.* He exhibited his drawings at the Royal Institution of Liverpool, where he was declared an American genius. In Edinburgh he received a regal reception and was elected to its Royal Society. Many honors came to him during his stay in England, including his election to the Fellowship in the Linnean Society. While in Great Britain he obtained enough subscribers to meet the cost of production for *Birds in America,* done in double elephant folio—27 by 40 inches—and the largest books ever published. All of the engravings were set in copper, life-size and in color. More than a thousand individual birds as well as thousands of American flowers, trees, shrubs, insects, and animals from Labrador to Florida and from Louisiana and Maine to the Great Plains were included.

By 1830 Audubon had teamed with Scottish naturalist William MacGillivray to write the text for *Birds of America,* called *Ornithological Biography.* The work was issued in five large volumes; the last release appeared in Edinburgh in May of 1838. Some of Audubon's original subscribers included Daniel Webster, Henry Clay, the kings of France and England, and many important libraries of the Western world. By the summer of 1839 his *Synopsis of the Birds of North America* was released. Audubon's reputation was established internationally as a first-rate naturalist and artist, and he was acclaimed the foremost naturalist in the United States (Elman 1977:100–107; Fisher 1949:70–71).

In his fifty-ninth year Audubon undertook an 8-month expedition to the upper Missouri River and the Yellowstone country. His comprehensive notes were published at a later date by his granddaughter in *Audubon and His Journals.* After this trip he published the "miniature" *Birds of America* (1844). He teamed with his friend Dr. John Bachman, minister and naturalist, to write a companion book on mammals. Bachman wrote the text while Audubon and his sons did the artistic work. The first edition of *The Viviparous Quadruples of North America* consisted of two volumes of 150 lithographic colored plates and was published twice, in 1845 and 1848. It was the first book of its kind in America and without rival in Europe. Naturalists immediately accepted it as a standard and authoritative work (Fisher 1949:74).

Renowned ornithologist Elliott Coues said, "Audubon and his work are one; he lived in his work, and his work will live forever" (Fisher 1949:76). The National Audubon Society was formed in 1886 in Audubon's honor by George Bird Grinnell, editor of *Forest and Stream.*

Attracting the distinguished support of John Greenleaf Whittier, Oliver Wendell Holmes, and others, some fifty thousand members joined within a 2-year period (Fox 1981:152). Audubon's enjoyment of the physical process of exploring the wilderness, tracking down each new species of bird and observing, recording, and cataloging it, marks him as one of the finest artist-naturalists of the romantic era in America, earning him his nickname, "The American Woodsman."

John Muir (1838–1914)

John Muir was born in Scotland and immigrated with his father, brother, and sister to Wisconsin at the age of eleven. The rest of his family came to America later. His mother, kindly and compassionate, and his father, an unbending Puritan, brought the family to the United States to seek a less discordant religious environment. The eldest son and the third in a succession of five daughters and three sons, John was expected to do heavy farm work from dawn to nightfall (Sargent 1971:7; Teale 1954:27). In his book *The Story of My Boyhood and Youth* (1913), Muir recounted his harsh experience while digging a 90-foot-deep well. After the first 10 feet he struck sandstone, and his father was advised to blast the rock. Lacking the skills to blast the sandstone, he decided to send his son down in a bucket to do the work with mason's chisels. Chipping from morning to night, day after day for months, in a space about 3 feet in diameter, Muir finally hit water 80 feet deep, but carbonic acid gas had settled at the bottom which nearly killed him. Even though his farm life was harsh, Muir found his surroundings inspiring and beautiful. He described the Wisconsin groves of oak as a summer paradise for song birds, saying, "Nature's fine love touches, every note going straight home into one's heart" (Muir 1975:137–38).

Inventive and hungry for knowledge, Muir made an arrangement with his father that he could read early in the morning before it was time for his chores. The zero-degree weather made a fire necessary. Fearing that his father might object to the cost of firewood, which took valuable work time to chop, he invented a self-setting sawmill. Encouraged by his neighbors to take some of his inventions to the State Fair in Madison, Muir had a successful showing, which brought him to the favorable notice of the university authorities. At the University of Wisconsin he selected a practical course of studies and disregarded the regimen required for a degree. Between work and study he had only 4 hours each night in which to sleep. He invented a bed that set him on his feet every morning at the hour desired. At his desk he arranged his books in order and so that they would automatically set themselves up on a rack and then close at a set time. After closing, each book would reposition itself in the appropriate stall as the next would open.

After leaving the university Muir took a long botanical and geological excursion through Canada, Wisconsin, Iowa, Illinois, and Indiana. Taking on odd jobs, he earned quick promotions in factories due to his inventions of labor-saving equipment. After an industrial injury nearly cost him the sight in one of his eyes, he was convinced that he should be true to himself by following nature and "the inventions of God" (Muir 1975:247–48, 260, 274–86; Teale 1954: 75, 99, 106, 163).

During his travels Muir began to keep a journal. His journal writing continued for the rest of his life. The journal he kept during his walk to the Gulf of Mexico contained observations on the forests, flora, and geography. He also wrote of his experiences with the inhabitants and of his personal reflections on human responsiveness toward nature. Edited posthumously, his observations appear under the title *A Thousand-Mile Walk to the Gulf* (1916). His next trip took him to San Francisco, where Muir immediately sought directions into the wilderness of the Yosemite Valley. He decided to remain in the area and work on a ranch while continuing his studies and explorations. His reflections, written at the age of thirty-one, appeared four decades later as *My First Summer in the Sierra* (1911). In his book *The Mountains of California* (1894) he shared his enthusiasm for the unknown. He described his climb on Mount Ritter, located in the middle portion of the High Sierra, as follows:

> Its height above sea-level is about 13,300 feet, and it is fenced round by steeply inclined glaciers, and canyons of tremendous depth and ruggedness, which render it almost inaccessible. But difficulties of this kind only exhilarate the mountaineer. . . . In so wild and so beautiful a region was spent my first day, every sight and sound inspiring, leading one far out of himself, yet feeding and building up his individuality. Now came the solemn, silent evening. Long blue, spiky shadows crept out across the snow-fields, while a rosy glow, at first scarce discernible, gradually deepened and suffused every mountain-top, flushing the glaciers and the harsh crags above them. This was the alpenglow, to me one of the most impressive of all the terrestrial manifestations of God. At the touch of this divine light, the mountains seemed to kindle to a rapt, religious consciousness, and stood hushed and waiting like devout worshipers. Just before the alpenglow began to fade, two crimson clouds came streaming across the summit like wings of flame, rendering the sublime scene yet more impressive; then came darkness and the stars.

Muir learned of Emerson and Thoreau at the University of Wisconsin. He read their books and often marked the margins with his own thoughts. When Emerson visited Yosemite, Muir acted as his interpreter of the natural history of the region. Two years later he named a mountain in the Yosemite region in Emerson's honor. Muir began to write articles for well-known journals, and he took the job of caretaker of a Yosemite hotel. He became the first non-Native to climb Mt. Whitney's east side and the recognized expert on Western trees. He wrote about the significance of glaciers in shaping the land after making five trips to Alaska, and he and S. Hall Yound became the first two white men to explore the Alaskan glaciers.

He married Louie Wanda Strentzel and leased and later bought a part of the Strentzel fruit ranch. After 10 years of prudent farming, he saved $100,000 which was enough to support his wife and two daughters while he devoted his time to his true ambitions, his hikes and observations. Muir is known to have taken 10 hours to walk 10 miles because he stopped so frequently to study or ponder. With no feeling for haste he could sit for hours studying the flowers (W.F.B. 1934:315 and Ford 1989:42).

Muir campaigned with Robert Underwood Johnson, an editor of *Century Magazine,* for the preservation of Yosemite National Park, which was ceded to the state of California in 1864. He also introduced bills to save the sequoias. After Muir spent 17 years trying his hardest to convince both the federal and state governments of the merit of the idea, President Theodore Roosevelt reacquired Yosemite for the federal government. By 1890 Yosemite, Sequoia, and General Grant, now King's Canyon, were all national parks. Muir credited Johnson as the "originator of Yosemite." Muir himself is credited with saving the Grand Canyon and the Petrified Forest, and with assisting in the establishment of Sequoia, Yosemite, Mount Rainier, Crater Lake, Glacier, and Mesa Verde national parks, and twelve national monuments including the Grand Canyon and the Olympic Peninsula, which later became national parks. Founder of the Sierra Club, he presided over it for 22 years (Ford 1989:40–43). Muir's work toward preservation later became the mission of the National Park Service.

Although a man of deep reverence, Muir shunned churches and felt that a journey into Yosemite Valley, in itself, was a religious experience. His deepest insight was in finding the inner oneness in all of nature, pointing out that no particle of nature is ever wasted. In the wilderness, he believed, one could appreciate fellow creatures, realizing everyone's part in a harmonious whole. John Muir said, "In God's wildness lies the hope of the world, the great fresh, unblighted, unredeemed wilderness" (Grossman and Beardwood 1961:201). Other books written by Muir were: *Our National Parks* (1901), *Stickeen* (1909), and *The Yosemite* (1912). Published posthumously were *Travels in Alaska* (1915), *A Thousand-Mile Walk to the Gulf* (1916), *The Cruise of the Corwin* (1917), and *Steep Trails* (1918).

Rachel Carson (1907–1964)

Writer and scientist Rachel Carson was employed by the United States Fish and Wildlife Service from 1936 to 1952. She authored *The Sea Around Us* (1951) and *The Silent Spring* (1962), which touched off an international controversy over the long-range effects of pesticides. By shocking the world with her presentation of the disasters brewing in the immediate future, she magnified public environmental awareness.

Born in Springdale, Pennsylvania, Rachel Louise Carson came to love the natural environment on her family's farm. She claimed in a biological sketch of herself that in large measure she owed her love of nature to her mother who "taught her as a tiny child joy in the out-of-doors and the lore of birds, insects, and residents of the streams and ponds" (Rothe 1952:101). In later years the study of birds became a hobby. She became an associate member of the American Ornithologists Union and a director of the Audubon Society of the District of Columbia. Carson's writing career began at the early age of ten when she won an award for her contribution to *St. Nicholas* magazine. She entered the Pennsylvania College for Women (now Chatham College) in Pittsburgh with the intent to become a writer. Her interest was redirected to science, however, after taking a course in biology. Graduating with a degree in zoology in 1929, Carson entered Johns Hopkins University for postgraduate study which led to her M.A. degree in 1932. In addition she taught summer school at Johns Hopkins and spent several summers at the Marine Biological Laboratory in Woods Hole, Massachusetts. During this period she also wrote feature articles on scientific topics for the *Baltimore Sunday Sun.* In 1931 Carson joined the zoology staff at the University of Maryland, where she remained for 5 years.

In 1936 Carson accepted a position as aquatic biologist with the United States Bureau of Fisheries (later the Fish and Wildlife Service) in Washington, D.C. She wrote bulletins, leaflets, and other informative literature. In 1947 she was assigned to the bureau's editor-in-chief position (Rothe 1952:101). It was her publication "Undersea," which appeared in *Atlantic Monthly,* that captured the attention of a publisher from Simon and Schuster who asked her to write a full-length book concerning the sea. Her first book, *Under the Sea-Wind,* was published in 1941. The book, subtitled "A naturalist's picture of ocean life," was critically and scientifically praised but sold only 1,400 copies in its first year (De Bruhl 1981:109). During the 1940s she brought in extra money by writing magazine articles while caring for her mother and her late sister's two daughters. She elected not to marry, and her devotion to her family continued throughout her life. While in her fifties, she adopted a niece's son left as an orphan. Work on her second book progressed slowly, taking 3 years. In preparation for the book she learned deep-sea diving at shallow depths and went on a 10-day voyage on a research ship.

In 1949 she was given a Eugene F. Saxton Memorial Fellowship and in 1950 the George Westinghouse Foundation award for outstanding magazine writing in the field of science. Her chapter "Birth of an Island" from her second book, *The Sea Around Us,* appeared in the *Yale Review* in 1950 before the book was published. This work became the basis for the award. In *The Sea Around Us* the reader is taken through successive periods of geological time and warned of the dangers of polluting the oceans with atomic wastes. Published in 1951, it went into a ninth printing and placed on the nonfiction best-seller lists throughout the country. In her chapter "The Long Snowfall," Carson shares scientific insight and emotional sensitivity:

> Every part of earth or air or sea has an atmosphere peculiarly its own, a quality or characteristic that sets it apart from all others. When I think of the floor of the deep sea, the single, overwhelming fact that possesses my imagination is the accumulation of sediments. I see always the steady, unremitting, downward drift of materials from above, flake upon flake, layer upon layer—a drift that has continued for hundreds of millions of years, that will go on as long as there are seas and continents. For the sediments are the materials of the most stupendous "snowfall" the earth has ever seen. . . .

A Guggenheim Fellowship followed and allowed Carson the opportunity for a year's sabbatical from the Fish and Wildlife Service to begin her third book, *The Edge of the Sea* (1956), also a best-seller, which explored the border zone where sea meets land. According to Brooks (1972:8), Carson spent hours preparing for the book by studying minute sea creatures under her binocular microscope. In so doing she felt a spiritual closeness to the individual creatures about whom she wrote. Her fourth book, the landmark *Silent Spring,* appeared in 1962. It set into motion one of the great movements of the century: environmentalism (De Bruhl 1981:109). Carson's grim warning was instrumental in bringing about awareness of the dangers of pesticides and herbicides which could kill everyone and everything if humanity failed to check their use. Her text ended on the following note:

> The "control of nature" is a phrase conceived in arrogance, born of the Neanderthal age of biology and philosophy, when it was supposed that nature exists for the convenience of man. The concepts and practices of applied entomology for the most part date from that Stone Age of science. It is our alarming misfortune that so primitive a science has armed itself with the most modern and terrible weapons, and that in turning them against the insects it has also turned them against the earth.

Attacks on the book reflected the alliance that had developed between science and industry. Monsanto Chemical Company responded, for example, with a report to advise the public of the horrors of a pesticide-free world (De Bruhl 1981:109). But public outcry could not be ignored. President John F. Kennedy read the best-seller with its call to prove "our mastery, not of nature, but of ourselves" (Steinbauer 1990:18). A special presidential advisory committee was appointed to study the issue. It called for more research into the potential health hazard of pesticides and warned against their indiscriminate use. Eventually many pesticides, including DDT, were banned, and others were brought under stricter controls.

After Carson's death by cancer, her books continued to reach new audiences. According to Graham (1970:270), Carson would have preferred to be remembered for her sea books, and it is there that the grandeur of her style is visible. She was not by nature a scolder, but her reverence for life called her to bring the message of modern crisis to public attention in *Silent Spring.* Her unusual blend of science and art was acknowledged through her reception of the Burroughs Medal, an honor that associated her with immortals in nature such as Henry David Thoreau (Gartner 1983:2). In 1990 she was listed by *Life* magazine as one of the most important Americans of the twentieth century.

THE PRACTITIONER PIONEERS

The mere description of nature and the advocacy to preserve it would not have saved it if it were not for the efforts of the practitioners, those who worked in the parks and wilderness areas and struggled to indeed preserve their pristine qualities. Among those are Frederick Law Olmsted, Gifford Pinchot, Stephen Mather, and Aldo Leopold.

Frederick Law Olmsted (1822–1903)

In the early years of the nineteenth century New York City had a number of pleasure gardens which gradually gave way to buildings. By 1855 there were no gardens left, and city residents began visiting cemeteries for their foliage, lawns, and parklike amenities (Olmsted and Kimball 1970:21). Although other cities of America at that time may have had open space and/or small parks, it was the establishment of New York's Central Park under the watchful eye of its architect, Frederick Law Olmsted, that signalled the birth of city parks in the United States.

As complaints about insufficient open space in New York continued, the Common Council of the city acquired an 840-acre parcel of rocky swampland just north of the city's boundaries. In 1857 a nonpartisan board was appointed to develop the park. A design competition was conducted in which Frederick Law Olmsted and Calvert Vaux participated. Their design, nicknamed "Greensward," was awarded top prize in April 1858, a year after Olmsted was appointed superintendent of the yet undesigned Central Park (Doell and Twardzik 1979:42).

Born on April 26, 1822, Frederick Law Olmsted tried his hands at farming, writing, and other professions before embarking on a career as a landscape architect, the profession he created. His upbringing in the New England countryside must have contributed to his interest in extending the natural environment into urban life-style. According to Havard (1989:29), Olmsted had been by all accounts a rather lonely lad. Having the tendency to take long walking trips, he rambled in the country. Jubenville (1976:31) relates the following story about Frederick Law Olmsted:

> Olmsted had an intense interest in the out-of-doors and had developed skills in boating, camping, and so on. As a young man, he spent many hours thinking, dreaming, and studying the outdoors and how it affected man. He also devoted much time to reading about people and nature, philosophy and agriculture, the science and art of landscape gardening. He then became a farmer, raising the traditional agricultural and horticultural crops, and practiced landscaping gardening as well.

Olmsted's first profession was writing. He produced a number of books, the most influential of which were *Journey in the Backcountry* (1860) and *The Cotton Kingdom* (1861), both published by Mason Brothers of New York. His writing was based on his dispatches as a *New York Times* correspondent in the pre-Civil War South. He also helped launch *The Nation,* the respected liberal journal still in circulation today.

Olmsted's second career as environmental planner and designer began with his appointment in 1857, at the age of 35, as the superintendent of Central Park. He had to be politically astute to get such an appointment at a time when New York City was having many political battles over the potential park development. The state legislature passed an act for "the Regulation and Governance of Central Park in the City of New York." The act was a reaction to the lack of progress in developing the park coupled with the corruption and inefficiency of the politicians in charge (Jubenville 1976:31).

Central Park was Olmsted's first and most famous work. The design, which he and British-born architect Calvert Vaux called Greensward, suggested that the development of the park revolve around a number of concepts that are still used in the planning of outdoor recreation areas. The two planners felt that a park is a single, coordinated work of art that should be framed upon a single, noble motive. The park should allow for some relief from the confinement of urban life. Yet uses of the park are not necessarily compatible, and accordingly different areas of the park should be spatially separated to reduce conflict and confusion.

Moreover, the primary purpose of the park is to provide the best practicable means of healthful recreation for the inhabitants of all classes (Olmsted and Kimball 1970).

In 1861 the United States Sanitary Commission, which became the American Red Cross, asked Olmsted to serve as its general secretary. In that capacity he was charged with providing the troops with medical and sanitary supplies. Two years later he was offered the position of general manager of the Mariposa Company, a gold mining company near Yosemite in California. A year later he became Commissioner of Yosemite and Mariposa Big Tree Grove. He was asked to provide a plan for the campus of the new University of California at Berkeley and the Golden Gate Park in San Francisco. He returned a year later to the East Coast to undertake a number of landscaping projects, among which were Prospect Park in Brooklyn, Fairmont in Philadelphia, and Lincoln Park in Chicago.

One of Olmsted's innovative concepts was the idea of a string of green spaces around a city to bring recreation areas close to every citizen. In 1888 he introduced this concept in Boston, with Charles Elliot. The park was nicknamed the "Emerald Necklace." The idea was adapted by many cities.

According to Havard (1989:32) the success of Central Park set off a mania for park building, and Olmsted's trademark sprouted up in the Midwest also, in Belle Isle Park in Detroit, Cherokee Park in Louisville, and Lake Park in Milwaukee. His idea of a commuter village, a suburb of an urban center, such as Riverside is to Chicago, is still regarded as a model for suburban design.

Among many of Olmsted's contributions aimed at underscoring the natural environment in the lives of those who live surrounded by buildings were landscape plans for many campuses and private estates. The Amherst, Trinity, West Point, George Washington, and Stanford campuses have his stamp. Biltmore, the estate of George Vanderbilt in Asheville, North Carolina, was designed by Olmsted. He was also selected to improve the grounds of the Capitol in Washington, D.C., in 1874.

As an advocate of comprehensive city planning, Olmsted urged that a city plan "would make provisions for physical and mental health, safety and transportation needs in commercial and residential district, proper housing and recreation" (Fisher 1986:2). We must point out that Frederick Law Olmsted had no patience with requests for organized recreation. "He saw his parks as places for walking, riding and relaxing in a naturalistic retreat from the harshness of the city" (Knudson 1984:164). This attitude may have caused the friction that led to the rise of the playground and recreation movement of Joseph Lee, Jane Addams, and Luther Gulick which will be discussed later. Today the park and recreation movements have come together.

Gifford Pinchot (1865–1946)

Gifford Pinchot, forester, conservationist, and politician, was born in 1865. Raised in New York City and at his family's wooded estate in Pennsylvania, he was offered a life of luxury and ease. Instead he chose to travel wilderness trails and camp the wooded countryside. Deciding on a career in forestry, Pinchot arranged his own course of study at Yale, since no American university offered a course of instruction in forestry. After graduation, Pinchot studied European forests while doing postgraduate work at the French National Forestry School at Nancy. Upon his return to the United States he began to explore the nation, observing the relationship of people and forests. He noted that forests were facing a desperate and losing struggle to loggers. Trees were vanishing along the eastern seaboard; also the hardwood forests of the South and the pine forests of the Midwest had been decimated. Recognizing that it was only a matter of time before timberlands in the West would disappear, Pinchot advocated the regulation of the commercial use of public and private forests. This included selective cutting, planning for future growth, and the establishment of fire prevention measures (Hirsh 1971:96–98; Wellman 1987:77).

According to James Penick, Jr. (1974:663–64), Pinchot applied principles of scientific forestry in the private North Carolina forest of George W. Vanderbilt. Shortly thereafter, Pinchot became a consultant forester in New York City. At that time he also made surveys of the forest lands of New Jersey and drew plans for two private tracts in the Adirondacks. Greatly affecting Pinchot's future was congressional passage in 1891 of a bill providing that forest reserves could be set aside as government land through a presidential proclamation, since these lands were eventually under his supervision.

In 1896 Pinchot was appointed to the National Forest Commission of the National Academy of Science, which was created to make recommendations on the national forest reserves in the western states. Pinchot joined the majority, which supported U.S. Army protection to defend the reserves from poachers. He voiced his objectives, which favored regulated use through a forest service whose members had received scientific training. Since he was the first American to make forestry a profession, Pinchot presumably saw himself in a leading position (Fox 1981:110–13). The National Forest Commission's study helped bring about authorization for commercial use of these reserves through passage of the Forest Management Act of 1897 (see Chapter 7).

In 1898 Pinchot was named chief of the small Federal Division of Forestry. He immediately began to put into effect his concepts of scientific forestry, establishing a decentralized organization with built-in flexibility. His employees were loyal, dedicated, and competent. With the firm support and backing of President Theodore Roosevelt, he campaigned for Congress to transfer the forest reserves from the General Land Office of the Interior Department to the Department of Agriculture. In 1905 the division was renamed the Forest Service. Pinchot's philosophy can be summed up as follows: "to make the forest produce the largest amount of whatever crop or service will be most useful, and keep on producing it for generation after generation of men and trees" (Penick 1974:664).

Application of Pinchot's conservation policy—using the land and its resources to best serve the people—caused the loss of the support of the preservationist wing of the conservationists. In the Hetch Hetchy debate, for example (see Chapter 7), John Muir supported preservation of the Hetch Hetchy Valley in Yosemite National Park for its beauty. Pinchot supported San Francisco's request to acquire the area as a reservoir. Pinchot's view was brought before congressional hearings in 1913. When asked if he knew of John Muir and his criticism of the bill, he replied:

> Yes, sir; I know him very well. He is an old and a very good friend of mine. I have never been able to agree with him in his attitude toward the Sierras for the reason that my point of view has never appealed to him at all. When I became Forester and denied the right to exclude sheep and cows from the Sierras, Mr. Muir thought I had made a great mistake, because I allowed the use by an acquired right of a large number of people to interfere with what would have been the utmost beauty of the forest. In this case I think he has unduly given away to beauty as against use (Nash 1970:88).

With President Roosevelt's help, Pinchot organized a White House Conference on the Conservation of Natural Resources to which all the nation's governors and other leading figures were invited. Also organized was a National Conservation Commission under Pinchot's chairmanship. The movement declined after Roosevelt left office. Pinchot's conservation policies went under the direct attack of Richard A. Ballinger, appointed Secretary of the Interior by President William H. Taft. Ballinger ended interdepartmental cooperative agreements that had allowed for smooth functioning of the Forest Service. The eventual struggle between the two led to a split in the Taft administration. In 1910 Taft dismissed Pinchot from government service for his public criticism of the president's decision to support Ballinger. His years as a close presidential adviser and molder of public policy influenced Pinchot to turn from forestry to politics. In 1914 he made his first of several unsuccessful attempts at election to the Senate, and that same year he married at the age of 49. In 1922 Pinchot was elected governor of Pennsylvania. Barred from succeeding himself, he tried again for the Senate. In 1930 he was elected to a second term as governor (Penick 1974:664-65).

Pinchot wrote *The Fight for Conservation* in 1910, and his autobiography, *Breaking New Ground,* was published posthumously in 1947. A major heart attack hampered his activities in 1939. He died of leukemia in 1946 at the age of 81. Throughout his years Pinchot was a leader in matters involving conservation. In 1909 he founded the National Conservation Association, which he directed from 1910 until it dissolved in 1923. He was involved in the passage of the Weeks Act in 1911, which provided for the expansion of forest reserves by purchase. A founder of the Society of American Foresters, he served as its president from 1900-1908 and 1910-1911. He continued his interest in forestry by serving as a nonresident lecturer and professor at the Yale School of Forestry, established through a lectureship grant awarded by his father (Penick 1974:665-66).

Gifford Pinchot, the utilitarian champion, viewed conservation as a demand for the welfare of the present generation first, and future generations later. Eventually this view gave way. Forest Service leaders such as Aldo Leopold shifted from a dominance of nature, in the Pinchot tradition, to a more cooperative harmony with nature. As such the foundation was laid for stronger recreation and wilderness values. Pinchot's legacy remained, however, molding Forest Service culture and values of conservation leadership, public service, responsiveness, integrity, a strong land ethic, and professionalism characterized by people who know their jobs and do them well. These values are the bedrock on which the Forest Service stands (see Chapter 7).

Aldo Leopold (1887–1948)

Prominent wildlife ecologist, conservationist, and environmental philosopher Aldo Leopold was born the eldest of four children in Burlington, Iowa. That Mississippi River community afforded him the opportunity to become acquainted with wildlife at a young age. He recognized the steady decline of the wood-duck population and the forest lands. His father, who owned a thriving desk factory, enjoyed the outdoors and nature. Setting an example of sportsmanship for the younger Leopold, he refused to hunt waterfowl during the nesting season, even though such practices had not yet been enacted as laws. While in high school, Leopold kept a journal of his observations of nature, which he continued to do throughout his life. Expected to take over the family business, he instead entered Yale University's Sheffield's Scientific School, where he received his B.S. in 1908. The following year he entered the Yale School of Forestry and received his Master of Forestry degree. After graduation he was employed as a forest assistant in the Apache National Forest in Arizona. He was quickly promoted to supervisor of New Mexico's Carson National Forest. He married Estella Bergere, with whom he had five children, all of whom built their own careers as conservationists and scientists (Rogers and Ford 1989:185-87; Nash 1974:482).

Leopold's career was placed on hold for 16 months when he suffered from a near-fatal attack of Bright's disease, probably as a result of overexposure while camping during an assignment. During his convalescence he read widely including, most likely, the writings of Thoreau, which he had received as a wedding present. Returning to the service he was assigned to the Office of Grazing in Albuquerque, New Mexico, where he led the game protection movement in the Southwest. He received a medal from the Permanent Wildlife Protection Fund, and founded and edited *The Pine Cone,* a quarterly newspaper of the New Mexico Game Protective Association. Although he was once an advocate of the elimination of predators such as wolves and mountain lions, in order to preserve game species such as deer, he changed his opinion, later advocating ecological balance. He warned that overhunting predators allowed for overpopulation and starvation of game species (Flander 1974; Rogers and Ford 1989:187).

After Congress recognized the importance of recreation on national forestlands, Leopold was assigned a leadership role in recreational planning, and he recognized the possible negative impact of recreational use of natural land. In 1918 he interrupted his Forest Service career to become secretary of the Albuquerque Chamber of Commerce. Hopeful that Forest Service management had become less utilitarian in their management of forest resources, he rejoined in 1919. He began to call for the protection of wilderness lands within the national forests. Through his efforts, the Gila Wilderness Area in New Mexico became the first wilderness designated for recreation in 1924. Camping and backpacking were permissible activities in the wilderness area, but tourist campgrounds were not to be provided. This novel plan was articulated 40 years later in the Wilderness Act, thus marking Leopold a "Pioneer of Wilderness" (Rogers and Ford 1989:188; Wellman 1987:137). Devoting the rest of his life to wilderness preservation, he embraced the concept that wilderness preserves were not simply for recreational use. Leopold believed that wilderness preservation symbolized self-restraint in the developing society, served as a reminder of our pioneer legacy, and provided an undisturbed ecosystem for environmental study (Nash 1974:48).

In 1924 Leopold moved to Madison, Wisconsin, to become the assistant director of the Forest Products Laboratory of the Forest Service. Continuing his efforts toward wilderness preservation, he wrote a 1925 article entitled "Wilderness as a Form of Land Use," which developed the notion that Americans no longer needed to conquer the wilderness, but that they needed to set aside large portions of it for posterity. As a speaker at the second National Conference on Outdoor Recreation in 1926, he called wilderness a fundamental recreation resource and urged the development of a national wilderness preservation policy. William B. Greeley, U.S. Forest Service Chief, endorsed his idea, and an inventory of roadless land areas in the United States was conducted and reported at the third National Conference on Outdoor Recreation in 1928. By 1929 the pathfinding L-20 Regulations directed the Forest Service districts to preserve undeveloped land; thus began the movement to establish "primitive areas" within national forests (Rogers and Ford 1989:187–89).

Leaving the Forest Service again in 1928 to conduct game surveys for the Sporting Arms and Ammunition Manufacturers' Institute, Leopold published one of the first intensive studies of game population ever undertaken in the United States, which was given in his *Report on Game Survey of the North Central States* in 1931. During this period, he developed a game management policy for the American Game Protective Association and became known as one of the country's finest authorities on native game. He was referred to as the "Father of Game Management." In 1933 Leopold assumed a newly created chaired professorship of wildlife management at the University of Wisconsin. He held this position until his death (Rogers and Ford, 1989:189). According to Nash (1974:483), Leopold's most important publication was *Game Management* (1933). Leopold's concepts, based on the emerging science of systems ecology, synthesized the most progressive knowledge of population dynamics, food chains, and habitat protection. Basic to his beliefs was the idea that the environment is not a commodity for humans to control but a community to which they belong. This idea stimulated the development of Leopold's most important concept, the "land ethic," which he wrote of in his most widely read book, *A Sand County Almanac*:

> A land ethic, then, reflects the existence of an ecological conscience, and this in turn reflects a conviction of individual responsibility for the health of the land. Health is the capacity of the land for self-renewal. Conservation is our effort to understand and preserve this capacity. . . . It is inconceivable to me that an ethical relation to land can exist without love, respect, and admiration for land, and a high regard for its value. By value, I of course mean something far broader than mere economic value; I mean value in the philosophical sense. Perhaps the most serious obstacle impeding the evolution of a land ethic is the fact that our educational and economic system is headed away from, rather than toward, an intense consciousness of land. . . . In short, land is something he has "outgrown" (Leopold 1966:236).

Leopold's work has been compared to that of Henry David Thoreau and John Muir. *A Sand County Almanac,* published just after his death in 1949, contained a lifetime of his observations of nature and the development of his ideas. It became a classic in environmental literature and a bible for the environmental movement of the past few decades. Before his death Leopold had been active in a number of conservation endeavors which included: member of the council of the Society of American Foresters (1927–1931); elected fellow 1946; appointed by President Franklin D. Roosevelt to the Special Committee on Wild Life Restoration in 1934; director of the National Audubon Society; vice president of the American Forestry Association; founder with Robert Marshall and others of the Wilderness Society in 1935; president of the Wilderness Society in 1939; president of the Ecological Society of America (1947); and member of the Wisconsin Conservation Commission from 1943 until his death (Nash 1974:484).

Although he had no religious affiliation of his own, many consider Leopold's "land ethic" a religious act of consequence to the future of life on earth (Nash 1974:484). While in Wisconsin the Leopold family retreated to their farm in the sand counties and each spring they planted the cropped-out land with pine seedlings, planting as many as six thousand pine trees a year. He said, "We abuse land when we regard it as a commodity belonging to us. When we see land as a community to which we belong, we may begin to use it with love and respect" (Hirsh 1971:150).

Stephen Mather (1867–1930)

Stephen Mather was a staunch conservationist, and he was among the first to urge the United States Congress to set aside areas that are of scenic, historic, and scientific significance. Born in San Francisco, California, he developed at an early age a great affection for the natural beauty of the great Sierras. After his graduation from the University of California, Berkeley, in 1887, he moved to the East Coast and worked as a reporter for the *New York Sun* for 5 years. He returned to California, after his marriage to Jane Floy, to serve as an executive in a borax mining business.

Concerned about the deteriorating condition of the national parks, Mather wrote to this effect to his acquaintance Frank Lane, the secretary of the interior. Lane invited him to direct the national parks, since they did not have a national director, only individuals as superintendents. In 1916 the National Park Service was established, and for 15 years Stephen Mather ran the service as its first director. Up until Mather's appointment there was no federal office charged with this responsibility. In fact the management of the thirteen national parks and eighteen national monuments that were under the auspices of the U.S. Department of the Interior at the time of his arrival "was accomplished by a loose organizational coalition of the Departments of Interior, War, and Agriculture" (Simpson

1989:95). Moreover, the pool from which park superintendents were selected was far from being a professional pool, for most of the appointments were political in nature.

Mather realized that the system needed a vast overhaul, which he set forth to accomplish. The plan was to tackle the problem on five fronts (Shankland 1970:56):

1. Get Congress interested enough in the national parks (a) to make vast increases in their appropriations and (b) to authorize a bureau of national parks.
2. Authorize a bureau and start it functioning.
3. Get the public excited about the national parks.
4. Make park travel easier by promoting wholesale improvements in hotels, camps, and other concessions and in roads and transportation facilities both inside the national parks and outside.
5. Sell national park integrity to the point where Congress would (a) add to the system all appropriate sites possible, (b) keep out inappropriate sites, (c) keep the established sites safe from invasion, and (d) purge the established sites of private holdings.

The first task was not an easy one, since previous attempts to get the U.S. Congress to establish a federal bureau had failed. Mather crusaded, using his own money, to convince Congress of the need for such an office. According to Simpson (1989:96), Mather hired a former newspaper person to start a public relations campaign. He also invited influential persons such as newspaper publishers and editors, railroad executives, and interested congresspersons to tour the parks at his own expense. He personally conducted the tours. Public awareness increased as articles in prestigious magazines such as *National Geographic* and *Saturday Evening Post* as well as in prominent newspapers exalted America's natural beauty and supported the need for its preservation.

In August of 1916 President Woodrow Wilson signed the bill to establish the National Park Service that became Public Law 64–235. The purpose of the National Park Service is "to promote and regulate the use of federal areas known as national parks . . . and to conserve the scenery and the national and historic objects and the wildlife therein . . . and to provide for the enjoyment of the future generations" (Everhart 1972:57).

SUMMARY

This chapter deals with the visionaries and practitioner pioneers who foresaw the need for preservation of areas, establishment of programs, and development of concepts that enhance the pursuit of leisure in natural resources. The transcendentalists, Ralph Waldo Emerson and Henry David Thoreau, venerated nature and called on citizens of this country and the world to respect and preserve it. The depth of their commitment is only overshadowed by the depth of the meaning behind their words. Both men were among the literary giants of the last century.

The scientist-naturalists, John Audubon, John Muir, and Rachel Carson, observed nature and recorded their observations, which were eventually shared with millions of people. Wilderness to them was a place of awe and worship. Their life work spearheaded a preservation movement that gained momentum in the mid 1900s and is in the mainstream of society activity today.

The pioneer practitioners put into practice the concepts gained from the transcendentalists and scientist-naturalists. They laid the foundations for our nation's fledgling institutions that manage our recreational resources. They helped to shape the roles of the park rangers and foresters who manage the natural resources for multiple use or limited use. Frederick Law Olmsted is called the father of the American park, Aldo Leopold was a promoter of wilderness areas and a founder of the Wilderness Society, Gifford Pinchot was the pioneer of American forests, and Stephen Mather was the first director of the National Park Service.

REFERENCES

Atkinson, B., editor (1950) *The Selected Writings of Ralph Waldo Emerson.* New York: Modern Library.

Audubon, J. J. (1960) *Audubon and His Journals,* Vol. I, II. New York: Diver Publications.

Benet, L. (1966) *Famous English and American Essayists.* New York: Dodd, Mead.

Bolton, S. (1954) *Famous American Authors.* New York: Thomas Y. Crowell.

Brooks, A., editor (1950) *The Complete Essays and Other Writings of Ralph Waldo Emerson.* New York, Random House.

De Bruhl, M. (1981) "Carson" in *Dictionary of American Biology, Supplement Seven, 1961–65.* New York: Charles Scribner's Sons.

Doell, C., and L. Twardzik (1979) *Elements of Park and Recreation Administration.* Minneapolis, MN: Burgess.

Elman, R. (1977) *First in the Field.* New York: Mason/Chartu.

Everhart, W. (1972) *The National Park Service.* New York: Praeger.

Fisher, C. (1949) *The Life of Audubon.* New York: Harper and Brothers.

Fisher, I. D. (1986) *Frederick Law Olmsted and the City Planning Movement in the United States.* Ann Arbor, MI: UMI Research Press.

Flander, S. (1974) *Thinking Like a Mountain.* Columbia, MO: University of Missouri Press.

Ford, P. (1989) "John Muir" in *Pioneers in Leisure* H. Ibrahim, editor. Reston, VA: American Alliance for Health, Physical Education, Recreation and *Dance (AAHPERD).*

Fox, S. R. (1981) *John Muir and His Legacy: The American Conservation Movement.* Boston: Little, Brown.

Gartner, C. (1983) *Rachel Carson.* New York: Frederick Ungar.

Gilbert, A. (1914) *More Than Conquerors.* New York: Century.

Graham, Jr., F. (1970) *Since Silent Spring.* Boston: Houghton Mifflin.

Grossman, A., and V. Beardwood (1961) *Trails of His Own.* New York: Longmans, Green.

Harding, W. (1954) *Thoreau: A Century of Criticism.* Dallas, TX: Southern Methodist University Press.

Havard, R. (1989) "Frederick Law Olmsted" in *Pioneers in Leisure and Recreation,* H. Ibrahim, editor. Reston, VA: AAHPERD.

Hirsh, C. S. (1971) *Guardians of Tomorrow.* New York: Viking.

Jubenville, A. (1976) *Outdoor Recreation Planning.* Philadelphia, PA: W. B. Saunders.

Knudson, D. (1984) *Outdoor Recreation.* New York: Macmillan.

Leopold, A. (1966) *A Sand County Almanac.* New York: Oxford University Press.

M.V-D. (1931) "Emerson" in *Dictionary of American Bibliography,* Vol. VI. New York: Charles Scribner's Sons.

Muir, J. (1977) *The Mountains of California.* Berkeley: Ten Speed Press. Reissue.

Muir, J. (1975) *The Story of My Boyhood and Youth.* Dunwoody, GA: Norman S. Berg. Reissue.

Nash, R. (1970) *The Call of the Wild (1900–1916).* New York: George Braziller.

Nash, R. (1974) "Aldo Leopold" in *Dictionary of American Biography.* Supplement Four, 146–50. New York: Charles Scribner's Sons.

Olmsted, F., and T. Kimball (1970) *Frederick Law Olmsted, Landscape Architect, 1822–1903.* New York: Benjamin Blorn.

Penick, Jr., J. (1974) "Gifford Pinchot" in *Dictionary of American Biography.* Supplement Four, 1946. New York: Charles Scribner's Sons.

Rogers, S. E., and P. Ford (1989) "Aldo Leopold" in *Pioneers in Leisure and Recreation,* H. Ibrahim, editor. Reston, VA: AAHPERD.

Ronald, A. (1987) *Words from the Wild.* San Francisco: Sierra Club Books.

Rothe, A., editor (1952) *Current Biography: Who's New and Why, 1951.* New York: H. W. Wilson.

R.W.A. and H.S.C. (1936) "Thoreau" in *Dictionary of American Bibliography,* Vol. XVIII. New York: Charles Scribner's Sons.

Sargent, S. (1971) *John Muir in Yosemite.* Yosemite, CA: Flying Spur Press.

Shankland, R. (1970) *Steve Mather of the National Parks,* 3d ed. New York: Alfred A. Knopf.

Simpson, R. (1989) "Stephen T. Mather" in *Pioneers in Leisure and Recreation,* H. Ibrahim, editor. Reston, VA: AAHPERD.

Steinbauer, M., editor. "The Life of 100 Most Important Americans of the 20th Century." *Life* 13:12 (Fall 1990).

Teale, E. (1962) *The Thoughts of Thoreau.* New York: Dodd, Mead.

Teale, E. (1954) *The Wilderness World of John Muir.* Boston: Houghton Mifflin.

Thoreau, H. (1965) *The Maine Woods.* West Haven, CT: College and University Press. Reprint.

Vickery, J. (1989) "Wilderness Visions." *Backpacker* 17(5):45.

Wellman, J. (1987) *Wildland Recreation Policy.* New York: John Wiley and Sons.

W.F.B. (1934) "John Muir" in *Dictionary of American Bibliography,* Vol. XIII. New York: Charles Scribner's Sons.

Wolf, W. (1974) *Thoreau, Mystic Prophet Ecologist.* Philadelphia, PA: Pilgrim Press.

4 Psychology and the Natural Environment

This chapter concerns itself with the psychology of the outdoor experience. A short presentation of the field of psychology will be given, followed by a presentation of the different attempts to explain the outdoor experience in psychological terms. Attempts at analyzing leisure activities as a unit have not been very fruitful in producing a unified psychology of leisure. Ingham (1986:276) suggested that these attempts can be classified into two approaches: the experiential approach, which emphasizes the subjective qualities of the leisure experience, relying extensively on self reporting with little attempt at discovering the underlying physiological bases that accompany these experiences, and a second approach that includes the reported motivation, satisfaction, and attributes of the leisure experience. While it seems that the two schools do not see eye to eye, since few mutual citations appear in their research, they both tend to agree that perceived freedom (from obligation) and intrinsic motivation (an activity for its own sake) are two concepts to which they can subscribe.

LEISURE AS A STATE OF MIND

The difficulty in viewing leisure as a state of mind only, lies in the fact that leisure is a complex phenomenon. Its physiological, social, and psychological dimensions usually overlap. Analyzing the psychological side of the leisure experience is of interest to a small number of psychologists, who suggested a number of criteria for a bona fide leisure experience to occur.

1. Perceived Freedom. To John Neulinger, at least early in his career, the primary psychological factor in a leisure experience is perceived freedom. This is "a state in which the person feels that what he is doing, he is doing by choice and because he wants to do it" (1974:15). What is relevant is that the person perceives the activity as being freely chosen. Neulinger later added two more criteria: motivation for the leisure activity and the quality of its outcome. According to Kelly these two criteria are attitudinal, criteria which "can be found in almost any context since there is no necessary condition for the perception outside the individual" (1987:26).

2. Autotelic Activities. These are activities that are meaningful in, and by, themselves. Does greater freedom always lead to greater leisure? asked Mannell and Bradley (1986). In their study of freedom and leisure they found that externally oriented subjects were less absorbed in their leisure experience than the internally oriented subjects. Their findings add support to the contention that it is perceived freedom that is critical in determining the experience of leisure.

Perception continues to be of importance in the work of Mihalyi Csikszentmihalyi (1975). To him, the individual's perception of the activity is what matters, not the mere perception of freedom. If the participant perceives the activity as too difficult to handle, anxiety will occur. On the other hand if the activity is perceived as too easy, boredom will result. He labeled the optimum condition for a meaningful experience of an activity as "flow."

3. Beneficial Outcome. The work of B. L. Driver, H. E. A. Tinsley, and their associates concentrated on studying the benefits derived from leisure experiences. B. L. Driver employed a series of scales to measure the outcomes of the recreational use of natural resources (1976). Thirty-nine psychological benefits representing nineteen domains were identified, and the Recreation Experience Preference (REP) scales were constructed to measure these benefits. According to Driver's model, a person will partake of a leisure activity because of his or her expectations for a positively valued benefit.

Driver and Brown (1978) later developed a system that would assist managers of leisure delivery systems to use the information gained from REP scales, which they entitled the Recreation Opportunity Spectrum (ROS). The system presents the leisure environment as a spectrum of opportunity available to the individual. It identifies six levels of "naturalness": primitive, semiprimitive nonmotorized, semiprimitive motorized, roaded natural, rural, and urban. For ROS, the more primitive the setting, the more one can experience solitude, tranquility, self-reliance, and closeness to nature.

There will be more discussion of the psychological benefits of outdoor experiences later in this chapter. Let us first examine the question of whether certain traits in some individuals make them inclined to partake of leisure experiences.

TRAITS AND THE LEISURE EXPERIENCE

Personality traits can be looked upon as continuous dimensions on which individual differences can be observed. Thus different leisure preferences may be arranged quantitatively or qualitatively. Traits are dispositions that may determine leisure behavior. Perhaps the most intriguing trait pertaining to outdoor recreation is the one labeled the type T personality, belonging to the thrill seekers, risk takers, and adventurers who seek excitement and stimulation, giving activity providers great worry and undue headaches.

Leisure and the Type T Personality

According to Farley (1986), the type T personality is on one end of a continuum. At the opposite end of that continuum is the type t personality (with a lowercase "t"), belonging to those who cling to certainty and predictability. Most people fall in between these two extremes. One with a type T personality has a low physiological arousability and therefore seeks excitement. Humans normally seek to adjust to some middle ground between high and low arousals. Some are born with unusually low arousability and are not very responsive to mental or physical stimuli, and these are big T persons who may seek highly stimulating experiences and environments. The precise biological bases for their low arousability is not yet known. Coupled with biological differences are personality traits that set big T persons apart from others: they tend to be more creative, more extroverted, and more experimental, and they tend to take more risks. Activity providers will find more men and younger persons in this category. They are the balooners, mountain climbers, and sky divers.

The number of women in this category is increasing (Mills 1986). The Explorers Club, perhaps the most prestigious organization for adventurers in the world, began admitting women in 1981 and now includes eighty-five women among its 3,000 members. Among the risk activities partaken by women are crossing the Australian outback alone on a camel for five months covering 1,700 miles, ascending Ana Purna's 26,000 feet, and crossing Papua New Guinea alone on foot. Why did Jan Reynolds climb up to 25,000 feet to ski off peak Mustagata in western China? She answers: "The deep smooth satisfaction I felt after I skied off Mustagata, under the golden, fading light of day was something that I will feel very seldom, if ever again, and that I will treasure like a precious jewel" (Mills 1986:27).

Leisure and Personality Traits

In studying personality, theorists describe it as being composed of trait dimensions along a series of continua. These traits affect behavior, including leisure choices. Driver and Knopf (1977) used the Personality Research Form (PRF) to investigate the traits of fifty recreationists and arrived at the following conclusions:

1. Personality traits probably influence the choice of the recreational activity in which a person engages the most frequently. Direct associations were weak in this study, and further research is needed.
2. Selected personality variables are significantly related to the amount of participation in a preferred activity once the choice has been made.
3. Personality traits do influence how important different types of desired consequences (or experiences) are to a recreationist when they decide to engage in preferred activities.

A criticism of the dependence on traits to try to understand leisure behavior is based on the exclusion of the role of the environment, both physical and social. A relatively new interest in environmental psychology helps in discovering the role it plays in leisure behavior.

ENVIRONMENT AND THE LEISURE EXPERIENCE

What role does the environment, particularly the natural environment, play in the motivation for, attitudes towards, and satisfaction with a leisure experience? Stokols and Altman (1987), two experts in environmental psychology, suggested that the emphasis in psychological research in the past concentrated on personal traits and interaction as seen in Table 4.1. The study of traits looks for universal laws, and the study of interaction focuses on the relationships among the elements.

Table 4.1 deals with the units of analysis used in arriving at conclusions concerning the motivation for, and the satisfaction with, certain behaviors. For our purposes neither the trait nor the interactional approach produces a theoretical framework that is useful for the understanding of leisure behavior. We agree with Stokols and Altman (1987:36–37) that in examining the transactional approach, a better understanding of the role of the environment in human behavior will occur. Needless to say, such an approach is also relevant to the

TABLE 4.1 General Comparison of Trait, Interactional, Organismic, and Transactional World Views

SELECTED GOALS AND PHILOSOPHY OF SCIENCE

	Unit of Analysis	Time and Change	Causation	Observers	Other
Trait	Persons, psychological qualities of persons	Usually assume stability: change infrequent in present operation: change often occurs according to preestablished teleological mechanisms and developmental stages.	Emphasizes *material causes,* i.e., cause internal to phenomena.	Observers are separate, objective, and detached from phenomena: equivalent observations by different observers	Focus on trait and seek universal laws of psychological functioning according to few principles associated with person qualities: study prediction and manifestation of trait in various psychological domains.
Interactional	Psychological qualities of person and social or physical environment underlying entities, with interaction between parts.	Change results from interaction of separate person and environment times occurs in accord with underlying regulatory mechanisms, e.g., homeostasis; time and change not intrinsic to phenomena.	Emphasizes *efficient causes,* i.e., antecedent consequent relations, causation.	Observers are separate, objective, and detached from phenomena; equivalent observations by different observers.	Focus on elements and relations between elements seek laws of relations between variables and parts of system: understand system by prediction and control and by cumulating additive information about relations between elements.
Organismic	Holistic entities composed of separate person and environment components, elements or parts whose relations and interactions yield qualities of the whole that are "more than the sum of the parts."	Change results from interaction of person and environment entities. Change usually occurs in accord with underlying regulatory mechanisms, e.g., homeostasis and long range directional teleological mechanisms, i.e., ideal developmental states. Change irrelevant once ideal state is reached, assumes that system stability is goal.	Emphasizes *final causes,* i.e., teleology, "pull" toward ideal state.	Observers are separate, objective, and detached from phenomena; equivalent observations by different observers.	Focus on principles that govern the whole, emphasize unity of knowledge, principles of holistic systems and hierarchy of subsystems; identify principles and laws of whole system.

Transactional	Holistic entities composed of "aspects," not separate parts or elements; aspects are mutually defining: temporal qualities are intrinsic features of wholes.	Stability/change are intrinsic and defining features of psychological phenomena; change occurs continuously; directions of change emergent and not preestablished.	Emphasizes *formal causes,* i.e., description and understanding of patterns, shapes and form of phenomena.	Relative: Observers are aspects of phenomena; observers in different "locations" (physical and psychological) yield different information about phenomena.	Focus on event, i.e., confluence people, space, and time; describe and understand patterning and forms of events; openness in seeking general principles, but primary interest in accounting for event; pragmatic application of principles and laws as appropriate to situations; openness to emergent explanation principles; prediction acceptable if not necessary.

Source: D. Stokols and I. Altman, *Handbook of Environmental Psychology* (New York: John Wiley and Sons, 1987), 75. (Reprinted with permission.)

understanding of the leisure experience in a natural setting, which is the focus of this volume.

Attempts at finding answers to the question posed earlier on the role that the environment plays in the motivation for, attitudes towards, and the satisfaction with certain experiences, including leisure experiences, were made by a new type of psychologists. According to Williams (1986), a shift in the approach of social psychology from examining the person independent of his or her setting to examining the person within his or her setting took place in the late 1960s. Research conducted on the relationship between the individual and the setting can be roughly divided into three perspectives. The first approach, called experimental aesthetics, addresses the meaning of the setting in the person's experience. The second approach, environmental cognition, addresses the meaning of the setting in the experience, which is a reflection of one's perception of the setting. The third approach, called behavioral ecology, concentrates on directly observable behavioral patterns in the natural setting. Williams summarized the findings of each approach as follows:

Experimental Aesthetics. Research in this area focuses on structural or organizational qualities of the natural environment, for example, how manicured is the park? An aesthetic experience takes place following an affective event which is based on a certain level of arousal. This level is dependent on the structural or organizational qualities mentioned. Physiological arousal is experienced as an euphoric feeling and is seen as a major source of intrinsic motivation (Ellis 1973). Yet arousal alone is not a sufficient condition for a leisure experience to take place—arousal could occur at work, for example. And, in fact, too much arousal, even in leisure activity, may end the perception of the activity as leisure. An activity which started as leisure may become too structured.

Environmental Cognition. According to Williams (1986:MIA) the emphasis here is on the perception of the environment, which is looked upon as a source of information rather than a source of stimulation. Interpreting the attributes of a natural setting could give clues as to the recreationally significant conditions and outcomes, for example, a fully packed slope will provide for an exhilarating skiing experience. Since human beings tend to categorize and label their experiences, accumulation of categories and labels could be useful, particularly to the manager of a leisure delivery system. Tversky and Hemenway (1983) applied this technique to natural environments: they identified their attributes and asked the subjects to identify the activities that were appropriate to each category, a process which could prove helpful to planners and managers, as will be presented under a subsequent section on the experience of nature.

Behavioral Ecology. This approach is concerned with how people experience and behave in everyday settings, including natural settings and not in research-contrived settings. Settings become the basic units that are used in analyzing behavior within a given space and for a specific time span, for example, studying behavior within a park at a particular season takes into consideration not only the physical attributes of the setting but also the psychological and social dimensions of behavior in the recreation place. This approach could prove helpful to managers and providers of leisure experiences including experiences in natural settings.

THE EXPERIENCE OF NATURE

Rachel and Stephen Kaplan (1989:ix) tried to answer a number of questions on the effect of the natural environment on human behavior:

1. Is the effect of nature on humans as powerful as it intuitively seems to be?
2. What lies behind the power of environments that not only attracts the appreciation of individuals but that makes them able to restore some people to healthy and effective functioning?

3. Are some natural patterns, such as meadows, more effective than others such as lakes?

Using the findings of research conducted in the area of environmental psychology, these authors came to a number of conclusions on the experience of nature. To them, humans, who are very sensitive to the spatial property of the environment, tend to categorize environments on the basis of their perception. This process produces a number of coherent perceptual categories. For example, research shows that wide-open, undifferentiated vistas as well as dense, impenetrable forests fail to provide information about one's whereabouts. These two settings tend to fall within a distinct category. Scenes that convey a sense of orderliness, such as manicured settings, are a second category, and a third category includes forests that are transparent, allowing sunlight to filter down, providing information on both accessibility and direction. These last two categories are preferred, which means that to attract the most people, a natural setting must include informational patterns that are readily interpretable. These informational patterns are, in many instances, provided by nature itself, and not necessarily by humans, as seen in the case of the transparent forest.

Natural Setting and Information Rate

Mehrebian and Russell (1974:84) suggested that since an outdoor natural setting is characterized by having a smaller density and slower pace of change than does an artificially created setting, whether outdoor or indoors, a natural setting has a lower information rate, which is preferred by many recreationists. The concept of information rate can be explained by comparing two paintings, one containing two colors, the other eight colors, which means that the latter has four times as much "information" to deal with than the former. But the idea behind information rate is much more complicated and requires the use of mathematical formulas that are beyond the scope of this volume. Suffice it to say that the number of colors in the above examples is not the only variable to be considered in calculating the information rate. The space that each color covers and its location on the painting are taken into consideration as well.

According to Mehrebian and Russell, the acceleration of information input triggers the General Adaptation Syndrome suggested by Selye (1956). The syndrome begins with a burdensome physiological arousal and a concomitant feeling of displeasure. A high rate of information input takes place in crowded, condensed areas. As a result, "understandably, those residing in congested urban areas express unrelenting desires to visit simple and rural settings such as national parks" (Mehrebian and Russell 1974:205). These two authors concluded that the relationship between internal behavioral patterns and external rhythms suggests a mechanism that directly relates arousal to information rate from the environment. It is not surprising therefore that the tempo of work, and even recreation, in an urban setting far exceeds that in a natural setting.

Preference for Natural Settings

Kaplan and Kaplan (1989:49) suggest that in the context of natural settings, those with human intrusions are less preferred than those where nature dominates. In the meantime in very open as well as in blocked areas, where it is difficult to anticipate what might happen, preference tends to be very low. In other words, humans respond negatively to both a high rate of information and to a paucity of information. This suggests that preference for a setting is related to how effectively a person can perceive himself or herself functioning in it. Humans prefer a setting where they feel safe, comfortable, and competent. Nonetheless, a natural setting could pose an enticing challenge to some persons or to others under their charge who may have low arousability. A challenge of nature may help some people to achieve optimal arousability (see the section on leisure and the type T personality).

Wilderness as a Challenge

In the past, the wilderness posed a challenge to human beings in their quest for survival. Although survival in the wilderness is rarely a concern in modern life, programs in wilderness survival abound and are used to experience self-discovery and enhance self-concept. Burton estimates that there are over 300 wilderness programs in the world today, many of which are directed toward special populations such as juvenile delinquents, the handicapped, and psychiatric patients. These programs are conducted for young people, adults, and seniors (1981). Outward Bound was established by Kurt Hahn and is considered a prototype wilderness challenge program (Ewert 1989). The first Outward Bound school started in Wales in 1941 to train merchant marines to withstand the challenge they had to face during World War II. The school was later moved to the United States. Burton listed five features of Outward Bound and similar programs:

1. A contrasting or novel physical environment.
2. A challenging set of problem-solving tasks.
3. A duration of at least 7 days.
4. A leader or instructor.
5. A group of at least four participants.

A longitudinal study of outdoor challenge programs was conducted for a period of 10 years, 1972–1981, by the U.S. Forest Service's North Central Forest Experimental Station in Michigan's Upper Peninsula. Table 4.2 shows the types and numbers of participants.

Most of the features in the program remained constant over the 10 years. The practice hike on the first evening led to instruction in map reading and compass orientation. The participants went through dense, trackless forest for the first few days. A 48-hour solo hike followed, which ended with a hike on one's own back to base camp to continue the program with others. Although the program lasted for 2 weeks in its first 8 years, it was reduced to 9 days in the last 2 years. The research tools used to evaluate the program remained the same: questionnaires were filled out on the first day and at various times, including the end of the program, and participants kept journals to record their feelings and reactions.

A number of pertinent questions were raised by Kaplan and Kaplan (1989:147): Does it re-

TABLE 4.2 Outdoor Challenge Participants

Year	No. groups	Boys	Girls	Adults	Total
1972	2	10			10
1973	2	12	8		20
1974	1	8			8
1975	3	13	6	4	23
1976	3	6	12	8	26
1977	2	6	3	3	12
1978	3	6	7	6	19
1979	3	5	3	3	11
1980	6	11	11	13	35
1981	2		3	9	12
Total	27	77	53	46	176

Source: R. Kaplan and S. Kaplan, *The Experience of Nature* (Cambridge: Cambridge University Press, 1989), 124. (Reprinted with permission.)

quire a wilderness setting to experience self-discovery and enhance self-concept? Does it take 2 weeks to achieve such gains? Are there shortcuts to achieve a sense of tranquility and a feeling of oneness with nature? Kaplan and Kaplan stated that Thoreau wrote of nature as a source of spiritual renewal and inspiration. A surprising outcome of wilderness research that they reviewed has been the remarkable depth of spiritual impact wilderness experiences have on those who participate in them. Yet the participants spent much less time in the wilderness and were engaged in less overtly cerebral activities than those of Thoreau. His quest for tranquility, peace, and silence was called a quest for *serenity* by Kaplan and Kaplan. In addition, the researchers seem to find two more quests occurring among the participants, *oneness* and *integration.* Kaplan and Kaplan concluded that they had not anticipated this research program would provide them with an education in the ways of human nature. They felt they had been introduced to some human concerns that are bound to broaden the conception of human motivation and priorities.

What is intriguing about the aforementioned results is that they correspond with what Aristotle suggested in the remote past—that the greatest of leisure experiences is contemplation, which he placed at the top of the hierarchy of leisure experiences. Human life has become so complicated that contemplation is rarely a priority in human affairs. Understanding the nature of human motivation as it relates to human needs may shed more light on the nature of the leisure experience.

MOTIVATION, HUMAN NEEDS AND LEISURE

Among the many attempts to understand human behavior, including leisure behavior in the natural setting, is the attempt to answer the question, what motivates a person to partake of a certain activity? The question of motivation has been a major part of research in psychology from the beginning. Researchers concentrated their efforts on finding a single factor that is responsible for human behavior. The terms *instinct* and *drive* were used to describe this single factor.

Early Motivational Theories

According to Levy (1979), the term instinct was used to describe a variety of human behaviors in the pre-World War I era. In his classical textbook *The Principles of Psychology,* William James defined instinct as the capability to act so as to bring about a certain event. Human beings possess many instincts, among which is the one (or ones) that motivate(s) us to play, recreate, and participate in leisure activity. The question became, which instinct? Although the scholars who attempted to answer this question at that time agreed that humans are instinctually motivated to play and recreate, they did not agree on the nature of the instinct. Accordingly, four classical theories were forwarded, which could lead to contradictory outcomes given the same circumstances (Levy 1979:155). The *surplus energy theory,* which explains play as based on leftover energy, contradicts the *relaxation theory* and the *teleological theory,* which explain leisure behavior in terms of the future, and all three contradict the *recapitulation theory,* which explains leisure behavior in terms of our past. Although these theories have been, in general, discarded by the leisure scholars, they served as precursors to some of the recent interpretations that there is a biological basis for play and recreation (Eisen 1988).

The concept of drive was adopted by psychologists after World War I and was used to explain human behavior as attempts to reduce certain needs. An essential group of needs were termed primary needs, which were deemed necessary for survival. Human beings attempt to reduce the need for food, warmth, exertion, sex, and security and accordingly achieve homeostasis, a state of physiologic equilibrium. Another group of needs were called secondary needs, which stem from the circumstances that surround our attempts to satisfy the primary needs. Among these needs are achievement, affiliation, creativity, curiosity, gregariousness, risk, self-abasement, and self-assertion. Later the terms basic needs and acquired needs were used to describe primary and secondary needs, respectively. A working session on needs and leisure held at the University of Illinois on May 22, 1977, generated the following list of seventeen needs or groups of needs deemed important to leisure behavior (Crandall 1980):

1. Enjoying nature, escaping civilization
2. Escape from routine and responsibility
3. Physical exercise
4. Creativity
5. Relaxation self-improvement, ability
6. Social contact
7. Meeting new people
8. Contact with prospective mates
9. Family contact
10. Recognition status
11. Social power
12. Altruism (helping others)
13. Stimulus seeking
14. Self-actualization (feedback, self improvement, ability utilization)
15. Challenge, achievement, competition
16. Killing time, avoiding boredom
17. Intellectual aestheticism

Crandall suggested that behavior, including leisure behavior, is caused by the interaction of the person and the situation (1980:51). According to Levy (1979:159), Murray advocated that behavior is a function of the interaction of needs (of persons) and pressure (from the environment). This interactive model was used to identify a number of environmental contexts. In the area of leisure behavior the person-environment interactive model was used to explain the need for a leisure experience. Levy (1977) reported that the need for relaxation is one of the leading motives for engaging in leisure behavior, a position which supported Dumazedier's claim to the same (1967). A few years later Ruskin and Shamir (1984) identified relaxation as a key motivation in leisure behavior. Does this mean that if pressure (from the environment) ceases and the need (of the person) to relax subsides, that he or she will decline any further engagement in leisure activities? Perhaps the answer lies in the fact that human needs are much more complicated than simple responses to primary and secondary drives, as shown in the following study.

London et al. (1977) found that the respondents in their study viewed leisure activities in terms of three need dimensions: liking, feedback, and positive interpersonal involvement. In order to develop a psychologically meaningful categorization of leisure activities, the authors took three elements into account simultaneously: the activities, the needs they satisfy, and individual differences in perceiving the activity. Factor analyses were applied, and the findings seem to replicate activity dimensions found in previous studies. These activity dimensions as well as need dimensions are shown in Table 4.3.

While leisure activity in a natural setting is not listed in Table 4.3, the data in the table show that a leisure activity may fulfill a multitude of needs: feedback, liking, and positive interpersonal involvement. Tinsley and Kass (1978) found their results to be in substantial agreement with previous studies. Needs such as catharsis, independence, advancement, getting along with others, reward, understanding, activity, ability, utilization, exhibition, and sex appear to be most leisure activity specific.

Need, as a concept, became central to the attempts to give psychological meaning to leisure behavior. But what is a leisure need? While most of the studies cited here treated it as being stable, Iso-Ahola and Allen (1982:142) suggested that the need for leisure is not stable but is

TABLE 4.3 Core Matrix Based on Rotated Factors

		NEEDS FACTORS		
Individual Factor	**Activities Factors**	**Feedback**	**Liking**	**Positive Interpersonal Involvement**
I	Sports	60.1	45.5	9.9
	Cultural-Passive	−53.2	58.0	−16.4
	Productive-Intellectual	59.9	38.3	−34.5
II	Sports	−17.1	37.0	−35.4
	Cultural-Passive	−94.3	25.3	−66.1
	Productive-Intellectual	−8.1	8.9	−86.4
III	Sports	77.2	65.8	64.0
	Cultural-Passive	−47.7	40.6	−14.9
	Productive-Intellectual	61.3	29.4	−10.9

Source: M. London et al., "The Psychological Structure of Leisure Activities, Needs, People," *Journal of Leisure Research* (National Recreation and Park Association, 1977):260. (Reprinted with permission.)

always changing. They refer to a leisure need as a perceived reason for participating in a variety of activities. One of the assumptions in their approach to the leisure need involves change across situations under which needs change from before to after participation (1982:142). After testing this hypothesis they concluded that leisure needs seem to be sensitive to the influence of the leisure experience itself. Does this mean that the need to participate in leisure activity is changing? Or is the way that it is fulfilled changing? For example, the need to survive motivates humans to eat. Varieties in foods have nothing to do with the need to survive, but food does. On that very basic level, survival is supreme whether we like the food or not. Whether the eating companions were stimulating or not, humans will have to eat to survive. Is (are) the leisure need(s) that powerful? The answer may lie in the hierarchy of needs.

The Hierarchy of Human Needs

Although the idea of placing human needs in a hierarchy is credited to Maslow (1968), the concept was forwarded by a medieval Arab scholar, Ibn Khaldun, who talked about human desires as being hierarchical, beginning with bodily appetite and progressing to the desires for security, companionship, and superiority and on to the final desire for leisure. The original conceptualization of Maslow included a need (desire) for leisure, as shown in Figure 4.1.

Levy presented the classification of Maslow's five prepotent need sets as shown in Figure 4.2. The idea of prepotency proposes that these five levels of needs are arranged in a hierarchical order.

Self-actualization has been presented by Maslow as a positive ideal of mental health. It has been suggested that leisure experiences, particularly in a natural setting, can help in achieving such an ideal (Scott 1974). Young and Crandall (1984) tested such a claim by comparing wilderness users to nonusers in their self-actualization scores. Using Shostrom's Personal Orientation Inventory (1974), which is the most validated measure of self-actualization as defined by Maslow, the authors concluded that while wilderness activities may be used by some individuals as self-actualizing experiences, the relationship between self-actualization and wilderness use is very weak.

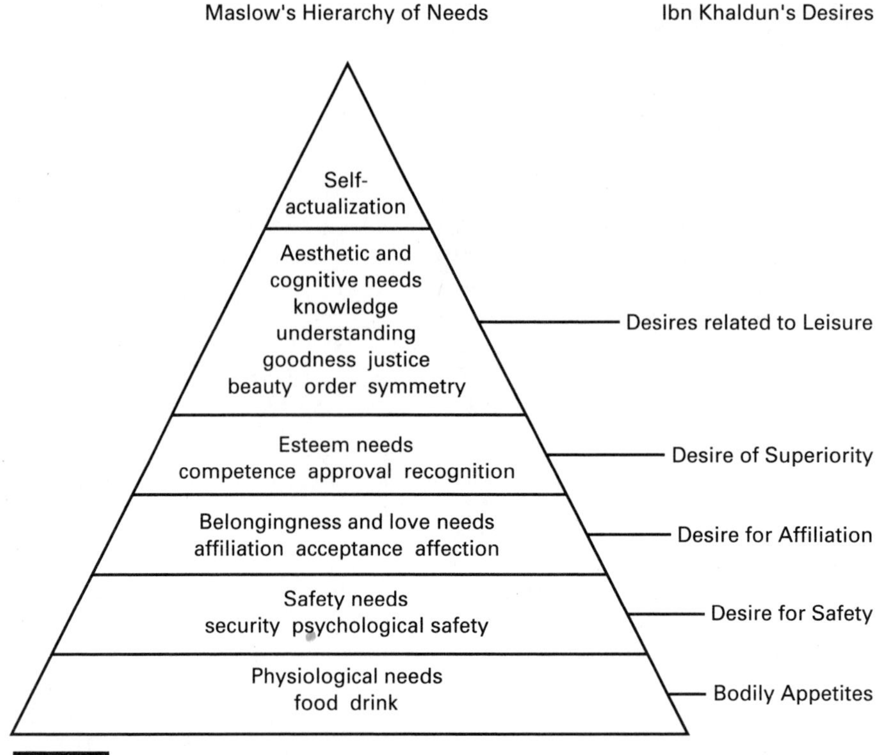

FIGURE 4.1 Representation of Ibn Khaldun's list of human desires versus Maslow's hierarchy of needs.

SATISFACTION, ATTITUDES, AND THE LEISURE EXPERIENCE

If the need for a leisure experience is satisfactorily met, does satisfaction then become the causative factor in further participation in the same leisure experience? Does this lead to a positive attitude toward the leisure experience?

Satisfaction and Leisure

The National Academy of Science Report (1969) suggested that in order to understand recreation better, research should be directed at the analysis of satisfactions sought in it. Hawes (1979) sought to study satisfactions derived from participation in leisure activity in an attempt to steer away from the traditional head count. His nationwide exploratory study utilized fifty selected leisure pursuits along with twelve "satisfaction" statements. A sample of 603 females and 512 males was used for analysis. Of interest is Hawes' finding that individuals can relate their participation in outdoor, active, group-oriented pursuits more readily to satisfactions than they can participation in indoor, passive, primarily individual pursuits.

According to Ingham (1986), leisure satisfaction is very much linked to motivation. He quoted Calder and Shaw as stating that "satisfaction derives from an activity which is perceived as intrinsically motivated because of a person's need to feel a sense of personal causation in his or her action" (1975:599). This brings us back to the notion of perceived freedom as being crucial to a bona fide leisure experience. Graef et al. (1983) found that intrinsically motivated

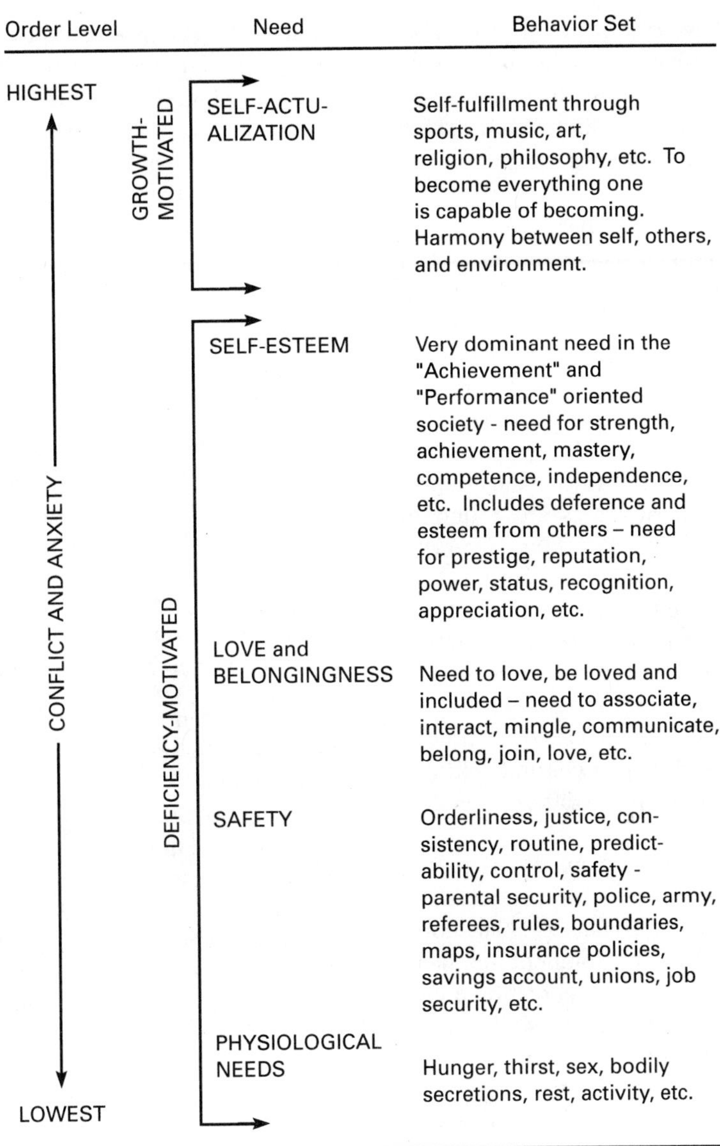

FIGURE 4.2 A schematic representation of Maslow's hierarchy of human needs.

activities, be they leisure activities or otherwise, lead to a state of happiness. Their study supports the proposal that satisfaction with an activity depends on perceived intrinsic motivation, which relies on a freedom in its choice.

Attitudes Toward Leisure

A concept which is much related to, and in fact to some extent dependent on, satisfaction is attitude, which is defined as a learned predisposition to respond in a constantly favorable or unfavorable manner to a given object (Crandall 1979). Implicit in this definition is the fact that attitudes can predict behavior. This requires that attitudes be measured. Attempts at measuring attitudes toward leisure activities are found in Burdge (1961), Neulinger (1974), and Crandall and Slivken (1979). Not only have applications of the scales constructed by these scholars been very limited, but the one constructed by Burdge has deteriorated considerably over time, as per the author himself (Yoesting and Burdge, 1976). Neulinger (1974) suggested that leisure attitudes manifest themselves clearly in cultural settings, a point that will be covered in a different section of this volume.

Studies in leisure attitudes could be useful for managers and providers of leisure programs, as shown by Wohlwill and Heft (1977). In comparing attitudes towards development and facilities in two contrasting natural recreation areas, the authors suggested that one-time study would not suffice in providing information on leisure preference. A feedback model was suggested, the basis of which is the interaction of three separable factors: objectives of the agency, attitude of visitors (to the natural areas), and the impact of visitations.

Another use of attitudinal studies is the effect of leisure participation on the attitude towards the environment. Jackson (1986) found that participants in "appreciative" activities (for example, cross-country skiing and hiking) hold more pro-environmental attitudes than participants in "consumptive" activities (for example, snowmobiling and trail biking). He also found that participation in outdoor pursuits is strongly related to attitudes towards those specific aspects of the environment necessary in pursuing the activities than to general issues of environmental concerns.

PSYCHOLOGICAL BENEFITS OF LEISURE EXPERIENCE

Societies sanction activities that are deemed beneficial to the membership collectively and individually. Leisure activities provide many sorts of benefits. Some are economic, others are social, and many are psychological. Tinsley (1986) lists the psychological benefits derived from leisure experiences as measured by the Recreation Experience Preference scale as follows:

- Achievement
- Leadership/autonomy
- Risk-taking
- Successful use of equipment
- Family togetherness
- Social contact
- Meeting/observing new people
- Learning/discovery
- Relationships with nature
- Reflection on personal values
- Creativity
- Nostalgia
- Exercise/physical fitness
- Physical rest
- Escape personal and social pressures
- Escape physical pressure
- Security
- Escape family
- Enjoyment of temperature

Earlier Tensley and his associates (1977) identified forty-four psychological benefits derived from leisure experiences. Utilizing the Leisure

Activities Questionnaire (LAQ), information from over 4000 respondents participating in eighty-two activities produced the following two lists:

I. Leisure Activity Specific Benefits that can be gained to a significantly greater degree through participation in some leisure activities than by participation in other leisure activities.

Ability utilization	Cooperation	Security
Achievement	Creativity	Self-esteem
Activity	Dominance	Sentience
Advancement	Exhibition	Sex
Affiliation	Independence	Social service
Aggression	Nurturance	Social status
Authority	Play	Supervision
Catharsis	Responsibility	Understanding
Compensation	Reward	Variety

II. Leisure Activity General Benefits that are gained to approximately the same degree from leisure activities.

Abasement	Justice	Self-control
Autonomy	Moral values	Succorance
Counteraction	Order	Task generalization
Deference	Recognition	Tolerance
Harm avoidance	Rejection	
	Relaxation	

The authors derived the following psychological benefit factors that can be used in distinguishing among leisure activities:

Self-expression
Companionship
Compensation
Security
Service
Intellectual aestheticism
Solitude

Psychological Benefits of Outdoor Experience

So far what has been listed refers to leisure experiences in general, be they active, passive, indoor, or outdoor. Does the leisure experience that takes place outdoors have its own characteristic benefits? Brown (1981) identified a number of highly valued experiences gained during outdoor recreational activities which came from many sources, covering research conducted in many sections of the United States, as follows:

Relationship with nature
Escape from physical pressures
Escape from social pressures
Achievement/challenge
Autonomy/independence/freedom
Reflection on personal values
Recollection/nostalgia
Risk-taking/action/excitement
Meeting/observing other people
Use and care of equipment
Exercise/physical fitness
Being with one's recreation group
Learning/exploration
Family togetherness
Privacy
Security
Physical rest

As can be clearly seen, relationship with nature was one of the most valued experiences in a natural setting, along with being with one's recreation group, a topic to be discussed in the next chapter.

Despite the tremendous desirability of an outdoor recreation experience, there are reasons why many individuals may not participate. Barriers to participation in outdoor experience can be psychological. Examples are the different types of phobias. These exaggerated fears may include fear of dogs, snakes, insects, and other animals which could render an outing miserable. A social phobia triggered when one is exposed to possible scrutiny by others would render group camping difficult. Other barriers are cultural, which fall within the parameters of the next chapter.

SUMMARY

This chapter discusses the psychological elements of an outdoor experience. As defined, leisure is predicated as a state of mind, which by its nature impacts one's psychological orientation. Yet there are personal traits that may affect one's involvement in a leisure experience. Additionally, the external environment plays a decisive role in the enjoyment of such an experience. For instance, humans prefer places where they feel safe and comfortable and where they believe they can function effectively.

When the leisure experience is taken in the out-of-doors, a new set of elements is taken into consideration. In general, the average natural setting with a lower information rate, that is, with a low number of stimuli, has relatively limited appeal to humans. Sometimes a natural setting has too few stimuli, as in a barren area, which may lead to boredom. On the other hand, too many stimuli may lead to anxiety. Thus humans seek natural areas with optimum stimuli.

What motivates a person to participate in an outdoor activity in the first place is discussed in relationship to the prevailing theories of motivation. The psychological benefits from such participation as reported in the literature are presented. While fulfilling primary needs may serve to reduce physiological disequilibrium, secondary needs may include the need for achievement, affiliation, curiosity, self-assertion, and the like. Leisure pursuits provide opportunities to fulfill these needs.

REFERENCES

Brown, P. (1981) "Psychological Benefits of Outdoor Recreation" in *Social Benefits of Outdoor Recreation* by J. Kelly. Champaign, IL: University of Illinois.

Burdge, R. J. (1961) *The Development of A Leisure Orientation Scale.* Unpublished thesis. Columbus, OH: Ohio State University.

Calder, B. J., and B. M. Shaw (1975) "Self Perception of Extrinsic Motivation." *Journal of Personality and Social Psychology* 31:599–605.

Crandall, R. (1979) "Attitudes Toward Leisure" in *Leisure: A Psychological Approach,* H. Ibrahim and R. Crandall, editors. Los Alamitos, CA: Hwong Publishing.

Crandall, R. (1980) "Motivations for Leisure." *Journal of Leisure Research* 12:45–54.

Crandall, R., and K. Slivken (1979) "Leisure Attitudes and Their Measurement" in *Social Psychological Perspectives On Leisure and Recreation,* S. Iso-Ahola, editor. Springfield, IL: C. Thomas.

Csikszentmihalyi, M. (1975) *Beyond Boredom and Anxiety.* San Francisco: Jossey-Bass.

Driver, B. L., H. Tinsley, et al. (1976) "Quantification of Outdoor Recreationists' Preferences" in *Research, Camping and Environmental Education,* B. Vander Smissen, editor. University Park, PA: Pennsylvania State University. HPER Series No. 11.

Driver, B. L., and R. C. Knopf (1977) "Personality: Outdoor Recreation and Expected Consequences." *Environment and Behavior* 9:169–195.

Driver, B. L., and P. Brown (1978) *The Opportunity Spectrum Concept and Behavioral Information in Outdoor Recreation Resource Supply Inventories.* Fort Collins, CO: Rocky Mountain Experiment Station of the U.S. Forest Service.

Dumazedier, J. (1967) *Toward a Society of Leisure.* New York: Free Press.

Eisen, G. (1988) "Theories of Play" in *Understanding Leisure* by G. Gerson et al. Dubuque, IA: Kendall and Hunt.

Ellis, M. (1973) *Why People Play.* Englewood Cliffs, NJ: Prentice Hall.

Ewert, A. (1989) "Kurt Hahn" in *Pioneers in Leisure and Recreation,* H. Ibrahim, editor. Reston, VA: AAHPERD.

Farley, F. (1986) "The Big T in Personality." *Psychology Today* (May):44-50.

Graef, R., M. Csikszentmihalyi, and S. M. Gianimo (1983) "Measuring Intrinsic Motivation In Everyday Life." *Leisure Studies* 2:155-68.

Hawes, D. K. (1979) "Satisfaction Derived from Leisure Pursuits: An Exploratory Nationwide Survey." *Journal of Leisure Research* 10:247-64.

Ibrahim, H. (1988) "Leisure, Idleness and Ibn Khaldun." *Leisure Studies* 7:51-58.

Ingham, R. (1986) "Psychological Contribution to the Study of Leisure, I." *Leisure Studies* 5:255-79.

Iso-Ahola, S. C., and J. Allen (1982) "The Dynamics of Leisure Motivation: The Effect of Outcome on Leisure Needs." *Research Quarterly for Exercise and Sport* 53:141-49.

Jackson, E. (1986) "Outdoor Recreation Participation and Attitudes toward the Environment." *Leisure Studies* 5:1-23.

Kaplan, R., and S. Kaplan (1989) *The Experience of Nature: A Psychological Perspective.* Cambridge: Cambridge University Press.

Kelly, J. (1987) *Freedom To Be: A New Sociology of Leisure.* New York: Macmillan.

Levy, J. (1977) "Leisure Module: A Multidimensional Approach to the Study of Leisure Behavior." Paper presented at the Symposium on Leisure Research, Congress of the National Recreation and Park Association, Las Vegas, NV. October, 1977.

Levy, J. (1979) "Motivation for Leisure: An Interactionist Approach" in *Leisure: A Psychological Approach,* H. Ibrahim and R. Crandall, editors. Los Alamitos, CA: Hwong Publishing.

London, M., R. Crandall, and D. Fitzgibbons (1977) "The Psychological Structure of Leisure Activities, Needs, People." *Journal of Leisure Research* 9:252-63.

Mannell, R., and W. Bradley (1986) "Does Greater Freedom Always Lead to a Greater Leisure?" *Journal of Leisure Research* 12:215-30.

Maslow, A. (1968) *Toward a Psychology of Being.* Princeton, NJ: Van Nostrand.

Mehrebian, A., and J. Russell (1974) *An Approach to Environmental Psychology.* Cambridge, MA: MIT Press.

Mills, J. (1986) "Living on the Edge." *Women's Sports and Fitness* (March):24.

National Academy of Science (1969) *A Program For Outdoor Recreation Research.* Washington, D.C.: National Academy of Science.

Neulinger, J. (1974) *The Psychology of Leisure.* Springfield, IL: C. C. Thomas.

Ruskin, H., and B. Shamir (1984) "Motivation as a Factor Affecting Males' Participation in Physical Activity During Leisure Time." *Society and Leisure* 7:141-61.

Scott, N. (1974) "Toward a Psychology of Wilderness Experience." *Natural Resources Journal* 14:231-37.

Selye, H. (1956) *The Stress of Life.* New York: McGraw-Hill.

Shostrom, E. (1974) *Manual for the Personality Orientation Inventory.* San Diego, CA: Educational and Industrial Testing Service.

Stokols, D., and I. Altman (1987) *Handbook of Environmental Psychology.* New York: John Wiley and Sons.

Tinsley, H. (1986) "Motivations to Participate in Recreation: Their Identification and Measurements" in *The President's Commission on Americans Outdoors: A Literature Review.* Washington, D.C.: U.S. Government Printing Office.

Tinsley, H., T. C. Barrett, and R. A. Kass (1977) "Leisure Activities and Need Satisfaction." *Journal of Leisure Research* 9:110-120.

Tinsley, H., and R. A. Kass (1978) "Leisure Activities and Need Satisfaction: A Replication and Extension." *Journal of Leisure Research* 10:191-202.

Tversky, B., and K. Hemenway (1983) "Categories of Environmental Scenes." *Cognitive Psychology* 15:23-42.

Williams, D. (1986) "Psychological Perspectives on the Environment. Experience Relationship: Implications for Recreation Resources Management" in *The President's Commission on American Outdoors: A Literature Review.* Washington, D.C.: U.S. Government Printing Office.

Wohlwill, J. F., and H. Heft (1977) "A Comparative Study of User Attitudes Towards Development and Facilities in Two Contrasting Natural Recreation Areas." *Journal of Leisure Research* 9:264-80.

Yoesting, D. R., and R. J. Burdge (1976) "Utility of a Leisure Orientation Scale." *Iowa State Journal of Research* 50:345-56.

Young, R., and R. Crandall (1984) "Wilderness Use and Self Actualization." *Journal of Leisure Research* 16:149-60.

5 The Social Aspect of Outdoor Experiences

The last chapter concentrated on the individual as an individual, on his or her traits, needs, attitudes, and satisfactions as they relate to leisure pursuits, with an emphasis on outdoor experiences. This chapter will look at the individual as a member of a society and as a member of its subgroups. The roles of culture and subculture are probed as they pertain to leisure behavior. These considerations are important to both managers and recreation participants.

THE NATURE OF HUMAN SOCIETY

As a system, the human society is composed of different structures and performs certain functions. Regardless of their historical time or geographical locations, all human societies are, to a great extent, similar when it comes to social structures and social functions. Following are the basic social institutions of society.

The Family

The family could be nuclear, referring to a male, a female, and their offspring, or extended to include blood and marriage relatives. The family performs the following social functions:

1. Sexual satisfaction
2. Reproduction
3. Socialization
4. Psychological sustenance
5. Economic support

Religion

Religion is the second most important major social institution in almost all human societies. Durkheim (1915) suggested that religion is the outcome of the collectivity of ritual. As indicated, rituals played and still play a very important role in the lives of individuals and societies. One view is that ritual was and is the cement that holds the society together. Such is the Durkheimian view, which was challenged by Victor

Turner (1982), who believes that in addition to its role in maintaining the social order, the ritual was the locus for rudimentary forms of leisure pursuits.

An important function of religion is that it determines that which is sacred and that which is profane. In other words, it dictates what is acceptable human behavior. The role of religion, then, is very important in leisure pursuits. An example comes to us from colonial America, when the Puritans and Quakers prohibited horse racing and frowned on mixed dancing.

Political Institutions

The political structure of any society revolves around the source of power and its allocation. According to Mayhew (1971:127), the organization of political power can produce the following functional capacities in a population:

1. Internal peace
2. External protection and expansion
3. Goal attainment
4. Interest alignment

The Economic System

In economic systems we see an evolution from the very simple systems of barter to the complex system of the stock market, long-term financing, and multinational corporations. One way of looking at the level of economic sophistication of a given society or region is through a tripartite classification based on the location of the bulk of the labor force, as follows:

1. Primary economy: agriculture and extractive business dominate
2. Secondary economy: industry and manufacturing dominate
3. Tertiary economy: most of the labor force in services and trade

American society has reached a tertiary economy in that most of its labor force is in services and trade. In the leisure sector of the economy, this means an increasing number of workers and professionals are seen in the leisure delivery systems, be they public or private.

Technology

Technology is both a social and a material institution. It refers to the organization, dissipation, and utilization of knowledge in the service of societal goals. Social technology includes formal and informal education, the media, and voluntary education. Material technology, on the other hand, includes science and industry.

Beside the five social institutions of the family, religion, government, the economy, and technology, secondary institutions such as play and work groups play important roles in our lives. Accordingly a number of social processes help the individual learn the roles he or she is supposed to play in these institutions. Foremost among these social processes is socialization.

SOCIALIZATION AND LEISURE BEHAVIOR

A human being is born socially neutral. Socialization is a process through which the culture of the community and/or society is instilled in the individual. This process, which begins at birth and continues throughout life, helps the individual to correctly play his or her assigned roles in the culture. Playing the role, as expected by the social groups with which the individual interacts, not only gives the needed admission to these groups, but also serves as the threshold to self-esteem. Humans play many roles in their lifetime, among which are leisure roles. Leisure roles include, but are not limited to, being a player on a sports team, an actor in a school play, or a member of the church choir.

The Age of Socialization into Leisure

As previously stated, socialization is a continual process, yet social scientists agree that there is a certain age when socialization is so powerful that the activity partaken could become a lifelong practice. There are a number of studies that focused on the age of socialization into outdoor recreational activities. Bevins et al. (1968) found that childhood participation in hunting and fishing was highly correlated with adulthood participation in the same activities. Hendee (1969) found that 70 percent of the adult participants in wilderness camping had taken their first camping trip before the age of 15. Bradshaw and Jackson (1979) investigated socialization into leisure activities in general and concluded such socialization takes place before age 13. Yoesting and Burkhead (1973) found that individuals who were active in outdoor recreation continued to be active in outdoor life during their adult years, and that the opposite was true, inactive children continued being inactive in these activities as adults. Their finding does not support Kelly's (1983) study that humans could be socialized into new activities in adulthood. On the other hand, it is possible that the recreationally inactive persons were not exposed to outdoor recreational activities. Had they been, they may have become active in them.

Agents for Socialization into Leisure

The family seems to be the most influential agent of socialization into leisure generally, and also into outdoor recreational activities. Kelly (1974) found that of the 744 activities reported in his study, 63 percent began with the family, most of which were either sports or outdoor recreational activities.

The school is considered by many as another socializing agent for leisure. Yet there is a paucity of studies on the role of the school as a socializing agent into outdoor recreational pursuits. As early as 1936, Neumeyer and Neumeyer suggested that in preparation for leisure, the school should include in its curriculum nature studies and activities for the exploration of the out-of-doors. Many of the school districts in the United States provide for some form of outdoor experiences, but the impact of these offerings has not been investigated. One of the early studies conducted in the United States showed that the less educated go more often to parks, but how much they appreciate nature is not known (White 1955). Also, do the less educated go to the park because it is the only leisure outlet available, compared with the theatre, the movies, and the zoo where the middle and upper classes tend to go more often because they can afford them?

Few empirical studies have been conducted on the role of youth serving agencies (YMCA, Boy Scouts, Campfire Girls, and the like) in experiences in the outdoors. Kleiber and Rickards (1981) suggested that the outdoor experiences provided by these agencies serve as a theatre. Experiences in that theatre, according to Shepard (1977), enhance the process of gathering and consolidating a range of skills at the end of childhood in preparation for the emancipation from the parental home. Outdoor activities also serve to prepare the young for initiation into puberty.

Places of worship, whether they are churches, synagogues, or temples, have been providing outdoor recreational activities for many years for both youth and adults, yet there is hardly any empirical study on their role in enhancing, or reducing, the leisure experience in natural settings. According to MacLean et al. (1985:262), outdoor experiences are so valued by the sponsors that they assume part of the expense and provide volunteer counselors. A recent trend in the provision of these activities is to organize family camping.

Private and publicly sponsored camps are also agencies for outdoor experiences. The private camp may be operated by a nonprofit organization such as the YMCA or for profit by an entrepreneur. In the second case, only the well-to-do can afford to attend. Public recreation and park agencies also conduct both day and resident camps for the young. While day camps are found in almost every region of the United States, resident camps operated by public agencies are found mainly in the West. Here, too, there is little empirical research conducted on the role of day or resident camps in the socialization into outdoor leisure experiences or the benefits derived from such experiences.

Family outings such as this one among the giant sequoias of Kings Canyon National Park in California were once reserved only for the well-to-do. Today they are within reach of the majority of citizens.

Enjoying the view from a picnic table in Biscayne National Park in Florida, this couple has increased leisure time during retirement.

Leisure as a Socializing Agent

Csikszentmihalyi (1981) advocated that socialization into leisure, or more precisely into expressive activities, is important because these activities could serve as the criteria by which instrumental activities are evaluated. In general, an instrumental activity is one in which the end-product is supreme (fishing commercially for the purpose of selling the fish) as opposed to an expressive activity in which the process is more important (fishing for sport). Although most leisure pursuits are to some extent expressive, Csikszentmihalyi's notion does not pertain solely to leisure activities. Work could be expressive to some. His point, though, is that expressive activities are used in the growing years as criteria by which other activities are evaluated.

Humans are socialized into a number of leisure roles in their lives. They might move from being young athletes to adult poker players to senior RV campers. In the process they become acquainted with the requirements for playing any of these roles. In the evolution of societies, leisure roles were not crucial to the society's welfare or to its members' survival. These roles are becoming increasingly important to the members of industrial/bureaucratic societies. According to Kelly (1983:115), leisure may be found to be central rather than residual in some phases of life, mainly in the growing years and in retirement.

Two spheres that affect human behavior are leisure behavior in primary and secondary groups, discussed in the following sections.

PRIMARY GROUPS AND LEISURE PURSUITS

Human dependency on others, which is witnessed from birth, tends to continue throughout life. Dependency is greater in the early years of life and remains at a high rate during childhood. Having the longest childhood among animals, including primates, makes humans more dependent on others for a longer period than are other animals. Humans are by necessity social, and they enter a greater number of social circles of different sizes and importance in their life course. The smallest of these circles consists of only two persons and is called a dyad. Other circles include primary face-to-face groups such as family and peers and secondary groups such as schoolmates, neighbors, and coworkers. Dyads, primary groups, and secondary groups are all socializing agents as well as providers of outdoor recreational opportunities.

Vacationers experience the out-of-doors from the luxury of an ocean liner in Milford Sound, New Zealand.

Dyads and Outdoor Pursuits

Perhaps the first dyadic relationships to occur are mother-infant, father-infant, and two-siblings dyads. It was Eric Erikson who brought to our attention the importance of the mother-infant dyad in the particular relationship of ritualization (Erikson 1977). Manning pioneered a theoretical study on backpacking and the basic needs of infants that included information on how to plan for toddlers and how to make hiking acceptable to children (1975). Empirical studies on the roles of dyads in outdoor pursuits are lacking, yet studies on their impact on organized sport exist (Eitzen and Sage 1989:83–93).

Another form of dyadic relationship begins in the late teens and early adulthood, and these partnerings can lead to sexual intimacy, which could be enhanced through leisure pursuits. It is no wonder that commercial advertisements use outdoor and leisure scenes intimating closeness between lovers.

Other than sexual dyads, dyadic friendships also exist in the form of two-person long-term relationships. The role leisure pursuits, including outdoor experiences, play in dyadic relationships is unknown, but one often sees two unattached men or women engaging in camping, hiking, and picnicking. The role of leisure pursuits in enhancing, or destroying, their friendship remains to be investigated. Intimacy is not limited to dyads—it can be seen in small primary groups of family and peers.

The Family and Outdoor Pursuits

Despite the changes that have taken place in the family structure, its main function as the dominant socializing agent in human societies remains the same. This is despite the encroachment of school, church, and peers on this particular function, let alone the most recent assault by the powerful medium of television. The family provides both the physical setting and the social setting for leisure activities. Glyptis and Chambers (1982) reported that not only is most free time spent at home, but the home is a physical source for many leisure pursuits, providing space and equipment. The backyard as a space for outdoor pursuits has not been thoroughly studied, but it is evident that many pursuits take place there. Suffice it to say that gardening is one of the most participated in outdoor activities in this country (see Table 5.1).

According to Orthner (1976) leisure, in general, contributes to marital cohesion. In an earlier study, West and Merriam (1970) found that outdoor recreational activities lead to family cohesiveness. According to Kelly (1981:47), the critical variable for the building of family cohesion is the nature of the interaction. He suggested that the work of B. L. Driver indicates that the perceived benefits of outdoor experiences include two elements for effective interaction: the strengthening of significant relationships and the enjoyment of companionship.

Peers and Outdoor Pursuits

According to Cheek (1981:49), leisure literature, both professional and investigatory, describes outdoor recreational activities as taking place in a group of around four persons. And although escaping urban pressure is an important motivational factor in participating in a wilderness

TABLE 5.1 Adult Participation in Leisure-Time Activities, by Selected Type: 1985

Type of Activity	Number (Millions)	Percent
Flower gardening	77	44
Swimming	72	41
Fishing	60	34
Bicycling	58	33
Bowling	44	25
Jogging	40	23
Softball	39	22
Camping	37	21
Weight training	33	19
Billiards	33	19
Aerobics	32	18
Motor boating	28	16
Volleyball	28	16
Calisthenics	26	15
Basketball	26	15
Hunting	25	14
Golf	23	14
Baseball	23	13
Tennis	23	13
Table tennis	21	12
Canoeing	16	9
Rollerskating	16	9
Horseback riding	16	9
Target shooting	16	9
Skiing	14	8
Racquetball	14	8
Waterskiing	12	7
Touch football	11	6
Sailing	9	5

Source: U.S. Bureau of the Census, *Statistical Abstracts of the United States: 1987* (107th edition) (Washington, D.C.: U.S. Government Printing Office, 1986), 215.

experience, hardly anyone does it alone. The solitude sought is usually a communal, not a solo, solitude. Based on the findings of the research conducted in the 1960s and 1970s, Cheek concluded that it is either kinship or friendship that is the basis of the social group of an outdoor leisure pursuit. Earlier, Cheek and Burch (1976) reported that members of an outdoor leisure pursuit group tend to remain physically together and to share decision-making, two elements that add to cohesion and intimacy.

Cheek also suggested that outdoor pursuits offer a unique opportunity for a human being to behave as a human being, a condition denied him or her in the too-rational industrial society. He asked;

> When may humans exalt their natures in addition or perhaps in contrast to their exactedness? . . . Only under very limited conditions; for limited periods of time; and with very few others of their kind. Outdoor recreation activities appear to offer the unique combination of these conditions in modern industrial societies (Cheek 1981:51).

To Cheek the most important use of outdoor settings is the all-too infrequently recognized function—to feel and exchange indications of special caring and liking.

LEISURE AND SECONDARY GROUPS

Other than the primary groups where frequent face-to-face interaction takes place, secondary groups play important roles as agents for leisure. Among secondary groups are schoolmates, youth groups, and adult groups.

Outdoor Pursuits with Schoolmates

It seems the first programs that provided outdoor experience through the school were made possible by the Kellogg Foundation of Battle Creek, Michigan, in the early 1930s (Smith et al. 1970). The Clear Lake Camp and its staff were made available to three Michigan schools. Students from grades 4 through 12 went to the camp for a period of 2 weeks. The program was enhanced when an act was passed by the Michigan legislature in 1945 which enabled school districts to acquire camps and operate them as a part of the regular educational and recreational programs of the schools.

According to Burrus-Bammel and Bammel (1990), there is sufficient evidence to conclude that outdoor/environmental education programs have the potential to produce benefits for both the participants and society. And although results of specific program evaluation have very little generalizability, the results have a remarkable consistency of demonstrative positive change. Malsam and Nelson (1984) reported an increase in the trust and respect for teachers, leaders, and other students after a 4-day residential program for sixth graders. According to Burrus-Bammel and Bammel (1990), programs do not have to be of long duration in order to promote lasting effects.

Outdoor Pursuits with Youth Groups

Youth groups include members of youth-serving organizations, young church members, and members of youth clubs. The idea of organizing activities for the young under the tutelage of adults is an old idea which emanated, most probably, from the need to socialize them in a manner acceptable to the elders. Neumeyer and Neumeyer (1936) wrote of Junglingsverein, a club of young unmarried men in Bremen, Germany, in 1709. By 1863, when George Williams organized his first YMCA in London, England, many of these Junglingsverein existed (1949:328). The YMCA and YWCA were urban youth centers concentrating on serving youth and saving them from urban decay.

According to Turner (1985:29), YMCA camping experience could go as far back as 1867, but actual records show that the Brooklyn, New York, YMCA took thirty boys on a trip described as camping out in 1881. In April 1884 the first encampment took place by Orange Lake, New Jersey, when YMCA boys went boating and fishing there. Bible study took 1 to 2 hours each day. A year later, some YMCA boys went to an encampment by Lake Champlain, New York, under the leadership of Sumner Dudley, after whose death it was named Dudley Camp. In 1908 the camp was moved to Westport, New York. Today there are 275 YMCA resident camps encompassing approximately 100,000 acres. In addition, the YMCAs administer close to 1300 day camps reaching approximately 1.5 million young people annually (Turner 1985:36).

The youth group that conducted its activity in natural settings from its inception was the paramilitary Boy Scouts, initiated by Lord Robert Stephenson Smyth Baden-Powell in London in 1908 at the heel of the British defeat in the Boer War in South Africa. His idea was to utilize the outdoors in developing physical fitness, self-reliance, and patriotism. According to Rosenthal (1986:162), the notion of the scout as a serviceable citizen trained to follow orders in wartime is at the heart of scouting. Yet Baden-Powell tried from the very beginning to define the movement as antimilitaristic (Rosenthal, 1986:190). In fact Baden-Powell was much influenced by Ernest Thompson Seton, one of the great artist/naturalists of this century. Seton founded the Woodcraft Movement after his immigration to America in the 1880s. Rosenthal states, "For Seton the natural wisdom of the woods was the highest available to man: individuals had to learn to trust their instincts and open themselves to the prompting of nature in order to achieve their full realization as human beings" (1986:65). Today the scout movement, for both boys and girls, has touched the lives of many young Americans. The numbers speak for themselves, as shown in Table 5.2.

According to Butler (1961:7), Dr. Luther Gulick and his wife, who were instrumental in establishing the Boy Scout movement in America in 1910, became interested in having a similar movement for girls. Moreover the Gulicks were convinced that the scouts' educational curriculum at the time was inadequate: "The solution was the establishment of the private camp which could teach all the topics the directors felt might be missing in the stringent but stagnating curricula of the day" (Ford 1989:87). The

TABLE 5.2 Boy Scouts and Girl Scouts, Membership and Units: 1960 to 1985 (in thousands)

Item	1960	1965	1970	1975	1978	1979	1980	1981	1982	1983	1984	1985
Boy Scouts												
Membership	5,165	5,733	6,287	5,318	4,493	4,285	4,318	4,355	4,542	4,689	4,755	4,845
Boys	3,783	4,231	4,683	3,933	3,303	3,176	3,207	3,244	3,244	3,245	3,567	3,657
Tiger Cubs	x	x	x	x	x	x	x	x	84	124	145	169
Cub Scouts	1,865	2,064	2,438	1,997	1,788	1,716	1,696	1,643	1,609	1,569	1,493	1,499
Boy Scouts	1,647	1,850	1,916	1,503	1,123	1,058	1,046	1,101	1,126	1,116	1,078	1,063
Explorers	271	317	329	434	392	402	477	499	606	758	941	1,024
Adults	1,328	1,502	1,604	1,385	1,190	1,109	1,110	1,111	1,117	1,122	1,098	1,090
Total units (packs, troops)	130	145	157	150	134	129	129	130	132	134	135	134
Girl Scouts												
Membership	3,419	3,647	3,922	3,234	3,084	2,961	2,784	2,829	2,819	2,888	2,871	2,802
Girls	2,646	3,030	3,248	2,723	2,511	2,389	2,250	2,276	2,247	2,281	2,247	2,172
Daisies	x	x	x	x	x	x	x	x	x	x	x	61
Brownies	x	1,072	1,259	1,160	1,245	1,206	1,115	1,110	1,120	1,163	1,172	1,128
Juniors	x	1,416	1,509	1,188	977	926	894	916	874	847	801	735
Cadettes	x	443	395	301	218	193	172	170	169	176	170	151
Seniors	x	99	85	74	57	52	46	45	41	40	40	40
Adults	773	617	674	511	573	572	534	553	572	607	624	630
Total Units (troops)	164	153	164	159	159	157	154	157	160	165	166	166

Source: U.S. Bureau of the Census, *Statistical Abstracts of the United States: 1987* (107th edition) (Washington, D.C.: U.S. Government Printing Office, 1986), 220.

Gulicks encouraged William Chauncy Langdon, a poet and a consultant on pageantry, to organize an outing experience for a dozen girls from Thetford, Vermont. The girls were called Camp Fire Girls, and they were set up in three ranks of achievement—Wood Gatherers, Fire Makers, and Torch Bearers—ranks that are still in use today. The philosophy of Ernest Thompson Seton was more influential in this movement than in the scout movement. The Woodcraft Ranger approach, teaching youngsters to use their hands as rangers do, with its strong American motif, Indian Lore, is very clear in the Camp Fire Girls. Now, after admitting boys, the organization is called simply Camp Fire.

From a single club in Hartford, Connecticut, in 1860 the Boys' Club grew to a nationwide organization with over one million boys in more than 700 clubs across the United States. The club is designed to serve boys of urban centers. A similar movement for girls started in 1945. Both Boys' Clubs and Girls' Clubs offer outdoor experiences for their members whenever possible (MacLean et al. 1985).

Outdoor Pursuit with Adult Groups

For the lack of a better word, the term adult groups is used to include the stable membership of voluntary associations, the makeshift groups that form around an outdoor experience, and workplace-centered groups.

Voluntary associations include both instrumental and expressive groups. The instrumental associations usually revolve around professions and occupations and are concerned with specific outcomes for their members, usually of extrinsic value such as wage increases and fringe benefits. Sometimes they also offer the membership some leisure and expressive activities. On the other hand, expressive voluntary associations revolve around activities that are of intrinsic value. The following are some of the expressive associations that deal with nature: American Camping Association, American Youth Hostels, National Audubon Society, Save-the-Redwood League, and the Sierra Club.

DEMOGRAPHIC CORRELATES OF OUTDOOR PURSUITS

The demographic factors that have an affect-effect relationship to leisure behavior include age, life course, gender, occupation, and residence. Although these factors provide a moderate basis for outdoor recreation participation (Manning 1985), nonetheless they should be presented and discussed.

Leisure Pursuits and Age. Play is witnessed among the upper orders of the class mammal of the animal kingdom. Play activities of young humans seem to go through stages that are universal despite differences in race, ethnicity, or cultural background. These activities are usually very simple and become increasingly complex as the society itself becomes more complex. Play may seem to be so natural that learning to play seems unnecessary, but learning to play helps one appreciate the intrinsic values of certain activities which may reflect on instrumental activities (activities that may lack the element of play) (Csikszentmihalyi 1981).

Leisure education is a recently coined term which describes the acquisition of skills for the enjoyment of leisure activities both now and in the future. Leisure counseling, also a recently coined term, is used to describe the process used by a professional to help a person choose and become involved in a leisure pursuit. While a young age is ideal for the acquisition of a desire for lifelong leisure pursuit (Bevins et al. 1968, Hendee 1969, and Bradshaw and Jackson 1979), leisure counseling would be useful to the adult who needs help in selecting a meaningful leisure pursuit.

Leisure Pursuits and Life Course. As life progresses we assume new roles, including leisure roles. Also, some roles are given up, sometimes by choice and sometimes not by choice.

Examples of the taking on and abandoning of leisure roles are provided in Snyder and Spreitzer (1978:57–62). Young men and women were found to assess their own competence as athletes, and if they believed that their competencies were below group expectations, they tended to withdraw from the leisure activity. Kelly (1983:50) suggested that participants in leisure pursuits evaluate not only their satisfaction with the activity but also its long-term benefits. Accordingly they form attitudes, either negative or positive, toward the activity. This process of evaluation goes on throughout the course of life.

As life progresses, new leisure roles should be taken on and old ones abandoned. Examples of leisure roles in different phases of life are given in Bammel and Burrus-Bammel (1981), Kelly (1983), and Gerson et al. (1988) and are shown in Table 5.3.

Leisure Pursuits and Gender. Although the gap separating the two sexes has been narrowed somewhat in recent times, recent studies show that they still play differently. DiPietro (1981) reported on his experiments when three young girls and three young boys, age four and half years, were compared as they organized themselves to play together. The boys' play was rougher and more aggressive. Does this mean that society still expects boys to be more aggressive? Or indeed is there is a biological difference in the type of play imprinted in the brain of the human male as opposed to the imprint in the brain of the female? In their study of 75 adolescents, Csikszentmihalyi and Larson (1984) found that the males spent over six hours a week on sports while the females spent half that time on sports. Also, the girls spent 31 percent of their waking hours on the arts (music, painting, drawing) while the boys spent half that much time on these activities. Is the difference in in-

TABLE 5.3 Leisure Pursuits and Age Groups

Kelly	Bammel and Burrus-Bammel	Gerson et al.
I. *Preparation Period*: (Birth to early 20s)	*Teens*: Active participation in vigorous form of recreation activity both outdoors and indoors.	*Birth-2*: Individual play, expanding horizon, becoming aware of environment. *2-3*: Beginning of imitative and creative play.
Play in childhood varies with age and sex and is a means of interaction and a way of self-discovery.		*3-4*: Parallel and symbolic play, social play, begin aquatics.
	Twenties: Active participation, especially in outdoor activities. Wilderness backpacking, canoeing, etc.	*5-7*: Large muscle development. Family activities important. *8-9*: Greater desire to participate and to succeed. *9-12*: Team sport. Sexual differences in play.
II. *Establishment Period* (Mid 20s to mid 40s)	*Thirties*: Less active and less frequent participation in outdoor recreation. Camping replaces backpacking.	*13-18*: Group influence, instant gratification, need to accept socially acceptable activities.
Leisure roles complement family and community roles. Investment in leisure pursuits increases after children are grown.	*Forties*: Less active participation, more spectating. Car or van camping replaces tent camping.	*19-22 (Identity)*: Testing intimate relationships. Test self through high-risk activities. *23-30 (Intimacy)*: Peak of physical prowess. Active in sports and high-risk activities.
	Fifties: Greater emphasis on spectating for the great majority. For a minority, renewed attempt at physical conditioning. Bowling.	*30-38 (Establishment)*: Activities of couples, social and community services. Children may be used as prestige symbols.
III. *Culmination Period*: (Mid 40s on)	*Sixties*: Spectating and decrease in physical character of activities. Gardening.	*38-55 (Adjustment)*: Less physical activity. Participation more spontaneous. Preference in smaller and family groups.
More choices in leisure pursuit are seen. Reestablishment of marital dyad occurs.		*55-65 (Mellow)*: Enjoyment of cultural and creative activities. Expansion to large groups for entertainment.
	Seventies: Some new sport activities may begin with retirement. Golf, swimming, shuffleboard, etc.	*65+ (Seniors)*: Physical fitness paramount. Preference for activity with same age group.

terests biologically based? Or is it a product of cultural orientation? Society and societal values seem to play an important part in determining interests, at least when it comes to considering the time freed from familial and civic obligation, as shown in the next study.

According to Bialeschki and Henderson (1986), despite the emancipation of the American woman and her entry into the work world, she is still expected to keep family and home together. In cross-cultural studies, men were found to have more time for leisure in Egypt (Ibrahim

More expensive outdoor vacations may include snorkeling in the Caribbean. A pool on Cozumel Island parallels the azure blue waters with just a strip of white sand separating them. Day trips to ancient Mayan ruins on the Yucatan are favorite adventures for a break from snorkeling or scuba diving.

et al. 1981), Israel (Shamir and Ruskin 1983), the USSR (Moskoff 1984), Norway (Fasting and Sisjord 1985), and Canada (Shaw 1985). How the imbalance of leisure time between genders is reflected in outdoor pursuits has not been empirically investigated. Are there more men recreating outdoors than women? According to Kelly (1983:38), while gender differences in the type of leisure activities pursued are negligible, women tend not to participate in hunting and drinking.

Leisure Pursuits and Occupation. Among the early studies conducted on the relationship between occupation and leisure is Clarke's (1956). He used five levels of occupational groupings: professional, managerial, clerical, skilled, and unskilled workers. Members of the top occupations tend to go to theatres, concerts, lectures, and art galleries and to read, study, and play bridge more often than do members of other occupations. Greater attendance at sports events and commercial recreation is witnessed among members of the middle occupations. Members of the lower occupations tend to attend bars and watch television more often than do the members of the higher occupations. Burdge (1969) used the same classification of occupations and concluded that members of higher occupations seem to participate in greater variety of leisure pursuits, including more participation in outdoor recreational pursuits. Bultena and Field (1978) found occupations to be significantly related to participation in outdoor activity, supporting Burdge's conclusion that persons occupying higher-paying positions tend to participate in more leisure pursuits, including outdoor ones.

Roberts (1970:28–29) suggested that occupations affect leisure pursuits and are affected by them as follows:

1. Manual occupations demand a great deal of time and energy, leaving manual laborers unable to cultivate active leisure pursuits.
2. Manual occupations are physically arduous and therefore may result in a need to spend leisure simply relaxing or recuperating.
3. Less financially well-off persons do not have substantial incomes to invest in leisure interest outside the home and do not have discretionary money to spare for club subscriptions, recreational equipment, and the like.
4. White-collar families have a greater opportunity to travel abroad, and this exposure may stimulate other leisure interests. Certain leisure activities appear to trigger participating in others.

5. Education awakens white-collar people to leisure interests found outside the sphere of the manual worker.
6. A white-collar worker's job may create more opportunities for one to acquire skills that can be exploited during leisure time.
7. Leisure habits emerge as status attitudes, which are generated at work and spill over into and influence people's leisure lives.

Tied somewhat to one's occupation is one's income, which affects affordability of certain leisure pursuits. Data from the United Media study (1983) show that households where income is $40,000 or more have 70 percent book readers, 29 percent other material readers, and only 1 percent nonreaders in comparison to 35 percent book readers, 54 percent other material readers, and 11 percent nonreaders in homes with incomes of $11,000 or less. Is income a factor in the selection of outdoor pursuits? According to Burdge (1969) the more expensive outdoor activities seem to appeal to the person in the higher levels of occupation with higher incomes, which agrees with the studies cited.

Leisure Pursuits and Residence. To what extent does the rural-urban dichotomy affect one's leisure pursuit? A study by Knopp (1972) showed that the urban male is more inclined to seek solitude and exercise than is his rural counterpart. Bammel and Burrus-Bammel (1981) stated that urban residents tend to watch TV, go to the movies, and enjoy swimming more often than do rural dwellers who appreciate the amenities provided in a natural setting, such as solitude and sentience. Rural dwellers also like to hunt. Allen et al. (1987:33) surveyed rural households to determine their satisfaction with their leisure activities. Their neutral responses led the authors to conclude that rural residents may be seeking more leisure opportunities than the ones provided in nearby areas. Their conclusion confirms Foret's conclusions (1985) drawn when she investigated the relationship between life satisfaction and leisure activities of rural and urban residents. Her data show that age and residence caused no significant differences in leisure satisfaction. However, urban dwellers were more recreationally active than were rural residents.

Sessoms (1963) reviewed most of the studies on age, residence, and occupation conducted up until 1963 which had to do with demographic characteristics and concluded the following:

1. Active participation in outdoor pursuits declines with age.
2. Greater participation is witnessed with higher income.
3. Varied participation increases with higher occupational prestige.
4. More participation is observed among urban residents.
5. Less participation is seen by families with small children.

According to Manning (1985:17), research conducted on the demographic correlates since 1963 has tended to corroborate Sessoms' findings. The studies cited by Manning show near uniformity in who is using the outdoor recreation resources: younger persons of higher socioeconomic status. This does not mean persons from a particular social class. In fact, the whole concept of social class is being replaced by another concept: life-style.

LEISURE PURSUITS AND LIFE-STYLE

It seems that the combined effect of all the demographic variables listed above—age, life course, education, occupation, and residence—produce a certain life-style. According to Bradshaw (1978:2) life-style refers to "the generalized ways people act and consume, that is somewhat more fine grained than subcultures—but more general than specific groups or experiences." Gattas et al. (1986) believe that to ask what one does in one's free time is not as important as asking with whom one spends one's free time. They believed leisure research should focus on groups and not activities.

An elaborate study of life-styles in America was conducted by Mitchell (1983). Through a survey of 800 questions, 1600 persons over 18 years of age, living in the contiguous forty-eight states, were divided into four comprehensive groups and subdivided into nine life-styles as follows:

I. NEED-DRIVEN GROUPS

1. *Survivor Life-style:* Terrible poverty marks these 6 million survivors of whom only 22 percent made over $5,000 in 1979. Their daily activities are heavily influenced by their high age, low education, and limited resources. They are absent from pursuits requiring a high level of physical energy such as active, and even spectator, sports. They score high on watching television and cigarette smoking.
2. *Sustainer Life-style:* Angry and combative, sustainers have not given up hope. Living on the edge of poverty with an income about $11,000 in 1979, the 11 million sustainers are heavily eschewed to machine, manual, and service occupations. Sustainers attend horse racing more than any other group, watch nature on TV, like to go fishing, read tabloids, and see a lot of X-rated movies.

II. OUTER-DIRECTED GROUPS

3. *Belonger Life-style:* Generally regarded as middle-class America for whom soap opera and romance magazines were created to fill their emotional needs, belongers watch their spending and are not given to faddish activities. These 57 million Americans have a deep-seated desire to fit in rather than stand out. They prefer home and family activities and such pursuits as gardening, baking, and watching television.
4. *Emulator Life-style:* The emulators are intensely striving people seeking to be like the achievers (see item 5). Despite their young age, a median of 27 years, they had an average income of over $18,000 in 1979. Their activities show they are second in conformity to belongers and tied with achievers. The 16 million emulators like bowling and pool, visit night clubs and arcades, and eat at fast food establishments.
5. *Achiever Life-style:* These are the driving and the driven people of the American system. Most of the 37 million persons in this group are the professionals such as teachers, lawyers, and physicians. They score high in such activities as playing golf, attending cultural events, drinking cocktails, traveling for pleasure, and reading magazines and newspapers.

III. INNER DIRECTED GROUPS

6. *I-am-me Life-style:* A shift from an outer to an inner focus of attention brings a discovery of new interests that redirect life goals. Here active sports participation, artistic work, and readership of specialized magazines is distinctive. I-am-mes, 8 million of them, have the highest of ownership of recreational gear such as backpacking, exercising, and bicycling equipment.
7. *Experiential Life-style:* The experientials, 11 million in toto in 1979, seek direct and vivid experiences. They are well educated with good earning power (over $25,000 in 1979). They love swimming, racquet sports and snow skiing. They engage in yoga and eat health food. They attend lots of movies and like to entertain. They drive European cars and own racing bicycles and backpacking equipment.
8. *Societally Conscious Life-style:* Feeling that they have attained positions of affluence, hence no longer feeling the need for self-display, members of this

group of 14 million engage in healthful outdoor sports such as bicycling, jogging, swimming, and sailing as well as chess. They, like the achievers, watch many sports programs on television.

IV. **COMBINED OUTER- AND INNER-DIRECTED GROUPS**

9. *Integrated Life-style:* The author estimated that 3.2 million persons in 1979 had reached maturity, balance and a sense of what is fitting, the prime characteristics of the integrated life-style. Since only 33 persons (2 percent of the sample) were identified in this group, the author declined to generalize. Another reason is that the integrateds are highly diverse, subtle in their response, and complex in their outlook. All of these make generalization difficult.

OUTDOOR PURSUITS AND SPECIAL POPULATIONS

Kennedy et al. (1987) state that there are many shortcomings in the labeling of the members of special populations, yet labels must be used to emphasize their special needs. Special populations refer to groups of individuals with special needs which should be attended to by specially trained and qualified personnel. Examples of special populations are the physically handicapped, the mentally retarded, and the mentally ill. Select information is needed on the conditions of each group so that special programs may be provided for them in the outdoors. While the data on their conditions are readily available, data on the numbers of the members in each special population are not available. O'Morrow (1980:9) gave the following reasons for the difficulties in gathering such data. First, the line of demarcation between members of special populations and others is not very clear and cannot be agreed upon by the people concerned. Second, definitions change from time to time and from place to place. This is particularly true in legislative enactments. Third, since there are no central agencies, governmental or otherwise, a uniform reporting procedure is lacking. Fourth, reporting varies so much that even within one region, classification is difficult. Accordingly it is difficult to estimate how many persons are in each category. Perhaps the most reliable source would be the *Statistical Abstracts of the United States, 1989.* Tables 5.4 and 5.5 show some of the figures on some special populations.

The data available show that there were over 4 million persons under the age of 22 who were in need of special education in the period from 1978 to 1987. In addition, there are two more special populations that need special attention, the poor and the elderly. Figure 5.1 shows that in 1990, 12 percent of Americans or some 30 million people were 65 years of age or over. The poor are estimated to be about 32 million people. Although there is much overlap between all these groups, nonetheless there is a need to serve the impaired, handicapped, destitute, and aged, and outdoor experiences prove to be a very useful tool.

The Mentally Challenged and Outdoor Experiences. The mentally retarded suffer from a number of impairments in cultural conformity, interpersonal relations, and responsiveness as well as in motor skills and speech skills. Sometimes the mentally retarded suffer from auditory and visual limitations. It is estimated that there are about six million such persons in the United States, most of whom are mild cases (educable), followed by moderate cases (trainable), and only 5 percent severe and profound cases (custodial) (Kraus 1983:230). Studies show that outdoor experiences for the mentally retarded are quite useful and beneficial. Table 5.6 lists these benefits.

In addition to camping, Kennedy et al. (1987:19) state that through activities such as rock climbing, white-water rafting, spelunk-

TABLE 5.4 Population in Institutions and Other Group Quarters, by Sex and Type of Quarters: 1960 to 1980

[In thousands. As of April 1. Based on sample data and subject to sampling variability; see text, section I and Appendix III. See *Historical Statistics, Colonial Times to 1970*, series A 359–371, for inmates of institutions.]

Type of Quarters	1960	1970 Total	1970 Male	1970 Female	1980 Total	1980 Male	1980 Female
Total	4,902	5,786	3,438	2,349	5,738	3,153	2,586
Institutional inmates	1,887	2,127	1,126	1,000	2,492	1,231	1,261
Homes for the aged and dependent	470	928	299	629	1,426	422	1,004
Mental hospitals and residential treatment centers	630	434	245	189	255	157	99
Correctional institutions	346	328	314	15	466	439	27
Tuberculosis hospitals	65	17	12	5	8	6	1
Chronic disease hospitals (excl. TB and mental)	42	67	38	29	61	36	25
Homes and schools for the mentally handicapped	175	202	114	88	149	85	65
Homes for the physically handicapped	24	23	16	6	27	15	12
Homes for dependent and neglected children	73	48	28	19	38	24	14
Homes for unwed mothers	3	4	(z)	4	2	—	2
Training schools for juvenile delinquents	46	66	53	14	42	34	8
Detention homes	11	10	7	4	17	14	3
College dormitories	829	1,765	891	874	1,994	989	1,006
Military quarters	868	1,025	1,005	20	671	613	58
Rooming and boarding houses	634	330	191	139	176	107	69
Other	684	539	224	315	404	212	192

—represents or rounds to zero. z fewer than 500

Source: *Statistical Abstracts of the U.S.*, 1989. Bureau of the Census, U.S. Government Printing Office, Washington D.C.

ing, and backpacking the retarded are faced with personal challenges as they are involved in interpersonal interaction and small group cooperation.

The Physically Challenged and Outdoor Experiences. It is estimated that close to 68 million Americans have some limitation that could prevent them from participating in regular recreation programs (Kraus 1983:263). Many of these people's limitations are not profound, but facilitation to their participation must be provided. These cases include the orthopedically impaired, the cerebral palsied, the blind, the deaf, and persons suffering from muscular dystrophy, multiple sclerosis, and cardiac malfunction. Depending on the case, the outdoor experience should be modified accordingly. Kennedy et al. (1987:142) suggested the following guidelines:

1. Change as little as necessary. For example, try to keep the structure of the activity as close as possible to the

TABLE 5.5 Public Elementary and Secondary Students in Educational Programs for the Handicapped, by Type of Handicap: 1978–1987

[For school year ending in year shown. For persons under 22 years old. Funds appropriated are for three grant programs based on the counts of handicapped children; Education of handicapped children in State operated of supported schools; handicapped State grants; and handicapped pre-school incentive grants. Excludes outlying areas.]

Item	1978	1979	1980	1981	1982	1983	1984	1985	1986	1987
Federal funds appropriated (million dollars)	700.5	953.9	1,044.5	1,055.8	1,101.3	1,189.4	1,241.7	1,314.3	1,335.7	1,669.3
All conditions	3,751	3,889	4,005	4,142	4,198	4,255	4,298	4,315	4,317	4,374
Percent distribution										
Learning disabled	25.7	29.1	31.9	35.3	38.6	40.9	42.0	42.4	43.1	43.6
Speech impaired	32.6	31.2	29.6	28.2	27.0	26.6	26.6	26.1	26.1	25.8
Mentally retarded	24.9	23.2	21.7	20.0	18.7	17.8	16.9	16.1	15.3	15.0
Emotionally disturbed	7.7	7.7	8.2	8.4	8.1	8.3	8.4	8.6	8.7	8.7
Hard of hearing and deaf	2.3	2.2	2.0	1.9	1.8	1.7	1.7	1.6	1.5	1.5
Orthopedically handicapped	2.3	1.8	1.6	1.4	1.4	1.3	1.3	1.3	1.3	1.3
Other health impaired	3.6	2.7	2.6	2.4	1.9	1.2	1.2	1.6	1.3	1.2
Visually impaired	.9	.8	.8	.8	.7	.7	.7	.7	.6	1.6
Multihandicapped	(NA)	1.3	1.5	1.6	1.7	1.5	1.5	1.6	2.0	2.2
Deaf-blind	(NA)	.1	.1	.1	.1	.1	.1	.1	(z)	(z)

NA Not available   z Less than .05 percent

Source: *Statistical Abstracts of the U.S.*, 1989. Bureau of the Census, U.S. Government Printing Office, Washington, D.C.

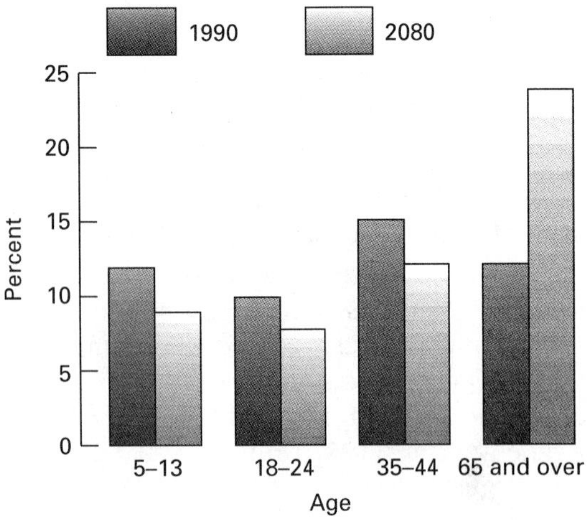

FIGURE 5.1 Percent distribution of the population by age.

existing activity. It is better to undermodify so as to challenge the individual and to provide normalized experiences.

2. Where possible, involve the person in the selection and activity modification process. Many times the user is a good source of information. Trails for the physically challenged are based on this phenomenon. All of the modifications have historically needed the approval of the participants.
3. There may be elements of competition to consider when working with groups of children and adults. For instance, in ski competitions, past performance, age, and sex of the participant are usually taken into consideration when pitting one person against another.

TABLE 5.6 Benefits of Camping for Handicapped: A Codified Statement

Primary Benefits	Functional Benefits
Attitudes	**Educational**
independence/self-confidence	learning opportunities
motivation	learn new skills and activities
self-awareness	opportunity for success
heightened morale	improved verbalization
improved behavior	higher academic achievement
improved discipline	creativity
improved cooperation	**Physical**
respect for others	activities of daily living
Social	increased opportunity for participation
socialization/informal group participation	improved coordination and physical fitness
group identity	**Vocational**
relationships with adults of a nonprofessional nature	organizing own activities
get along with others	camping as possible future employment
opportunity for sharing	initiating own activities
Environmental	**Recreational**
expanded environment	activities
heightened community interest/ awareness	fun
opportunity for normal experiences	education for leisure
adapt to community	
adapt to family	

Source: C. C. Hansen, "Content Analysis of Current Literature on Camping for Handicapped Children" in *Training Needs and Strategies in Camping for the Handicapped* by Nesbitt et al. (Eugene, OR: University of Oregon Press, 1972), 34–35. (Reprinted with permission.)

4. Try to offer activities that are characteristic of those individuals who are in the mainstream of society. That is, offer to persons with disabilities the same leisure opportunities that exist in society. The normalization principle should be emphasized, and the idea of inventing activities should be deemphasized.
5. Where possible, activities should have common denominators, especially if they are modified. For example, in ski competitions everyone follows the same rules. The physical impairment and the fact that everyone follows the same rules are the common denominators for equality in participation.
6. In many instances the person with a disability is cast in the role of spectator. The authors of this volume strongly feel that individuals should be provided opportunities to participate in, and in some cases be "nudged" into, participant-based activities.
7. Although the authors do *not* devalue cooperative and other noncompetitive leisure experiences, the person who is disabled should have ample opportunities to participate in equitable competitive situations.
8. Start at the level where the participants are currently functioning. This does *not* mean starting at the lowest level.
9. Individuals should be given opportunities for free choice. This may enhance the feeling of control and reduce feelings of "learned helplessness."

The Socially Deviant and Outdoor Experiences. While sociologists look at deviancy as the outcome of cultural and environmental factors, psychologists tend to view it as the result of some personality disorganization. Whatever the case, the two million or so individuals who are in the correctional system may benefit from recreational experiences in natural settings. In some instance the experience is used as a form of rehabilitation, as is the case with the deep-sea diving program in the men's colony in Chino, California. If these men were Type T personalities, risk-takers, such a program would provide the challenge they need. In other cases, the activity is deemed somewhat preventive, as with provisions of outdoor experiences in the Outward Bound program for the juvenile delinquent. Here the activity is thought to keep the person from deteriorating into further deviancy.

The Elderly and Outdoor Experiences. As shown earlier in the section on leisure pursuits and life course, the interests of the elderly will change due to a number of factors. According to Burdman (1986), the reduction in the number of muscular and nerve cells is accompanied by a loss of elasticity. Also the person suffers from less efficiency in all body systems. The outcome is an increase in ailments such as cardiovascular, respiratory, and musculoskeletal problems, diabetes mellitus, and hypothermia. Moreover the elderly could suffer from some psychological problems such as depression, dementia, and alcoholism. Recreation programs including outdoor experiences have proven beneficial. For instance, Owens (1982) found that satisfaction with leisure contributed significantly to life satisfaction of the 205 elders he studied. According to Leitner and Leitner (1985:16), the leisure patterns of the elderly, although diverse, are dominated by television viewing and reading. A possible reason for this could be their physical limitations. This may add to the feeling of loneliness as shown by the studies of Creecy, Wright, and Berg (1982). On the other hand popular outdoor activities which include gardening and camping may decrease loneliness through socialization (McAvoy 1982, Leitner and Leitner 1985).

SUMMARY

In this chapter on the social aspects of outdoor experiences, the roles played by the socializing agents are taken into consideration. The family is one of the most important in that respect, as is religion. Both agents could determine what is acceptable, and what is not, as a recreational activity. While there are enough empirical studies on the role that the family plays in this regard, there is a paucity of empirical evidence on the role of religion. Still, it is clear from the study of rituals that some elements of leisure pursuits may have evolved thereof. For example, Shrove Tuesday activities in Chester, England, were the starting point for soccer, which has evolved into the world's most popular sport.

Three other social institutions affect leisure behavior, namely the political structure, the economic system, and the technological level of the society at hand. The political structure controls leisure offerings through legislation on the local, state, or federal levels. Details on these three levels will be given in Chapters 7, 8, and 9. In the next chapter, the relationship between the economic structure and leisure is presented. Technology is presented here as divided into two aspects, material and social technology. Material technology refers to scientific advances as well as industrialization. Their impact on outdoor pursuits is exemplified in the increasing number of snowmobiles in North America. Social technology refers to education and the mass media. The introduction of nature documentaries on television has helped to make people aware of the importance of conservation.

Other than primary and secondary groups, demographic factors such as age, gender, occupation, and residence have been studied by various researchers. The result of these studies are presented in this chapter. For instance, early socialization into outdoor pursuits has been shown to be desirable. Also, it's been found that men seem to have more free time than women, and that the higher-paying one's occupation, the greater the participation in outdoor pursuits. Rural dwellers seem to enjoy more nature activities than do urban dwellers.

The relationship between life-style and leisure pursuits is another important area of study. Life-style refers to the unique combination of age, educational attainment, and income that results in a certain way of living. Life-style is reflected in outdoor pursuits in the choice of activities. For example, professionals might travel for pleasure, while semiskilled workers might instead tend to go fishing. The role that recreational activities play in the lives of special populations is presented here also. It seems that outdoor recreational activities help the mentally retarded person's self-awareness, the physically challenged person's self-confidence, and the social deviant's self-expression.

REFERENCES

Allen, L., et al. (1987) "The Role of Leisure: Satisfaction in Rural Communities." *Leisure Today* (April):5-8.

Bammel, G., and L. Burrus-Bammel (1981) *Human Behavior and Leisure.* Dubuque, IA: Wm. C. Brown.

Bevins, M., R. Bond, T. Concorn, K. McIntosh, and R. McNeil (1968) "Characteristics of Hunters and Fishermen in Six Northeastern States." *Vermont Agriculture Experimental Station Bulletin* 565.

Bialeschki, M., and K. Henderson (1986) "Leisure in the Common World of Women." *Leisure Studies* 5(3):299-308.

Bradshaw, R., and J. Jackson (1979) "Socialization for Leisure" in *Leisure: A Psychological Approach,* H. Ibrahim and R. Crandall, editors. Los Alamitos, CA: Hwong.

Bradshaw, T. K. (1978) *Lifestyle in the Advanced Industrial Societies.* Berkeley, CA: Institute of Governmental Studies, University of California.

Bultena, G., and D. Field (1978) "Visitors To National Parks: Test of the Elitism Argument." *Leisure Sciences* 1, no. 4.

Burdge, R. J. (1969) "Levels of Occupational Prestige and Leisure Activity." *Journal of Leisure Research* 1(3)202-24.

Burdmen, G. M. (1986) *Healthful Aging.* Englewood Cliffs, N.J.: Prentice Hall.

Burrus-Bammel, L., and G. Bammel (1990) "Outdoor/Environmental Education: An Overview For the Wise Use of Leisure." *Leisure Today* (April):17-22.

Butler, G. (1961) *Introduction to Community Recreation.* New York: Macmillan.

Cheek, N., and W. Burch (1976) *The Social Organization of Leisure in Human Society.* New York: Harper and Row.

Cheek, N. (1981) "Social Cohesion and Outdoor Recreation" in *Social Benefits of Outdoor Recreation,* J. Kelly, editor. Champaign, Il: Leisure Behavior Laboratory, University of Illinois.

Clarke, A. C. (1956) "The Use of Leisure and Its Relation to Levels of Occupational Prestige." *American Sociological Review* 21:301-7.

Creecy, R. F., R. Wright, and W. E. Berg (1982) "Correlates of Loneliness Among the Black Elderly." *Activities Adaptation and Aging* 3(2):9-16.

Csikszentmihalyi, M. (1981) "Leisure and Socialization." *Social Forces* 60 (December):2.

Csikszentmihalyi, M., and R. Larson (1984) *Being Adolescent.* New York: Basic Books.

DiPietro, J. (1981) "Rough and Tumble Play: A Function of Gender." *Developmental Psychology* 12:50-58.

Durkheim, E. (1915) *The Elementary Forms of Religious Life.* London: George Allen and Unwin.

Eitzen, D. S., and G. Sage (1989) *Sociology of North American Sport.* Dubuque, IA: Wm. C. Brown.

Erikson, E. (1977) *Toys and Reason: Stages in the Ritualization of Experience.* New York: Norton.

Fasting, K., and M. K. Sisjord (1985) "Gender Roles and Barriers to Participation in Sport." *Sociology of Sport Journal* 2(4):345-51.

Ford, P. (1989) "Luther Gulick" in *Pioneers in Leisure and Recreation,* H. Ibrahim, editor. Reston, VA: AAHPERD.

Foret, C. M. (1985) *Life Satisfaction and Leisure Satisfaction Among Young-Old and Old-Old Adults with Rural and Urban Residence.* Unpublished Ph.D. dissertation. Denton, TX: Texas Women's University.

Gattas, J. T., et al. (1986) "Leisure and Lifestyle: Towards a Research Agenda." *Society and Leisure* 9(2):524-37.

Gerson, G., et al. (1988) *Understanding Leisure: An Interdisciplinary Approach.* Dubuque, IA: Kendall/Hunt.

Glyptis, S., and D. Chambers (1982) "No Place Like Home." *Leisure Studies* 1:247-62.

Hendee, J. (1969) "Rural-Urban Differences Reflected in Outdoor Recreation Participation." *Journal of Leisure Research* 1:333-41.

Ibrahim, H., et al (1981) "Leisure Behavior Among Contemporary Egyptians." *Journal of Leisure Research* 13:89-104.

Kelly, J. (1974) "Socialization Toward Leisure: A Developmental Approach." *Journal of Leisure Research* 6:181-93.

Kelly, J. (1981) "Family Benefit From Outdoor Recreation" in *The Social Benefits of Outdoor Recreation,* J. Kelly, editor. Champaign, IL: Leisure Behavior Laboratory, University of Illinois.

Kelly, J. (1983) *Leisure Identities and Interaction.* London: George Allen and Unwin.

Kennedy, D., D. Austin, and R. Smith (1987) *Special Recreation: Opportunities For Persons with Disabilities.* Philadelphia, PA: Saunders.

Kleiber, D. and W. Rickards (1981) "Outdoor Recreation and Child Development" in *Social Benefits of Outdoor Recreation,* J. Kelly, editor. Champaign, IL: Leisure Behavior Laboratory, University of Illinois.

Knopp, T. (1972) "Environmental Determinants of Recreation Behavior." *Journal of Leisure Behavior* 4:129-38.

Kraus, R. (1983) *Therapeutic Recreation Service: Principles and Practices.* Philadelphia, PA: Saunders.

Leitner, M., and S. Leitner (1985) *Leisure in Later Life.* New York: Hawthorn Press.

Maclean, J., J. Peterson, and W. D. Martin (1985) *Recreation and Leisure: The Changing Scene.* New York: Macmillan.

Malsam, M., and L. Nelson (1984) "Integrating Curriculum Objectives." *Journal of Physical Education, Recreation and Dance* 55(7):52-54.

Manning, H. (1975) *Backpacking: One Step at a Time.* New York: Vintage Books.

Manning, R. (1985) *Studies in Outdoor Recreation: Search and Research for Satisfaction.* Corvallis, OR: Oregon State University Press.

Mayhew, L. (1971) *Society: Institutions and Activity.* Glenview, IL: Scott, Foresman and Company.

McAvoy, L. H. (1982) "The Leisure Preference Problems and Needs of the Elderly." *Journal of Gerontology* 11(1):40-47.

Mitchell, A. (1983) *The Nine American Lifestyles: Who We Are and Where We're Going.* New York: Macmillan.

Moskoff, W. (1984) *Labor and Leisure in the Soviet Union.* New York: St. Martin's Press.

Neumeyer, M., and E. Neumeyer (1936 and 1949) *Leisure and Recreation.* New York: A. S. Barnes.

O'Morrow, G. (1980) *Therapeutic Recreation: A Helping Profession.* Reston, VA: Reston Publishing.

Orthner, D. (1976) "Patterns of Leisure and Marital Interaction." *Journal of Leisure Research* 8:98-116.

Owens, D. J. (1982) *The Relationship of Frequency and Types of Activity to Life Satisfaction in Elderly Deaf People.* Doctoral dissertation, New York University. *Dissertation Abstracts International* 42:311A.

Roberts, K. (1970) *Leisure.* London: Longman.

Rosenthal, M. (1986) *The Character Factory: Baden-Powell's Boy Scouts and the Imperative of the Empire.* New York: Pantheon Books.

Sessoms, H. D. (1963) "An Analysis of Selected Variables Affecting Outdoor Recreation Patterns." *Social Forces* 42(October):112–15.

Shamir, B., and H. Ruskin. (1983) "Sex Differences In Recreational Sport Behavior and Attitudes: A Study of Married Couples in Israel." *Leisure Studies* 2(3):253–68.

Shaw, S. (1985) "Gender and Leisure: Inequality in the Distribution of Leisure Time." *Journal of Leisure Research* 17(4):266–82.

Shepard, P. (1977) "Place and Human Development" in *Children, Nature and the Urban Environment.* U.S. Forest Service General Technical Report. Washington, D.C.: U.S. Government Printing Office.

Smith, J., R. Carlson, G. Donaldson, and H. Masters (1970) *Outdoor Education.* Englewood Cliffs, NJ: Prentice Hall.

Snyder, E., and E. Spreitzer (1978) *Social Aspects of Sport.* Englewood Cliffs, NJ: Prentice Hall.

Turner, V. (1985) *100 Years of YMCA Camping.* Chicago, IL: YMCA of the USA.

United Media Enterprises. (1983) *Where Does the Time Go?* New York: Newspaper Enterprise Association.

U.S. Bureau of the Census (1987) *Statistical Abstracts of the United States.* Washington, D.C.: U.S. Government Printing Office.

U.S. Bureau of the Census (1989) *Statistical Abstracts of the United States.* Washington, D.C.: U.S. Government Printing Office.

West, P., and L. Merriam (1970) "Outdoor Recreation and Family Cohesiveness." *Journal of Leisure Research* 2:251–59.

White, C. (1955) "Social Class Differences in the Uses of Leisure." *American Journal of Sociology* 61:145–50.

Yoesting, D., and D. Burkhead (1973) "Significance of Childhood Recreation Experience on Adult Leisure Behavior." *Journal of Leisure Research* 5:25–36.

6 The Economics of Outdoor Pursuits

Why is it that in a society with such a capitalistic orientation, many American politicians and naturalists argue for the preservation of large chunks of government land for outdoor enjoyment? Why do they also fight for the provision of programs and activities on those lands? Perhaps because some of them feel that Americans should be rewarded for their hard work. Work is necessary because although unpleasant, it is important to life. Leisure, on the other hand, is not only pleasant, it could be meaningful (Kelly 1987). Meaningful activities are those with which a person can easily identify. Some claim that leisure in a natural setting is more than pleasant and meaningful, it is important to human welfare and could be therapeutic if not euphoric.

Many believe the claim that leisure is beneficial to human welfare is exaggerated (Olson 1961), yet the provisions for outdoor experiences continue to exist even though the number of those who participate in genuine outdoor pursuits may seem too small to warrant the expense of maintaining vast outdoor recreation opportunities (Simmons 1975:5). The support for providing areas and allocating funds for programs to be conducted in these areas will not subside. Perhaps because outdoor pursuits have become an integral part of the total leisure scene in the countries of the Western world, particularly the United States and Canada. In fact, natural areas and related programs are provided in many Third World countries such as Egypt and India, not necessarily for the citizens but for badly needed hard currency coming from foreign tourists (Ibrahim 1991:95,100). In other words, leisure has become a source of income for the producers of its goods and services as well as a source of pleasure and meaningfulness for the ones who consume these goods and services.

How did this come about, in a country that was not long ago straddled with a puritanical ideology so ingrained that at the time of the writing of the Constitution a proposal was forwarded to include in its articles a prohibition against horse racing, gambling, and all extravagance (Dulles 1965:65)? A presentation on the nature of the economic system and the changes that have taken place will shed some light on this development.

THE NATURE OF THE ECONOMIC SYSTEM

The work of Rostow (1960) shows that there are certain requirements that have to be met and certain steps to be taken before leisure spending can become an important ingredient in society's economic system. In essence the society should be at the stage of high consumption (see Figure 6.1)—that is, when most of its citizens could become high consumers of goods and services including leisure goods and services. At an earlier stage of economic development, it is possible that only a few privileged citizens become high consumers. These were the members of the leisure class in past eras (Veblen 1953). Today most of us are members of that leisure class; most of us are high consumers.

Figure 6.1 shows that in the 1920s the American economy entered the high mass consumption phase, which includes leisure spending. The figures for such spending are shown in Table 6.1.

Figure 6.2 shows spending trends for leisure in the United States for 1962–1982. The amounts in Figure 6.2 do not include government spending, nor do they include the spending of some private and public agencies on recreation.

According to the data presented in Table 6.1 and Figures 6.1 and 6.2, two thirds of the American economic output consists of goods and services to be consumed by individuals, households and groups, a good share of which are included under leisure spending. In 1962 leisure spending

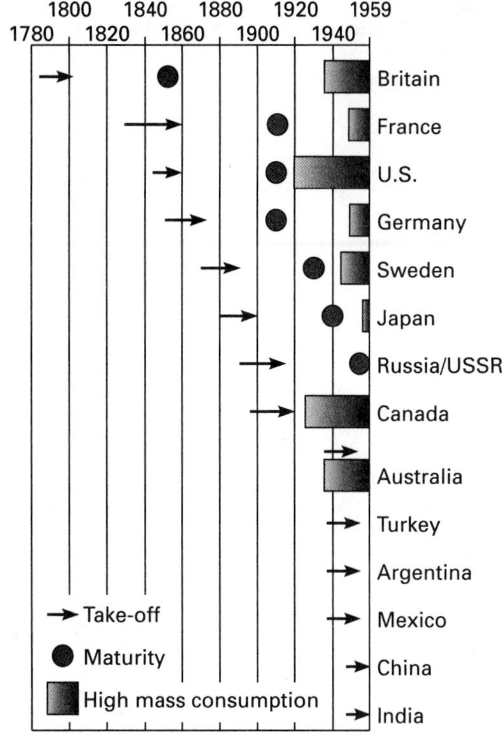

FIGURE 6.1 Five stages of economic growth.

was about $48 billion, and in a quarter of a century the figure jumped to $320 billion. What made leisure such a potent force in the American economy? MacLean et al. state that the following three important factors are responsible for making leisure play a leading role in the economy of this society (1985:58-60):

1. Productivity The productivity of a given market today is eight times what it was 140 years ago. The gross national product (GNP), which is the total market value of goods and services, has increased at an average rate of 3 percent per year for many years. Also, the labor force has grown steadily in the past few years. Increased productivity means that more goods and services are provided to be consumed. This requires a concomitant increase in income.

TABLE 6.1 Personal Consumption Expenditures for Recreation, U.S.: 1970–1985 (in Millions of Dollars)

Type of product or service	1970	1975	1980	1981	1982	1983	1984	1985
Total recreation expenditure	42,718	70,233	114,972	128,625	138,321	152,052	165,291	176,289
Percent of total personal consumption	6.7	6.9	6.6	6.7	6.7	6.8	6.8	6.8
Books and maps	2,922	3,570	5,595	6,174	6,551	7,185	7,823	7,972
Magazines, newspapers, sheet music	4,097	6,356	10,438	11,012	11,445	11,967	12,695	13,196
Nondurable toys and sport supplies	5,498	8,954	14,633	16,005	16,826	18,004	19,796	20,350
Wheel goods, durable toys, sports eqpt.	5,191	10,514	17,185	18,727	19,336	20,419	23,423	26,727
TV's, radios, records, musical instruments	8,540	13,489	19,888	22,020	24,515	28,182	31,280	35,119
Radio and TV repair	1,383	2,229	2,555	2,659	2,774	2,834	2,837	3,100
Flowers, seeds, and potted plants	1,798	2,659	4,047	4,413	4,495	4,806	5,217	5,549
Admission to spectator amusements	3,269	4,317	6,490	6,929	7,799	8,601	9,403	9,661
Motion picture theaters	1,829	2,197	2,671	2,853	3,326	3,583	3,938	3,678
Operas and nonprofit institutions	531	787	1,786	2,049	2,141	2,389	2,678	2,991
Spectator sports	1,136	1,333	2,033	2,027	2,332	2,629	2,787	2,994
Clubs and fraternal organizations	1,465	1,921	3,020	3,430	3,842	4,154	4,430	4,752
Commercial participant amusements	2,367	4,858	9,666	11,677	12,471	13,606	14,132	14,554
Parimutuel net receipts	1,096	1,662	2,095	2,229	2,240	2,269	2,462	2,605
Other	5,065	9,704	19,360	23,350	26,027	30,025	31,973	32,802

Source: *Statistical Abstracts of the U.S.*, many editions. Bureau of the Census, U.S. Government Printing Office, Washington, D.C.

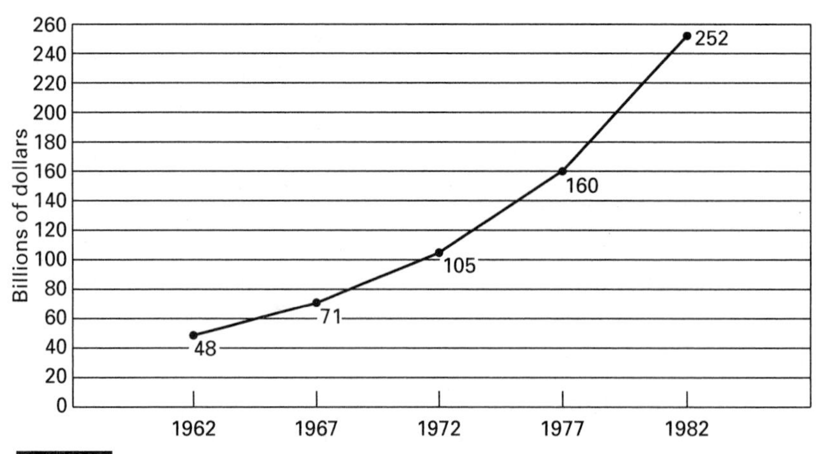

FIGURE 6.2 Spending trends for leisure in the United States, 1962–1982. *Source: Bureau of the Census, Statistical Abstracts of the U.S.,* many editions.

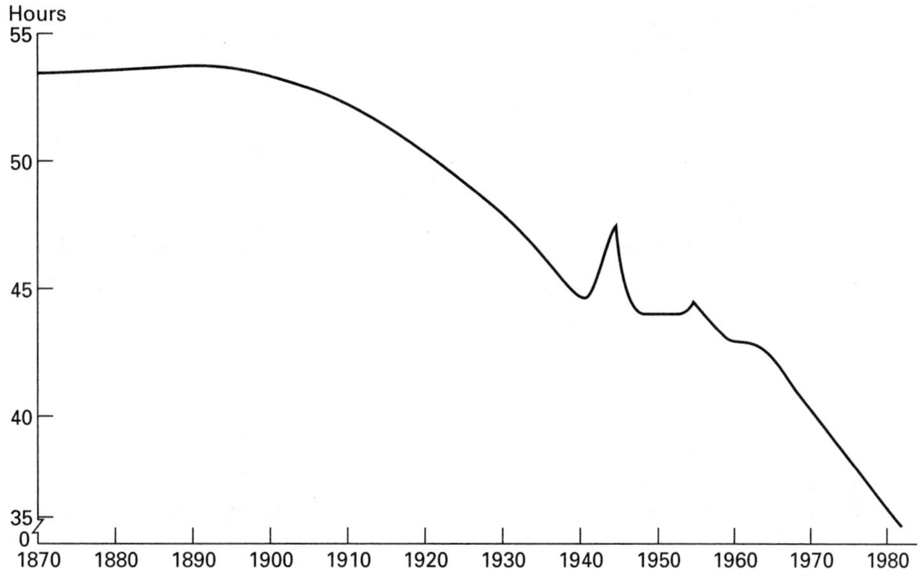

FIGURE 6.3 Average weekly hours per worker, U.S., 1869–1983. Other studies do not agree with Jensen's and United Media's research that work hours declined in the 1970s. *Source: Bosserman, P. "The Evolution of and Trends in Work and Non-Work Time in the United States Society (1920–1970)," Society and Leisure* 7(1):94. (Reprinted with permission.) Modified to 1983.

2. Increased Income A substantial increase in income above and beyond what is needed to purchase essential goods and services becomes necessary for the consumption of "the nonessentials," that is, leisure services and equipment, whether provided by the private or public sector. This increase is called discretionary income. An increase in productivity and a viable discretionary income might not, in themselves, have led to the increase in leisure pursuits that has been witnessed in the last few decades in the United States. Another ingredient was at work, an increase in free time.

3. Increased Free Time In order for leisure to become an important facet of a society it was crucial to have time freed from familial, civil, and work obligations—time in which a person could partake of an activity for its own sake, for its intrinsic value. Societal values play important roles in how one perceives time as being free from all obligations, and a study of the value system in American society is necessary. The American value system has gone through drastic changes since the early settlement of the country. There were attempts to include in the U.S. Constitution provisions that prohibit gambling, horse racing, and the like. Today some of these activities are sponsored by government agencies. Also, Americans have witnessed a change in their attitude towards work. Changes in work time are shown in Figure 6.3. The drop in work time from 50+ hours per week to 30+ hours per week in 100 years allowed for an increase in free time to about 32 hours per week (Jensen 1985 and the United Media Enterprises 1983). Jensen's figures are based on a summary of previous time-budget studies, and the United Media Enterprises work is based on interviews of 1,024 persons from the general public, 101 newspaper editors, 105 cable television directors, and 116 network television news directors.

In addition to increased productivity, increased income, and increased free time, the high level of mobility of Americans played an important role in the phenomenal increase in leisure pursuits in this country. The automobile, which facilitated business and trade, became an important element in leisure pursuits as well. It provided access to the vast recreational resources in this country. More recently, the new American invention, the RV, began taking people of all ages into areas that had been inaccessible to anyone a generation ago. There, they found another American invention, the campground, which has evolved in a short time into a very convenient recreational facility provided with such amenities as flush toilets and hot showers. The convenience of the campground is surpassed only by the convenience of the RV, which has been recently described as the great indoors in the great outdoors.

While these four variables, productivity, discretionary income, discretionary time, and mobility, are still affecting leisure behavior in the United States and other industrial societies, the rate of population growth, which at one point was instrumental in increased demand for leisure services, leveled off a few years ago. In fact, both discretionary income and discretionary time are leveling off also (see Table 6.1). In addition, the rate of increase in productivity is not as high as it used to be a decade or two ago.

Nonetheless, spending on leisure goods such as pleasure boats, RVs, snowmobiles, athletic equipment, and sportswear continued to climb in the last few years, as shown in tables 6.1 and 6.2.

Recreation Expenditure

The exact expenditures on leisure pursuits either by individuals or by agencies are hard to obtain. This may be due to the lack of precise definition of what a leisure pursuit is. How can pleasure travel be separated from business travel? Another factor is the overlap in the categorization of leisure spending. Should vacationing in a recreational vehicle be classified as travel or outdoor recreation? Nonetheless, estimates show that spending on leisure pursuits, in total, has steadily increased over the years. *U.S. News and World Report,* which monitored spending for many years, estimated leisure spending by individuals, households, and groups at $50 billion in 1965, which rose to $300 billion in the late 1980s (Ibrahim 1991:175). MacLean et al. (1985:62–67) classified leisure spending in five categories:

1. Recreation Supplies and Equipment This category includes durable items such as recreational vehicles and motorcycles; televisions, radios, and tape recorders; camping and sports equipment; musical instruments and art supplies; and garden supplies.

2. Travel and Vacation Businesses With the marked improvement in transportation, travel and vacationing have become very large businesses in this country. Although ownership of a second home (for vacations) is not as prevalent as it used to be, the concept of timeshare purchase of vacation accommodation is gaining ground. Many states, such as Florida, are becoming dependent on travel as their most important source of income. Also many countries today are becoming dependent on tourism, for example Egypt, Greece, and Mexico. MacLean et al. (1985:63) estimate that $70 billion are spent annually by Americans in this category.

3. Sport and Outdoor Recreation Next to travel and vacationing, outdoor recreation and sports account for the largest expenditure on leisure activities. Sports have been an important part of the leisure scene in America for many years. In addition, the recent increased interest in wellness and fitness has added to the expenditure in this

TABLE 6.2 Sporting Goods Sales, by Product Category: 1980–1986, U.S. (In Millions of Dollars)

Selected product category	1980	1981	1982	1983	1984	1985	1986 (proj.)
Sales, all products	16,691	18,725	18,684	23,111	26,401	27,446	29,119
Percent of retail sales	1.7	1.8	2.0	2.0	2.0	2.0	na
Athletic sport clothing*	3,127	3,201	3,014	3,226	3,432	3,376	3,503
Athletic sport footwear	1,731	1,785	1,900	2,189	2,381	2,610	2,791
Gym shoes	465	616	659	639	669	656	675
Running shoes	397	372	421	557	591	572	572
Tennis shoes	359	284	287	340	371	470	507
Aerobic shoes	na	na	10	29	54	178	266
Basketball shoes	86	80	81	119	159	185	198
Golf shoes	68	78	99	115	110	109	116
Baseball shoes	56	58	48	66	87	103	108
Athletic equipment	6,487	6,762	7,114	7,925	8,317	8,922	9,311
Firearms and hunting	1,351	1,454	1,567	1,666	1,620	1,699	1,716
Fishing tackle	539	689	586	606	616	681	715
Camping	646	663	735	790	699	724	775
Golf	386	413	493	633	630	730	767
Snow skiing	379	307	332	386	502	593	650
Optics	na	na	na	na	294	309	327
Tennis	237	254	277	293	315	273	287
Archery	149	169	168	179	212	212	212
Baseball and softball	158	157	154	173	153	176	187
Water skis	123	123	106	133	146	125	131
Billiards	173	146	124	199	100	117	125
Bowling accessories	107	107	103	106	108	106	106
Recreational transport	5,345	6,977	6,656	9,771	12,271	12,539	13,514
Bicycles and supplies	1,233	1,299	1,148	1,638	1,840	2,109	2,109
Pleasure boats	2,718	3,656	3,684	4,612	6,209	6,753	7,428
Recreational vehicles	1,178	1,820	1,701	3,368	4,082	3,515	3,807
Snowmobiles	216	202	123	153	140	162	170

na= not available
*Category does not cover all sales
Source: *Statistical Abstracts of the United States, 1986.* Bureau of the Census. U.S. Government Printing Office, Washington, D.C.

category. A quarter of a century ago, the Bureau of Outdoor Recreation predicted a 141 percent increase in outdoor pursuits from the year 1965 to the year 2000. And it is estimated that millions of Americans flock to water resources, mountains, and deserts to pursue their leisure activities. Total communities around these areas have been established, and their economy depends entirely on the sport aficionado and outdoor enthusiast.

4. Cultural Activities This category includes music, drama, dance, arts and crafts, books and other publications, and museums. Not only are televisions, radios, cassettes, and digital recordings selling in record numbers, but attendance at musical and dramatic plays has also increased. Even in the area where growth was once slow, as in opera and symphony performances, attendance is increasing. Expenditure on arts and crafts supplies has also increased. The same is witnessed in books and other publications. Also, attendance at museums has increased significantly in the last few years.

5. Home Expenditure As previously stated, the home is the most important center for leisure activity. Not only are most homes equipped with a backyard, but some are also equipped with a recreation room, a hot tub, and a swimming pool. Home expenditures on leisure include playground equipment, hobby shops, and entertainment equipment, including computerized games. Away from home, family spending on leisure includes going to movies, amusement parks, and theme restaurants.

The expenditures on travel, vacationing, and outdoor recreation are important facts of our economy. Clearly, as seen in tables 6.1 and 6.2 and as suggested by many authors (MacLean et al. 1985, Jensen 1985, and Knudson 1984), these are the largest expenditures on leisure pursuits. They are supplemented by government expenditures in the provision of outdoor recreation areas, as discussed next.

Government Expenditure

All three levels of government, local, state, and federal, are involved directly in outdoor recreation. Their major contribution is in the provision of areas such as parks and forests, and they also provide programs in many of these areas. It is difficult to find out how much the government spends on recreation because, in many instances, these expenditures are not listed under a separate category. Nonetheless, Jensen (1985:72–74) tried to elucidate the government's involvement in outdoor recreation as follows:

Federal Government Expenditure. Two federal departments are directly involved in the outdoor pursuits of Americans as they take place on federal lands: the Department of Agriculture through the management of national forests and the Department of the Interior through the management of national parks spend large sums on maintaining these areas. Moreover, other federal agencies provide recreation for millions of Americans on their lands. Clearly it is hard to estimate the federal government's expenditure on outdoor recreation. In Chapter 7 the role of the federal government in outdoor recreation will be discussed.

State Expenditure. The fifty states spend close to $1 billion in financing outdoor recreation. Most of this money is raised through taxes. Sometimes a certain tax is specified for recreation expenditure, such as the cigarette tax in Texas. Another source of income to be used for recreation purposes is licensing fees, for example fees for hunting and fishing licenses. State bond elections have been used very successfully in park development and natural resources expansion. User fees are also required in many locations.

Local Government Expenditure. While Jensen (1985:74) suggests that local governments spend, on the average, 2.3 percent of their income on recreational facilities and programs, MacLean et al. suggest 3.7 percent (1985:82). The total amount spent by local governments could reach $2 billion. Chapter 9 is devoted to local government and outdoor recreation.

Other Expenditures

Other than leisure pursuit expenditures by individuals, households, and governments, there are expenditures by both public and private agencies that should be included in the estimates of the total expenditure picture. For instance the camps of the different youth service organizations are an example of nonprofit organizations spending on leisure pursuits and a school camp is an example of what a public agency spends on leisure pursuits.

Spending on, and for, leisure pursuits is only half of the total picture, the other half being the incomes accrued from these activities. These incomes have strong impact on the economy of the nation, a region, and/or a state.

NATIONAL ECONOMIC IMPACT

It is estimated that private recreation business provides nearly 7 percent of the total employment in the United States (Walsh 1986:1). When the number of those employed in the recreation services provided by the public sector is added to the above, the impact of leisure spending on the American economy becomes clearer. In addition, foreign tourists account for 4 percent of the total exports of American goods and services, which helps in addressing the problem of trade deficit in the U.S. economy.

Demand and Supply

Knudson (1984:10) suggested that the outdoor recreation system could be looked upon as composed of four elements that correspond to four economic parallels, as follows:

Visitors and their characteristics	→ Demand
Recreational resources	→ Supply
Plans and policies	→ Pricing
Tools for implementation	→ Management

These four economic parallels affect outdoor pursuits as follows: In the American economic system the concepts of demand and supply are used to determine economic policy. Demand is based on the ability and willingness of consumers to buy specific quantities of goods and services at a given time (Kelly 1985:38). To what extent is the American consumer able and willing to buy goods and services pertaining to outdoor pursuits? It is clear that he or she has the purchasing power, as depicted in a discretionary income of about 6.9 percent to do so. She or he is willing, as a consequence of value inculcation and life-style, to pursue leisure activities. What comes next is the matter of supply. According to Kelly (1985:3), there are two types of supply mechanisms in the leisure business. The first is direct supply, which includes the manufacturing, wholesaling, and retailing of equipment and apparel, as well as the provision of services. In direct supply, the supplier deals directly with the consumer. In the second type of supply, some suppliers deal indirectly with the consumer, such as the writers who write the books we read in our leisure time, or the actor in the movies we watch. Other suppliers, the service providers, deal with our leisure experiences directly, such as the ones from whom we rent our fishing boat, or the ones who fix and maintain our recreation vehicle.

Clawson and Knetsch (1966) pioneered a study of demand in outdoor recreation in America. They used a single exploratory variable, the average direct cost of auto operation times the distance, as a proxy for the price the consumer is willing to pay for an outdoor leisure experience. Over the years researchers agreed that other nonprice variables are an important determinant in the demand for recreation goods and leisure services. Walsh (1986:157) lists them as follows:

1. Socioeconomic characteristics of the consumer.
2. Attractiveness and quality of the recreation site.
3. Availability of substitute service.
4. Travel time.
5. Congestion or crowding.
6. Taste and preference of the consumer.

The supply side of the demand-supply continuum in outdoor recreation includes the recreation resources that are available to the consumer. Clawson and Knetsch (1966) suggested the following simple classification of these resources which is still in use:

User Oriented Areas. The primary consideration is easy accessibility for the recreation consumer. Most local public and private facilities would fall into this category.

Intermediate Areas. The resource partially dictates the accessibility into these areas. Most regional and state-run facilities would fall into this category.

Resource-Oriented Areas. The resource determines to a great extent the accessibility of the area to the consumer. National parks, forests, and wildlife refuges would fall into this category.

PRICING AND MANAGING

It is hard to determine the price that a leisure consumer should pay for the use of a government-run recreation facility, due to the absence of competitive markets. Walsh states that "as a result, the efficient operation of recreation programs by public agency is likely to depend on the ability of managers to adopt the correct least-cost price policy" (1986:503). Accordingly, the user fee should be set at the intersection of the demand curve with the marginal cost and average cost curve. The demand curve shows how the quantity demanded of some recreation activity during a specific period will change as its price changes. Average cost includes the cost of investment plus the cost of operation. When and if the demand is equal to the supply, marginal cost will equal average cost. If the demand exceeds the supply, marginal cost will increase and profits will result. If the supply exceeds the demand, marginal cost will decrease and subsidy will be needed.

It is clear how difficult it is to set user fees for a government-run recreation facility. Suffice it to say that one of the most difficult decisions to make concerning fees, as based on the above formula, is the cost of investment: what is the monetary value of a national park or a national forest? Adding to the difficulty is the inverse relationship between the demand for outdoor recreation and the supply of natural resources, as shown in Figure 6.4. The supply of these resources is abundant in areas that are located far from population concentration where the demand is great.

The problem of the inverse relationship between location of public lands and population centers was recognized in the report of the Outdoor Recreation Resources Review Commission (ORRRC) in 1962. It was recommended in that report that the individual states develop comprehensive plans detailing their outdoor recreation supply and demand and providing recommendations for improvement of the situation. The plan was to be repeated every 5 years. A nationwide plan for outdoor recreation was prepared by the Bureau of Outdoor Recreation in 1973. Another plan was issued in 1979. Further details are provided in Chapter 7.

Another factor that plays an important role in the economic aspects of an outdoor experience is management. Knudson (1984:18) suggested that a large number of conceptual, biological, legal, and organizational skills are needed to effectively manage these areas and the programs provided in them. Successful programs are an economic asset to their sponsoring agency. If success in management of outdoor recreational resources is to be attained, it must be preceded by an attempt to improve management.

The Economic Benefits of Outdoor Recreation

Outdoor recreation programs along with their facilities and lands, being a service to the public, may appear to involve expenditures only. In fact, there are economic benefits to the general public, which is the actual owner of the lands involved. Peterson and Brown (1986:Vii) suggested that economic benefits are generally defined relative to two basic economic objectives. First, efficiency is seen when the monetary value of the benefits exceeds the monetary value of the costs. Second, equity is seen when the distribution of purchasing power among individual citizens is fair. There are many concerns related

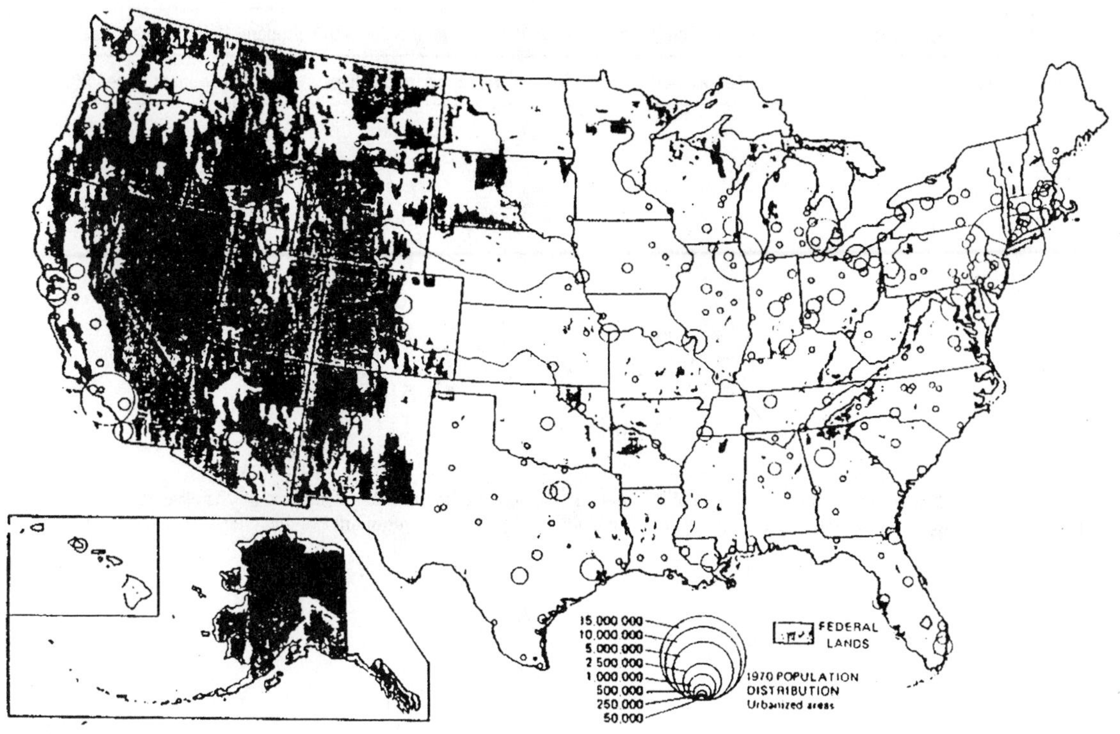

FIGURE 6.4 Distribution of public land to population in the United States.

to efficiency and equity. Granted, the interest on the national level is in seeing that growth in national assets occurs and that the wealth of Americans improves, "however, our national concern in the international scene is not so much for efficiency at a world scale as it is for a favorable national balance of payment" (Peterson and Brown 1986:V13). The same may be applied to state and local governments, where each jurisdiction tries to become internally efficient by maximizing internal net gain within their own boundaries.

Another important concern, expressed by Walsh and Loomis (1986, V37), is how much should government spend on outdoor recreation projects? Will these projects contribute to national economic development (NED)? The NED objective is to increase the value of the output of goods and services. The contribution of outdoor recreation to NED is defined in terms of the net willingness of the consumers to pay for the goods and services. Payments are done in the form of taxes to be approved by the citizens and in fees to be paid by the recreationists. It is only recently that economists began to estimate the contribution of outdoor recreation to NED. Walsh and Loomis (1986:V40) provided us with an estimate based on the direct consumption benefits of on-site leisure activities and the indirect consumption of the flow of information about these activities and sites and the preservation and protection of the sites. The authors offered information shown in tables 6.3, 6.4, and 6.5 to illustrate the contribution of outdoor recreation to national economic development.

Table 6.3 summarizes the contribution of park and recreation programs to NED in 1982. The total government expenditures of about

TABLE 6.3 Benefits and Costs of Recreation and Park Programs by Federal, State and Local Government, United States, 1982

Level of Government	Recreation Visitor Days	Net Economic Value	Government Expenditures
All Government, Total		$26,268	
Million	3,100	$305	$8,876
Per Household	36		$103
Municipal and County		$9,363	
Million	2,200	$109	$6,140
Per Household	26		$72
State		$6,387	
Million	300	$74	$1362
Per Household	3		$16
Federal, Total		$10,518	
Million	600	$122	$1,375
Per Household	7		$16

Source: R. Walsh and J. Loomis "The Contribution of Recreation to National Economic Development" in *The President's Commission on Americans Outdoors, Literature Review* (Washington, D.C.: U.S. Government Printing Office, 1986), 46.

TABLE 6.4 Net Economic Value of Fishing and Hunting, United States, 1980

	Recreation Days (millions)	Value per day	Total Value (Millions)	Approximate Number of Studies
Type of Fishing				
Freshwater	1,103	$22.60	$24,928	8
Trout	160	$16.50	$2,640	18
Anadromous	85	$46.87	$3,984	8
Saltwater	147	$40.81	$5,999	5
Type of Hunting				
Deer	102.5	$31.73	$3,252	14
Elk	5.0	$35.18	$176	5
Antelope	0.5	$31.16	$16	3
Other Big Game	16.1	$45.64	$735	2
Small Game	246.7	$26.17	$6,456	6
Migratory Birds	58.8	$41.30	$2,430	6
Other Animals	51.7			
Nonconsumptive	377.5	$3.00	$1,333	2
Total or Average	2,353.8	$22.00	$51,748	

Source: R. Walsh and J. Loomis "The Contribution of Recreation to National Economic Development" *The President's Commission on Americans Outdoors, Literature Review.* (Washington, D.C.: U.S. Government Printing Office, 1986), 46.

TABLE 6.5 Federally Provided Recreation. Generally Excluding Fishing and Hunting, United States, 1982

	RECREATION VISITOR DAYS				
Activity	**U.S. Forest Service (millions)**	**Bureau of Land Management (millions)**	**Value Per Day**	**Total Value (Millions)**	**Approximate Number of Studies**
Camping and Picnicking	66.1	7.0	$14.20	$1,381	10
Motorized Travel	67.4	5.0	$6.70	$645	1
Hiking and Horseback Riding	16.4	1.0	$20.76	$481	6
Water Related Activities	9.6	1.8	$20.27	$307	14
Winter Sports	14.1	0.2	$13.98	$267	2
Cabins and Organization Camps	14.9	N/R	N/R		
Other	10.5	3.3			
Wilderness	11.2		$29.99	$447	5
National Park Service	106.3		$21.92	$3,099	2
Corps of Engineers	146.9		$4.99	$975	4
Bureau of Reclamation	45		$20.67	$1,237	2
Tennessee Valley Authority	6.6		$4.99	$44	3
Total or Average	680.4		$9.82	$8,883	

Source: R. Walsh and J. Loomis "The Contribution of Recreation to National Economic Development" in *The President's Commission on Americans Outdoors, Literature Review* (Washington, D.C.: U.S. Government Printing Office, 1986), 46.

$9 billion are offset by a net income of over $26 billion. The largest beneficiary of the three levels of government is the federal government, which netted over $10 billion, as against slightly over $1 billion in expenditures.

Table 6.4 summarizes some studies conducted over the years on the contribution of wildlife recreation programs to NED in 1980. The reason for the concentration on fishing and hunting is that these two activities were subject to more study than were other outdoor recreation activities.

Table 6.5 summarizes contributions to NED by other types of outdoor recreation. There is, of course, some overlap between activities which is unavoidable.

THE ECONOMICS OF TOURISM

Included in the economics of outdoor recreational activities is the economics of tourism. Granted some tourists may not engage in outdoor pursuits, but since most do, the impact of this fast-growing leisure pursuit should be included in our discussion.

Jafari (1983:3) estimated that tourism has become a strong economic institution of global significance. He estimated that it comprises about $700 billion, or 6 percent of the world gross national product (GNP). According to Lerner and Abbott (1982:2), between 1975 and 1980 international travel increased by 75 percent, at an average of a 15 percent increase per year. Yet international business did not increase by an equivalent amount during that period. In fact that period witnessed an increase in vacation days globally.

The United States' share in this bonanza is quite sizeable. Hunt estimates that this country received 20.8 million tourists in 1984, or 6.9 percent of total international arrival, and captured 11.4 percent of international receipts (1986:V-60). Most of these tourists came from Canada, Mexico, Japan, and Great Britain. These foreign tourists spent less money here than did American tourists visiting other lands. In other words, international tourism is not economically beneficial to the national economy. Most of the American tourists go to Canada and Mexico (58 percent), followed by Europe. Maybe the U. S. government should have an office to promote tourism to the United States, as many countries do. In fact, some Canadian provinces have offices abroad to promote tourism to their particular region of Canada. Most of the efforts of state tourism officers in the United States are directed to attract tourists from within the country. Their efforts are indeed successful.

Of the total travel expenditure of $234 billion spent by Americans in 1984, $217 billion, or 92.7 percent were spent on domestic travel (Hunt 1986:V-61). Nine out of ten of the trips taken by Americans are for pleasure. Three-fifths of these trips are long-term vacations, and two-fifths are weekend trips. The economic impact of pleasure travel is sizeable, accounting for 7 percent of the American GNP. Travel generates 4.7 million jobs, with a payroll of $50.9 billion and tax revenues of $13.6, $8.9, and $2.7 billion for federal, state, and local treasuries, respectively.

Within the United States, the interstate promotion of tourism is faring rather well. According to Spandoni (1986:1), state campaign budgets totaled about $82.8 million dollars for 1985, an increase of about 11.8 percent from the previous year. In the same year, 554.4 million trips were taken within the United States, about 30.2 million more than the previous year.

Air travel dominates travel in the United States, but other modes are being used. The sale of recreational vehicles peaked at 540,000 in 1972, leveled off, dropped to 200,000 in the early 1980s, and saw an increase to 300,000 in 1985.

Studies show that Americans travel to national forests and parks and to national, state, and local recreational areas to pursue a number of outdoor pursuits. As shown earlier, walking for pleasure is the most participated in leisure activity, followed by swimming, visiting zoos, picnicking, driving for pleasure, and sight-seeing.

Researchers are finding out that leisure pursuits are an essential part of tourism. Vacationers select a destination where they can participate in certain activities, and not just a particular destination (Epperson 1983:31). According to Rubenstein (1980), who surveyed 11,000 persons as to their reasons for taking a vacation, rest and relaxation topped the list (63 percent), followed by escaping routine (52 percent), visiting friends and relatives (45 percent), renewal (45 percent), and exploring new places (35 percent).

REGIONAL AND LOCAL ECONOMIC IMPACTS

This section deals with the economic activities generated in a region or locality by the recreational use of natural resources within its boundaries. Many regions, states, and local communities establish their own economic development projects. Although an outdoor recreation project may look economically beneficial, Millard and Fischer (1979) suggested that the planners take into consideration the loss of the natural resource to activities other than recreation, the increase in medical and other assistance to nonlocal tourists, and the increase in local prices due to the willingness of the tourists to overpay.

According to Alward (1986), the economic effects of investing in recreational development projects are divided into two categories. The first category includes the direct impact of transactions intimately related to the project or activities. The second category encompasses the chain of consequences that result from the direct effect. These secondary economic impacts go beyond the recreation site. For example, recreationists visit motels and restaurants on their way to and from recreation sites, and gas stations supply the recreationists with fuel to make the trip. While most, if not all, the direct economic impacts will take place at or close to the recreation site, the indirect impacts may be felt far from the site due to the predominance of interregional trade links.

Spatially, Stevens and Rose (1985) propose a hierarchical conceptualization of the impacted region, as shown in Figure 6.5. In the figure the smallest spatial unit is the recreation site. Most of the direct economic impact of recreation activities occurs in the second unit, the support area. This area encompasses the retail outlets where the recreationists buy services and goods. A third area includes the travel corridors where there are impacts on transportation, food, and lodging services. The fourth area includes the residences of the recreationists along with the businesses which will provide them with the goods needed for the activities—the recreational clothing, equipment, and supplies. The fifth and final area extends beyond the fourth into the rest of the United States and possibly the world where most, if not all, of the clothing, equipment, and supplies purchased in the fourth area may have been manufactured.

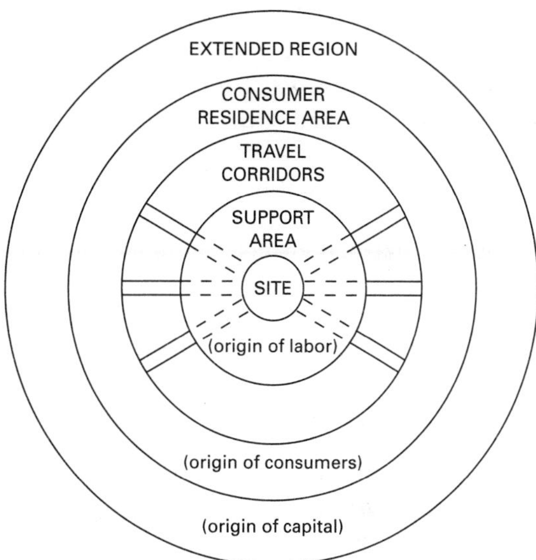

FIGURE 6.5 Regions impacted by recreation. *Source: Stevens, B., and A. Z. Rose. (1985). "Regional Input-Output Methods for Tourism Impact Analysis." Assessing the Economic Impacts of Recreation and Tourism,* D. Propst, ed. USDA Forest Service, Southeastern Forest Experiment Station, Asheville, NC.

It is clear how complicated the economic impacts of outdoor recreation are, and how difficult it is to assess them. The task is easier when the recreation site is small, serving a small circle of recreationists. But when the recreation site is large, the analysis of its economic impact becomes more difficult. The situation is complicated once the site becomes nationally and internationally renowned, as is true of some of the national parks. For example, tourists from abroad may have purchased their camping equipment outside the United States.

Empirical Findings

The National Environmental Policy Act (NEPA) requires under certain circumstances that project plans include information on social and economic effects. Environmental impact studies have yielded important information on the economic impact in the vicinity of a large recreation site. Large in this case means that the construction of the site would have an environmental impact. If there are no such impacts, information on the economic and social impact would be lacking, since the construction will have no significant effect on the quality of the environment. According to Walsh (1986:375), these studies include the estimated changes in direct and indirect output of each industry and business, income and employment, population shifts, and tax revenue and expenditure for social services in the region. Also included are the effects on environmental quality such as air and water pollution. The studies also show the distribution of economic gains and losses of industry and businesses resulting from the construction of the recreation site.

Walsh stated that studies of regional economic impacts have tended to emphasize gains and have failed to count losses, particularly of secondary nature. He reviewed Millard and Fischer (1979), which was previously cited, and showed the following:

1. Development of a recreation site usually means that the natural resource cannot be used for other purposes.
2. An increase in local services will occur to provide for the influx of tourists and recreationists.
3. The site will be overutilized during the season and underutilized otherwise.
4. Higher prices may result as the influx of out-of-towners increases, who are willing to pay more for goods and services.
5. Congestion may result on roads and in the local businesses, which may alter the locals' life-style.
6. It is possible that the average resident, who is not employed in an industry or business having to do with the recreation site, will be the one affected negatively by the change.

The Multiplier Effect

According to Knudson (1984:79), the money that stays in a community or region increases the spending ability of those who receive the wages and profits. The multiplier effect is a term used to indicate that the effect of one dollar spent at one point will be more than merely one dollar. In a small region, one dollar spent may produce the effect of $1.53. And if the whole nation is considered, each dollar spent in a national park considered with the multiplier effect would reach $3.02. But one dollar spent in a small community does not remain within its boundaries, since a good portion of it will be spent on supplies and goods imported to the region.

The economic impact of large recreation sites is both considerable and far-reaching, as shown in the case of Olympic National Park (Knudson 1984:79). Visitors to the park spent $21.8 million, of which $18.3 million were spent in the state of Washington, and only $8 million were spent on the Olympic Peninsula, where the park is located. The $21.8 million spent had a multiplier effect of $66 million across the United States.

Walsh (1986:378) suggested that a formula be used to assess the multiplier effect of a recreation site. The multiplier for a recreation business is equal to one divided by the inverse value added, as expressed in percentage of direct sales:

$$\text{Multiplier} = \frac{1}{1 - \text{Value Added (in percent)}}$$

Value added is defined as the proportion of total sales taking place in the region. The more business in the region, the higher the multiplier. For instance, if 40 percent of the sales took place in the region, then the multiplier is expressed as $\frac{1}{1 - .40}$ or 1.67. But if regional sales were 50 percent, the multiplier would be

TABLE 6.6 Regional Output of Sales Multipliers for Expenditures on Recreation Goods and Services, United States

Regions	Sources	Types of Recreation Development	Output of Sales Multipliers
Teton County, Wyoming	Rajender et al.	Tourism	1.46
Southwest Counties, Wyoming	Kite and Schultz	Fishing, Flaming Gorge Reservoir	2.07
Sullivan County, Pennsylvania	Gamble	Summer homes	1.60
Itasca County, Minnesota	Hughes	Summer resorts	2.23
Ely County, Minnesota	Lichty and Steinnes	Boundary Waters Canoe Area, tourism	2.23
Wadsworth County, Wisconsin	Kalter and Lord	Tourism	1.87
Baldwin County, Alabama	Main	Tourism	2.58
Montana	Haroldon	Winter resorts	2.40
Grand County, Colorado	Rhody and Lovegrove	Hunting and fishing	2.00
Colorado Counties	McKean and Nobe	Hunting and fishing resident and nonresident	1.75 2.60
Yaquina Bay, Oregon	Stoevener et al.	Fishing	2.06
United States	National Marine Fisheries Service	Saltwater fishing	1.90

Source: R. Walsh *Recreation Economic Decisions* State College, PA: Venture Publishing, 1986, 380. (Reprinted with permission.)

$\frac{1}{1-.50} = 2.0$, and at 60 percent the multiplier would be $\frac{1}{1-.60} = 2.5$. Needless to say, if no sales took place in the region the multiplier will be $\frac{1}{1-0} = 1$, or no multiplier at all.

Walsh (1986:380) summarized the results of several regional economic impact studies, as shown in Table 6.6. The multipliers for these recreational activities across the United States varied from 1.46 to 2.60, with an average of 2.00. The main reason for the variation in the multiplier's effect is attributed to the size of the area from which the participants are drawn. Also the type of services and industries located in the region as related to the activities provided in the recreation site will affect the size of the multiplier.

OUTDOOR RESOURCES AND TAXATION

Land is a good source of income to the government if it is privately owned and taxed. Once private land is acquired by a government agency, taxes are lost. Knudson (1984) believes that the reduction in government income in such cases is negligible when the piece of land is small and the acquisition is gradual. Moreover, fees, licensing, and sales tax on the site, once developed, usually compensate for the lost property tax. He cited Rosner's study (1977) in northwestern Wisconsin, which reported that public land acquisition by the National Park Service and Wisconsin Department of Natural Resources (over 17,000 acres) did not affect the local tax rate for the following reasons:

1. The county tax loss represented less than 1 percent of the valuation in the two counties that were affected.
2. An increase in school aid offset lost school revenue.
3. Shared state taxes as well as tax credits compensated for other local losses in revenue.

COMMERCIAL/PRIVATE OUTDOOR RECREATION

Commercial/private outdoor recreation enterprises vary in size from a small pond opened for fishing on weekends to Disneyland and Disney World. Bullaro and Edginton (1986:70) estimate that the share of the outdoor recreation system, both private and public, would be $85 billion of the $300 billion in leisure spending in this country. There are over 130,000 private suppliers of outdoor recreation services and businesses in the United States. The economic impact of these enterprises will vary according to the size, type, and orientation of each.

Knudson cites the economic impact of Disney World as including the construction of close to 20,000 hotel/motel rooms along the interstate highway leading to the site, which displaced orange groves. Also, commercial campgrounds are located within easy driving distance, and another theme park, Sea World, is close by (1984:84). Negative impacts include serious water pollution problems, congested traffic, and high prices for local residents. The Disney Corporation tried to benefit from its experience in Disneyland in Anaheim, California, where the site was smaller and control over adjacent land was difficult. For Disney World, the corporation acquired a much larger parcel, with the intention of controlling the area surrounding the site. It was successful in preserving many species of birds, mammals, and plants. Nonetheless the control could not be exerted over the hotels, motels, restaurants, and campgrounds built outside Disney's 27,000-acre property, a sign of overcommercialization.

The problem of overcommercialization is greater in the case of Niagara Falls, where commercial enterprises grew on both sides of the river, as soon as the area gained fame and tourists began to visit the falls in the early 1900s. Both the Province of Ontario and New York state tried certain controls which proved difficult to implement. According to Knudson (1984:86), the honky-tonk atmosphere still prevails there as well as in the Great Smokey Mountains National Park, Gettysburg National Military Park, and the Rocky Mountain National Park. While the multiplier effect is at work in these areas, Knudson decries the lack of quality and appropriateness of some of these commercial enterprises.

CAREERS IN OUTDOOR RECREATION

It has only been recently that most people work and play indoors. In the past most human endeavors took place outdoors. Working outdoors is not a new thing. Today, many people long for an outdoor career where there is plenty of fresh air and natural light.

Outdoor careers are found in many fields other than outdoor recreation, such as agriculture, anthropology, archeology, botany, conservation, and construction. Careers in engineering, geology, marine biology, meteorology, mining, seamanship, and surveying can also be outdoor careers. This section will be limited to presenting some of the career possibilities in outdoor recreation.

Foresters

Foresters manage and protect forests. They also estimate the potential growth of areas under their jurisdiction. Jobs are available in local, state, and the federal government as well as in private companies. The duties of the forester vary significantly from wildlife protection to providing information to the public. A bachelor's degree in forestry is a minimum educational requirement for an entry-level job in forestry.

Forestry Technicians

Foresters are supported in their work by forestry technicians, who usually have one or two years of college education. Forestry technicians may take part in the maintenance of recreation areas in forests, as well as inspect trees for disease and engage in fire fighting and flood control.

Game Wardens

Game wardens are the professionals charged with the protection of natural wildlife resources. State conservation departments as well as federal agencies employ most game wardens. A college degree plus some experience in outdoor life is required.

Naturalists

Naturalists are the interpreters of nature in outdoor recreation sites. Skill in oral communication is needed, as well as a college degree. Jobs are found in the federal and state governments and also with private companies that outfit recreationists for outdoor experiences into remote areas such as the Everglades. Knowledge and skill in the use of equipment needed for the outings are desirable.

Nature Photographers

Most nature photographers are free-lancers who work in harsh and sometimes hazardous environments in pursuit of unique photographs of animals, plants, or nature scenes. Other than technical training, certain personal traits are required for success in this field, including dedication, patience, and perseverance.

Park Rangers

Park rangers, particularly the ones at small parks, are jacks- and jills-of-all-trades. Their work varies from recreation planning to park administration. A park ranger supervises aides, gives out information, serves as an interpreter of nature, and checks on public safety. He or she may act as a police officer in many instances.

Range Managers

Range managers are professionals charged with the management and protection of range resources in determining the degree of their multiple use: grazing, lumber cutting, fishing, hunting, and other outdoor recreational activities. Most range managers are employed in federal and state government agencies.

Recreation Specialists

National parks and forests as well as state and local parks need the services of recreation specialists in planning and executing different outdoor recreational activities, which may be of a general nature or highly specialized.

The following are some of the highly specialized careers in outdoor recreation:

1. **Deep-Sea Sport-Fishing Guide** These guides organize excursions for sport fishing at offshore locations. Knowledge and experience in deep-sea sport fishing are needed in this job, as well as the ability to operate a boat. A license from the U.S. Coast Guard is required. The license is obtained by taking a test.
2. **Hang Glider Instructor** Needless to say, a special skill and lengthy prior experience are needed for this career. Since this activity is relatively new, there are not that many career opportunities.
3. **Hunting and Fishing Guide** Knowledge of the fish and game habitats and hunting and fishing techniques in the region is needed by a successful guide. This means

that substantial experience in fishing and/or hunting in the particular territory are needed before embarking on this career.

4. Scuba Diving Instructor The recent growth in recreational diving has led to the increased demand for scuba diving instructors. Certification is needed for such a job, and it is offered through professional organizations.

5. Ski Instructor Skiing is also a growing recreational activity, and the need for ski instructors is increasing. While there is certification for one to become a ski instructor, some ski areas conduct their own clinics for the purpose of preparing instructors.

6. White-Water Rafting Guide These are the professionals who take parties through rapids, over falls, and around boulders. They use large rubber rafts, rowing through churning white water. Substantial experience in white-water rafting is needed.

7. Back-Country Adventure Guide These individuals generally operate adventure tours through scenic areas. An intimate knowledge of special sites ranging from native petroglyphs to spectacular waterfalls is necessary. Frequently transportation via four-wheel drive vehicles, horses, or mules is provided, so training in these specialized areas is needed as well. Most guides are self-employed or work for a small outfitter, although there are outfitters that are growing rapidly into bigger organizations due to the popularity of the adventures.

The National Association of State Park Directors published a list of salaries for five levels of personnel who work in state parks across the United States. This list is shown in Table 6.7.

TABLE 6.7 Salaries of Personnel in State Natural Resources

	Field Unit Employee (1)		Field Unit Manger (2)		Field Supervisor (3)		Operations Chief (4)		State Park Director (5)	
	Annual Salary Range		Annual Salary Range		Annual Salary Range		Annual Salary Range		Annual Salary Range	
	Minimum $	Maximum $	Minimum $	Maximum $	Minimum $	Maximum $	Minimum $	Maximum $	Minimum $	Maximum $
AK	26,892	42,694	35,580	48,276	40,728	55,260	53,292	73,248	59,232	81,240
AL	10,618	17,830	21,715	45,370			31,278	47,658	43,134	65,780
AR	15,054	25,064	15,058	34,450	22,074	36,712	26,676	43,264	47,191	
AZ	13,660	22,906	20,556	33,654	29,549	44,716	32,284	48,859	42,500	64,320
CA	23,196	33,396	33,396	56,016	58,944	64,812		75,144		90,520
CO	21,576	32,556	31,860	49,419	39,576	53,028	43,632	58,464	43,632	58,464
CT	18,965	22,317	26,459	43,910	51,035	62,648			41,947	51,486
DE	14,960	32,683	22,453	42,843	29,430	49,050	33,694	56,156	54,280	
FL	12,685	20,372	16,613	34,924	26,970	45,445	35,000	61,040	42,000	73,030
GA	12,444	24,870	17,394	33,456	30,708	43,206	33,456	51,492		
HI	16,332	18,624	19,524	21,540	30,948	45,336	36,936	49,848	39,496	56,928

TABLE 6.7 Continued

	Field Unit Employee (1)		Field Unit Manger (2)		Field Supervisor (3)		Operations Chief (4)		State Park Director (5)	
	Annual Salary Range		Annual Salary Range		Annual Salary Range		Annual Salary Range		Annual Salary Range	
	Minimum $	Maximum $	Minimum $	Maximum $	Minimum $	Maximum $	Minimum $	Maximum $	Minimum $	Maximum $
IA	16,275	21,091	22,076	30,695	32,128	40,636			42,607	53,846
ID	18,262	24,461	24,461	34,445	31,242	41,870	36,171	48,485	46,176	61,900
IL	18,036	32,544	20,736	47,232	31,764	53,772			36,288	61,896
IN	9,594	26,997	17,706	29,796	22,807	33,722	25,697	38,350	34,944	54,392
KS	21,564	31,860	23,788	36,888	38,896	42,708	38,736	54,492		65,000
KY	6,780	18,024	15,072	35,688			27,072	49,992	52,500	
LA	10,428	15,432	14,652	21,900	21,216	30,756	22,620	32,028		
MA	15,879	20,541	19,740	31,788	26,914	45,243	33,569	45,243	42,466	53,190
MD	17,261	28,232	23,157	41,065	33,762	44,350	32,264	51,730	45,513	51,730
ME	15,225	19,905	15,683	26,395	24,356	33,820	28,059	39,166	38,542	56,555
MI	20,790	25,780	22,605	41,450	36,955	52,100	42,010	57,940	50,610	67,685
MN	22,404	28,626	22,404	43,034	33,137	44,621	33,137	44,621	47,940	63,684
MO	12,852	21,636	17,148	27,612	25,428	32,688	35,616	46,380	41,570	57,945
MS	8,448	20,028	16,572	32,640	24,840	35,712	29,412	44,040	35,356	52,972
MT	10,223	16,425	14,433	27,437	23,466	32,490	25,587	35,380	30,508	40,416
NC	14,436	24,252	18,420	34,704	25,884	41,700	29,508	47,976	37,176	60,648
ND	17,688	27,264	19,512	32,952	24,888	37,992			36,768	55,752
NE	15,085	21,119	26,902	37,663			33,421	46,789	55,000	75,000
NH	13,000	19,400	16,600	25,400	23,400	33,100	30,300	36,100	37,800	48,100
NJ	21,435	40,212	24,708	48,685	42,266	59,178	50,000	70,000	59,471	83,261
NM	13,125	21,778	17,268	28,819	21,755	36,517	25,025	42,115	41,280	53,192
NV	18,653	24,983	21,106	28,430	24,983	33,932	29,707	40,611	40,276	
NY	13,400	19,425	19,300	39,000	55,800	85,992		88,115		87,076
OH	15,205	34,590	21,237	39,603	33,343	43,659	40,394	52,936	43,867	64,251
OK	10,704	19,358	21,821	26,438	31,277	41,612	34,411	45,774	48,000	48,000
OR	17,784	24,468	18,804	33,696	29,136	43,056	39,072	49,836		58,884
PA	14,025	21,672	18,543	28,186	32,411	50,093	37,262	57,487	49,291	60,988

TABLE 6.7 Continued

	Field Unit Employee (1)		Field Unit Manger (2)		Field Supervisor (3)		Operations Chief (4)		State Park Director (5)	
	Annual Salary Range		Annual Salary Range		Annual Salary Range		Annual Salary Range		Annual Salary Range	
	Minimum $	Maximum $	Minimum $	Maximum $	Minimum $	Maximum $	Minimum $	Maximum $	Minimum $	Maximum $
RI	16,423	16,994	19,618	21,492	22,969	26,273	33,068	37,432	38,388	43,503
SC	12,767	20,716	14,937	35,876	26,906	40,359	29,102	43,653	41,425	59,744
SD	14,352	21,507	16,931	25,376	23,088	34,611	29,036	43,555	32,718	49,067
TN	13,154	23,280	17,124	29,724	25,416	37,248	25,416	37,248	40,668	60,444
TX	10,572	20,448	18,540	32,412	30,336	38,184	36,948	46,560		51,987
UT	16,200	26,100	19,900	38,300	30,700	44,800	34,000	49,600	38,000	55,500
VA	13,881	18,962	19,817	29,595	25,903	35,368	30,953	42,280	40,434	55,231
VT	13,395	21,050	15,517	24,461	25,522	40,539	28,850	45,822	34,840	55,515
WA	12,264	25,572	22,164	37,536	34,032	43,440	39,876	51,060	70,032	72,132
WI	16,136	28,132	20,134	42,032	32,679	45,562	32,679	45,562	42,170	62,980
WV	9,012	25,207	12,768	33,184	20,856	38,135	23,952	43,843	47,600	
WY	15,683	25,064	22,152	35,463	24,460	39,166	32,905	52,665	40,143	64,167

VI. PERSONNEL—B. Salaries

(1) **Field Unit Employee (Park Ranger)**—the entry-level park employee with broad contact, interpretive, and facility maintenance duties.

(2) **Field Unit Manager (Park Superintendent/Manager)**—the senior on-site employee who manages the park and supervises subordinate park rangers or other classes.

(3) **Field Supervisor (District Manger/Supervisor)**—the employee with responsibility for overseeing the operation of a number of parks in a given region or part of the state.

(4) **Operations Chief (Central Office Line Supervisor)**—the one employee in the central office whose principal task is the day-to-day direction of park system operations; normally the position to which field units report and which, in turn, reports to the director of the parks agency.

(5) **State Parks Director**—head of state park system overseeing all other personnel.

Source: National Association for State Park Directors (1991) *Annual Information Exchange* (Tallahassee, FL).

SUMMARY

This chapter deals with the economics of outdoor pursuits and begins with a question: Why does the national policy of a capitalistic-oriented society include the preservation of a large part of public lands for outdoor pursuits? Moreover the policy calls for the provision of costly programs and facilities to be provided on these lands. Despite the appearance of these provisions and activities as being mere expenditures, the fact is that outdoor pursuits represent an important part of national, regional, and state economies.

A delicate balance between consumption and production takes place as the economic system evolves. Personal expenditure on leisure pursuits is calculated in the total economic picture, which reached $48 billion in 1962. In a quarter of a century the figure jumped to $320 billion, making leisure a potent force in the American economy. Productivity, increased income, increased free time, and mobility are suggested as the reasons for making leisure play a leading role in the economy. Americans are spending good sums of money on recreation supplies and equipment, travel and vacations, sports and outdoor pursuits, cultural activities, and home entertainment.

It is hard to estimate the exact amounts of governmental expenditure on the provision of areas, facilities, and programs in recreation. It is also hard to estimate the expenditure of non-profit organizations on similar activities. But expenditure is only half of the picture of the relationship between leisure and the economy. The other half is the economic impact of such expenditure. The economy of the outdoor recreation system revolves around four elements: demands of the recreationists, supply of natural resources and programs, plans and policies concerning the use of these resources and programs, and the management and implementation of these plans and policies.

The economic impact of leisure is exemplified in the tourism business. It is estimated that tourism now represents 6 percent of the world gross national product (GNP). The United States share is quite sizeable. Regional and local economic impacts are felt in that if one dollar is spent locally, its impact is felt regionally and even nationally. Yet there are some negative impacts from the use of an indoor recreational site which include overuse during the season, higher prices for locals, and congestion on roads and in local businesses.

The expansion in the provision of outdoor recreational pursuits has helped in the creating of new specialties, some of which require rigorous and professional training. The career possibilities in outdoor recreation include, but are not limited to, foresters, forestry technicians, game wardens, naturalists, nature photographers, park rangers, range managers, and recreation specialists.

REFERENCES

Alward, G. (1986) "Local and Regional Economic Impacts of Outdoor Recreation Development in the President's Commission of Americans Outdoors" in *A Literature Review.* Washington, D.C.: U.S. Government Printing Office.

Bullaro, J., and C. Edginton (1986) *Commercial Leisure Services.* New York: Macmillan.

Clawson, M., and J. Knetsch (1966) *Economics of Outdoor Recreation.* Baltimore, MD: Johns Hopkins University Press.

Dulles, F. R. (1965) *A History of Recreation.* New York: Appleton-Century-Croft.

Epperson, A. (1983) "Why People Travel." *Leisure Today* (April):31.

Hunt, J. D. (1986) "Tourist Expenditure in the United States" in *The President's Commission on American Outdoors, Literature Review.* Washington, D.C.: U.S. Government Printing Office.

Ibrahim, H. (1991) *Leisure and Society: A Comparative Approach.* Dubuque, IA: Wm. C. Brown.

Jafari, J. (1983) "Tourism Today," *Leisure Today* (April) 3–5.

Jensen, C. (1985) *Outdoor Recreation in America.* Minneapolis, MN: Burgess.

Kelly, J. (1985) *Recreation Business.* New York: Macmillan.

Kelly, J. (1987) *Freedom To Be: A New Sociology of Leisure.* New York: Macmillan.

Knudson, D. (1984) *Outdoor Recreation.* New York: Macmillan.

Lerner, E., and C. B. Abbott (1982) *The Way To Go.* New York: Warner Books.

MacLean, J., J. Peterson, and D. Martin (1985) *Leisure and Recreation: The Changing Scene.* New York: Macmillan.

Millard, F., and D. Fischer (1979) "The Local Economic Impact of Outdoor Recreation Facilities" in *Land and Leisure: Concepts and Methods in Outdoor Recreation,* C. Van Doren et al., editors. Chicago, IL: Maaroufa Press.

National Association of State Park Directors (1990) *Annual Information Exchange.* Tallahassee, FL: NASPD.

Olson, S. (1961) "The Spiritual Aspects of Wilderness" in *Wilderness: America's Living Heritage,* D. Brower, editor. San Francisco, CA: Sierra Club.

Peterson, G., and T. Brown (1986) "The Economic Benefits of Outdoor Recreation" in *The President's Commission on Americans Outdoors, Literature Review.* Washington, D.C.: U.S. Government Printing Office.

Rosner, M. (1977) *Impact Upon Local Property Taxes of Acquisitions Within the St. Croix River State Forest in Burnett and Polk Counties.* Madison, WI: Department of Natural Resources, Technical Bulletin. No. 101.

Rostow, E. (1960) *The Stages of Economic Growth.* Cambridge, MA.: Harvard University Press.

Rubenstein, C. (1980) "Vacations" *Psychology Today* May: 62-67.

Simmons, I. G. (1975) *Rural Recreation in the Industrial World.* New York: John Wiley.

Spandoni, M. (1986) "Special Report: Travel and Tourism." *Advertising Age.* 14(July):6.

Stevens, B., and A. Z. Rose (1985) "Regional Input-Output Methods For Tourism Impact Analysis," in *Assessing the Economic Impacts of Recreation and Tourism,* D. Propst, editor. Asheville, N.C.: USDA Forest Service, Southeastern Forest Experiment Station.

United Media Enterprises. (1983) *Where Does the Time Go?* New York: Newspaper Enterprises Association.

Veblen, T. (1953) *The Theory of Leisure Class.* New York: New American Library.

Walsh, R. (1986) *Recreation Economic Decision: Comparing Benefits and Costs.* State College, PA: Venture Publishing.

Walsh, R., and J. Loomis (1986) "The Contribution of Recreation to National Economic Development" in *The President's Commission on Americans Outdoors. Literature Review.* Washington, D.C.: U.S. Government Printing Office.

PART *two*

Outdoor Resources

This part consists of five chapters that examine the locations of outdoor recreational areas and places. Chapters 7, 8, and 9 cover the recreational areas and facilities owned and operated by the federal, state, and local governments, respectively. Chapter 10 is devoted to looking at the role played by commercial enterprises and private individuals, and Chapter 11 is devoted to outdoor opportunities in other countries. Considerable attention is given to Canada in this chapter. Availability of data and information was instrumental in selecting the five countries for inclusion in this volume.

7 Federal Resources and Recreation

The United States has assembled a world-class system of public outdoor recreation lands, beginning with the protection of Yosemite Valley in the 1860s and Yellowstone, the first national park, in 1872. The system has been carved mostly from the old "public domain," the unregulated expanses of Western open space acquired by the United States through treaty, purchase, and the forcible eviction of earlier inhabitants. By the late nineteenth century, private enterprises had come to regard the public domain as common property and spoils for the bold. They had profitably stripped its timber, mined its substrates for minerals, and diverted and dammed its rivers, often leaving behind a burned, scarred, and eroded landscape. Though the public owned the resources, the exploiters paid little or no fee for the booty. Prodded by some foresighted Americans, Congress acted, though in piecemeal fashion, to limit the abuse and stop future exploitation. Thus were born the first national park (1872), the national monuments (1906), and the National Park System (1916), all managed by the Department of the Interior. Congress "withdrew" these lands from the public domain, and preserved them because they exhibited special values. Most of the remaining public domain, still vast, stayed with the Department of the Interior under what is now the Bureau of Land Management. Other segments became national wildlife refuges.

In addition, Congress created the National Forest Service in 1905 and endowed it by transferring 85 million acres to the Department of Agriculture for management. The National Forest System embodies the Forest Service's tradition of regarding timber as a crop, to be harvested according to the principle of *sustained yield,* that is, to cut and grow wood at equal rates over the long term.

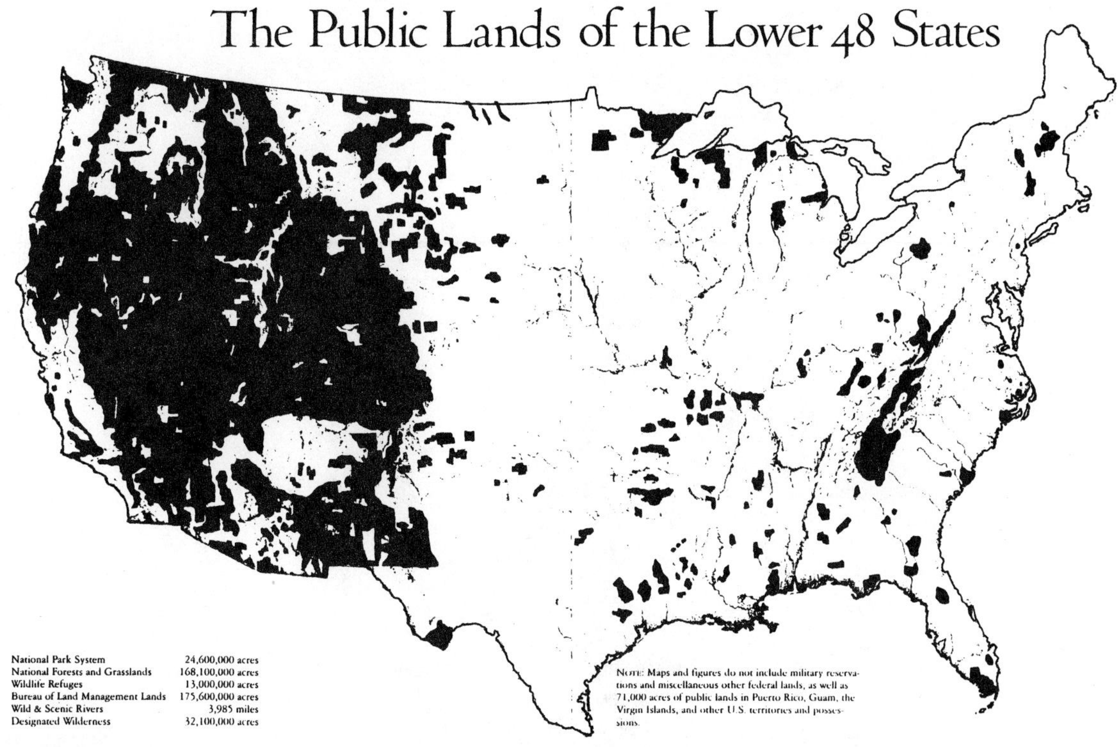

FIGURE 7.1 Public lands of the lower forty-eight states.

The extent of public domain is shown in Figure 7.1. At the federal level the National Forest Service and the National Park Service represent two types of agencies. The Forest Service practices *multiple use,* where the primary challenge is to balance economic use and conservation. Figure 7.2 illustrates the diverse uses of a resource.

Multiple-use management takes advantage of the resource's ability to provide a greater combined bundle of uses and benefits from the same parcel of land. The Forest Service, for example, has a special legislative mandate to implement multiple-use management on National Forest Systems by administering the national forests for outdoor recreation, range, timber, watershed and wildlife and fish. Passage of the *Forest and Rangeland Renewable Resources Planning Act of 1974* directed the secretary of agriculture to prepare a Renewable Resources Assessment (RRA) by December of 1975 with an update in 1979 and each 10-year period thereafter. The 1990 RRA program renewed the Forest Service's commitment to multiple-use management, but the resources were better rounded out and implemented with greater environmental sensitivity. To round out its multiple-use role the Forest Service (1990:1–2) listed the following high priorities:

1. Enhance recreation, wildlife, and fisheries resources.
2. Ensure that commodity production is environmentally acceptable.
3. Improve scientific knowledge about natural resources.
4. Respond to global resource issues.

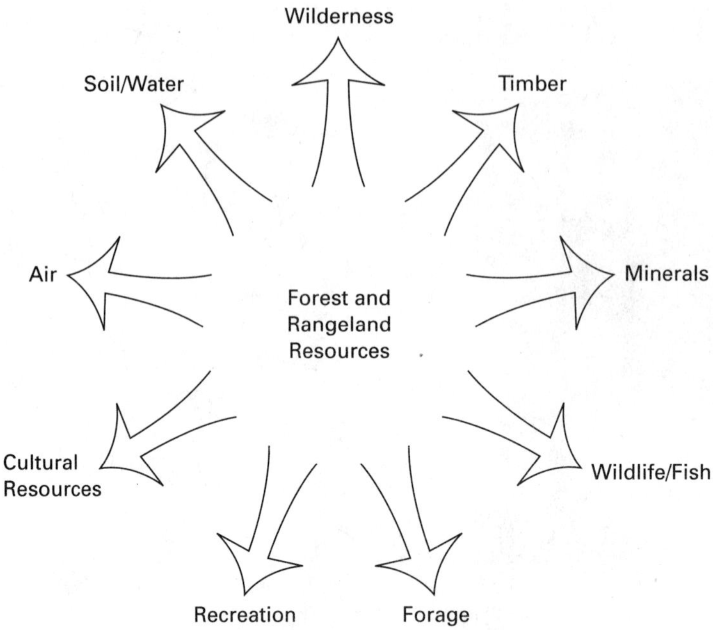

FIGURE 7.2 Multiple-use management provides the opportunity to simultaneously produce a number of resource benefits from the same parcel of land. *Source: The Forest Service, U.S. Department of Agriculture, Program for Forest and Rangeland Resources: A Long-Term Strategic Plan.* (U.S. Government Printing Office, 1990), 1–3.

The Forest Service multiple-use and increased environmental sensitivity role will be expanded to the state and private forest landowners through assistance programs. Other multiple-use agencies include the Bureau of Land Management, Bureau of Reclamation, Army Corps of Engineers, Tennessee Valley Authority, and National Marine Fisheries Service.

The National Park Service represents the *single-use,* or restricted use, concept. National park areas are to be preserved in virtually their present state for the "benefit and enjoyment of people now and in the future" (Jensen 1985:328). According to Jensen, the resources are not there to be exploited for profit such as by harvesting or milling; but since the resources are protected for the enjoyment of the people, recreation is permitted as long as the activity is not destructive to the unique values of the park unit. Another single-use agency is the U.S. Fish and Wildlife Service. Wild and scenic rivers and wilderness areas are also managed under the single-use philosophy.

From the purist sense any recreation use on wilderness lands is disruptive to the wild ecological system. Therefore decisions involving recreational use on these lands are critical (Jensen 1985:328–29). The distinction between various agencies' land management philosophies is narrowing, and this trend is expected to continue. For instance, generally hunting has not been permitted in national parks, but it is permitted on designated areas of national forests and BLM lands. Today, hunting occurs in one national park, several national riverways, seashores, and trails, and all national preserves administered by

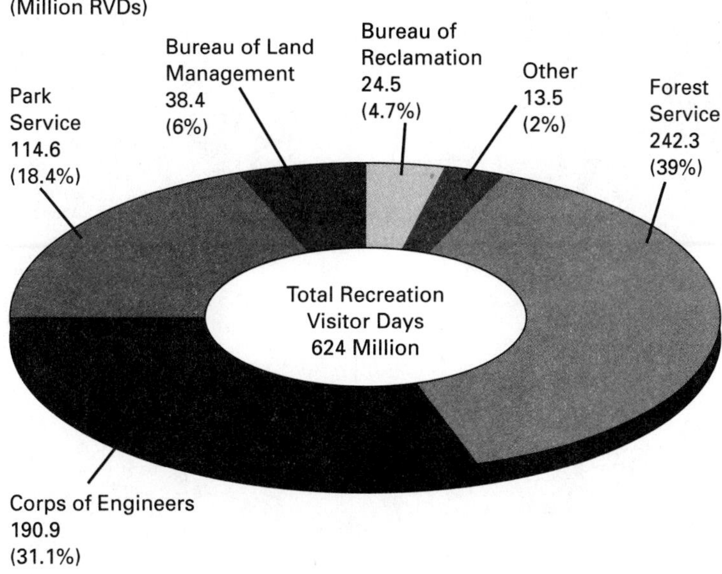

FIGURE 7.3 The number of recreational visitor days (RVDs) by federal agency in 1988. *Source: The Forest Service, U.S. Department of Agriculture, Report of the Forest Service* (U.S. Government Printing Office, 1990), 35.

the National Park Service (Craig 1991:43). Recreation usage, regardless of land management philosophy, is a major concern of each federal agency, as seen in Figure 7.3, which shows recreational visitor days by agency.

These two philosophies, single use and multiple use, led to a split between two early outdoor leaders, John Muir and Gifford Pinchot (refer to Chapter 3 for their biographies), who were once allies in the crusade to redeem the public domain from uncontrolled exploitation. Their differences surfaced over the Hetch Hetchy Valley controversy in which the proponents of multiple use won the right to create a water reservoir in a spectacularly beautiful valley next to the Yosemite Valley, both contained within Yosemite National Park. This reservoir would serve the water needs of the growing city of San Francisco. Pinchot, the spokesperson for the emerging doctrine of conservation, argued for damming the Hetch Hetchy. He believed that the strict preservation creed of the park bureau supporters was unnecessarily limiting of the nation's resources. As such he believed that the preservation of the Yosemite Valley in its pristine state met the needs of the park, and that a more practical use of the neighboring valley allowed for multiple use of this land. Both aesthetic and economic uses were permitted.

An outraged Muir, a major proponent of the preservationists, claimed that the argument of the dam builders was devised for destruction. He believed that the entire park should be preserved in its natural state, including both spectacular valleys. In his preservationist outlook, there was no room for compromise. This dispute was closely followed by the San Francisco media, and because of this, a schism between the conservationists and preservationists was in full view of the public.

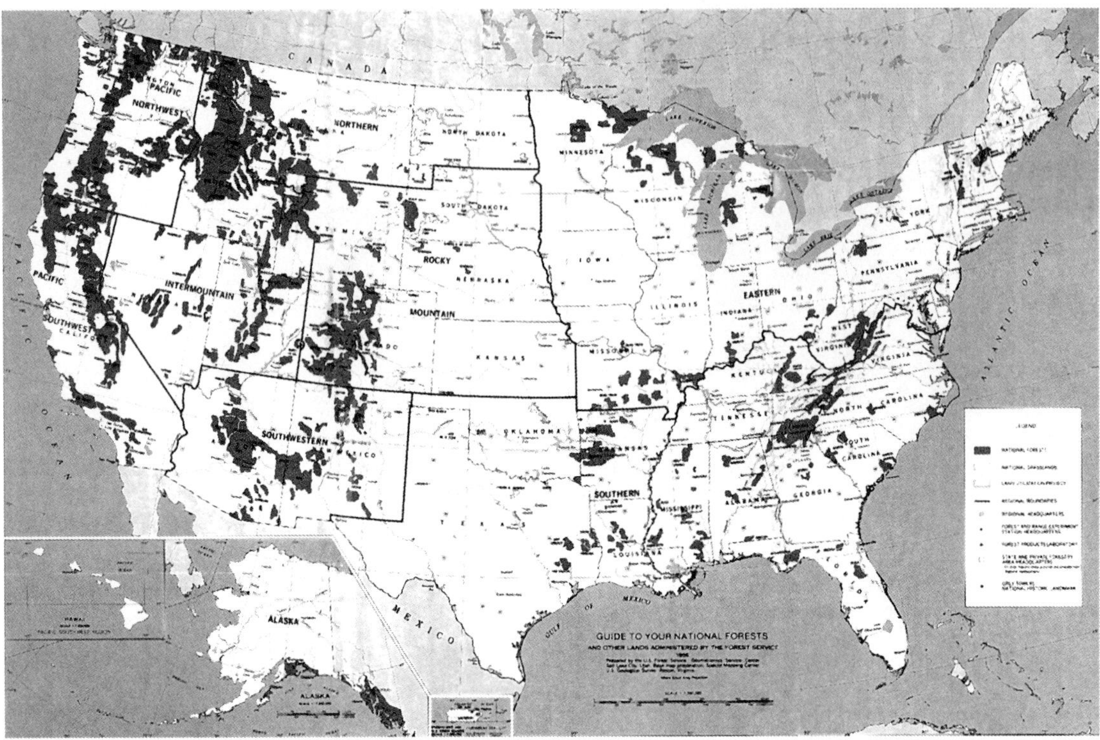

FIGURE 7.4 Forest Service lands in the United States. *Source: The Forest Service, U.S. Department of Agriculture, A Guide to Your National Forests* (U.S. Government Printing Office, 1988), 418.

THE NATIONAL FOREST SYSTEM

The National Forest System contains over 191 million acres of public land dispersed throughout all but seven states in America (see Figure 7.4). The system includes 156 national forests and grasslands administered by 630 district ranger offices in nine regions. More outdoor recreation takes place in the national forests than on any other public lands. Over 108,000 miles of trails and over 10,000 recreational sites including campgrounds, picnic areas, ski areas, and visitor centers are available. Portions of 67 rivers on the forest lands are managed as wild and scenic rivers. Nineteen national recreation areas, scenic areas or monuments, and 376 national recreation trails are found in the national forests.

Roughly 17 percent of national forest land, or 32 million acres, is congressionally designated wilderness, offering a more primitive recreational experience in some of the country's most spectacular scenery.

History of the National Forest

The Creative Act of March 3, 1891, authorized the president to establish forest reserves from forest and rangelands in the public domain. The impetus for the establishment of these reserves came from recreation and conservation groups who believed strongly that forested areas should be placed under official governmental protection (Tweed 1980:iii). By 1897 the *Organic Administration Act* was passed, which, however, provided for the right of entry to persons for prospecting, locating, and developing mineral resources, and for the use of water and timber resources found on forest reserves. On February 1, 1905, President Theodore Roosevelt signed the *Transfer Act,* which transferred the nations's forest reserves from the Department of the Interior to the Department of Agriculture. That same day, Secretary of Agriculture James Wilson endorsed Gifford Pinchot's conservation philosophy establishing that the forests were to be utilized and not merely reserved. The forest reserves, later renamed the national forests, were to be managed for the greatest good for the greatest number of people on a long-term basis. Local questions were to be decided by local officials—a philosophy that has made the Forest Service one of the most decentralized and responsive agencies in the federal government.

Recreational development Recreational use of forest lands grew slowly at first, then more rapidly as automobiles became numerous and roads penetrated into previously remote and inaccessible areas. Increased prosperity and more free time encouraged recreational improvements. The first official report recognizing the prominence of recreational use in the national forests was made in the U.S. Department of Agriculture's 1919 edition of the annual *Report of the Forester.* Tweed (1980:1-26) researched early recreation use in the national forests to World War II and found that recreation was one of the major activities with the granting of temporary leases for summer cottages and camp sites. Thousands of recreation permits were issued in 1913 for pleasure resorts and boathouses, and there were over one million day visitors, 231,000 campers, hunters, anglers, boaters, swimmers, and climbers, and 191,000 guests at houses, hotels, and sanitariums. Early budget limitations and priorities precluded recreation spending by the federal government, so to a large extent these visitors depended upon privately owned facilities for their basic needs. Forest rangers cleared inflammable material from around heavily used camp spots and built crude rock fireplaces, erected toilets, dug garbage pits, and developed sources of water supply.

According to Tweed (1980:1-26), the initial areas of concentration of summer visitors were in the Angeles National Forest of southern California, the Oregon (later Mt. Hood) National Forest in northern Oregon, and the Pike and San Isabel National Forests of central Colorado, all in mountains near cities. Holders of summer-home permits often formed cooperative associations to provide common facilities and services. In 1915 forester Henry Graves recommended to the secretary of Agriculture that the Columbia Gorge Park be developed in the Oregon National Forest. This became the first time that the Forest Service dedicated an extended area for purely recreational use, prohibiting timber sales and the distribution of permits for homesites. Soon the Eagle Creek campground and Eagle Creek trail were developed by the Forest Service, and by 1919 the North Pacific District created a recreation office.

It may have been that a broader interest in recreation resulted from the constant creation of national parks out of national forests. Mt. Rainier National Park had been created from part of the Mt. Rainier Forest Reserve in 1899, Crater Lake National Park from part of the Cascade Forest Reserve in 1902, Glacier National Park from part of the Blackfoot National Forest in 1910, Rocky Mountain National Park from parts of the Arapaho and Colorado National Forests in 1915, and Lassen Volcanic National Park from part of the Lassen National Forest in 1916. More transfers followed.

Pinchot and his division, the Bureau of Forestry (later renamed the Forest Service), had campaigned to assume the administration of the national parks. But by 1910 another campaign had developed to create a separate Bureau of National Parks within the Department of the Interior. Supporters of the park bureau concept, such as John Muir and Robert Underwood Johnson, based their rejection of possible Forest

Service management largely on fears of Pinchot's controversial support of the Hetch Hetchy reservoir project within Yosemite National Park. Pinchot and his successor, Henry Graves, viewed strict preservation by supporters of the park bureau to be unnecessarily limiting and wasteful of the nation's resources. It is probably safe to assume that at least a portion of the Forest Service's recreation interest in the second decade of this century resulted from the service's hope of preventing the creation of (or limiting the growth of) a new parks bureau which had as a major purpose the development of recreation facilities.

Because of their role in the development of the nation's urban parks, various landscape architects looked upon themselves as the logical agents to develop professionally planned recreation facilities in the national forests and parks. As early as 1910 proposals for a parks bureau had included a role in the new agency for landscape architects. And by 1916 it became apparent to the Forest Service that if it were to compete successfully with the newly created National Park Service, it ultimately would have to develop professionally planned recreation facilities. Early in 1917 the service employed Frank A. Waugh, professor of landscape architecture at Massachusetts Agricultural College in Amherst, to prepare a national study of recreation uses of the national forests. In his report Waugh suggested that certain parts of the forest be developed as scenic reservations, allowing no use that would significantly detract from the recreation values present. He discussed briefly the recreation potential of the national monuments, then under Forest Service control, explaining their status as scenic or scientific preserves. He argued that recreation must be considered one of the major uses of the national forests, equal in importance to timber harvesting, watershed protection, or grazing. It was his belief that nearly all national forest lands had potential for public recreational use. Under these circumstances he felt that it would be impossible for one agency to manage all of the recreational development while another looked after other resource management problems. Either the Forest Service and the National Park Service would have to merge, or each would have to develop its own recreation program. The latter was preferable. His report concluded that there was a need for the Forest Service to hire trained, professional personnel for its recreation program.

World War I to the Great Depression

As soon as World War I ended, the Forest Service hired landscape engineer Arthur H. Carhart to work in the Rocky Mountain District. At the same time the North Pacific District made forester Fred Cleator its recreation specialist. Carhart designed a foot trail for tourist use on Pikes Peak. Since Congress had appropriated no funds for recreation, the Commerce Club of Pueblo (Colorado) raised money and cooperated with the city to erect a few shelters, toilets, and fireplaces in Squirrel Creek Canyon, 30 miles from town. It was Carhart's belief that recreation planning for the national forests would inevitably have to pass beyond the construction of single campgrounds to comprehensive general planning. By late 1919 he began work on such a plan for the San Isabel National Forest.

Financially backed by the San Isabel Public Recreation Association, Carhart's plans for an extensive system of campgrounds, picnic grounds, roads, and trails were implemented. This collaboration served as a model for other communities and continued until the Great Depression. Similar cooperation eventually produced a significant number of national forest recreation areas at a time when the Forest Service chose not to, or could not, expend much of its regular appropriation on such work. Carhart helped to develop the idea of wilderness, or limited recreational development, in certain superb natural environments. One result was a landmark policy statement on wilderness from Secretary of Agriculture William M. Jardine in 1926, which pledged 1,000 square miles of wilderness in the Superior National Forest, the forerunner of the Boundary Waters Canoe Area.

Convinced that important progress had occurred, Carhart asked Chief Forester William B. Greeley to seek $50,000 for recreation work in the national forests for 1922. The request was made, but the money was not approved. Carhart made a similar request for funding for fiscal year 1923. Again funding was denied, and instead Congress reluctantly provided $10,000 for simple facilities required by recreationists for fire and sanitary protection. Carhart responded with his resignation, which vacated the single position in the Forest Service dedicated wholly to recreation. The Forest Service generally held that the recreational role of the national forest was to provide space for recreation. Publicly financed recreation facilities in these forest areas remained limited in number and simple in nature.

For nearly a decade after Carhart's resignation two groups, foresters and collaborators, handled all Forest Service recreation problems. Most of the responsibility fell to the foresters, who assumed responsibility for the design, construction, and administration of recreation sites. In the meantime, H. R. Francis of New York State College of Forestry at Syracuse University developed a general course for forestry students in the basic concepts and requirements of forest recreation. Whether academically trained in recreation work or not, foresters carried out the Forest Service recreation program. It was these foresters who received the first congressional appropriations for recreational development beyond fire prevention and sanitary facilities. As campgrounds improved, recreational use rose by 38 percent in the mid 1920s. A few positions specializing in recreation work began to develop as the Forest Service found itself year after year getting deeper into the recreation business. But just as it became apparent that the hiring of technically trained personnel in recreation was necessary, the Great Depression forced Congress to cut rather than increase recreational spending.

The Great Depression to World War II

A policy statement in the 1930s reaffirmed that the responsibility for recreational planning still rested entirely on regional foresters and forest supervisors. A cautious, conservative site development policy continued. This policy fit the budget and goals of the Hoover administration. This modest level of national forest recreation development ended, however, with the election of President Franklin Delano Roosevelt in 1933. A decade of frenzied activity followed that was checked only by World War II. During the height of the New Deal, the Forest Service received recreation funds and support far beyond its wildest dreams. These changes in the magnitude and scope of the Forest Service recreation program resulted in inevitable changes in its recreation policy. To cope with the severe national economic crisis, authorization and funds for public works in forest, water, and soil conservation were provided. With Executive Order 6101 Roosevelt created the Emergency Conservation Work (ECW) program to carry out specified activities. The Civilian Conservation Corps (CCC) was viewed by FDR as primarily a forestry organization dedicated to fighting fires, planting trees, thinning timber stands, and stopping soil erosion and floods. But the field personnel of the state and federal agencies soon realized that CCC labor might also be directed toward the construction of forest improvements—particularly roads, trails, buildings, and recreation sites. Through its provisions for public works spending, the National Industrial Recovery Act of June 16, 1933, provided yet another opportunity for Forest Service recreation facilities to be built.

Permanent recreation improvements were encouraged and erected from coast to coast. The level of development of some of the more popular national forest areas in the Northwest even surpassed that of the national parks of the region. Public Works Administration (PWA) funds were made available for the building of the Timberline Lodge on Mt. Hood, which became known as one of the wonders of the Northwest. By 1935 it became apparent that a central office for recreation was needed to oversee recreation planning and development in the National Forest System. Ernest E. Walker, a trained landscape architect, was hired for the Washington office. In 1937 the Recreation and Lands Division received a chief, Robert Marshall.

A forester and wilderness enthusiast, Robert Marshall had previously served as the chief forester for the Indian Service, U.S. Department of the Interior. Marshall had a strong and long-lasting influence on Forest Service recreation policy and development, despite the fact that his career was cut short by an early death after only 30 months in office. He worked tirelessly to establish a secure position for recreation on an equal footing with the other traditionally more dominant phases of national forest management such as timber and range use. An ardent outdoorsman, indefatigable hiker, and persistent advocate of wilderness and primitive areas, he was a strong advocate for adequate camping, outing, scenic, and other recreation areas. He had written the recreation section of the National Plan for American Forestry in 1933. Independently wealthy, he helped to found and endow the Wilderness Society. By the late 1930s, recreation, under Marshall's charge, had been established as a major priority of the Forest Service. Under his direction, the service built a number of camps, along with substantial facilities designed primarily for the use of low-income adults, 4-H clubs, and similar youth groups. Downhill skiing areas began to appear as interest increased. Expansion of facilities had become impressive, and by 1939 the Forest Service's first book on recreation, *Forest Outings,* appeared.

The 1940s brought a decline of the CCC program recreation projects and employment of technical personnel. Entry of the United States into World War II in December 1941 caused national defense to take priority. Rebuilding of a recreational staff took many years, although work continued on overnight individual family camping and picnic units. Never again however did the service look at recreation as a mere designation of a few roadside camping areas with tables and privies. National forest recreation had become a part of life for millions of Americans (Tweed 1980:1–26).

The *Multiple Use-Sustained Yield Act of 1960* supplemented the purpose for which the national forests were established to include outdoor recreation, watershed, range, timber, and wildlife and fish purposes. Meeting increased demands for recreational opportunities is a major aim of forest land managers. Because each acre of the National Forest System has recreation potential, it is mandated that recreation be considered when planning or executing resources management programs. Containing some of the nation's greatest assets, almost all National Forest System lands are available for outdoor recreation.

In 1974 Congress enacted the *Forest and Rangeland Renewable Resources Planning Act* (RPA), which directed the secretary of Agriculture to periodically assess the nation's forest and rangeland resources and to regularly submit recommended long-range Forest Service programs. The first program, submitted in 1975, recommended an increase in the supply of outdoor recreation opportunities and services. The new programs would emphasize *dispersed recreation,* that is, forest- and rangeland-oriented recreation that makes use of sites other than ones already designed for concentrated recreational use.

In meeting its recreation responsibilities, the Forest Service coordinates with the private sector and government agencies to avoid duplication of efforts. Where appropriate, as determined through joint land use planning, National Forest Service recreation resources are used to complement opportunities on other public lands. Where economically feasible, the private sector is encouraged to develop and maintain recreation facilities for the public as long as the long-term public interest is served.

The Forest Service role in outdoor recreation is to strive toward the following:

1. *Cooperation* The Forest Service cooperates with private interest, local and state governments, and federal agencies by sharing its knowledge, resources, and capabilities.
2. *Land Planning and Management* The Forest Service develops, administers, and protects National Forest System lands in a manner that produces opportunities for quality recreation experiences.
3. *Research and Information* The Forest Service conducts research to aid effective recreation management on all forest and range lands and provides information that enhances the national forest visitors' experiences.

Despite the fact that more people recreate in the national forests than anywhere else, the national forests have not reached their full potential in meeting the growing outdoor recreation needs of the American people. In developing their management plans for the next 10 to 15 years, the Forest Service conducted the most comprehensive citizen participation effort ever attempted by a federal agency. The result was a clear message for more and better opportunities to enjoy the national forests. The Forest Service is challenged to unify the American people and their lands in a manner that best meets the public's ever-changing needs. In 1987 a new plan, the *National Recreation Strategy Project,* was developed. The plan calls for a strategy to manage recreation on national forest lands within the context of multiple-use management. The strategy offers many opportunities for recreation by developing the following (Forest Service 1988:3):

1. An expression of willingness to try new ideas and new approaches.
2. Partnerships to help stretch the federal dollar in order to offer high-quality outdoor recreation.
3. A study of customer needs and the ability to discover new customers.
4. A trusting approach with its employees by encouraging some calculated risk-taking, even if there are mistakes, in order to do a better job.

The strategy called for the development of several marketing plans that focus on customer satisfaction. The importance of meeting the needs of urban populations through recreational opportunities in nearby national forests was emphasized (see Figure 7.5). The strategy allows the service the flexibility to reach its outdoor recreation potential without dictating policy. It encourages creative and imaginative thinking, increases opportunities for professionals in recreation, builds on cost-sharing programs, and promotes interpretation and environmental education as an important part of outdoor recreation.

Recent Recreational Trends

The Forest Service (1990:33–43) reported in 1989 that recreationists spend 252.5 million recreational visitor days (RVDs) on National Forest System lands, a 4 percent increase over 1988. Recent data show that the national forests and grasslands account for 39 percent of the total RVDs of use that take place on federal lands—more outdoor recreation than on any other

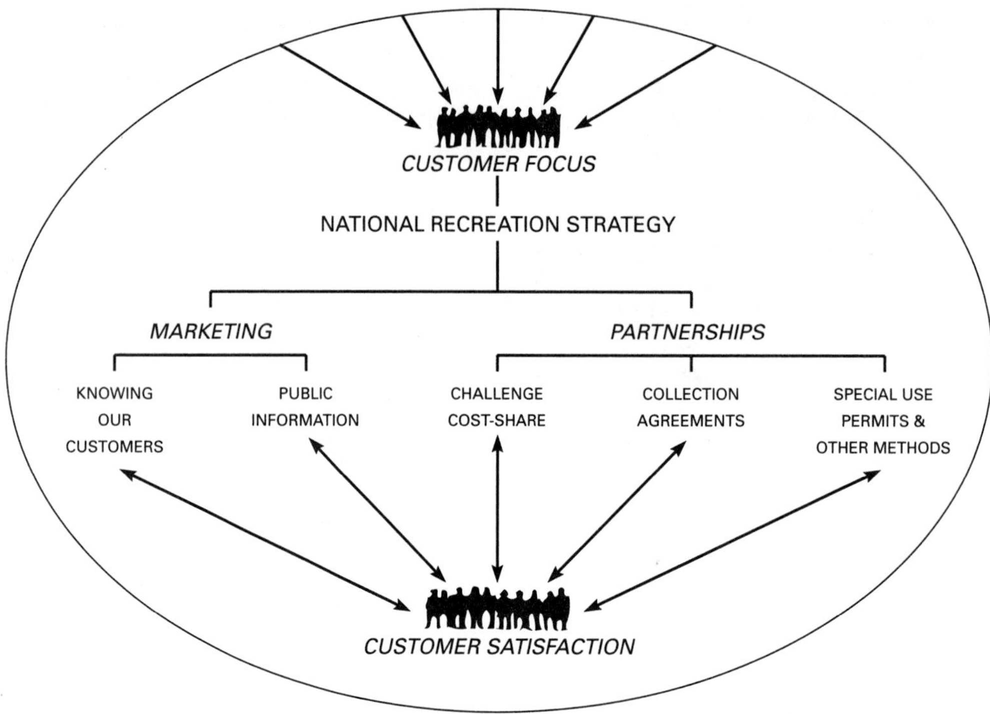

FIGURE 7.5 The Forest Service strategy to meet the needs of the people. *Source: The Forest Service, U.S. Department of Agriculture, A Guide to Your National Forests* (U.S. Government Printing Office, 1988).

federal landholding (see Figure 7.6). The Forest Service trail system is the largest in the nation, with more than 108,381 miles of trails on which to hike, ride, or cross-country ski. The national forests have 3,338 miles of the National Wild and Scenic River System, 354 wilderness areas in 36 states covering 32.5 million acres, 14 national recreation areas, and many geologic, scenic, and botanical areas. The forests also contain valuable historic and prehistoric archeological resources, and more than 4,400 campgrounds, 1,400 picnic grounds, 50 major visitor centers, and hundreds of Forest Service offices throughout the United States. In cooperation with the private sector, the forests provide more than 40 percent of the downhill skiing in the nation, as well as sites for many lodges, resorts, and more than 15,000 summer homes.

The Forest Service is involved in a wide spectrum of recreational activities. There are 360,000 miles of road and an extensive trail system for motorized vehicles that provide access to these activities. Most national forest visitors use these lands, roads, and trails for unstructured dispersed recreation, such as hiking, hunting, and driving for pleasure. This accounts for an equivalent of 148 million RVDs, or approximately 59 percent of total use. Five percent of the total use of 11.6 million RVDs occurred in wilderness and primitive areas.

The National Forest System contains the greatest diversity of wildlife, fish, and plant species of any single land ownership in the country. With goals to maintain ecosystem diversity, the service responds to recreational and commercial uses of fish and wildlife. Fish and wildlife

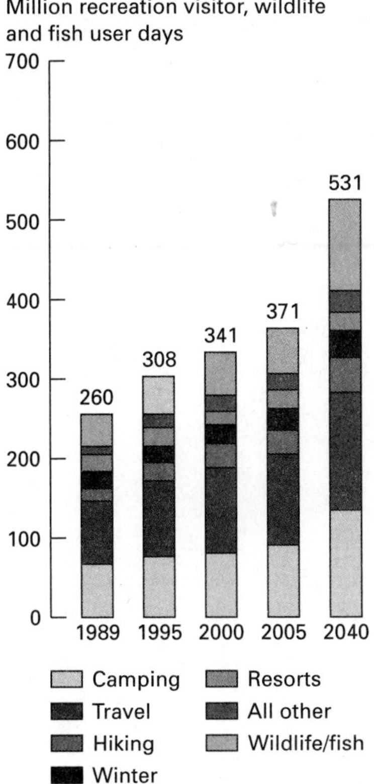

FIGURE 7.6 National Forest Service recreation projections. *Source: The Forest Service, U.S. Department of Agriculture, The Forest Service Program for Forest and Rangeland Resources: A Long-Term Strategic Plan* (U.S. Government Printing Office, 1990), 6–7.

resources of the National Forest System provided over 41 million user days of recreation for anglers, hunters, and nonconsumptive fish and wildlife users representing about 17 percent of all recreation in national forests. Forest land recreational development has continued to expand in scope and significance, showing no sign of diminishing in our time.

Partly as a result of the National Recreation Strategy Project, the Forest Service has over the past few years developed partnerships with local, county, state, and federal government, private interest groups, senior citizen groups, disabled youth groups, correction facility inmates, high schools, colleges, universities, utility companies, recreation industry corporations, timber operators, interpretive associations, and private businesses. Projects provide barrier-free access to recreation facilities, improved hiking trails, rehabilitated and modernized campgrounds, interpretive signing, summer youth employment in recreation site operation and maintenance, vegetation management for scenic resources, development of the 1988 Scenic Byways program for vehicular recreation, renovation of historical buildings for interpretation, and the production of a video on river safety. Partnerships with private cruise lines in Alaska pay Forest Service interpreters. In the eastern United States a partnership between the Forest Service, the National Park Service, and the Appalachian Trail Conference helped make the Appalachian Trail world renowned. These and other successes resulted in the president's 1989 budget proposal to direct $3 million to Challenge Cost-Share projects to encourage more partners to join the program (Forest Service 1988:5–11).

THE NATIONAL PARK SYSTEM

National Park Service (NPS) holdings comprise 80 million acres of land in forty-nine states, the District of Columbia, American Samoa, Guam, Puerto Rico, Saipan, and the Virgin Islands (see Figure 7.7). A national park is of such national significance as to justify special recognition and protection, and it takes an act of Congress to create it. Additionally the president has authority, under the *Antiquities Act of 1906,* to proclaim *national monuments* on lands already under federal jurisdiction. This distinction has been given to great natural reservations, historic military fortifications, prehistoric ruins, fossil sites, and to the Statue of Liberty. The secretary of the interior is usually asked by Congress for

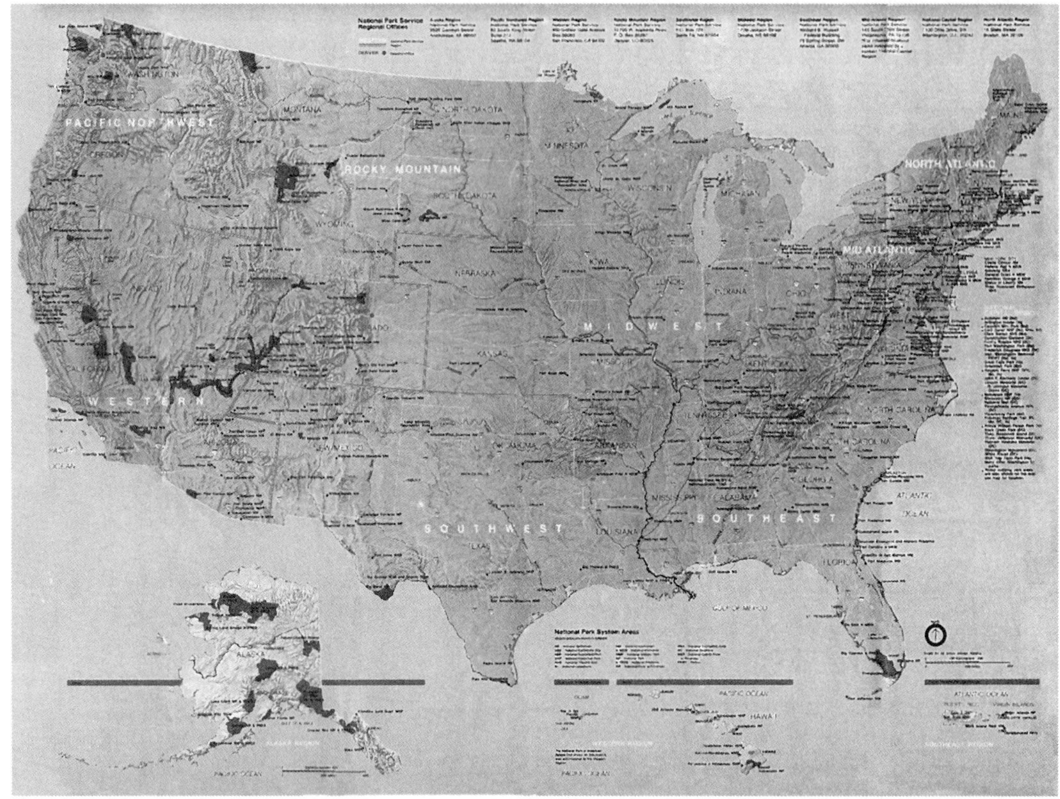

FIGURE 7.7 The National Park system. *Source: U.S. Department of the Interior, The National Parks: Index* (U.S. Government Printing Office, 1989), 10–11.

recommendations on proposed additions to the system. The secretary is counseled by the National Park System Advisory Board, which is composed of private citizens who offer advice on possible additions to the system and policies for its management.

Areas added to the NPS for their natural values are expanses or features of land or water of great scenic and scientific quality and are usually designated as national parks, monuments, preserves, seashores, lakeshores, or riverways. Such areas contain one or more distinctive attributes such as forest, grassland, tundra, desert, estuary, or river systems; or they may contain "windows" on the past for a view of geological history; or they may have imposing landforms such as mountains, mesas, thermal areas, and caverns. They may also be habitats of abundant or rare wildlife and plantlife. Components, known as units, of the National Park System are listed in Table 7.1.

Tilden, recognized in 1954 by Conrad L. Wirth, director of the National Park System, for his perceptive and spiritual interpretation of the scenic and scientific areas of the system, wrote,

> The national parks are not merely places of physical recreation. If finer and more re-creative recreation can be found anywhere in the world, the spots have not yet been revealed. But the word *recreation* covers a host of activities, and many of them can be had in municipal, state or other areas, in the national forests, and in Lake

TABLE 7.1 Classification, Number, and Acreage of National Park Service Areas

Classification	Number	Acreage
International Historic Site	1	35.39
National Battlefield	11	12,771.90
National Battlefield Park	3	8,767.39
National Battlefield Site	1	1.00
National Capital Park	1	6,468.88
National Historic Site	69	18,467.71
National Historic Park	29	151,632.86
National Lakeshore	4	227,244.37
National Mall	1	146.35
National Memorial	23	7,949.16
National Military Park	9	34,046.72
National Monument	79	4,844,610.12
National Park	50	47,319,321.07
National Parkway	4	168,618.32
National Preserve	14	22,155,497.84
National Recreation Area	18	3,686,923.39
National Rivers	5	360,629.91
National Scenic Trail	3	172,202.61
National Seashore	10	597,096.47
National Wild and Scenic River and Riverway	9	292,596.82
Park (Other)	10	40,120.70
White House	1	18.07
Totals	355	79,997,167.05

Source: U.S. Department of the Interior, *National Parks: Index 1989* (Washington, D.C., U.S. Government Printing Office, 1989), 13.

> Mead, Millerton, Coulee Dam. . . . I cannot understand why anyone should travel long distances to the national parks for physical recreation as such, but if they represent a special dividend, deriving from a larger appreciation a higher use, then visiting them becomes a most desirable thing (Tilden, 1959:14).

National Park History

After America won its independence from Britain, the country had few unique sites of natural beauty that had been recognized as recreation areas, the most prominent of which, Niagara Falls, had been exploited commercially to its detriment. After the western expansion, the giant sierra redwood trees of California were rediscovered in Yosemite Valley. America finally had a claim to antiquity; the huge trees had been growing before the time of Christ, and they certainly made up for the lack of old castles found in the European countryside. The magnificence of the Yosemite Valley displaced all claims that the European countryside was more scenic. By 1864 a park to preserve the nation's greatness was established when the U.S. government ceded lands in Yosemite Valley to California to protect the redwoods. Specifically, in the conditions of acceptance, the federal government stated the retention of the land was for "public use, resort, and recreation" and the lands were to be held "inalienable for all time" (Runte 1987:29–30).

Granite peaks and domes rise high above broad meadows in the heart of the Sierra Nevada.

Visitors climb the stairs to one of the well-preserved cliff dwellings at Mesa Verde National Park in southwestern Colorado.

Later, in 1872, Yellowstone National Park was established. This was the first time the term *national park* appeared, although the earlier Yosemite protection had embodied the concept. The artist George Catlin is the first person credited with articulating the need for a wildland park for the nation. In 1832, after traveling through Sioux Indian lands and foreseeing their eventual destruction, he proposed that a park be established to preserve the Sioux culture and the bison on which they were so dependent (Wellman 1987:51–52). Catlin's idea did not come to fruition, and even after Yellowstone was created in 1872, it was almost twenty more years before another national park was created. In 1890, at the urging of John Muir and Robert Underwood Johnson, bills were passed in Congress providing for the protection of additional lands that would eventually become Sequoia, General Grant, and Yosemite national parks. Soon after, Mount Rainier National Park and Crater Lake National Park were added.

During these early years a policy had evolved in Congress that only "worthless" lands could be set aside as parks. This meant that it would be necessary to first exhaust any possibility of economic viability of the land before Congress would act to set land aside. Repeatedly in congressional hearings, exhaustive lists of the unsuitability of the land for development and profit, save for scenic beauty, were established (Runte 1987:30).

In 1891 the passage of the Forest Reserve Act gave the president unilateral authority to proclaim forest reservations, which permitted the lengthy congressional debates to be avoided. By 1893 President Benjamin Harrison proclaimed 13 million acres in the West as forest reserves. This amount was increased to 46 million acres by presidents Grover Cleveland and William McKinley. Theodore Roosevelt, the naturalist and conservationist, more than tripled the forest lands to nearly 150 million acres during his administration. Many additional national parks were eventually carved from these holdings. Roosevelt also made expansive use of the Antiquities Act of 1906, which empowers the president to preserve all "objects of historic or scientific interest" as national monuments if the land is already under the jurisdiction of the federal government. Until then national parks had only been established to preserve scenic wonders; Roosevelt interpreted "scientific" to mean of geological significance as well, and as such he designated the first scientific national monument, a basalt monolith rising 865 feet in the air, Devils Tower, Wyoming. The Petrified Forest, Montezuma Castle, El Morro, other Indian cliff dwellings, and Lassen Peak soon followed as national monuments. All were relatively modest in size until 800,000 acres were set aside around the Grand Canyon and 600,000 acres around Mount Olympus as national monuments (Runte 1987:65–81).

During this time it was still important that the lands be considered useless or worthless for economic gain in order to be set aside. And unique scenic beauty was the criterion for designation as a national park. A dismal failure of conservation was a result of this narrow policy. Next to Yosemite Valley lay Hetch Hetchy Valley which was, to some, as magnificent as Yosemite. However, since it was right next to Yosemite it could hardly be considered unique, which resulted in its demise. After a bitter struggle by preservationists to save the area, San Francisco won the right to flood the valley to create a reservoir for the city. Since the economic worth of the land was established, its park status was removed. The loss of Hetch Hetchy Valley in 1913 highlighted the need for unified management and protection of the parks and resulted in the passage of the Organic Act of 1916, thus creating the National Park Service. Prior to this act, management of the parks, monuments, and forests was distributed among numerous government agencies with no one clear protector of the lands. Stephen Mather, a skilled promoter and eventually the first director of the NPS (see Chapter 3, Visionaries and Pioneers), appealed to the utilitarian conservatives in Congress in his cause to establish a bureau to protect the parks. He vigorously promoted the "See America First" campaign, designed to keep tourists in the United States rather than going abroad. This established that the parks too had economic worth measured in tourism dollars. Economic mandates prevailed in Congress again, and the valuable asset of the national parks was recognized and protected by the 1916 act (Runte 1987: 51, 81, 95).

Over one hundred twenty nations have followed the United States' lead in creating the world's first National Park Service (Craig 1991:41). And the original mission of the NPS is still valid today (Ridenour 1991:22): "To conserve the scenery and the natural and historic objects and the wildlife . . . and to provide for the enjoyment of the same in such manner and by such means as will leave them unimpaired for the enjoyment of future generations."

The preservationists' idea of protecting and preserving parklands through annexation of areas within the park ecosystem did not take hold for years. Not until 1934, with authorization of the Everglades National Park, was there a clear pledge to preservation of this kind. This marked a departure from the scenic vista that characterized previous parks. Flora and fauna in a fragile ecosystem were protected for the first time, although the boundaries of the park were not large enough to protect against the damage from residues of farming and urban populations.

In that same year, 1934, the Great Smoky Mountain National Park was authorized, and in 1935 Shenandoah National Park joined the system, both largely as a result of donations from private citizens, including $5 million from John D. Rockefeller, Jr. Earlier, in 1927, because the area around Yellowstone was blighted by gas stations and tourist traps, Rockefeller began acquiring approximately 35,000 acres near Jackson Hole, Wyoming, to supplement the expansion of Yellowstone National Park. Although the purchase was completed by 1929, Congress did not expand the park status for another 20 years. Instead, in 1929 they authorized Grand Teton National Park, which comprised only mountaintops that were clearly economically inviable. Congress viewed the Jackson Hole Valley area connecting Grand Teton to Yellowstone as too valuable to be set aside, even though the land would be donated. In essence, Congress continued to ignore the preservation of the wildlife that wintered in this lower elevation area and were therefore open game during hunting season. Finally, in 1950, Congress annexed a large segment of the valley to Grand Teton National Park. A strip of forest land between Grand Teton and Yellowstone was omitted from park protection to appease the hunters.

During the twentieth century it became increasingly difficult and costly to set aside land for national park status. This was evident in the establishment of Everglades National Park, where private holdings dot the parklands. Protection of an entire ecosystem was again thwarted, although recognition of the need for protection had taken root. The movement to protect the Everglades was paralleled by the Save the Redwoods movement, which began as early as 1852. Major groves were set aside as state parks and Muir Woods National Monument was authorized, but the movement to protect the redwoods' coastal ecosystem from the lumberman's axe was not achieved until the 1960s when Redwood National Park was designated. Three state parks were adjoined in 1968 through the federal purchase of contiguous private lands, but only after neighboring lumbering activity caused the toppling of over three hundred redwoods (Runte 1987:138–54).

Independence Hall was constructed between 1732 and 1756 and is part of Independence Hall National Historical Park.

The Land and Water Conservation Fund of 1965 (see Chapter 12, Management Policies) provided the majority of funds to acquire additional lands for the park system. Revenues come from off-shore drilling leases for oil and gas, admissions and user fees at federal recreational sites, surplus-land sales, and excise taxes on motorboat fuel (Jensen 1985:187 and Knudson

The best way to see the prehistoric ruins and beautiful red rock canyons of Canyon de Chelly National Monument is to take a whole- or half-day guided tour from an approved Navajo guide onto the reservation lands.

Historic reenactments occur at the national historical parks much like the one depicted here.

1984:368). A 1988 study, *The National Park System Plan,* concluded that 69 percent of all natural parks need their boundaries expanded in order for the National Park System to preserve them for future generations (Craig 1991:42). Much of this expansion is necessary because of the lack of understanding of ecosystems at the time the parks were established. Ecosystem management took a lead in park service activities in the 1960s.

In 1963 a team of distinguished scientists chaired by A. Starker Leopold wrote in *Wildlife Management in the National Parks,* "The major policy change that we would recommend to the National Park Service, is that it recognize the enormous complexity of ecologic communities. . . ." (Runte 1987:198). In 1964 President Lyndon B. Johnson signed the *Wilderness Act* into law. Nine million acres were immediately designated as wilderness, but it was not until 1970 and then 1976 and 1978 that additional lands were set aside.

With Alaska achieving statehood in 1959, it offered the last frontier in which complete ecological preserves could be set aside as national parks, wilderness areas, and wildlife refuges. This fertile setting created a long, controversial debate which culminated in President Jimmy Carter and Secretary of the Interior Cecil D. Andrus taking action to force Congress to finally protect more than 100 million acres, or 28 percent of the state. This 1980 act more than quintupled the acreage of protected lands (see Figure 7.8).

National Park System	54,900,000 acres
National Forests	22,300,000 acres
Wildlife Refuges	78,200,000 acres
Bureau of Land Management Lands	70,000,000 acres
Wild & Scenic Rivers	3,352 miles
Designated Wilderness	56,600,000 acres

Note: Maps do not show the Alaska Maritime National Wildlife Refuge—a collection of offshore islands and islets that includes St. Matthew Island in the Bering Sea and most of the Aleutian Islands chain.

FIGURE 7.8 The public lands of Alaska.

The *Alaska Land Act of 1980* set aside 43.6 million acres for new national parks, 53.8 million acres for wildlife refuges, and 1.2 million acres

Petrified Forest National Park was first protected as a National Monument in 1906.

for the National Wild and Scenic Rivers System. However, even with the vast amount of land protected, preservationists gradually learn that ecosystems have been severed by economic interests. For instance, significant amounts of land were protected as "preserves," areas which permit hunting, fishing, and mining, where evidently a compromise had been struck to accommodate the economic interests of tourism and mining (Runte 1987:236–58).

Not Only Parks and Monuments

Many nontraditional national areas were established in the 1960s and 1970s, including Cape Cod National Seashore, Indiana Dunes National Lakeshore, and Gateway National Recreation Area on the outskirts of New York. Many of

Narrow high-walled gorges cut through a 70-mile uplift of sandstone cliffs with highly colored sedimentary formations. Dome-shaped white-cap rock along the Freemont River in Utah accounts for this national park's name, Capitol Reef.

these acquisitions were funded by the Land and Water Conservation Fund (discussed in Chapter 12, Management Policies). The Wild and Scenic Rivers System was established with 1968 legislation, and passage of the National Parks and Recreation Act of 1978 created the National Trails System. The passage of the National Parks and Recreation Act of 1978 provided for a host of even more new and expanded park areas, including Santa Monica Mountains National Recreation Area near Los Angeles and New River Gorge National River in western Virginia. In all, fifteen units were added to the National Park System by the 1978 act.

Recreational Opportunities and Park Nomenclature

The National Park Service offers some of the world's greatest camping areas, backcountry camping, camping modifications for handicapped persons, especially those in wheelchairs or those who have difficulty walking, and concessions for tourists. Park diversity impacts the recreational opportunities available, and a wide range of special activities from horseback riding to canoeing to studying wildlife is available for visitors. Most park rangers conduct interpretive programs and evening programs around

Ruins of a large pueblo of the Salado Indians who flourished in the Verde Valley between A.D. 1100 and 1450 can be seen at Tuzigoot National Monument near Clarkdale, Arizona.

the campfire. To understand the opportunities one must understand park nomenclature. In recent years Congress and the National Park Service have attempted to simplify the nomenclature and to establish basic criteria for use of the different official titles. Brief definitions of the most common titles as described by the National Park Service (1989:7–8) follow:

National Park Generally a *national park* contains a variety of resources and encompasses large land or water areas to help provide adequate protection of the resources. For example, Hawaii's Haleakala National Park preserves the outstanding features of Haleakala Crater on the island of Maui and protects the unique and fragile ecosystems of the Kipahulu Valley.

National Monument A *national monument* is intended to preserve at least one nationally significant resource. It is usually smaller than a national park and lacks its diversity of attractions. For example, New York's Fort Stanwix National Monument is a complete reconstruction of the fort where the Americans withstood British invasion and the site of the treaty with the Iroquois.

Pecos National Monument protects two Spanish missions and the ruins of the ancient pueblo of Pecos, which was a landmark along the Santa Fe Trail.

National Preserves The category of *national preserve* is established primarily for the protection of certain resources. Activities such as hunting and fishing or the extraction of minerals and fuels may be permitted if they do not jeopardize the natural values of a site. In 1974 Big Cypress and Big Thicket were authorized as the first national preserves. Big Cypress National Preserves (Florida) adjoins the Everglades National Park, providing a freshwater supply crucial to the park's development. Big Thicket Nature Preserve (Texas) offers an excellent opportunity to study and research a great number of plant and animal species in this "biological crossroads of North America" (National Park Service 1989:71).

National Lakeshore and National Seashore Preserving shoreline areas and off-shore islands, the *national lakeshore* and *national seashore* focus on the preservation of natural values while at the same time providing water-oriented recreation. Although national lakeshores can be established on the shore of any natural freshwater lake, the existing four are all located on the shores of the Great Lakes. Sleeping Bear Dunes National Lakeshore and Indiana Dunes are both on Lake Michigan, and Pictured Rocks and Apostle Islands are both on Lake Superior. The national seashores are on the Atlantic, Gulf, and Pacific coasts. They include Assateague Island National Seashore (Maryland and Virginia), Gulf Islands National Seashore (Mississippi), and Point Reyes National Seashore (California).

National River and Wild and Scenic Riverway These designations preserve ribbons of land bordering on free-flowing streams that have not been dammed, channelized, or otherwise altered by humans. Besides preserving rivers in their natural state, these areas provide opportunities for outdoor activities such as hiking, canoeing, and hunting. The Merced River (California), Alatna Wild River (Alaska), and Delaware National Scenic River (Pennsylvania) are examples of rivers preserved in these categories.

National Scenic Trails These trails are generally long-distance footpaths winding through areas of natural beauty. The Appalachian National Scenic Trail, for example, follows the Appalachian Mountains from Mount Katahdin, Maine, through New Hampshire, Vermont, Massachusetts, Connecticut, New York, New Jersey, Pennsylvania, Maryland, West Virginia, Virginia, Tennessee, and North Carolina, to Spring Mountain, Georgia for approximately 2,000 miles. National scenic trails (described later in this chapter) are administered by the National Park Service. The NPS encourages other public and private agencies to develop, maintain, and protect trails; expand and designate trails; and, where feasible, cooperate with and support the efforts of the trails community nationwide.

National Historic Site These sites preserve places and commemorate persons, events, and activities important in the nation's history. They range from archeological sites associated with prehistoric Indian civilizations to sites related to the lives of modern Americans. Historical areas are customarily preserved or restored to reflect their appearance during the period of their greatest historical significance. A wide variety of titles—*national military park, national battlefield park, national battlefield site,* and *national battlefield*—have been used for areas associated with American military history. But other areas such as national monuments and national historic parks may include features associated with military history. *National historic parks* are commonly areas of greater physical extent and complexity than *national historic sites.* The lone international historic site, International Peace Garden (North Dakota and Manitoba), refers to a site relevant to both U.S. and Canadian history.

National Memorial The title *national memorial* is most often used for areas that are primarily commemorative. But they need not be sites or structures historically associated with their subjects. For example, the home of Abraham Lincoln (Illinois) is a national historic site, but the Lincoln Memorial (in Washington, D.C.) is a national memorial. Several other areas administered by the National Capital Region whose titles do not include the words national memorial, such as the Washington Monument (Washington, D.C.) are, nevertheless, classified as memorials.

National Recreation Area Originally, *national recreation areas* such as Coulee Dam National Recreation Area (Washington) were units surrounding reservoirs impounded by dams built by other federal agencies. The National Park Service manages many of these areas under cooperative agreements. The concept of recreational areas has grown to encompass other lands and waters set aside for recreational use by acts of Congress and now includes major areas in urban centers such as Gateway National Recreation Area (New York). There are also national recreation areas outside the National Park System that are administered by the U.S. Forest Service. For example the latter two units of the Whiskeytown-Shasta-Trinity National Recreation Area are administered by the Forest Service.

National Parkway *National parkways* encompass ribbons of land flanking roadways and offer an opportunity for leisurely driving through areas of scenic interest. They are not designed for high-speed travel. Besides the areas set aside as parkways, other units of the National Park System include parkways within their boundaries. The Blue Ridge Parkway (North Carolina and Virginia) is a 470-mile parkway that follows the crest of the Blue Ridge Mountains.

National Wilderness Area Congress designated *national wilderness areas* (discussed later in this chapter) in many units of the National Park System as well as within units managed by other federal agencies. This designation does not remove wilderness lands from the parks, but it does ensure that they will be managed to retain the "primeval character and influence, without permanent improvements or human habitation . . ." (National Park Service 1989:8).

Two areas of the National Park System have been set aside primarily as sites for the *performing arts.* These are Wolf Trap Farm Park for the Performing Arts (Virginia), America's first such national park, and the John F. Kennedy Center for the Performing Arts (Washington, D.C). Two historical areas, Ford's Theatre National Historic Site (Washington, D.C.) and Chamizal National Memorial (Texas), also provide facilities for the performing arts.

Parks in the nation's capital are administered by the National Park Service under the *Reorganization Act of 1933,* which was the first major expansion of the park service holdings. Most parklands in the capital are included in the federal holdings, although the District of Columbia also operates parks, playgrounds, and recreational facilities. The National Park Service also administers several units in Maryland, Virginia, and West Virginia.

Besides the National Park System, the Wild and Scenic Rivers System, and the National Trails System, there are areas known as *affiliated areas.* These are areas that are neither federally owned nor directly administered by the NPS but that utilize NPS assistance. They comprise a variety of locations in the United States and Canada that preserve significant properties outside the National Park System, such as the David Berger National Memorial in Ohio. The memorial honors the memory of the eleven Israeli athletes who were assassinated at the 1972 Olympic Games in Munich. Some affiliated areas have been recognized by acts of Congress, others have been designated national historic sites by the secretary of the interior under authority of the *Historic Sites Act of 1935.* All draw on technical or financial aid from the National Park Service.

The National Park Service in the Twenty-First Century

As the National Park Service looks to the twenty-first century, the following issues must be addressed (Craig 1991:42–43; Ridenour 1991: 22–23):

1. Environmental challenges These are some of the most serious challenges facing the NPS. However, these problems go beyond park boundaries. For example, air

Yosemite Valley was the first federal expanse set aside for the enjoyment of the people when it was ceded to the state of California. Today the national park is inundated with visitors in the busy summer months.

pollution and water pollution may be generated hundreds of miles away from the parks but still contaminate the park environments (see Chapter 16, The Environment).

2. Parkland boundaries There is a need for a buffer zone between private and public interests. Some artificial boundaries cut across natural boundaries such as geological formations and drainage basins.

3. Biodiversity Biodiversity must be protected or more sensitive species will disappear as invasive or exotic species take over (see Chapter 16, The Environment).

4. Education National park administrators must demonstrate the highest environmental ethics and must continue to teach the public about preservation if the parks are to survive ecologically. They will need to keep the public informed of the desirability of individual units. The parks are great reservoirs of science and should be utilized for environmental research.

5. Poaching Poaching takes place throughout the system and must be curtailed. Hunting, cacti rustling, and artifact collecting are examples.

6. Visitation Visitation is on the rise and is expected to hit over a half billion by the year 2010. The NPS must search for a balance between use and preservation.

7. Rangers Better pay, housing, and job mobility must be provided to park rangers. There will be a stronger need for bilingual interpreters in the future.

8. Repair and additions Many of the parks have deteriorated due to lack of funds and are in need of repair. Additional facilities

Hubbard Glacier, one of the great tidewater glaciers protected in Alaska by the National Park Service.

for the handicapped and aged should be provided. Bilingual interpretive markers will be needed in many units.

9. Urban parks The National Park Service has recognized the need for the creation of urban parks, usually designed for recreation. Such parks must be worthy of the name "National Park."

10. Inspiration The National Park Service will need to offer community outreach programs.

11. Joint-efforts Close working relationships with other federal agencies and state and local governments need to be forged. The creation of recreation areas outside of the National Park System will be vital so that park overuse can be mitigated.

WILDERNESS LANDS

The passage of the Wilderness Act in 1964 formalized the nation's desire to protect its wilderness resource. Wilderness has been defined by the act as areas that:

- Are affected primarily by the forces of nature, where humans are visitors.
- Possess outstanding opportunities for solitude or primitive and unconfined types of recreation.
- Are undeveloped, federally owned, and generally over 5,000 acres in size.
- Are protected and managed so as to allow natural ecological processes to operate freely.
- May contain ecological, geological, scenic, or historic value.
- Are formally designated by Congress as wilderness.

Wilderness History

The early national parks were intended to provide an outdoor experience in relative comfort. Visitors enjoyed transportation by train or carriage, and plush resorts awaited them after a day's sojourn in the spectacular scenery. But there was a growing issue between recreationists who wanted comfort and facilities and those who wished to rough it in a wilderness environment. The current federal concept of wilderness—land left essentially wild and free from human impact—originated with the Forest Service (Cordell et al. 1990:4). In the 1920s the Forest Service's Aldo Leopold, Arthur Carhart, and others advocated the preservation of large areas in an undisturbed state. In 1921, Leopold (see Chapter 3, Visionaries and Pioneers), defined wilderness as "a continuous stretch of country preserved in its natural state, open to lawful hunting and fishing, big enough to absorb a two-week's pack trip, and kept devoid of roads, artificial trails, cottages, or other works of man" (Wellman 1987:132). According to Wellman (1987:132-34), Leopold advocated that for a minority of people, preservation of wilderness would be the greatest priority, and that these views should be represented when possible. His proposal in 1921 for a wilderness area in New Mexico's Gila National Forest, supported by local hunters, won support the following year, and in 1924 the area was designated the Gila Roadless Area. The nation's first wilderness preserve consisted of approximately 500,000 acres. Soon five other roadless areas were established within the National Forest System, and several more were under consideration. In the meantime, Arthur Carhart was also making progress toward establishing a roadless area in the Superior National Forest in Minnesota. His proposal for a lakeland wilderness area was approved by the secretary of Agriculture in 1923. Supported by later legislation, his plan provided the foundation for the million-acre Boundary Waters Canoe Area Wilderness (Wellman 1987:133). Soon the National Park Service had to respond to the pressures of preservationists. Scientific research parks were established, one of the earliest being a 4,480-acre "primitive" area in Yosemite National Park.

Responding to this National Park Service challenge and to Leopold and others within the Forest Service, the Forest Service developed the "L-20" regulations of 1929 which directed national forest staffs to protect "primitive" undeveloped lands. This represented one of the first attempts to establish wilderness as a general classification of land use with specific management guidelines. Under these regulations, some sixty-three primitive areas encompassing nearly 8.5 million acres were established. But protection was tenuous, boundaries could be changed by administrative order, and many wilderness areas contained state or private lands that were subject to development. Wilderness advocates, especially Robert Marshall, then chief of the Forest Service's Recreation and Lands Division, pressed for stronger measures. The result was the "U-Regulations" of 1939, which established three land categories: U-1 "wilderness" (areas of more than 100,000 acres to be left undeveloped), U-2 "wild" (5,000–100,000 acres to be managed as wilderness), and U-3 "recreation" (roadless areas where timber harvest and some other development were permitted) (Cordell et al. 1990:4).

Following World War II, wilderness proponents, led by Howard Zahnisher of the Wilderness Society, pressed for congressional action to provide greater protection. With impetus provided by the Outdoor Recreation Resources Review Commission (ORRRC), the *Wilderness Act* became law in 1964 (P.L. 8-577) (see Chapter 15, Outdoor Recreational Activities). Passage of the act created the *National Wilderness Preservation System* (NWPS), which required affirmative action by Congress on each addition to the wilderness system. It shifted the process of wilderness designation from the Forest Service to Congress.

Marshall's 1939 definition became the basis for the legislative definition of wilderness, and his equal emphasis on human use and preservation of the primitive environment carried through to current wilderness management guidelines. The Wilderness Act applied to the national forests, national parks, and national wildlife refuges. Its early effects were felt mainly by the Forest Service, which already possessed large areas of protected wilderness (Cordell et al. 1990:4). The National Park Service had utilized a zoning system to protect wilderness values in undeveloped areas more than a half mile from roads. The Fish and Wildlife Service had not managed any area specifically for wilderness purposes, because manipulation of habitat to enhance wildlife values often resulted in substantial modification of areas, thereby conflicting with wilderness values. Nevertheless once charged with wilderness responsibilities, Congress designated Great Swamp Wildlife Refuge in New Jersey as the first refuge to be admitted to the National Wilderness Preservation System (Hendee et al. 1978:67). Lands managed by the Bureau of Land Management were not subject to the Wilderness Act until passage of the *Federal Land Policy and Management Act of 1976.*

The Wilderness Act accorded statutory protection specifically to lands that met the wilderness definition: an area where the earth and its community of life are untrammeled by humans, where humans themselves are visitors who do not remain. It was the Wilderness Act which did much to alter the concept of wilderness as a residual resource or useless land to wilderness as a primary resource central to national recreation policy. Prior to the act's passage, the first wilderness bill was introduced in Congress by Senator Hubert H. Humphrey in 1956. Subsequently sixty-four additional wilderness bills were introduced and considered by Congress before passage (Browning et al. 1988:1).

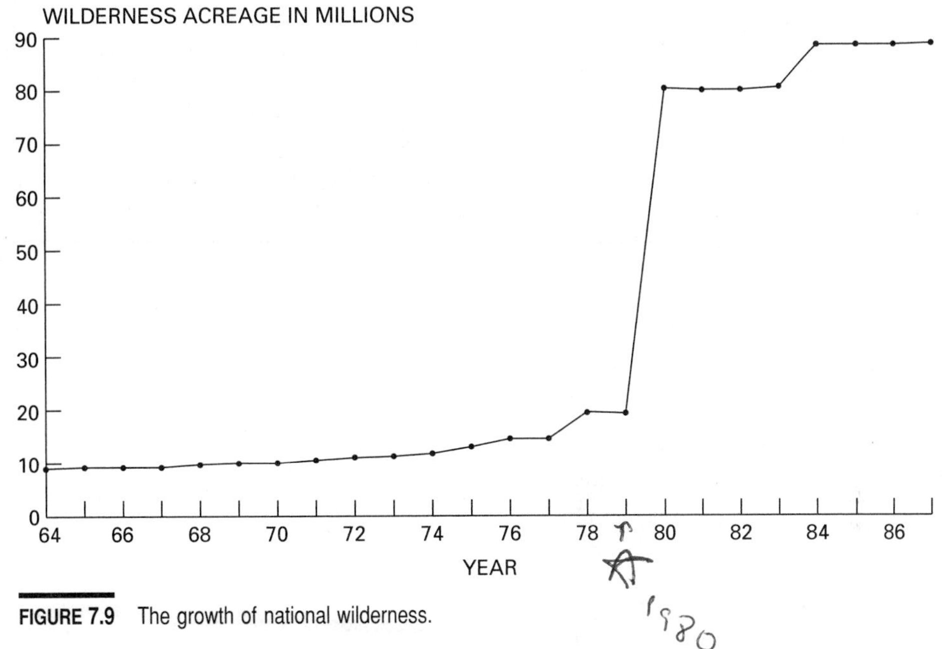

FIGURE 7.9 The growth of national wilderness.

90.7 million acres total

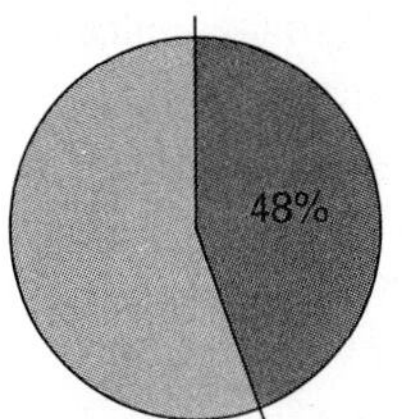

National Park System
38.5 million acres of wilderness
System totals 80 million acres

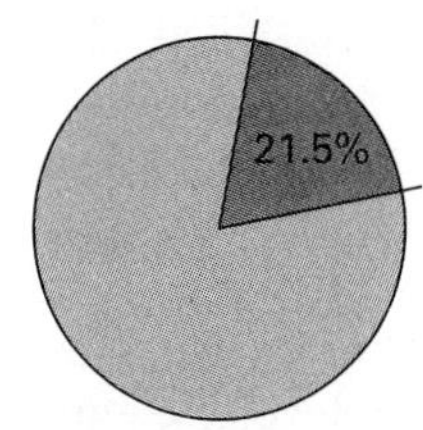

National Wildlife Refuge System
19.3 million acres of wilderness
System totals 90 million acres

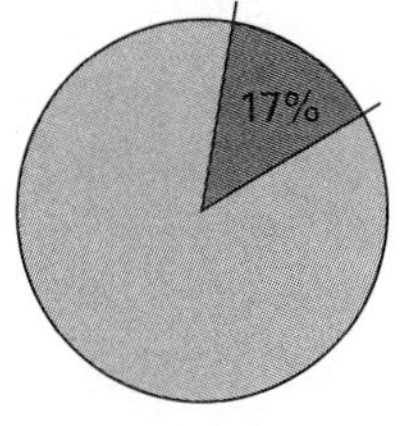

National Forest System
32.4 million acres of wilderness
System totals 191 million acres

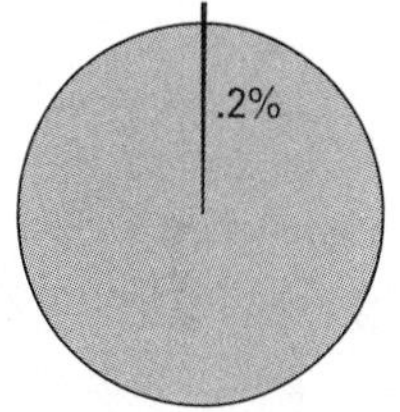

Bureau of Land Management Lands
0.5 million acres of wilderness
System totals 250 million acres*

*BLM holdings after settlement of state and native claims under the Statehood Act of 1958 and the Alaska Native Claims Settlement Act of 1971.

FIGURE 7.10 The wilderness system.

The 474 units totaling nearly 91 million acres that make up the National Wilderness Preservation System are the crown jewels of America's public lands heritage. They stand as living testimony to the wisdom and foresight of Congress and the American people to preserve the lands of past generations for the enjoyment of future generations. Accordingly, wilderness areas are protected from development—the construction of roads, dams, or other permanent structures, timber cutting, the operation of motorized vehicles and equipment, and, since 1984, new mining claims and mineral leasing. Figures 7.9 and 7.10 show the growth of national wilderness and the present holdings.

High-Priority Issues for Wilderness Preservation

According to Cordell et al. (1990:6) the following are high-priority issues for wilderness preservation:

1. Allocation The appropriate criteria or agenda that determines the final size and composition of the NWPS is much debated. Aside from the obvious recreational demand, advocates of increasing the NWPS point to the need to protect representative ecosystems and areas to monitor environmental changes, among other reasons. Those who argue against enlarging the NWPS are concerned that wilderness restrictions on water use, grazing, mining, and energy extraction do not contribute to the national economic growth.

2. Nontraditional wilderness A related issue is whether the NWPS should be expanded to include aquatic and underground wilderness units. In addition to amending the Wilderness Act, Congress would need to resolve a number of potential problems, including determining surface rights.

3. Wilderness degradation The characteristics important to a wilderness area are vulnerable. Even the Wilderness Act itself sets up a tension between human use and preservation of wilderness character. Some wilderness areas are heavily used for recreation, resulting in soil erosion, plant loss, water pollution, disruption of wildlife, and loss of opportunities for solitude. Wilderness areas are also threatened from outside sources including aircraft overflights, air pollution, and the introduction of exotic plant species (see Chapter 16, The Environment). Furthermore, wilderness areas may be threatened from such global influences as ozone depletion, acid precipitation, and deforestation.

4. International cooperation. The National Wilderness Preservation System is unique in the world in terms of its purpose. With appropriate international cooperation, it could serve as a component of a larger global system of wild areas for resource protection.

5. Management coordination and consistency According to the Wilderness Act, wilderness is a supplemental purpose in forests, parks, wildlife refuges, and public lands. Because each agency has a somewhat different mission, the management of wilderness areas is not entirely coordinated or consistent.

6. Funding and training The designation of wilderness by law does not ensure the preservation of an area in its original condition. Inadequately trained wilderness managers and understaffed and poorly funded wilderness management programs seriously hamper the mandated responsibility to preserve wilderness character.

7. Education Wilderness managers alone cannot prevent the degradation of the wilderness resource. The public must also understand wilderness values and how to use wilderness with respect and restraint, so the wilderness does not lose its character. The development of effective educational and interpretive techniques and material to teach the public low-impact use skills will be a continuing challenge (see Chapter 15, Outdoor Recreational Activities).

Wild and Scenic Rivers System

The *Wild and Scenic Rivers Act of 1968* provided for the establishment of a system of rivers to be preserved as free-flowing streams accessible for public use and enjoyment. According to the National Park Service (1989:92), components of the system, or portions of component rivers, may be designated as *wild, scenic,* or *recreational* rivers. Rivers are classified according to the natural qualities they possess and the evidence, as viewed from the river, of human presence in the area. Rivers have been classified as wild, scenic, or recreational on the basis of the following traits:

- A wild river displays little evidence of human presence in the area. The river is free of impoundments (dams), and it is generally inaccessible except by trail.
- Scenic rivers have relatively primitive shorelines and are largely undeveloped, but they are accessible in places by road.
- Recreational rivers have more development, are accessible by road or railroad, and may have been dammed.

Once a river area is designated a component of the Wild and Scenic Rivers System, the objective of the managing agency—local, state, or federal—is to preserve or enhance those qualities which qualified the river for inclusion within the system. Recreational use must be compatible with preservation. Wild and Scenic River designation provides the following important protection (Hendee et al. 1978:129):

1. It provides complete protection against dam construction and other water development projects.
2. It prohibits construction of power transmission lines.
3. It permits administering agencies to condemn private land, if less than 50 percent of the entire river area is owned by federal, state, or local government. However, land within a city, village, or borough cannot be condemned if valid zoning ordinances protecting the river areas are in effect.
4. It calls for complete withdrawal from mineral entry of lands within 1/4 mile of the bank of any river designated for management under the "wild" category.

Rivers administered by the National Park Service are units of the National Park System. Those administered by the U.S. Fish and Wildlife Service are components of the National Wildlife Refuge System. State rivers and streams may become units of the Wild and Scenic Rivers System when established under state laws and developed with river management plans acceptable to the secretary of the Interior. Federally managed components of the system are designated by act of Congress. Usually Congress first requires, by law, a detailed study to determine the qualification of a river area for the system and then makes the decision.

Passage of the Wild and Scenic Rivers Act established an important milestone in the conservation of our nation's great natural resources. It recognized the value of rivers and their environs as an outstanding natural feature which must be preserved for future generations to enjoy. The search continues for outstanding rivers that should be included in this prestigious system now containing seventy-five rivers.

The National Trails System

According to the National Park Service (1989:103) the *National Trail System Act of 1968* calls for establishing trails in both urban and rural settings for persons of all ages, interests, skills, and physical abilities. The act established four classes of trails: congressionally designated long-distance national scenic trails, national historic trails, side or connecting trails, and national recreation trails. The act promotes public access to, enjoyment of, and appreciation for those trails. The law designated the Appalachian National Scenic Trail and the Pacific Crest National Scenic Trail as the first long-distance trails winding through some of the most striking natural beauty in the country. Fourteen other trails were proposed for study to determine whether they met the criteria for congressional designation as national scenic trails. So far, eight national scenic trails and eight national historic trails have been designated (see Figure 7.11). Other potential routes are being studied to determine whether they are suitable for designation as units of the system.

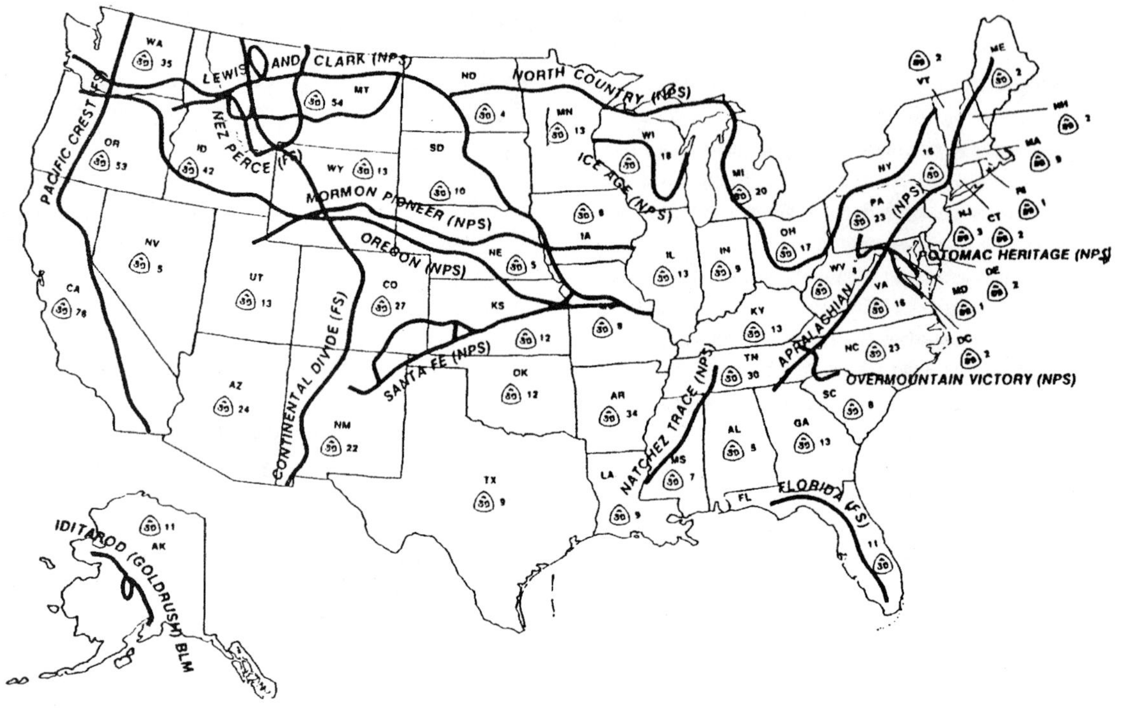

NATIONAL SCENIC TRAILS

FACTS ON LONG-DISTANCE TRAILS
December, 1989

(Listed by date of Congressional destablishment:)

	Year Estab.	Expected Miles	No. of Miles Certified
Appalachian National Scenic Trail	1968	2110	2110
Pacific Crest National Scenic Trail	1968	2600	2522
Continental Divide National Scenic Trail	1978	3200	700
North Country National Scenic Trail	1980	3200	1000
Ice Age National Scenic Trail	1980	1000	450
Florida National Scenic Trail	1983	1300	650
Potomac Heritage National Scenic Trail	1983	704	200
Natchez Trace National Scenic Trail	1983	694	25

FIGURE 7.11 The national trails system.

National recreation trails are managed by public or private agencies and are designated by the secretary of the Interior, or, if they are within national forests, by the secretary of Agriculture. A national recreation trail must be fully developed and ready to be used at the time of designation. This is certified by the administering agency that also must assure that the trail will be open for public use for at least 10 years following designation.

The 774 national recreation trails that have been designated throughout the country are located in every state, the District of Columbia, and Puerto Rico, with a total length of more than

8,400 miles. The majority of the trails, 508, are on federal lands, 80 are on state property, and 29 are on private lands; 145 are local trails, and 12 are under joint sponsorship. Successful attempts to create new trails have resulted in the designation of old aqueducts, abandoned railroads, and old logging trails for public use.

There are numerous trail users that benefit from the designation of trails, including hikers, horseback riders, bicyclists, motorcyclists, ski tourers, snowshoers, snowmobilers, all-terrain-vehicle riders, joggers, and mountain bicyclists. Because trails are utilized by diverse groups, the potential for conflict exists. Management has attempted to designate trails for specific use, for instance, separating motorized users from hikers.

While trail use is on the increase, resources have not been provided by either the Department of the Interior or the Department of Agriculture to effectively develop programs (Harvey and Henley 1989:2, 23). A cooperative research and lobbying group, the National Trails Coalition, was established in 1985, and one of its missions is the protection of trails on public lands. Recently, Congress has resumed the trails funding effort. Also, citizen groups have been organized to offer support and to work on trails. However, the task of building national trails is a difficult one, since they pass through private and government land, with the latter managed by various federal and state agencies. In a study done by the American Hiking Society (1990:1–3) it is estimated that the federal government will need to spend $202 million to bring existing hiking trails in the national forests up to standard. This estimate is $7 million more than the General Accounting Office calculated in its survey of the national forest trails. In either case, it is clear that funds are needed to bring existing trails up to standard, and there is also an urgent need for more trails as well as for the development of opportunities for pleasure walking and hiking because of overcrowded conditions on existing trails.

U.S. FISH AND WILDLIFE SERVICE

The U.S. Fish and Wildlife Service is the principal agency through which the federal government carries out its responsibilities to conserve, protect, and enhance the nation's fish and wildlife and their habitats for the continuing benefit of people. The service's major responsibilities are for migratory birds, endangered species, certain marine mammals, and freshwater and anadromous fisheries.

The service's origins date back to 1871 when Congress established the U.S. Fish Commission to study the decrease of the nation's food fishes and recommend ways to reverse the decline. Created as an independent agency, it was placed under the Department of Commerce in 1903 and renamed the Bureau of Fisheries. Meanwhile, in 1885, Congress created an Office of Economic Ornithology in the Department of Agriculture. The office studied the food habits and migratory patterns of birds, especially the ones that have an effect on agriculture. This office gradually grew in responsibilities and was renamed the Bureau of Biological Survey in 1905. In addition to studying the abundance, distribution, and habitats of birds and mammals, the survey managed the nation's first wildlife refuges, controlled predators, enforced wildlife laws, and conserved dwindling populations of heron, egrets, and other waterfowl and migratory birds.

The Bureau of Fisheries and Bureau of Biological Survey were transferred to the Department of the Interior in 1939. One year later, in 1940, they were combined and named the Fish and Wildlife Service. Further reorganization came in 1956 when the *Fish and Wildlife Act* created the U.S. Fish and Wildlife Service and established within the agency two separate bureaus—Commercial Fisheries, and Sport Fisheries and Wildlife.

The Bureau of Commercial Fisheries was transferred to the Department of Commerce in 1970 and is now known as the National Marine Fisheries Service (described later in this chapter). The Bureau of Sport Fisheries and Wildlife remained in the Department of the Interior. In accordance with a 1974 act of Congress, the "Bureau" was dropped and the agency was called simply the U.S. Fish and Wildlife Service. Today the service employs approximately 6,500 people at facilities across the country, including a headquarters office in Washington, D.C., eight regional offices including one for research, and over seven hundred field units and installations. Among these are national wildlife refuges and fish hatcheries, research laboratories, field offices, and law enforcement agents.

The Fish and Wildlife Service leads the federal effort to protect and restore animals and plants that are in danger of extinction both in the United States and worldwide. It maintains major research laboratories and field stations, as well as cooperative research units at universities across the country. It provides biological advice to other agencies and members of the public concerning the conservation of habitat that may be affected by development activities. Rachel Carson (see Chapter 3, Visionaries and Pioneers), once a service employee, awakened the American public in her book *Silent Spring* to threats to fish and wildlife from highly toxic and long-lasting pesticides such as DDT. The service is making major efforts to restore nationally significant fisheries, depleted by overfishing, pollution, or other habitat damage. The service is responsible for the conservation of over 800 species of migratory birds. In addition the service regulates hunting of bird populations and acquires and manages many national wildlife refuges to provide secure habitats for migratory birds.

Federal Aid and International Programs

Two laws administered by the Fish and Wildlife Service—the *Federal Aid in Wildlife Restoration Act* and the *Federal Aid in Sport Fisheries Restoration Act*—have created some of the most successful programs in the history of fish and wildlife conservation. Known as *Pittman-Robertson* (wildlife) and *Dingell-Johnson* (fish) after their congressional sponsors, these programs provide federal grant money to support specific projects carried out by state fish and wildlife agencies. The money comes from federal excise taxes on sporting arms and ammunition, archery equipment, and sport fishing tackle. In 1984 the sport fisheries restoration legislation was supplemented by new provisions known as the *Wallop-Breaux* amendments. These provisions increased revenue for sport fish restoration by extending the excise tax to previously untaxed items of sporting equipment, and by channeling into fisheries restoration a portion of the existing federal tax on motorboat fuels and import duties on fishing tackle and pleasure boats. Funds are used to acquire land for wildlife habitat and for fishing and recreation, for research to provide access to hunting, to develop fishing and boating areas, to manage and maintain fish and wildlife habitats, and to carry out hunter safety training and aquatic education.

Cooperating with other countries on wildlife research and management programs, the Fish and Wildlife Service also has a variety of international responsibilities under some forty treaties, statutes, and agreements. When requested it offers technical assistance to foreign countries. Additionally it seeks to stem the global loss of wetlands and establish guidelines for wise use of wetlands through the international wetlands convention.

The National Wildlife Refuge System

The National Wildlife Refuge System is a network of U.S. lands and waters managed specifically for wildlife. Vitally important, refuges provide habitat for approximately sixty endangered species and hundreds of species of birds, mammals, reptiles, amphibians, fish, and plants. Over 450 refuges, encompassing about 90 million acres in forty-nine states and five trust territories, now comprise the system. Units of the

The National Wildlife Refuge System

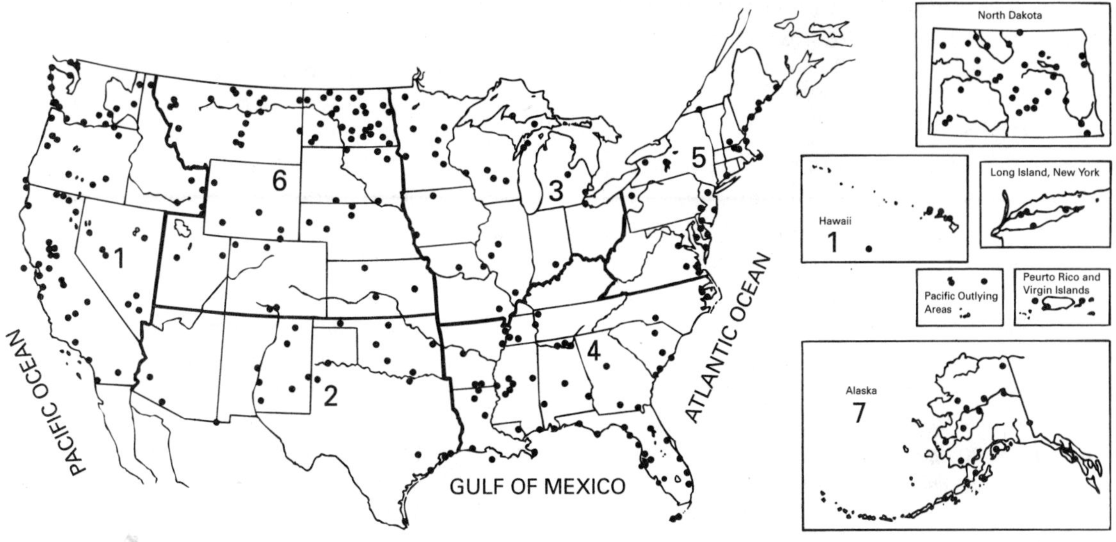

FIGURE 7.12 Growth of the National Wilderness Preservation System, 1964–1987.

system stretch across the continent from the north shore of Alaska to the Florida keys and beyond to islands in the Caribbean and South Pacific. These units range in size from Minnesota's tiny Mille Lacs, less than an acre, to Alaska's Yukon Delta, almost 20 million acres (see Figure 7.12).

At the turn of the century, ladies' fashions contributed to the need for establishment of the first refuges. Herons and egrets were killed in large numbers for their plumes, used for hats. Other human and natural calamities also played a part. In 1903 President Theodore Roosevelt signed an executive order protecting the herons, egrets, and other birds on Florida's Pelican Island, making it the first "national" wildlife refuge. This was part of a concerted effort on the part of the American people to actively protect and manage their irreplaceable wildlife resources. A succession of federal laws and international treaties continued to protect wildlife and ensure the acquisition, establishment, and maintenance of secure lands and waters. These laws were the *Migratory Bird Conservation Act of 1929,* the *Migratory Bird Hunting Stamp Act of 1934,* the *Fish and Wildlife Act of 1956,* the *National Wildlife Refuge System Administration Act of 1966,* the *Endangered Species Act of 1973,* and the *Alaska National Interest Lands Conservation Act of 1980.*

Today the refuge system is a unique collection of diverse areas administered by the U.S. Fish and Wildlife Service. Many refuges are located along the major north-south flyways, providing feeding and resting areas for the great semiannual migrations of ducks, geese, and other birds. Other areas serve as sanctuaries for endangered or unusual species. For example, the Aransas Refuge in Texas is the winter home of the whooping crane, and the Hawaiian Islands Refuge provides the only habitat for a number of endangered species including the Hawaiian monk seal and green sea turtle.

Archeological artifacts and areas of historical significance located on refuge lands are preserved along with wildlife habitat. DeSoto

Refuge in Iowa, for instance, maintains an exhibit and collection of items reclaimed from the historic steamship *Bertrand,* which sank in the Missouri River in 1865.

Recreation

National wildlife refuges offer a wide variety of recreational opportunities. An estimated 27 million people visit these lands annually. Although public uses are regulated so they do not interfere with the wildlife purposes of the refuge, many activities are available. Recreational uses may include wildlife observation, photography, nature study, hiking, boating, hunting, and fishing. Some refuges provide visitor centers, special study areas, environmental education programs, interpretive trails and drives, wildlife observation towers, photographic blinds, and other public facilities. Activities vary with each refuge and may depend on the season of the year. Visitors are advised to check with refuge personnel prior to a visit to determine which activities are allowed and what regulations apply toward the consideration of the wildlife. Every visit to a refuge is different, and each person has an individual experience.

The prevailing refuge management philosophy for many years was a commitment to anonymity, the belief being that the fewer who knew about refuges, the better. People have discovered, however, that refuges are natural treasures (see Chapter 15, Outdoor Recreational Activities). The U.S. Fish and Wildlife Service is meeting and must continue to meet the challenge of tourists by providing more extensive outdoor experiences while protecting the wildlife for which the refuges were created.

Riley and Riley (1979:4–7) suggest appropriate etiquette and methods to make visits to refuges more productive and enjoyable, as follows:

1. Visit early or late in the day when most birds and other wildlife are more active.
2. Follow walking trails and automobile tour routes when viewing wildlife.
3. Remember that refuges are not parks. They do not offer non-wildlife-related recreational activities.
4. Always inquire in advance before coming to see a certain creature or natural event to be certain it is appearing on schedule.
5. Before visitation, it is wise to acquire some understanding of the wildlife to be observed.
6. Field guides, binoculars, and insect repellent may improve a trip.
7. A simple rule for good wildlife viewing is to stop and look back every so often. Both mammals and birds freeze as visitors pass, but they tend to continue their activity soon after.
8. Human activity on refuges must be consistent with wildlife welfare and habitats.

In addition, wildlife should be observed from a distance through binoculars, spotting scopes, and telephoto lenses; wildlife should be allowed to keep the visitor in view; wildlife should not be followed or chased; and wildlife should be viewed for a limited time.

OTHER FEDERAL AGENCIES

Other federal agencies, because of the resources they manage, have a significant impact on outdoor recreation. These include the Bureau of Land Management, the Bureau of Indian Affairs, the U.S. Army Corps of Engineers, the Bureau of Reclamation, the Tennessee Valley Authority, and the National Oceanic and Atmospheric Administration.

The Bureau of Land Management

The Bureau of Land Management (BLM) is responsible for managing the nation's public lands and resources in a combination of ways that best serves the needs of the American people (see Figure 7.13). Management is based on the

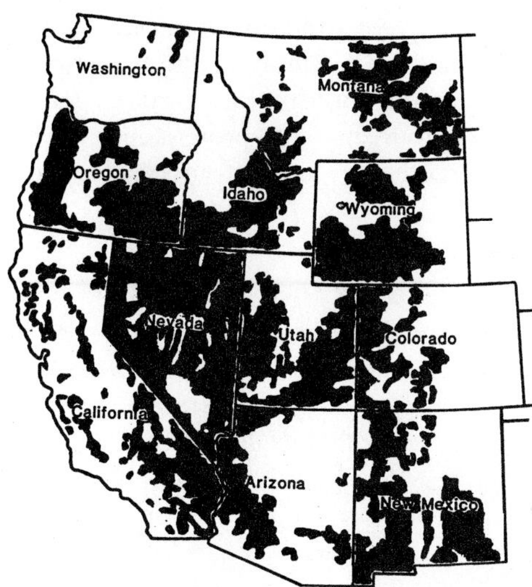

FIGURE 7.13 Public land in the western states. *U.S. Department of the Interior, Bureau of Land Management.*

Unusual erosion has formed innumerable highly colored and bizarre pinnacles, walls, and spires in Utah's Bryce Canyon National Park (top) and Cedar Breaks National Monument (below).

principles of multiple use and sustained yield, combining uses and balancing needs of future generations for renewable and nonrenewable resources. These resources include recreation, range, timber, minerals, watershed, fish and wildlife, and wilderness. The headquarters of the BLM national office is in Washington, D.C. There are 12 state offices, 58 district offices, and 140 resource area offices. Most of the BLM's 9,650 employees work in field offices in the western United States. Many skills and talents are required for positions such as recreation specialists, foresters, range conservationists, wildlife biologists, archeologists, surveyors, and engineers.

History In 1812 Congress established the General Land Office to administer the public domain. The passage of the *Taylor Grazing Act* in 1934 established the U.S. Grazing Service to provide active range management on public domain lands. In 1946 the Presidential Reorganization Plan No. 2 merged the Grazing Service with the General Land Office to create the Bureau of Land Management within the Department of the Interior. When Congress enacted the *Federal Land Policy and Management Act of 1976,* it established a coherent legislative mandate for managing the public lands, making the BLM a true multiple-use agency.

Today the bureau administers what remains of the nation's once vast land holdings—the *public domain.* The public domain once included nearly 2 billion acres of land. In the course of our national expansion and development, public lands were sold or deeded by the federal government to the states and their counties and municipalities, to educational institutions, to private citizens, and to industries. Other lands were set aside as national parks and monuments, forests, wildlife refuges, and military installations. The remaining public lands, about 300 million acres located primarily in the west and in Alaska, comprise about one-eighth of our nation's land area. The public lands are a vast storehouse of fossil fuels, other important minerals, and timber. Livestock forage on more than 170 million acres leased to ranchers. Public land provides homes for hundreds of thousands of pronghorn antelope, deer, elk, and caribou, millions of smaller creatures, and about sixty thousand wild horses and burros. Most of these public lands are available for a full range of recreational activities, including hiking, camping, hunting, fishing, skiing, off-road travel, cave exploration, rockhounding, watching wildlife, and enjoying solitude.

Recreation Offering a greater diversity of outdoor recreation opportunities than national parks and national forests, the BLM accommodates about 58 million recreation visits each year. This includes national conservation areas, a national recreation area, about 2,000 miles of the Wild and Scenic River System, about 1,700 miles of national trails, and twenty-five wilderness areas in eight states. In addition, the BLM manages 85,000 miles of streams containing trout, salmon, and other sport fish in more than 470 developed recreation sites, as well as thousands of areas open to a wide variety of recreational uses.

The bureau prepared *Recreation 2000: A Strategic Plan* in 1988 to set forth its commitment to the management of outdoor recreation resources on public lands. The plan presents a revitalized approach to managing the outdoor recreation resource as one of the principal multiple uses of public lands. Through the plan, the bureau hopes to create a better awareness and understanding on the part of the public of the importance of outdoor recreation resources, and the role the public lands play in providing recreational opportunities. The plan calls for diversity, resource dependency, resource protection, visitor service and interpretation, partnerships, maintenance, construction of recreation facilities, recreational planning, limitations, permits, fees, increased opportunities through loan adjustments, tourism, and professional development of recreation and resource management specialists.

The Bureau Of Indian Affairs

The mission of the Bureau of Indian Affairs (BIA) is to act as the principal agent of the United States in carrying on the government-to-government relationship that exists between the United States and federally recognized Indian tribes. The BIA is to carry out the responsibilities that the United States has, as trustee, for property it holds in trust for federally recognized tribes and individual Indians. The first goal of the bureau, under a U.S. policy of Indian self-determination, is to encourage and support tribal efforts to govern themselves and to provide needed programs and services on the reservations (see Figure 7.14).

One of the principal programs of the BIA is administering and managing some 53 million acres of land held in trust by the United States for Indians. The program is designed to help tribes not only protect but also develop their forest, water, mineral, and energy resources. Additionally the bureau spends more than $10 million a year to develop Indian recreational enterprises. The BIA is headquartered in Washington, D.C., but most of its employees work in 12 area offices, 84 agencies, and 180 schools throughout the country. More than 80 percent of the employees are Native Americans. This is, in part, due to a strict Indian preference requirement in hiring.

Recreation Not so many years ago, remote reservations were generally inaccessible to the public. Today they are open to visitors and offer numerous recreational facilities. In fact, many tribes have built recreational facilities on their lands to attract tourists, to bolster tribal income.

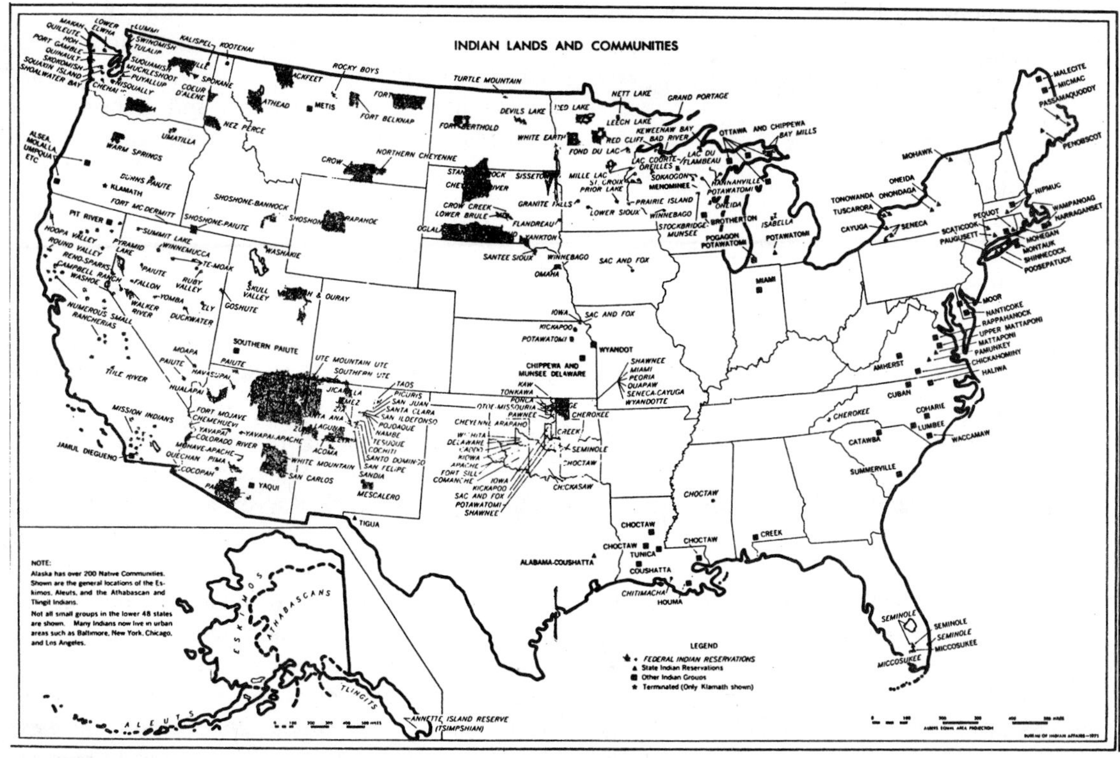

FIGURE 7.14 Indian lands and communities in the United States. *Source: Bureau of Indian Affairs, Department of the Interior, American Indians Today* (U.S. Government Printing Office, 1987).

Some tribes have established camping facilities, and others have invested in luxurious resorts. Because of their economic potential, the Bureau of Indian Affairs has supported commercial recreational developments with financial and administrative assistance. Tourism efforts have promoted job opportunities on reservations with Indians operating facilities, supervising campgrounds, and working as rangers similar to rangers in the national parks and forests.

Many reservations have spectacular scenery, and most offer hiking opportunities and hunting and fishing facilities. Others offer horseback riding, boating, and skiing. Major reservations conduct motor tours to archeological sites and areas of scenic interest. Powwows, dance ceremonials, crafts sales, and museums also attract many visitors. The most successful developments are those of the White Mountain Apaches of Arizona, the Mescalero Apaches of New Mexico, and the Confederated Warm Springs Tribes of Oregon. Navajo Tribal Park in Monument Valley of Arizona and Utah abounds with ancient ruins and spectacular vistas. A corps of Navajo rangers runs the park and offer interpretive services.

According to the United States Commission on Civil Rights (1973:1), a state cannot enforce its game and fish laws within the boundaries of an Indian reservation; therefore, permission to hunt or fish on reservations must be received from the tribe.

When visiting reservations visitors should:

1. Remember that they are guests in a place where cultural attitudes, social customs, and often language are distinctive.
2. Visit public areas only and not enter areas that are private or off-limits.
3. Be prepared to pay a fee if required for photography.
4. Ask permission to photograph individuals.
5. Avoid photographing restricted areas or events.
6. Seek permission to observe private or sacred dances.
7. Seek permission for backcountry travel.

U.S. Army Corps of Engineers

The U.S. Army Corps of Engineers, located in the Department of Defense, traces its origins to the American Revolution. On June 16, 1775, when the Continental Congress established the army, it provided for a chief engineer to direct fortifications during the Battle of Bunker Hill. By 1802 the Corps of Engineers was made permanent, and the U.S. Military Academy was established at West Point, New York, under the chief of army engineers as the only engineering college in the nation.

The corps has maintained a tradition of responding to the nation's military and civil engineering needs. In earlier times, those needs included coastal fortifications and lighthouses, surveying and pathfinding on the frontier, construction of public buildings, clearing of river channels, and operation of such early national parks as Yellowstone and Yosemite. Today's needs include operation of complex military facilities, flood control, comprehensive water resources management, fish and wildlife conservation, development of recreation resources, environmental restoration, and management of toxic wastes, energy resources, and the space program.

The corps employs 48,000 military and civilian members and more than 1,000 architect-engineer and construction firms. It has a network of thirteen regional headquarters, thirty-nine district offices, four major laboratories and research centers, and hundreds of offices at projects throughout the country.

Recreational Development The army engineers, as explorers and mapmakers for pioneers, were among the first to advocate protection of natural resources, according to Turhollow (n.d.:11–18). Among the first to explore the Yellowstone area, they urged that it be set aside and protected. Eventually the roads they designed, built, and maintained opened the wonders of the area to the public. Army engineers along with the U.S. Geological Survey also explored and mapped the Yosemite Valley. After John Muir and other conservationists persuaded Congress in 1890 to declare it a national park under joint control of California and the federal government, the army was asked by the Department of the Interior to take administrative charge of the park until 1911. Besides policing the park, army engineers also laid out trails, produced a map for tourists, and preserved the fauna and flora from destruction by tourists and private owners of land in the park. Army engineer Hiram M. Chitenden, who had helped preserve Yellowstone and published the first book-length study of that area, *Yellowstone National Park,* was selected to oversee the new park. Based on recommendations from Chitenden's commission, the park boundary was established to include 1200 square miles that became the Yosemite National Park that we know today.

In 1876 Congress assigned the corps the task of reengineering the Washington Monument. Originally the monument had been the work of a privately funded organization to honor the memory of the first president. A massive cornerstone was laid in 1848, but technical problems and bankruptcy caused a half-finished eyesore to stand for almost 30 years. The corps, after twelve years of construction, completed the monument with a lightning rod placed on top made of a strange new metal called aluminum.

Roosevelt Dam near Globe, Arizona, is the world's highest masonry dam at 273 feet high, 220 feet thick, and 1,125 feet across. Behind the dam spreads 30-mile-long Roosevelt Lake, which offers good bass fishing and cabins.

The monument, as part of the National Park System, is still the tallest load-bearing masonry structure in the world.

The *Federal Water Project Recreation Act of 1965* requires that the planning of all projects by the corps give consideration to the inclusion of facilities for swimming, boating, fishing, camping, and sight-seeing wherever appropriate. In developing plans for recreational facilities, the corps seeks the cooperation of all federal and state agencies concerned. In addition, the corps bears responsibility for the environmental protection of the sources for various recreational activities.

Bureau of Reclamation

The Bureau of Reclamation (BuREC) is housed in the Department of the Interior. Its head office is in Washington, D.C., and it has seven regional offices throughout the United States. The bureau is best known for its great dams and powerplants, among them Grand Coulee Dam on the Columbia River and Hoover Dam on the Colorado River. These huge projects and their forerunners made a significant impact on settlement in the West. Chartered in 1902, Reclamation's name comes from its original mission to reclaim the arid lands of the western United States for farming by providing a secure, year-round supply of water for irrigation. Impetus for the great dams came from farmers and townspeople who repaid the costs of construction many times over through production of food, fiber, jobs, energy, and other investments that contributed to America's prosperity.

As the West grew and water resource needs increased, Reclamation's mission expanded as well. In addition to irrigation, its responsibilities include hydroelectric power generation, management of municipal and industrial water supplies, river regulation and flood control, development and management of outdoor recreation, enhancement of fish and wildlife habitats, and research.

Recreational Development Reclamation reservoirs provide millions of visitors with facilities for fishing, swimming, picnicking, and sight-seeing on its 333 reservoirs and other bodies of water throughout seventeen western states. Today recreation resource management is a vital part of the service's multipurpose water and power resource development program. BuREC encourages development of recreation facilities to provide maximum recreation opportunities for today's public while protecting the natural resources under its control for tomorrow's future. The majority of recreation areas on Reclamation lands are managed by local, county, or state agencies and by federal agencies such as the U.S. Forest Service or the National Park Service. A few are managed directly by the BuREC. Each recreation area offers different attractions, often in a variety of natural environments. Reservoir shorelines and newly created wetlands provide habitat for fish, waterfowl, and other wildlife.

In 1987 the Bureau of Reclamation made a commitment to the enhancement of recreational opportunities through Reclamation projects to meet growing public demands. The bureau intends to pursue legislation that will give it broader authority to manage public recreation on its facilities.

The Tennessee Valley Authority (TVA)

The Tennessee Valley Authority (TVA) is a government-owned corporation created by an act passed May 18, 1933. All functions of the TVA are vested in its board of directors, whose members are appointed by the president with the consent of the Senate. Offices of the board and general manager are in Knoxville, Tennessee.

The TVA conducts a unified program of resource development for the advancement of growth in the Tennessee Valley region. The TVA provides technical assistance in areas including industrial development, regional waste management, tourism promotion, community preparedness, and vanpool organization. At Muscle Shoals, Alabama, it operates a national laboratory for the development of new and improved fertilizers and processes. In cooperation with other agencies, the TVA conducts research and development programs in forestry, fish and game, watershed protection, health services related to its operation, and economic development of Tennessee Valley communities.

A system of dams built by the TVA on the Tennessee River and its larger tributaries provides flood regulation on the Tennessee and contributes to regulation of the lower Ohio and Mississippi rivers. The system maintains a continuous 9-foot-draft channel for navigation for the length of the 650-mile Tennessee River main stream. The dams harness the power of the rivers to produce electricity. They also provide other benefits, including potential for outdoor recreation (Henderson 1991:715).

Recreational Development From its beginning, the TVA has worked to encourage development of a wide variety of outdoor recreation facilities and opportunities in the Tennessee Valley, particularly on TVA lakes and shorelines. To secure the involvement of those most affected, the TVA structured its recreation policy so that its activities would stimulate, support, and complement the actions of concerned agencies and individuals. This policy includes identification of recreation resources available throughout the valley, encouragement for development by other public agencies and private investors, technical assistance where needed to achieve this development, and the provision of basic facilities where needed to assure safe access to the lakes and to protect the shoreline from misuse.

The TVA has set aside a large tract of reservoir shoreline for wildlife management and hunting areas, for wildlife refuges, and for duck and geese feeding areas to be managed by the state game and fish agencies and the U.S. Fish and Wildlife Service. Also, over 100,000 acres of reservoir lands have been transferred to the National Park Service and the U.S. Forest Service, which administer them largely as natural forest lands.

Since 1969 the TVA has provided basic recreation improvement including picnic facilities, boat-launching ramps, access roads, and sanitary facilities along many of its reservoir shorelines. By 1978, use of these facilities grew to such an extent that it was evident to the TVA board of directors that a new policy for facility management was needed. Implementation began in 1979 of specific management plans for TVA facilities on reservoir properties. The new policy maintained TVA's long-standing recreational goals—to provide a quality outdoor experience, to encourage state and local government agencies to develop parks and other recreation facilities wherever feasible, and to assist in the growth and development of quality private recreational opportunities in the valley. In management of its own facilities, the TVA designated certain areas for specific uses (day use, overnight camping, etc.), began employing onsite resident caretakers, and charged a modest fee for camping on developed grounds.

One of the most effective ways the TVA supports its recreation commitment is to make suitable portions of its shoreline lands available to others for development. Land and land rights have been transferred or conveyed for a nominal consideration to federal, state, and local governmental agencies for the development of public parks and access areas. Lands have been leased, licensed, and sold to quasi-public groups and organizations for group camps. With the increased popularity of canoeing, river fishing, hiking, and biking, the TVA is working with various groups to promote protection of streams while providing for their use. Concentrating its trail development on agency lands near population centers and developed recreation clusters, the TVA plans are carried out on a regional basis to assure that trail development meets the larger goals of state and national programs. In addition to these activities on reservoir lands, the TVA has provided a wide range of technical assistance to others to help them improve their own recreational programs.

Land Between the Lakes (LBL) is a center for outdoor recreation, environmental education, and resource stewardship managed by the TVA as a demonstration in maximum utilization of a region's available resources. An Army Corp of Engineers project, the 170,000-acre peninsula is located between Kentucky Lake and Lake Barkley in western Kentucky and Tennessee (see Figure 7.15). LBL receives more than 2 million visits annually from a wide variety of users ranging from hikers and campers to hunters and anglers. There are special areas provided for offroad vehicles, campers with horses, and field archers. LBL also offers interpretive centers, roadside exhibits, over 200 miles of trails, and an outdoor school located in its environmental education area. Methods and principles for demonstration, development, and operation of the area are being tried and tested to help establish criteria for managing multiple-use facilities and resources throughout the United States.

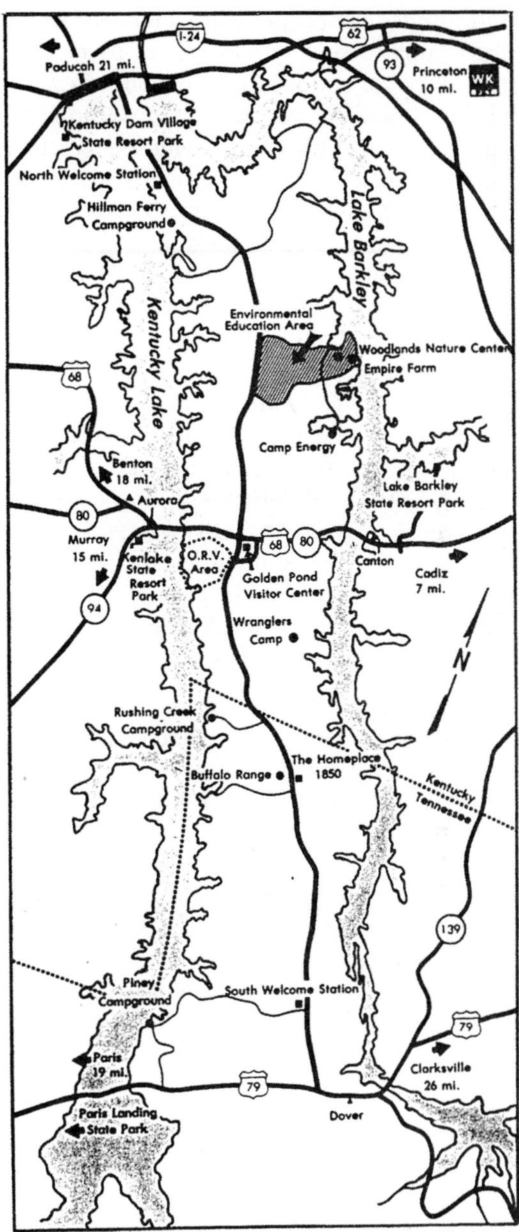

FIGURE 7.15 TVA's land between the lakes. *Source: Brochure: Recreation on TVA Lakes.* Tennessee Valley Authority, 1984.

National Reservoir Areas According to Knudson (1984:281–82), more recreationists visit large flood control reservoirs than national parks, and these areas receive more individual visits than do national forests. With 68,000 dams in the United States, there are abundant water-related recreational opportunities. In general, reservoirs are popular recreation sites for fishing, boating, water-skiing, swimming, camping, picnicking, hiking, sight-seeing, and a variety of other activities. Large dams built under the direction of the U.S. Army Corps of Engineers, the Bureau of Reclamation, and the Tennessee Valley Authority offer recreational attractions. These agencies, however, had no official responsibilities for recreational planning and management before 1962, when John F. Kennedy approved *Senate Document 97,* which specified the need for outdoor recreation and fish and wildlife enhancement in planning for water projects. With the passage of the *Federal Water Projects Recreation Act of 1965,* procedures for developing multipurpose water resource projects were established, and plans for recreation use were required. The act provided that:

1. Recreation, fish, and wildlife enhancement be considered a purpose of federal water resource projects, though not to exceed 50 percent of the benefits or costs of such multipurpose projects.
2. Recreation possibilities be considered for existent and planned federal, state, and local public developments.
3. Recreation, fish, and wildlife enhancement features must be administered by nonfederal administration.

The benefits of recreation bolstered the justification of new projects, but a provision requiring state and local cooperation gave veto power to these groups which, on occasion, stopped projects. Implementation of the act, however, clearly made the federal government the nation's largest provider of inland water-related opportunities. Conversely, while these projects created new water-related recreational opportunities, previous recreational opportunities were impaired due to the destruction of excellent trout streams, scenic canyons, and archeological remains. Public concern for natural diversity has caused public resistance to many new dam projects.

National Oceanic and Atmospheric Administration

The National Marine Sanctuary Program

The National Oceanic and Atmospheric Administration (NOAA) is an agency of the United States Department of Commerce. Title III of the *Marine Protection, Research and Sanctuaries Act of 1972* authorized the secretary of Commerce to designate discrete marine areas of special national significance as national marine sanctuaries in order to provide comprehensive, protective management of their conservation, recreational, ecological, historical, research, educational, or aesthetic value. The sanctuary program is administered by the NOAA. A select number of marine areas in the country have been given this special protected status because of their nationally significant natural and cultural resources. These national marine sanctuaries are the aquatic counterpart of our national parks—the unique areas designated as national marine sanctuaries are meant to be managed for the long-term benefit and enjoyment of the public. Specifically, resources are to be protected, the public is to be given a better awareness of the marine environment, and scientific research and ecological monitoring are to be encouraged. Traditional commercial activities, which are mostly banned in national parks, are allowed in national marine sanctuaries as long as they do not undermine the fundamental health and integrity of the area.

In 1980, a 1252-square-mile portion of the waters surrounding Anacapa, Santa Rosa, Santa Cruz, San Miguel, and Santa Barbara islands was designated the Channel Islands National

Marine Sanctuary. The sanctuary and the Channel Islands National Park combine to provide comprehensive protection to an extraordinary combination of land and sea.

Likewise, in order to protect the spectacular marine ecosystem of the Florida Keys, the *Florida Keys National Marine Sanctuary and Protection Act* was enacted by Congress and signed into law by President George Bush on November 16, 1990. According to the Coral Reef Coalition, the act first and foremost creates the Florida Keys National Marine Sanctuary, which encompasses approximately 2600 square nautical miles, making the sanctuary the largest of its kind in the United States. Additionally the act calls for the NOAA to prepare a comprehensive management plan for the sanctuary after consulting with the public and with federal, state, and local government authorities. A broad-based advisory council will assist in developing and carrying out the plan.

Certain rules for the sanctuary are laid out by the act itself. Oil and gas development are prohibited, and commercial vessel traffic is restricted with an internationally designated "Area To Be Avoided." The act also places particular emphasis on improving water quality throughout the area. The act incorporates the Key Largo and Looe Key National Marine Sanctuaries, established in 1975 and 1981, respectively, into the Florida Keys National Marine Sanctuary. According to the Coral Reef Coalition the large size of the newer sanctuary offers the opportunity to set up differing regulations for separate areas within the sanctuary, similar to a system already in place at the Great Barrier Reef Marine Park of Australia. Some areas can continue to be used in the accustomed ways, while other areas can be designated for preservation, restoration, or scientific research. This system provides for multiple uses within the sanctuary while also making certain its natural resources are protected for the future (see Chapter 16, *The Environment*).

The National Marine Fisheries Service The National Oceanic and Atmospheric Administration Fisheries, also known as the National Marine Fisheries Service (NMFS), is the federal agency that manages the sea's living resources between 3 and 200 miles off the U.S. coast. Organized in 1970, the NMFS is composed of headquarters offices, five regional offices, and four regional fisheries. It administers federal regulations designed to assure that fishing stays within sound biological and economic limitations and that U.S. commercial and recreational anglers have the opportunity to harvest all the fishery resources within these limitations. The service regulates foreign fishing in the U.S. Exclusive Economic Zone (EEZ). It also protects marine habitats and marine animals such as the great whales, porpoises, and sea turtles. The NMFS shares with the U.S. Fish and Wildlife Service the administration of the *Marine Mammal Protection Act,* which protects marine mammals. In addition the NMFS collects data on commercial and recreational catch.

In 1979 the NMFS began a new comprehensive Marine Recreational Fishery Statistical Survey. Surveys are conducted in the Atlantic, Gulf of Mexico, Pacific, Western Pacific, and Caribbean. The component survey findings are combined to produce estimates of recreational catch, fishing effort, and participation.

Recreational Development The NMFS is committed to the promotion of increased opportunities for marine recreational fishing through its *Action Plan* (1990). According to the NMFS (1990:2), in the period between 1980 and 1985 the value of marine recreational fishing grew from $7.5 billion to $13.5 billion. From 1955 to 1985 the number of anglers increased from 5 million to 17 million. Since 1985, however, there has been no substantial increase. Perhaps the greatest concern for the NMFS is the need for healthy fisheries resources. To keep this commitment the NMFS is increasingly consigned to rebuilding and conserving marine fishery resources and habitats. For example, the NMFS research center reviews, evaluates, and, if needed, upgrades its stock assessment capabilities to ensure that assessments for species of recreational importance, and for forage species upon which these fish depend, are provided. In the Southwest Region a research project on the estuarine dependence of the California halibut, a prized recreational species in southern California, was recently completed. The 2-year study revealed that the halibut depends upon shallow-water bays and lagoons for nursery areas for the first year of life. Studies of this nature serve to protect the species.

The Action Plan calls for sufficient staffing and effective, cooperative partnerships with other federal and state agencies, Regional Fishery Management Councils, interstate commissions, and public and private sector interests. Through partnerships the service promotes angling ethics, conservation, and aquatic information.

SUMMARY

The U.S. government plays a crucial role in outdoor recreation in America. The government still owns one-third of the land in this country, that is, 700 million acres of a total 2 billion acres. Two federal agencies, the United States Forest Service and the National Park Service, provide numerous resources and varied programs for the nature aficionado. The historical development of these two agencies and the extent of their offerings are covered in this chapter.

Attention is given to the provision of wilderness areas on federal land. The idea of preserving areas in their pristine condition has been gaining support, and a number of federal acts were passed underscoring the importance of these areas to the American people. Accordingly a number of systems are now provided for the enjoyment of the recreationist, for example, the Wild and Scenic Rivers System and the National Trails System.

Several federal agencies are involved in the offerings of outdoor pursuits. Among these are the U.S. Fish and Wildlife Service, the Bureau of Land Management, the Bureau of Land Reclamation, the Tennessee Valley Authority, and the National Oceanic and Atmospheric Administration. Their offerings are detailed in this chapter.

REFERENCES

American Hiking Society (1990) *American Hiker* (June). Washington, D.C.

Browning, J., J. Hendee, and J. Roggenbuck (1988) *Wilderness Laws: Milestones and Management Direction in Wilderness Legislation, 1964–1987.* Bulletin No. 5. Moscow, ID: University of Idaho.

Bureau of Indian Affairs, U.S. Department of the Interior. (1987) *American Indians Today.* Washington, D.C.: U.S. Government Printing Office.

Coral Reef Coalition (no date) *Inside the New Florida Keys Natural Marine Sanctuary.*

Cordell, H., J. Bergstrom, L. Hartmenn, and D. English (1990) *An Analysis of the Outdoor Recreation and Wilderness Situation in the United States: 1989–2040.* Fort Collins, CO: United States Department of Agriculture Forest Service General Technical Report RM-189.

Craig, B. "Diamonds and Rust." *National Parks* 65, no. 5-6 (May/June 1991). Washington, D.C.: National Parks and Conservation Association.

Forest Service, U.S. Department of Agriculture (1990) *The Forest Service Program for Forest and Rangeland Resources: A Long-Term Strategic Plan.* Washington, D.C.: U.S. Government Printing Office.

Forest Service, U.S. Department of Agriculture (1988) *The National Forests: America's Great Outdoors National Recreation Strategy.* Washington, D.C.: U.S. Government Printing Office.

Forest Service, U.S. Department of Agriculture (1990) *Report of the Forest Service Fiscal Year 1989.* Washington, D.C.: U.S. Government Printing Office.

Harvey, T., and S. Henley (1989) *The Status of Trails in National Forests, National Parks, and Bureau of Land Management Areas.* Washington, D.C.: The American Hiking Society.

Hendee, J., G. Stankey, and R. Lucas (1978) *Wilderness Management.* Forest Service, U.S. Department of Agriculture. Washington, D.C.: U.S. Government Printing Office.

Henderson, G. (editor) (1991) "TVA" in *The U.S. Government Manual (1990–1991).* Tanham, MD: Bernan Press.

Jensen, C. (1985) *Outdoor Recreation in America.* Minneapolis, MN: Burgess.

Knudson, D. (1984) *Outdoor Recreation.* New York: Macmillan.

National Marine Fisheries Service (1990) *Marine Recreational Action Plan.*

National Park Service, U.S. Department of the Interior (1989) *The National Parks: Index 1989.* Washington, D.C.: U.S. Government Printing Office.

Ridenour, J. "Building on a Legacy." *National Parks* 65, no. 5-6. (May/June 1991). Washington, D.C.: National Parks and Conservation Association.

Riley, L., and W. Riley (1979) *Guide to the National Wildlife Refuges.* Garden City, NJ: Anchor Press/Doubleday.

Runte, A. (1987) *National Parks: The American Experience.* Lincoln, NE: University of Nebraska Press.

Tennessee Valley Authority (1984) *Recreation on TVA Lakes.* Knoxville, TN.

Tilden, F. (1959) *The National Parks: What They Mean to Me.* New York: Alfred A. Knopf.

Turhollow, A. (undated) *Do You Know?* Los Angeles: U.S. Army Corp of Engineers.

Tweed, W. (1980) *Recreation Site Planning and Improvement in National Forests 1891–1942.* U.S. Department of Agriculture. Washington, D.C.: U.S. Government Printing Office.

United States Commission on Civil Rights (1973). *Staff Memorandum: Constitutional States of American Indians.* Washington, D.C. March 1973.

Wellman, J. (1987) *Wildland Recreation Policy.* New York: John Wiley and Sons.

8 State Resources and Recreation

Prior to the establishment of the United States of America, the Massachusetts Bay Colony set aside 90,000 acres for fishing and fowling. The *Great Ponds* Act of 1641 protected about 2,000 sites of freshwater bodies, each 10 acres or more in size. The hunting and fishing that took place at these ponds were for survival, not recreational, purposes. Nonetheless, the Great Ponds Act could be looked upon as the genesis of state involvement in preserving natural resources (Foss 1968:223).

After independence and the establishment of the United States, the federal government in 1832 granted the territorial governor of the Arkansas Territory the right to hold the Arkansas Hot Springs and Washita River Salt Springs from private ownership. The governor had the right to lease these areas, which were considered valuable because of their healing power (Fazio 1979:214). Arkansas Hot Springs was taken back by the federal government and made into a national park in 1921 in a manner similar to what happened to the Yosemite Valley, which was granted to California in 1864 but was taken back to eventually become the nation's second national park in 1875. These actions by the states and the federal government were not intended to enhance recreational opportunities, but rather to preserve some of the nation's natural resources.

Fazio (1979:214) credits the state of New York with the earliest significant, lasting contributions to state action concerning recreational resources. Its action came as a response to the deplorable conditions and uncontrollable commercial development of the areas surrounding Niagara Falls, which led Frederick Olmsted to decry the loss of beauty around the falls. In 1885 the U.S. Congress placed these areas under the care of the state of New York as the New York

State Reservation of Niagara. Conditions at Niagara may have improved slightly after that. According to Knudson (1984:86), "It was difficult to see the falls because of all the hucksters and makeshift commercial shops that lined the sides of the scenic wonder."

At the time Niagara was put under its care, New York was considering the creation of another open-space area, the Adirondack Wilderness. A total of 715,000 acres of lakes and mountains were dedicated as the state's "Forest Preserve." Although it was the fear of water shortage that prompted the action initially, Nash (1967:118) argues that recreational rationale had finally achieved legal recognition when the Adirondack and Catskill regions became "forever wild" as stipulated in the New York state constitution.

State park legislation increased at the turn of the century. Minnesota developed Itasca State Park when it received a federal grant to protect the headwaters of the Mississippi River. Illinois initiated the nation's first state agency for state parks in 1903. Its first park was Fort Massac, which led to the establishment of the state's park system.

Stephen Mather, director of the National Park Service since 1916, became interested in helping states develop their own systems of parks. He organized the first National Conference on State Parks in Des Moines, Iowa, in 1921. At that time only nineteen states had state park systems or similar arrangements such as state forests and preserves. The National Conference on State Parks became a permanent organization known today as the National Society for Park Resources, an affiliate of the National Recreation and Park Association.

The Depression years brought about greater cooperation between the states and the federal government. The *Park, Parkway and Recreational Area Study Act* of 1936 produced numerous inventories which were developed by NPS personnel on states' situations. The states became aware of their needs for natural resources. Two more acts helped the states acquire more natural resources, the *Surplus Property Act* of 1944 and the *Recreation and Public Purposes Act* of 1954. And with the passage of the *Land and Water Conservation Act* of 1965, the states were able not only to acquire lands but also to receive technical assistance in expanding their natural resources.

THE STATE AND OUTDOOR RECREATION

The Tenth Amendment to the Constitution of the United States (also known as "the states rights"), which passed in 1925, clarified the role of the state vis-à-vis the role of the federal government in providing services to its residents. The amendment specifies that "the powers not delegated to the United States by the Constitution, not prohibited by it to the states, are reserved to the states respectively, or to the people." The Tenth Amendment became the authority by which state governments began to provide services that had been provided by private agencies. The earlier services included education, health, and welfare. Eventually recreation became a recognized function of state government.

In the *Third Nationwide Outdoor Recreation Plan* (Heritage 1979:74-75), the state is described as having several unique powers that give it a dominant role in providing recreation service, as follows:

1. The state has a repository of police powers for land use control which is the basic tool for land preservation or designation for recreation.
2. The state can finance recreation through bond issues, special taxes, and fees. It is also responsible for the administration of the monies allocated to local authorities for recreation through the Land and Water Conservation Fund. The

enactment of these funds requires a Statewide Comprehensive Outdoor Recreation Plan (SCORP), which makes it clear that the state could play an important role in outdoor recreation.

According to the *Plan* (Heritage 1979) public visitations to outdoor recreation areas managed by the state increased drastically from the 1960s to the 1970s. From the inception of the Land and Water Conservation Fund in 1965 until the year 1978, close to $2 billion have been given, on a matching basis, to state and local governments. This means that close to $3.9 billion were spent in 14 years to enhance outdoor recreation opportunities on state and local natural resources. About 1.77 million acres of new recreation land were acquired nationwide during this time.

During the period from 1965 to 1978, approximately 22,000 different recreation units were assisted through the Land and Water Conservation Fund. The units ranged from small neighborhood parks to large regional or state recreation areas. Local projects utilized 58 percent of funding and accounted for 16,779 projects and 312,000 acres. The states utilized the remaining 42 percent of funding and accounted for 5,272 projects and 1.46 million acres. The states provided guidance and technical assistance to the local authorities in their quest for enhancing recreation services.

Today the states own about 78 million acres of land and water that are used, or have the potential to be used, for outdoor recreation. These areas constituted approximately 5 percent of the nation's resources. The 78 million acres owned by the states are classified roughly into state forests (26.5 million acres), fish and wildlife areas (9 million acres), state parks (5.5 million acres), and other areas (37 million acres) which include nature preserves. Table 8.1 shows the classification of state lands.

The state forests, which constitute the largest segment in the lands owned by the states that can be used for outdoor recreation, include 1.6

TABLE 8.1 State Lands Classification

Use Classification	Acreage
Forests	26,503,389
Fish and Wildlife Areas	9,005,445
Parks	5,528,030
School Land	430,807
Unclassified	36,400,000
Total	77,867,671

Source: Bureau of Land Management, U.S. Department of the Interior, *Public Land Statistics.* (Washington, D.C.: U.S. Government Printing Office, 1977).

million acres in the southeast, 3.3 million acres in the south central region, 9.9 million acres in the northeast region, and 11.8 million acres in the north central region. The thirteen western states have the most state-owned acreage, and the twelve southern states the least, as shown in Table 8.2. Alaska and California have the most acreage in state parks, Washington and Minnesota in state forests, and Mississippi and Pennsylvania in state fish and wildlife areas.

State Functions and Recreation

Today most of the fifty states see recreation as an important service to be provided for their residents. Although there is no universal agreement as to what constitutes a good package in leisure and recreation services to be offered, facilitated, or enhanced by the state government, the following eight functions are considered sufficient by MacLean et al. (1985:104–106):

1. Enactment of Permissive Legislation Permissive legislation refers to state laws that allow local public bodies to finance and operate services. Certain qualification of personnel involved in the service may be required. Education, health, welfare, as well as recreation are enacted by local authorities according to permissive legislation. The first enabling act in recreation was passed in 1915 in New Jersey. Today all states have such acts.

TABLE 8.2 State-owned Land Distribution by Region

Region	Total State-Owned Land (Acres)	Percent of State-Owned Land	Percent of U.S. Population in Region
West	51,225,102	65%	17%
North Central	12,492,490	16%	28%
Northeast	9,524,583	12%	24%
South	4,595,583	6%	31%

Source: Heritage Conservation and Recreation Service, *The Third Nationwide Outdoor Recreation Plan* (Washington, D.C.: U.S. Government Printing Office, 1979), 75.

2. Service to Local Recreation Authorities Many states have established offices or departments of recreation, one function of which is to assist the local authority in providing adequate service to the local residents. Assistance could come in many ways, among which are studying needs, providing information, conducting programs, conducting in-service training, developing standards, allocating grants-in-aid, and coordinating and monitoring federally funded programs.

3. Provision of Areas, Facilities, and Programs Although the acreage of the lands provided for recreation by the state is dwarfed by the acreage of the lands provided by the federal government, the state lands' proximity to population centers makes them more accessible. The total acreage of state lands available for recreation is about 41 million acres, which is approximately 6 percent of the amount of federal lands available for the same purpose. On state lands the states have developed roads, trails, swimming pools, beaches, picnic grounds, playgrounds, and campgrounds. In addition, recreation is offered in state-run institutions such as hospitals, prisons, colleges, and universities.

4. Management of Plants and Wildlife The propagation, distribution, and protection of living things, plant or animal, fall under the joint concern of the state and federal governments. The latter is concerned with wildlife that crosses state and international boundaries, such as migratory birds. Within its boundaries, each state manages plants and wildlife through a number of activities such as reforestation; protection of rare trees, plants, flowers, and endangered species; setting aside of reserves; improvement of wildlife habitat; and regulation of hunting and fishing.

This vantage point from Dead Horse State Park in Utah overlooks the geological wonderland of the Colorado Plateau cut by canyons formed by the Green and Colorado rivers.

5. Research and Education Most of the above functions require the backing of research. In many instances, research units are established within the concerned department. Social research is conducted in relationship to the use and the need for areas, facilities, and programs. Scientific research is conducted in relationship to the

Newspaper Rock State Historic Monument, north of Monticello, Utah, protects one of the finest panels of rock art in the world. Literally hundreds of figures have been depicted on a smooth rock over the last 3,000 years.

management of plants and wildlife. Recreation education is provided by the state in a number of ways: education that prepares a recreation professional is offered through the state colleges and universities; recreation education for the layperson is offered through publications, films, videos, exhibits, and lectures. Media education could be provided by the state department of parks and recreation directly or through assistance given by the state to local recreation authorities.

6. Promotion of Tourism Tourism has become a leading business for some states, which, along with many other states, are waging campaigns to attract tourists. Special efforts are exerted to provide the tourist with the necessary conveniences in improved roads, adequate accommodations, and necessary services.

7. Standards and Regulations The state endeavors to protect both the recreationists and the resource through standards and regulations. The recreationist is protected through safety and health standards and regulations that are observed in beaches, camps, resorts, restaurants, and swimming pools. The resource is protected through inspection, licenses, and permits.

8. Cooperation with Federal Agencies As previously stated, there are a number of federal laws pertaining to recreation in the natural environment that have some bearing on state and local offerings either directly or indirectly. Cooperation with federal agencies, as has been shown, enables all fifty states to expand their recreation resources, facilities, and programs. Moreover, since most states have counterparts to federal agencies, it makes sense that agencies of the same orientation should cooperate and coordinate their efforts in achieving what seems to be similar goals. For instance, the National Park Service and the state park department, also the U.S. Forest Service and the state forestry service, should enhance their offerings through cooperation and coordination.

State Recreation Services

The states have become increasingly involved in providing recreation services. Although the structures through which these recreational services are provided may vary, the services themselves are similar.

State Recreation Commissions/Boards

Thirty-four of the fifty United States have commissions or boards to monitor and promote the recreation offering by the state.

State Department of Parks and Recreation

Not all states will have a department entitled as such, but all have an agency that serves as a liaison for recreation. This service is required in the administration of the Land and Water Conservation Act funds provided by the 1965 act, which led to the next service.

State Outdoor Recreation Plan In order to become eligible for federal money from the Land and Water Conservation Act, the state is required to designate an agency to handle the funds, to prepare an outdoor recreation plan, and to develop a procedure for raising the matching funds required of the local community. This requirement led to an increase in the number of local park and recreation commissions/boards which will be discussed later. It also made each state take a serious look at its natural resources.

State Recreation Resources

Most of state recreation lands, whether they are forests or parks, were originally acquired as gifts, tax-delinquent lands, original holdings since colonial time, or federal land turned over to the states. As the demand for recreation increased after World War II, states began to purchase lands using bonds or earmarked taxes. While the bonds were the main sources for acquiring lands, special taxes on cigarettes and gasoline were also used for that purpose.

Some federal laws made acquisition of recreation lands easier on most states by applying the concept of matching funds. The first of these laws was the Pittman-Robertson Act of 1937, which allowed federal funds to be used in wildlife management. In 1950, the Dingell-Johnson Act was used to improve fisheries. But it was the Land and Water Conservation Act of 1965 that allowed for matching funds to be used for the acquisition of lands for recreation and as open space.

Today state resources that can be used for outdoor recreation are classified into four categories: parks, forests, preserves, and fish and wildlife areas. Table 8.1 shows the acreage of some of the state lands, including land that can be used for recreation.

STATE PARKS

The impetus for establishing state parks which resulted in the First National Conference in Des Moines, Iowa, in 1921 was provided by the desire of members of the federal government to get the states to develop their own systems. The two criteria for park site selection suggested then by Richard Leiber, a leader in that movement, were scenic value and/or historical significance. Yet the state park was to be dedicated to the public for the intelligent use of its leisure time (Knudson 1984:197).

Today all fifty states have some form of state park, although the parks vary in number, size, and administrative affiliation. They range in type from highly developed, with lodges and marinas, to completely primitive, without roads or signs. The numbers and sizes of parks are so disproportionately distributed that 53 percent of state park lands are in only three states: Alaska, California, and New York. New York's Adirondack State Park is the largest park in the United States with its 6 million acres. Most state parks are of medium size and are close enough to population centers for the enjoyment of outdoor activities such as boating, camping, and hiking along with the organized activities of golf and tennis. While New York has the largest acreage of state parks, located mainly in the Adirondacks, California has over 1 million acres of state park land and Alaska has a little less than 1 million acres.

The organizational structures under which these parks are administered vary according to each state's administrative setup. While the State Park Department oversees the state parks in Arizona, Georgia, Idaho, and Kentucky, the Department of Conservation oversees them in Alabama, Illinois, Iowa, and New York. The Department of Natural Resources has a park system to manage the state parks in Alaska, California, Hawaii, Indiana, Michigan, and Utah. In Arkansas and South Carolina state parks are charged to the Tourism Division. In some states, the state parks are administered by the highway department.

STATE FORESTS

Of the fifty states, only four do not have state forests: Kansas, Nebraska, Oklahoma, and Texas (Knudson 1984:192). According to Jensen (1985:125), state forests are better developed in the eastern, southern, and midwestern states where the forests are of high quality. The forests in the plains states and western states are of poor quality and are less developed.

When state forests were acquired, the major thrust was to protect the land from erosion, to develop areas for timber, and to provide experimental and demonstration areas. Recreation as such was not considered until after World War II. Today outdoor recreation is an acceptable activity in most state forests. Although many specific areas have been designated for recreation, attempts are made to keep these areas as primitive as possible while still providing comfortable accommodations and, in many instances, interpretive service.

The activities that take place in state forests typically include, but are not limited to, boating, camping, fishing, horseback riding, hunting, nature study, and picnicking. Campsites, with or without modern conveniences, are provided in many of the nation's state forests.

NATURE PRESERVES

Among the many nonprofit organizations that promote the enjoyment of the aesthetic aspects of outdoor recreation (such as the National Wildlife Federation, the National Park and Conservation Association, the Izaak Walton League, the Audubon Society, and the Sierra Club), the Nature Conservancy is unique in that it directs its efforts to acquiring and preserving land. The Conservancy buys endangered natural areas and turns them over to other agencies for protection and management. Its Heritage Program is conducted in cooperation with state governments in identifying, locating, and inventorying natural areas, endangered species, and unusual physical phenomena which could become the basis for acquisition.

Many states have followed the concept of preserving lands that have outstanding natural significance. According to Knudson (1984:195), Illinois' efforts in this direction started as early as 1858. Cook County, Illinois, has more dedicated natural areas—areas to be preserved for posterity—than any other county in the state. They are not all administered by one agency; some are still held privately or run by industry.

FISH AND WILDLIFE AREAS

Each of the fifty states has a department charged with the management of fish and wildlife or a division in an agency for the same purpose. The responsibilities of such a department or agency are to propagate fish and wildlife, to distribute game animals, game birds, and game fish, and to manage fisheries and refuges. In the areas administered by such a department or agency, fishing, hunting, and trapping take place according to the state laws and regulation and with the licensing obtained from the department or agency.

According to Knudson (1984:196), wildlife management by regulation began during the colonial period. In fact, bounty was imposed on some wildlife. By the mid 1800s the concept of seasons was used to protect big game animals as land clearing and wetland drainage were threatening many habitats. Still, human population expansion continued to threaten many wildlife species. It was not until the opening years of the twentieth century that recreational hunters and fishermen set aside refuges and preserves for exotic and threatened species.

Despite, or maybe because of, the primitive nature of wildlife and fish areas, recreation has become popular there. While fishing and hunting are on top of the list of activities that take place in wildlife and fish areas, other outdoor recreation activities are observed there also; in fact, camping, hiking, nature study, and picnicking are more popular because their seasons are longer when compared to the fishing and hunting seasons. Interpretive services are also provided in many of these areas along with facilities for observation of wildlife.

REGIONAL DIFFERENCES

The National Association of State Park Directors publishes an *Annual Information Exchange,* the latest of which was published in April of 1990. The data collected by the association detailing the total acreage of outdoor resources in each of the fifty states (excluding state forests and state trails) is shown in Table 8.3.

According to Chubb and Chubb (1981), there are regional differences not only in the number of units but also in their characteristics. The Pacific Region of the United States (Alaska, California, Hawaii, Oregon, and Washington) is the leading region, accounting for approximately 20 percent of the total state park acreage. The Middle Atlantic Region, another leading region, accounts for 11 percent of the total state park acreage. That region includes New York, Pennsylvania, and Rhode Island. The West South Central Region (Arkansas, Louisiana, Oklahoma, and Texas) has the least acreage in state parks, approximately 2.5 percent of the national total (see Figure 8.1)

The degree of development varies from state to state and park to park as do the types of activities that take place in each park. Some parks adhere to the original concept of a state park as suggested by Richard Leiber, a leading authority on state parks, in 1928:

> A typical portion of the state's original domain; tract of adequate size, preserved in primeval, unspoilt, "unimproved," or "beautified" condition. It is a physical expression of life, liberty, and the pursuit of happiness.
>
> A state park must have either scenic or historic value or both, and is dedicated to the public for the intelligent use of its leisure time (Michaud 1966:561).

TABLE 8.3 Total Acreage Of State Outdoor Resources (except state forests and trails)

	Total of All Categories Other Than (2) and (8)						
	Number of Units Total	Number of Units Operational	Total Acreage		Number of Units Total	Number of Units Operational	Total Acreage
AK	123	123	3,237,032	MT	313	240	51,208
AL	24	23	48,985	NC	49	49	128,698
AR	49	45	47,309	ND	30	27	17,186
AZ	25	22	39,470	NE	86	83	148,666
CA	280	245	1,287,067	NH	70	66	32,967
CO	99	95	230,400	NJ	98	88	91,787
CT	94	93	31,889	NM	39	39	118,951
DE	23	23	11,898	NV	22	21	141,610
FL	146	108	418,930	NY	181	166	258,400
GA	63	58	61,734	OH	72	72	207,682
HI	75	68	24,861	OK	70	60	95,332
IA	87	87	52,000	OR	233	173	89,935
ID	26	20	46,808	PA	114	108	276,322
IL	218	218	384,229	RI	85	73	9,223
IN	21	21	56,767	SC	57	48	79,308
KS	25	24	30,219	SD	92	81	92,421
KY	46	46	41,842	TN	81	75	133,044
LA	52	21	38,903	TX	129	112	433,366
MA	124	117	59,651	UT	49	45	115,333
MD	50	43	96,112	VA	38	38	51,078
ME	143	117	70,303	VT	60	33	46,706
MI	93	84	262,454	WA	215	185	231,498
MN	64	64	200,000	WI	63	52	70,697
MO	73	71	109,184	WV	43	43	126,885
MS	28	27	22,795	WY	48	47	119,424
				TOT	4,396	3,898	10,079,684

Source: National Association of State Park Directors, *Annual Information Exchange* (Tallahassee, FL, 1990).

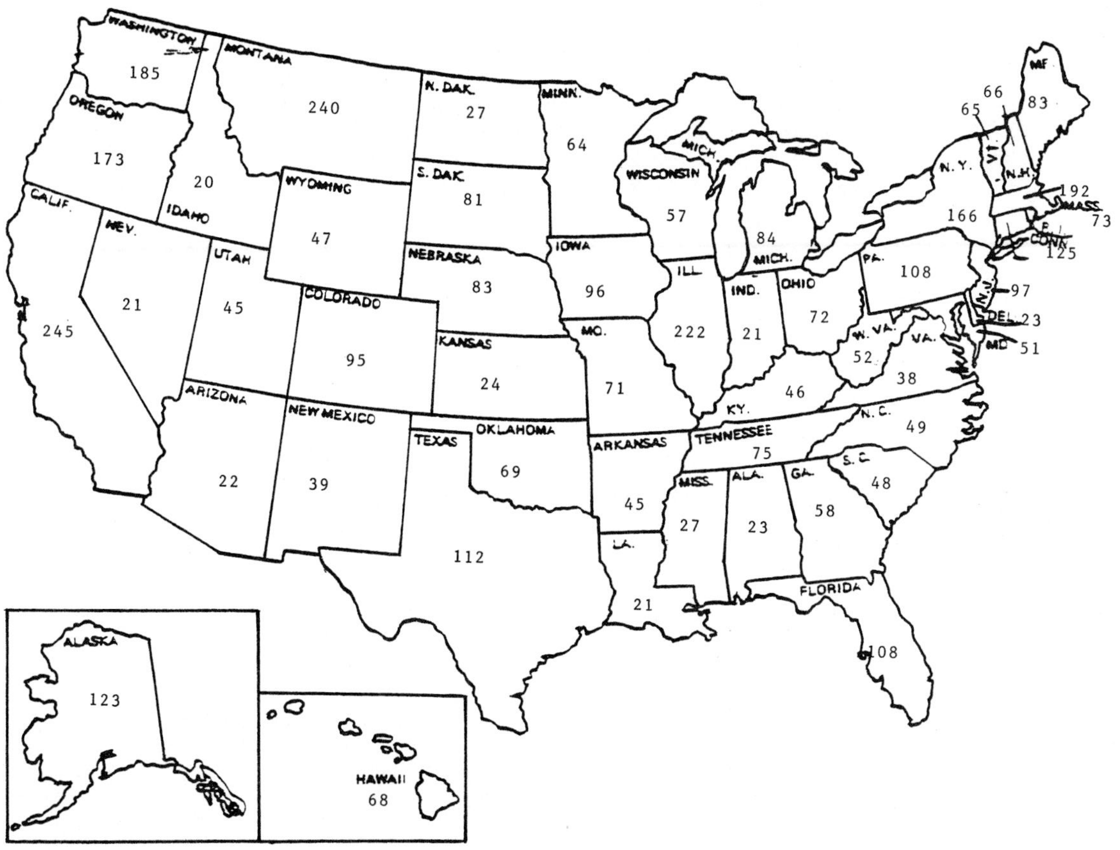

FIGURE 8.1 Operational recreational areas in the 50 states.

The early state parks were oriented toward providing for contemplative leisure. The features that were commonly protected or displayed were waterfalls, river gorges, picturesque coastlines, beautiful lakes, cave systems, mountain peaks, mature forests, undisturbed swamps, paleontological sites, geologic phenomena, and important historic sites (Chubb and Chubb 1981:468). As the demand for recreative leisure increased, so did the types of facilities to accommodate their users: picnickers, beach users, horseback riders, and winter sport enthusiasts. Lodges were provided in the early era when there was both a lack of commercial accommodations outside parks and when reaching many parks required a long trek by automobile traveling slowly on undeveloped roads.

Recently attempts have been made to classify state parks according to use. The idea is to limit the use of the term "state park" to rustic areas as the original concept indicated and to give names such as "state recreation area" to spots where there is more active participation in various outdoor sports than in actual contemplation of rustic nature.

Spending on state parks varies from state to state, as shown in Table 8.4 which shows that West Virginia spends 1.195 percent of its budget on state parks, followed by Oklahoma, New York, and California.

TABLE 8.4 Spending on State Parks and Its Percentage of State Budgets

	Total State Park Operating Budget $	Total State Government Operating Budget $	Percent of Government Budget Spent on State Parks		Total State Park Operating Budget $	Total State Government Operating Budget $	Percent of Government Budget Spent on State Parks
AK	4.784,100	2,400,000,000	0.1993	MT	2,475,600	1,896,944,962	0.2257
AL	24,738,998	5,400,932,150	0.4581	NC	6,826,703	6,250,000,000	0.1092
AR	17,320,341	3,905,348,264	0.4435	ND	1,807,289	1,400,000,000	0.1291
AZ	6,395,727	3,200,000,000	0.1999	NE	6,585,445	1,554,076,440	0.4238
CA	150,329,000	17,035,359,000	0.8825	NH	7,752,492	1,358,604,483	0.5706
CO	9,440,880	4,446,182,262	0.2120	NJ	23,857,657	12,380,334,000	0.1927
CT	7,800,000	6,328,234,760	0.1233	NM	7,612,472	2,543,257,700	0.2993
DE	4,928,044	1,044,368,000	0.4719	NV	3,844,875	1,500,000,000	0.2563
FL	36,019,564	18,525,112,154	0.1944	NY	106,341,800	11,102,000,000	0.9579
GA	22,519,934	6,400,000,000	0.3519	OH	41,197,279	18,582,138,617	0.2217
HI	5,716,293	2,766,372,000	0.2066	OK	19,965,133	2,000,000,000	0.9983
IA	8,304,000	3,273,776,000	0.2537	OR	19,400,000	6,500,000,000	0.2985
ID	3,040,710	1,564,300,000	0.1944	PA	39,700,000	11,839,032,000	0.3596
IL	27,476,500	22,616,809,700	0.1215	RI	4,805,931	1,434,393,284	0.3550
IN	11,999,976	8,074,865,585	0.1486	SC	14,785,049	7,326,409,942	0.2018
KS	5,406,725	1,963,300,502	0.2756	SD	5,010,813	1,062,183,948	0.4717
KY	53,744,800	7,497,472,860	0.7166	TN	33,116,900	7,396,042,000	0.4478
LA	5,668,096	5,200,000,000	0.1090	TX	37,979,801	19,233,771,903	0.1974
MA	19,787,700	12,391,503,750	0.1597	UT	11,043,227	2,513,818,100	0.4393
MD	19,576,656	9,871,845,732	0.1983	VA	9,459,608	11,343,357,205	0.0831
ME	3,797,197	1,416,790,659	0.2680	VT	3,937,127	1,216,898,000	0.3235
MI	21,416,100	15,636,670,000	0.1370	WA	25,029,051	8,018,074,700	0.3122
MN	13,232,600	5,400,000,000	0.2467	WI	11,321,436	5,067,258,546	0.2234
MO	16,072,895	7,136,625,407	0.2252	WV	17,304,420	1,464,866,970	1.1950
MS	9,887,145	5,415,388,112	0.1826	WY	3,480,573	1,590,000,000	0.2189
			Totals		974,330,500	323,924,533,627	

Source: National Association of State Park Directors, *Annual Information Exchange* (Tallahassee, FL, 1990).

CALIFORNIA AND OUTDOOR RECREATION: A CASE STUDY

Article I, Declaration of Rights, Section I of the Constitution of the State of California (1849) reads as follows:

> All men are by nature free and independent, and have certain inalienable rights, among which are those of enjoying and defending life and liberty; acquiring, possessing, and protecting property and pursuing and obtaining safety and happiness.

Pursuit of happiness through leisure and recreation started with the first settlers in California and became part of the state and local government beginning at the turn of the century. Although the federal government gave Yosemite to California in 1864, it was eventually taken back to become the second national park after Yellowstone, so the California state park system actually began with the creation of the Redwood Park at Big Basin in 1902. In 1909 California passed the *Park and Playground Act,* the purpose of which was to enable local authorities to establish such facilities. But it was not until 1939 that the state park system was formalized with the establishment of the State Park Commission (State of California Recreation Commission 1950:111).

In 1961, Edmund G. Brown, governor of California, adopted a recreation policy for the state of California. At the time of the adoption of the policy, the California Department of Natural Resources had four divisions, one of which was called the Division of Beaches and Parks. The division was to be administered by a chief, appointed by the director (of the Department of Natural Resources) upon nomination by the State Park Commission.

The State Park Commission was established in 1947 and consisted of five members appointed by the governor with the advice and consent of the state senate. Members are selected because of their interest in park and conservation matters and serve for terms of 4 years.

The Department of Natural Resources, through the State Park Commission, has control of the California Park System. The commission is to administer, protect, and develop the system for the use and enjoyment of the public. In its annual report to the governor, it should gather, digest, and summarize information concerning the state park system, including suggesting means for conserving, developing, and utilizing the scenic and recreational resources of the state. The commission is authorized to receive and accept in the name of the people of California any gift to be added or used in connection with the state park system. The commission, whenever in its judgment it is practicable to do so, shall collect fees, rentals, and other return for the use of parks. The state of California created in its treasury a state park fund to be used for improvement and maintenance of the state parks.

California Recreation Policy The California Public Resources Code (Section 540b, 1977 and 1981) states that the commission (now called the California Park and Recreation Commission)

> . . . shall formulate, in cooperation with other agencies, interested organizations and citizens, and shall recommend to the Director (of the Department of Parks and Recreation) a comprehensive recreational policy for the State of California.

The policy statement of 1974 was reviewed and another statement was approved by the commission and issued on July 15, 1981, which indicated the general scope and direction for all recreation and recreation-related programs and actions undertaken or funded by the state. It gives clear indication of the objectives desired for federal and local agencies, as well as for private-sector activities in the recreation field. This policy has been put into effect through a planning process, as indicated in the following section.

California Recreation Planning Program

California's statewide recreation planning program calls for a continuous process of identifying, analyzing, and solving the problems of providing recreation opportunities for the state's citizens and visitors. Under direction of the California Department of Parks and Recreation, the planning program provides leadership, policy guidance, program direction, and information to public and private recreation suppliers. This effort helps suppliers offer the facilities and programs best suited to the needs and desires of recreationists.

The major objectives of this program are as follows:

- To identify, on a statewide basis, the recreation needs of Californians.
- To examine critical recreation problems related to providing needed recreation opportunities.
- To provide a policy and program framework in which the various public and private recreation suppliers can work together to meet the public's recreation needs.
- To have government agencies and the private sector work together to devise solutions, mobilize resources, and resolve conflicts related to recreation matters.
- To maintain California's eligibility to receive money from the federal Land and Water Conservation Fund.

In both its concept and execution, this approach to statewide recreation planning is new in California and the nation. This program is innovative in its orientation toward future trends, its emphasis on process and continuity, its wide variety of activities and products, its overall unity, and its process of making state agencies accountable for following the plan.

The state of California, in order to receive federal grants, must publish a recreation plan every five years. The purposes of this document are to periodically examine the current recreation environment in California; to evaluate existing programs and planning materials; to rethink current state recreation policy and objectives; and to recommend or direct relevant public and private recreation involvement in the subsequent 5-year planning period.

At any given time, the California Outdoor Recreation Plan is the summary of all current materials and efforts. The Outdoor Recreation Plan does not specify programs as such. The California Recreation Action Program Reports, when approved by the governor, direct recreation efforts of all state agencies and regulate their relationships with other suppliers of recreational opportunities from the private sector.

Leisure Pursuits of Californians

The Department of Parks and Recreation conducted a survey in 1987 of 2,140 randomly selected California residents. The survey shows that Californians devote more than a billion participation days per year to the pursuit of outdoor recreation. A participation day reflects the engagement of one person in a recreation activity for any amount of time on any one day. The average household in California for purposes of statistics consists of 2.4 persons. The survey contained thirty-eight recreation pursuits, as shown in Table 8.5.

The California Department of Parks and Recreation interpretation is that the activities in which the highest percentages of California's population participated were among the simplest and least expensive. Examples are walking, picnicking, and beach activities. These same activities have also been consistently identified as most popular since such research began in the early 1960s.

Water activities seem to play an important role in California. More than two-thirds of all Californians engage in beach activities, and more than half go swimming each year. More than 20 percent of all household activities are directly related to water and beaches.

TABLE 8.5 Outdoor Activity Participation (1987 Survey)

	Percent of Total Population Participating	Average Days Per Participant	Total Estimated Household Participation Days (Millions)
Walking	76.6	52.2 Days	149.6
Driving for pleasure	75.5	33.4	81.8
Visiting museums, zoos, etc.	72.0	10.1	31.7
Beach activities	67.9	24.5	69.0
Picnicking-developed sites	64.4	14.4	31.6
Use of open turf areas	64.4	28.1	69.1
Swimming-lakes, rivers, ocean	59.0	18.8	42.6
Attending sports events	50.4	16.2	28.1
Attending cultural events	49.7	7.9	15.1
Birdwatching, nature study	47.4	23.4	31.5
Camping-developed sites	46.1	12.5	18.3
Trail hiking/mountain climbing	37.7	10.0	14.8
Freshwater fishing	36.3	19.5	19.5
Play equipment/tot lots	34.0	24.7	35.1
Swimming pools	31.1	31.5	33.3
Softball, baseball	25.6	21.0	19.2
Sledding, snow play, ice skating	25.0	7.6	5.4
Camping-primitive/backpacking	24.9	10.4	8.2
Bicycling	23.0	32.9	46.0
Power boating	19.8	16.6	9.7
Saltwater fishing	18.5	13.7	9.6
Tennis	17.6	21.4	18.2
Downhill skiing	17.5	8.4	4.9
Golf	16.4	30.7	16.8
Kayaking, rowboating, etc.	15.7	7.2	4.1
Water skiing	14.6	12.0	5.6
Four-wheel driving	14.3	23.1	8.3
Target shooting	14.0	9.4	4.2
Off-road vehicles	13.0	22.4	9.6
Jogging/running	12.6	58.3	55.1
Horseback riding	12.5	16.3	6.1
Hunting	12.2	15.0	3.9
Basketball	11.5	23.1	10.3
Sailing, windsurfing	10.3	11.5	4.2
Cross-country skiing	9.5	6.3	2.2
Football	9.1	15.8	6.0
Soccer	7.4	43.8	9.5
Surfing	4.1	25.7	5.5

Source: *California Outdoor Recreation Plan* (Sacramento, CA: Department of Parks and Recreation, 1988), 25.

The less popular activities among Californians tend to require expensive and specialized equipment, a high degree of skill or proficiency, or physical prowess. These activities involve smaller numbers of people who participate more frequently in them. For example, soccer players constitute only about 7.4 percent of the population, with a very high degree of participation.

Providers of State Recreation

A number of state agencies play one or more roles in the provision of outdoor recreation opportunities, as described in the following paragraphs.

Department of Parks and Recreation This department manages four distinct programs, as follow:

1. *The California State Park System* includes 281 units totaling 1,251,400 acres. Recreation facilities provided at these units include over 12,000 campsites and almost 10,000 picnic sites, as well as 57 boat ramps, over 2,300 boat slips, and over 2,700 miles of trails. Many of the units offer interpretive programs and facilities including visitor centers, museums, and interpretive panels and displays. There are more than 700 historic structures within the units of the State Park System. A series of subunits within the system offers increased protection to designated areas. Currently, there are ten cultural preserves, thirty-three natural preserves, and seven state wildernesses.

   Of the State Park System's 281 units, 240 units are classified according to appropriate levels of development, resource protection, and uses, as shown in Table 8.6.

TABLE 8.6 Classification of California State Park System

Classification	Number of Units
State parks	69
State beaches	73
State historic parks	41
State historical monument	1
State reserves	17
State recreation area	36
State urban recreation area	1
Wayside campgrounds	2
Total Units	240

Source: *California Outdoor Recreation Plan* (Sacramento, CA: Department of Parks and Recreation, 1988), 0–42.

Over 60 million visits are made to the State Park System each year. Day-use visitation to the system has continued to increase modestly. The most reliable figures are for paid attendance, as opposed to free day use. Combining the known and estimated use, the growth was roughly 15 percent over the last 7 years. Table 8.7 shows recent estimates of use at state-operated units.

The number of visitors seems to increase as the population increases around the state's major population centers along the Pacific coast. The problem with expanding facilities to serve the increased number of visitors is that it not only costs more to buy near-urban land, but it is also more expensive to operate recreation facilities near such areas.

An important factor in the state's growing and changing population is the large increases in Hispanic and Asian people immigrating to California. These groups have different recreation preferences and habits than those of the Anglo clientele of the past. Both groups tend to prefer family-oriented facilities,

TABLE 8.7 Day Use in California State Park System in Number of Visitors

Year	Paid use	Free use
1980–81	11,469,108	45,767,937
1981–82	11,854,906	44,654,965
1982–83	12,886,433	41,418,420
1983–84	14,423,720	43,049,451
1984–85	15,309,276	42,961,980
1985–86	15,679,440	45,775,191
1986–87	15,631,926	50,298,887

Source: *California Outdoor Recreation Plan—1980* (Sacramento, California: Department of Parks and Recreation, 1988).

activities, and programs. These demographic changes are forcing the State Park System to reevaluate its program and rethink its role as a recreation provider. To this end, in 1987 a departmental operations task force held a series of meetings to gather input on key issues and concerns, and to suggest how these matters should be dealt with.

2. *The Off-Highway Motor Vehicle Recreation (OHMVR) Program* has been established by law as a separate program entity within the Department of Parks and Recreation. A seven-member OHMVR Commission, with three members appointed by the governor and two members each appointed by the Senate Rules Committee and the Speaker of the Assembly, oversees the program. A deputy director manages the program with a staff of about 70 full-time and 40 part-time employees. The program includes two major components:
   - The state OHMVR system
   - Assistance to other agencies for OHMVR facilities

   The law establishing the state's OHMVR program expired January 1, 1988. New legislation passed in the 1987 session of the legislature that extended the program for another 5 years. The legislation mandates that 33 percent of the program's budget be allocated to pay for conservation and law enforcement measures. This provision is designed to assure a solid resource management program that includes law enforcement and wildlife enhancement.

   The OHMVR system includes seven state vehicular recreation areas (SVRAs) covering approximately 40,000 acres serving about a million and a half visitors each year. There is a growing demand due to the strong attraction of backcountry off-roading for people who feel constrained by their urban existence, and also due to the limitations being placed on this type of recreational use in many open-space areas in the state. In addition to the visitors to the state areas, over four and a half million off-highway visitor-days of use are estimated to take place at federal and local off-road facilities each year.

3. *The Historic Preservation Program* helps to ensure that examples of California's diverse cultural heritage are preserved. The program's scope includes preserving historic buildings, archeological sites, artifacts, records, and traditions. Many of these historic materials are an integral part of many types of outdoor recreation, offering scenery for many urban walks and providing backdrops for outdoor recreation such as picnicking, playing ball, sunbathing, photography, painting, and nature study. Visiting museums and historic sites are popular outdoor

recreation activities for which there is a great deal of public support.

The program has two major components, federal historic preservation in California and state financial assistance for historic preservation. Under the federal program, the department identifies historic properties, places outstanding examples on the National Register, and takes further action to help preserve many of them. This may include granting of federal monies for restoration or rehabilitation. State financial assistance has been provided by the 1984 State Park Bond Act, which included $10 million for this purpose. Also, $4 million was appropriated in 1987 to assist major historic preservation projects. Park bond issues currently under consideration would provide $20 million for historic preservation projects.

4. *Financial Assistance to Local Park and Recreation Agencies* as well as a limited amount of technical advice and consultation have been available through the Department of Parks and Recreation. Most of the money has come from state general obligation bonds approved at periodic intervals by the California voters. Also a small amount of money is made available from the federal Land and Water Conservation Fund. This money is administered by the department under the supervision of the National Park Service, which dictates firm guidelines on how these funds can be distributed and used. The money is used for acquisition of park properties and development of new facilities, but not for park operation and maintenance. In recent years, the lack of such money has served to restrain enthusiasm for grants acquisition and development. This factor could become critical in the coming years.

   In addition to the Land and Water Conservation Fund money, which has been reduced in recent years to only $2.5 million in 1986–87, most local grant funds come from the following two recent state bond acts:

   a. The California Park and Recreational Facilities Act of 1984 authorized $150 million for grants.
   b. The Community Parklands Act of 1986 authorized $100,000 for grants to be made available on a per capita basis to qualifying local agencies.

The Department of Boating and Waterways This department has the responsibility for developing and improving boating facilities throughout the state. This is accomplished through loans to various agencies and jurisdictions for small-craft harbors and marinas, as well as by providing launching-facility grants and capital outlay investment in boating facilities at State Park System units and facilities.

The department's financial assistance for boating facilities for fiscal year 1987–88 amounts to approximately $23 million. The department also promotes boating safety and conducts beach erosion control efforts in cooperation with federal and local agencies.

The department is concerned that the demand for additional boating facilities is outstripping the supply. This problem is aggravated by a growing inability or unwillingness of many client agencies to assume responsibility for the operation of more facilities. Many existing facilities are not being kept in proper condition for the intensive use they receive.

The Department of Fish and Game This department manages the state's game and nongame species for scientific, economic, as well as recreational purposes. It owns about 350,000 acres of land and water, most of which offers opportunities for a wide variety of wildlife-associated recreation activities such as hunting and fishing. Recently, the numbers of hunters and anglers have declined, with a significant increase in more nonconsumptive wildlife recreation such as bird-watching, nature photography, sketching, and painting. To offset the drop in hunting and fishing license fees and to help cover the cost of maintaining the facilities needed for the nonhunting and nonfishing activities, the department is charging a fee at some of its wildlife areas for these activities.

Department of Water Resources This agency manages California's vast complex of dams, aqueducts, pumping plants, and other appurtenant structures that store and transport water. Although these facilities are designed primarily to generate power and deliver water to contracting agricultural, industrial, and residential users, they have great recreation potential. Unfortunately the department is experiencing a problem of meeting public expectations for recreation and an inability of other public agencies to supply funds for this purpose. Also, the department is having problems with water quality at some reservoirs as a result of the poor hygienic practices of recreationists. Growing liability problems are reflected in an increasing number of lawsuits brought by people who claim they've been injured while recreating at water project facilities. Large awards have been made to claimants in many cases, which may force the department to close some of its sites to recreationists.

Department of Forestry and Fire Protection This department's primary responsibility is to provide fire protection and watershed management services for private and state-owned forests, deserts, and grasslands. The department is finding that operating its recreational offerings is a growing problem because of drug and alcohol abuse, vandalism, theft, and the presence of an increasing number of homeless people. Also, off-highway vehicle operators tear up the terrain, contributing to higher patrol and training costs. In addition the department finds that many recreationists fail to understand that their behavior leads to a less-than-pristine appearance of the forests. Accordingly the department is experiencing increasing costs in operating its recreation sites.

Coastal Commission This regulatory agency for California's coastal resources is concerned with the provision of access to recreational opportunities, protection of the marine environment, promotion of land use policies, and regulation of various types of development. The commission does not operate any recreation lands or facilities; it depends entirely on other agencies to assume this responsibility. Tighter operating budgets for those agencies, stricter staffing limitations, expenditure ceilings, and liability concerns are hampering the commission's mission.

State Coastal Conservancy Under its Public Access Program, the conservancy grants awards to public agencies or nonprofit organizations to provide coastal accessways, acquire land for public access to significant coastline resources, and accept dedication of lands to provide public access to recreation and resource areas.

The conservancy is authorized to receive sites for parks, recreation, fish and wildlife habitat, historical preservation, or scientific study. It can acquire excess lands, open-space lands, and areas needed to undertake enhancement.

The conservancy does not manage or operate lands on a long-term basis. It turns over its properties to cities, counties, state or federal agencies, or nonprofit organizations for operational responsibility.

The conservancy has a role in effecting urban waterfront restoration and in providing funding for parks, open space, coastal access, and other public areas and facilities. It plans and coordinates federal surplus land sales in the coastal zone.

Wildlife Conservation Board The Wildlife Conservation Board acquires property to preserve or restore wildlife habitat, and it develops or improves facilities for wildlife-associated recreation on land owned by itself and local government agencies. These facilities may include fishing piers and floats, boat ramps, jetty access walkways, lake or reservoir improvements, boardwalks, nature trails, and interpretive areas. These projects are generally undertaken in coordination with local agencies which operate and maintain the facilities for public use.

The board has acquired or developed 467 state and local units. Each unit offers some type of wildlife-associated recreation. The lands acquired or dedicated to this purpose by the board comprise most of the 350,000 acres owned by the Department of Fish and Game. These lands are managed by the department, either directly or by agreement with local agencies.

As project operators, local agencies are being allowed to impose user fees or to develop revenue-generating related facilities, such as campgrounds, at their cost, to help offset operation and maintenance costs. The board is aware of the public pressure for more urban and suburban recreation opportunities, as well as the emerging interest in barrier-free design for disabled accessibility wherever possible.

Tahoe Conservancy The conservancy was established to implement the $85 million Lake Tahoe Acquisition Bond Act through land acquisition, land management, resource protection, and public access and recreation. At present, the conservancy is managing 2,900 acres at Lake Tahoe, focusing on erosion control in the lake basin. Grants are provided to local jurisdictions to provide lake access and recreation opportunities, and to state and federal agencies for wildlife management. The overriding concern for the conservancy is the deterioration of the quality of Lake Tahoe's water.

Santa Monica Mountains Conservancy This agency implements the Santa Monica Mountains Comprehensive Plan by acquiring, restoring, and consolidating land in the Santa Monica Mountains Zone for park, recreation, or conservation purposes. To accomplish this, the conservancy acquires property to protect the natural environment, manages the lands on an interim basis, and works with established land management agencies to take over these lands. Its acquisition program is focused on the most critical open space and recreation land in the area. In addition, the conservancy is providing grants to local agencies for acquisition and development of their own park and recreation lands.

The conservancy has identified a number of concerns. Primary among them is the need to link existing park units through development of a trail system. The State Department of Parks and Recreation owns 35,000 acres and the National Park Service owns about 15,000 acres, while the conservancy itself owns 10,000 acres. These lands need to be tied together. Other concerns include the increasing use of trails, the need for additional camping facilities, and the need to improve public access to the land already in public ownership.

SUMMARY

This chapter is concerned with the development and role of state government in outdoor recreation areas and offerings. While the initial involvement was through the development of parks, other functions, such as coastal conservation and desert preservation, were added over the years. In addition, state structures dealing with recreation directly were established in many states. As the recreation services increased, areas that are owned and run by the state came into being. Today there is hardly a state in the Union that does not have a state park, a state forest, or a historical monument.

A number of federal acts that were passed during the last three decades increased the pressure on the states to develop comprehensive outdoor recreation plans. A plan is required if the state is to receive federal funds. Typically the plan covers the state policy on recreation and describes the issues the state faces where recreation is concerned. Planned actions for the next five years are included.

There are regional differences in what the states offer in the way of outdoor recreation. An example of state offerings is given with a case study of California, along with an examination of the state's role in regional and local recreational offerings. The study of what Californians like to do plays an important role in developing comprehensive plans for the state.

REFERENCES

Chubb, M., and H. Chubb (1981) *One Third of Our Time? An Introduction to Recreation Behavior and Resources.* New York: John Wiley and Sons.

Department of Parks and Recreation (1981) *Recreation in California: Issues and Actions: 1981-1985.* Sacramento, CA: Department of Parks and Recreation.

Department of Parks and Recreation (1988) *California Outdoor Plan—1988.* Sacramento, CA: Department of Parks and Recreation.

Fazio, J. (1979) "Parks and Other Recreational Resources," in *Leisure Emergence and Expansion,* H. Ibrahim and J. Shivers, editors. Los Alamitos, CA: Hwong Publishing.

Foss, P. (1968) *Recreation: Conservation in the United States, A Documentary History.* New York: Chelsea House.

Jensen, C. (1985) *Outdoor Recreation in America.* Minneapolis, MN: Burgess Press.

Knudson, D. (1984) *Outdoor Recreation.* New York: Macmillan.

Heritage Conservation and Recreation Service (1979) *The Third Nationwide Outdoor Recreation Plan.* Washington, D.C.: U.S. Government Printing Office.

MacLean, J., J. Peterson, and W. Martin (1985) *Recreation and Leisure: The Changing Scene.* New York: MacMillan.

Michaud, H. (1966) "State Parks," in *Natural Features of Indiana,* A. Lindsey, editor. Indianapolis, IN: Indiana Academy of Science.

Nash, R. (1967) *Wilderness and the American Mind.* New Haven, CT: Yale University Press.

National Association of State Park Directors (1990) *Annual Information Exchange.* Indianapolis, IN: Division of State Parks.

State of California Recreation Commission (1950) *Recreation in California.* Sacramento, CA: State of California Recreation Commission.

9 Local Resources and Recreation

In colonial America, the dominance of puritan values kept recreational activities from being a local concern. Localities were settlements built on land that was granted to homogeneous groups who agreed to participate in their community affairs, which were handled in town meetings. As communities increased in size, a committee was selected to run the affairs of each community. Recreation was not a concern then, but open space was.

The town common played an important role in providing public open space. The earliest common was established in Boston in 1634. William Penn decreed a 10-acre common in the center of Philadelphia in 1682. Another common of Philadelphia's size was provided in Savannah, Georgia, in 1733. Earlier, in the area settled by Spain in the New World, it was required that the new cities include a plaza or a city square, as was the case in Saint Augustine, Florida.

It is questionable whether recreational activity motivated the establishment of these open spaces. According to Fazio (1979:207), most of the commons then were meant to be meetinghouse lots, used as an equivalent to a church, except in open air. And according to Knudson (1984:149), a common served many other purposes, including being a cow pasture, a military training field, and a public hanging post where pirates, witches, and Quakers met their earthly end. Also the common served as America's version of Hyde Park, London, for public speakers and their hecklers. The common later became

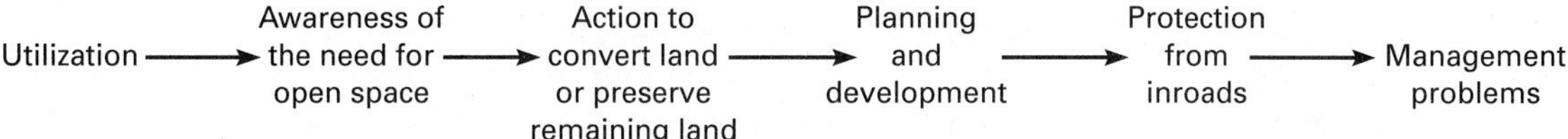

FIGURE 9.1 Stages of park development.

the site for parades and celebrations, the place for music and sport, and the spot for strolling and picnicking.

The Boston Public Garden was founded in 1852 across the street from Boston Common; it included the first botanical garden in America. Arnold Arboretum was established there in 1876. Boston also saw the first children's sand garden, which was promoted by Dr. Maria Zakzrewska. A large sand pile was placed in the yard of the Children's Mission on Parmenter Street, where fifteen children spent 3 days a week for 6 weeks during July and August of 1885. In 1887 paid matrons were hired to observe the children; a supervisor was hired in 1893 and organized play was introduced. Funds for operating the playground were provided by the Massachusetts Emergency and Hygiene Association. In 1899, the City Council allocated $3,000 toward meeting the playground operating costs.

The concept of urban parks was promoted by Charles Elliot and Frederick Law Olmsted (Knudson 1984:149). The first planned park, New York's Central Park, was authorized in 1853 by the City of New York, and it took many years to complete. The park set the standard for municipal parks in the United States. In 1888 Boston set aside a string of green spaces on the city outskirts which were nicknamed the "Emerald Necklace." According to Haines (1977:159), William Cullen Bryan began to emphasize the need for a park in New York City in 1836. In fact there was an earlier complaint by a citizen to the city's mayor in 1785 about the lack of a "proper spot where the inhabitants (of New York) could enjoy the benefits of exercise necessary for health and amusement" (Foss 1968:304). The city acquired 740 acres of swamps and brambles for open spaces. But Frederick Law Olmsted advocated that human existence would be more bearable if parks rather than swamps and brambles were provided. He believed that parks are facsimiles of rural landscapes which provide tranquility and rest to the mind (Gans 1974:16). His adoption of the natural style in this urban park served as the model for America's city parks in the future. According to Fazio (1979:208), parkland development follows certain steps, as shown in Figure 9.1.

Many city parks were built in the second half of the nineteenth century, except for during the Civil War years. While the first three decades of the twentieth century saw some growth in state and national natural resources, the Depression years led to a phenomenal growth in urban parks. Many of the anti-Depression public works programs provided by the federal government proved to be very beneficial to city parks.

According to Caro (1974), in 1932 New York City had about 15,000 acres of parkland and 119 playgrounds. By 1939, 20,000 acres were added to the city parks, along with 255 new playgrounds and 10 new swimming pools. Despite the growth, many of the city's poorer areas did not benefit from it.

After World War II, a number of federal acts helped in the development of urban open space and recreational resources. Notably, the Land and Water Conservation Fund Act of 1965 led to considerable growth in urban and suburban parks.

LOCAL GOVERNMENT STRUCTURE

All states empower their local governments to provide services to their citizens. The states do so through enabling legislation or by allowing the local governments to use their charters and special laws. An enabling law is an act by the state legislature that does the following, according to Knudson (1984:151):

1. Empowers the local government to establish, operate, and maintain parks and recreation programs and agencies.
2. Provides for the establishment of a board to govern the operations.
3. Empowers the board to acquire lands and other real properties and to develop them, to employ a staff, and to issue bonds.
4. Establishes the mechanisms for operations in subordination to the local government.

MacLean et al. (1985:82) suggest that state enabling acts include the following:

1. A method of establishing the managing authority and board.
2. A listing of powers of the administrative authority and executive.
3. A description of fiscal procedures to be followed, including how money can be obtained, accounted for, and spent.
4. Cooperative agreements among existing government agencies.
5. Guidelines for qualification and selection of personnel.

Enabling acts allow the local government to provide services to its constituency. Structurally, there are three types of local governments in the United States, county, city, and district.

County Government There are 3,043 counties in the United States, varying in number from 3 counties in Rhode Island and Hawaii to 254 counties in Texas. Technically there are no counties in Louisiana, where the term parish is used instead, or in Alaska, where the term borough is used.

There are three basic forms of county government: 1) The Commission form of government began in Pennsylvania in 1724 and spread widely; it is the most dominant form today. The governing body is elected specifically for that purpose and fulfills both the executive and legislative functions in county government. The commissioners (called supervisors in some states, including California and Iowa), serve on a commission that is usually composed of three to five members; 2) The supervisor form, another type of county government, evolved in New York and differs from the commission form in that the governing body is made up of persons who were first elected as township supervisors. There the typical size of the governing body is about twenty supervisors; and 3) The executive form in county government revolves around a county manager who reports to a county board which serves as the policy-making body.

Most American county governments superimpose a number of special boards or commissions for special purposes among which are park, recreation, and leisure services.

City Government It is estimated that there are over 18,000 municipalities in the United States, varying in the number of residents from less than a hundred to several millions.
There are basically three types of government in American cities: 1) The mayor-council type of government is the oldest and most common. Usually voters at large vote for the mayor and voters by wards vote for the council; 2) The commission form of government allows the commissioners to perform both legislative and executive functions. Each commissioner will oversee a department or more. Voters at large vote for the board of commissioners; and 3) The council-manager type of government gives the legislative power to the council and the executive power to the manager.

FUNCTIONS OF LOCAL BOARDS/ COMMISSIONS

A local board or commission typically performs the following functions:

1. Approves the acts of the department under its jurisdiction. As the governing board responsible for the results of the work of the department, the board/ commission receives work reports through the superintendent and records its approval of them.
2. Acts as a court of final appeal. Any disagreement arising among employees or between the public and employees, if not satisfactorily resolved by the superintendent, may be considered by the commission, whose decisions are final.
3. Advises the superintendent on problems of administration. All superintendents need advice in the performance of their managerial duties and in carrying out the policies set by the commission. The advice of the commission should not be interpreted as instructions or regulations unless given such force by action of the commission as a whole.
4. Interprets the department and the general operation of the system to the public. The commission fulfills this responsibility by published actions, by public discussion and address, and by planned use of available means of public communication. The members of the commission often symbolize the aims and objectives of the department, for the character of the department is reflected in the members, who are appointed commissioners, no less than by the employees.
5. Represents the general public. Commissioners should conduct meetings that are open to the public and should permit individuals or delegations to address them on pertinent subjects. Most frequently the matter brought before a commission in this way is such that an immediate answer is not always possible or expedient. Often the petitioner is not in agreement with the commission. It should be remembered that the prerogative of the petitioner is only to state views and not to participate in the action. The responsibility for the action, if any is taken, rests with the commission which, after giving a respectful hearing to the petitioner, makes its own decision based on the facts involved. The decision need not be made at the time the matter is brought before the commission; the subject may be taken under advisement and a decision announced in due course.
6. Represents the department at official occasions. Commissioners often act as spokespersons for the department at public ceremonies, public hearings on problems concerning the department, and conferences on recreational programs, policies, or other relevant issues.
7. Negotiates advantages for the department. Because of their individual and collective prestige, commissioners are often in a better position than the superintendent or others to negotiate advantages for the department with the local governing authority, other public officials, and the general public. Among these advantages might be an adequate budget for departmental operations. The layperson who does not derive pecuniary gain from the appropriation for the department is usually more effective than a salaried employee in such negotiations.
8. Appoints standing and ad hoc committees. When the work of the

Sedona, Arizona, when incorporated as a city, had as one of its first official actions a resolution to protect the city's juniper and pinyon pine trees from unauthorized destruction by bulldozers.

department becomes extensive, the commission may appoint a special committee, usually consisting of only one person. A standing committee makes it convenient to assign to a commissioner, for further investigation and consideration, any matter on which the commission may not be ready to act. Committees will not have administrative powers in the matters referred to them. No committee or individual member has any authority except by referral to and through the entire body.

9. Separates managerial from policy-making activities. Execution of policy is delegated to the superintendent and the employed staff. Although there is no lack of interest in all phases of departmental operations by commission members, creation of an administrative department to handle such matters provides for a sharp delineation between formulation and administration of policy.

LOCAL GOVERNMENT AND LEISURE SERVICES

Leisure services, which include the provisions for outdoor recreation opportunities, were not among the services provided by local governments initially. The dominant puritanical outlook of colonial America viewed play as sinful. The puritans adopted a harsh work ethic emphasizing the virtue of simplicity of living and industry in working. To create God's kingdom on earth, they believed recreation was to be negated. The councils or commissions that were set up to run local affairs had nothing to do with the establishment of facilities or the provision of programs in recreation. Eventually the local government became involved in the provision of open space and the building of parks, but it was voluntary associations that became concerned with the provision of recreation, particularly for the young.

Some years after the Boston experiment of the Sand Garden of 1885, Chicago Hull House became involved in the creation of a children's playground in 1892. Hull House, which began as a center for improvement of the conditions of slum dwellers, became involved in recreation. More playgrounds sprang up in the east and midwest. The Playground Association of America was formed by concerned citizens such as Jane Addams, Henry Curtis, and Luther Gulick. The association's magazine, *Playground,* voiced their concern over the lack of recreational opportunities for the young. With the change of its name, the *Playground and Recreation Association of America* in 1911 was voicing concern over recreation for everyone. This voluntary association was named the National Recreation Association in 1926. In 1965 the name was changed to the National Recreation and Park Association. The addition of the word park signalled an emphasis on the role that the outdoors played in American recreation as well as in the work of this voluntary association.

It was not until the early 1900s that local governments began to show interest in providing local leisure services. Butler (1940:407) suggested that municipal recreation started in large metropolitan areas with the provision of children's playgrounds. This took place before local governments were empowered by the states to do so through enabling legislation. General welfare laws and/or police powers in state constitutions or local charters were used as bases for the provision of these early recreation services.

As suggested by Rainwater (1922:192), the playground movement which started as a philanthropic deed went through the following nine distinct transitions from its inception in the 1880s until the end of World War I:

1. The limited provisions of activities to little children expanded to all ages.
2. The summer-only programs expanded to year-long programs.
3. The offerings expanded to include indoor activities, instead of outdoor activities only.
4. The program expanded to rural areas, rather than existing merely in congested urban centers.
5. The support shifted from philanthropic groups to total community support.
6. Play became organized instead of being free, with schedules provided for activities.
7. The projects became rather complex and varied.
8. The philosophy shifted to include varied activities, and not just the provision of facilities.
9. Community and group activities were considered before individual interests.

These transitions are witnessed in seven distinct stages through which the playground movement evolved, accompanied by the expansion in the number of local parks (Rainwater 1922:60):

1. The sand garden, 1885–1895
2. The model playground, 1895–1900
3. The small park, 1900–1905
4. The recreation center, 1905–1912
5. Civic art and welfare, 1912–1915
6. Neighborhood organization, 1915–1918
7. Community service, 1918–1922

Hjelte (1940:16) suggested that between 1922 and 1940, five additional transitions took place:

1. The play movement became a recreation movement.
2. The movement became more than just municipal; it became a state and national movement.
3. The program became integrated with public education curriculum and systems.
4. The organization expanded into rural as well as urban areas.
5. The organization eventually came under the public sector in place of the previously subsidized quasi-public control.

The new social conscience of the 1930s helped to increase understanding of the need for the provision of municipal recreation assisted by the much welcomed role of the federal government in alleviating the scourge of the Depression. To combat the rampaging unemployment at that time, federal projects were organized, among which were the building of many local parks under the auspices of the Works Projects Administration.

Originally these local parks were organized under a department which became responsible

Commission or Board
Governing Authority
Director
Park Foreman
Recreation Supervisor
Sr. Pk. Caretaker
Sr. Recreation Ldrs.
Park Caretaker
Recreation Leaders
Asst. Pk. Caretaker
Asst. Recreation Ldrs.

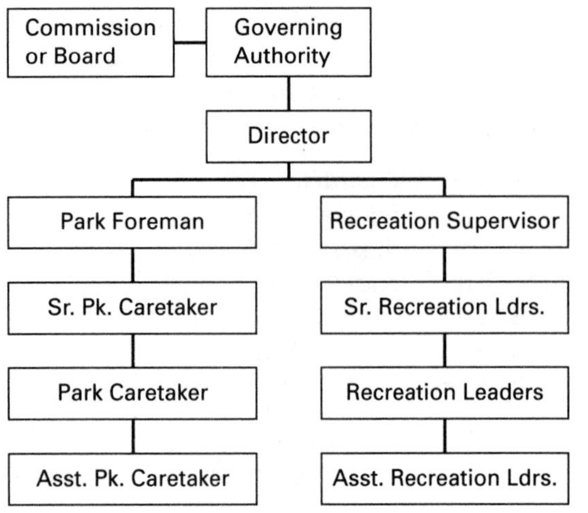

FIGURE 9.2 Small city park and recreation structure.

for the acquisition, development, and maintenance of parks and outdoor resources. Eventually another function, that is, recreation, evolved to provide various activities initially for children and later for adults. In many instances, a separate department for recreation was established; otherwise, parks and recreation went hand in hand. Today, more than two-thirds of the local governments have a combined department of parks and recreation (see Figures 9.2, 9.3, and 9.4).

A study conducted by the National Recreation and Park Association in cooperation with the International City Management Association showed that nine out of ten local governments in the United States have a year-round, full-time

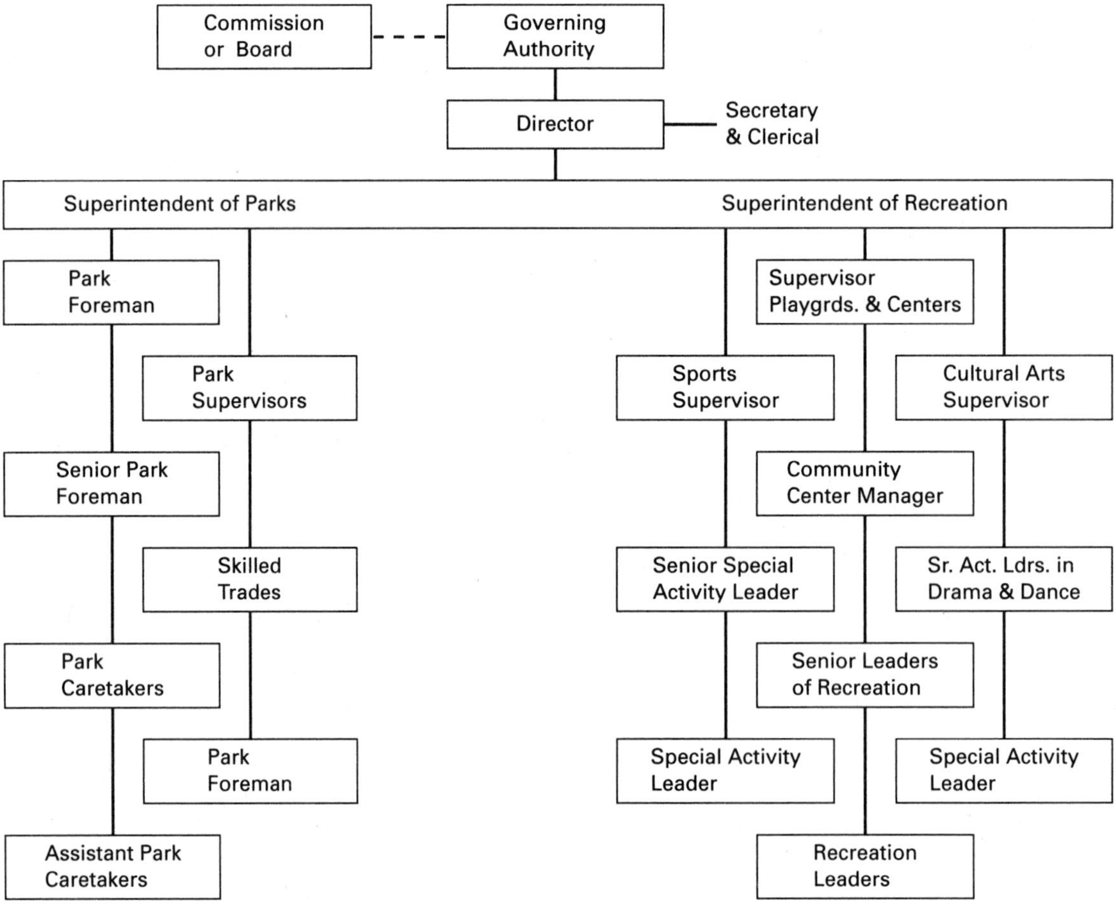

Commission or Board
Governing Authority
Director
Secretary & Clerical
Superintendent of Parks
Superintendent of Recreation
Park Foreman
Park Supervisors
Senior Park Foreman
Skilled Trades
Park Caretakers
Park Foreman
Assistant Park Caretakers
Supervisor Playgrds. & Centers
Sports Supervisor
Cultural Arts Supervisor
Community Center Manager
Senior Special Activity Leader
Sr. Act. Ldrs. in Drama & Dance
Senior Leaders of Recreation
Special Activity Leader
Special Activity Leader
Recreation Leaders

FIGURE 9.3 Medium-size city (over 50,000) park and recreation structure.

park and recreation agency to fulfill the following functions (Heritage Conservation and Recreation Service 1979:76):

- Planning, acquiring, developing, and maintaining parkland and recreation areas and facilities.
- Providing services for groups and individuals with special leisure service needs.
- Providing education for attainment of specific leisure skills.
- Sponsoring special community events and celebrations.
- Sponsoring social, cultural, and athletic programs on a continuing basis.

The structure of the agency providing leisure services may vary greatly, as shown in Figure 9.2, 9.3, 9.4.

Special Districts

In some states, enabling laws allow for the formation of a special district that allows two or more municipalities to establish a joint park and recreation service. While there are numerous metropolitan districts of this sort, there are rural ones as well. The board controlling some of these park and recreation districts is elected directly by the constituents.

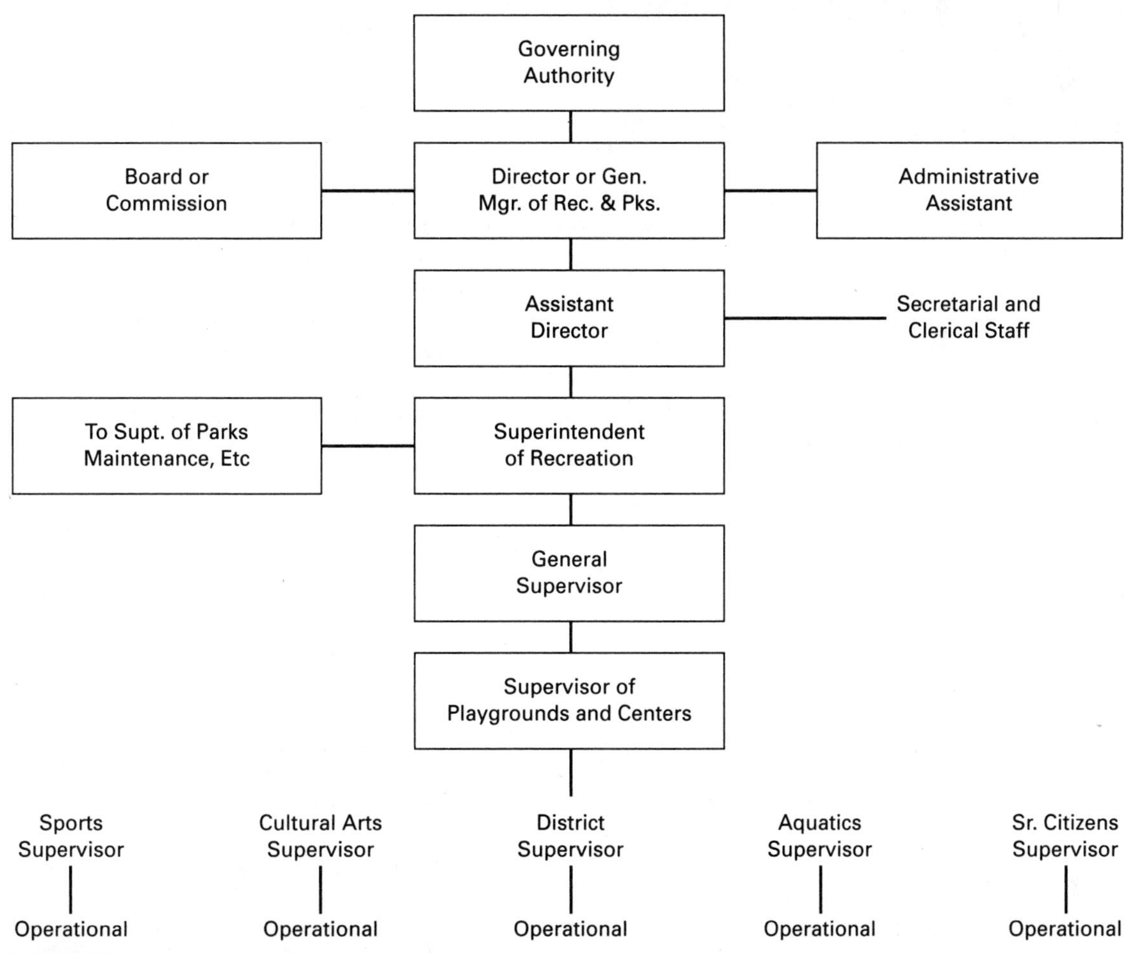

FIGURE 9.4 Large city (over 100,000) park and recreation structure.

Boardwalks over marshy wetlands are creating parks out of previously inaccessible areas within easy access for the public in large cities.

Miramar Lake, a reservoir for the city of San Diego, has a 5-mile path around its perimeter which is frequented by nearby city dwellers.

Recreation through School Districts

In many instances, local recreation offerings are provided through the education board. According to Hjelte and Shivers (1972: 122), this is neither the major administrative organization for park and recreation services, nor the most desirable one, since it tends to exclude, necessarily by design, the adult population.

Recreation through a Single Local Agency

Ibrahim et al. (1987:77–79) listed the advantages and disadvantages of combining parks and recreation under one local agency as follows:

Combined Recreation and Parks Department

Advantages:

1. Consolidation of all related activities under one municipal department.
2. Development of a comprehensive and diversified program of both passive and leadership-oriented activities.
3. Reduction of dual development of facilities and areas.
4. Central control.
5. Flexibility of budget.
6. Even distribution of workload.
7. Improved communication.
8. Better understanding by public.
9. Elimination of duplication of efforts.
10. Scope of leisure philosophy not splintered within a personal framework.

Disadvantages:

1. Park or recreation development might be seriously subordinated to opposite ideology, depending on interest or background of administrator.
2. School facilities are not automatically utilized.

Separate Recreation Department

Advantages:

1. Selection of recreation specialists as staff members.
2. Orientation toward activity; planning of facilities accordingly.

3. Assurance that a recreation board can coordinate efforts on recreation.
4. Recreation budgets specifically set aside for that purpose and not sacrificed for other services.
5. Broad perspective for providing programs and services.
6. Easier placement of responsibility for success or failure of recreation administration.
7. Emphasis on studying recreational needs and interests of a community.
8. Effective recreation service rendered.

Disadvantages:

1. Overlapping and duplication of effort.
2. Public confusion over responsibility.
3. Duplication impedes planning.
4. Overlapping with schools.
5. Additional administrative machinery needed.
6. Difficulty in defining recreation role and jurisdiction.
7. Recreation cannot work in a vacuum, cuts across the work of other departments.
8. Facilities used are under control of a second agency.
9. Lack of coordination between parks and programs.

Separate Park Department

Advantages:

1. Development and maintenance of park facilities under own auspices.
2. Experience in dealing with large numbers of patrons.
3. Large budgets usually allocated.
4. Park board is less likely to be politically influenced.
5. Parks lend prestige to recreation.
6. Trained staff in horticulture, construction, and maintenance of parks.

Disadvantages:

1. Major attention on physical properties and natural resources.
2. Buildings needed for recreation are in the jurisdiction of park departments, which means that the parks department may refuse to allow certain activities in the park.
3. Boards burdened with property problems.
4. Attitude of park authorities toward recreation is conservative and hesitant.
5. Recreation is of secondary importance.
6. Lack of motivation to insist on high-quality recreation leadership.
7. Great difficulty in securing school buildings.
8. Budget cuts affect recreation more than park services.

A study was conducted in 1976 by the National Recreation Association on the degree of involvement of cities with populations of 10,000 and more in municipal recreation. The study showed that of the responding cities, 66 percent provided leisure services under a combined park and recreation department, 96 percent cooperated with local school systems in providing recreation opportunity, and 88 percent provided full-time, year-round programs.

FINANCING LOCAL RECREATION

The principal sources of funds for the current operation of local services, which are different from capital development funds, are as follows:

1. Appropriation from general fund
The monies collected for local services can be appropriated as needed by the governing body, be it the city council or the county board of supervisors. These are usually tax monies collected for services such as police, fire, and public works. In most cases, the park and recreation board or commission reviews the needs, as presented by the head or heads of the departments concerned. The request for funds is then sent to the city council or board of supervisors for approval.

2. Special Recreation Tax Some states authorize the levying of a tax for a special purpose such as recreation. In this case the money is, by law, allocated for that very purpose and only that purpose. This provides a form of stability from year to year, and the advisory body does not have to sell its program to the city council or board of supervisors year after year. It also provides the local park and recreation boards with some independence. This special tax is usually expressed in so many cents of the valuation of the local community to be served. For instance, if the amount needed to administer a program is $200,000 and fees and charges will bring in $80,000, the amount to be levied would be $200,000–$80,000=$120,000. And if the total valuation of the community equals $60,000,000, the special tax rate would be $120,000/60,000,000=$.20 per $100 assessed valuation. This means that the owner of a property worth $100,000 in that community will pay $200 a year to support the local recreation program.
3. Fees And Charges According to Waters (1982:1), park and recreation departments used to attempt to provide their programs at either low cost or no cost at all. The budget crisis has altered the situation recently, and more and more departments are increasing their fees and charges. An alternative would be that fees and charges be a percentage of total expenses.

Fees and charges for use of recreation areas, including outdoor recreation facilities, fall in one of six categories: entrance fees are charged for large areas such as zoos and botanical gardens; admission fees are charged for entry into a building having a program or event; rental fees are used for the exclusive use of a facility; user fees are charged for participation in an activity; permit fees are for the privilege of participation; special service fees are applied for specific uses. Higher fees could be charged nonresidents.
4. Other Sources According to Kraus and Curtis (1982:256), beginning in the mid 1960s many municipal recreation and park departments began calling on major companies for more significant forms of help. Among the types of help are outright gifts, sponsorship of programs and events, adoption of a facility or area, and provision of technical assistance. To stimulate giving of this type of assistance, some park and recreation departments have developed gift catalogs which itemize and illustrate the specific needs of the department. Among the plans that enhance outdoor recreation is the adopt-a-park idea. Usually the adoption is for a specified period of time, such as 3 years. Friends-of-the-park is another idea which revolves around forming a tax-exempt organization for the purpose of maintaining and improving the facility.

SOURCES FOR CAPITAL DEVELOPMENT

The adding of facilities and areas may come from funds raised for this particular purpose and could include the following:

1. Bond Issues The money accrued from a bond, which is to be paid along with interest in the future, is to be used for building costly projects that the current budget could otherwise not afford. Although a bond is a liability, it is a reasonable means for expansion of areas and facilities. General obligation bonds are paid off by additional assessments on property. Revenue bonds are paid off by the revenues accrued from the use of a facility or area built by bond monies.
2. Federal Funds Federal acts in the 1960s and 1970s such as the Land and Water Conservation Fund assisted many localities in

acquiring and developing open space and outdoor recreation areas. Community development block grants were used in 7.7 percent of local recreation facilities and programs. General revenue-sharing (GRS) grants provided millions of dollars to local recreation, which ranked fifth among all local government expenditures of GRS funds.

Unfortunately federal funds were drastically reduced in the 1980s. A direct mail survey was conducted by the California Department of Parks and Recreation in 1987 to obtain basic information about the status of local recreation services. When the respondents were asked to list the most critical issues facing their agency during the coming 5 years (1988–1993), they responded as follows:

Issue	Percentage
Declining public funds	100
Increasing insurance cost	48
Development of new parks	40
Deterioration of existing parks	35
Provision of special-use recreation	31

3. Donations and Gifts Decreasing federal funding led local park and recreation agencies to seek donations and gifts as means of capital development. Among the examples given by the Heritage Conservation and Recreation Service (1979:14–15), some took place before the burgeoning federal deficit became public. For instance, Catalina Island Company donated a 41,000-acre open space to Los Angeles County, the Irvine Company gave 2 acres and a yacht club structure to the city of Irvine, California, for a youth center, and the Janss Corporation donated a golf course to the city of Conejo, California.

4. Special Assessment This is the least used, and least recommended, method in financing capital development for park and recreation services. The assessment is to be paid by those who use the facility or area among the property owners in the community. If the facility or area is needed in a well-to-do neighborhood, the residents might be persuaded to vote for the special assessment, but in a poor area, even if the residents are persuaded to support a special assessment, it might represent a hardship for many of them. Accordingly this method is not used by many agencies (MacLean et al. 1985:85).

EXAMPLES OF LOCAL OFFERINGS

Recreational offerings in Los Angeles County, California, and Tacoma, Washington, will now be examined as examples of what a county or city can provide.

Los Angeles County Los Angeles has the largest county government in the United States. A board of five supervisors serves both the legislative and executive functions. It is the governing body for the benefit of the citizens of the unincorporated county area. It enacts ordinances and establishes rules for the administration of the county's departments and special districts. The board is assisted by the chief administrative officer, who is responsible for making recommendations concerning procedures and actions.

Los Angeles County, as a subdivision of the State of California, is charged with the responsibility of providing services to all its citizens, if such services are not provided by the municipalities in which they live. There are eighty-three cities in the county, whose residents totaled over seven million in 1988. Along with the one million residents of the unincorporated area, Los Angeles County population reached over eight million in 1988. The county's largest city, the

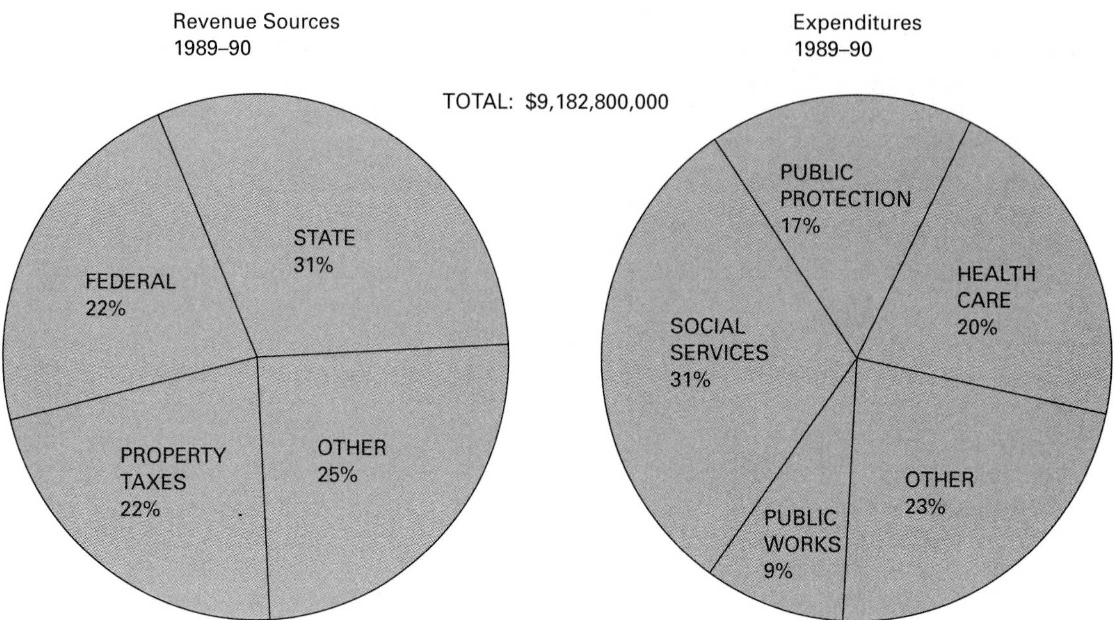

OTHER SOURCES: Contract Cities, Sales Tax, Courts, Vehicle License Fees, Forfeiture, Deed-Transfers, Parking/Traffic Violations, Public Health Licenses.

FIGURE 9.5 Los Angeles County revenues and expenditure, 1989–1990. *Source: L.A. County Board of Supervisors, County of Los Angeles Department of Parks and Recreation Guide* (1990).

city of Los Angeles, had 3,311,544 residents in 1988, and the smallest city, Vernon, accounted for 92 residents in the same year.

The 1989-1990 Los Angeles County budget totalled over $9 billion. Of that amount, 74 percent was earmarked for mandated and/or special projects such as health and welfare services, roads, and flood control. Law enforcement used 6 percent of the budget, as did parks and recreation. Figures 9.5 and 9.6 show revenues and expenditures of the Los Angeles County budget.

The Los Angeles County Department of Parks and Recreation seeks to meet the needs of the eight million people who live in the county. The prime responsibility of the department is to serve the one million residents of unincorporated areas. To do so, it operates a network of major regional parks to provide specialized outdoor recreation for county residents. County parkland totals about 72,000 acres. While this may seem to be adequate acreage per capita (10 acres per 1000 residents), most of this land, 41,000 acres, is on Santa Catalina Island, which is 27 miles offshore. The county provides over 150 miles of hiking trails and 76 miles of beaches (administered by the Department of Beaches). The Department of Parks and Recreation administers five nature study centers which provide interpretive programs. Each of these centers is located in a natural wild area.

There are thirty-five regional parks and recreation areas run by the county. Santa Catalina

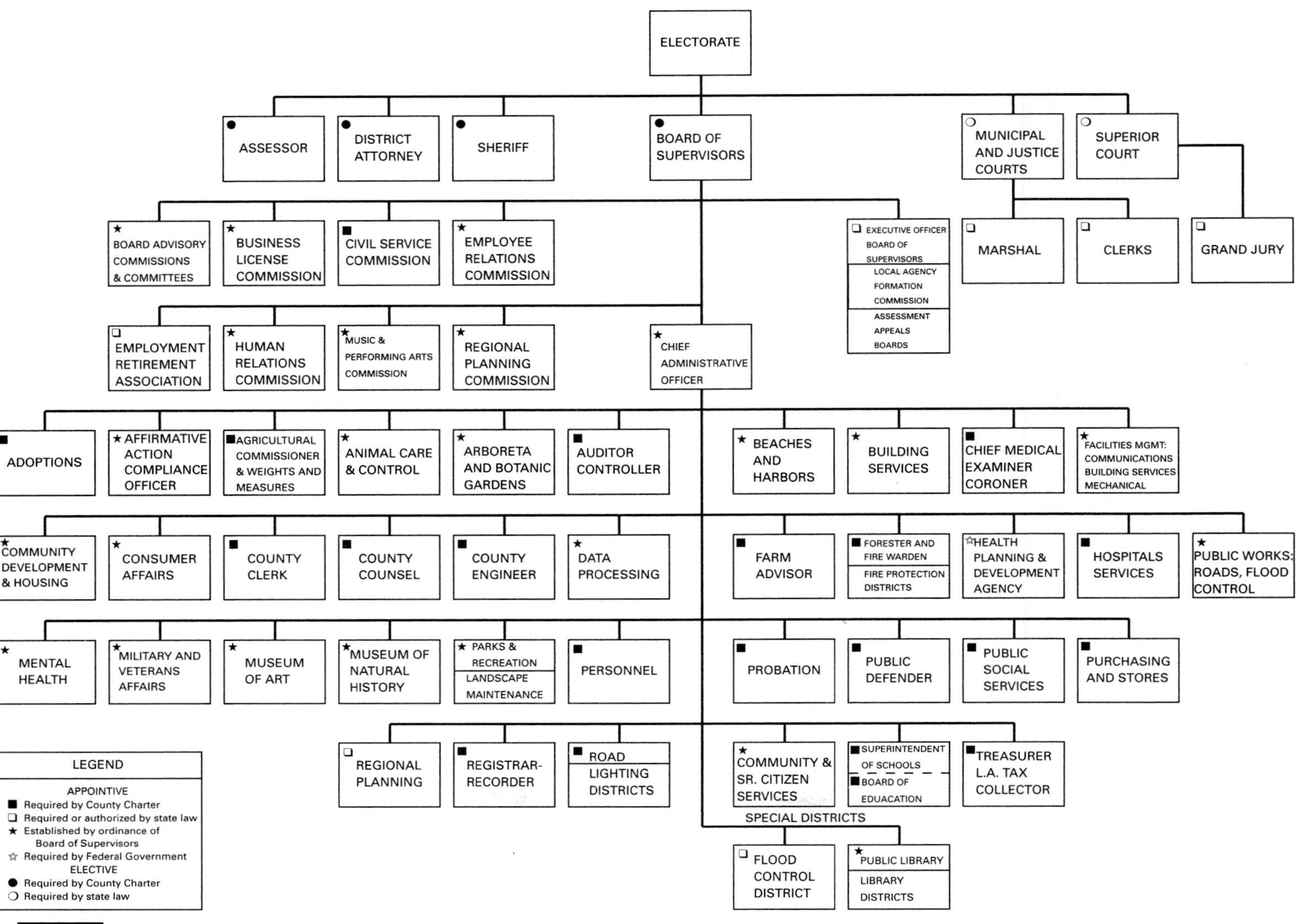

FIGURE 9.6 Los Angeles County government organization. *Source: L.A. County Board of Supervisors, County of Los Angeles Department of Parks and Recreation Guide* (1990).

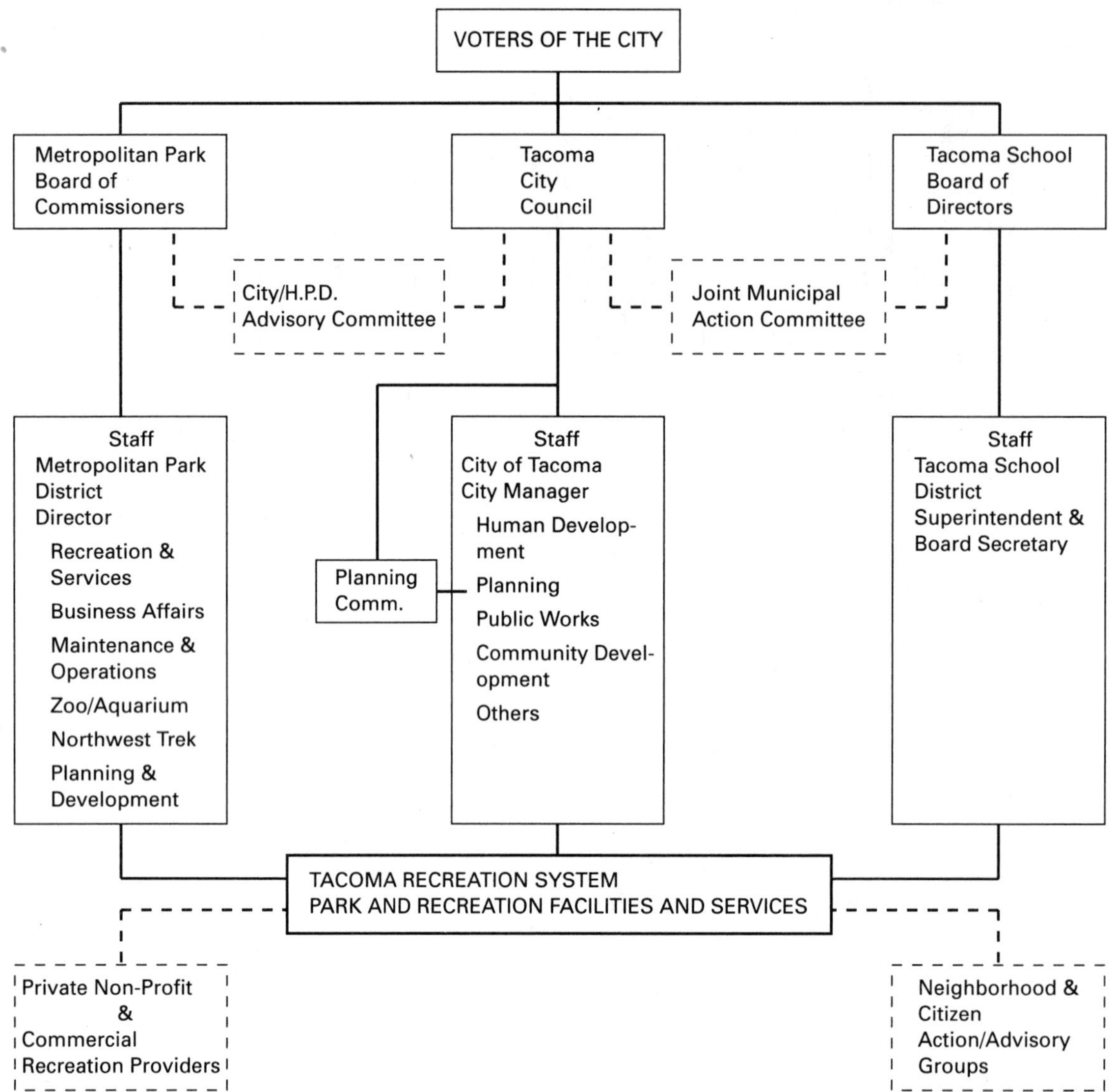

FIGURE 9.7 Tacoma recreation system. *Source: City of Tacoma, Five Year Recovery Action Program (1982), 1–10.*

Island has the largest acreage of unspoiled land for backpacking, hiking, and camping. Peck Road Water Conservation Park, one of the smallest regional parks in Los Angeles County, has an 80-acre lake which provides shoreline fishing in a flood control basin that was converted for outdoor recreation use.

There are 126 neighborhood and community parks administered by Los Angeles County. The county has turned over more than fifty parks to cities that incorporated around these parks. These neighborhood and community parks vary in size from .6 acre to 40 acres.

Tacoma, Washington With a population of 170,000, this city is expecting to reach 183,000 by the year 2000. It is located in Pierce County, which has a population of about 673,000. Three local government agencies are responsible for the majority of public park and recreation offerings, as follows:

1. Metropolitan Park District The parks and recreation facilities and programs for the city are primarily the responsibility of the Metropolitan Park District. The five board members are elected directly by the voters of the district. The board appoints the director, who is responsible for the development and maintenance of the district's parks and recreation facilities and programs. As a separate governmental agency, the Metropolitan Park District has taxing authority for special levies and bonds.

2. City of Tacoma Since 1953, Tacoma has had a council-manager government. The council is directly elected by the voters of the city electoral districts with three at-large positions. These positions, as well as that of mayor, are part-time positions. The Tacoma City Council has the responsibility for establishing city policy, formulating annual budgets, appointing the city manager and director of public utilities, as well as appointing citizens to various citizens' boards and commissions. At least four major city departments are actively engaged in planning, maintaining, and implementing recreation opportunities. City departments outside the public utilities department are the responsibility of the city manager.

3. Tacoma School District The Tacoma School District has five board members elected by the district at large. The superintendent of schools, appointed by the board, is responsible for implementation of policies established by the board and for fulfilling criteria mandated by state education requirements. The Tacoma School District makes gymnasiums, athletic fields, and playgrounds available for public recreation purposes. District recreation facilities are the responsibility of the assistant superintendent for school facilities. The Tacoma Recreation System is comprised of three agencies of the public sector which individually and collectively provide recreational opportunities to the people of Tacoma: although the Metropolitan Park District is charged with the primary responsibility of providing parks and recreational opportunities to the city's residents, the Tacoma School District as well as the City of Tacoma, through several departments, also contribute to the overall recreation system. In addition to the formal governmental structure, advisory committees such as the City/Metropolitan Park Board and the Joint Municipal Action Committee (composed of members of the Tacoma School Board and the Tacoma City Council) meet on matters of mutual interest.

Recreation and open space planning is a function of the Tacoma City Planning Department under the direction of the Tacoma Planning Commission and in close coordination with the Metropolitan Park District and the Tacoma School District. Implementation is primarily the responsibility of the Metropolitan Park District.

Under the direction of the Metropolitan Park Board and the Tacoma Planning Commission, the respective staffs of the three agencies are preparing a Recreation and Open Space Facilities Plan. This plan will be a guide for the location, acquisition, development, and improvement of recreation and open space in Tacoma.

Staffs of the Metropolitan Park District, the Tacoma School District, and the City of Tacoma work closely in planning programs and services to provide recreational opportunities to the people of Tacoma. This cooperative planning aims at providing efficient service and effectively using public dollars.

PROBLEMS IN LOCAL OFFERINGS

In studying the recreation resources, behaviors, and evaluations of people in the Detroit region, Marans and Fly (1981) compared those living in the inner city to those in its suburbs. Low levels of participation in leisure pursuits characterize residents of the city of Detroit, where only one in ten children play in the public park. Most of the children play in backyards or on sidewalks.

Although recreation resources are unevenly distributed in Detroit, favoring the suburban resident over the inner city resident, local parks are available to the city dweller. There is a park within a mile for eight out of ten households in the inner city. Yet their use is limited due to the same problems found in other inner cities: gangs, vandalism, alcoholism, stray dogs, and other unsafe conditions. Marans and Fly suggested that the municipal department of recreation consider the qualitative as well as the quantitative dimensions of recreation resources under its jurisdiction.

In a relatively recent study, Lawrence (1984) compared public recreation opportunities in central Los Angeles to the opportunities in its affluent suburbs. The study revealed a series of gaps, as follows:

1. The inner city community has less public recreation land than the suburban communities studied.
2. The suburban staff put in 59 percent more hours per week than did the inner city staff.
3. Community support was very limited in most inner city recreation areas, while the suburban areas enjoyed volunteer support.
4. The inner city areas seem to suffer from special problems of gangs and vandalism.

The author concluded that two distinct and separate systems of recreation offerings seem to be emerging in Los Angeles. She suggested that the commissioners and the Department of Parks and Recreation examine their policies, allocate more resources, and train personnel to reduce the gap between inner city and the suburbs in recreation offerings. She called on the department to involve the local community in its efforts by organizing advisory councils to help in planning the strategies to meet local needs.

SUMMARY

The evolution of offerings in outdoor recreation at the local level, be it municipal or county, is traced from the mere provision of open space to the establishment of highly complex recreational organization. The leaders in this respect, Frederick Law Olmsted and Charles Elliot, are presented first along with the philosophy that guided them in designing parks that represented the American way of life.

Local government structures, as they relate to the establishment of natural resources and the provision of outdoor programs, are investigated. So is the role of citizens in overseeing the services provided to the local citizens. Sources for the financing of areas, facilities, and programs are enumerated. Sources for operations include appropriations for the general fund, special recreation taxes, fees and charges, as well as gifts. These are distinguished from sources for capital development which include, but are not limited to, bond issues, federal funds, donations, and special assessment.

Two examples of local offerings in outdoor recreation are cited. The offerings of the county of Los Angeles, California, as well as the city of Tacoma, Washington, are given. Some of the problems facing local authorities where public recreation is concerned include low level of participation, uneven distribution of resources, and unsafe conditions in the recreation place. Suggestions for improvement of leisure services offerings are given.

REFERENCES

Butler, G. (1940) *Introduction to Community Recreation.* New York: McGraw Hill.

Caro, R. (1974) *The Power Broker.* New York: Vintage Press.

City of Tacoma (1982) *Five Year Recovery Action Plan.* Tacoma, WA: City of Tacoma.

County of Los Angeles (1990) *Los Angeles County Almanac: A Guide To Government.* County of Los Angeles.

Fazio, J. (1979) "Parks and Other Recreational Resources" in *Leisure: Emergence and Expansion,* H. Ibrahim and J. Shivers, editors. Los Alamitos, CA: Hersny Publishing.

Foss, P. (1968) *Recreation: Conservation in the United States, a Documentary History.* New York: Chelsea House.

Gans, H. (1974) "Outdoor Recreation and Mental Health" in *Land and Leisure: Concepts and Methods in Outdoor Recreation,* D. Fischer, T. Lewis, and G. Priddle, editors. Chicago: Maaroufa Press.

Haines, A. (1977) *The Yellowstone Story.* Yellowstone, WY: Yellowstone Library and Museum Association.

Heritage Conservation and Recreation Service (1979) *Fundraising Handbook.* U.S. Department of the Interior. Washington, D.C.: U.S. Government Printing Office.

Hjelte, G. (1940). *The Administration of Public Recreation.* New York: Macmillan.

Hjelte, G., and J. Shivers (1972) *Public Administration of Recreational Services.* Philadelphia, PA: Lea and Febiger.

Ibrahim, H., R. Banes, and G. Gerson (1987) *Effective Park and Recreation Boards and Commissions.* Reston, VA: AAHPERD.

Knudson, D. (1984) *Outdoor Recreation.* New York: Macmillan.

Kraus, R., and J. Curtis (1982) *Creative Management in Recreation and Parks* St. Louis, MO: C. V. Mosley.

Lawrence, D. (1984) *The Recreation Gap.* Los Angeles: University of Southern California.

MacLean, J., J. Peterson, and W. Martin (1985) *Recreation and Leisure: The Changing Scene.* New York: Macmillan.

Marans, R., and J. Fly. *Recreation and The Quality of Urban Life.* Ann Arbor, MI: Institute of Urban Research, University of Michigan.

Rainwater, C. (1922) *The Play Movement in the United States.* Chicago: University of Chicago.

10 Other Outdoor Recreation Resources

The natural resources used for outdoor recreation that are discussed in the last three chapters are owned by governmental agencies. This chapter will discuss nongovernmental resources.

In the United States, nongovernmental land that can be utilized for outdoor opportunities exceeds 740 million acres, of which 217 million acres of noncorporate land are now designated by their owners as open for recreation. In addition, there are about 40 million acres of noncorporate forest and open space that are used for the same purpose (Heritage 1979:77). Of corporate lands, 13 percent is designated for either employee or special groups recreation.

While most of the governmental lands open for outdoor recreation are located in the western United States, 90 percent of nongovernmental lands with recreational potential are located in the eastern and southern United States, with considerable recreational opportunities in rural areas. The Federal Energy Regulatory Commission requires that recreation facilities be provided at hydroelectric sites. This policy enhances the potential for outdoor recreation opportunities provided through the private sector. Among the notable achievements are:

- Private and nonfederal public utility companies have funded public recreation facilities.
- Waterways are used both for power generation and public recreation.
- Improved management techniques have been incorporated into recreation plans on hydroelectric project sites.
- Development of hydroelectric project lands and waters has fostered the growth of recreation facilities and support services on adjacent properties.

The 1973 Nationwide Outdoor Recreation Plan included a recommendation to allow charitable deduction for the donation of recreation lands. Many nonprofit organizations sought the benefits of making these charitable donations, including the Nature Conservancy, which purchased threatened lands and held them temporarily to be publicly auctioned off. In another example, wildlife refuges were expanded through a donation from the Union Camp Corporation of 16,000 acres to the Okefenokee National Wildlife Refuge and 2,850 acres for the endangered species program in Florida (Heritage 1979:78). In Oklahoma City, many city and state parks were established as a result of a 1976 transfer of 157 acres formerly used as a sandpit by the Dolese Company. Development money was pledged by civic groups and the Kerr Foundation. Another example is the acquisition of several recreation areas by the Greater Kansas City Resource Foundation. A group of business and community leaders in Missouri donated an 8,500-acre tract, 60 miles south of St. Louis, for a state park.

These are all examples of what charitable donations can do for outdoor recreation opportunities. Other than land donation, a business could become involved in the protection of wildlife. A tract of 480 acres containing Idaho's Silver Creek, a renowned trout stream, was protected by the Nature Conservancy with funds raised by Boise Cascade Corporation and the Union Pacific Railroad. In Wisconsin, four county recreation departments around Milwaukee now administer some 20 miles of utility right-of-way and plan many more, in cooperation with the Wisconsin Electric Company.

For the purpose of this work, nongovernmental outdoor recreation resources are classified into five categories, as follows:

1. Personal resources that have an impact on outdoor pursuits include second homes, cottages, RVs and trailers, time-share facilities, houseboats, and hunting lands.
2. Private organization resources include social and athletic clubs, hiking and mountaineering groups, and traveling associations.
3. Semipublic organization resources such as youth organizations and preservation associations have an impact on outdoor pursuits.
4. Industrial and business resources are sometimes used by employees for their outdoor recreation activities.
5. Commercial recreation resources include amusement parks, campgrounds, marinas, farms, ranches, and resorts.

PERSONAL RESOURCES

Personal resources that allow for outdoor recreation opportunities include the provision of certain facilities in one's primary residence as well the ownership of other facilities such as vacation homes, trailers, campers, and houseboats.

Primary Residence Resources

The family home remains the major setting for recreational activities in general (Glyptis and Chambers 1982). In addition, the American home is equipped with a backyard which provides for outdoor recreational outlets including the traditional family barbecue on summer evenings. The *Statistical Abstracts of the United States, 1987* shows that 48 percent of a sample interviewed in 1983 listed picnicking as an outdoor recreational activity, and only walking for pleasure, swimming, and visiting zoos surpassed the picnic as desirable outdoor activities (these activities were listed by 53 percent, 53 percent, and 50 percent of interviewees, respectively). Some of the picnics may have taken place away from participants' backyards, but the fact that the picnic ranks so high as an outdoor activity shows the importance of having a facility for it at home.

Another important home facility for outdoor recreation is the family swimming pool. According to MacLean et al. (1985:210), there are over two million swimming pools in America's backyards. Chubb and Chubb estimate that 85,000 swimming pools are built in America's backyards each year (1981:329). Most of these swimming pools are located in the sunbelt states. As previously stated, swimming is a dominant outdoor pursuit, ranked equal with walking.

The spa has become a popular addition to many American homes. Although it can be installed indoors, many spas are installed outdoors in the southern and western United States and Canada.

In residences that lack backyards or side yards, balconies and flat roofs function as resources for outdoor recreation activities, including sunbathing, growing plants and flowers, and eating outside. Most residences where balconies and roofs are used for recreation are found in the inner cities. According to Chubb and Chubb (1981:330), architectural styles are modified to accommodate the residents' needs for outdoor outlets by maximizing the amount of usable balcony and/or roof space.

Second Home Resources

The idea of having a vacation home, which was limited to the very rich in earlier times, gained popularity in Great Britain during the Victorian era (Ibrahim 1991:234). In the United States, the Forest Service began as early as 1915 to lease summer home sites. Although this practice is now de-emphasized, it became a big business in the 1960s. Real estate companies offered millions of acres of forest land and/or water front land by mail or telephone to customers who sometimes acquired the land without even seeing it. Large real estate companies offered free trips to willing customers to inspect their future vacation home.

According to Ragatz (1974), five to seven million American families own a vacation home or land for their trailer. Only one third of second homes are as fully equipped as the owners' primary residences are. Most are small cottages or cabins, approximately 7 percent of which are shared between two or more families (Chubb and Chubb 1981:331). About 8 percent of these second homes are utilized by the owners as rentals.

Locations of these second homes vary greatly. Originally, when the British middle class began to imitate the wealthy stratum, second homes were places in the country away from the crowded, industrial cities of late-1800s England. These were retreats for the well-off to enjoy open space, socialize with friends, or work on a hobby. Second homes located in the country are not dominant in the United States or Canada.

Water-oriented second homes are in the majority in Canada and the United States (Chubb and Chubb 1981:331). Most of these homes are modest structures that are extensively used in summer months along the Atlantic, Pacific, and Great Lakes shorelines. Entire communities of such homes are found in Florida and southern California. Naturally aquatic recreation activities are dominant along these shorelines.

Desert second homes are used in the winter months by owners whose primary homes are in areas with cold climates. These homes are located in the southwestern United States.

Mountain second homes are usually cabins that are used primarily during the hunting season and are located away from lakes or rivers. In addition, fishing, snowmobiling, and skiing could take place while vacationing at a mountain second home.

Outright ownership of a second home proved to be a difficult undertaking for many people, and the alternative to individual or family ownership of a second home involves property sharing. This is an arrangement which allows the family to enjoy the full benefits of a personal second home without having to carry the whole financial burden. When a second home is owned by two or more individuals or families, a *shared whole ownership* is in practice. *Time-sharing* is another concept for second homes which is practiced in two ways. In the *membership plan,* the developers continue to own the property and give the person and/or the family the right to use it for a specific period of time. In the *interval-ownership plan,* the buyer receives the title to the property for a particular period. According to Chubb and Chubb (1981:334), more than half a million American families have time-sharing properties in twenty-six states.

Other Personal Resources

Some people in North America use houseboats as second homes (Chubb and Chubb 1981:335). Houseboats are less expensive than many traditional second homes. In addition, they can be moved from one location to another. Scarcity of berths and high docking and berthing fees are making this alternative increasingly difficult.

Recreational trailers and recreational vehicles (RVs) are also used as second (and sometimes first) homes. Sales of recreational vehicles, in general, peaked in 1972 in the United States at 549,000 units, then leveled off, and then dropped to about 200,000 in 1980. Interest in RVs increased during the mid 1980s when over 300,000 units were sold (Barker 1986:15).

Another personal resource which can be used for outdoor pursuits is land. Farms, ranches, woodlands, ponds, and laneways can be used for hunting, fishing, swimming, boating, horseback riding, snowmobiling, or simple walking.

PRIVATE ORGANIZATION RESOURCES

Humans tend to organize themselves into groups to fulfill specific functions. Private organizations are witnessed in almost all human societies and should be distinguished from semipublic organizations. Membership in private organizations is usually more restricted than is membership in semipublic organizations. Private organizations can generally be divided into two groups. The first—instrumental organizations—emphasize the achievement of certain goals. Examples of instrumental associations are professional organizations and labor unions. In contrast, the emphasis of the second group—expressive organizations—is associational and interactional. Examples are social, sport, and hobby clubs. The concept may have started with Saint Andrew's Golf Club in Scotland in the 1500s, but the idea did not reach North America until 1888 when Brookline Country Club was established near Boston (Dulles 1965:242).

Social Clubs

Today in the United States and Canada there are hundreds of social clubs catering to all kinds of expressive activities, some of which have little to do with outdoor pursuits. Social clubs vary from small, informal groups that meet to play table games or to discuss topics of interest to highly structured, substantial groups whose interests are political, religious, or ethnic in nature. A large club might own a building that is equipped for indoor recreation. Members of social clubs sometimes organize outdoor pursuits on regular or semiregular bases.

Sport and Athletic Clubs

Like social clubs, sport and athletic clubs vary in size from small, loosely organized teams which do not own a facility to the powerful, sometimes elitist, country clubs with their expansive grounds and facilities. The most frequently found types of sport/athletic clubs in Canada and the United States cater mostly to those who play golf, tennis, and racquetball. Curling clubs are found in Canada, and soccer clubs are popular in the United States. Indoor tennis has been gaining here as well. There are approximately forty private ski clubs that not only own the slopes and the lifts, but are also equipped with a clubhouse with all the needed amenities (Chubb and Chubb 1981:339).

Sportspersons Clubs

The emphasis in sportspersons clubs is usually on fishing, hunting, and shooting. The size and structure of these clubs vary significantly. According to Chubb and Chubb (1981:339), there are thousands of these clubs with little or no recreation resources that are open to virtually anyone willing to pay the modest membership fees. Some clubs are formed by middle-income individuals who acquire a few acres of land with a potential for outdoor activities. The more affluent outdoor aficionados purchase or lease prime areas and sometimes employ a warden to manage the fish or game. There are also a number of private rifle and skeet shooting clubs where demonstrations and competitions are held.

Boat and Yacht Clubs

Boat and yacht clubs purchase or lease waterfront property, the development of which varies according to the financial resources of the club members. The basic service provided is the mooring and/or storing of vessels. Services may expand to include a clubhouse, an extensive marina, and a restaurant. Boating was listed as the favored recreation of 28 percent of the persons interviewed (U.S. Bureau of Census 1988:218). In 1980 there were 11.8 million boat owners in the United States who spent $7.4 billion on their activity. Although many of these owners do not belong to a boating club, their sheer number provides us with an idea of the impact this activity has on society.

Hiking and Mountaineering Clubs

Although most hiking takes place on publicly owned land in Canada and the United States, shelters are provided on leased land by hiking and mountaineering clubs. According to Chubb and Chubb (1981:341), ninety-three such clubs are organized into the Appalachian Trail Conference, which provides shelters along the 2000-mile Appalachian Trail from Georgia to Maine. The Appalachian Mountain Club of Boston has nine huts that are situated about a day's hike apart in the White Mountains region of New Hampshire. The club is the biggest and oldest affiliate of the Appalachian Trail Conference.

Similarly, the Adirondack Mountain Club owns and operates two lodges in the Adirondack Mountains, and the Alpine Club of Canada owns and operates similar facilities in Alberta and British Columbia.

SEMIPUBLIC ORGANIZATION RESOURCES

Semipublic organizations are those that depend on public donations and/or government grants. Although the line of demarcation is blurred between purely private organizations and semipublic ones, the latter are open to public scrutiny more than are the former, since they receive and accept public funds. Accordingly semipublic organizations must abide by the law of the land—for example, they cannot tolerate discrimination on any grounds.

In this section two types of semipublic organization are presented: youth-serving organizations and preservation organizations.

Youth-Serving Organizations

Some youth-serving organizations own an outdoor recreation resource; others do not own one but are involved in outdoor recreational activities.

The Boy Scouts were organized in England in 1908 by Lord Baden-Powell who, during the Boer War, had seen the English soldiers in need of outdoor survival skills. He set about to help boys secure this essential training. William D. Boyce, a Chicago publisher, and other enthusiastic supporters organized the Boy Scouts of America in 1910. The movement has spread throughout the world, with an international structure representing about 110 countries with headquarters in Switzerland. The Boy Scouts of America has over four million members, about a fourth of whom are adult leaders. Since its inception, the Boy Scouts' membership has included more than 70 million persons.

Scouting is open to boys of all religions and races, and scout leaders encourage members to do their "duty to God." Troops are sponsored by religious institutions, civic groups, schools, and parent-teacher organizations.

According to Chubb and Chubb (1981:349), most of the 58,569 scout troops in the United States have access to one or more of the 600 scout camps operated by the 417 local scout councils. The national scout headquarters administers six high-adventure camps located in Minnesota, Florida, Kentucky, Maine, Wisconsin, and New Mexico. The Philmon Scout Camp and Explorer base is on 137,493 acres and is well equipped for outdoor pursuits in hiking, camping, and wilderness survival.

The Girl Guide/Girl Scout movement was started in Great Britain by Lord Robert Baden-Powell and his sister, Lady Agnes Baden-Powell, in 1909. There are ninety-three other nations that have developed their own scouting association for girls. These organizations form the World Association of Girl Guides and Girl Scouts and maintain world centers in Switzerland, England, Mexico, and India. These centers offer Girl Scouts and Girl Guides opportunities to meet members of scouting movements in other countries. In the United States, the first Girl Scout troop was formed in 1912 in Savannah, Georgia, by Juliette Gordon Low, who organized the troop in her hometown. She had been active in the Girl Guide movement in England and in Scotland, and she patterned the American troops accordingly. Today, the Girl Scout movement provides girls with opportunities to develop their potential to make new friends, to take active leadership roles in their communities, and to learn outdoor survival skills.

The Girl Scout movement has day- and resident-camp properties that are shared by troops for their outdoor programs and for leader-training sessions. There are national centers in Wyoming, New York, Maryland, and Georgia. The Girl Scout National Center West in Wyoming provides a wide variety of outdoor-living opportunities for older scouts. The Rockwood Girl Scout National Center is a year-round 93-acre facility in Potomac, Maryland, that serves as a hostel for Girl Scouts from the United States and other nations. The center is also used for a variety of programs concerning nature conservation.

The Young Men's Christian Association (YMCA) began with George Williams in London, England, in 1844 for the purpose of instilling Christian morals among youth. The first American YMCA was formed in Boston in 1851. Today the National Council of the Young Men's Christian Association of the United States has about 1800 member associations employing close to 6,000 professionals. There are over 9494 YMCAs world-wide, with facilities that include 1364 swimming pools, 1621 gymnasia, 680 hostels, and 1000 cafeterias (Chubb and Chubb 1981:351).

American YMCAs operate more than 400 resident camps and more than 1200 day camps. Forty-four YMCAs in thirty-nine cities across the United States operate 12,000 low-cost rooms to encourage less affluent travelers to "Visit U.S.A."

In addition to facilitating outdoor pursuits and travel, one YMCA program is designed to strengthen family relationships through parent-child clubs and activities. Over half a million parents and children are involved in: Y-Indian Princesses (6- to 9-year-old girls and their mothers) and Y-Trailblazers (boys over 9 years of age and their fathers).

The Young Women's Christian Association (YWCA) began in London, England, in 1855 to meet the needs of working women. By 1894 a worldwide YWCA was in the making, with eighty-three nations represented in its membership. In 1866, the first American YWCA formed in Boston. Although there is some emphasis on outdoor pursuits, the program revolves around the formation of groups allowing for new person contacts, sharing of ideas, discovering and rediscovering values, acquiring employment and leisure skills, and providing community services. Classes include homemaking, consciousness-raising, career readiness, job training and placement, money management, teen parenting, and stress management. Recreation includes music, arts and crafts, dramatics, tennis, swimming, archery, aerobics, volleyball, and bowling. Programs of physical fitness and health education are emphasized.

The *Smith-Lever Act of 1914* provided for cooperative extension work in agriculture and home economics. It included boys' and girls' 4-H Clubs, with "4-H" standing for Head, Heart, Hands, and Health. The 4–H idea has spread to more than eighty countries. Through the International Four-H Youth Exchange, young Americans visit other countries and young foreigners may live and work with American families for months at a time. Other international programs include travel seminars, agricultural training, and rural youth leaders exchange. In the United States, 4-H has nearly five million members from 3,150 U.S. countries, with 143,000 clubs and special-interest groups guided by 568,000 adult and teenage leaders. Only 20 percent of the members live on farms; 40 percent live in towns with less than 10,000 population and in open country, and the remainder live in larger towns, suburbs, and cities.

Although the name may indicate an exclusively outdoor orientation, the Camp Fire organization serves youth in a variety of ways. The organization was started as the Camp Fire Girls by Luther Gulick in 1910. In 1975 admission of boys to this once-upon-a-time all-girls organization led to a change in the name. Today Camp Fire is a national organization with 500,000 members, both boys and girls. Its purpose is to provide a program of informal education and opportunities for youth to realize their potential to function effectively as caring, self-directed individuals. The organization also seeks to improve conditions in society that affect youth. A nonprofit agency for youth ages birth through 21, Camp Fire is open to all without regard to race, creed, ethnic origin, sex, or income level.

Two more youth-serving organizations, the Boys' Club and the Girls' Club, have no outdoor resources to speak of. According to MacLean et al. (1985:194), the Boys' Club movement originated in response to the plight of boys in the crowded slums of New England cities. The emphasis in the program for boys and girls is on the enhancement of the youngsters' life-style, which includes day and overnight camping experiences.

Preservation Organizations

Although the main objectives of preservation organizations is the preservation of natural areas and historical sites, numerous outdoor pursuits can take place on their premises. Not all organizations concerned with preservation own the property to be preserved; many of these organizations work to encourage other organizations, agencies, and individuals to preserve property for future generations. Following are some of the nonprofit organizations that deal with outdoor pursuits.

The *Nature Conservancy* is the largest preservation organization in the United States. It owns close to a half million acres of land. The land is either purchased, donated, or acquired because it is ecologically significant. Sometimes the land acquired by the conservancy is turned over to governmental agencies to manage. The organization's holdings are managed by its 60,000 volunteers. Among the most popular recreational areas of the conservancy are the Virginia Coast Reserve and California's Santa Cruz Island. The Virginia Coast Reserve consists of thirteen barrier islands which, along with their tidal pools, amount to 35,000 acres. California's Santa Cruz Island has 55,000 acres which are home to many rare and endangered species. The conservancy provides an interpretive center, overnight accommodations, hiking expeditions, and boating trips.

The *National Audubon Society* manages sixty-four wildlife refuges totaling 200,000 acres. This 400,000-member organization emphasizes the protection of wildlife populations, particularly birds. The permanent staff in some of these sanctuaries serve as interpreters of wildlife and conduct hikes through the refuges (see Chapter 14, Education and the Outdoors).

The *National Trust for Historic Preservation* owns and operates nine museums and ten historical sites. It also encourages and assists agencies, organizations, and individuals to undertake historic preservation. It has close to 160,000 corporate and individual members. Other organizations that are involved in nature preservation include the *Brooks Bird Club, Bass Anglers Society, Sport Fishing Institute,* and the *Garden Club of America.* The Third Nationwide Outdoor Recreation Plan (Cordell et al. 1979:79) lists the following advantages as the basis for the potential role of the nonprofit sector in outdoor recreation:

- Nonprofits provide a variety of services that the state cannot provide. State forests within metropolitan areas are currently underutilized. Nonprofit organizations could provide interpretive services and educational programs for urban residents using the state forests for activities such as nature walks and cross-country skiing.
- Nonprofits have expertise in specific areas of land management that would enhance state programs. For example, because of limited resources, little attention has been given to certain nonprofits that have the expertise to provide the necessary leadership in development and management of a state trails system.
- Nonprofits can provide a model for the provision of quality services. Nonprofit agencies could better train field personnel in the management of public land and the provision of services, and they could be effective in involving volunteer groups to carry out these functions.
- Nonprofits can bring special-needs groups to state properties. Nonprofits can provide the required expertise and labor to provide access to public lands and special site-related programs for special populations.
- Nonprofits can attract a variety of user groups to a site because of the diversity of programs offered. In Massachusetts, for example, Franklin Park in Boston, Forest Park in Springfield, and the Heritage Park in Fall River are cited as examples of sites that attract diverse elements of each city's population.
- Nonprofits can promote the use of open space as a means of encouraging people to use community services located in close proximity to recreation areas. For example, establishment of the State Heritage Park in Lawrence, Massachusetts, involved the rehabilitation of a town common adjacent to a city hall.

INDUSTRIAL AND BUSINESS RESOURCES

In this section, two concepts will be discussed: the provision of recreation by industry and business for their employees and the utilization of industrial lands for outdoor recreation.

Employee Recreation

Provision of recreational opportunities by industry and business for their employees began at the heel of the advent of industrialization in the mid 1800s. Peacedale Manufacturing Company of Rhode Island is credited with providing library resources and singing classes as early as 1854. Other companies followed suit when the Pullman Company, the National Cash Register Company, and the Metropolitan Life Insurance Company provided recreation centers and golf courses and organized picnics and outings for their employees.

A 1913 survey by the U.S. Bureau of Labor Statistics shows that more than 50 percent of the fifty-one companies surveyed offered some form of employee recreation. In 1918 San Francisco established the first citywide industrial recreation association. A significant increase in this sort of offering was witnessed in the late 1930s, when the international recreation department was established by the United Auto Workers. In 1941 the National Industrial Recreation Association was created.

MacLean et al. describe a sample employee recreation program established in Columbus, Indiana. The Cummins Employees Recreation Association has received national recognition in this regard. The program is financed through fees and income from commissions on sales from the company's vending machines. A 345-acre facility is owned and operated by the association. At the facility, varied programs are offered, among which are outdoor activities. Picnicking, camping, boating, and fishing seem to head the list of the most popular activities (1985:219).

Industrial Land and Outdoor Recreation

According to Cordell et al. industrial land provided a significant portion of outdoor recreational opportunities in the United States in the past, when 72 percent of corporate land was open for some form of recreation. Forty-four percent of the land was open to the general public for recreation use without permission. Most of the 68 million acres used for that purpose were in the southern states (1979:38-83). Knudson (1984:136) listed the following four types of industries where lands are either utilized in outdoor pursuits or have potential for such use:

1. Wood-Using Industries Weyerhaeuser Corporation was the first of the large wood-using companies to start a tree farm in 1941. By 1975, its farms were open to the public for a nominal fee as recreation resources mainly for hunting and fishing. Other activities provided on Weyerhaeuser lands are cross-country skiing and hiking. The company provides vacation homesites for its employees. Weyerhaeuser hires professional staff to protect and manage wildlife and to supervise and conduct activities on its natural resources.

In addition to its two primary objectives of providing vital wood fiber to be used in the making of paper and protecting the water sources, Weyerhaeuser's efforts to preserve scenic beauty, increase recreation opportunities, and enhance game and wildlife on its natural resources point to the degree of the company's involvement in outdoor pursuits.

2. Utility Companies Electric power derived from hydroelectric plants is monitored by the Federal Energy Regulatory Commission. Among the commission's requirements is the development of recreational opportunities and utilization of each plant's reservoir as a recreation site. An example of such an arrangement is the Pacific Gas and Electric Company in California, which derives most of its electric power from hydroelectric plants in California mountains. Additionally, since power company profits are limited by California laws, excess income goes to recreation and park projects.

3. Land-Holding Companies Louisiana Land and Title Company and Gulf and Western Corporation have recreational resources that are open to the public. Other companies have donated land as public preserves.

4. Other Manufacturing Companies Included among these companies are steel and mining companies. For example, the United States Steel Company has opened a large parcel of its land to the public for outdoor pursuits.

There are motivating factors behind the involvement of profit-oriented corporations in sponsoring outdoor pursuits. Profit does not seem to

TABLE 10.1 Selected Industry Donations to the Nature Conservancy

Donor	Acres	Year
American Can Company		
Big Rib River, WI	720	1981
Dravo Corporation		
Coffee Island, AL	794	1981
Federal Paperboard		
Green Swamp, NC	13,850	1977
Huber Corporation		
Crystal Bog, ME	3,795	1975
International Paper Co.		
Richmond Hill, GA	26,154	1977
Clark Creek, MS	427	1978
Mississippi Sandhill, MS	26	1979
Ogeechee River, GA	8,865	1980
Appalachian Trail, ME	1,216	1980
Camel's Hump, VT	315	1980
Time-Life		
Roy E. Larsen's Sandylands, TX	2,138	1977
Union Camp		
Great Dismal Swamp, VA	49,097	1975
Chowan Swamp, NC	4,729	1976
Okefenokee Swamp, NC	14,849	1978
Silico Ricefields, GA	1,517	1978
Weyerhaeuser		
Great Dismal Swamp, VA	10,957	1978

Source: D. Knudson, *Outdoor Recreation* (New York: Macmillan, 1984), 142 (reprinted with permission).

be the dominant factor (Knudson 1984:138). Some companies open their land to recreationists because it was always open before the land was acquired. The company may feel that the best public relations can occur if the land is left open for recreation use.

On the other hand, the opening of private land to public use may lead to difficulties, one of which is the cost of operation. In order to provide adequate service, the operating company may find it necessary to provide facilities, collect trash, control fire hazards, and build roads, among other things. Another problem the operating company may face is legal liability. Real or imagined damage may occur on the land, and legal action may be taken. Knudson cited a case in California in which, because of one judge's decision favoring the recreationist, the California Redwood Association suspended its carefully developed recreation program (1984:141).

Donation of Land

Land is sometimes donated by companies, corporations, or individuals in order to save income tax, capital gains tax, or both. Other times the motivational factor behind the donation is public good. The largest receiver of these lands is the Nature Conservancy. Knudson presented the material shown in Table 10.1 to show the amount of land received by the Nature Conservancy in 1975–1981.

COMMERCIAL ENTERPRISES

The leisure market is one of the largest and fastest-growing economic sectors in the United States and Canada. Heading the list are high-adventure and high-risk leisure activities, according to Bullaro and Edginton (1986:7). The authors cited white-water rafting, rappelling, spelunking, hang gliding, wind surfing, and soaring as some of the activities that have increased in popularity lately. Travel and tourism have also become popular in recent years.

Interest in outdoor pursuits by Americans, as well as Canadians, could be traced to the fact that the United States and Canada had to be built before they could be lived in, and this took lots of energy and necessitated dealing with elements of nature. Venturing into wilderness was done for purely practical reasons, to find food and build shelter. When contact with nature decreased somewhat with the building of settlements, love for the outdoors did not subside.

In the United States, the first entrepreneurial attempt involving natural resource may have taken place in the Yellowstone Territory in 1870. A group of individuals who were sent by the federal government to study the natural wonders and beauty of that area discussed the possibility of forming a private corporation to develop Yellowstone. Despite the American orientation toward an entrepreneurial style of life, that territory was made into a public park, the first of its kind in the world. Nonetheless the entrepreneurial spirit found its way into other outdoor recreational areas. Commercial enterprises in the leisure sector are service-oriented and should be concerned with providing services that are not only useful or beneficial, but also satisfactory. According to Bullaro and Edginton (1986:13), leisure experience at the beach, mountain, river, desert, or lake must provide for aesthetic pleasure, spiritual awareness, awe, risk, excitement, and physical challenge.

Commercial enterprises having to do with outdoor pursuits come in many types, sizes, and orientations, as seen in the following descriptions.

The high-risk activity of bungee jumping has had a meteoric rise in popularity in the last decade. Private operators are now providing opportunities for thrill-seekers to jump in many parts of the United States, including jumps from hot air balloons.

Commercial Campgrounds

The National Campgrounds Owners Association estimates that private campgrounds provide 1.2 million individual campsites in 13,000 campgrounds. Since there are close to 5,500 public campgrounds providing 330,000 individual campsites, the individual campsites of commercial enterprises (1,200,000) provide 78 percent of total campsites in the United States (1,530,000). According to Jensen (1985:250), the size of the average private campground has grown recently. The average campsites per campground increased from 41 to 98 in 10 years (1975–1985).

According to Knudson (1984:123), the recent trend is towards the development of franchises and condominium campgrounds. For a franchise in Kampgrounds of America, the potential owner of a site purchases the name of the company and its services. He or she will be guaranteed a certain territory. The condominium campground entails one of two approaches. The individual owns a specific lot located in the campground. The site can be rented out when the owner chooses, or the owner can own an undivided interest in the entire property. Examples of campground condominiums are Bryn Mawr Camp Resorts and Yogi Bear Jellystone Parks.

Membership campgrounds sometimes offer a time-sharing arrangement at other campgrounds. Such an arrangement allows the member to use other sites at affiliated campgrounds across the United States and Canada. For example, Camp Coast to Coast coordinates visits among 150 campgrounds in North America.

While most of the commercial campgrounds cited have elaborate facilities such as swimming pools and tennis courts, a small number of campgrounds still are rustic and provide traditional outdoor pursuits such as hiking and nature walks. A smaller number provide roadside overnight camping with hardly any promise for outdoor pursuits.

Campground associations have been formed in many states and provinces to promote business, affect governmental decisions, and provide the needed information and education for members and others. On the national level the National Campground Owners Association was formed for the same reasons.

According to Chubb and Chubb (1981:387), commercial campgrounds are more desirable than public ones because of the following special features:

- Acceptance of advance reservations, thus making it possible to plan an itinerary that includes a series of popular destinations without constantly worrying about campsite availability.
- Availability of more amenities, such as electric, water, and sewer hookups; paved camping spaces; bathhouse and laundromat facilities; recreation halls; and well-lit, patrolled campsite areas.
- A policy of remaining open in the off-season, thus making it possible for people to camp while enjoying such activities as snowmobiling, ice fishing, hunting, and cross-country skiing.
- Provision by some campsites of fully equipped tents or recreation vehicles so that campers traveling by air and others not wishing to bring their own equipment may still enjoy the advantages of camping. This also allows noncampers to try camping and see how they enjoy the experience before investing in equipment of their own.

In a Gallup poll camping was found to be pursued by 21 percent of the 1,500 households investigated (Ibrahim 1991:233). A study by Cerullo and Ewen (1982:17) showed that America's minorities—blacks, Jews, and Hispanics—barely exist in the camping world.

Ski Areas

While Jensen (1985:251) reports that there are 700 ski areas in the United States, Chubb and Chubb (1981:390) report 1300 such areas. Jensen also states that the number of skiers has been increasing by about 10 percent a year to a total of 10 million people who go skiing in America's ski areas. According to Jensen (1985:251), half of the areas he reported on are of medium size, ranging between 50 and 200 acres, while 25 percent are small and therefore limited. The remainder are large and elaborate and other features could be easily added, such as tobogganing, sledding, snowmobiling, and cross-country skiing. Chubb and Chubb (1981:390) state that 50 of the ski areas in the United States are regarded as world-renowned major resorts. The Chubbs report that American ski developments are located in 41 states. They provided the material shown in Table 10.2.

TABLE 10.2 Characteristics of U.S. Ski Regions

Characteristics	The East	The Midwest	The Rocky Mountains	The Far West
Range	Northern Georgia and western North Carolina to Maine.	Michigan, Wisconsin, Minnesota, parts of Illinois, Ohio, and Indiana.	Mountain areas of New Mexico, Colorado, Utah, Idaho, and Montana.	Pacific coast mountain areas of California, Oregon, Washington, and Alaska.
Elevation (above sea level)	Modest; 460–1400 meters (1500–4500 ft.).	Minor; glacier-produced hills reach 490 meters (1600 ft.) at most.	High; between 1500–3300 meters (5000–11,000 ft.); some resorts at 2400 meters (8000 ft.).	Similar to Rocky Mountains region.
Skiing opportunities	Enormous variety; some of the most interesting and stimulating skiing; most trails are carved through forests and are narrower than elsewhere; good cross-country skiing opportunities.	Less variety; ideal learner and intermediate slopes; runs are often cut through woods; lacks rugged terrain; drops 60–180 meters (200–600 ft) at most; excellent slalom course and ski jump facilities; competitions numerous; exceptional cross-country skiing.	Best skiing for expert skiers; some runs are through forest; many open slopes are 300 feet or more in width; satisfying long runs; greatest vertical drop in United States; status-skiing opportunities; some gentle slopes permit use by less than expert skiers.	Exceptional bowl and panoramic skiing; excellent opportunities for learners as well as experts; sheer scale of High Sierra skiing unsurpassed; some ski areas are close to urban centers in Northwest.
Major resort areas	Intensive development along mountainous spine of Vermont; most challenging areas are in New Hampshire; one big mountain (Whiteface) is in New York along with 100 smaller areas; Sugarloaf area in Maine is well known and impressive; several popular resorts in Pennsylvania.	Clusters of centers ideal for learners around Detroit, Chicago, Milwaukee, Minneapolis-St. Paul metropolitan area; chain of resorts bordering Great Lakes from Lutsen, Minnesota, across Wisconsin to Boyne City, Michigan; Boyne Country ski development is leader in Midwest—first in world to install a quadruple chairlift.	Contains nation's most prestigious resorts (Colorado in particular); even small resorts match largest resorts elsewhere in skiable area but not necessarily in facilities; subregional differences not substantial, but southern resorts have drier powder snow, whereas northern areas have greater snow depths.	Two concentrations in southern California—areas within 160 km (100 miles) of Los Angeles and the High Sierra resorts of Lake Tahoe region; prime ski area in northern California is Mt. Shasta; three areas on flanks of Mt. Hood near Portland, Oregon; three areas in Snoqualmie Pass near Seattle, WA; more than 30 areas in Oregon and Washington designed primarily as day areas.
Advantages or disadvantages	Closest to heaviest concentrations of potential skiers; most areas readily accessible by car; best areas seriously overcrowded at times; many areas have distinctive atmospheres and many loyal users.	Many resorts within a 1- or 2-hour drive of large urban centers; midwestern skiers known for their enthusiasm and dedication; excellent ski services and instruction opportunities.	Many resorts not readily accessible; cost and altitude problems for non-Westerners; some of the most beautiful settings in the world; great diversity of winter sports and après-ski opportunities.	Access often difficult in Sierra Nevadas; evening and weekend opportunities excellent in some areas; best areas are away from usual vacation routes; some cost and altitude problems for skiers from the East; exotic settings available on highest slopes.

Length of season	Usually 3 or 4 months; extended and made more reliable by heavy use of snow-making equipment; occasional mild winter can be disastrous, especially in the South.	Similar to the East but colder temperatures an asset; adequate skiing almost a certainty throughout season where snow-making equipment is used.	Longer season than East or Midwest; depends on latitude and elevation.	Longest season; year-round skiing possible in some high northern locations.
Skiing conditions	Winds occasionally strong.	Often extremely cold temperatures, sometimes accompanied by strong winds.	Most comfortable climatic conditions; mostly skiing below timberline, which provides wind-protected trails; more sunny days than other regions.	Threat of storms; risk of being snowed in.
Snow and trail conditions	Unpredictable; extreme cold periods alternate with devastating thaws; snow on trails often packed hard because of heavy use.	Heavy snowfalls supplemented by use of snow-making equipment; has most uniform conditions of all regions.	Large quantities of snow in average season; dry-air conditions produce snow that rarely packs into hard snow or ice; best consistency in world—better even than in European Alps; danger of avalanches; problems with whiteouts and flat light.	Heavy snowfalls—often too much; reaches depths of 5 m (15 ft) in Sierra Nevadas in average season; snow very persistent—comes early and stays late; unfortunately often damp, sometimes wet conditions.
Examples of major resort developments	Stowe, Vt., considered to be the ski capital of the East; steep, narrow trails provide challenge; 660 m (2150 ft) vertical drop; 58 different lodge facilities.	Boyne Country, Michigan, largest privately owned ski development in U.S.; foremost complex in the Midwest; best racing slopes in region; 190 m vertical drop; can accommodate 1500 people in deluxe lodge, inn, and villa facilities.	Aspen, Co., considered by many to be the ski capital of the world; includes 4 huge mountain slopes; one just for beginners; 1160 m vertical drop; 95 places to stay, providing 1608 rooms and 1469 condominium facilities.	Heavenly Valley, California-Nevada border, largest ski area in the world; 5200 hectares (20 sq. miles) of lift-served terrain; 1100–1200 m (3600–4000 ft) vertical drop; 24 places to stay.

Source: M. Chubb, and H. Chubb, *One Third of Our Time: An Introduction to Recreation Resources and Behavior* (New York: Wiley, 1981), 391–92. Reprinted with permission.

Although ski areas are developed and managed by large corporations, most of the areas are located on national forest land. Because of the increased demand, the National Forest Service is guiding the development and operation of the ski resorts located within its jurisdiction. For example the number of skiers on a slope, in a given day, is controlled. Construction of ski trails is also controlled in order to reduce land disturbance.

Commercial ski resorts supply a variety of services, programs, and facilities, described as follows by Chubb and Chubb (1981:394):

- Lighted slopes and trails (especially at resorts close to metropolitan areas) to extend the skiing day and accommodate after-work skiers.
- Reasonably priced equipment rentals and ski schools with ample beginners' slopes to attract new participants.
- Rope tows, chairlifts, gondolas, and trams to transport skiers rapidly and effortlessly to the skiing areas.
- Snow-cat or helicopter transportation and guide services to make skiing in backcountry areas feasible.
- Iceskating rinks, toboggan runs, sleigh rides, and heated swimming pools to provide other outdoor activities and to attract nonskiers.
- Indoor swimming pools and tennis courts to attract nonskiers and to please the skiers, most of whom swim and about 65 percent of whom play tennis.
- Après-ski programs, including movies, live entertainment, and parties involving the use of resort-provided lounges, gamerooms, discotheques, restaurants, bars, and nightclubs.

Resorts

Resorts, other than ski resorts, include beauty and health resorts, which probably started with the Romans and were founded around hot springs. Also there are warm-weather resorts ranging from simple to luxurious and sport resorts which provide instruction and practice activities.

Health and beauty resorts are more prevalent in Europe than in North America; they are found around Czechoslovakia's Karlsbad, France's Vichy, and Germany's Bad Pyrmont. According to Chubb and Chubb (1981:395), while the emphasis in Europe is on mineral water therapy, the emphasis in North American resorts was initially on beauty but has shifted to fitness. The typical resort gives daily facials, massages, manicures, and pedicures to its guests. Fitness, which is emphasized in middle-class spas has become an important feature of the health and beauty resort. A recent trend is the resort-spa which offers a combination of health and recreation. Most of the recreational activities are not of an outdoor nature.

The warm-weather resort started in the 1950s with Club Mediterranean, which now boasts a one million member organization. The original idea was to help single people who wanted to go tenting. Today that club operates 82 resort villages in 29 countries. Most of these resorts are beach oriented, and a few are skiing oriented. Modern distractions such as radios, televisions, telephones, or newspapers are not allowed. As per its name, many of the resort locations are around the Mediterranean Sea, but there is a year-round resort at Copper Mountain in Colorado (Chubb and Chubb 1981:395). Although most of the participants are French (47 percent), Americans and Canadians constitute 12 percent of the participants. Over the years the clientele has changed—married couples, older individuals, as well as singles come to these resorts.

Sport resorts have expanded rapidly, particularly those that emphasize tennis and golf. These resorts provide opportunities for receiving instruction in the sport as well as practicing it. Other than organized sport, some of the resorts provide for outdoor pursuits such as horseback riding and hiking. For example, North

Carolina Pinhurst Club has a 200-mile trail for horseback riding. In addition, it has very attractive features that have no bearing on outdoor recreation—a health spa, a trap-and-skeet shooting facility, an olympic-size swimming pool, and a lake for boating are enjoyed by club members.

According to Jensen (1985:251), over 50 percent of American resorts are owned by recreation enterprises. Some are built on small sites providing limited activities, while others are built on sites of 1,000 acres or more. Forty percent of American resorts are owned by families, while the remaining 10 percent are owned by clubs or nonprofit associations. Three-fourths of the land included in resorts is dedicated to recreation. Water sports are by far the most popular activities at resorts. Fishing, boating, and water skiing take place, and swimming is the favorite single activity (Jensen 1985:251).

Amusement Parks

A small, private park, Jones Wood, provided entertainment on Manhattan Island as early as 1850. But it was the building of Coney Island on the southwestern end of Long Island, New York, that may have signalled the birth of amusement parks in America. The idea was copied from the world-famous Luna Park in Paris.

Today there are approximately 400 amusement parks in the United States (U.S. Bureau of Census 1987:220). The annual income of these parks is over $4 billion (Grover 1987:30). These parks vary from small ones, where rides, games, and shows are all together, to the gigantic Disneyland and Disneyworld. Disneyland recorded its 250-millionth admission in August of 1986. Both Disney parks draw one-third of the total attendance at amusement parks, with Disneyworld attracting 15 million visitors annually.

According to Jensen (1985:253), many of the major amusement parks are developed on large parcels of land with enough open space and natural features to contribute to a genuine outdoor experience.

Guest Ranches and Vacation Farms

Guest (dude) ranches are working farms that acquire additional income by opening them to guests. In fact, accommodating guests often becomes the main source of income, with livestock and the production of crops as secondary interests. Most of these ranches are 1,000 acres or more. Horseback riding is the main outdoor activity of the guests, along with fishing, hunting, and swimming. The life-style is western, since most of these ranches are in the west (Jensen 1985:253).

In the midwest many small farmers have opened their farms for outdoor pursuits, particularly for fishing, as a means of augmenting their income. Hunting is also allowed for a fee on farms with pastures and woodlands. Some farms are providing swimming pools and golf courses.

SUMMARY

Private outdoor recreation opportunities could come from personal, nonprofit, semipublic, and industrial and business resources. Their offerings not only supplement public offerings, but they could serve as models in a number of cases. While the personal resources may include residences, second homes, boats, RVs, and the like, private organizations include social, sport, and athletic clubs, boat and yacht clubs, as well as nature clubs. Semipublic organizations such as the YMCA, the Boy Scouts, and preservation organizations offer members many outdoor pursuits. In the meantime, a number of industries are seeking to provide their employees with these opportunities.

Commercial enterprises have been in the business of providing outdoor recreation activities for many years. Campgrounds, ski areas, and resorts accommodate many a recreationist. Amusement parks have played important roles in providing outdoor outlets for young and mature alike.

REFERENCES

Barker, W. (1986) "On The Road to Recovery: RV Makers Rev up to a Strong Year." *Barrons* 24 (February):15, 28-30.

Bullaro, J., and C. Edginton (1986) *Commercial Leisure Services.* New York: Macmillan.

Cerullo, M., and P. Ewen (1982) "Having a Good Time: The American Family Goes Camping." *Radical America* 16 (1-2):13-43.

Chubb, M., and H. Chubb (1981) *One Third of Our Time: An Introduction To Recreation Behavior and Resources.* New York: Wiley and Sons.

Cordell, H., H. Legg, and R. McLellan (1979) "The Private Outdoor Estate." *The Third Nationwide Outdoor Recreation Plan.* Washington, D.C.: U.S. Government Printing Office.

Dulles, F. (1965) *A History of Recreation* 2d ed. New York: Appleton-Century-Crofts.

Glyptis, S., and C. Chambers (1982) "No Place Like Home." *Leisure Studies* 1(2):247-62.

Grover, R. (1987) "Theme Parks: This Slugfest Is No Fancy." *Business Week* (23 March):38.

Heritage Conservation and Recreation Service (1979) *The Third Nationwide Outdoor Recreation Plan.* Washington, D.C.: U.S. Government Printing Office.

Ibrahim, H. (1991) *Leisure and Society: A Comparative Approach.* Dubuque, IA: Wm C. Brown.

Jensen, C. (1985) *Outdoor Recreation in America.* Minneapolis, MN: Burgess Publishing.

Knudson, D. (1984) *Outdoor Recreation.* New York: Macmillan.

MacLean, J., J. Peterson, and D. Martin (1985) *Recreation and Leisure: The Changing Scene.* New York: Macmillan.

Ragatz, R.(1974) *Recreation Properties.* Springfield, VA: Council on Environmental Quality.

U.S. Bureau of the Census (1986) *Statistical Abstracts of the United States, 1987* (107th Edition). Washington, D.C.: U.S. Government Printing Office.

U.S. Bureau of the Census (1988) *Statistical Abstracts of the United States, 1989* (109th Edition). Washington, D.C.: U.S. Government Printing Office.

11 Outdoor Recreation in Other Countries

Many countries showed interest in providing natural resources for the enjoyment of their citizens at about the same time that the United States did. Two such countries are Canada and Australia, and their park systems are addressed in this chapter. The development of their outdoor pursuits differs from development in the European countries included in this chapter. Additionally, the system that prevailed in the USSR before its dissolution is discussed, since it followed economic, political, and social systems that were in contrast with the ones espoused by the United States, Canada, Australia, Great Britain, or France. The impact on recreation due to the political upheavals of the early 1990s in the former USSR and eastern Europe will be of interest to follow in the new political entities that have emerged. The strong trend to establish national parks and preserves in many Third World countries is explored in the last section.

OUTDOOR RECREATION IN CANADA

Canada is a vast country that extends from the Atlantic Ocean to the Pacific Ocean and from the Arctic to the northern border of the United States. Located so far north, Canada has harsh winters in addition to its diverse topographic features, which include the maritime provinces of Newfoundland, Prince Edward Island, New Brunswick, and Nova Scotia, followed by the densely forested regions of Quebec and Ontario that eventually turn into fertile lowlands. As one continues westward, one finds an industrial region, followed by the Canadian shield, a central depression of hard, old rocks. The vast prairie region of southern Manitoba, Saskatchewan, and Alberta is followed by the mountains and forests of British Columbia. North of this expansive land is the Arctic region, where most of the Eskimos live. The native Indians live across the southern tier, a strip of land 250 miles wide, north of the midwestern United States. The two European communities that settled in Canada—the French and the English—live in different areas across Canada.

It is assumed that the ancestors of both the Eskimos and Indians came by the northwestern route across the Bering Strait. Despite the hazards of life in the Arctic region, the Eskimos subsisted on whatever they were able to extract from their harsh surroundings. Eventually they established a life-style which was somewhat playful (Blanchard and Cheska 1985:142). Most of their playful activities were related to survival techniques. According to Johnson (1979:338), most, if not all, Eskimo activities that might have had an impact on leisure in general, and outdoor recreation in particular, disappeared with the advent of the white people.

But this was not the case with the activities of Native Indians. While many of their activities that had some bearing on outdoor recreation disappeared, some were adopted by the Europeans. An example would be Baggataway, which was practiced by the Algonquin and Iroquois people. Baggataway was a military scrimmage, infused with a religious ceremony designed to obtain the blessings of the gods, who would grant health and fertility on the victorious team. Baggataway's new name, lacrosse, was given to it by the French settlers because the implement used in the activity has a curved, netted neck which resembles a bishop's crosier (crooked staff).

But the Native Indian implement that was adopted by European settlers that had a real impact on outdoor recreation in Canada (and elsewhere) in later years was the canoe. According to Johnson (1979:337), 14 percent of all Canadians participate in the outdoor recreational activity of canoeing.

The first Europeans to settle in Canada around the mid 1500s were French adventurers who landed on the shores of Nova Scotia and Newfoundland. They ascended the St. Lawrence River to where Montreal now stands and on today's site of Quebec. They sold knives and hatchets to the natives and began the fur trade. The country of New France was founded in 1627, and it became engaged in a war with the Iroquois tribe a decade later. A quarter of a century after that New France was in war with England. Although there were periods of peace between New France and England, the struggle continued. By 1763 most of Canada became a British dominion. Nonetheless there are still two European communities in Canada, English and French.

French Canada According to Johnson (1979:342–45), the Catholic church played a decisive role in the lives of early French Canadians. Strict puritanical behavior was expected of every French Canadian, with gambling and dancing prohibited. Another important factor that affected recreational activities was the climate. Long winters required that the settler be physically fit in order to survive. Accordingly, the French Canadians developed proficiencies in outdoor activities which served as the nucleus of their recreational activities later. They became skillful at canoeing, hunting, and snowshoeing. During the severe Canadian winter they participated in races on the snow and frozen rivers. One of their favorite races was in the horse-drawn carriole (sleigh). Summer, on the other hand, was the time for hard work on the land.

After the building of a few French settlements in New France, three distinct life-styles evolved. The affluent, earlier settlers lived in the larger population centers and imitated the French aristocracy. Douville and Casanova (1967:193) suggest that during their lavish ceremonies and elaborate banquets, one could easily have imagined oneself breathing the atmosphere of Versailles rather than the air of Quebec.

The more typical French Canadian lived in the outlying settlements and depended on kin and neighbors to extract a livelihood. Life in the linear villages along the St. Lawrence had none of the pomp of life in the larger settlements. The inhabitants lived according to what the church and the seigneur allowed or disallowed. Recreational activities revolved around their close-knit communities.

A third type of a French Canadian was the *Coureur de Bois,* the lover of nature who imitated the ways of the natives. These people not only abandoned European values, they adopted the habits, customs, and recreational activities of the native people. They lived in the wilderness and removed themselves from the moral dictates of the settled French and their authority.

English Canada The same hard conditions faced English Canadians, and the settlers had to rely on communal activities to get certain tasks done. This cooperative spirit led to the rise of the bee, a group working together to harvest, raise a barn, and the like. Eventually the bee included a social element in which the host supplied food, drink, and amusement. The drink was usually whiskey, and the amusement included a hoe-down and contests. The bee as a way of accomplishing a communal task eventually died out when the play element dominated the work element.

English villages of Canada began to provide for recreational outlet through the inn and the tavern, which were patterned after the English pub. Traveler and resident alike began to participate in the infamous blood sports, which were also seen in Great Britain: cockfighting, bear and bull baiting, and dogfighting.

Imitation of the British extended to the upper class of English Canada. In their attempts to emulate the English aristocracy of the old country, the life-style of the wealthy in the New World was filled with organized and informal outdoor activities. They became "fond of horse racing, and field sports, fishing and sailing in the summer, and skating and carrioling in the winter . . ." (Guillet 1933:323).

According to Baker (1982:160), curling was introduced to Canada by Scottish immigrants as early as 1807. An annual festivity was held called bonspiels, which featured the sliding of a round, flattened stone on a frozen lake. In the meantime ice hockey was being practiced by the English troops stationed in Kingston in 1855. A few years earlier, in 1842, some of the English settlers began to compete with the natives in their Baggataway. Soon a set of rules and standards for fields and equipment were drawn, and the game was renamed lacrosse by the Europeans.

Settlement of western and northern Canada by Europeans was very slow. Once it started, a true mix of people came to live in compact communities, each having its own traditions, amusements, and recreational activities. In the North particularly, communities were far apart.

At the end of the 7-year war in Europe in the 1750s, most of Canada was ceded to Great Britain. Quebec was to retain a French civil law to protect the position of the Catholic church. A hundred years later, the Dominion of Canada came into being on July 1, 1867. At that time the early dominance of garrison towns came to an end and the strong class distinction in both French and English Canada began to break down. Canada was turning into a modern industrial society. Canadians began to seek other forms of recreational activities, especially the mechanized forms of bicycling and motoring. The negative reaction of the conservatives to such activities was swift, and the federal government's Lord's Day Act of 1906 was meant to keep the purity of the Sabbath. But in contrast, some civic-minded organizations were aware of the need for, and the value of, leisure pursuits, particularly among the young.

Canadians had at that time a reasonable acreage of dedicated open space, but it was not necessarily play space. In fact, as early as 1859, the Toronto City Council had regarded parks as "breathing spaces where citizens might stroll, drive or sit to enjoy the open air" (McFarland 1970:14). Other cities had their designated open spaces. In a manner not dissimilar to what occurred in its neighboring country, the United States, three levels of government became involved in outdoor recreation in Canada, as described in the following sections.

The Angel Wing Glacier found on Mount Edith Cavell in Alberta, Canada, is one of many protected by national parks in Canada.

The Cabot Trail along the coast of Nova Scotia is one of the most scenic drives in North America.

Role of the Federal Government

Prior to the 1900s, the role of the federal government in outdoor pursuits was limited to the provision of open space. In the meantime some cities were involved in providing open space. A century later, as will be shown, many federal agencies have direct impact on the recreational activities of Canadians, and some agencies have indirect influences.

One of the federal agencies that has direct impact on leisure pursuits in Canada is the Ministry of National Health, which oversees fitness and amateur sports. One of the ministry's two departments has a direct impact on leisure pursuits, and it is called Recreation Canada. The other section, Sport Canada, promotes national and international competition in the country. Recreation Canada is decentralized in that it provides funds and offers assistance to organizations in the provinces. Demonstration projects are given wherever needed, and attention is directed to the recreation needs of special populations. Recreation Canada encourages businesses and industries to provide all forms of recreation, including outdoor pursuits, for their employees.

Environment Canada-Parks, an agency of the Ministry of Indian and Northern Affairs, also has a direct impact on outdoor recreation. Environment Canada-Parks has three branches, the National Parks Branch, the National Historic Parks and Sites Branch, and the Policy and Research Branch. The first branch oversees Canada's twenty-eight national parks (see Figure 11.1), which cover 50,000 square miles or close to 32 million acres, making Canada's national parks one of the largest park systems in the world. These are areas that have significant scenic, geologic, geographical, and biological elements that are to be preserved for future generations. There are five huge national parks in Canada which amount to 82 percent of the total acreage of Canada's national park system: Wood Buffalo, Kluane, Jasper, Glacier, and Banff, totalling over 26 million acres. Small units constitute the remaining 6 million acres in the system. According to Chubb and Chubb (1981:524), these smaller units have been established primarily because of their historical significance. There are over 75 such sites that are operated like parks.

Almost half of Canada's national parks are located in the prairie provinces of Alberta, Manitoba, and Saskatchewan. Twenty percent of park lands are in the far west in British Columbia and the Yukon Territory, and 20 percent more are in the Northwest Territory. The four Atlantic

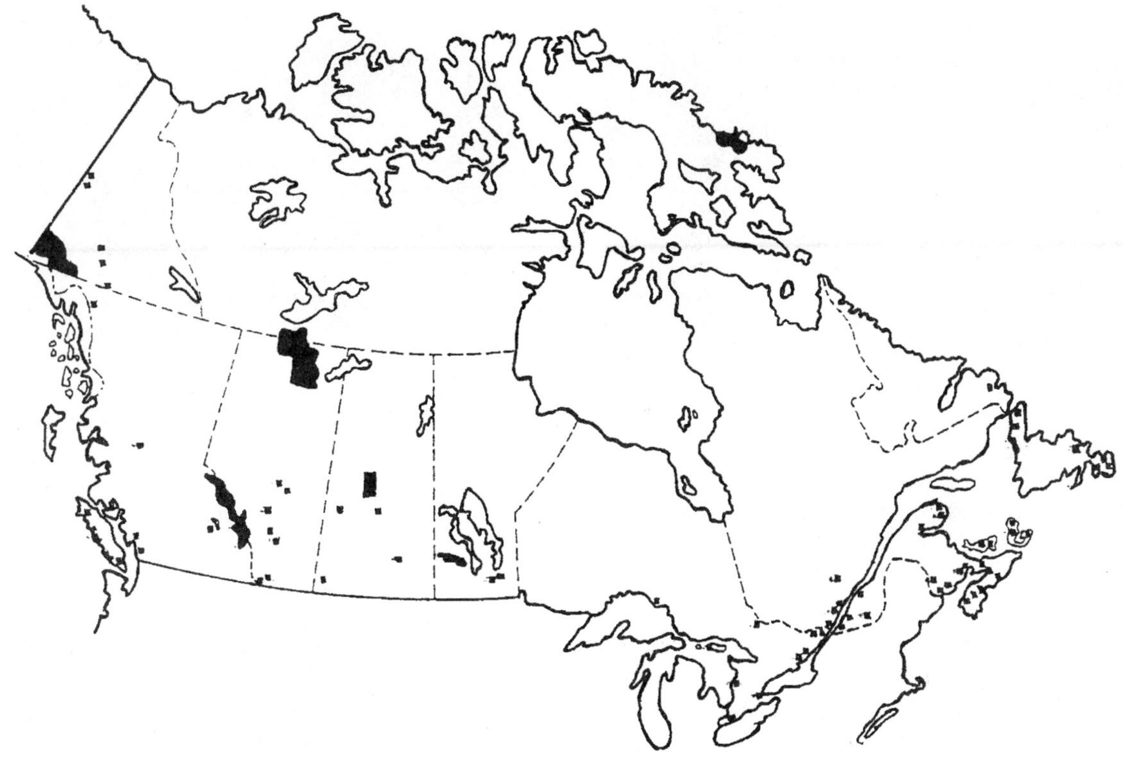

FIGURE 11.1 National parks of Canada.

provinces of New Brunswick, Newfoundland, Nova Scotia, and Prince Edward Island contain 3.2 percent of Canada's national parks, leaving populated Ontario and Quebec with a mere 2 percent of the system's land (Chubb and Chubb 1981:526). Fortunately these two provinces are able to compensate for the lack of federal recreation resources because of the nature of the role of the provinces.

Role of Provincial Government

There are ten provinces in Canada, and each has its own government. Ten percent of Canadians, or 2.5 million people, live in the four Atlantic provinces, New Brunswick, Newfoundland, Nova Scotia, and Prince Edward Island. Further west, 25 percent of Canadians live in Quebec and 30 percent live in Ontario. The prairie provinces west of Ontario have a population that lives in a wedge which broadens westward. This means that most of Canada's national parks are in the least populated areas. This makes the role of the provincial government, particularly in the East, an important one when it comes to outdoor recreation offerings.

Unlike the situation in each state in the United States, the provincial government is less dependent on the federal government where land and/or open space are concerned. Unsettled public land in Canada, known as the Crown lands, are under the control of the provinces. Individual U.S. states do not control public land, and their involvement in outdoor recreation has been somewhat limited by this factor. In Canada,

Ontario, Canada's Niagara Falls ranks as a natural wonder of the world. On March 30, 1885, the Ontario legislature passed the Niagara Falls Park Act establishing Ontario's first Provincial Parkland. The Queen Victoria Niagara Falls Park Act in 1887 officially established the Niagara Parks Commission, and in May of 1888 the park was officially opened to the public.

Nautical scenes like this one in Peggy's Cove, Nova Scotia, are the rewards for the many cyclists who tour through the province.

the provinces have found that it is easy, politically and financially, to allocate large pieces of land as parks and forests. Following are examples of provincial outdoor resources in Canada.

Ontario Queen Victoria Park in Ontario is part of the Niagara Parks System, which extends for 32 miles between Lake Erie and Lake Ontario. This is a chain of parks along the Niagara River with views over Niagara Falls and adjacent natural vistas. The facilities in the chain include picnic areas, playing fields, horticulture displays, and amphitheaters.

The Ontario park system originated with a single park in 1893, Algonquin Provincial Park. Other parks were added during the next half century until the Provincial Parks Act of 1954 officially made Ontario's system the largest provincial park system in Canada. The system totals nearly 10 million acres with an annual attendance of over 11 million visitors, of which one-fourth are for overnight camping (Ibrahim 1991:156). The system consists of 130 units that include 20,000 campsites, 73 miles of beaches, 3000 miles of canoe routes, and 1000 miles of trails. Ontario Parks, which constitutes 5 percent of the province's land, is administered by the Ministry of Natural Resources, which controls all open space in Ontario, a 230-million-acre estate. Most of Ontario's parks are either surrounded by or are adjacent to Crown lands, which makes it very easy to expand the system.

The Ministry of Natural Resources of Ontario uses a five-class system of parks, as follows:

1. Primitive parks, which are large undeveloped areas.
2. Nature reserves, which feature distinctive land forms or ecosystems.
3. Natural environment parks, which have outstanding recreational landscapes.
4. Recreation parks, which offer a wide range of activities.
5. Wild rivers, which are undeveloped rivers.

The Ministry of Natural Resources of Ontario also administers the province's forests. Chubb and Chubb estimate that 75 million recreation occasions take place in these forests each year (1981:501). Visits to vacation cottages represent

33 percent of these occasions, camping represents 21 percent, fishing 15 percent, swimming 8 percent, boating 6 percent, hiking 6 percent, snowmobiling 6 percent, hunting 4 percent, and canoeing 2 percent.

British Columbia This province's park system began with the Stratcona Park on Vancouver Island in 1911. Today the park system is administered by the Park Branch of the province's Department of Recreation and Conservation. The park acreage is close to 8.5 million acres, with one park, Tweedsmuir, representing 7 percent of the total. Tweedsmuir is Canada's largest provincial park and is dominated by spectacular Rainbow Mountain (Knudson 1984:203). The British Columbia Park Act classifies its parks into the following six groups:

Class A:	Preserves offering outstanding features.
Class B:	Parks providing public outdoor recreation opportunities.
Class C:	Locally controlled parks.
Class D:	Public Recreation Areas.
Class E:	Wilderness conservancy.
Class F:	Nature conservancy.

While class A parks are the most numerous, comprising two-thirds of the system, class B parks are fewer yet larger in size. The locally controlled parks in British Columbia are smaller in size (Chubb and Chubb 1981:493).

Saskatchewan The Saskatchewan Department of Culture and Youth provides grants of up to 50 percent of cost to municipalities to help in the development of recreational facilities and programs. Fieldhouses and community centers as well as skating and curling rinks have been developed under this program in this prairie province. The department also encourages heritage and historic conservation and interpretation. Some of these activities have direct bearing on the pursuit of outdoor activities (Ibrahim 1991:157).

Quebec According to Knudson (1984:202), the Quebec provincial park system is larger than the entire national park complex, having 52,000 square miles of parks. Most of Quebec parks are in the Laurentian Mountains and contain hundreds of lakes, many miles of fishing streams, elaborate skiing facilities, and numerous holiday resorts. Quebec still owns huge areas classified as Crown lands which are adjacent to or surrounding its provincial parks.

Role of Municipalities

Local self-government was slow in developing in Canada due to the dominance of the provincial government, particularly in New Brunswick, Nova Scotia, Quebec, and Ontario. Nonetheless the establishment of municipal parks began in earnest with the beginning of the settlements. For instance, as early as 1763 Halifax Commons was granted to the city. Montreal had its first public square in 1821, and Hamilton built its Gore Park in 1852. As the provinces began to enact enabling laws empowering their municipalities to build parks, set procedures for acquisition of land, and establish standards for the management of natural resources, Montreal established its Mount Royal Park in 1860. Twenty years later, Vancouver built Stanley, London-Victoria, and Saint John-Rockwood parks.

According to McFarland (1970:37), the Canadian citizenry became aware in the late 1800s of the importance of recreation in their life-style and the role that natural resources could play in the pursuits of outdoor activities. Voices were raised proclaiming the importance of providing recreational opportunities, particularly in urban slums where poor families lived as early as the 1860s. A resolution passed by the National Council of Women spoke to this very point.

In a manner not dissimilar to what happened in the United States, concern among social reformers led to the formation of a playground association in 1914. This led to the establishment of municipal park boards in the large cities of the eastern provinces. Another development by

TABLE 11.1 Percentage of Canadians 18 Years and Over Participating in Selected Recreation Activities

Activity	1967	1969	1972	1976
Tent camping	13	12	19	19
Trailer camping	6	6	10	12
Camping with pick-up truck	—	2	4	9
Swimming (non-pool)	—	—	—	42
Canoeing	5	8	10	14
Bicycling	—	13	19	28
Walking or hiking	13	37	38	54
Wilderness tripping	—	—	—	17
Cross-country skiing	—	—	2	10
Driving for pleasure	—	67	63	66
Sightseeing from vehicle	—	—	37	49
Picnicking	40	54	52	57
Canal use				
Commercial boat	—	—	2	5
Private boat	—	—	6	9
Non-boating	—	—	8	12
Visiting historic sites	16	37	35	43
Visiting national parks (during past 12 months)	13	—	22	29

Source: R. Johnson, "Leisure in Canada" in *Leisure: Emergence and Expansion,* H. Ibrahim and J. Shivers, editors (Los Alamitos, CA, 1979), 350. (Reprinted with permission from Hwong Publishing.)

civic-minded individuals in the prairie and western provinces led to the establishment of community leagues which promoted playgrounds and parks alongside community centers and swimming pools. The community league is a merger of more than one civic organization, each of which is concerned with the development of the local community (Kraus 1984:127).

Outdoor Pursuits of Canadians

Canada is well endowed in natural resources, and its citizens enjoy outdoor recreational activities. This is reflected in the data shown in Table 11.1.

The data in Table 11.1 show that driving for pleasure was the most pursued outdoor activity for the period studied, 1967–1976. Picnicking and hiking followed, and hiking showed an increase from 13 percent participation by persons over 18 years of age in 1967 to 54 percent by 1976. Visiting historical sites increased 400 percent in the same 9-year period. Attendance at national parks continued to increase into the mid 1980s, as shown in Figure 11.2. Visitations to national parks by regions in 1984 are shown in Figure 11.3. The figure shows that the western region is the most popular (64 percent), followed by the Ontario region (7 percent) and the Quebec region (3 percent).

While it is hard to define what percentage of tourism actually involves outdoor activities, tourism to and from Canada is on the increase. Many U.S. citizens take trips to Canada for the enjoyment of its natural resources as well as other attractions. Canada accounts for the second-largest share of Americans traveling abroad, with 18 percent in 1986 in comparison to 22 percent of Americans traveling to Mexico and 8 percent to Great Britain. Tourism in Canada is an important economic factor in the reduction of deficits in travel accounts. *Statistics Canada* (1986: vii) shows that 40.4 million trips

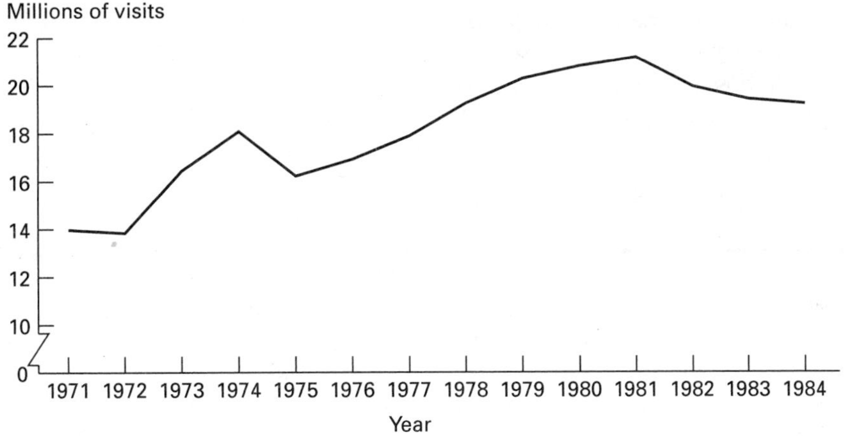

FIGURE 11.2 National park attendance, Canada, 1971–1984.

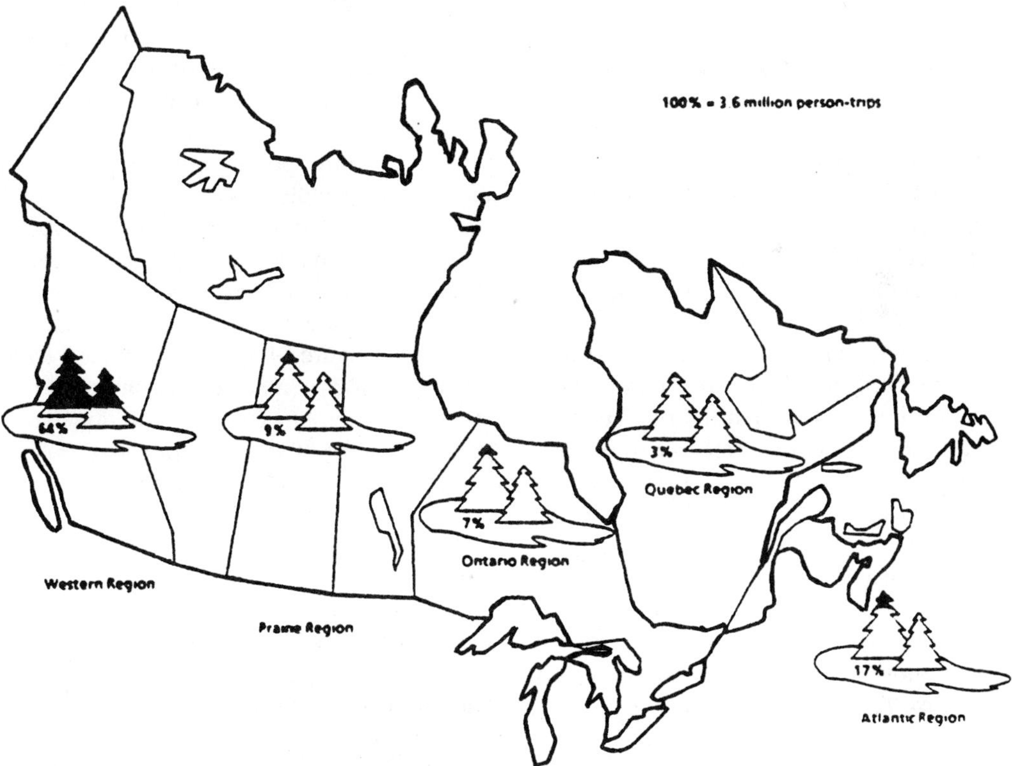

FIGURE 11.3 Visitation to national parks by Parks Canada regions, 1984.

were taken by Canadians abroad and 40.5 million trips by Americans and others were made to Canada. A trip of 24 hours or more conforms to the international definition that is used in tourism statistics.

OUTDOOR RECREATION IN GREAT BRITAIN

The leisure pursuits of Britons originated in two sources. The first is the rituals and traditions inherited from the Saxons and the Normans. The other source is the life-style of British nobility. Strutt (1970) wrote of the great parades of the Saxons and the tournaments of the Normans. His work was first published in 1801 and points out that in the pre-Reformation days, feasts and frolics were associated with religious events. Some of the activities of the commoners, which were needed for survival, became pastimes of the rich. Hunting is a good example: the masses were allowed to hunt for rabbit and vermin, but the wealthy were allowed the prizes such as fox and bear. Despite their attempts to protect their vast estates from the encroachment of the commoners, members of the aristocracy were eventually forced to share their game with the masses.

The commoners in Britain were by no means serfs, like the poor people on the continent. They were free men and women, although poor. They had a reasonable sense of freedom from the dominance of an elite class, which may have been a factor in the growth of what is now called blood sports such as cockthrowing, which consisted of throwing missiles at a tethered cock until it died. Or soccer, which was in actuality a battle of 1,000 villagers pitted against another 1,000 from another village. The melee took place on Shrove Tuesday, supposedly a religious holy day.

The commoners' activities led to severe criticism by the clergy, who failed to cause reform in the Britons' leisure behavior at that time. It was the Industrial Revolution that eventually led to change. Emphasis on production ended the riotous and cruel blood sport of the countryside, since most of the men were lured to the city in search of their fortunes. The Industrial Revolution created many changes, including a drastic reduction in the number of holy days, thus days off.

In the nineteenth century a revolution took place in the leisure habits in Great Britain. A clear distinction between work and leisure was obvious, as free time was regularized into weekly and annual blocks. Discussions on the need for constructive use of free time took place and involved not only men of the cloth, but also social reformers.

Changes were also taking place in the social structure among the residents of the British Isles. A middle class was on the rise, a class that was bent on imitating the aristocracy, which traditionally lived in the country and enjoyed open space. Rich gentlemen started what Lowerson and Myerscough call "Consumer Town" resorts which led to the popularization of seaside holidays for the middle class. A train excursion was organized on Easter day of 1844 that took the passengers from London to the seaside resort of Brighton. It created great popular excitement (1977:32). Seaside trips, which began in the 1840s (see Figure 11.4), have become a national institution—75 percent of British vacations are spent this way. "In fact, the traditional and ritualistic aspects of the trip appears to be an essential ingredient for most of the participants," write Chubb and Chubb (1981:129).

Interest in sport also grew in the Victorian era, when it was believed that sport was the best method of converting people from destructive leisure habits such as drinking and gambling. Alcoholic consumption continued to go hand in hand with sport, however, as had happened in the previous century. The public house, or pub, was the center of the social lives of the poor. Pubs provided amusement, warmth, and lavatories. Some pubs became the "easies," the precursors of the music hall.

NORTH EASTERN RAILWAY

NIDDERDALE FEAST.

CHEAP EXCURSION TO THE SEA-SIDE.

On TUESDAY, Sept. 20th, 1870,

A Special Train will leave PATELEY BRIDGE, and Stations as under, for

SCARBRO

LEAVE	A.M.
Pateley Bridge	6 0
Dacre Banks	6 8
Darley	6 12
Birstwith	6 17
Hampsthwaite	6 21
Ripley	6 30
Starbeck	6 40
Knaresbro'	6 50

FARE THERE AND BACK.
COVERED CARRIAGES.

Children under Twelve Years of Age, Half-fare.

The Return Train will leave Scarbro' at 5.30 p.m. same day.

NO LUGGAGE ALLOWED.

☞ The Tickets are only available for Scarbro' in going, and for the Stations at which they were issued on return.

As only a limited number of Carriages can be allotted to this Train, the following Regulations will be strictly observed, in order, as far as possible, to secure the comfort of the public, and to avoid delay:—The number of Tickets supplied for issue will only be equal to the amount of Carriage accommodation, and no persons except holders of Tickets for this Train will be permitted to travel by it, *and any person attempting to travel without a Ticket will be charged the full ordinary fare both ways. The Tickets are at the Stations ready for issue;* and persons who intend to travel by this Train must apply early enough to enable the Station Clerks to procure any additional Tickets that may be required.

York, August, 1870. W. O'BRIEN, General Manager.

EDWARD BAINES AND SONS, GENERAL PRINTERS, LEEDS.

North Eastern Railway excursion handbill, 1870.

FIGURE 11.4 North Eastern Railway excursion handbill, 1870.

Punting along the Cam River in Cambridge, England, is a favorite outdoor pastime of students at the university.

Backpacking in England along the Cotswold Way is a favorite activity. This 97.5-mile trail follows the top of a steep escarpment and has beautiful views.

Outdoor Pursuits

Despite the sudden expansion in leisure pursuits of Britons at the beginning of the twentieth century, outdoor activities were not dominant among activities pursued. Like other European countries, and unlike Canada or the United States, Great Britain was unable to establish publicly owned parks. Its first national park was established in 1950. In fact the parks shown in Figure 11.5 are still predominantly privately owned. The first attempt at providing outdoor recreation through legislation took place in 1844 when a bill was introduced in Parliament to permit public access to open land. During World War II a similar bill was introduced, but it was not till 1949 that the National Parks and Access to the Countryside Act was passed. A National Parks Commission was set up under the Minister of Housing and Local Government and was charged with the duty of ". . . exercising the function conferred on them by the following provisions of this Act—a) for the preservation and enhancement of natural beauty in England and Wales, and particularly in the areas designated under the Act as National Parks or as Areas of Outstanding Natural Beauty; b) for encouraging the provision or improvement, for persons resorting to National Parks, of facilities for the

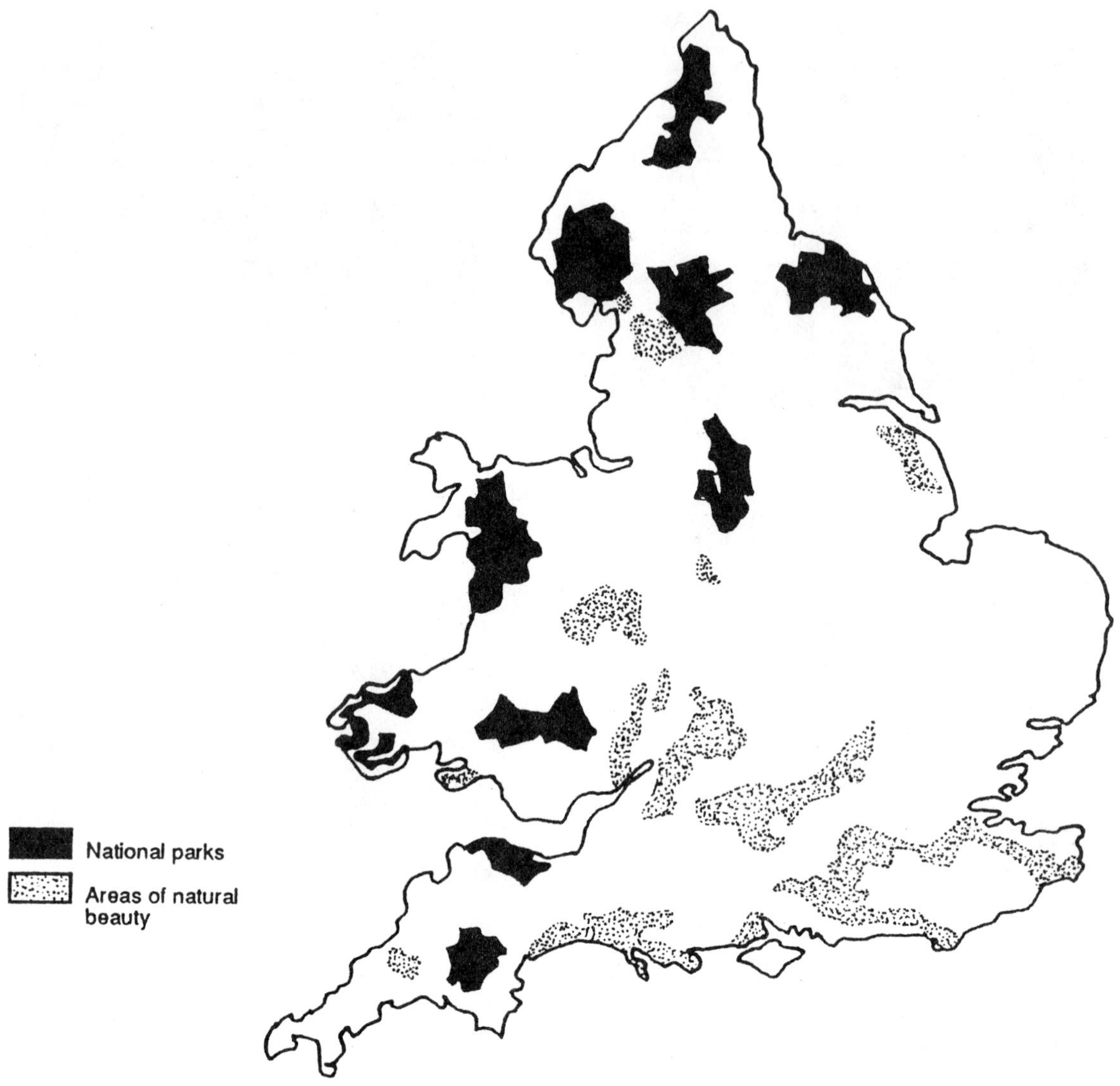

FIGURE 11.5 National resources in England and Wales.

enjoyment thereof and for the enjoyment of the opportunities for open air recreation and study of nature afforded thereby . . ." (Section 1, National Parks and Access to the Countryside Act, 1949).

According to Chubb and Chubb (1981:527), national parks represent one-tenth of the land in England and Wales. Most of them are more or less pastures which were originally hardwood forests. Within these areas are state forests designated for outdoor activities such as pleasure driving, walking, picnicking, fishing, camping, and orienteering. The National Parks Commission's name has changed to Countryside Commission, but it still performs the same functions (see Figures 11.6 and 11.7).

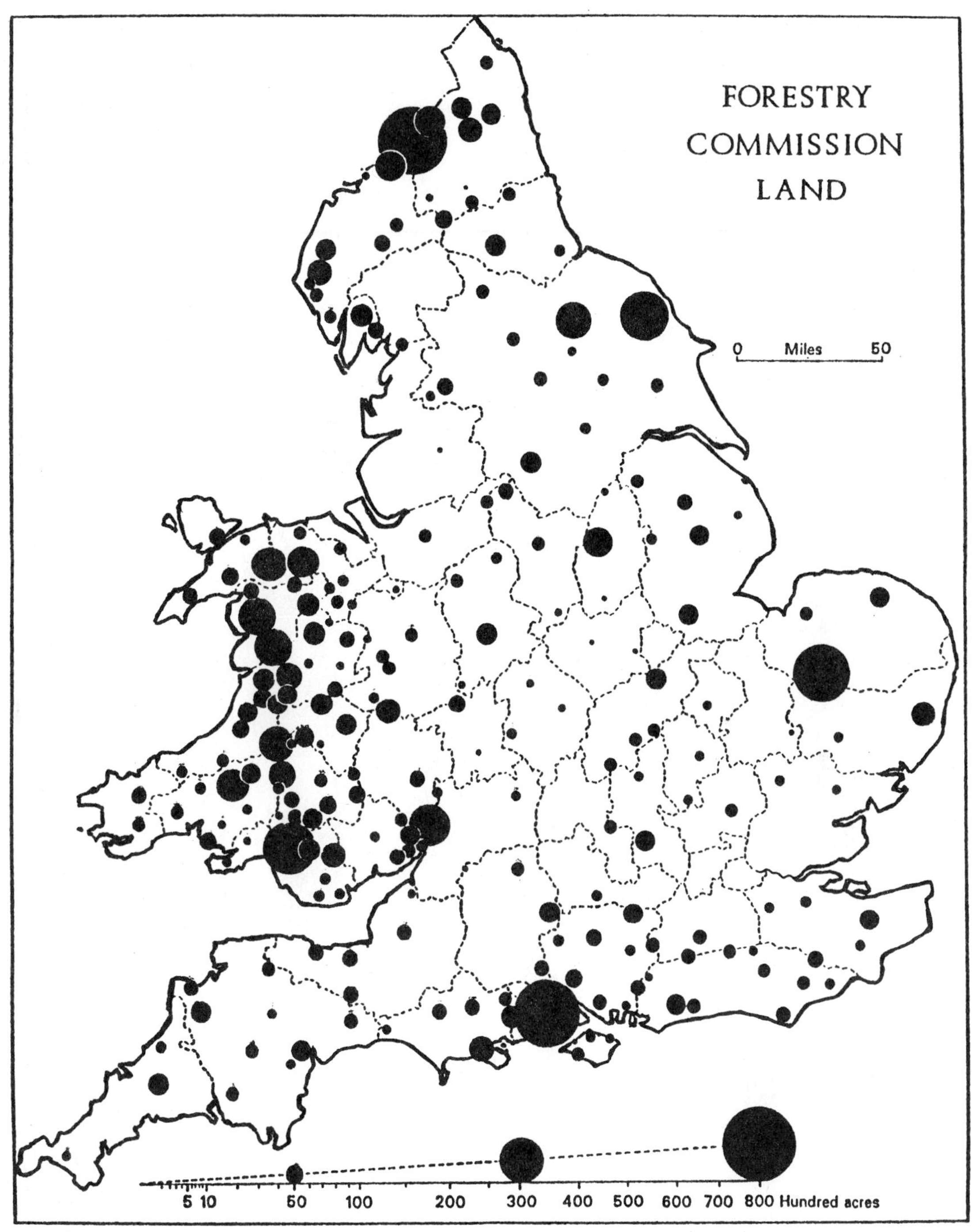

FIGURE 11.6 Forestry Commission land.

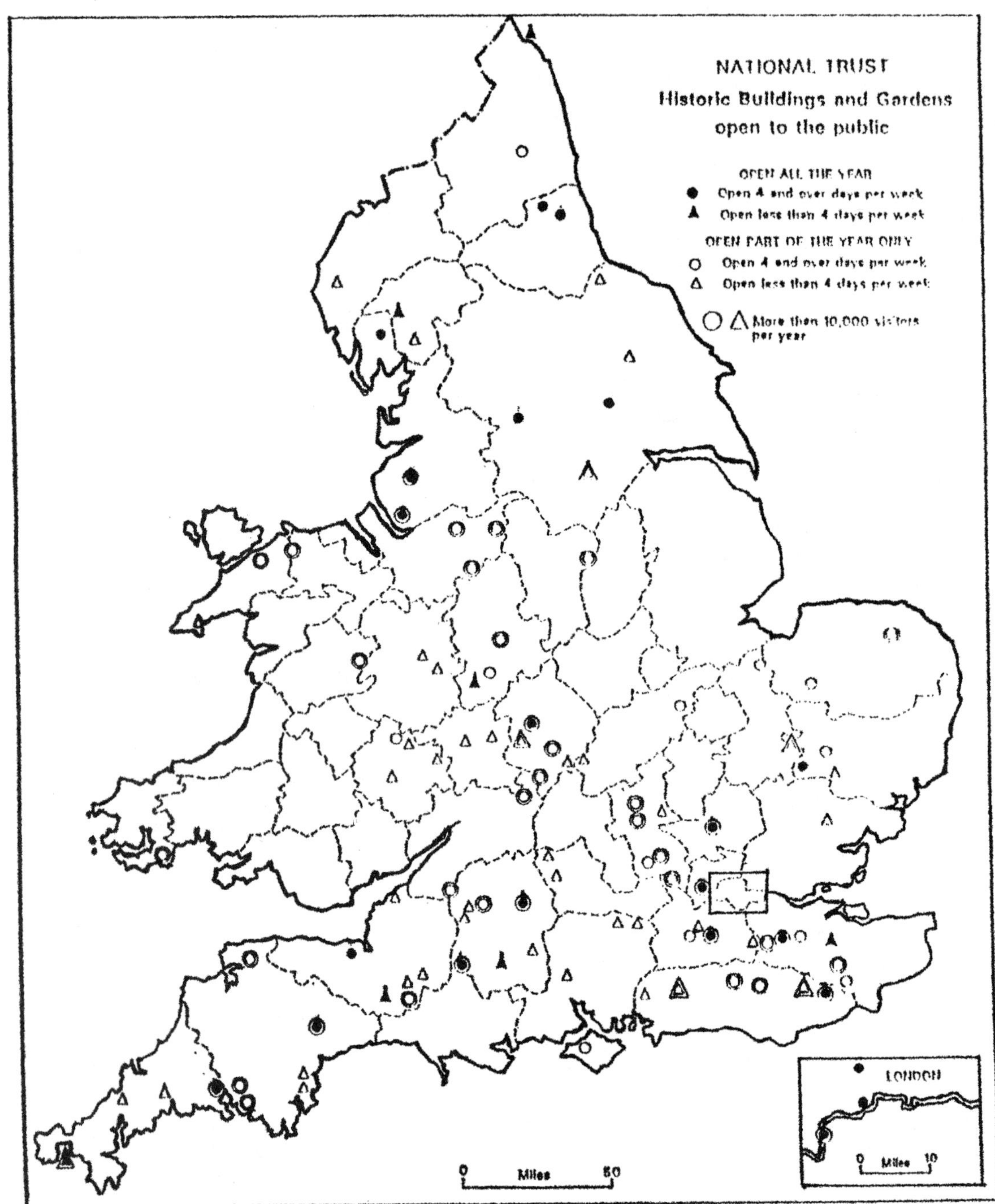

FIGURE 11.7 Properties owned by the National Trust.

Three surveys were conducted by the government's Office of Population Census and Surveys, in 1973, 1977, and 1980, which included queries about leisure activities. The General Household Survey (GHS) was administered on 20,000 persons aged 16 and over. Veal (1984) analyzed the data and concluded that walking for pleasure is dominant in outdoor pursuits, and that darts and snooker/billiards, the usual English pub pastimes, are dominant among indoor activities.

Tourism is also very popular among Britons; the data of the GHS reveal that 17 percent of the sample visited historical buildings in the 4 weeks before the interview took place. Tourism would be the second most popular out-of-the-home or out-of-the-park activity after walking for pleasure (17 percent and 21 percent, respectively).

OUTDOOR RECREATION IN FRANCE

Although the concept of a public garden may be traced back to Mesopotamia's Hanging Gardens of Babylon, Rome added to the concept a millennium later by providing gardens around villas. The Persians developed the concept of *paradeisos,* from which the word paradise was derived. The Greeks added a term to describe the concept of open space, *agora,* but it was the Normans who provided the *park,* the unruffled hunting estate which remained out-of-bounds to the commoners until recently. While the concept of a "natural" park developed in the British Isles, the preference was for a manicured garden on the continent, particularly in the estates of the French aristocracy.

Although the French aristocracy may be credited with the development of manicured gardens such as the Tuileries and Versailles, it was the Italian aristocracy that first opened up its private estates for the commoners to enjoy. The French aristocracy built grounds for themselves that are characterized by topiary work, aviaries, and fish ponds. Grand mansions were built for the owners' enjoyment. For instance, in Versailles, the terrace of the main building was adorned with ornamental basins, statues, and vases. The garden included a grand canal 200 feet wide and a mile long, complete with gondolas. The artificial lake was filled with waterfowl and was connected to a waterfall.

Initially these pleasure gardens were limited to the aristocracy, which eventually succumbed to public pressure and opened the gardens to the public. Later, open space along the ramparts of the Seine in Paris was provided for Parisian citizens. Today the French people enjoy these resources for their outdoor pursuits.

Among the many leisure pursuits that the French enjoy is traveling. It is reported that 77 percent of Paris residents take a vacation; 45 percent of vacationers choose to visit the countryside, 25 percent the sea, and 15 percent the mountains. The remaining 15 percent stay at home for lack of means (Ibrahim 1991:142). The study conducted by Szalai et al. (1972) shows the French sample spending 9.9 percent of its free time in outdoor activities compared to 16 percent for the American sample and 13.3 percent for the Russian sample.

OUTDOOR RECREATION IN THE CIS

The USSR, until recently a group of republics ruled by traditional communism, is undergoing rapid political change. Today eleven of the original fifteen republics are struggling to remain together as the Commonwealth of Independent States (CIS). Outdoor recreational programs will probably reflect the impact of these political upheavals to some extent. To understand the full ramifications of these changes it is necessary to look at outdoor recreation as it existed at the time the USSR was composed of fifteen republics ruled by communism.

Under communism, the former USSR treated leisure pursuits as important elements in increasing the productivity of labor, and the control over free time was greater than what was seen under other systems. Treated from an

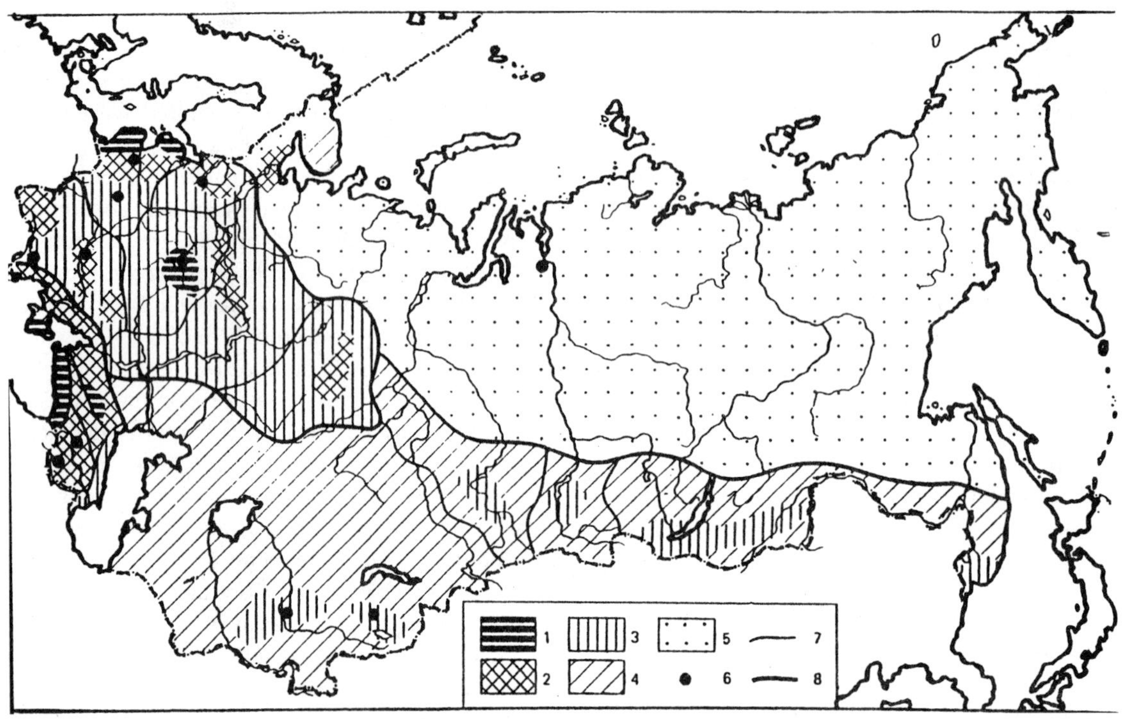

FIGURE 11.8 Recreational zoning of the CIS (Commonwealth of Independent States). Regions and localizations with the density of institutions: 1—very high; 2—high; 3—average; 4—low; 5—very low; 6—excursion centers; 7—boundaries of recreational regions; 8—boundaries of recreational zones.

economic point of view, free time was used for the regeneration of the labor force. In a study of the recreational geography of the USSR which was translated to English, the original editors emphasized the role of health resorts in maintaining or increasing the productivity of the labor force (Preobrazhensky and Krivosheyev: 1982).

The authors divided the country into five recreational zones based on the density of the recreational offerings and facilities (see Figure 11.8). These five zones were in turn divided into twenty regions. The recreational facilities range from a very high concentration (Zone 1), to high concentration (Zone 2), to average concentration (Zone 3), to low concentration (Zone 4). Zone 5 has hardly any facilities at all.

The classification of land under communism did not include land for recreation. Nature preserves, as a class, were strictly scientific research areas sometimes used for recreation. A new addition to these areas, Moose Island National Park, is now 5 years old. According to Gorokhov and Vishneveskaya (1988) the founding of Moose Island National Park coincided with the beginning of *perestroika* and *glasnost.* Although there were attempts to make Moose Island a national park as early as 1912, World War II wrecked the plan. It is by no means the only national park in the USSR: the first one was established in Estonia in 1971 and is called Lahemaa National Park. The exciting thing about Moose Island is its proximity to Moscow, a city of 10 million people.

TABLE 11.2 Relative importance of several nonwork-time activities in large cities in European parts of the USSR, various years (hours per week)

	1923–24	1936	1963	1965–68	1967–70
1. Housework and work in the private plot (excluding the care of children)	35.0	24.0	21.2	19.5	18.5
2. Daily cultural life					
(a) leisure, including	6.7	5.5	12.4	16.0	17.3
Reading books and magazines	2.1	1.0	2.3	2.1	3.3
Reading newspapers	2.9	1.8	1.4	1.6	2.5
TV and radio	-	1.0	5.1	6.2	7.5
Movies, theater and other public performances	0.6	0.7	0.9	1.3	1.3
(b) studying		.0	.6	.0	.3
(c) amateur talent activities and other kinds of nonprofessional creative works	1.1	-	0.1	0.8	0.4
3. Physical culture (i.e., education), sports, hunting and fishing, going to the country	0.2	0.3	0.7	0.7	1.6
4. Meeting with friends, guests, and dances	6.2	7.6	5.8	5.2	5.8
5. Occupied with children	5.6	4.3	3.0	5.0	3.1
Caring for children	5.0	-	1.9	2.9	1.5
Upbringing of children	0.6	-	1.1	3.0	1.6

Source: W. Moskoff, *Labour and Leisure in the Soviet Union* (New York: St. Martin's Press, 1984), 83. (Reprinted with permission.)

Outdoor Pursuits

The average work week decreased gradually in the former Soviet Union, from 58.5 hours before World War II to 47.8 hours in 1955 to 41.8 hours in 1965, to 39.4 hours in 1990 (Ibrahim 1991:113). But the great gain was in the 2-day weekend. Time budget studies showed that the average Soviet citizen spent more time on the same leisure activities he or she enjoyed before the advent of the 2-day weekend: they watched more television, read more books and magazines, and went to the movies more frequently. Weekends away from home were limited by the lack of accommodations, the availability of which was controlled by the government. This limited availability persisted despite the fact that not only weekend time but vacation time also increased in the Soviet Union (Table 11.2).

Although vacations were eliminated altogether during World War II, the policy of giving a 2-week vacation after 6 months of employment was resumed after the war. In 1955 a 1-month minimum vacation was granted to workers aged 16–18. The 2-week vacation for older workers was increased to 3 weeks. Scientific researchers and educators have up to 48 days of vacation.

Vacations can be spent in a state-run facility or a rented *dacha,* or country cottage. To do the former, the worker must be a member of a group granted permission to use the state-run facility. These are houses of rest, sanitoria, or pensions. Workers on vacation are allowed into houses of rest. Pensions are, to some extent, similar to the houses of rest with a little more freedom on the part of the resident. A sanatorium is used for workers referred by medical professionals who need treatment and therapy.

TABLE 11.3 Sixteen recreational activities by order of number of participants, selected years between 1940 and 1970, in the USSR

Sport	1940	1945	1955	1960	1965	1970
1. Athletics	3	3	1	1	1	1
2. Tourism	14	18	14	11	4	2
3. Volleyball	5	6	2	3	2	3
4. Skiing	2	1	3	2	3	4
5. Pistol shooting	6	7	5	6	5	5
6. Football	7	9	7	8	7	6
7. Basketball	11	12	9	7	8	7
8. Chess	1	2	4	4	6	8
9. Draughts	–	4	6	5	9	9
10. Fishing	–	–	–	–	–	10
11. Table tennis	–	–	12	10	10	11
12. Shooting	–	–	–	–	–	12
13. Swimming	8	8	11	13	11	13
14. Cycling	9	10	10	12	12	14
15. Gymnastics	4	8	8	9	13	15
16. Speed skating	10	13	13	14	14	16

Source: J. Riordan, "Leisure, the State and the Individual in the USSR," *Leisure Studies* 1(1):89. Reprinted with permission.

Dachas were important in citizen life and will probably continue to be popular in the new system. Their popularity stems from the fact that they allow an extended family to stay together. Although few of them exist, the demand for the *dachas* is so strong that private ownership was allowed under the previous strict socialistic period. There are also individual enterprises that own and operate some of the *dachas.*

Changes in the leisure patterns of citizens over the years are shown in Table 11.3. Outdoor sports such as hunting, fishing, and hiking increased eightfold from the 1940s to the 1970s. Table 11.3 shows that tourism moved from the fourteenth rank of recreational activities in 1940 to the second position among the same sixteen activities in 1970.

Preobrazhensky and Krivosheyev (1982:208) recognized the dilemma of the Soviet citizen when it came to recreational offerings. The authors point out the discrepancy between the changing patterns of recreational activities and existing facilities. For instance, hiking and mountaineering were becoming the most popular recreational activities in the USSR, yet there were not enough facilities for the recreationists. The need for the availability of more natural resources is evident in the poll that was cited by these two authors. Persons between the ages of 16 and 60 indicated that they prefer to spend their vacations in forests (35 percent), by a river or lake (30 percent), by the sea (28 percent), in the mountains (5 percent), or near a mineral spring (2 percent). On the other hand, Shaw (1980) believes that as long as there is central control of land and means of production, easy solutions to problems and/or good planning in recreation will not be found. Riordan (1982:74) believes that the Soviet leaders had opted for the following, which was a hindrance to any improvement on the leisure scene:

1. The organization of working people in their leisure time to the maximum possible extent within the framework of a tidy hierarchical and functional structure.

2. The cultivation of competitive activities, as in sports (a leisure-time analog of the competition between people at work designed to raise work tempos), and material rewards for victors, which more effectively improve people's readiness for work and pretrain soldiers for the Soviet nation state.
3. Using leisure, specifically, as a means of obtaining a fit, obedient, and disciplined work force needed for achieving economic and military strength and efficiency, in particular, in order to:
   a. Raise physical and social health standards, the latter meaning to simply educate people in the virtues of bodily hygiene, regular exercise, and sound nutrition, but also combat unhealthy, deviant, antisocial (and therefore anti-Soviet) behavior: drunkenness, delinquency, prostitution, "sexual perversions," even religiosity and intellectual dissidence.
   b. Develop general physical dexterity, motor skills, and other physical qualities useful for "labor and defense."
   c. Socialize the population into the establishment system of values such as loyalty, conformity, team spirit, cooperation, and discipline.
   d. Encourage a population in transition from a rural to an urban way of life to identify with wider communities, such as the work place, the neighborhood, the town district, the region, the republic, and, ultimately, the whole country.

By associating leisure activities or organizations with the work place, the Party leadership and its agencies were able to better supervise, control, and "rationalize" the leisure time activities of employees.

The policies stated do not correspond to the Western view of leisure. Whether there will be any change with *glasnost, perestroika,* and the fundamental political and economic changes that have occurred will be an interesting area of study.

OUTDOOR RECREATION IN AUSTRALIA

Some Australian writers claim that the concept of a national park was realized in Australia first. They say that Yellowstone, which is claimed to be the first national park ever, did not receive the official name of National Park until 1890. By that time the Royal National Park at Port Hacking, Australia, had already been set aside in 1881 for "the purpose of a National Park" during a citizen and parliamentary campaign for better recreation provision (Mosley 1978:27).

The demand for such natural areas began with hiking groups in Sydney just before the turn of the twentieth century. The idea of hiking and walking clubs grew very quickly. The idea was to protect the wilderness from the incursions of the motor car and the motorist. When Aldo Leopold pressed for wilderness areas within the U.S. National Forest, the concept had already been adopted by the conservationists of New South Wales. The National Park and Primitive Areas Council was formed in 1932, and it proposed a two-pronged approach: open areas for tourists and limited-access primitive areas. Things worked well until the mid-1940s, when a rift formed between the naturalists and recreationists on the percentage of land to be preserved and closed to recreation. The naturalists were successful in passing a legislative provision for a state system of floral reserves in 1948. In 1967 another bill, the National Park and Wildlife Act, provided for nature preserves within national parks. In 1975, the Common Wealth National Parks and Wildlife Conservation Act provided for the declaration of the whole or part of a national park as a wilderness zone. Mosley (1978:32) states that the wilderness reserve

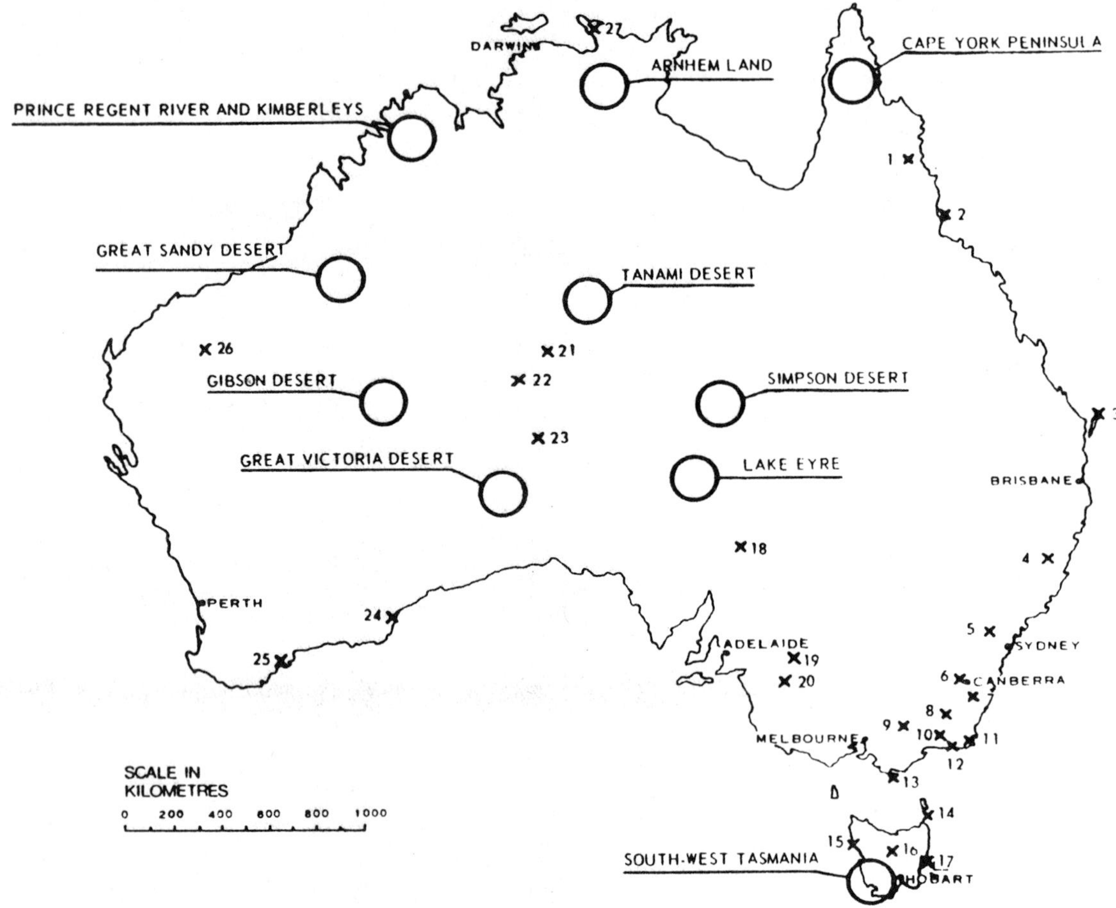

FIGURE 11.9 Australian outback.

movement in Australia developed as a result of local needs, "but owes something to an awareness of the success of this method in the U.S.A."

A Sample of Leisure Pursuits

A study of the recreational use of the Baw Baw Alpine Reserve was conducted in 1975. Baw Baw is a natural preserve that is widely used by different interest groups (see Figure 11.10). It is about 20,000 acres in size and is about 100 miles east of Melbourne. Two questionnaires were mailed to a stratified sample of Victorian households, and 1400 were received back. The questionnaires explored the respondents' attitudes towards, and perceptions of, wilderness areas; and sought details of recreational patterns and preferences along with personal data.

Table 11.4 summarizes the findings of these studies. Bushwalking (hiking) is practiced by 70 percent of all recreationist, regardless of their reasons for being at the reserve and is followed in popularity by sight-seeing (58 percent) and downhill skiing (43 percent). Activities

TABLE 11.4 Activities Suited to the Reserve: Visitor Preference Profiles

5 Most Preferred Activities in Reserve Include . . .	Visitor Group							
	All visitors	Mountain Ranges Sightseers	Snow Sightseers	Trail Bike/4WD Vehicle Enthusiasts	Bushwalkers	Downhill Skiers	Ski Tourers	Conservation Group Members
Bushwalking	70	84	66	56	100	54	80	94
Sightseeing	58	82	75	41	44	19	12	31
Downhill skiing	43	17	31	25	21	100	41	15
Barbeques and/or Picnics	34	44	47	28	25	7	8	12
Frolicking in snow	32	23	44	40	23	16	11	12
Ski touring	29	6	20	8	24	57	85	37
Climbing mountains	28	44	26	23	47	14	32	57
Photography	27	27	25	23	31	33	18	42
Tobogganing	26	17	34	35	17	19	4	9
Nature Study	22	31	21	7	30	16	19	51
Camping in open	20	37	14	31	45	6	34	50
Staying overnight in Village	20	10	12	13	9	50	18	6
Socializing in Village	19	9	14	10	8	43	19	9
Driving for pleasure	13	19	15	11	9	6	4	4
Riding on chairlift	12	10	15	18	7	10	6	2
Trail bike riding	10	15	12	71	10	1	3	2
Horseback Riding	9	9	11	20	7	4	4	4
Camping in huts	8	10	10	18	11	0	6	12
Riding in 4WD vehicles	7	9	10	41	6	1	4	4
Ski orienteering	7	1	6	3	3	11	32	9
Camping in snow	7	3	6	9	16	3	30	28
Fishing	6	11	6	23	11	1	1	4

Source: F. Mosley, editor, *Australia's Wilderness* (Hathorn, Victoria, Australia: Australian Conservation Foundation, 1978), 40. (Reprinted with permission.)

participated in by fewer recreationists include fishing (6 percent), tent camping (7 percent), ski orienteering (7 percent), and driving a 4WD vehicle (7 percent). Bushwalking is also listed as the second-most-preferred activity by those visitors whose main reasons for coming to the reserve were sight-seeing, skiing, and motoring. Figure 11.10 shows that the greatest number of visitors (16,000 a year) came for snow sightseeing, followed by mountain ranges sightseeing and downhill skiing (4,500) and bush camping (3,000). Only 300 visits a year were paid to the reserve with motoring on a bike or in a 4WD vehicle in mind.

A few years ago, the Australian Labor government created the Ministry of Tourism and

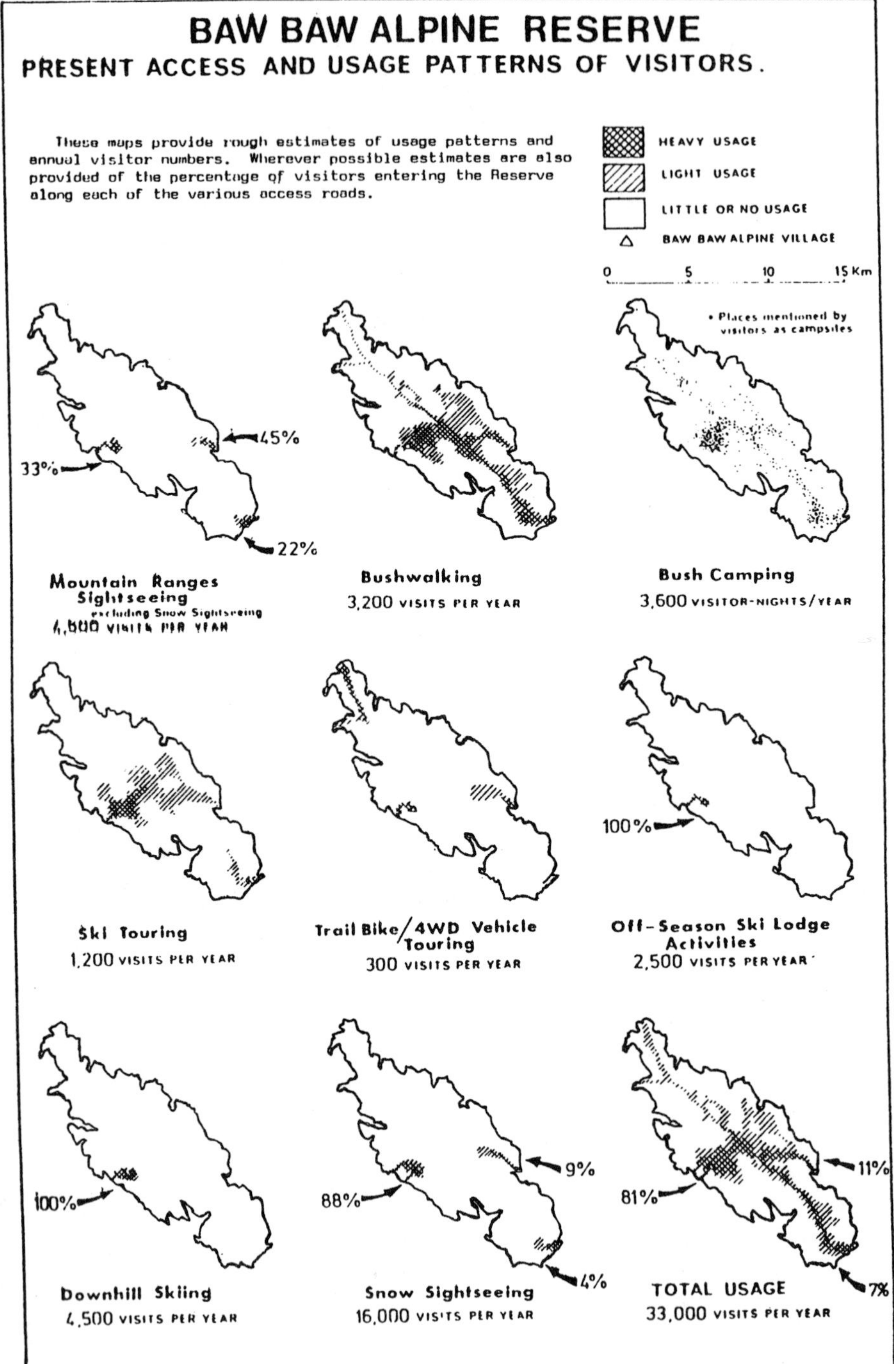

FIGURE 11.10 Patterns and volumes of recreational use of the Baw Baw Alpine Reserve.

Recreation in accord with the following general principles underlying the National Recreation Program:

1. That prime emphasis be placed upon the enrichment and advancement of recreational participation at the local community level.
2. That the entire population, whether rich or poor, young or old, physically adept or inept, be encouraged to participate in some form of constructive regular recreational activity.
3. That recreation programs be coordinated with all types of associated agencies in the community.
4. That recreation be recognized as an essential part of life in this age and in the future, and that citizens be educated to cope with the subsequent changes in their life pattern.

National park systems are growing in many South American countries, serving a dual purpose of protecting the natural treasures and providing for a healthy tourism industry.

Unfortunately the ministry was short-lived. The Cabinet decided to eliminate such a federal office, but the Australian love for outdoor pursuits continues.

OUTDOOR RESOURCES AND THE THIRD WORLD

In countries outside the Western and Eastern blocs, the tendency to preserve natural resources for either conservation and/or recreation is catching on (National Geographic Society 1989).

Many African countries have taken the necessary steps to establish national parks and conservation areas. Tanzania, for example, has set aside the Ngorongoro Crater conservation area, which borders Serengeti National Park. Tanzania has also acted to preserve another national

Angel Falls, in Venezuela's Parque National Canaima, is the highest waterfall in the world at around 3,000 feet.

Native hammocks are available for overnight stays in the jungle regions of the Amazonas.

Tropical birds and lush tropical forests are enjoyed by river runners in the Amazonas region of South America.

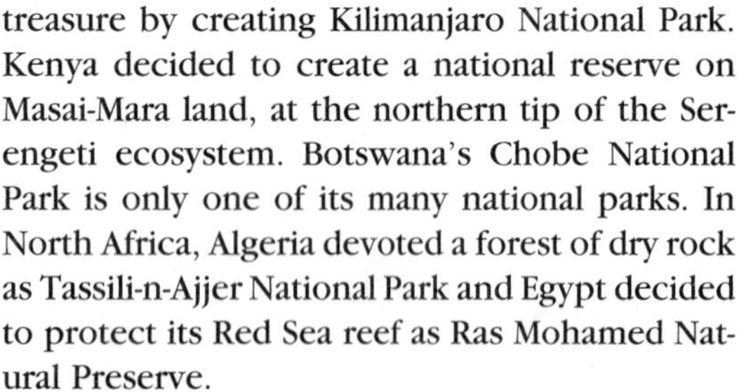

treasure by creating Kilimanjaro National Park. Kenya decided to create a national reserve on Masai-Mara land, at the northern tip of the Serengeti ecosystem. Botswana's Chobe National Park is only one of its many national parks. In North Africa, Algeria devoted a forest of dry rock as Tassili-n-Ajjer National Park and Egypt decided to protect its Red Sea reef as Ras Mohamed Natural Preserve.

In Asia, China dedicated large areas of primitive forests, hillsides of flowers, and hundreds of lakes as Jiuzhaigou National Park. Nepal gave the mountain whose peak touches the sky national park status as Sagarmatha National Park. Taal Volcano Island in the Philippines was dedicated as a national park, as was Bromo-Tenger-Semeru in Indonesia. Ranthambhore National Park in India is where the almost extinct tiger now roams.

The Iguazú National Park of Argentina is adjacent to the Iguaçu National Park of Brazil. The world's widest waterfall is found here, surrounded by many miles of subtropical rain forest. Venezuela's Angel Falls, the highest waterfall in the world, is protected in Canaima National Park. In Guatemala, pre-Columbian pyramids in a sea of green are protected as Tikal National Park. Ecuador preserved the famed Galápagos, the natural laboratory of evolution, as a national park; and near the southern reaches of the Andes, Chile created the Torres del Paine National Park. Peru, on the other hand, selected Manu Biosphere as a natural preserve where previously jaguar were hunted almost to extinction.

These are but a sample of the international trends to preserve and protect natural resources for everyone's enjoyment.

SUMMARY

While the United States may be a leader in providing outdoor resources to its citizens for their leisure pursuits, other countries are interested in doing the same. Canada has been a pioneer as well in many respects. It also has a three-tier government structure, local, provincial, and federal, and all three levels of government are involved in providing facilities and programs in outdoor recreation. In Europe, Great Britain was able to convert a number of privately owned lands into public use. France's contribution was in opening the manicured gardens of the past aristocracy to the public.

Outdoor offerings in the former Soviet Union suffered from too many bureaucratic obstacles. There is hope that fresh ideas and modified policies will prevail in the new federation of republics.

The wilderness movement in Australia is traced to the beginning of the century, along with a description of the conflicts that ensued between naturalists and recreationists. Specific uses by each recreationist group are discussed.

Also presented are some of the national parks and natural preserves that are now seen in Africa, Asia, and Latin America as evidence of an international trend to provide outdoor opportunities for everyone.

REFERENCES

Baker, W. (1982) *Sports in the Western World.* Totowa, NJ: Rowan and Littlefield.

Blanchard, K., and A. Cheska (1985) *The Anthropology of Sport: An Introduction.* South Hadley, MA: Bergin and Garvey.

Chubb, M., and H. Chubb (1981) *One Third of Our Time: Introduction to Leisure Behavior and Resources.* New York: Wiley and Sons.

Douville, R. and J. Casanova (1967). *Daily Life in Early Canada.* New York: MacMillan.

Gorokhov, V., and S. Vishneveskaya (1988) "The Soviet Experiment, Creating a National Park in the Midst of Moscow." *National Parks* (Nov/Dec):16–17.

Guillet, E. (1933) *Early Life in Upper Canada.* Toronto: University of Toronto Press.

Ibrahim, H. (1991) *Leisure and Society: A Comparative Approach.* Dubuque, IA: Wm. C. Brown.

Johnson, R. (1979) "Leisure in Canada," in *Leisure: Emergence and Expansion,* H. Ibrahim and J. Shivers, editors. Los Alamitos, CA: Hwong Publishing.

Knudson, D. (1984) *Outdoor Recreation.* New York: Macmillan.

Kraus, R. (1984) *Recreation and Leisure in Modern Society.* Glenview, IL: Scott, Foresman.

Lowerson, J., and J. Myerscough (1977) *Time to Spare in Victorian England.* Hassocks, Sussex: Harvester Press.

McFarland, E. (1970) *The Development of Public Recreation in Canada.* Ottawa: Canadian Parks and Recreation Association.

Moskoff, W. (1984) *Labour and Leisure in the Soviet Union.* New York: Saint Martin's Press.

Mosley, F. (Editor) (1978) *Australia's Wilderness.* Hathorn, Victoria, Australia: Australian Conservation Foundation.

National Geographic Society (1989) *Nature's Wonderlands: National Parks of the World.* Washington D.C.: National Geographic Society.

Preobrazhensky, V., and V. Krivosheyev (Editors) (1982) *Recreational Geography in the USSR.* Moscow: Pregress Publishers.

Riordan, J. (1982) "Leisure, the State and the Individual in the USSR." *Leisure Studies* 1, 1:65–79.

Shaw, D. (1980). Achievements and Problems in Soviet Recreational Planning. In *Home, School and Leisure in the Soviet Union.* Edited by J. Brine et al. London: Allen & Unwin.

Statistics Canada (1986) *Tourism and Recreation.* Ottawa: Ministry of Supplies and Services.

Strutt, J. (1970) *The Sports and Pastimes of the People of England.* New York: Augustus Kelly.

Szalai, A. (Editor) (1972) *The Use of Time: Daily Activities of Urban and Suburban Population in Twelve Countries.* The Hague, Netherlands: Mouton.

Veal, A. (1984) "Leisure in England and Wales: A Research Note." *Leisure Studies* 2(2):221–29.

PART *three*

Management, Education, and Participation

The chapters in this part are concerned with the policies, procedures, and problems of management in outdoor recreation as well as with outdoor education. Management policies on wilderness, acquisition, and interpretation are presented in Chapter 12. Management procedures on carrying capacity, fees and charges, financing outdoor programs, and visitor and area management are discussed in Chapter 13. The education of participants and the training of managers are discussed in Chapter 14. In Chapter 15 some of the activities that human beings partake of in their quest for outdoor adventure are given. Our environment is faced with many problems that may have implications for outdoor recreation, and these are presented in Chapter 16. Not only overuse but also carelessness by recreationists are factors to be considered when thinking of environmental problems.

12 Management Policies in Outdoor Recreation

Can Americans continue to pursue their outdoor recreational activities without destroying America's natural resources? According to Cole (1986:M-1), recreation impact increases as one moves from the urban and developed end of the recreational opportunity spectrum toward its primitive and wild end. Washburne and Cole (1983) reported that vegetation impacts are a problem in 71 percent of wilderness areas and soil impacts are a problem in 61 percent of them. A discussion on the policies toward American natural resources will provide the needed background for understanding current strategies that are intended to keep natural resources available for recreational use for many years to come.

There are two management policies that govern the natural areas used for recreation in this country. The first policy is based on the preservation principle, which is followed in most of America's federal parks and is followed somewhat in state and local parks. The second policy, which is based on the multiple-use principle, is followed in federal, state, and private forests.

PRESERVATION POLICY

The legislation that established the first national park, Yellowstone, is important in that it provided the basis for the concept that federal land would be "dedicated, and set apart as a public park or pleasuring ground for the benefit and enjoyment of the people" (Frakt and Rankin 1982:17). The park was established by an act of Congress in 1872. By the turn of the century four more national parks had been established. The executive branch of the federal government had the authority to reserve land from the public domain and preserve it in its current status. Prior to 1910, this authority was exercised repeatedly for purposes which included the establishment of wildlife reserves. Other purposes included the establishment of Indian and military reservations, reservation of timber land, and withdrawal of land from its current use pending classification. In 1906 the Antiquity Act was passed, which authorized the president of the United States to reserve lands with scientific beauty and scientific importance. In 1916 Congress established the National Park Service. The act creating this agency specified its purpose as follows:

> To conserve the scenery and the natural and historic objects and the wildlife therein and to provide for the enjoyment of the same in such manner and by such means as will leave them unimpaired for the enjoyment of future generations.
>
> (Everhart 1972).

According to Nash (1978:13), the passage of the National Park Service Act did not change the original concept of public enjoyment. It is clear in hindsight that pleasure-seeking people could (and did) impair nature despite the legislative stipulation that the parks' scenery and wildlife should be left "unimpaired." Nash writes of how Stephen Mather, the first director of the National Park Service, was instructed by his boss, the secretary of the Interior, in a letter dated May 13, 1918, to let the public enjoy the parks in the manner that best satisfied the individual taste. In other words, no attempts were made then to define what kind of enjoyment is appropriate in a natural setting.

Nash believes that the concept of preservation was set aside at that time, and efforts were directed toward having the National Park Service stand on its own feet in its early years. A circus image of parks was generated, with drive-through sequoias, soap-sudded geysers, bear feedings, and caged wildlife as the techniques used to attract visitors. The firefall replaced the chicken fall in Yosemite where a giant wood fire on top of Glacier Point, 3,000 feet above the valley floor, was pushed over the cliff as music was played. This activity was not questioned until the late 1960s.

Grand Canyon National Park focuses on the world famous canyon of the Colorado River. The park encompasses 177.7 miles of river with adjacent uplands which expose an immense variety of formations that illustrate vast periods of geological history.

The results of these amusive activities were on the minds of those who legislated the Everglades National Park in 1934. Their bill specified that no development of the project or plan for the entertainment of visitors should be undertaken that would interfere with preservation of the natural conditions (1978:31-32). Nash cites the work of two persons, George Wright and Lowell Sumner of the National Park Service, who brought the agency's attention to the need for preservation. Sumner urged the establishment of a recreation saturation point or a carrying capacity, which he defined as the maximum degree of the highest type of recreational use which a wilderness can receive, consistent with its long-term preservation (1978:33).

The Division of Forestry of the Department of Agriculture became the U.S. Forest Service in the early years of the nineteenth century. Soon thereafter recreation was added as one of the multiple uses of the national forests. Preservation was not a priority, and roads and structures grew all over national forests. Two foresters, Arthur Calhart and Aldo Leopold, were instrumental in setting aside large blocks of acreage which became the United States', and perhaps the world's, first designated wilderness (see Chapter 7, Federal Resources). Preservation of these wilderness areas revolved around limiting the modes of travel permitted in them, but not the number of visitors to them. Later preservation was underscored with the establishment of research reserves, which included virgin forests of scientific importance. Today these are called experimental forests.

Another pioneer in the preservation of wilderness areas was Robert Marshall who, as director of the Forestry Division of the U.S. Office of Indian Affairs, crusaded the curtailment of road building in primitive areas. Both he and Aldo Leopold were instrumental in forming the Wilderness Society, whose effort was directed toward keeping adverse effects out. The Wilderness Society intervenes directly with government officials to halt projects that may threaten wilderness. The society has found it necessary to go to court for this very purpose.

Preservation through management became the focus of attention of the Sierra Club in the late 1930s. Proposals were numerous, including the curtailing of buildings and use of trails, certification of outdoorsmen, and limits on overnight camping. The Sierra Club sponsored the High Sierra Wilderness Conference in 1949, which grew to today's Biennial Wilderness Conference. The idea of a National Wilderness Preservation System did not materialize until 1964 with the passage of the Wilderness Act. But this took hard work on the part of the preservationists fighting those who wanted to dam wild rivers and exploit the wilderness.

The Wilderness Act (Public Law 88–577) directed the secretaries of Agriculture and the Interior to review lands within their jurisdictions, that is, national forests and national parks, respectively, and to recommend their suitability as wilderness areas. Currently close to 90 million acres are so classified and are the basis of the primitive areas within national forests and the roadless areas of national parks. According to Nash (1978:39), while the earlier legislation emphasized pleasuring and enjoyment, this time the law specified that the protected land was to be enjoyed *as wilderness.*

The Wilderness Act defines wilderness as an area where the earth and its community of life are untrammeled (uninterrupted) by humans and where each person is a visitor who does not remain. If wilderness is not managed according to this definition, the alternatives are either to prohibit all use of wilderness areas or to permit an open-door policy that will eventually lead to the destruction of wilderness areas.

In 1975, the Eastern Wilderness Act allowed select Forest Service areas east of the 100th meridian to be included as wilderness areas although they did not meet the criterion of being free from human influence. They were to be allowed to revert to their natural condition. A few years later a large section in Alaska was added to the system (see Table 12.1).

Table 12.1 shows that by 1981 the National Wilderness Preservation System occurred on lands of four federal agencies, the Forest Service (31.5 percent), the National Park Service (44.3 percent), the Fish and Wildlife Service (24.1 percent), and the Bureau of Land Management (.1 percent).

By the mid-1980s the system consisted of 445 areas totaling about 89 million acres, most of

TABLE 12.1 Area of the National Wilderness Preservation System by Location, Managing Agency, and Year

Managing Agency	Contiguous States and Hawaii (1964) (millions of acres)	(1979)	Alaska (1981)	United States (1981)	(1981)
Forest Service, USDA	9.1	15.3	19.7	5.4	25.1
National Park Service, USDI	0.0	2.8	3.0	32.4	35.4
Fish & Wildlife Service, USDA	0.0	0.7	0.6	18.7	19.3
B. of Land Management, USDI	0.0	0.0	0.01	0.0	0.0
Total	9.1	18.8	23.31	56.5	79.8

Source: D. Knudson, *Outdoor Recreation* (New York: Macmillan, 1984), 435. (Reprinted with permission.)

which are in Alaska. This is expected to increase as stipulated in the Federal Land Policy and Management Act of 1976, under which the Bureau of Land Management must submit areas in its jurisdiction as wilderness candidates.

According to Knudson (1984:434–37), nine states have wilderness policies and two have legislation that meets the same standards of federal wilderness: California has two areas totaling 97,000 acres and New York has sixteen areas totaling about one million acres.

Principles of Wilderness Management

Hendee et al. (1978:137–48) suggested the following eleven principles for wilderness management:

1. Wilderness is one extreme of the outdoor recreation opportunity spectrum. Recreationists in America have the wide choice in a continuum of settings ranging from the paved to the primeval. Recreational demands that are inconsistent with the intended character of wilderness can be met elsewhere. And there is (are) plenty of elsewhere(s).
2. Management of wilderness areas must be viewed in relationship to the management of adjacent lands. This principle is also based on the outdoor recreation opportunity spectrum. Heavy recreational use in the area adjacent to wilderness is bound to affect the wilderness area. The creation of a buffer zone between the two areas to absorb the impact may be a good solution, as would the creation of zones for different uses.
3. Wilderness is a distinct, composite resource with inseparable parts. This principle necessitates that wilderness be managed in toto, with no separate managements, one for vegetation, another for wildlife, and a third for recreation. Here the focus is on the protection of the naturalness of relationships between the wilderness ecosystem parts.
4. The purpose of wilderness is to produce human value and benefits. Wilderness is set aside not for its flora and fauna, but for the people. Recreational, therapeutic, and scientific benefits are to be derived from wilderness. (This view,

known as the anthropocentric position, takes the "use and enjoyment" phrase in the Wilderness Act literally. The other view, the biocentric position, calls for the natural ecological process to operate as freely as possible, which eliminates humans from wilderness.)

5. Wilderness preservation requires management of human use and its impact. Recreational use of wilderness area has the greatest impact if contrasted to scientific use. Accordingly, it is the management of recreationists that is becoming crucial.
6. Wilderness management should be guided by objectives set forth in area management plans. Without such a plan, management will be uncoordinated, even counterproductive. (Wilderness management plans will be discussed later.)
7. Wilderness preservation requires carrying capacity constraints. The level of tolerance a wilderness area can sustain before unacceptable impact occurs must be specified. (Carrying capacity will be discussed in detail later.)
8. Wilderness management should strive to reduce the physical and social-psychological impacts of use. This principle calls for selective restrictions which focus on certain impacts. Kind, timing, and location of use could be regulated. For instance, the number of persons in a camping party, the length of a hike, and the use of fire should be regulated.
9. Only minimum regulation necessary to achieve wilderness management objectives should be applied. In order that the recreationist may benefit from leisure experience, restrictions should be at a minimum so that the salient characteristics of such an experience (freedom, spontaneity, etc.) may be felt.
10. The management of individual areas should be governed by a concept of nondegradation. This idea calls for not only the maintenance of the present environmental levels, but also restoration from below-minimum levels. In other words the management should strive to elevate some conditions to at least a minimum level.
11. Wilderness-dependent activities should be favored. From scientific study to leisure pursuits, wilderness should provide the place for some of these activities, but not necessarily all of them. Laboratories are places of scientific study and pools are places for swimming; accordingly, only the activities that require and depend on wilderness should be allowed there.

MULTIPLE-USE POLICY

The multiple-use policy is applicable in most national forests, the lands administered by the Bureau of Land Management, and most state forests. Many activities are allowed under this concept, including grazing, timber cutting, and of course recreation. The concept was reaffirmed in the Multiple-Use Sustained-Yield Act of 1960, Public Law 86–517. Congress emphasized that the national forests are established and shall be administered for outdoor recreation, range, timber, watershed, and wildlife purposes.

Multiple use means that the management of all renewable surface resources are directed to meet the multiple needs of the American people. Sustained yield means the achievement and maintenance in perpetuity of a high-level output of these renewable resources. According to Knudson, the concept of multiple use is a slippery one and it is difficult to define to the satisfaction of each group that uses the land (1984:473). The concept applies to the two largest land-management agencies in the United States: the Bureau of Land Management and the U.S. Forest Service. In application, certain areas of these two agencies may be administered under a single-use concept, but they should fit within the broad concept of multiple use within the agency. For example a campground would be restricted to recreational use and a watershed to wildlife protection, and both would fit under the multiple-use concept.

The lands under the jurisdiction of the Bureau of Land Management are managed under multiple use as described in Public Law 94–579, the Federal Land Policy and Management Act. The act was passed in 1976, 16 years after the Multiple-Use Sustained-Yield Act of 1960 which regulated the use of national forests. The language of the 1976 act is similar to the language of the 1960 act in that it is stipulated that the lands under the jurisdiction of BLM should be managed according to the multiple-use and sustained-yield principles. The 1976 act required that certain areas of BLM lands that are qualified as wilderness areas be included under the National Wilderness Preservation System. BLM was given 15 years (until 1991) to review its potential wilderness candidates.

Although multiple use seems to be a sound policy, its application is met with difficulties. At the core of these difficulties is the fact that different groups view America's natural resources differently. For instance, Knudson (1984:474) gave the following five views of the American forest:

American Indians (nineteenth century and before):	The forest was home, and nature was a force that could be used but not dominated. Small areas could be used up, but there was always more.
Pilgrims and pioneers:	The forest was a wilderness and the home of a hostile enemy, but it produced food, shelter, and export capital. Though the forest was a necessity, it was believed that the forest must be reduced by a substantial amount.
Lumbermen (at the turn of the nineteenth century):	The forest was a timber mine, a resource. (The forest was not yet treated as a renewable resource.)
Foresters:	The forest is a renewable resource. It must be protected and nurtured; the timber harvest must be rationalized.
Recreationists:	The forest is a service environment. Romantic and esthetic aspects predominate.

It is clear that these interests are in many instances incompatible and the management of lands designated for multiple use should carry the burden of upholding the law. Philosophically and legally the multiple-use concept centers on the greatest total benefit over a long period of time. This makes the task of the contemporary manager very difficult indeed.

CLASSIFICATION OF RECREATION RESOURCES

The total area of the United States is 3.62 million square miles, 98 percent of which is land and 2 percent inland water. These are the two basic recreation resources.

Land Resources

Of the 2.2 billion acres of land in the United States, 58 percent is privately owned, 34 percent is owned by the federal government, 5 percent by the states, 2 percent by Indians (reservations), and 1 percent by local governments. There are many ways of classifying recreation resources on these lands, among them the Clawson and Knetsch (1966) classification, as follows:

- *User-oriented areas* are located and designed with the access and use by the visitor as the principal but not the only consideration. This classification includes most city and county recreation areas and many commercial areas.
- *Intermediate areas* are located and planned to meet the needs of users, but in areas dictated partially by the resource. These areas are managed with resource maintenance and use as balancing considerations; they include most state parks, forests, and reservoir projects, many fish and wildlife areas, and some commercial recreation areas.
- *Resource-oriented areas* are located and planned with the resource base as the key criterion, with recreation use coming as a result of the resource. The large areas of national forests, most national wildlife refuges, national parks, national resource lands, and some large state properties fall in this category, as do forest industry lands.

Knudson (1984:299) suggested a method of classification based on identifying the source of the recreation resource. He suggested five methods of classification, as follows:

1. Ownership or jurisdiction classes This approach was used in Section Two of this book, relating recreation offerings to the firms, individuals, or public agencies that own and manage them. This system does much to describe in a few words the goals and policies affecting the property.

2. Designation classes Properties are called parks, forests, wildlife areas, nature preserves, memorials, recreation areas, parkways, trails, or scenic rivers, lakes, or reservoirs. There are specific facility designations, such as wilderness, golf course, country club, arboretum, ski area, and camp, that help define the character and features of the area. The most commonly understood classes are combinations of the jurisdiction and facility designation, quickly describing the resource to people who have any familiarity with the resource system.

3. Service area classification For people concerned primarily with planning, this classification approach defines the parks and open spaces by size and service areas of public facilities, regardless of the agency managing them. This system is used to define the character of supply and to point out the kinds of resources most needed. Variations of this approach have been used for years by the National Recreation and Park Association. A number of states and cities have adopted similar categories, referring to facilities in terms of whether they serve a neighborhood, community, or region, for example.

4. Orientation classification This classification was described earlier. It defines management and policy purposes in rough groupings as to whether they are user-oriented, intermediate, or resource-oriented. This merely identifies management emphasis. It is most valuable in explaining the policies of an agency to interested visitors or in interagency discussions of proper roles for various resources.

5. Resource classification Within a property, the land base can be classified into various resources related to its purpose and intensity of development.

Six classes of resources were proposed by the Outdoor Recreation Resources Review Commission (ORRRC). This commission was established by the president of the United States in 1958. Its report in 1962 suggested the following classes of outdoor recreation resources:

I. High-Density Recreation Areas
Intensively developed and managed for mass use.

Facilities:	Heavy investment concentrated in relatively small areas, many facilities usually present.
Use:	Exclusively for recreating: heavy peak load pressures (e.g., weekends).
Land Use:	Often competes with residential construction and commercial uses, due to location near urban centers.
Examples:	Beaches, boardwalks, swimming pools, highly developed trailer camps, some mass-use picnic/game areas.

II. General Outdoor Recreation Areas
Areas subject to substantial development for specific recreation uses.

Facilities:	Many, but usually fewer than in high-density recreation areas—always some human-built facilities.
Use:	Accommodates the major share of all outdoor recreation day, weekend, and vacation use. Use is concentrated, but not as much as in category I. Zoning may be needed.
Land Use:	Competes with a wide variety of uses, due to locations in both urban and rural settings.
Examples:	Campsites, picnic areas, ski areas, resorts, coastal areas, hunting preserves.

III. Natural Environment Areas
Areas suitable for recreation in natural environments, intermediate between categories II and IV.

Facilities:	Few and simple; user enjoys resources "as is" in an environment where humans fend largely for themselves; management emphasis is on the natural rather than the human-made. Access roads, trails, primitive camping areas, and safety and fire provisions are present.
Use:	Generally dispersed, not concentrated; hunting, birding, fishing, canoeing, rustic camping, sight-seeing, snowmobiling, ORV use (family style).
Land Use:	Often multiple-use lands; largest class in acreage.
Examples:	Most national forest and BLM lands, buffers in national parks. Most of state and county forests, most fish and wildlife areas, most reservoirs.

IV. Unique Natural Areas
Areas of outstanding scenic splendor, natural wonder, or scientific importance.

Facilities:	Few—acceptable only if they enhance protection of the natural feature.

Use: Limited to observation and study in many cases. Management focuses on preservation of feature, not public demand.
Land Use: Areas often small, special; incompatible uses excluded.
Examples: Old Faithful geyser, Old Man of the Mountain, Bristlecone Pine area of Inyo National Forest, nature preserves.

V. Primitive Areas
Undisturbed roadless areas in a natural wild condition.

Facilities: None except trails, no structures, no machines.
Use: Goal is to provide solitude from evidence of civilization; commercial uses prohibited except guide service. Use may be restricted in order to:
a) provide opportunity for solitude by user, and
b) preserve primitive conditions.
Land Use: Competes with several other wildland uses—timber production, grazing, power dam construction, mining. These uses and roads are generally excluded from primitive areas. (For reasons found acceptable by Congress, mining and grazing have been allowed to continue temporarily in some areas.)
Examples: Gila Wilderness Area; most of Rocky Mountain National Park; portions of Porcupine Mountain State Park, Michigan; Quetico-Superior Boundary Waters Canoe Area, Minnesota-Ontario; Wood Buffalo National Park, Alberta.

VI. Historic and Cultural Sites
Sites of major historic or cultural significance, local, regional, or national.

Facilities: Emphasis is on restoration and preservation of the historic features; facilities usually relate to protection of features during visitor use and interpretation of the historical significance, providing suitable access.
Use: Varies considerably, depending upon type and fragility of features; always appropriate to the historic feature. Overuse is prevented, not accommodated.
Land Use: Exclusively for appreciation of history and culture and associated recreation values of the site.
Examples: Mt. Vernon, Russell Cave (Ala.), Tippecanoe Battlefield.

Jensen classifies the land mass in the United States into four categories: forest lands, grasslands, deserts, and tundra. The features and resources of each are varied, as described in the following paragraphs.

Forest Lands America was covered with forests initially, but consumptive use of timber over the past two centuries has reduced the area of forest to only one-third of the nation. Today there are 748 million acres of forest land, most of which (420 million acres) are privately owned. The U.S. Forest Service controls 187 million acres, the National Park Service 30 million acres, and state and local agencies 38 million acres. Forests vary in terrain, elevation, and type of trees that they support. Forests are a good source for many types of outdoor recreation.

Grasslands The grasslands that supported grazing animals in the past have become America's food basket in the last two centuries.

Attempts are now being made to recover as much of America's grasslands as possible for scenic, scientific, and recreational purposes. Heavy vegetation around water resources have high recreation potential. A Great Plains Grasslands National Park has been proposed.

Deserts Lands receiving less than 10 inches of annual precipitation are generally classified as desert. These range from sand dunes and dry lake beds to plateaus, mountains, and canyons. Despite the prevailing concept that deserts are inhospitable, they have become a significant source for outdoor recreation. Traditional outdoor pursuits have been augmented with newer ones: parachuting, sand sailing, and hang gliding. The Bureau of Land Management controls most of the U.S. desert lands that have recreational potential.

Tundra This natural ecosystem around the arctic and alpine zones stretches across the northern section of the continent, with Alaska accounting for most of it. Smaller regions of tundra are found in the Rocky Mountains, the Sierra Nevada, and the Cascades. Tundra lacks trees but contains grasses, hedges, herbs, and shrubs. Its harsh winter makes recreation pursuits rather limited. In addition, its vegetation is too delicate to allow for mass leisure pursuits. The Bureau of Land Management and the National Park Service own most of the lands that are classified as tundra in the United States.

Water Resources

Water resources that are utilized for recreation can be classified into rivers, wetlands, shorelines, lakes, and reservoirs.

Rivers Although most American rivers are found in segments of 25 miles (40 kilometers) or less, these rivers have served as transportation routes with adjacent trails. There are approximately 3.25 million miles (5.24 million kilometers) of rivers in the United States, some of which are free-flowing through natural settings. Accordingly rivers provide unique opportunities for a variety of leisure pursuits. Among these are swimming, boating, and fishing as well as rafting, kayaking, and canoeing.

Wetlands This term describes marshes, swamps, bogs, wet meadows, and shallow ponds. It is estimated that there are 75 million acres of wetlands in the United States today. Examples of wetlands are the Everglades, Hackensack Meadowlands, the Great Dismal Swamp, and the Okefenokee Swamp. The recreational opportunities provided in wetlands include fishing, hunting, trapping, bird watching, hiking, canoeing, and photography.

Shorelines The coastlines around and within the United States total around 100,000 miles, or 161,000 kilometers. Most of the American coastline is developed; 70 percent of the continental U.S. coastline is privately owned. The federal government controls 11 percent of the coastline; state and local governments control 19 percent. This does not mean that the 30 percent of coastline controlled by government is available for public recreation. Topographically only 10 percent of American coastline, or only 10,000 miles, is available for public recreation, including aquatic activities such as swimming, boating, sailing, fishing, and diving. Also camping, hiking, and picnicking take place along the coast.

Lakes There are close to 100,000 natural lakes in the United States, varying in size from a prairie pond to the expansive Great Lakes. The leisure pursuits on these lakes vary from swimming and fishing to sailing, boating, and water skiing. Also at the shores of these lakes, recreationists camp, hike, picnic, jog, walk, and watch birds. The surface acreage of fresh water available for recreation is about 22 million acres, comprised of both natural lakes and human-made reservoirs.

Reservoirs There are close to 50,000 reservoirs in this country which have been constructed by government agencies and private individuals for the purpose of flood control, generating electricity, or providing water for irrigation. Most of these reservoirs are small, some are medium size, and a few are large. The medium ones were built with the help of the Soil Conservation Service or the Fish and Wildlife Service. The larger ones were built under the direction of the Bureau of Land Management, the U.S. Army Corps of Engineers, or the Tennessee Valley Authority.

PLANNING FOR OUTDOOR RECREATION

Planning takes into consideration the general purpose related to the kind of service being offered or suggested. In the case of outdoor recreation, the objective is to provide constructive leisure pursuits in a safe, natural environment. The work of the scholars who were concerned with leisure in the early years of the twentieth century set the tone for such an objective. The formation of the Playground Association of America was in conjunction with advocacy. Local, state, and federal agencies as well as private organization began programs in fulfillment of this objective. As industrialization, automation, and urbanization increased, so did the demand for organized leisure pursuits, including outdoor recreation experiences.

By the middle of the twentieth century, public interest in recreation was heightened when the demand for expanded facilities led to a crisis in outdoor recreation. According to La Page (1988:127), that crisis was responded to by massive state and federal reinvestment in our public outdoor recreation estate. The response included numerous state bond issues, the Forest Service's Operation Outdoor and the National Park Service's Mission 66. Most important was President Eisenhower's decision to appoint the Outdoor Recreation Resources Review Commission (ORRRC). It became clear from analyzing past offerings and considering present programs that planning is important for the future of outdoor recreation.

Planning Procedure Planning should be based on the policies, regulations, and plans of the agency or agencies involved. In addition the public should be involved in the planning procedure. Jensen (1985:311) suggested the following six methods of public involvement:

1. Public meetings where people have a chance to hear proposals and voice their support or resistance.
2. Coverage in the news media. This exposes ideas and alternatives to the public and stimulates involvement.
3. The appointment of advisory committees to represent the public.
4. Public surveys or polls to provide information for the planning process.
5. Agency sensitivity to views of members of the public.
6. Presentations at the meetings of service clubs, political groups, and auxiliary organizations.

There are four levels of recreation plans in the United States today:

1. Nationwide plans
2. State comprehensive plans
3. Local (city, district or county) plans
4. Project or site plans

Regardless of the level of the plan, Jensen (1985:304) suggested that the following twelve principles be observed:

1. Park and recreation areas should provide opportunities for all persons regardless of race, creed, age, gender, or economic status.
2. To meet the needs in a particular geographic area, consideration should be made of all the resources available,

including lakes and streams, woodlands, marshes, mountains, historical and archeological sites, areas of scenic value, and areas of special interest.

3. Multiple use can often add to the total use of an area; therefore, multiple use should be considered, even though it is not always accepted.
4. Early acquisition of land based on a comprehensive recreation plan is essential. Unless sites are acquired well in advance of demand, land costs often become prohibitive.
5. Timely evaluation should be made of present recreational needs and future trends to accurately project for the future.
6. Insofar as possible, recreation areas and facilities should be properly distributed in accordance with the population, so that all of the people have approximately equal availability of recreational opportunities.
7. The design of individual park and recreation sites should be as flexible as possible to accommodate changing patterns of recreation in the given area.
8. Barriers should be avoided whenever possible to provide for easy access to recreation areas by the elderly, the handicapped, and others with mobility restrictions.
9. There should be citizen involvement in planning whenever possible because this results in good ideas and added enthusiasm toward using the areas once they are developed.
10. Responsibilities should be defined and agreed upon by the various governmental and private agencies so that the duplication of areas, facilities, and services will be avoided and so the public will receive the best return possible on the dollars spent.
11. Park and recreation lands should be protected in perpetuity against encroachment and nonrecreation purposes. These areas should not be considered the path of least resistance for highways, public utilities, and buildings.
12. The plan for a particular recreation area or the plan for a system of areas and facilities should be carefully integrated with the total master plan for the particular agency or area. Park and recreation planning is not an isolated function. It should be integrated with the total plan.

NATIONAL OUTDOOR RECREATION PLANS

There were unsuccessful attempts to develop some comprehensive national plans for outdoor recreation after World War I. President Calvin Coolidge called a National Conference on Outdoor Recreation in 1924 where 128 public and private agencies were represented. The final report, which appeared in the Senate document number 158 of May 1928, made recommendations for future outdoor recreation pursuits. But the recommendations were set aside with the coming of the Great Depression. With the establishment of the Works Progress Administration to ward off unemployment at that time, many facilities and programs were built on federal, state, and local lands. Nash (1978:36) believes that because of lack of planning, roads were built in wild places in national parks and forests by thousands of job-hungry men. Federal care threatened to divide and conquer the last really large wilderness areas in the country.

After World War II, different federal agencies responded to the increasing demands for outdoor recreation pursuits by developing their own individual plans such as Mission 66 of the National Park Service and Operation Outdoor of the U.S. Forest Service. The first comprehensive planning effort on a national level was done by the Outdoor Recreation Resources Review Commission in the 1960s.

Outdoor Recreation Resources Review Commission

Upon the suggestion of President Eisenhower, Congress established the Outdoor Recreation Resources Review Commission, known as ORRRC, in 1958. Eight members of Congress and seven private citizens were appointed by the president of the United States to serve on the commission, chaired by Lawrence Rockefeller. The commission was charged to survey the outdoor recreation needs of the American people for the following four decades and to recommend a plan of action to meet those needs.

The commission surveyed America's stock of outdoor recreation areas, both actual and potential, and conducted interviews, giving questionnaires to a cross section of the American public in an attempt to discern recreational needs and demands on the natural resources. ORRRC's recommendations were included in its final report to Congress in 1961; the report included 27 volumes, each written on a separate topic.

The ORRRC report defined a policy framework which divided the responsibilities for outdoor recreation in the United States along the following lines:

1. Local and state governments are to take the basic responsibility for supplying recreational opportunities.
2. The federal government is to preserve areas of national significance.
3. The federal government is to offer financial and technical assistance, provide leadership in getting all states to supply increased opportunities, and manage existing federal lands for broad recreation benefits.
4. Individual and private efforts are expected to continue providing places and activities, equipment, services, and other products, and to lead preservation of land through nonprofit groups.

The commission recognized that demand will exceed supply in outdoor recreation opportunities in the following years unless certain actions were taken immediately. The problem was compounded by the fact that the extant facilities for outdoor recreation were not only overtaxed, but also antiquated. According to Knudson (1984:329), ORRRC's recommendations have been implemented to a remarkable degree. Most important was the establishment of the Bureau of Outdoor Recreation, which provided a federal focus on national outdoor recreation planning including the 1973 and 1979 nationwide outdoor recreation plans. The bureau changed its name to the Heritage Conservation and Recreation Service in 1978 and was discontinued in 1981.

Other outcomes of the commission's recommendations include the following:

1. Expansion of the National Park System.
2. Establishment of the National Wilderness System.
3. Inauguration of the Land and Conservation Fund Program.
4. Establishment of the Wild and Scenic Rivers System.
5. Establishment of the National Trail System.
6. Authorization of state and local land acquisition programs.

Public Land Law Review Commission Report (1970)

Congress decided in 1964 that there was a need for a bipartisan commission to review the nation's land use, laws, and policies. The Public Land Law Review Commission (PLLRC) was to report to Congress the status of land use, the problems associated with such use, and the changes needed for more effective use. Its report of 1970 contained 452 recommendations based on the input of hundreds of economists, planners, and managers. The recommendations related to the recreational use of land were commensurate with ORRRC recommendations, as follows:

1. Role of the federal government The federal government should be responsible for the preservation of scenic areas, natural wonders, primitive areas, and historic sites of national significance; for cooperation with the states through technical and financial assistance; for the promotion of interstate arrangements, and for management of federal lands for the broadest recreation benefit consistent with other essential uses.
2. Role of state governments The states should play a pivotal role in making outdoor recreation opportunities available by effecting the acquisition of land; by developing sites; and by providing and maintaining facilities of state or regional significance; by providing assistance to local governments; and by providing leadership and planning.
3. Role of local governments Local governments should expand their efforts to provide outdoor recreation opportunities, with particular emphasis upon securing open space and developing recreation areas in and around metropolitan and other urban areas.
4. Role of the private sector Individual initiative and private enterprise should continue to be the most important force in outdoor recreation, providing many and varied opportunities for a vast number of people, as well as the goods and services used by people in their recreation activities. Government should encourage the work of nonprofit groups wherever possible. It should also stimulate desirable commercial development, which can be particularly effective in providing facilities and services where demand is sufficient to return a profit.

Other recommendations of the PLLRC included the following:

1. Emphasis on the preservation concept for the public land under the jurisdiction of the National Park Service.
2. Continuation of the multiple-use policy of the public lands under the jurisdiction of the Forest Service and the Bureau of Land Management with recreation as a primary use.
3. Purchase of private lands that could provide for right-of-way corridors or access to otherwise inaccessible recreation areas.
4. Expansion of the National Park System, wilderness areas, seashores, and the Wild and Scenic Rivers System.
5. Improvement in the land classification and acquisition program as related to recreation with the use of advanced methods of financing acquisition and allocating funds for development.

Despite its significance to outdoor recreation, the report of the PLLRC has not received much attention because the commission chair, Wayne Aspinell, was not reelected and because there was no single program for implementation (Knudson 1984:332). Nonetheless the report raised a number of national and regional issues pertaining to recreation policy and planning in the United States.

Nationwide Outdoor Recreation Plan of 1973

Public Law 88–29, known as the Organic Act, required that the secretary of the Interior should:

> . . . formulate and maintain a comprehensive nationwide outdoor recreation plan, taking into consideration the plans of the various Federal agencies, States, and their political subdivisions.

> The plan shall set forth the needs and demands of the public for outdoor recreation and the current and foreseeable availability in the future of outdoor recreation resources to meet those needs. The plan shall identify critical outdoor recreation problems, recommend solutions, and recommend desirable actions to be taken at each level of government and by private interest.
>
> (Jensen and Thorstenson 1977:247).

In 1973 the Bureau of Outdoor Recreation of the Department of the Interior published a national plan entitled *Outdoor Recreation: A Legacy for America.* It was a policy document on the roles of the three levels of government. According to Knudson (1984:332–33), a draft of the plan was presented to President Richard Nixon earlier with a strong urban emphasis and a multi-billion-dollar price tag. The plan was printed for the record by the Senate Interior Committee under the title "The Recreation Imperative." It recommended that 30 percent of the Land and Water Conservation Fund go to urban centers and that grants should be allowed for operational expenses such as implementing recreational programs. This nationwide recreation plan was based on surveys of over 4,000 persons across the country. The data showed that participation in leisure pursuits had increased sharply since the previous ORRRC study. In the meantime, recreation resources did not increase at the same rate. The report called for quick action on part of all three levels of government and the private sector to aid in increasing resources. The report also pointed to the increasing problem of pollution of America's natural resources that provide for recreational outlets. Carrying capacity determinants were suggested as an important managerial tool to reduce abuse.

According to Jensen (1985:316–17), the 1973 plan specified the following functions for the federal government:

1. Complete a program of identification, selection, and planning for acquisition of those superlative areas needed to round out the federal recreation estate.
2. Continue to use the Land and Water Conservation Fund to acquire needed federal recreation lands and assist the states in doing the same.
3. Open to the public directly or through state and local entities those underused portions of federal properties or facilities having public recreation values, when such lands are not available for transfer.
4. Accelerate evaluations of proposed trails, wild and scenic rivers, wilderness areas, wetlands, and historical properties to ensure that those unique lands are preserved by federal, state, or local governments or private interests for the benefit of the public; and accelerate the evaluation of federal land holdings to determine if beaches, shorelines, islands, and natural areas can be made available for increased public recreation use.

Further, the plan stated that to improve the management and administration of recreation resources and programs, the federal government will:

1. Accelerate the identification and no-cost transfer of surplus and underused real property to state and local governments for parks and other recreation sites.
2. When the land is not available for transfer, and direct federal management is not necessary or desirable, take necessary steps to transfer management responsibility for existing recreational units to state and local governments.
3. Promote recreation developments on or near federal lands on the basis of regional land-use plans. Whenever possible, private investment should be used for the provision of these services.
4. Undertake preparation of recreation land-use plans for all management units and coordinate such planning with all

interested federal, state, and local government agencies and private entities.

Nationwide Outdoor Recreation Plan of 1979

The Nationwide Outdoor Recreation Plan of 1979 was quite different from the plan of 1973 in that it was developed from a series of task force reports on specific issues which were reviewed by the public and revised accordingly. It also included surveys on recreation preference and participation. The report followed two major themes—an assessment of outdoor recreation and a suggested action program (Jensen 1985:317).

Assessment of Outdoor Recreation The assessment provides a summary of trends, needs, and opportunities along with benefits accrued from participation in recreation activities. Included were the demographic variables affecting participation and agencies providing facilities and programs, along with a description of problems facing recreation.

Action Program A program of action was suggested to revolve around nine issues of national significance:

1. Federal land acquisition.
   a. A new and more effective planning and decision-making process will be instituted to identify and select lands eligible for the federal portion of the Land and Water Conservation Fund.
   b. A policy will be developed defining the federal role in protection and acquisition of land for conservation of natural, cultural, and recreational resources. This policy will encourage alternatives to outright acquisition.
2. Wild, scenic, and recreational rivers.
   a. New guidelines will be developed to shorten the time required to study potential wild, scenic, and recreational rivers.
   b. Federal agencies will develop guidelines to avoid adverse effects on potential wild and scenic rivers identified in the nationwide rivers inventory.
   c. Federal land-managing agencies will assess the potential of rivers identified in the nationwide inventory located in their lands and take steps to designate or manage these rivers as components of the National Wild and Scenic Rivers System.
   d. Administration of the Clean Water Act and the Wild and Scenic Rivers Act will be better coordinated to ensure that investments made to clean up rivers and waterways provide maximum public recreation benefits.
3. National trails and trail systems.
   a. The Forest Service will establish 145 additional national recreation trails in the National Forest System.
   b. Federal land-managing agencies will establish goals for creating additional national recreation trails on public lands other than national forests.
   c. The Department of the Interior will accelerate its efforts to encourage state, local, and private land managers to submit applications for new national recreation trails.
   d. A grass-roots effort will be undertaken across the country to assess national trail needs. This assessment will be made by representatives of state, local, and private trail interests in cooperation with federal agencies.
   e. States, localities, and private landholders will be more actively encouraged to develop trails on their lands and to participate with federal agencies and trail users in creating a national trails system to meet public needs.
   f. The accomplishments of the "rails-to-trails" program of the Railroad

Revitalization and Regulatory Reform Act will be evaluated and further recommendations made to eliminate outstanding problems.

g. State and local governments will be encouraged to develop appropriate types of bike-ways using existing federal programs.

4. Water resources.
   a. Federal water quality grants will be more closely examined to determine the degree to which they include recreation considerations.
   b. Nonstructural alternatives to flood control, including the preservation of open space for recreation, will be evaluated for their applicability in flood-prone communities.
   c. Actions will be taken to ensure that urban waterfront revitalization projects include considerations for recreation and public access.
5. Energy conservation.
   a. A program of energy conservation will be developed for all recreation lands, facilities, and programs, and guidelines will be issued for all federal recreation grant programs to state and local governments.
6. Environmental education.
   a. Guidelines will be prepared for all Department of the Interior agencies and coordinated with other federal agencies.
7. The handicapped.
   a. The Department of the Interior will provide improved access to recreation facilities.
   b. The Department of the Interior will establish procedures to involve disabled citizens in the development of recreation policy and programs.
8. The private sector.
   a. The feasibility of cooperative agreements between the private sector and public recreation agencies will be explored as an alternative method of improving public recreation opportunities, and appropriate demonstrations will be undertaken.
9. Research.
   a. A comprehensive national recreation research agenda will be prepared.

In order to ensure continuous planning, a division for this purpose was established in the National Park Service. Its mission is:

1. To define and monitor the annual action programs.
2. To update the 5-year assessment.
3. To conduct nationwide recreation surveys and coordinate more specialized federal surveys.
4. To compile and update a national research agenda for recreation.
5. To promote long-range planning for the future of recreation in America.

STATE OUTDOOR RECREATION PLANS

The role of the state in outdoor recreation activities was detailed in Chapter 8. In this chapter the discussion is limited to the states' plans for outdoor recreation pursuits. Prior to the passage of the Land and Water Conservation Fund Act in 1965, individual states had no incentive to prepare an outdoor recreation plan. With the passage of the Land and Water Conservation Fund Act, an incentive was provided. For a state to receive financial assistance from the fund, it must have a current plan that spells out the ways in which it, the state, will help satisfy the recreational needs of its residents. A new plan must be prepared every 5 years. From 1965 to 1980 every state in the Union prepared a comprehensive outdoor recreation plan that was renewed every 5 years as required. With the attempts at reducing federal spending in 1981, some states stopped the practice of developing a new plan every 5 years.

The state is empowered through the U.S. Constitution to assume the responsibility for services that were not specified as federal government responsibility. Recreation is one of these responsibilities, and the planning for it was encouraged by the Land and Water Conservation Fund Act.

The typical state outdoor recreation plan revolves around three areas: demand, supply, and future projection. Problems and issues are addressed in some plans. The department charged with overseeing state parks and recreation offerings is usually the department responsible for developing the state's outdoor recreation plan and the coordination of its implementation with the agencies of the federal government and with the state's political subdivisions such as counties and cities.

The guidelines require that, in preparing the plan, citizen input must be considered. The state must seek the views of both public officials and interested citizens. Public meetings are encouraged. The following information is required in the plan:

1. A brief description of factors—such as climate, topography, wildlife, history, populations, and urbanization—that influence outdoor recreation in the state.
2. A list of the federal and state agencies that are responsible for creating, administering, and financially assisting publicly owned recreation areas.
3. An inventory of recreation areas that are publicly or privately owned, summarized by region or county, and a list of historic sites.
4. An estimate of the number of people who participate in each of several recreational activities, now and in the future, and an estimate of the frequency with which they participate.
5. A statement of recreation needs that will be met by the state, county, and local governments.
6. A statement of recreation needs of special populations, such as the elderly, the handicapped, and the poor.
7. A description of actions proposed for the next 5 years to provide more outdoor recreation opportunities, such as proposals for acquisition and development, legislation, financial and technical assistance, and research.

LOCAL OUTDOOR RECREATION PLANS

The local outdoor recreation plan addresses the demand and supply of local recreation opportunities and a prediction of future demands and the suggested answers to these demands. The same information that is to be included in a state plan should be included in a local plan except that it would be limited to the locality. Most local governments, whether county, city, or township, have planning departments that can help in providing some of the needed information. Sometimes the planning department prepares the whole document, if the department charged with parks and recreation would prefer not to prepare it because they lack staff. In other instances outside consultants are hired to prepare the local outdoor recreation plan.

According to Jensen, while there is no single best method of developing a plan, planners generally agree that the procedure can be divided into the following three major phases (1985:330):

1. Collection of data about past history and present status.
2. Projection of future park and recreation needs.
3. Formulation of realistic proposals for both near and long-term future.

In implementing the plan, cooperation of public agencies and private citizens must be secured. Input of all concerned must be sought during the different phases of preparing the document. Also, adequate financial support needed for implementation must be secured in advance. To be effective, the implementation of the plan must proceed according to an approved timetable.

Knudson (1984:334) stated that time frames of 5 to 20 years are commonly used in the preparation of local outdoor recreation plans. While 5 years is adequate, 20 years seem to be a long time. Many changes, both demographic and spatial, take place in a span of 20 years. Not only would young adults become middle-aged persons in two decades, but many new residents could move into the community, altering it considerably in less than a 20-year period. The altering of open space must be taken into consideration.

PROJECT PLANS

On the macro level, nationwide plans for outdoor recreation were discussed, and on the intermediate level, statewide and local plans were presented. On the micro level, the level of a single project, whether campground, waterfront, or ski resort, public or private, certain steps should be observed.

First, a master plan should be prepared that includes a description of the need for the development of the site based on demographics and predicted participatory figures. An inventory of existing (even if limited) resources would support the need for the proposed site. Also data on the physical characteristics of the site will be needed. How the site will be managed, in general terms, should be included. An important part of the master plan of a site is the preparation and submission of an environmental impact statement. The statement should be submitted, in conjunction with requirements of the Land and Water Conservation Fund Act, to the liaison office in each state.

It is imperative that the public become involved, not only because it is required in the case of public projects, but also because the public is, after all, the consumers to be served by the project. Market researchers for private enterprises conduct surveys to find out interest and preference of consumers. Such a process lacks interactive debate, which is explicitly required in public projects.

While each public agency dealing with projects for outdoor recreation may have its own way of developing a project, Jensen (1985:322) and Knudson (1984:339) suggested that the approach used by the Forest Service may serve as a model. The approach entails four major steps, as follows:

1. *Drafting of a detailed site map,* including:
   - Land lines and boundaries as well as ownership.
   - A permanently established baseline and reference points.
   - The map scale (usually no smaller than 1:600).
   - Contour lines with an interval of 1 or 2 feet (0.3–0.6 m).
2. *A narrative report,* consisting of three main parts:
   - Analysis and discussion of the physical characteristics of the site as they may influence design and construction.
   - Analysis and discussion of the physical and aesthetic requirements of the use or uses and the desired level of experience of users.
   - Statement of design objectives—that which you intend to do with design to accommodate the desired uses within the capability of the site to withstand the use.

3. *A general development plan,* usually made by tracing the detailed site map and adding proposed improvements. It would contain the following:
   - An overall design scheme.
   - The type and placement of all facilities but not layout details.
   - Road plan.
   - Survey control baseline and description.
   - Map showing the site and surrounding area.
   - Orientation.
   - Legend.
   - Aerial photo coverage.
4. *A final construction plan,* which conveys instructions to the contractor and includes:
   - Road design.
   - Water and sewage system designs.
   - Grading plans, including all contour modifications.
   - Family unit layout and construction details.
   - Construction drawings of all facilities and structures.
   - Layout information for the location of all site improvements.
   - All necessary specifications.

SUMMARY

In order that the managers of outdoor recreational areas and programs be able, not only equitably but also wisely, to provide adequate opportunities to all their recreationists, certain management policies should be followed. The two basic policies of preservation and multiple use are detailed in this chapter.

The preservation policy, which seeks to set apart certain lands for the benefit of all, and as applied particularly to wilderness areas is discussed in light of some eleven principles. The multiple-use policy which allows for certain forms of exploitation of natural resources is applicable to the national forests and is met with difficulties, at the core of which is the fact different users view American natural resources differently.

Outdoor recreation resources are classified into two basic categories, land and water, and both in turn are classified into small units such as forests, grasslands, deserts, and tundra; and rivers, wetlands, shorelines, lakes and reservoirs. The policies to be followed in the utilization of each are presented along with the process of planning.

National outdoor recreation plans, as required by law, are detailed in this chapter. Also presented are state comprehensive plans which were prompted by the passage of a number of federal acts. State plans for outdoor recreation are conducted every 5 years. Local outdoor recreation plans address the demand and supply of local offerings. On a micro level, the plan for a single local project is detailed from the master plan to the environmental impact report.

REFERENCES

Clawson, M., and J. Knetsch (1966) *Economics of Outdoor Recreation.* Baltimore, MD: Johns Hopkins University Press.

Cole, D. (1986) "Resource Impact Caused by Recreation," in The President's Commission on Americans Outdoors, *Literature Review.* Washington, D.C.: U.S. Government Printing Office.

Everhart, W. (1972) *The National Park Service.* New York: Praeger.

Frakt, A., and J. Rankin (1982) *The Law of Parks, Recreation Resources and Leisure Services.* Salt Lake City, Ut: Brighton Publishing Co.

Hendee, J., G. Stankey, and R. Lucas (1978) *Wilderness Management.* Forest Service, U.S. Department of Agriculture. Washington, D.C.: U.S. Government Printing Office.

Jensen, C., and C. Thorstenson (1977) *Issues in Outdoor Recreation* Minneapolis, MN: Burgess.

Jensen, C. (1985) *Outdoor Recreation in America.* Minneapolis, MN: Burgess Publishing.

Knudson, D. (1984) *Outdoor Recreation.* New York: Macmillan.

La Page, W. (1988) "Recreation Management: Physical Resources and Environment," in *Leisure Today: Selected Readings,* Vol. IV, S. H. Smith, editor. Reston, VA: AAHPERD.

Nash, R. (1978) "Historical Roots of Wilderness Management," in *Wilderness Management* by J. Hendee, G. Stankey, and R. Lucas. Forest Service, U.S. Department of Agriculture. Washington, D.C.: U.S. Government Printing Office.

Outdoor Recreation Resources Review Commission (1962) *Outdoor Recreation For America.* Washington, D.C.: U.S. Government Printing Office.

Washburne, R., and D. Cole (1983) *Problems and Practices in Wilderness Management: A Survey of Managers.* Research Paper INT-304. Ogden, UT: Forest Service, U.S. Department of Agriculture.

13 Management Procedures in Outdoor Recreation

Management is both a science and an art. It has become increasingly important in recent years as social organizations became more complex. Managers need experience in order to help an organization achieve its goals and run smoothly. The accumulation of ideas from early managers led to a body of knowledge that is supported by theories borrowed, sometimes, from other fields, including sociology, psychology, economics, and business administration. A growing number of managers are depending on scientific knowledge to make decisions, but these decisions should be tempered by personal judgment, intuition, and inspiration, making management an art as well as a science.

While the information in this chapter is drawn from past experiences and accumulated knowledge of the best possible procedures to follow in the management of outdoor recreation resources and activities, needless to say, managers must depend on their own best judgment to arrive at sound conclusions.

BASIC CONCEPTS OF MANAGEMENT

There are a number of fundamental concepts that should be kept in mind in the management of outdoor recreation resources and activities. The science and art of management were born out of the business and industrial sectors of society and not from its service sector. While there are very useful ideas emanating from business and industry, outdoor recreation opportunities are, nonetheless, offered as a service to the individual citizen, and they should be kept this way. Accordingly not all basic concepts in business and industrial management are applicable to the outdoor recreation sphere.

Management by Objectives MBO, as it is now known, requires that the manager and her or his staff become involved in both the establishment and/or the crystallization of the agency's objectives. Glover (1979) suggested the following guidelines for such endeavors:

1. Objectives must be quantifiable, so they can be used as criteria for future evaluation.
2. Each objective should be given a precise time limit for accomplishment.
3. Although objectives must fit within the framework of overall departmental policy and objectives, personnel at each level should play a role in setting their own goal(s).
4. A limited number of major objectives, usually three or four, are appropriate for each unit or individual, rather than too many.
5. Although the objectives may be challenging, they must also be both realistic and attainable.
6. Quantified performance criteria should be used in measuring the success in achieving each objective and should also be used in the personnel evaluation process as a measure of accountability.

Strategy Management This approach entails following a continual process to effectively relate the agency's objectives and resources to the available opportunities (Kraus and Curtis 1982:36–37). The approach revolves around three types of objectives:

1. The mission of the agency, which should be clearly defined.
2. The social/psychological objectives as based on the agency's perceived role.
3. The financial objective, which in the case of a nonprofit organization is to perform a service rather than to make money.

According to Kraus and Curtis (1982), the key element of successful strategy management is that it is always changing. Adaptation to new needs and opportunities is part of the strategy.

PPBS The planning, program, budgeting system (PPBS) calls for the careful development of goals, evaluation of the program or programs intended to reach these goals, and the establishment of a budget for that very purpose. The system involves the following steps:

1. Careful identification and description of objectives and the range of programs to achieve them.
2. Projection of needs to future years.
3. Explicit, systematic identification of alternative ways of reaching the objectives.
4. Estimation of the total cost implications of each alternative, including capital and noncapital costs, as well as nondirect charges such as employee benefits, replacement costs, and maintenance costs.
5. Estimation of the expected results of each alternative.
6. Presentation of the resulting major cost and benefit trade-off among the alternatives, along with the identification of major assumptions and uncertainties, over the period of time ahead.

PERT The program evaluation review technique (PERT) uses mathematical formulas and computer simulations to identify all key activities designed to achieve the stated goals of the agency. A flow sequence showing time, resources, and performance for each task is prepared. This process is called PERT-Time, and it attempts to do the following:

1. Present an organized plan for the project's completion.
2. Provide an estimated time of completion.
3. Identify the critical activities.
4. Identify those activities whose completion can be stretched out and the maximum time they can be extended.

5. Provide a means for making economic trade-offs between the cost penalties of being late, and the cost penalties for reducing the scheduled time.

The financial aspect of the PERT strategy is termed PERT-Cost, and it spells out the cost as related to each step and/or element. The PERT approach is useful in both the planning and implementation of projects. Since it is expensive, PERT is rarely used by park and recreation agencies.

Conflict Resolution Conflict is no longer viewed as always harmful or counterproductive. Conflict, in fact, may be an important vehicle for change. It is its resolution that should be handled with utmost care. According to Kraus and Curtis (1982:37), two broad approaches are utilized in conflict resolution:

1. Use of group process to examine the problem and arrive at an appropriate solution.
2. Development of a scientific approach using the PERT method to select the appropriate solution.

Either approach requires that a decision be made as shown in the following section.

Decision-Making Decision-making is probably the central activity of management, because its effectiveness is measured by the quality of its decisions. Decision-making should be a conscious act, the purpose of which is to choose from a number of alternatives. When and if a decision is made that pertains to a routine problem, the decision should be programmed into everyday and/or continuous operations. Decisions made for nonstructured situations require special consideration. There will be situations when no decision is needed. According to Zeigler and Bowie (1983:182), when the following situations arise, a decision is needed:

1. A discrepancy between the present state and the desired state exists.
2. The discrepancy is large enough to require special attention.
3. The decision-maker(s) are adequately equipped to deal with the situation.
4. There is enough motivation to attempt to reach a decision.

Zeigler and Bowie suggested that the following steps be taken in decision-making:

1. Identification of the problem.
2. Generation of alternatives.
3. Selection of an alternative.
4. Acceptance of decision and plan of action.
5. Implementation of the decision.
6. Evaluation.

Following are some of the situations that occur in outdoor recreation settings which require decision-making.

CARRYING CAPACITY

One of the most important decisions to be made by the management of an outdoor recreation resource is the carrying capacity of the resource. The idea behind carrying capacity is that when the resource encounters heavy use, its capacity to sustain recreation without deterioration should be determined (Fogg 1975:13). The idea can be traced back to the mid 1930s, but the interest in it peaked in the 1960s and 1970s, when the demand on the outdoor recreation resources increased dramatically. Fogg (1975:14) suggested that the design load of a resource is dependent on several factors which should take carrying capacity into consideration. These factors include:

1. The general attractiveness of the area.
2. The site in relation to population distribution.
3. The economic level of the tributory population.
4. The degree of urbanization of the tributory population.
5. The influence of an area of similar characteristics.

Many studies have been conducted on carrying capacity and its application in outdoor recreation areas (Stankey and Manning 1986:M-47). Some studies show that there are difficulties in adopting the concept, and other studies show difficulties in implementing it. Washburne and Cole (1983) found that managers of two-thirds of national wilderness areas believe that their use exceeds their capacity by far, and only one-half of these managers reported some progress in establishing carrying capacities.

According to Hendee et al. (1978:171), recreation resources are used by many different people, seeking many different, and sometimes conflicting, experiences. And if carrying capacity is designed to maintain the resource for as long as possible, research has shown that capacity is a function of more than simple numbers of users: intensity of use, habitat type, seasonality, and location play decisive roles in carrying capacity. Some researchers have criticized the term as inappropriate, inadequate and misleading for recreation resource management. Hendee et al. suggest that the emphasis should be on the intent behind the concept of carrying capacity. They suggested the following four criteria for carrying capacity:

1. The determination of carrying capacity is ultimately a judgmental decision.
2. Carrying capacity decisions depend on clearly defined objectives.
3. The range of available alternative opportunities must be taken into consideration.
4. Carrying capacity is a probabilistic concept and not an absolute measure.

Knudson (1984:315) discussed the factors that affect carrying capacity and grouped them into three major types.

1. Characteristics of the Resource Base The geology and soil of the resource are important factors in determining carrying capacity. Good soil has high carrying capacity which, in turn, is dependent on its drainage and depth. If the resource is dry enough to allow for reasonable use during the season, this will add to its capacity. Too dry or too muddy soil reduce capacity. Texture of the soil, its depth, and the type of underlying rocks play important roles in determining these factors.
Topography is an important factor in determining carrying capacity: while rough topography does not allow for many campsites, smooth topography does. Slopes facing north hold snow longer, providing longer skiing seasons but shorter seasons for picnicking and swimming. Different types of vegetation differ in their ability to withstand use. Also vegetation can be used to provide special benefits such as windbreaking along beaches, which may increase carrying capacity by extending the season. Climate is an important factor in determining the length of the season. Rainfall patterns, fog, and storms determine to a great extent the length of the season and the type of activities. The existence of water, or lack thereof, determines the type of use, thus the carrying capacity of the resource, for both people and wildlife.

2. Characteristics of Management The philosophy and laws that govern the agency in charge determine, to a great extent, the elements of the carrying capacity of the source. Examples of both the philosophy and laws are seen in the number of campsites per acre and in the size of the campsite itself, which translates into a certain carrying capacity. The design of the resource determines its carrying capacity. Paved roads encourage more traffic in comparison to gravel roads. The addition of a beach to a lake would, possibly, increase use.

3. Characteristics of Users Some users visit an outdoor recreation area for the enjoyment of nature, and others may visit it to be with a group. For the first type of users, crowding would be more of a problem than for the second type. Some recreationists use large equipment such as boats in their outings, others are content with smaller equipment. Also the type of activity practiced while in an outdoor recreation setting is very much related to carrying capacity. For instance, still hunting allows more hunters in an area than stalk hunting.

Knudson concluded that increased use or congestion may lead to sociologic impairment of the recreation experience and/or ecologic deterioration of the recreation resource. He suggested the use of the limiting factor approach, creating a ceiling of carrying capacity, not necessarily permanently. The ceiling can be raised to the next limiting factor as needed.

On the other hand, Graefe et al. (1987:78) suggested that carrying capacity can be utilized within the framework of the Recreational Opportunity Spectrum (ROS). The ROS combines spatial allocations with activities for the purpose of providing for a range of recreational opportunities. Carrying capacity is determined through the interaction of the physical, social, and managerial settings. Following are the factors affecting carrying capacity:

1. Land type:
   a. height
   b. density
   c. resiliency
   d. productivity
   e. geologic size
   f. resistance to compaction.
2. Vegetation:
   a. height
   b. density
   c. resiliency
   d. reproducibility
3. Social:
   a. number of contacts with others
   b. types of encounters
   c. types of activities
4. Other:
   a. access
   b. length of season
   c. patterns of use
   d. occupancy length
   e. attractiveness of site for specific activities

Must carrying capacity be described in terms of standards for acceptable conditions? Washburne (1982) compared two standard-based approaches to carrying capacity. The traditional approach uses numerical capacity as being necessary to keep the desired conditions. This approach fails to recognize type, distribution, as well as the setting of the activities. He suggested an alternative approach by rearranging the sequencing and priorities and by focusing greater attention on a monitoring program. Numerical capacities are still used but are placed in perspective. In essence his suggestion is very similar to Graefe et al. He proposed Visitor Impact Management, which takes into consideration five major areas when dealing with carrying capacity and visitor impacts:

1. Impact interrelationships
2. Use-impact relationships
3. Varying tolerance to impacts
4. Activity-specific influences
5. Site-specific influences

Research Findings

Stankey and Manning (1986:M-49) summarized research findings on carrying capacity according to the following three sets of factors.

Natural resource factors There exists a curvilinear relationship between recreational use and the impact of such use. Most recreational use leads to an impact, but additional use causes little additional impact. Also, secondary effects must be taken into consideration. It is rather difficult to determine the most appropriate indicator of the impact on a natural resource, since many ecological impacts are subject to some degree of management control. In the meantime, most of the research done focused on vegetation and soil. Studies on water, air quality, and wildlife should be encouraged.

Social factors Managers should make a distinction between crowding and overuse. Presence of others may be a motivational factor in recreation participation. The central factor seems to be that when others are seen to be sharing the same experience, perception of crowding declines. Satisfaction with an outdoor recreational experience is a complex, multifaceted concept.

Managerial factors Management can use the following four basic strategies to handle carrying capacity:

1. Reduce use through restrictions.
2. Accommodate more use by providing more opportunities.
3. Modify the character of use to reduce impact.
4. Harden the resource base to increase its resilience.

Direct management techniques to control carrying capacity focus on visitor behavior and limit choice by using permits and regulations. Indirect techniques attempt to influence visitor behavior.

Stankey and Manning (1986:M-54) indicated that several important gaps exist in our understanding of how carrying capacity works. They suggested that there is a need for better understanding of the interrelationships between ecological and social factors in setting carrying capacities. Also needed is our understanding of the consequences, social and ecological, when such capacities are exceeded. An understanding of how effective, or ineffective, certain management action is at addressing carrying capacity would be useful. Finally, more knowledge is needed on what constitutes compatibility among different groups, a concept which could be useful in minimizing crowding and conflict.

ESTIMATING USE RATES

Data on the use of outdoor recreation resources are useful in many ways. They are useful in planning; facts are needed for the adequate preparation for future use of a park, a forest, or any outdoor recreation resource. Another reason for keeping data on the use rate of the resource is to trace the changes that are occurring in utilizing the resource. The data could also be used, when needed, in public relations endeavors, whether directed to laypersons or to officials. Accurate data are also used in conjunction with obtaining federal and state grants and subsidies. Such data undoubtedly have budgetary implications on the local level.

Units of measurement The 1973 Nationwide Outdoor Recreation Plan required that each federal land-managing agency report annually to the Bureau of Outdoor Recreation, in accordance with the Land and Water Conservation Fund Act of 1965, as amended, on recreation use at each management unit, using the recreation visitor-hour as the standard unit of measure. When available and appropriate, agencies also should include recreation visit and activity-hour data. The definitions of these terms are as follows:

- A recreation visitor-hour is the presence for recreation purposes of one or more persons for continuous, intermittent, or simultaneous periods of time aggregating 60 minutes.
- A recreation activity-hour is a recreation visitor-hour attributable to a specific recreation activity.

- A recreation visit is the entry of any person into a site or area of land or water for recreation purposes.

States and localities have begun to use the same terms in preparing their reports on recreational management units.

Another unit of measurement that has come into use is "activity day" or "recreation day," which gives the average number of hours of participation per day in a given activity.

Other than by making an actual count, which is not feasible in many instances, and pure guess, which is not accurate, Jensen (1985:332) suggested the following methods for keeping track of the use of a natural resource:

1. **Estimates based on observation** This method involves no counting or sampling. It is simply a manager's best judgment of the number of visits to a particular area during a specified time. Obviously with this method there is much room for error, and the errors tend to be on the high side.
2. **The sampling method** This involves either direct counts of people or counts of a related element, such as number of cars. Generally, the larger the sample the more reliable the data. There is the problem of whether the sample is representative of the total population.
3. **The pure count method** This is the most cumbersome, yet the most accurate method of counting either individuals or a related phenomenon such as cars, entry fees, user fees, number of boats, campsite occupancy, or one of a number of other related elements.

Characteristics of uses The characteristics of those using natural resource areas are described in Chapter 5. When, how, and with whom the participant uses the resource will be described in this section. According to Hendee et al. (1978:291), most visits to natural resource areas are short. Day use seems to prevail in small and medium-size areas. Day use in national park backcountry and national forest wilderness and primitive areas was 41 percent of total use. Length of stay for overnight campers in these natural resources varied from 1.6 to 5.9 days. The authors believe that length of stay has been the same for a number of years and that increased travel costs could lead to fewer trips in the future.

The parties of wilderness visitors are generally small, from two to four persons (Hendee et al. 1978:296). Parties of over ten persons account for 5 percent of all groups in most areas. This may be due, in part, to managerial regulation to reduce the impact of large groups on the environment and on other visitors.

Summer seems to be the preferred season for engaging in recreational activities in natural settings. Hunting continues into the fall in many areas, and skiing is enjoyed in the winter. Only in the southern and southwestern United States, particularly in low elevation areas, would outdoor recreational activities continue in the winter and spring. Weekenders attend these activities more so than do day participants, even in the summer.

Most natural settings in the United States draw visitors from all over the nation. Nonetheless, it seems that close-by residents seem to dominate the scene. For instance, 92 percent of the Yosemite visits are made by Californians, and residents of the state of Washington account for 78 percent of visits to the national parks in that state (Hendee et al. 1978:299).

FINANCING OUTDOOR RECREATION

Although both the public and private sectors deal with outdoor recreation opportunities, the former has much more to do with it than the latter. In turn, the public sector should be treated as comprising three subsectors when the subject is outdoor recreational resources and activities: the municipal (city/county), state, and federal subsectors. How do these sectors finance outdoor recreation?

1. **Taxes** General taxes are the most common form of revenues for a local program. There is usually a property tax in which an assessment is provided for a given fiscal year. The monies collected are used to provide municipal services such as education, sanitation, police, streets, health, recreation, and other local services by either a city, a township, or a county government. Sometimes more than one public body are joined to provide a service. In that case one, two, or more public bodies are empowered to establish special districts, for example a park and recreation district, with special taxes collected for such purpose. Sometimes a small part of the general tax, expressed in mills, is collected. A mill is one thousandth of a dollar ($.001). *Millage taxes* are allocated in some localities for a certain program, for example, a park and recreation program. In other instances, *special assessment taxes* are collected from those who stand to benefit from the activity and not from others.
2. **Bonds** Bonds are used to finance major capital developments such as the acquisition of land and the building of facilities. There are many forms of bonds. A *term bond* is paid in its entirety at the end of a given period of time, usually 10 to 30 years. A *callable bond* allows the agency to pay it off before the end of the term. A *serial bond* allows for a specific portion to be paid yearly. A *general-obligation bond* is paid from general tax revenue. An *assessment bond* is derived from special assessment on those who would benefit from the project. A *revenue bond* is paid off from the income derived from the facility that has been built.
3. **Fees and Charges** In public recreation, in general, there are seven common types of fees and charges (Warren 1986:F-5). All of these are applicable to areas used for outdoor recreation, be they local, state, or federal.
   a. *Entrance Fees* These are charges for the entrance into large facilities such as zoos, botanical gardens, or game reserves.
   b. *Admission Fees* These charges are collected for performances, exhibitions, museums, and the like.
   c. *Rental Fees* These are charges for the use of a property that is not consumed and is to be returned, such as boats or motorcycles.
   d. *User Fees* These charges are for participation in an activity usually done with others, such as skiing, swimming, or playing golf.
   e. *License and Permit Fees* Certain activities are allowed upon the payment of these fees, for example, hunting, fishing, and camping.
   f. *Special-Service Fees* These charges cover special and atypical events such as workshops, summer camp, and class instruction.
   g. *Sales Revenue* These monies are obtained from the operation of concessions, restaurants, and stores.

The philosophic basis for, or against, charging for public recreation will be discussed later in this chapter.

4. **Government Grants** Grants through the federal government and other governments have brought billions of

dollars to public recreation agencies. Although these have been drastically reduced in recent years, these funds allowed for an unprecedented expansion in outdoor recreation opportunities in the recent past.

a. *Land and Water Conservation Fund* Administered by the National Park Service, this fund assisted municipalities and states in acquiring and developing open space. Each state must prepare a State Comprehensive Outdoor Recreation Plan (SCORP) listing existing resources and identifying its future needs.
b. *Community development block grants* In the 1970s substantial sums were used from these grants to enhance outdoor recreation facilities, particularly within urban settings.
c. *Revenue-sharing grants* With no strings attached, expenditure of monies from revenue-sharing grants on recreation ranked fifth among all local government expenditure, after police, fire, transportation, and general expenditures. Most of the expenditure went to operating expenses rather than capital development in recreation.
d. *Labor Assistance Programs* Foremost among these programs is CETA, the Comprehensive Employment and Training Act, which was designed to provide short-term employment and training for unskilled workers. Grants monies were used, instead, to support operations and maintenance in recreation as well as other municipal services. The Job Training Partnership Act (JTPA) has replaced CETA.
e. *Urban Park and Recreation Recovery Program* This relatively small program was designed to help distressed communities rehabilitate rundown recreation systems. Indoor and outdoor facilities were included in the rehabilitation program.

There are grants, both federal and state, that can be used in outdoor recreation for both capital development and operating expenses. In Canada, the federal government provides considerable assistance to provinces and municipalities.

5. **Foundation Grants** Due to a shortage of public monies from both federal and state sources, many local park and recreation departments are approaching foundations and private citizens for grants and gifts. According to Kraus and Curtis (1982:252), there are several types of foundations, as follows:
   a. Special-purpose foundations are created for the purpose of meeting a special need. Sometimes recreation and sport are listed among those needs.
   b. Company-sponsored foundations are created for the purpose of corporate giving. Although a separate entity, this type of foundation is controlled by the mother company.
   c. Community foundations are established to serve a particular community, be it spiritual or residential.
   d. Family foundations are established by a person or a family for the purpose of reducing taxes.

Kraus and Curtis suggested the following strategy in approaching foundations for gifts or grants (1982:253):

a. Establish a foundations committee composed of capable, willing individuals.
b. Prepare a list of foundations that may be interested in recreation, particularly outdoor recreation.
c. Develop a proposal concept that may be used to sound out the foundation before beginning the next step.

d. Prepare a formal grant proposal, which should be brief and convincing.
e. Present the proposal to the foundation in a timely fashion according to their published schedule.
f. Follow up by requesting a meeting within 2 to 3 weeks.

Grantsmanship is a relatively new term which shows how important it is to skillfully present a case to donors. Kraus and Curtis (1982:254) suggested that in order to achieve maximum results in obtaining a grant, the following points should be observed:

1. Beat the crowd, develop contacts, know about new grants before they are fully announced.
2. Visit grant headquarters, meet the key people, personalize your approach. Remember, they are bored by the mountains of paper which flood them.
3. Invite "them" to your city, and make the visit memorable; have "them" visit all sites.
4. Contact local political party leaders for assistance; seek industry and business people with high contacts.
5. In your presentations, use films, displays, large sketches, and graphics.
6. At first refusal or resistance, question why and follow up; persist until successful.
7. If a grant is awarded, get full newspaper coverage.

FEES FOR OUTDOOR RECREATION

The types of fees charged for the use of outdoor resources were presented earlier. This section deals with the philosophy for or against charging for outdoor recreation. The use of fees and charges for outdoor recreation activities goes back to 1908, when Mount Rainier National Park instituted an automobile fee. Charges were levied in Central Park by its concessionaire. Fees were charged in Connecticut state parks in 1933. Yet the practice was not widespread. With the decline of governmental support, the need for new sources of financing became evident. This does not mean that the other methods of financing, described earlier, are to be abandoned or even reduced in importance. Taxes, bonds, and grants are, and will always be, very important sources of financing public recreation.

Arguments for and against Fees

There are numerous arguments against the collection of fees in public recreation, if it is to continue to be public recreation. The bases for both capital outlay and operational allocation should be taxes. The support for the stand against fee collection for recreation comes from the case of public education, where fees are not collected and everyone is admitted. The proponents argue that the same should be observed in recreation and at all levels of public enterprise, local, regional, state, and federal. Another objection to charging fees revolves around the fact that those who need recreation the most are generally the least able to pay. Recreation is a service that should be provided not only on the same basis as education, but also on the same bases as sanitation and police protection (Kraus and Curtis 1982:230). To charge for recreation means double taxes, which is not acceptable.

On the other hand, those who advocate the collection of fees in recreation argue that the public tends to appreciate more those services for which it pays. Moreover, charging fees can be a useful guide in that it points out the desired program and/or facility, which could be helpful in further planning.

Two additional arguments for charging fees in outdoor recreation are: 1) fees help control access to the natural setting, and 2) fees help to expand and improve current offerings.

In 1979, the Heritage Conservation and Recreation Service (HCRS), the successor to the Bureau of Outdoor Recreation (BOR), supported the collection of fees, suggesting that the American consumer is both willing and able to pay (1979:5).

As early as the 1960s Rodney (1964:256) suggested a series of useful guides in establishing and maintaining fees in public recreation, as follows:

1. All fees and charges for recreation services should be in conformity with the long-term program policy of the recreation system and should be consistent with the legal authorization governing such practices.
2. Fees and charges should be viewed as a supplemental source of recreation and park funds and not as the primary source. Therefore, the value of any proposed activity or facility should be judged with respect to its meeting public needs rather than its income-producing potential.
3. All services entailing fees or charges should be periodically reviewed by the department, and those facilities or programs meeting general and basic community-recreation needs should not have fees imposed on them.
4. Sound business procedures and administrative controls should be used in the collection and disbursement of special revenues.
5. Policies regarding concession operations or the lease of departmental facilities should be determined as part of the general administrative responsibility with respect to fees and charges.
6. In general, recreation facilities, when not being used for departmental programs, should be made available free or at minimal cost to nonprofit and nonrestricted community organizations, particularly character-building organizations serving school-age children.

Kraus and Curtis (1982:232) suggested a number of techniques in minimizing the impact of increased fees, as follows:

1. Public Relations Park and recreation facility users should be provided the courtesy of advance notice of fee changes, as well as an explanation of the need for the revenues collected and the basis for them.
2. Gradual Increases Gradual increases, clearly tied to rising costs, may be more acceptable to the constituency than sudden or drastic fee increases.
3. Fee-by-Fee Consideration Each type of activity or facility should be separately examined and an appropriate fee set, according to the level of demand, cost of the activity, types of fees asked at competing opportunities, possible cosponsorship of the activity, or similar factors. In some cases, activities or facilities which tend to yield a profit may be used to subsidize or partially subsidize the cost of others.
4. Annual Passes Agencies may also provide frequent visitors to parks with the opportunity to purchase annual passes or other special privileges. The method may be used to increase both visitation volume and user identification with the recreation and park system; it is typically used for community swimming pools.

VISITOR MANAGEMENT

When a visitor arrives at an outdoor recreation site or area, a number of methods should be utilized to make his or her visit as pleasant as possible, while at the same time maintaining and preserving the natural setting on which the activity is taking place.

The Physical Aspects of Visitor Management

In addition to providing roads and trails, the agency should place signs wherever necessary. Signs are a major form of communication in outdoor recreation. Douglass (1975:313) suggested that they give directions, identify areas, give warning, supply information, and provide posting of agency regulations. He classified signs into the following four categories:

1. Administrative signs. These signs are used to identify boundaries, offices, and areas.
2. Directional signs. The internal direction sign is meant to inform pedestrians, while the external direction sign is for motorists.
3. Interpretive signs. These are designed to highlight the attraction, tell a brief history, or give some interpretation of the area.
4. Restrictive signs. These signs post regulations, control visitor movement, and remind visitors of their responsibilities.

Two other important physical aspects of visitor management are pedestrian and vehicular circulation. Both should be studied and developed according to the needs of the visitors as well as crowd control principles.

Information and Education

Roggenbuck and Ham (1986:M-59) conducted a review of literature on information-education programs in natural recreational settings and found them to be important components of management by both users and managers. These elements can be effective in solving certain management problems. They suggested that managers should endeavor to achieve the following:

- Develop an understanding of recreationists' characteristics, behavior, and informational needs so that programs can be designed to provide information that is important to managers.
- Develop cost-effective media presentations, both personal and nonpersonal, that are targeted at user groups whose wants are not being met or whose behavior is potentially problematic.
- Develop means to provide accurate information to recreationists early in the trip-planning process (computerized information systems seem to have potential).
- Assist in the benefit-cost analysis of information-education programs, especially with regard to reducing physical impacts on recreation lands.

Hendee et al. (1978:323) noted that management actions are either direct or indirect. Direct action is authoritarian and allows little freedom of choice. Indirect action, which uses information and education, is more subtle and could be effective in modifying behavior. Ham (1984) found that campers' compliance with a park's efforts was related to the quality and clarity of instruction.

Instruction can be given via signs, in leaflets, or through personnel. Personnel-based technique can be costly (Martin and Taylor 1981:104), and as a result some managers resort to the use of volunteers. Table 13.1 shows some of the direct and indirect management techniques used in wilderness areas.

Interpretive Service

According to Knudson (1984:396), there are three visitor-oriented objectives of interpretive service:

1. Tell the story of the recreational place.
2. Shape the visitor's experience.
3. Involve the participant in the activities of the place.

According to Jensen (1985:359), appreciation of the environment is another goal of interpretive

TABLE 13.1 Direct and Indirect Techniques for Managing the Character and Intensity of Wilderness Use

Type of Management	Method	Specific Techniques
Indirect		
(Emphasis on influencing or modifying behavior. Individual retains freedom to choose. Control less complete; more variation in use possible.)	Physical Alterations	Improve, maintain, or neglect access roads. Improve, maintain, or neglect campsites. Make trails more or less difficult. Build trails or leave areas trailless. Improve fish or wildlife population or take no action (stock, or allow depletion or elimination).
	Information Dispersal	Advertise specific attributes of the wilderness. Identify range of recreation opportunities in surrounding area. Educate users to basic concepts of ecology and care of ecosystems. Advertise underused areas and general patterns of use.
	Eligibility Requirements	Charge constant entrance fee. Charge differential fees by trail zones, season, etc. Require proof of camping and ecological knowledge and/or skills.
Direct	Increased Enforcement	Impose fines. Increase surveillance of area.
(Emphasis on regulation of behavior. Individual choice restricted. High degree of control.)	Zoning	Separate incompatible uses (hiker-only zones in areas with horse use). Prohibit use at times of high damage potential (no horse use in high meadows until soil moisture declines, say July 1). Limit camping in some campsites to one night, or some other limit.
	Rationing Use Intensity	Rotate use (open or close access points, trails, campsites). Require reservations. Assign campsites and/or travel routes to each camper group. Limit usage via access point. Limit size of groups, number of horses. Limit camping to designated campsites only. Limit length of stay in area (max/min).
	Restriction on Activities	Restrict building campfires. Restrict horse use, hunting, or fishing.

Source: C. Gilbert, et al. "Toward A Model of Travel Behavior in the Boundary Waters Canoe Area," *Environment and Behavior.* 4:2(1972):131–57. (Reprinted with permission.)

service. The scope of the interpretation program includes nature hikes and tours led by trained interpreters. Sometimes self-guided activities are used on trails and in nature centers and demonstration areas.

Tilden (1962:67) suggested the following principles as the guidelines of nature interpretation:

1. Interpretation is revelation based upon information. Build a story into your presentation and incorporate the visitors into your stories. True interpretation deals not with parts but with the historical and spiritual whole.
2. Interpretation is art and can be taught. The story is art—not science. We are all poets and artists to some degree; images are adventures of the imagination. The interpreter must possess the skills of speaking and writing.
3. The chief aim is provocation, not instruction—to stimulate in the reader or hearer a hunger to widen his or her horizon of interests and knowledge. The national park or monument, the preserved battlefield, the historic restoration, and the nature center in a public recreation spot are all places where interpretation blooms and flourishes. First stimulate the visitor's interest, and then stimulate her or him to see and understand.
4. Interpretation should aim to present the whole to the whole person. Toward a perfect whole, the interpreter works for a complete experience, using all five senses. The visitor should leave with one or more pictures in mind.
5. Interpretation programs for children should use a different approach than those for adults. Children enjoy using superlatives, such as the largest this, the smallest that. They love to touch objects with their fingers and hands. Challenge their senses. The interpreter can help children relate to phenomena in terms they understand, without talking down to them.

Control of Undesirable Actions

Hendee et al. (1978:314) suggested that there are five undesirable actions, to which they suggested certain responses. The authors listed the following as categories of undesirable visitor behavior:

1. Illegal Actions with Adverse Impacts Examples are the illegal use of chain saws or motorbikes in wilderness. The manager should enforce the law in cases of illegal actions.

2. Careless or Thoughtless Violations of Regulation with Adverse Impacts Littering is an example, as are shortcutting a trail instead of walking on switchbacks, camping in closed areas, and building wood fires where they are not permitted. It is possible that informal education sessions could be useful in reducing careless and thoughtless behavior.

3. Unskilled Actions with Adverse Impacts Digging a drainage ditch around a tent is an example of an impact resulting from a lack of wilderness skills or knowledge. Perhaps a pre-activity session that is designed to go over basic skills for the activity would be in order. Also signs could be posted, both pictorial and with text, on how to pitch a tent.

4. Uninformed Behavior which Intensifies Use Impacts This is illustrated by large numbers of visitors who enter a wilderness at a few well-known access points during peak use periods when they might have dispersed themselves over a number of access points if they had been more informed about alternative places. Some form of educational sessions would be useful to combat this behavior. Another way to control access entries would be to close off that entry point with a physical barrier, posting signs (pictorial), and indicating the next entry point.

5. Unavoidable Minimum Impacts
Examples are when visitors step on plants, when vegetation under a tent is damaged, and so on. The manager may have to revert to reduction in the use of the facility or area.

Litter control Research shows that litter detracts seriously from wilderness experience (Stankey 1973 and Lee 1975). The amount of litter that could be left by visitors might reach between 100 and 200 pounds for each visitor (Hendee et al. 1978:333). Fortunately the "incentive system of litter control" has proven to be very successful (Clark et al. 1972). This is the system in which the rangers contact families to solicit their children's help in keeping the natural area clean in return for rewards such as badges and presents. In the backcountry, where there are few children, an "appeal system" seems to be working in which the adult users are reminded to do their own litter pack-out.

The permit system The use of mandatory permits to use special areas such as trails has the important benefit of providing communication between the user and the manager (see Figure 13.1). Information is provided that could improve the user's experience and reduce his or her impact on the area. According to Hendee et al. (1978:319), a self-issued permit could be used where the impacts are not high enough to require rationing.

In a recent article, Pfister (1990:28) blamed the restrictive permit system on the sharp decline in the number of backcountry users of nineteen California wilderness areas, as shown in Table 13.2.

Rationing of permits, suggested Pfister, could be the reason for the attitudinal change that has taken place among the enthusiastic backcountry backpackers who have adopted the concept of substitutability (Hendee and Burdge 1974). They now freely shift among various choices in outdoor activities, as shown in some market surveys. Pfister suggests that management policies should attempt to:

1. Remove rationing techniques in areas of low participation.
2. Remove control over most areas except for those witnessing growth.
3. Devise new approaches to control use.

AREA MANAGEMENT: SPECIAL CASES

Outdoor recreation takes place in many locations, some of which have special characteristics that require special attention. Special management attention should be given to wilderness areas, rivers, and trails.

Wilderness Management

Wilderness in the United States is defined by the Wilderness Act of 1964 (Public Law 88–77). Wilderness is an area where human interference is kept at a minimum, yet recreation is practiced in it to a high degree. The act created the National Wilderness System, which contains 445 separate areas totaling close to 90 million acres, most of which are in Alaska and the West.

Patterns of use of these wilderness areas vary greatly, although day use seems to be the dominant pattern (Lucas and Krumpe 1986:M-121). Hiking seems to be the most prevalent form of travel, followed by horseback riding and canoeing/boating. Along with hiking, fishing, photography, and nature study are also practiced in wilderness areas.

Visitors to these areas seem to be young, well educated, and mostly males. Most come in pairs or small groups. Wilderness areas are visited mainly in the summer, although visits in the spring take place in the desert wilderness of the southwestern United States. Intensity of use varies significantly.

WILDERNESS PERMIT
U.S. Department of Agriculture Forest Service

______________________ Wilderness or Primitive Area [1—2] (Code)

When signed below, this Permit authorizes

____
(Name)

____
(Address)

______________________________ [3–7]
(City) (State) (Zip Code)

to visit this Wilderness or Primitive Area and to build campfires in accordance with applicable regulations. from [8–9] [10–11] to [12–13] [14–15]
(Mo) (Day) (Mo) (Day)

The number of people in the group will be . . . . [16–17]

The number of pack or saddle stock used will be . . . . [18–19]
(Enter "0" if no stock will be used)

The place of entry will be ______________________ [20–21]
(Location)

The trip will end ______________________ [22–23]
(Location)

I agree to abide by all laws, rules, and regulations which apply to this area, and to follow the rules of behavior listed on, or attached to this permit. I will do my best to see that everyone in my group does likewise.

__________ (Date) ______________________ (Visitor's Signature)

__________ (Date) ______________________ (Issuing Officer's Signature)

The visitor must have this permit in his possession during his visit to the Wilderness

This section for optional use of issuing officer.
Planned travel route, duration, and location of camps.

Travel Zone (see map)	24 – 25	26 – 27	28 – 29	30 – 31	32 – 33	34 – 35	36 – 37	38 – 39	40 – 41	42 – 43
Nights of use by zone	44 – 45	46 – 47	48 – 49	50 – 51	52 – 53	54 – 55	56 – 57	58 – 59	60 – 61	62 – 63

Visitor receives white copy.
Send yellow copy to the Forest Service Regional Office in San Francisco.
Send pink copy to the Ranger District where the trip starts.

GPO 191 406 R5-2300-32 Rev. 3/72

FIGURE 13.1 The standard wilderness permit used in all National Forest wilderness and National Park backcountry areas.

TABLE 13.2 Backcountry Use for Nineteen California Wilderness Areas (Thousands of visitor-days)

Name	1976	1977	1978	1979	1980	1981	1982	1983	1984	1985	1986	Change Peak to 1986
Caribou	23.1	41.4	24.2	11.9	16.5	16.5	11.0	11.9	10.0	9.9	10.0	−76%
Cucamonga	17.5	8.9	50.1	24.0	48.9	14.3	14.2	26.1	36.3	39.9	3.46	−93%
Desolation	298.6	301.7	216.1	307.2	202.7	212.8	195.1	143.1	20.0	222.7	227.5	−26%
Dome Land	11.4	8.5	10.7	12.5	8.5	11.4	9.6	5.8	6.4	6.7	4.3	−66%
Emigrant Basin	156.1	244.3	207.1	209.2	258.0	257.8	195.4	117.5	216.9	62.4	59.9	−77%
Hoover	130.2	142.0	66.6	67.4	72.0	93.6	74.9	59.9	103.0	106.6	49.0	−66%
John Muir	812.9	903.2	848.2	827.4	688.5	791.6	602.2	358.8	449.9	397.5	451.9	−50%
Marble Mt.	92.6	91.7	87.7	89.4	90.8	68.3	58.8	48.4	60.1	64.1	67.5	−27%
Mokelumne	30.4	17.2	7.4	36.8	25.6	39.1	48.3	29.0	18.7	25.1	25.4	−48%
San Gabriel	34.9	41.9	46.4	73.5	53.3	33.3	33.6	28.8	28.8	26.7	23.5	−68%
San Gorgonio	253.8	246.8	273.7	260.1	280.2	299.2	317.3	239.3	191.7	190.3	190.6	−40%
San Jacinto	86.1	90.2	116.9	116.9	129.2	78.0	77.8	76.8	75.3	80.7	33.4	−74%
San Rafael	47.7	44.3	46.2	42.5	34.4	42.0	43.6	76.1	73.3	96.1	97.9	+64%
South Warner	29.8	11.4	14.2	14.3	21.5	12.1	13.0	14.4	14.7	14.9	15.3	−49%
Thous. Lakes	11.7	10.3	10.0	12.1	11.4	5.9	9.4	12.0	11.6	12.6	18.2	+36%
Yolla Bolly	24.7	23.3	20.2	42.1	44.9	31.8	36.4	33.8	36.5	29.6	33.4	−26%
Ventana	18.5	82.9	13.0	66.3	88.8	90.2	40.2	25.9	28.5	28.4	29.6	−67%
Golden Trout	—	—	—	72.7	114.1	122.5	104.6	92.6	97.5	104.7	69.6	−43%

Source: Forest Service, U.S. Department of Agriculture, *Use of National Forest Trails, National Wilderness Preservation System* (Washington, D.C.: U.S. Government Printing Office, 1988). (Reprinted with permission.)

According to Lucas and Krumpe (1986:M-129), research has been conducted on the management of wilderness areas, yet a large gap in knowledge still exists. Further research is needed. Nonetheless, they proposed the following recommendations, which are consistent with the recommendations suggested in another study (Frome 1985):

1. Reaffirm the goal of keeping wilderness distinctive. Preservation of natural processes and conditions should be the overriding goal, along with provision of opportunities for a unique visitor experience dependent on natural conditions.
2. Complement wilderness with provision of a variety of high-quality semiprimitive recreation opportunities on undeveloped public lands outside wilderness areas. This will meet diverse public recreation needs and desires, and reduce pressures on wilderness areas for types of recreational use that would diminish their distinctive and special character.
3. Further apply and test the limits of an acceptable charge system as the most promising way of managing wilderness carrying capacity. (This idea was discussed in the section on carrying capacity.)
4. Emphasize the monitoring of wilderness use and conditions to provide a foundation for management.
5. Stress educational/informational approaches as a means of visitor management and as a means for minimizing regulations that tightly control visitor movement and behavior.

6. Increase trail maintenance to control environmental damage and meet visitor needs.
7. Relocate and redesign trail systems to reduce damage and provide better experiences for visitors.
8. Measure wilderness recreational use in comparable ways for all wildernesses administered by the National Park Service, Forest Service, Fish and Wildlife Service, and Bureau of Land Management to provide comparisons and to identify trends.

River Recreation

River recreation has grown steadily over the past few years. There are close to three and a half million linear miles of rivers and streams in the United States. Some of these miles are fit for recreational settings, many of which have been protected as part of the Wild and Scenic Rivers System. According to Lime (1986: M-137), recreation associated with that system has become one of the fastest expanding segments in Forest Service management. Lime painted a picture of the river recreationists as follows:

1. River recreationists vary widely in their activities, use patterns, motivation, and attitudes.
2. Socialization seems to be the most-mentioned motivational factor behind choosing rivers as the loci for recreation.
3. Risk-taking seems to be a characteristic common to river recreationists.
4. River recreation seems to be a novice experience for many of those participating in it.
5. Group size of river recreationists seems to be considerably larger than for most other outdoor recreation activities in natural settings.
6. Most of river recreationists are young, many below the age of 30.
7. River recreationists begin their activities at a later age than do most other recreationists, with the exception of tubers.
8. Participants in river recreation are predominantly white collar workers with above average incomes.

Lime expects that the demand for river recreation in the future will produce a number of challenges that should be met. Not only will there be an increase in the demand for access to urban water resources, but there will also be an increase in recreational use of existing river corridors. As the number of river recreationists increases, so will the need for expansion in service, equipment, and related industries. Organizations and clubs are being formed to promote water-based recreation along with increased demand for these opportunities by minorities, women, and senior citizens. The manager of a water-based resource should expect longer participation, demand for high-quality trips, and requests for handicapped access. Instruction in safety, good public relations, and high tech equipment will be in demand on water-based resources. Demand will continue for outfitters, boat liveries, and other commercial establishments along river corridors.

Recreation Trails

Hiking on trails in a natural setting gained popularity as a form of recreation in the early 1960s. In addition to hiking, trails provide other forms of recreation such as opportunities for nature study, photography, drawing and painting, and solitude. Trails can also serve as access to hunting, fishing, and camping. The passage of the National Trails System Act of 1968 (Public Law 90–543) provided the needed boost for these forms of recreation. The use of trails by recreationists more than doubled from 1969 to 1983. Although most of the increase took place in the 1970s with a leveling-off period in the 1980s, the 1990s may witness a substantial increase in trail recreation (Krumpe and Lucas 1986:M-153).

Hiking, which takes place on the trail, is more or less a day use, and not much associated with overnight camping. The distances covered are modest. Hikers in wilderness areas desire solitude, low-level encounters, and unmodified natural setting. Other trail users desire other amenities which create conflicts. Horseback riders, bicycle riders, and motorcycle riders do not use trails in wilderness areas, and their interests clash with the interests of others on nonwilderness trails. Similarly, cross-country skiers' interests clash with those of snowmobilers. Krumpe and Lucas (1986:M-155) suggested separation of trail users whenever possible.

The impact on trail use is seen in littering, horse manure, and deterioration of trails generally. Most of the trails in the United States were built 50 years ago for administrative purposes. Time and inadequate finances have contributed to the problem of trail deterioration. Rationing of users of trails has been suggested as a possible remedy. Other suggestions include a lottery system, a merit system, and trail fees. Limiting the number in a group entering a trail is another means of control.

According to Krumpe and Lucas (1986:M-159), research has concentrated on remote backcountry settings and little was done to investigate the use of trails located near metropolitan areas. The relationship between trail systems and the broader spectrum of recreation opportunities should also be explored. For instance, trail use has grown recently with the increased interest in wellness and fitness.

RISK MANAGEMENT: SPECIAL CASES

According to Kraus and Curtis (1982:286), there were 190 visitor fatalities and 2483 visitor injuries in the National Park System in 1978. In the same year, 1505 employees of the NPS were injured. The authors suggested five guidelines to be used in accident reduction and risk management.

1. Systematic Reporting and Record Keeping The agency should maintain an accurate picture of trends for possible future control.

2. Facilities Inspection and Hazard Abatement Regular inspection should be made of all areas imposing special risks such as rockslide areas, sharp curves, thin-iced places, and similar hazards. Also all equipment should be regularly checked.

3. Participant Safety Procedure All visitors should be made aware of the possible risk taken in some outdoor recreational activities. Unsafe conduct and hazardous areas should be pointed out through bulletins, signs, and oral warnings.

4. Staff Training Safety awareness and precautions should be made an important part of staff orientation and training. Members of the staff should take it upon themselves to make visitors aware of risky behavior and to firmly apply rules and regulations related to such behavior. Moreover, the staff should be licensed in first aid.

5. Emergency Procedures Emergency procedures should not only be established but also made known to all members of the staff. Regular patrols should be organized along with a speedy and effective means of communication with remote areas. Transportation should be available, and evacuation and escape routes should be delineated.

The process of law enforcement in a natural setting includes the following five steps, according to Harmon (1979):

1. To recruit and train competent personnel experienced in and responsible for various specialized duties.
2. To provide organization and training of personnel to deal with varied emergencies and challenges as they may occur, including ongoing in-service training in methods of law enforcement, first aid, and similar functions.
3. To promote safe design and construction of facilities; while law-enforcement personnel are not usually involved in this process, they can contribute helpful information at the planning stage to prevent problems that may occur later.

4. To provide a sound public relations and interpretative program, in order to give the visitor a high-quality experience in the natural environment, improve the public image of the park system, and familiarize visitors with the rationale underlying park regulations and ecologically sound use of the park setting.
5. To carry out fair and thorough enforcement of the rules, with emphasis on a positive and pleasant approach to the public, stressing education and helping to build positive attitudes, rather than a punitive or threatening approach.

LAW AND OUTDOOR RECREATION

The following legal terms are useful in our discussion of law and outdoor recreation:

Act of God. An unavoidable incident due to forces of nature that could not have been foreseen or prevented.

Assumption of risk. Participation or involvement in an activity or situation where an element of risk is inherent. Voluntary participation can be interpreted as an acceptance of risk. In outdoor recreation there is an element of reasonable risk that the participant assumes through his or her decision to participate.

Attractive nuisance. A facility, area, or situation that attracts participation and is hazardous. Examples are a footbridge in poor repair, a designated swimming area that is unsupervised or improperly regulated, or children's play equipment in poor repair. Whether a situation would be legally declared an attractive nuisance would be influenced by the laws of the particular state, the age and competence of the injured person, and the various circumstances surrounding the incident.

Civil law. Civil action implies a noncriminal infringement upon the rights of a person, agency, or corporation. Tort and contract disputes are examples of civil suits. Civil law is different from criminal law in that it regulates private, ordinary matters.

Common law. That body of governing principles and rules of action derived from past practices, customs, and raditions.

Contributory negligence. Where an individual's action was not the primary cause of negligence, but it was a contributing factor to the negligent act.

Equal protection of the law. The right of equal treatment by the law and the law enforcement agencies for all persons under similar circumstances.

Foreseeability. The degree to which danger may have been expected or an accident foreseen.

Immunity. Freedom or protection from legal action. Sovereign immunity refers to the protection of the government or the ruling body against possible suit or blame. It is based on the concept that "the king can do no wrong."

Injunction. A prohibitive ruling issued by a court directing a person or agency to refrain from performing a specific act.

Liability. Being responsible for a negligent act or other tort; having legal responsibility which was not fulfilled and resulted in injury.

Liability insurance. Insurance policies that provide protection against financial loss from liability claims.

Mandatory legislation. Enacted legislation that must be observed. Its opposite is *permissive legislation.*

Negligent. Not exercising the proper care or following the procedures that a person of ordinary prudence would do under similar circumstances. It can take the form of either commission or omission of an act.

Permissive legislation. Legislation that legalizes an action but does not require or mandate it. Its opposite is *mandatory legislation.*

Proximate cause. The situation or factor that was the main cause of an injury or incident.

Prudent person. One who acts in a careful, discreet, and judicious manner in view of the particular circumstances.

Statutory law. Law that is made through legislative acts.

Tort. A civil wrong or injustice, independent of a contract, which produces an injury or damage to another person or to property.

Liability and Recreation Agencies

Not long ago liability was hardly a problem with which a recreation agency, public or private, had to contend. Today the recreation provider and the equipment manufacturer are subject to the threats of a lawsuit. Previously the tradition of sovereign immunity protected public agencies, a right of government inherited from the British legal system where the King cannot be wrong. Today, the government and its agents are not so immune, and neither is the manufacturer. Attention must be given to acquiring safe equipment and to conducting safe recreation.

Tort Laws and Negligence

Civil wrongs that are not criminal in nature, such as trespassing, nuisance, defamation, and negligence, fall under tort laws. Most cases related to outdoor recreation come under negligence, which means that the person in charge failed to perform his or her responsibilities at the expected level of a prudent person under the same circumstances. Even if the acts of the person are not intentional, good intentions are not safeguards against prosecution. In the case of negligence, prosecution is done by the injured person and not by a law enforcement person. The prosecutor must show by a preponderance of evidence (over 50 percent) that the defendant was negligent.

According to Jensen (1985:343), for a person to be declared negligent, the following elements must exist:

1. The defendant must have a *duty toward the plaintiff.* Employees of recreation-sponsoring agencies clearly have certain duties toward participants. In most states a person does not have a legal duty toward a stranger even when the stranger is in dire need of help. To encourage aid when needed, some states have passed *Good Samaritan laws,* which provide legal protection for a person who tries to assist another person.
2. The plaintiff must have been harmed by the tort or wrong committed by the defendant. This could be in the form of property damage, personal injury, or damage to one's character or reputation.
3. The individual having *duty* must have breached that duty by an act of omission (*nonfeasance*). This means that a person who does nothing when something should have been done is often as liable as one who responds incorrectly.
4. The breach of duty mentioned in the previous item must have been directly related to the damage done to the plaintiff. In other words, the breach of duty was the proximate cause of the damage.

The situations that could lead to possible negligence include, but are not limited to, the following:

1. *Impudence.* (This is known as the reasonable-man test.) A duty of care is decided upon in court which involves what a prudent individual should do to safeguard the persons under his or her care.

2. *Attractive nuisance.* This concept revolves around whether the facility or equipment therein are attractive, yet hazardous, unsecured, and/or unsupervised.
3. *Faulty equipment.* The malfunction of equipment or an instrument may lead to the injuring of a participant.

Visitors to outdoor recreation areas are subject to protection under tort law according to their status, which is decided upon by the courts. Knudson (1984:503) classified these visitors into three categories, as follows:

Trespassers A trespasser is a person who enters the property of another without permission and not for the benefit of the property owner. The landowner has only minimal responsibility for the protection of the trespasser, taking due care to avoid injuring the person, if the trespasser's presence is known. The trespasser should be notified of dangers. Traps set for the trespasser or intentional shooting at the trespasser would make the landowner liable.

Licensees A licensee is a person who enters a property with the consent, implied or stated, of the owners but not for the benefit of the owner. Examples of licensees are cross-country skiers who receive permission (no fee paid) to use company land or a farm, a person who asks permission to hunt pheasants in a cornfield, or a fisherman who is allowed to cross private land to reach a stream. The landowner is required to warn the licensee of hidden hazards (deep hole, snow-covered stumps, a violent bull) known to the owner, and the landowner is required to prevent willful harm to the licensee. Other than fulfilling those requirements, the owner has few responsibilities for injury to visitors. The landowner is not under obligation to inspect the premises for unknown dangers. The licensee cannot receive damages for injury to himself or herself, his or her vehicle, or equipment.

Invitees The invitee class includes any visitor to a public park, forest, lake, refuge, or other recreation area, or a business visitor to a commercial recreation area, or any visitor to industrial or other land for the benefit of the landowner. If both the visitor and the landowner receive mutual benefit, the visitor is usually classified as an invitee. The owner has an obligation to keep the premises (that portion that is designated for recreation use) safe and to prevent injury to the visitor. This requires:

1. Warnings of danger to the visitor.
2. Regular inspection of the premises and facilities.
3. Removal of dangerous conditions or installation of safety measures where practicable.

Despite the vulnerable position of recreation agencies, recent lawsuits are showing that these agencies are winning. According to Rankin (1990), there are two fundamental explanations for this. First, managers of outdoor recreation resources are upgrading equipment and facilities to meet accepted safety standards. Second, agency defense in court revolves around a statutory scheme that relieves the agency of duty to protect the participant. The Federal Tort Claims Act and similar state statutes, which allowed public agencies and their employees to be sued, left several exceptions in the law, for example, policy-level immunity. Accordingly when a lawsuit results from a questionable policy, the court will reinstate some immunity to insulate the agent from liability.

While the implied immunity applies mainly to public agencies, another method of defense is used by private, as well as public, recreation providers. A model statute was initiated in 1965 by the Council of State Governments entitled "Public recreation on private lands: limitations on liability." It became the basis for many state laws on this subject. If the owner allows for the recreational use of her or his land or facilities without charge, she or he owes no duty to keep the property safe or warn of dangerous conditions. But if fees are charged, or if the owner were to willfully and maliciously fail to warn against danger, then she or he is subject to a lawsuit.

Waivers/Release Agreements

There have been instances in which damage waivers were not upheld in court, but development in the past decade indicates differently (Rankin 1990:9). As a general rule, waivers are held up by the court unless there is a statute to the contrary. For instance, if the negligent act falls below the standard established by law, or if the case involves public interest. The decision as to what is of public interest is left up to the court. Also the court examines the language of the waiver to see that it is written in simple, clear, and unambiguous language understandable to lay persons.

Rankin (1990) reviewed a number of cases in risk recreation and suggested that although liability should be a concern of risk recreation providers, fear of unjust and excessive judgments by the courts is not justified. This claim is supported by the fact that in the case of Rubenstein v. United States (Kaiser 1986:147), the court ruled in favor of the defendant (the United States). Burrell Rubenstein brought action against the United States under the Federal Torts Claim Act to recover for injuries that a client suffered from a bear attack while camping at Yellowstone National Park. The plaintiff was warned through a brochure and signs that bears were dangerous animals. It was difficult to envisage what additional measures could have been taken by the park authorities to ward off a possible attack by a bear. The plaintiff knew or should have known of the risk of an unprovoked attack.

But in another case, Niddangh v. United States (Kaiser 1986:146), action was brought under the wrongful death statutes of the State of Wyoming. The plaintiff was acting on behalf of the estate of Stephan Athan who was killed by a falling tree at a campsite at Yellowstone National Park. Stephan Athan was an invitee to whom the United States owed the duty to keep the premise safe and to warn him of any danger. He was encouraged to enter the campground with a sense of assurance and did not assume the risk of camping. The United States was found negligent.

SUMMARY

This chapter provides an idea of how some management procedures can be utilized in outdoor recreation resources. The basic concepts in management such as Management by Objectives, Strategy Management, the PPB System, and PERT can be used in the management of outdoor recreation resources.

The management techniques that can be utilized in outdoor resources include the process to determine the carrying capacity of a facility, the process to estimate user rates, along with the units to be utilized to measure use.

Sources for financing outdoor recreation such as taxes, bonds, fees, and charges as well as grants are presented as the possible avenues of financing outdoor recreation. Arguments for and against charging fees for outdoor recreation pursuits on public lands were presented as well. While those who oppose fees use public education as their model, the proponents of fees argue that charging of fees will help control access to natural resources. Also, improvements could result from the use of fees for such a purpose.

Visitor management represents a problem for the manager of outdoor areas. Procedures for visitor control which has some bearing on carrying capacity are discussed along with the need for management of special areas such as wilderness, rivers, and trails. Among the many techniques to be used in visitor management are improvement of the physical appearance of the natural resource, provision of adequate information and education systems, control of undesirable activities, litter control, and the permit system.

Since some outdoor pursuits present risk for many recreationists, a section on risk management is included along with the basic laws that govern liability. Two court cases on agency liability are described.

REFERENCES

Clark, R., J. Hendee, and R. Burgess (1972) "The Experimental Control of Littering." *Journal of Environmental Education* 4(2):22–28.

Douglass, R. (1975) *Forest Recreation.* New York: Pergamon Press.

Fogg, G. (1975) *Park Planning Guidelines.* Alexandria, VA: National Recreation and Park Association.

Frakt, A. N. (1978) "Adventure Programming and Legal Liability." *Journal of Physical Education, Recreation and Dance* 49 (April):25.

Frome, M. (1985) *Issues in Wilderness Management.* Boulder, CO: Westview Press.

Gilbert, C. et al. (1972). "Toward a Model of Travel in the Boundary Water Canoe Area," Environment and Behavior 412:131–57.

Glover, J. (1979) "MBO: A Tool for Leisure Service Management." *Parks and Recreation* (March):26.

Graefe, A., F. Kuss, and J. Vaske (1987) *Recreation Impacts and Carrying Capacity*: A Visitor Impact Management Framework. Washington, D.C.: National Parks and Conservation Association.

Ham, S. (1984) "Communication and Recycling in Park Campgrounds." *Journal of Environmental Education* 15(2):17–20.

Harmon, L. (1979) "How to Make Park Law Enforcement Work for You." *Parks and Recreation* (Dec):20.

Hendee, J. C., and R. J. Burdge (1974) "The Substitutability Concept: Implication for Recreation Research and Management." *Journal of Leisure Research* 157–63.

Hendee, J., G. Stankey, and R. Lucas (1978) *Wilderness Management.* U.S. Forest Service. Washington, D.C.: U.S. Government Printing Office.

Heritage Conservation and Recreation Service (1979) *Fees and Charges Handbook.* Department of the Interior. Washington, D.C.: U.S. Government Printing Office.

Hines, T. (1968) *Budgeting for Public Parks and Recreation.* Washington, D.C.: NRPA.

Jensen, C. (1985) *Outdoor Recreation in America.* Minneapolis, MN: Burgess Publishing.

Kaiser, R. (1986) *Liability and Law in Recreation, Parks, and Sports.* Englewood Cliffs, NJ: Prentice Hall.

Knudson, D. (1984) *Outdoor Recreation.* New York: Macmillan.

Kraus, R., and J. Curtis, (1982) *Creative Management in Recreation and Parks.* St. Louis, MO: Mosby.

Krumpe, E., and R. Lucas, (1986) "Research on Recreation Trails and Trail Users," in *The President's Commission on Americans Outdoors, A Literature Review.* Washington, D.C.: U.S. Government Printing Office.

Lee, R. (1975) *The Management of Human Component in the Yosemite National Park Ecosystem.* Yosemite, CA: The Yosemite Institute.

Lime, D. (1986) "River Recreation and Natural Resources Management: A Focus on River Running and Boating," in *The President's Commission on Americans Outdoors, A Literature Review.* Washington, D.C.: U.S. Government Printing Office.

Lucas, R., and E. Krumpe (1986) "Wilderness Management," in *The President's Commission on Americans Outdoors, A Literature Review.* Washington, D.C.: U.S. Government Printing Office.

Martin, B. H., and D. T. Taylor (1981) *Informing Backcountry Visitors: A Catalog of Techniques.* Gorham, NH: Appalachian Mountain Club.

Pfister, R. (1990) "Participation and Management Policy: Backcountry Recreationists' New Preferences." *Leisure Today* (April):28–31.

Rankin, J. (1990) "The Risk of Risks: Program Liability for Injuries in High Adventure Activities." *Leisure Today* (April):7–10.

Rodney, L. (1964) *Administration of Public Recreation.* New York: Ronald Press.

Roggenbuck, J., and S. Ham (1986) "Use of Information and Education in Recreation Management," in *The President's Commission on Americans Outdoors, A Literature Review.* Washington, D.C.: U.S. Government Printing Office.

Stankey, G. (1973) *Visitor Perception of Wilderness Recreation Carrying Capacity,* INT-142. Ogden, UT: Ranger Experimental Station, U.S. Forest Service.

Stankey, G., and R. Manning (1986) "Carrying Capacity of Recreational Settings," in *The President's Commission on Americans Outdoors, A Literature Review.* Washington, D.C.: U.S. Government Printing Office.

Tilden, F. (1962) *Interpreting Our Heritage.* Chapel Hill, NC: University of North Carolina Press.

Warren, R. (1986) "Fees and Charges," in *The President's Commission on Americans Outdoors, A Literature Review.* Washington, D.C.: U.S. Government Printing Office.

Washburne, R. (1982) "Wilderness Recreational Carrying Capacity: Are Numbers Necessary?" *Journal of Forestry* 80(1):726–28.

Washburne, R., and D. Cole (1983) "Problems and Practices in Wilderness Management: A Survey of Managers. *Research Paper,* INTD-304. Intermountain Forest and Range Experiment Station. Washington, D.C.: U.S. Forest Service.

Zeigler, E., and G. Bowie (1983) *Management Competency Development in Sport and Physical Education.* Philadelphia, PA: Lea and Febiger.

14 Education and the Outdoors

Lloyd Burgess Sharp, an early leader in outdoor education, said, "In simple terms, outdoor education means all of that learning included in the curriculum in any subject matter area and at any grade level which can best be learned outside the classroom" (Rillo 1985:7). This statement suggests that outdoor education is not exclusionary. Rather outdoor education is inclusive of many subject areas that deal directly with the natural environment and life situations outside of the classroom. Outdoor education can take place in the school yard, on the playground, at a park, on a farm, or at camping facilities. An outdoor education experience can take place in minutes or overnight, or it may last for a week. Programs are sponsored through educational institutions, camps, recreation departments, and private entrepreneurs. Outdoor educators have varied professional backgrounds ranging from recreation to biology. According to Ford (1989:30), " . . . outdoor educators include those interested in the outdoor pursuits of a physical nature; those who are interested in high risk outdoor recreation; those who teach elementary school camping; the physical educator who is interested in fitness; the teacher who approaches education in a holistic manner—including mental, physical, and social aspects of learning; and, in fact, all teachers and leaders interested in incorporating the subject and the medium of the outdoors into their programs."

A comprehensive definition of outdoor education is set forth in an adaptation of a position paper on the definition and philosophy of outdoor education by the Council on Outdoor Education (COE) (1989:31) available from the Educational Resource Information Center (ERIC): "Outdoor education is education *in, about,* and *for* the out of doors." This is the most acceptable definition to the council because it expresses the place, the topic, and the purpose of outdoor education. It suggests that the location could be any outdoor setting that is conducive to direct experiences, allows contact with the topic, and permits participant interaction and socialization. The COE explains that the topic includes the outdoors and the cultural aspects related to the national environment. While any subject may be taught, learning must take place through the outdoor experience. Soil, water, animals, and plants make up the basic areas of study, but the student may also learn and practice outdoor activities pursued during leisure time. Outdoor education is a holistic approach to the study of the interrelationships of nature, humans, attitudes for caring about the environment, and skill development in using natural resources for survival as well as leisure pursuits. The purpose of outdoor education is to implement the cognitive, psychomotor, and affective domains of learning for the sake of the ecosystem (Council on Outdoor Education 1989:31–32).

TERMINOLOGY

Another early leader in outdoor education, Julian Smith (1974:23–24), explained the desire of many who were involved in outdoor education to keep terminology simple. But Gilbert and Chase (1988:26–28) found that it had become next to impossible to define outdoor education. They found, however, that definitions were necessary to continuing programs in outdoor education. One will undoubtedly hear the following terms associated with outdoor education: conservation education, environmental education, resource-use education, nature education, camping education, outdoor recreation, and others. Smith (1974:24) said:

> Whatever label is given to the outdoor 'thing' there seems to be some common agreement that the vitalization of learning and the guarantee of a healthful, beautiful and permanent natural environment for today's and tomorrow's generations are goals which should be and can be realized. To achieve such high purposes, there is a great need for better communication, but with fewer words and more cooperative action by those who would be educational leaders in these times.

In the adaptation by the Council on Outdoor Education (1989:32) the following definitions were given:

> *Environmental education* refers to education about the total environment, including population growth, pollution, resource use and misuse, urban and rural planning, and modern technology with its demands on natural resources. Environmental education is all-encompassing, while outdoor education is seen by some to relate to natural resources and not to include the wide sense of the world environment. Many people, however, think of outdoor education in its broadest sense and prefer the term outdoor/environmental education.
>
> *Conservation education* is the study of the wise use of natural resources. It tends to focus on animals, soil, water, and air as single topics in relation to their use for timber, agriculture, hunting, fishing, and human consumption. It is not usually concerned with preservation, recreation, or human relations and as such is more narrow than outdoor education. The use of this term has decreased since the 1960s.
>
> *Resident outdoor school* is the process of taking children to a residential camp during school time for a period of usually three to five days to extend the curriculum through learning in the outdoors. This process was originally called camping education. It was later referred to as school camping, but these phrases were discontinued when parents and taxpayers believed they meant the same thing as summer camp, which seemed to be more recreational than educational.

Outdoor recreation refers to a broad spectrum of outdoor activities participated in during leisure time purely for pleasure or some other intrinsic value. Included are hiking, swimming, boating, winter sports, cycling, and camping. In many countries, and to some extent in the United States, these activities are called *outdoor education,* particularly if they are taught in the school as part of the curriculum.

Outdoor pursuits are generally nonmechanized, outdoor recreation activities done in areas remote from the amenities of telephone, emergency help, and urban comforts. To many people, the terms outdoor recreation and outdoor pursuits are similar.

Adventure education refers to activities into which are purposely built elements perceived by the participants as being dangerous. The activities are not inherently dangerous as taught (under qualified instruction), but they appear to be so to the participant and thus they generate a sense of adventure. Adventure activities include such things as rope courses, white-water rafting, mountaineering, and rock climbing.

Experiential education refers to learning by doing or by experience. Many experiential education activities are synonymous with adventure activities and outdoor pursuits; however, experiential education can also mean any form of pragmatic educational experience. In many ways, outdoor education may be viewed as experiential, especially when learning takes place through outdoor experiences.

Environmental interpretation is a term usually associated with visitor centers administered by national park or forest service centers. The term refers to a technique used to help visitors understand the meanings of the phenomena on display, while simultaneously arousing curiosity for more information.

Nature education and *nature recreation* are learning or leisure activities related to natural resources. The terms were used from the 1920s to the 1950s, and the activities were not usually interrelated, nor did they focus on the overriding concerns of ecology and stewardship of the land. They were usually isolated, individual activities using natural resources for equipment and facilities, and involving knowledge of nature.

HISTORY

The origin of outdoor education is difficult to trace. Some believe its beginnings go back as far as Socrates and Plato. Others attribute the beginnings to the "outing trips" of private schools in the 1800s such as those taken by students of the Round Hill School, and still others trace the roots of outdoor education to summer recreation programs in California or to the out-of-classroom activities in the Atlanta Public Schools of the 1920s. But it is clear that industrialization of the early 1900s brought children from farms to crowded cities, and time and again participants in physical activities became spectators with physical health problems. An era in which tuberculosis frequently claimed the lives of citizens was upon the nation, and as a remedy, the enrichments of outdoor life were rediscovered. Like many other ideas, the notion of outdoor education did not bloom from a single advocate but grew from several movements and dedicated individuals. A closer look at two early programs and the thinking of several early leaders follows.

Round Hill School

Round Hill School of Northampton, Massachusetts, was a school for boys that existed from 1823 to 1834. The curriculum was unique in offering 2 hours a day of physical education and outdoor activities. Sharing an interest in nature, the outdoors, and hiking, the school's founders, Joseph Cogswell and George Bancroft, located their school on a round hill overlooking the scenic Connecticut River valley within view of the beautiful Berkshire Mountains. Joseph Cogswell is credited as the originator of school camping and outdoor education in the United States. (Bennett 1974:33–37).

Bennett's research uncovered the following proposal in the school prospectus:

> . . . and certainly in the pleasant days of Spring and Autumn, so far from compelling them to remain at home, we would encourage them [the students] to go abroad and learn to feel the beauty of creation and the benevolence of its Author. Short journeys, whether on foot or by other means of conveyance, might quicken their powers of observation, and by refreshing and strengthening their bodies, prepare their minds for more profitable application (Cogswell and Bancroft 1823:8–9).

Early after the school's opening in 1823, outdoor activities were made available. Cogswell took six of the students on a 100-mile round trip journey to Hartford. Changing off the entire way, they either walked or rode horses. Student letters refer to Cogswell leading other excursions to strawberry fields and gardens, on fishing and hunting trips, and on camping expeditions. Students participated extensively in outdoor activities such as skating, coasting, swimming, and horseback riding. Art lessons were sometimes taught at the bank of the river. Crony Village was constructed by the boys by burrowing into the hill and adding a chimney and door. Many evenings were spent around the fire cooking and telling stories. Reports indicate the pupils enjoyed excellent health (Bennett 1974:33–37).

Offering an excellent education in which camping and outdoor education played an essential part, Round Hill School was described by a student in later years as follows:

> When I left it in 1828 to enter my uncles' Boston office, I was strong, healthy, and self-reliant, though not remarkable in any degree; a fair swimmer, a good shot, and best of all a good rider; and I never can be grateful enough for the advantages which Mr. Cogswell conferred (Bennett 1974:37).

Boy Scouts of America

The Boy Scout movement (see Chapter 10) took off immediately in the United States and quickly became the nation's largest nonschool youth organization. Other outdoor youth organizations of the early 1900s such as Woodcraft Indians, Sons of Daniel Boone, and Boy Pioneers set the stage for the movement's acceptance. Ernest Thompson Seton, who established Woodcraft Indians, had the background and interest in youth to establish him as the logical choice for the position of first Chief Scout of the Boy Scouts of America in 1910. His many volumes on scoutcraft became an integral part of scouting, and his intelligence and enthusiasm helped turn an idea into reality. The handbook *Boy Scouts of America: A Handbook of Woodcraft, Scouting, and Life-craft* first appeared in 1910, and within the first 30 years of publication sold an estimated seven million copies (Nash 1970:19). In it, Seton listed nine pertinent principles necessary for achieving the joys of outdoor life. These principles were worded as follows (Nash 1970:21–22):

1. This movement is essentially for recreation.
2. Camping is the simple life reduced to actual practice, as well as the culmination of the outdoor life.
3. Camps should be self-governing.
4. The camp-fire is the focal center of all primitive brotherhood. We shall not fail to use its magic powers.
5. Fine character and physique can be developed through the knowledge of *woodcraft pursuits*—riding, hunting, camper-craft, scouting, mountaineering, Indian-craft, Star-craft, signalling, boating, and all good outdoor athletics and sports including sailing, motoring, nature-study, wild animal photography and above all Heroism.
6. Try not to "down the others, but to raise ourselves."
7. Personal achievements will receive decoration.

8. A heroic ideal leads to higher things.
9. The effect of the picturesque is magical. The charm of titles, costumes, ceremony, phrase, dance and song are utilized in all ways.

The Boy Scout movement continues today. Current programs are discussed later in this chapter.

Seton, who immigrated to America from Scotland in the 1880s, wrote:

> Sport is the great incentive to Outdoor Life; nature study is the intellectual side of sport. I should like to lead this whole nation into the way of living outdoors for at least a month each year, reviving and expanding a custom that as far back as Moses was deemed essential to the national well-being . . . it is not enough to take men out-of-doors. We must also teach them to enjoy it. . . .
> (Nash 1970:21).

In 1903, Liberty Hyde Bailey, another man of insight, wrote of the child's need to study nature. Borrowing some ideas from American philosopher, psychologist, and educator John Dewey's progressive education, Bailey wrote:

> Nature-study is not science. It is not knowledge. It is not facts. It is spirit. It is concerned with the child's outlook on the world . . . nature-study is studying things and the reason of things, not about things. It is not reading from nature-books. A child was asked if she had ever seen the great dipper. 'Oh, yes,' she replied, 'I saw it in my geography' (Nash 1970:65–66).

It is perhaps due to the influence of innovative thinkers and educational philosophers that outdoor education evolved. Two people, Lloyd B. Sharp and Julian W. Smith, are especially significant to the development of outdoor education in the United States.

Lloyd Burgess Sharp, known as "L.B." or as "The Chief," was born in Kansas in 1894. He was first called "Chief" by campers, but he eventually earned the title from others because he was an innovator, promoter, and chief in his field. Educated at Columbia University, Sharp received his B.S., M.A., and Ph.D. degrees at a time when Columbia was noted for its progressiveness. According to Vinal (1974:45–47), Sharp spent several years with the National Recreation Association and taught at Columbia. In 1925 he was named executive director of Life Camps, Inc., and by 1926 he led the organization away from the traditional camping program of centralized camping to decentralized camping with each group responsible for its own program. During the 1930s he continued pioneering in "camping education" at Life Camps. In 1940 Sharp established National Camp for the training of leaders, and by 1944, National Camp and Life Camps, Inc., had published *Extending Education.* Sharp's vision received national exposure in this publication and others, and his books and publications influenced many in the field of outdoor education.

Many methods and practices that have proven successful in outdoor educational instruction were evolved by Sharp and his associates. According to Conrad (1974:16), Sharp made the original proposition that subjects, topics, and courses that could best be learned outdoors be carried out in their own optimum sphere. This concept was the basis of his writing and teaching. Sharp explained (Rillo 1985:1), "That which ought and can best be taught inside the schoolroom should there be taught, and that which can best be learned through experience, dealing directly with native materials and life situation outside the school, should there be learned."

Julian W. Smith has been referred to as the Dean of American outdoor education. He served as professor of education at Michigan State University and director of the Outdoor Education Project of the American Association for Health, Physical Education and Recreation (now AAHPERD, discussed later in this chapter). According to Donaldson (1974:59–61), Smith's involvement with outdoor education began in 1940. As principal of Lakeview High School (Michigan), Smith arranged for the school to participate in one of the W. K. Kellogg Foundation school camping programs. In 1946 he became the head of a cooperative project between the Michigan

Department of Conservation and the Department of Public Instruction to promote outdoor education. The Kellogg Foundation provided partial financial support. During the period from 1946 to 1953, Michigan was known for its innovations in the field of outdoor education and became the nation's primary leader. The leadership was so strong that Michigan remains one of the leaders in the field today.

In 1953 Smith joined the faculty of the then Michigan State College. By 1955 his ambition of the 1940s was realized when his strongly felt need for an umbrella organization to encompass the many fields involved in outdoor education came into being. At that time he became the director of the far-reaching Outdoor Education Project. The project arranged many activities, including three national conferences and a newsletter, *A Newsletter for the Exchange of Ideas on Outdoor Education.* Smith's contributions made the newsletter preeminent among several such publications, and there was evidence that the project impacted and broadened the nation's concept of outdoor education. Eventually the Council on Outdoor Education and Camping was developed under the General Division of AAHPERD after more than 10 years of project status. Because of Smith's efforts, thousands upon thousands of American youth are better off. Smith proclaimed, "Outdoor education and camping are not frills to be scalloped around the curriculum. In the woods, fields, and streams children can see, feel, hear; they can even smell and taste. Here reality, with all its vividness, becomes both motivation and method for learning" (Donaldson 1974:59).

Smith described the significant developments of outdoor education in the United States (1974:27–30). Early development prior to 1940 began with such labels as field and camping trips, outings, recreation, and camping education. Organized camping, combined with the educational philosophies of Dewey, Kilpatrick, and others whose leadership gave rise to "progressive" education, influenced outdoor education. During the period from 1940 to 1950, resident outdoor schools grew in number, including those in the Battle Creek, Michigan, area conducted at the Clear Lake Camp; San Diego (California) City-County Camp Commission with a program at Cuyamaca; Tyler, Texas; Cleveland Heights, Ohio; and others. What occurred at resident outdoor schools was generally referred to by the term *outdoor education* during this period. An event of particular significance was the first state legislation, passed in Michigan, which allowed school districts to acquire and operate camps as a segment of a school program. To a great degree, outdoor education was strongly influenced by organized camping at this time, but developments in curriculum, professional training and programs were strong forces. Near the conclusion of this period a surge of interest in all forms of outdoor pursuits began to take hold.

The 1950s brought rapid growth in resident outdoor schools and greater emphasis on other out-of-classroom experiences. The Outdoor Education Project broadened the concept of outdoor education and further developed teaching of skills, attitudes, and appreciation for satisfying outdoor pursuits. The National Conference on Teacher Education for Outdoor Education was held at the Clear Lake Camp in Michigan in 1953, and the interdisciplinary approach to outdoor education was emphasized. During this period the Taft Field Campus was established by Northern Illinois University with its excellent leaders in outdoor education.

The 1960s brought about growth in a wide variety of outdoor education activities, particularly the use of outdoor settings by elementary schools, teaching of outdoor skills, and the increase in the in-service and pre-service preparation of teachers and leaders. Institutions that developed graduate study in the field included Indiana University, Pennsylvania State University, State University of New York, Northern Colorado University at Greeley, and New York University. Expansion of programs was the result of the influence of such organizations as the Outdoor Recreation Resources Review Commission and the Bureau of Outdoor Recreation and was assisted by federal legislation and a number of federal programs in education. By the late 1960s, terminology began to expand and an increased concern toward environmental education took root.

According to Burrus-Bammel and Bammel (1990:50), ever since the 1970s educators have recognized the need to provide environmental education programs throughout all academic levels and to integrate the subject with other subject matters. In 1970 public outcry led to passage of the Environmental Education Act, which specified state and federal partnerships in the areas of teacher training, curriculum development, and community education programs. More than 50 percent of the funding never materialized, however, and in 1982 Congress decided not to extend the act. After coming to a virtual standstill during the Reagan administration, new proposals were forwarded by environmentalists for future consideration. These are contained in the *Blueprint for the Environment* (Liddle 1989:3). Also making an impact on outdoor education in the 1980s and 1990s was the formation of the President's Commission on Americans Outdoors. This bipartisan commission was appointed by President Ronald Reagan in 1985 to look ahead for a generation to determine what Americans would want to do outdoors and how appropriate places to do these things could be provided.

Philosophy and Teaching Methodology

The practice of outdoor education has evolved as a result of years of experience of devoted individuals, outdoor centers, laboratories, and community agencies. The movement was ahead of its time in teaching interrelationships of various areas of the curriculum with the outdoors and the environment. Through outdoor education, urban children may learn about the earth. Observation is the theme, and the earth is the teacher. With the focus off the individual, some students blossom in ways they never could in the classroom. For example, students actually see erosion in process. They learn to problem solve and to cooperate with others. Outdoor education offers another means to teach and reach our children.

The primary goal, legal justification, and unique contribution of outdoor schools are found in the nurturing of understanding outdoor science and conservation. Other goals include social adjustments, work experience, and healthful living. Finally, students learn that life is more than mere existence. It is hoped that they discover things in our world that are beautiful.

Whatever the outdoor program, the philosophy for outdoor education may be based on the following four premises, according to the Council on Outdoor Education (1989:32):

1. A prime goal of outdoor education is to teach a commitment to human responsibility for stewardship or care of the land. The development of a land ethic that commands us to treat the land and all its resources with respect at all times and on all occasions is the first value for any outdoor education program. It is action-oriented and attitude-developing. It recognizes that whatever is taught in outdoor education must be translated into ethical ecological action.
2. Related to the goal of a land ethic or commitment to stewardship must be the belief in the importance of knowing certain facts or concepts. The cognitive purpose of outdoor education must be that of the interrelationship of all facets of the ecosystem. The interrelationship of natural resources with each other, and with humans and their societal customs, is the underlying curricular objective. The understanding of basic

ecological, sociological, and cultural principles is prerequisite to the commitment to an ethic of land stewardship. Concurrently, outdoor education does not mandate specific choices in ecological ethics. . . . It prepares people to choose carefully after weighing the impact of the action on the environment, culture, and humanity.

3. We not only need to know the natural environment for the survival of the species, but we need to know it as a medium through which we spend many hours of leisure. Just teaching people about the interrelationships of the resources will not enhance their leisure hours, nor save them from the miseries encountered in harsh environmental situations. Because we know that humans seek the outdoors for leisure pursuits, it is incumbent upon us to teach the recreator how to live comfortably in the outdoors and how to recreate with a minimum impact on the environment. The quality of the outdoor recreation experience is directly related to the quantity of the knowledge about the out-of-doors.
4. A fourth philosophical belief is that outdoor educational experience is not just one field trip, one week at outdoor school, or even a once-a-year event. It must be taught at all levels and pursued throughout life.

Contributions of outdoor education, according to Earl V. Pullias (1974:14), include the following:

1. A healing and growth-producing relationship with the natural world.
2. A promotion of sensitivity.
3. An assistance in the development of habits of withdrawal and renewal which are fundamental to physical, mental, and spiritual health in modern life.
4. To offset dealing with abstractions with simple direct experience.
5. At its best, nurturing of the spirit and bringing forth of communication with the earth.

To be an effective tool in the educational process, outdoor education must be planned, organized, and administered so that teaching and learning take advantage of the outdoor situation. The land itself provides the information and, with the assistance of a qualified teacher, the land does the teaching. Because children come to the out-of-doors to learn, they should spend as much time as possible learning in the outdoors. When inside, the instructor expects the attention of the students. When out-of-doors, students focus attention on nature.

Sharp helped to mold many of the methods and practices that have proven successful in outdoor teaching. These methods include discovery, inquiry, deliberation, and integration. Learning out-of-doors is a natural process with student and teacher developing a partnership. They observe objects together. Teachers serve as facilitators of the learning process. They must not attempt to be controlling, nor can they expect to have all of the answers. By learning together, students and teachers develop trust and confidence, both of which can often be carried back into the indoor environment. The methodology is simple and direct; it is learning by using the senses.

Discovery learning is the most appropriate method used to teach in outdoor education. Natural curiosity can be aroused in the out-of-doors. More important than knowing answers is the ability to ask questions. Children may be able to provide the answers, and answers can be provided through use of the five senses and through availability of reference materials at the outdoor site and in the classroom.

An example of a broad-based, in-depth training program for outdoor education was developed in Missouri during the late 1960s and early 1970s. This program for state classroom teachers allowed for regional workshops. Participating teachers returned to their classrooms and passed along skills and concepts to their students. By the mid 1970s statewide workshops were formed which were soon followed by the formation of the Missouri Coalition for Education in the Outdoors (MCEO). The coalition's board makes efforts to better serve and involve more Missourians in outdoor education and environmental concerns (Teeters 1989:3). Another good example of an outdoor education teacher-training program is conducted by Northern Illinois University. Students take three or four courses in outdoor education in block sequence, allowing for a variety of outdoor experiential learning-teaching situations at the Lorado Taft Field Campus. Students learn to teach in an outdoor setting for at least 2 weeks by teaching elementary school children (Rillo 1985:11).

According to Priest (1989:73–77) in an international survey, 5 experts ranked the importance of items of concern, attributes, and skills of outdoor leaders of adventure activities. They ranked the concerns of outdoor leadership as follows: enabling learning and enjoyment of participants and caring for safety and well-being of participants; protecting the natural outdoor environment; continuing good relations with resource managers; avoiding a situation involving litigation; maintaining the future existence of any organization; and creating professional outdoor leadership association. They ranked the attributes critical to outdoor leaders as follows: judgment based on experience; awareness and empathy for others; flexible leadership style; motivational philosophy and interest; healthy self-concept and ego; desirable personal traits and behavior; and physical fitness. They ranked the skills critical to outdoor leaders as follows: safety procedures and practices; group management; problem solving; technical activity and instructional skills; environmental skills; and organizational skills. North American experts commented that technical activity and safety skills were of paramount importance in preventing accidents to avoid possible litigation which might arise as a consequence.

There are various curriculum approaches to outdoor education, as follows (Rillo 1985: 15–16):

1. **Vertical Articulation** This approach encompasses the use of a broad theme or basic understanding which is introduced at the kindergarten level. Each grade level studies the theme but in a more refined and sophisticated manner.
2. **Horizontal Articulation** In this approach, outdoor activities are selected which correlate with basic concepts of each discipline in the curriculum. The study of art, for example, can be offered through opportunities to sketch in the natural environment.
3. **Modular Approach** This approach uses packaged instructional modules or planned units of study which are available through a variety of sources. For example, the National Environmental Education Development (NEED) program was developed by the National Park Service, the National Education Association, and the Association of Classroom Teachers in the early 1970s. Modular programs are particularly popular with recreation departments and park systems which organize programs for visiting groups of students. The modular approach is less time-consuming than the other approaches, but it does not allow for the careful curriculum correlation of the other approaches.

As with all programs in a curriculum, the outdoor education program must be evaluated.

Every participant of the program should be included in the evaluation process. It is important that the scope is broad-based to include not only the cognitive but also the other outcomes of the program, for example, social development, interpersonal skills, environmental awareness, and responsibility. Rillo (1985:25) recommends the following techniques: interest inventories, student narrative logs, attitude scales, subjective reports, anecdotal records, conferences, interviews, student opinion surveys, community opinion surveys, and professional opinions.

OUTDOOR EDUCATION IN SCHOOLS

Implementing the practice of studying in the out-of-doors varies by grade level. To date, outdoor education has had its largest impact upon the elementary school curriculum. Lower grade instructors tend to offer classroom-related field experiences and projects at parks, ponds, school sites, and the like. Teachers in the upper elementary levels and beyond may use camp settings. Students in higher grade levels tend to study the out-of-doors through activity and adventure programs. Some high schools arrange programs through outside agencies (see nonschool agencies). Outdoor education programs are also seen in higher education in interesting ways, for example, in interdisciplinary programs.

Objectives specifically related to school camping programs were approved as early as 1949 by the American Association of Health, Physical Education and Recreation at their Boston Convention (Los Angeles City Schools 1961:4–6). These include the following:

1. Consider the development of the whole child.
2. Ensure children's participation in the total program—planning, executing, evaluation.
3. Seek to integrate all of the educational activities around problems inherent in living together outdoors.
4. Make the setting the out-of-doors, and center all of the activities on outdoor traditions.
5. Make complete use of the country's natural resources and outdoor heritage.
6. Base methodology upon discovery, adventure, and direct experience.
7. Stress principles rather than detailed facts.
8. Emphasize the social process of cooperation rather than competition.
9. Make the education experience be essentially a group process.
10. Make the education be essentially an experiential process.

Outdoor Education in Preschool

A day camp program developed at Ohio State University was implemented at St. Andrew's Presbyterian Day School in Columbus. Shepard and Caruso (1988:28–29) organized the day camp for preschoolers, ages three to five. The camp fostered the development of a natural, curious, creative childhood by providing activities in which each child could explore the out-of-doors and learn to use senses without pressures. Preschool children, they found, are developmentally ready for sensory learning and want to feel and listen. The 2-day program, offered one weekend of each season of the school year, was designed to give children a chance to grow as total individuals through outdoor skills and shared experiences. A second aim was to provide a social interaction between children and adults during leisure time, and a third aim was to train education and recreation leaders from nearby colleges to work with preschoolers and their families in a nontraditional outdoor setting.

Children at the day camp participate in games that focus on cooperation and sharpen movement skills and coordination. They assemble items in a day pack for an upcoming hike. Staff

Nontraditional outdoor settings provide a stimulating environment.

leaders pack the first aid kit, but each child must carry an item important to the group as a whole. The hike includes a group trip of 15 to 20 feet into the woods, where opportunities to use the senses abound. Here children begin to develop an environmental vocabulary. A color-coded frame tent is put together, and children learn about campfire safety. They cook their own food over the fire and mix their own instant drink. Afterwards they wash their own dishes and put them away. The children are also encouraged to read a map and color-coded compass to aid in basic skill development and outdoor vocabulary.

Outdoor Education in Public Schools

Educators and interested citizens of San Diego city and county conducted an experimental community school camp at Cuyamaca State Park in California in 1946 to test the theory that camping could become an integral part of the educational program. Aims were twofold: first, to make democracy real and understandable through outdoor living, and second, to give every child of appropriate age a camp experience. The sixth grade level was selected for the experimental program, and 1201 campers plus some 300 parents, teachers, volunteers, and visitors participated in the experience. Afterward, San Diego's elementary school principals met to evaluate the project. They voted unanimously to continue and to expand the program (Pumala 1973:99).

Today hundreds of sixth grade girls and boys go with their classroom teachers to the outdoor education schools in the mountains of San Diego County. For 5 days and 4 nights the children live together in an attractive outdoor setting. The environment is explored with trained outdoor personnel. Students take an active part in planning their week, setting standards of behavior, and accepting the responsibilities that are necessary for group outdoor living.

The San Diego Office of Education is responsible for the administration of the Outdoor Education Program, for providing and maintaining facilities, and for hiring staff. Staff is hired at a 1 to 10 ratio of instructors to students, which includes a support staff consisting of maintenance and kitchen personnel, a nurse, and a clerk, all of whom work under the leadership of the director of outdoor education. The on-site principal and credentialed teachers prepare for a week of living and learning together in a new social and natural environment. Fees for attending are the same for each school and district, although costs to parents may vary, since some districts provide a portion of the cost from annual budgets or through district fund-raising activities.

The outdoor education experience is part of the regular school instructional program. Classroom teachers are responsible for correlating indoor classroom learning with outdoor school instruction. The outdoor school curriculum is a curriculum of action: exploring, discovering, investigating, evaluating, working, creating, conserving, and sharing. Outdoor classroom activities include studies in astronomy, geology, ecology, fire ecology, hiking, soil study, forest improvements, weather study, tree planting, animal tracking, survival skills, Indian study, orienteering, as well as preparing and cooking meals over an open fire. Around the campfire, students carve, sing, and dance. The outdoor environment includes hills, valleys, rivers, clear skies, and plants and animals. Campers learn to use maps, compasses, telescopes, binoculars, microscopes, and magnets while using scientific methods of research: exploring, discovering, collecting, recognizing problems, planning, cooperating, proposing, testing, investigating, and evaluating. In conjunction with work projects, students develop an appreciation for, and an understanding of, the complexity of the environment. They also learn the need to use natural resources wisely to ensure that they are available to provide a good quality of life in the future.

San Diego's Outdoor Education Program is the oldest in California and now operates on three sites. While outdoor education programs are not mandated in California, residential centers throughout the state influence more than 150,000 students a year. Environmental education received the strong support of California Superintendent of Public Instruction Bill Honig and Secretary for Resources Gordon Van Vleck in a joint policy statement on environmental education. They stated that instruction must be provided at all grade levels and in all appropriate subject matter areas. Supporting outdoor learning experiences, it was stressed that full use of services, materials, and expertise offered by resource management agencies, citizen conservation associations, business and industry, and others should be made. They emphasized that teachers must understand the importance of their role in environmental education, possess the necessary knowledge and skills in this area of instruction, and be provided with adequate instructional materials and equipment.

Many public schools, elementary and high school, form partnerships with nonschool agencies. These agencies are discussed later in this chapter.

Higher Education Programs

Prescott College in Arizona stresses experiential learning and self-direction within an interdisciplinary curriculum. The college expects its graduates to learn to adapt to a changing world. All students begin the process upon arrival through the college's Wilderness Orientation Program. Joining more experienced students, the novices are led on an outdoor backpacking expedition for 17 to 19 days. During the expedition, time is set aside for each person to spend 3 days in solitude for contemplation. Trips may include remote outings to the mountains and canyons of the Southwest or to the Grand Canyon. Students become acclimated to the Southwestern environment and are introduced to a variety of physical, social, and cultural conditions in which they learn the process of adaptation.

At Prescott College the curriculum is flexible to fit the students' needs; it is organized into multidisciplinary programs: Outdoor Action, Environmental Studies, Human Development, Cultural and Regional Studies, and Humanities. These are not isolated components but frequently support each other. Members of the faculty move freely from one study area to another, as do students. The goal is to blend experiential, theoretical, and interdisciplinary coursework. For example, in Environmental Studies, the course "Environmental Perspectives and Whitewater Rafting" is a 3-week expedition with a twofold intent: first, to learn rafting skills, techniques, and expedition leadership, and second, to study the basic natural history of the regions including vegetation, geology, and general historical aspects of Indian and non-Indian cultures of the region.

The Prescott College Outdoor Action Program is dedicated to an outdoor education curriculum. Graduates populate the faculties of U.S. Outward Bound schools and design similar programs in colleges and secondary schools throughout the country (Weisman 1990:39). The Outdoor Action curriculum includes the following courses:

Avalanche Forecasting for Backcountry Skiers
Kayaking, Basic Whitewater
Mountain Search and Rescue
Outdoor Education and Recreation
Rockclimbing, Basic
Sea Kayaking and Marine Landscapes
Ski Touring, Basic
Wilderness First Aid
Wilderness Leadership, Fall Quarter
Wilderness Leadership, Spring Quarter
Wilderness Orientation, Instructor's Course

Another interdisciplinary approach has been seen at Whittier College, where students may enroll in a pair of classes, "Outdoor Recreation" and "Spanish," which undertakes the study of the interconnections between recreation, language, and culture. It is a goal of the paired courses to contrast as well as explore the continuities between Latin American values and those of the United States with respect to recreation and leisure. In doing so, the Outdoor Recreation class emphasizes the cultures and recreational opportunities of the Southwest and Mexico. The Spanish class is activity-oriented. An innovative technique to teach language, called Total Physical Response (TPR), is utilized. Movement and actions associated with outdoor recreation provide the setting for learning the language. The classes are integrated in terms of both thematic content and approach. For example, the unit on "Fishing in Mexico" is approached as follows: the Outdoor Recreation class focuses on methods of deep-sea fishing, while the Spanish class concentrates on practical tasks such as how to rent a boat and equipment in Spanish, using the proper level of formality and respect and within the proper cultural contexts. Joint labs and field trips are included in the pair of courses. Laboratory classes include outdoor activities conducted in Spanish and in which both instructors participate. The field trips include visits to Baja California, Pio Pico State Park, and the Huntington Gardens in California (Cordes and Chabran 1988:17).

Indiana University has a 2,300-acre instruction center for leadership in outdoor education, outdoor recreation, and camping called Bradford Woods. The program is administered by the Department of Recreation in the School of Health, Physical Education and Recreation, with guidance from an advisory committee representing many of the major program constituents. As a satellite campus of the university, Bradford Woods has been a learning resource since the early 1950s.

The instruction center area, donated by John Bradford for the welfare of Indiana's children and for the professional preparation of leaders of youth, includes two artificial lakes, beach and boating facilities for camp programs, and over 1,800 acres of woods and hills for study and experiential leadership and professional development activities. One camp, James Whitcomb Riley, is managed and controlled by the university. It consists of year-round facilities with indoor accommodations for over 250 persons and is used for summer camp, outdoor education, and challenge education programs, and for weekend programs and conferences throughout the year. Available separately or in combination, three villages offer a broad range of lodging, including rustic cabins and tent areas. Other facilities on the property are leased to organizations that conduct their own programs, including the American Camping Association, which headquarters at Bradford Woods.

Year-round opportunities exist for persons to gain academic credit and practical experience in outdoor education, outdoor recreation, camping administration and leadership, resource management, therapeutic recreation, special education, and other areas. Major programs include a full residential summer camping season for children and adults with a variety of disabilities, outdoor education for elementary and special education children, adventure and challenge education programs, leadership conferences, seminars, professional development workshops, and weekend retreats.

Programs are conducted by a full-time, year-round staff of professionals and support personnel. Part-time and seasonal staff reaches about one hundred during the summer. In addition, Bradford Woods provides training opportunities and internships for students from universities throughout the United States, conducts a comprehensive forest management and wildlife habitat program, and provides national leadership in the development and evaluation of outdoor-based programs. In 1980, the Institute on Innovations in Camping and Outdoor Education for the Handicapped was established as an annual event at Bradford Woods. The Bradford Woods facility has hosted hundreds of international visitors and participants (Robb n.d.:v–vi).

Outdoor recreation schools across the country are growing in number as individuals seek the thrill and sense of accomplishment in learning new skills.

Extracurricular Activities

The Outdoor Program at the University of Oregon is the nation's largest and most active extracurricular program. It serves as a model for numerous other programs across the country and embraces all aspects of outdoor pursuits and wilderness activities. Unlike with traditional outing clubs, there are no membership dues, meetings, or administrative obligations. Serving as a cooperative, the program offers those interested in pursuing an outdoor activity a chance to find others with similar plans. Wilderness goals range from learning new skills to extended expeditions all over the world. Several hundred trips are arranged each year offering a wide range of activities at various skill levels. Most are fairly spontaneous and are arranged by volunteers. All responsibilities, chores, and decisions are borne equally among trip participants. There is no charge other than the shared cooperative costs of gas, food, and equipment rental if necessary. The Outdoor Program has a variety of resources available to launch just about any trip. Vehicles of all sizes are available through the state motor pool, and a variety of outdoor gear for trips is also available. Resource staff help in any aspect of trip preparation. Trips are open to students, staff, and the community. The

Rock climbing can be learned in adventure programs.

Desert environments require backpackers to learn specialized skills.

objectives are cooperative learning and fun. The Outdoor Program provides the community with an outdoor resource center, with libraries and files teeming with valuable resource material.

Typical program activities include backpacking, day hikes, canoeing, kayaking, rafting, bike touring, photography, mountaineering, sailboarding, ski touring, telemark skiing, winter camping, ocean kayaking, and other self-propelled wilderness activities. On-campus events include films, slide shows, speakers, equipment swaps, equipment sessions, instructional sessions, kayak pool sessions, environmental action projects, and environmental symposiums and conferences.

NONSCHOOL AGENCY CONTRIBUTIONS TO OUTDOOR EDUCATION

Many nonschool agencies including nonprofit organizations, federal and state agencies, local recreation and park departments, and special interest groups participate in outdoor education programs which complement the school setting. In some cases these programs actually become part of a school curriculum, or they may serve in the capacity of extracurricular activity. Examples of a few of such offerings are included below.

Boy Scouts of America

The history of the Boy Scouts of America (BSA) was presented earlier. BSA continues to teach boys skills for outdoor adventures, with camping playing a vital role in this process. Today the Family Camping Program, launched in 1984, is designed to give family members ample opportunity to share the outdoor experience. The Boy Scout Conservation Program incorporates educational activities throughout the scout program which build an awareness and understanding of wise and intelligent management of natural resources. Conservation awards were initiated as early as 1914 and continue to inspire scouts

Preparing for outdoor adventures requires appropriate dress and the right safety equipment.

Girl Scouts gather for a traditional camp meeting at the conclusion of the weekend's activities.

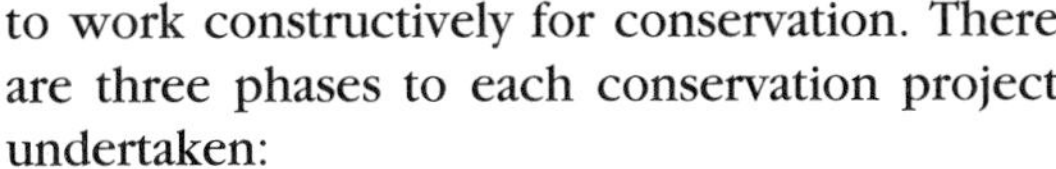

to work constructively for conservation. There are three phases to each conservation project undertaken:

1. Identification of need, such as environmental improvement, public awareness, and involvement in community decision-making groups.
2. Research, to study the need and to develop individual skills required to successfully carry out the project.
3. Action, which is the result of planning. Action involves knowing what needs to be done through research and the application of skills. Follow-up includes unit evaluation of the project—what was learned, what else could have been done, etc.

Some Explorer posts specialize in outdoor activities and conservation. Fields of study include camping, hiking, canoeing, ecology, mountaineering, field sports, fishing, conservation education, safety, survival, and proper outdoor living.

Girl Scouts of the U.S.A.

Outdoor activities have always been an integral part of Girl Scouting. Founder Juliette Low buffed the notion of the day that ladies do nothing strenuous. She believed that girls would be attracted to the out-of-doors for sports, camping, and nature study. Today camping experiences and facilities are an important part of the Girl Scouts' outdoor education experience. Outdoor education in Junior Scouting, for example, is divided into three categories (Ciraco et al. 1984:2):

1. Camping and Campcraft Skills Basic skills are developed; information is provided on readiness for camping, safety, and health in the outdoors and on how to select and care for camping equipment.

2. Scout Ceremonies Troop ceremonies are designed to be performed in local parks to inspired outdoor themes. These ceremonies promote participation, leadership, and cooperation.

3. Outdoor Education Activities According to the Girl Scout Public Relations Office (1990), outdoor education programs are autonomous, varying according to districts across the country. For instance, in Ohio the Buckeye Trails Girl Scout Council offers an outdoor program and activities in camp cooking, clean-up, wildlife, knots, compass, low-impact camping, fossil identification, hiking, group games, campfire building, and sky and weather interpretation.

Young Men's Christian Associations

Outdoor education programs were offered at 259 (14 percent) of YMCA units. An example is Camp Cosby, a branch of the Birmingham, Alabama, YMCA, which is located one hour from the city on 135 wooded acres along the shores of a lake formed behind Logan Martin Dam on the Coosa River. According to Abrahamson (1990:20–25), Camp Cosby has served as a summer camp since 1922. In 1981 it opened its small outdoor environmental education program. Starting as an overnight program, it offered canoeing, fishing, and forestry. Growth and interest were phenomenal. Today its expanded outdoor environmental program serves 1,200 summer campers and 4,900 students. Many schools in the area send their entire fifth- or sixth-grade classes to Camp Cosby each year as part of their academic curriculum.

A dramatic part of the outdoor program is "Living History." Dressed as pioneers and Indians, Y camp staff reenact life as it was conceived to be in the area in 1810, a time when Alabama was part of the Mississippi Territory and Birmingham was a sparsely populated wilderness. In this manner the students learn history, geography, and basic survival skills. They are taught Indian sign language and how to use silence and the five senses to enjoy nature.

Staff are young energetic teachers and recent graduates from college. Besides participating in Living History, the staff perform skits around the campfire, instruct parents, haul canoes, lead song and prayer, and teach 200 students a week. While camp staff teach nine classes, teachers from participating schools teach the other three. Volunteer parents may also teach. Schools select classes from a list of sixty offerings including: environmental education, animal activity, tight rope, climbing, recycling, tree diaries, candle making, and pioneer tools.

A nominal fee is charged for general stays of three days and two nights with food and lodging included. The Y offers a number of scholarships (camperships), and many schools raise money to help send children to camp. Those who pay the full price are supplemented with extra funding from United Way and from income earned from the regular summer camp. The aim is to enable everyone to participate. The success of the outdoor environmental education program at Cosby has renewed local interest in summer camp.

National Audubon Society

The National Audubon Society operates six education centers in Connecticut, California, Ohio, New Mexico, Maine, and Wisconsin. Professional naturalists and volunteers conduct outdoor classes, community outreach programs, and teacher-training workshops. Audubon's three summer ecology camps in Maine, Connecticut, and Wyoming offer adults intense natural history study sessions with optional college credit. The Maine camp also offers sessions for children ages 10 through 15. The Audubon Expedition Institute offers travel-study programs in the United States for high school and college students interested in examining firsthand the natural and social issues affecting the country. Field seminars focusing on specific skills and issues are held year-round.

Outward Bound

Outward Bound is an adventure-based educational program whose objective is leadership training and self-discovery through challenging activities in a wilderness setting. It is the largest adventure program in the world, with nearly 50 years of experience. Outward Bound is composed of a system of five wilderness schools and several urban centers located throughout the country. Instructors are skilled at providing safe outdoor education. Each course has regular on-site safety inspection, and external review teams audit each school's programs. Centering on a specific activity, each Outward Bound program offers extensive technical training. Activities include: mountaineering, canoeing, sailing, backpacking, sea kayaking, canyoneering, whitewater rafting, dog sledding, horse training, coastal trekking, skiing, rock climbing, bicycling, or some combination. Instructors teach the technical skills needed for the particular environment and activities of choice.

Each course offers opportunities to become proficient in basic campcraft, emergency care, wilderness navigation, food planning and preparation, and expedition planning. Care and protection of the environment are emphasized in all courses. During coursework, personal skills in leadership, problem-solving, decision-making, and communication may be augmented. Some high school programs have formed partnerships with Outward Bound to offer outdoor experiences for their students.

Outward Bound does not consider itself to be a survival school, although time alone or a solo experience is an important part of the program. This time is spent in a natural setting with minimum equipment so that reflection on the course can take place. Students do not have to be athletic or experienced outdoor persons to join in the wilderness challenges. Students should be in reasonably good physical condition because the courses are mentally, physically, and emotionally demanding. Nearly 600 courses are offered. College credit is an option if available through individual institutions. Courses are also available for professionals (see also the National Outdoor Leadership School, described in the following section).

U.S. Forest Service

The Forest Service's natural resource and environmental education program emphasizes involving educators, resource professionals, and citizens' groups in developing skills and techniques for teaching others about their environment. Information and involvement programs aim to inform the public about natural resource matters on both national and local levels. The Forest Service *Woodsy Owl* program creates public awareness of pollution and environmental improvement problems and suggests solutions.

The agency also administers and hosts programs that provide education, training, and work for youth, minorities, the economically depressed, the elderly, and the mentally and physically challenged. Through these activities, participants help themselves become stronger and more self-sufficient citizens. Example programs include the Youth Conservation Corps, Forest Service Volunteers, Touch America Project, Job Corps Civilian Conservation Centers, and Senior Community Service Employment Program.

PROFESSIONAL EDUCATION

Another responsibility of education is to serve the professional who will act as leader, organizer, interpreter, manager, and/or administrator in outdoor settings. Colleges and universities have a significant challenge to meet growing demands in coming years. The professional preparation curriculum should provide the combination of core content and specialization required by each branch of the recreational profession. According to Ford (1985:32), it is difficult to prescribe specific qualifications for the outdoor education/recreation professional curriculum because the field offers such a wide variety of positions. There are, however, some qualifications which may be expected of all employees working in outdoor-related programs. These include:

1. The ability to understand all types of people, and to understand their psychological needs.
2. The ability to understand basic physiological needs such as food, liquid, rest, health, exercise, warmth, and shelter from wind, rain, heat, and cold.
3. A knowledge of basic natural resource understanding such as reading signs of changing weather, and basic concepts of

ecology including the interrelationships of plants, animals, rocks, water, air, and humidity.

4. An understanding of one or more of the following: trees, flowers, mammals, birds, insects, reptiles, or rocks.
5. The knowledge of minimum-impact camping.
6. A knowledge of how to help prevent accidents and administer first aid.
7. An ability to lead songs, tell stories, teach games, express a sense of humor, display high energy, and possess an attitude of professionalism.

In summary, the leader needs the ability to see the world and interpret it to others who do not have the knowledge, and at the same time to teach the skills necessary for safe and successful enjoyment of activities in the out-of-doors. The following are examples of some of the organizations and schools that offer professional development opportunities.

American Association for Leisure and Recreation

The American Association for Leisure and Recreation (AALR) is a voluntary professional organization dedicated to the development of school and community programs of leisure services and recreation education. It is one of seven associations making up the Alliance for Health, Physical Education, Recreation and Dance. Through the implementation of program goals, the AALR hopes to meet the challenge of the intelligent use of leisure time and the acknowledgment of its importance to the citizenry. The goals are as follows (Ford 1985:2):

1. The encouragement of professional involvement and exchange.
2. The monitoring of recreation legislation and the rendering of consultation at the request of legislators.
3. The dissemination of information on topics of current interest in leisure and recreation.
4. The maintenance of liaisons with organizations having allied interest in leisure and recreation.
5. The ability to support, encourage, and guide members of the organization in the development programs of leisure services.
6. The facilitation of communication between professionals and the lay public, between the schools and the community.
7. The creation of opportunity for professional growth and development.
8. The ability to nurture the conceptualization of a philosophy of leisure through curriculum development and professional preparation.

The creation of *Leisure Today,* a biannual insert in the Alliance's *Journal of Physical Education, Recreation and Dance,* was designed to concentrate on single themes of contemporary leisure interests, including outdoor education. In addition, AALR maintains a continuing number of publications. According to Patricia Fehl and George Wilson (1985:100), the association will continue to support a cardinal principle of education—"Worthy Use of Leisure."

American Camping Association

The American Camping Association is a nonprofit, nonsectarian national association founded in 1910 with a membership of over 5,000. Membership includes all types of camps and professionals who help people experience the out-of-doors, including: camp owners, directors, executives, students, businesses, day and resident camps, private and not-for-profit camps, travel and trip camps, school programs, environmental education centers, special emphasis camps, and agency camps. The association's mission is to enhance the quality of the experience for youth and adults in organized camping, to promote high professional practices in camp administration, and to interpret the values of organized camping to the public.

The ACA offers education and training through conferences, educational events, study materials, and mentors. *Camping Magazine* is published seven times a year. Its certified Camp Director Program is built on education, self-assessment, evaluation, and professional involvement. To prepare for a career in camping, the association suggests that courses are taken in the areas of: Camp Counseling, Camp Administration, Outdoor Education, Business Management, Personnel Management/Human Relations.

National Outdoor Leadership School

Since 1965, the National Outdoor Leadership School has taught wilderness skills, conservation, and leadership to more than 28,000 students. Each area provides the fundamental knowledge, skills, and experiences essential for minimal-impact use and enjoyment of a wilderness environment by emphasizing safety, judgment, leadership, teamwork, outdoor skills, and environmental studies.

Educator courses are offered for outdoor recreation specialists, classroom teachers looking for new approaches, or those persons who would like to become wilderness educators. Courses offer opportunities to share ideas and to teach approaches and skills with colleagues and peers in an expedition setting. Most students bring significant experience to courses. Ideas are exchanged, and students are encouraged to teach class in an area of expertise. With the assistance of instructors, students alternate functioning as leader. Classes offer expedition planning, equipment selection, and student evaluation processes (see also *Outward Bound,* listed under nonschool agency contributions to outdoor education).

National Recreation and Park Association

The National Recreation and Park Association (NRPA) is an independent, nonprofit organization established in 1965. It originated as the Playground Association of America in 1911 and became the National Recreation Association in 1926. The association promotes the development of the recreation and park movement and the conservation of natural and human resources in the United States. It sponsors conferences and institutions and provides membership with reports and publications. In the late 1970s and early 1980s, NRPA offered public campaigns to provide information about the value of recreation and leisure. The association seeks to unify its diverse membership without permitting its primary concern for publicly sponsored outdoor recreation and open-space programs to monopolize. In 1985 NRPA studied and developed recommendations for the President's Commission on American Outdoors created by President Ronald Reagan. The organization publishes *Parks and Recreation.*

National Wildlife Federation

The National Wildlife Federation offers outdoor educational opportunities for teachers of preschool to high school, and to administrators and outdoor educators. The focus is a multidisciplinary approach to environmental education. Education programs, interpretive activities, and creative indoor/outdoor adventures are led by environmental experts. Each program demonstrates how nature studies can be readily incorporated into existing classes in the arts and humanities, global issues and current events, and science.

Special activities and highlights include an information activity exchange, a resource fair on environmental education materials, hands-on activities, field trips, and camaraderie with other teachers. A sampling of potential programs includes ecology, citizen action, environmental ethics, urban nature studies, and environmental issues. University credit is available. Course goals are as follows:

1. To increase awareness and understanding of environmental issues and ecology.
2. To acquaint the participant with the wealth of excellent resource material available.
3. To increase confidence in environmental education so that it can be incorporated throughout the entire curriculum.

Student Conservation Association

The Student Conservation Association (SCA) is a nonprofit, educational organization that provides college students and persons who are over 18 and out of school with the opportunity to volunteer their services for the better management and conservation of national parks, public lands, and national resources. SCA participants gain work experience, enhancing future employment opportunities.

Resource assistants work individually in a professional capacity for approximately 12 weeks. They complete a variety of resource management duties as equal members of the resource staff of cooperating agencies, which include the National Park Service, U.S. Forest Service, U.S. Fish and Wildlife Service, Bureau of Land Management, state park and wildlife agencies, and private natural resource agencies. The positions offer a variety of tasks, and generally each position has a main theme or subject matter in which the volunteer participates. Some of these subjects are: wildlife and fisheries, forestry recreation management, environmental education, interpretation, visitor assistance, trail maintenance and construction, and backcountry management. Some positions may require specific educational background, skill, or experience. Anyone participating in the program must be 18 years of age or older and out of high school.

OUTDOOR EDUCATION FOR ALL

Outdoor education programs in the United States and Canada have roots that some people trace to Europe. British tented schools were founded prior to World War I, and the German school country homes of the 1920s and early 1930s are only two examples. International outdoor education is probably best characterized by a great diversity in outdoor adventures. The diversity of programs is influenced by the immediate environment, time, and philosophy. While Americans may marvel at schools allowing 5-day camp experiences, Bavarian codes urge camp experiences of 2 weeks or more. Philosophical goals vary from country to country. According to MacKenzie (1974:155–59), primary goal emphasis varies from a social emphasis in New Zealand and Australia, to a conservation emphasis in Sweden and a physical fitness emphasis in Great Britain. In 1991 a new experimental program in Venezuela led by New Yorker Judy Myers took children from Maracaibo to the Andes for 1 week of outdoor camping activities. Whatever their goals, outdoor education programs were found to be on the rise worldwide. Each program offers learning experiences for Americans to study.

As a self-conscious movement in American education, outdoor education experiences have moved from elementary school camping to all age levels and outdoor settings. Preschoolers to adults are enriched by outdoor education courses. No longer a middle-class phenomenon, outdoor education has moved to a greater class-spread and to special groups. Schools without camps are seeking local settings within walking distance. Farms, forests, and gardens offer increasing possibilities.

This chapter highlighted only some of the thousands of programs that represent trends in outdoor education in communities throughout North America. Leisure time, and an awareness that the environment is threatened, have focused attention on the outdoors and heightened our appreciation for the precious beauty of an outdoor experience.

SUMMARY

Outdoor education has a multitude of objectives, some of which include: to help people live in harmony with the natural environment, to establish a basic understanding of others, to utilize an interdisciplinary approach to education, to learn to use all of the senses, to learn in the natural laboratory, and to arouse the natural curiosity of the student.

Outdoor education in America goes back to the eighteenth and nineteenth centuries and began to expand in reaction to the industrialization of North America. Among the early advocates were Ernest Thompson Seton, George Bancroft, Joseph Cogswell, Lloyd Burgess Sharp, and Julian Smith. Their efforts resulted in both formal offerings such as Round Hill School and informal ones through youth organizations. Traditional schools became involved in outdoor education through interdisciplinary programs and planned instruction.

On the college level, centers for outdoor education were established and extracurricular programs with outdoor orientation were organized, such as the center at the University of Oregon. Academic credit is given for students who are planning careers in education or recreation through institutions such as Bradford Woods at Indiana University.

A number of nonprofit organizations such as the National Audubon Society and the YMCA became involved in providing outdoor education, and other organizations such as the American Camping Association are concerned with the education and training of camp staff.

BIBLIOGRAPHY

Periodicals

CEO Newsletter. Council on Outdoor Education. Cortland, NY.

Journal of Environmental Education. Heldref Publications. Washington, D.C.

Journal of Experiential Education. Association for Experiential Education. Englewood, CO.

Journal of Outdoor Education. Lorado Taft Field Campus of Northern Illinois University. Oregon, IL.

The Outdoor Communicator. New York State Outdoor Education Association. Albany, NY.

Science Activities. Heldref Publications. Washington, D.C.

Modular Resources

Project Learning Tree (two volumes). American Forest Institute. Washington, D.C.

Man and His Environment. National Environmental Education Development, National Education Association. Washington, D.C.

Green Box. Humboldt County Office of Education. Eureka, CA.

Outdoor Biological Instructional Strategies. Regents of the University of California. Berkeley, CA.

Understanding Your Environment Series. U.S. Forest Service. Portland, OR.

Project Wild. Volume 1: *Elementary Activity Guide* and Volume 2: *Secondary Activity Guide.* Western Regional Environmental Council. Boulder, CO.

REFERENCES

Abrahamson, D. (1990) "Environment Education," *Discovery YMCA.* National Council of Young Men's Christian Associations of the U.S.A. Chicago, Winter, 1990.

Bennett, B. (1974) "Camping and Outdoor Education Began at Round Hill School," in *Perspectives On Outdoor Education,* G. Donaldson and O. Goering, editors. Dubuque, IA: Wm. C. Brown.

Burrus-Bammel, L., and G. Bammel (1990) "Outdoor/Environmental Education—An Overview for the Wise Use of Leisure," *Journal of Health, Physical Education, Recreation and Dance* (April).

Ciraco, C., G. Davies, J. Findutter, S. Hussey, C. Kennedy, C. Murphy, D. Nye, V. Simpkins, and K. Waite (1984) *Outdoor Education in Girl Scouting.* New York: Girl Scouts of the United States of America.

Cogswell, J., and G. Bancroft (1823) *Prospects of a School to Be Established at Round Hill.* Northampton, MA: Cambridge University Press.

Conrad, L. (1974) "Lloyd B. Sharp's Philosophy of Education," in *Perspectives on Outdoor Education,* G. Donaldson and O. Goering, editors. Dubuque, IA: Wm. C. Brown.

Cordes, K., and R. Chabran (1988) "Outdoor Recreation in the Southwest and Mexico and Spanish: A Paired Course Model." *Journal of Recreation and Leisure* 8:1 (Spring).

Council on Outdoor Education (1989) "Outdoor Education Definition and Philosophy." *Journal of Health, Physical Education, Recreation and Dance* 60:2 (February).

Donaldson, G. (1974) "Julian W. Smith," in *Perspectives on Outdoor Education,* G. Donaldson and O. Goering, editors. Dubuque, IA: Wm.C. Brown.

Donaldson, G., and O. Goering (editors) (1974) *Perspectives on Outdoor Education.* Dubuque, IA: Wm C. Brown.

Fehl, P., and G. Wilson (1985) "Recreation 1960–1985." *Journal of Physical Education, Recreation and Dance* 56:4 (April).

Ford, P., (1985) "Outdoor Education/Recreation," in *American Association for Leisure and Recreation Career Information.* Reston, Va: Association of the American Alliance for Health, Physical Education, Recreation and Dance.

Ford, P. (1989) "Outdoor Education." *Journal of Health, Physical Education, Recreation and Dance* 60:2 (February).

Gilbert, J., and C. Chase (1988) "Outdoor Education, the Malady and the Prescription," *Journal of Health, Physical Education, Recreation and Dance* 59:5 (May/June).

Liddle, J. (1989) "The Education President: Will the Bush Reform Include Environmental Education?" *CEO Newsletter.* Coalition for Education in the Outdoors. Spring, 1989.

Los Angeles City Schools (1961) *Outdoor Education and School Camping.* Los Angeles: Division of Instructional Services, Youth Services Section.

MacKenzie, N. (1974) "World Perspectives in Outdoor Education," in *Perspectives on Outdoor Education,* G. Donaldson and O. Goering, editors. Dubuque, IA: Wm. C. Brown.

Nash, R. (1970) *The Call of the Wild (1900–1916).* New York: George Braziller.

Priest, S. (1989) "International Experts Rank Critical Outdoor Leadership Components." *Journal of Health, Physical Education, Recreation and Dance* 60:2 (Feb.).

Pullias, E. (1974) "Better Education for Modern Man," in *Perspectives on Outdoor Education,* G. Donaldson and O. Goering, editors. Dubuque, IA: Wm.C. Brown.

Pumula, E. (1973) "The San Diego California Community School Camp," in *Outdoor Education: A Book of Readings,* D. Hammerman and W. Hammerman, editors. Minneapolis, MN: Burgess.

Rillo, T. (1985) *Outdoor Education: Beyond the Classroom Walls.* Bloomington, IN: Phi Delta Kappa Educational Foundation.

Robb, G. (n.d.) "Preface," in *Leadership and Professional Development Programs,* edited by J. Wilke and G. Robb. Bloomington, IN: Indiana University.

Shepard, C., and V. Caruso, (1988) "Kid's Play in the Great Outdoors," *Camping Magazine* 60:3 (January). Martinsville, IN: American Camping Association.

Smith, J. (1974) "Where We Have Been—What We Are—What We Will Become," in *Perspectives on Outdoor Education,* G. Donaldson and O. Goering, editors. Dubuque, IA: Wm.C. Brown.

Smith, J. (1974) "Words, Words, Words," in *Perspectives on Outdoor Education,* G. Donaldson and O. Goering, editors. Dubuque, IA: Wm. C. Brown.

Teeters, C. (1989) "The Missouri Coalition for Education in the Outdoors." *CEO Newsletter.* Coalition for Education in the Outdoors. Spring, 1989.

Vinal, W. (1974) "Still More Outdoor Leaders I Have Known," in *Perspectives on Outdoor Education,* G. Donaldson and O. Goering, editors. Dubuque, IA: Wm. C. Brown.

Weisman, A. (1990) "Prescott College," *Arizona Highways.* 67:3 (March). Phoenix, AZ: Arizona Department of Transportation.

15 Outdoor Recreational Activities

America's landscapes include mountains, deserts, woodlands, wetlands, prairies, swamps, and tundra. Its waterways form a web over most of the continent, and its coastline, if stretched, would reach halfway around the world. Its wildlife refuges are unparalleled, and its panoramic vistas are a source of American pride. More than a third of the United States is public land: federal, state, regional, county, and municipal property (President's Commission on Americans Outdoors 1987:1). While some of the land is not conducive to recreational pursuits, much of it is open to recreational use. The land available is a living statement of America's commitment to the outdoors, but recreational opportunities are not expanding to meet increasing needs.

In an analysis of outdoor recreation and wilderness, Cordell et al. (1990:3–4) explained that the demand for outdoor recreation grew after World War II, when the economy grew to support it. Many new families were started, and the population grew rapidly. The quality of automobiles and roads increased, fuel became cheaper, and the average work week declined to 40 hours over 5 days. Outdoor recreation opportunities were increasingly available to middle- and lower-income groups. Use of the public recreation lands expanded. By the mid 1950s it burgeoned, but many federal recreation sites were deteriorating. Park Service Director Newton Drury responded with Mission 66, a program to rehabilitate facilities and build new ones by 1966. Conservationists, led by Joseph Penfold of the Izaak Walton League, recommended additional action to meet the nation's outdoor recreation needs. The result was congressional action in 1958 establishing the Outdoor Recreation Resources Review Commission (ORRRC). The ORRRC was charged with assessing the nation's outdoor recreation needs to the year 2000 and recommending programs to address those needs. Information was gathered by the commission over a period of 3 years.

The ORRRC found that outdoor recreation was a major leisure activity growing in importance and that outdoor recreation opportunities were most urgently needed near metropolitan areas. While considerable land was available for outdoor recreation, it was not effectively meeting the need. The ORRRC's recommendations led to creation of the Bureau of Outdoor Recreation in 1963 to coordinate national recreation policy and programs, and influenced the development of the Land and Water Conservation Fund (1965), the Wilderness Preservation System (1964), the National Wild and Scenic Rivers System (1968), and the National Trails System (1968) (see Chapter 7, Federal Resources).

In the 1960s and early 1970s, demand for outdoor recreation opportunities dramatically increased again. Government at all levels responded to the demands. With money from the Land and Water Conservation Fund, states, cities, and counties expanded their park and open-space systems. Meanwhile, American society changed significantly. Its population increased by 63 million people and shifted southward and westward; the average American became older; the nation shifted from dependence on traditional heavy industry to high technology, communication, and services. Government, business, and residence became less centralized.

The 1980s brought major changes both in the demand for and the supply of outdoor recreation opportunities. Participation in many activities had surpassed the projections of the ORRRC. A growing population was putting increased pressure on recreation lands while development was subtracting from available open space in and near growing cities and towns. Technology had spawned a host of new activities, from hang gliding, to driving rugged vehicles off-road, to snowmobiling. The population changed toward an older citizenry, more women were working, and there were more single parents. The federal government and many states were finding it difficult to pay for many programs, including outdoor recreation.

A consortium of interest groups went to Laurance Rockefeller, the chairman of the 1960 ORRRC, and urged that he take the lead in stimulating a new ORRRC-like assessment of outdoor recreation trends and needs. He convened with a small group of conservation and recreation leaders. Rockefeller's Outdoor Recreation Policy Review Group concluded that there was evidence that outdoor recreation opportunities were contracting, rather than expanding to meet increasing need. These findings led the group to recommend that a comprehensive federal reappraisal of the nation's recreation policy and resources be made by a new commission patterned after the ORRRC.

When effort to have Congress enact legislation creating the commission stalled, President Ronald Reagan established, by executive order, the President's Commission on Americans Outdoors in 1985. President Reagan directed the commission to look ahead for a generation and determine what Americans wanted to do outdoors and what was needed to ensure that they have the necessary opportunities. The commission's report, *Americans Outdoors: The Legacy, the Challenge* (1987), contained more than sixty specific recommendations: it urged the establishment of "greenways," described as "corridors of private and public lands and waters to provide people with access to open spaces close to where they live"; it urged communities to shape growth so they could remain attractive places to live and work; and it recommended intensified efforts to maintain the quality of national resources and to increase recreation opportunities on federal lands. Partnerships between government agencies and the private sector were seen as a key to expanding outdoor opportunities. Finally, the commission recommended that Congress establish a dedicated trust fund to provide a minimum of $1 billion a year for outdoor recreation (Cordell et al. 1990:2–4).

According to the President's Commission on Americans Outdoors (National Geographic Society 1987:1–2), nearly 90 percent of North American people seek enjoyment in mountains, seashores, lakes, pathways, and playgrounds. The demand has grown faster than the population. Bicycling and camping have increased fivefold, boating has doubled, and skiing continues to climb in popularity. Risk sports such as rock climbing and white-water rafting have also grown. Cordell and Siehl (1989:4) estimate that Americans in 1987 spent some part or all of 28.2 billion personal days on outdoor recreational activities. Of the approximately 4.6 billion outdoor recreation trips Americans took, about 50 percent, or some 2.25 billion, were taken to participate in wildland activities such as camping, canoeing/kayaking, fishing, hunting, hiking, horseback riding, bicycling, wildlife observation, winter skiing, and visiting prehistoric sites. In general, activities which are physically demanding, involved risk and adventure, are educational, or are equipment oriented have been growing the fastest.

According to Ewert (1989:2), wildland recreation is no longer simply the domain of the white male fisherman and backpacker. Participants increased to include members of different cultures, particularly Hispanics and Asians. But according to Cordell and Siehl (1989:5), federal and state lands are mainly used by young to middle-aged white individuals who generally are well educated and possess a good income. The elderly, the less educated, members of racial minorities, the disabled, the economically disadvantaged, and those living in cities participate much less in wildland recreation. And according to Freysinger (1990:49), white, middle-class women participate significantly less than do men in outdoor recreation. Women's participation in all physical recreation, indoor and outdoor, tended to be less than men's participation. This may be because many adult women have received less exposure to physical activity than their male counterparts. This tendency may change in the future. Freysinger also found participation in all physical recreation activities tended to decline faster for single persons of either sex than among non single persons or persons with children. Fortunately, according to Cordell and Siehl (1989:5), identification and improvement of disproportionately available opportunities is becoming a priority.

All ranks of the government are involved in some aspect of providing for wildland recreation, from the local and county through the state and federal levels. Thousands of small and medium-sized businesses also contribute to high-quality recreational experiences in wildland settings. According to Cordell and Siehl (1989:5–6), estimates indicate that federal lands receive nearly 12 percent of all outdoor recreation participation, state lands receive about 14 percent, local recreation sites account for 60 percent, and private land and enterprises provide about 14 percent. From 1977 to 1987, the total number of visitor days (a measure of total visitation time) increased 4.0 percent. The difference in growth rates between total visitor time on sites and number of visits reflects more visits, each of shorter duration. This tells that for each visit to federal land, visitors are traveling less and staying for shorter periods of time. Many outdoor recreation activities need to take place closer to home in the future, due to decreasing leisure time and a decrease in family vacation time due to the prevalence of dual-income households.

While the nation's population is expected to grow at a slower pace in the future, it is still growing, and with the growth comes the call for more outdoor recreation opportunities. However, a changing society with new technological opportunities means varying interests. National polls indicate increasing popularity in the following outdoor pursuits: downhill skiing, outdoor swimming, canoeing/kayaking, water skiing, and cross-country skiing. Decreasing popularity is predicted for some forms of boating, driving vehicles off-road, sledding, ice skating, picnicking, and pleasure driving (see chapter 16, The Environment). It also appears that more active pursuits will reign over more passive activities. More growth is indicated for adventuresome and somewhat risky activities, for educational activities, and among activities that are not time intensive (Cordell and Siehl 1989:6).

Forecasts have also been made by Cordell and Siehl (1989:7–9) based on predicted future societal trends, which include: a redistribution of the population to non metropolitan areas, extensive growth in the coastal states, increased ethnic and cultural diversity, more low- and more high-income families, and a growing elderly population. They predict that the following wildland recreation activities will grow more quickly in future years: hiking, walking, running, bicycling, visiting museums, historic sites, and prehistoric sites, camping, and family gatherings. They also predict that all forms of water and snow activities will grow rapidly, including canoeing, rafting, swimming, and skiing. Ewert (1989) predicts that the future will also call for more high tech activities such as mountain biking, jet-skiing, and heli-skiing. Table 15.1 shows projected growth patterns to the year 2040 if recent resource availability trends continue.

Each type of outdoor adventure requires unique preparation, skills, training, and equipment, and all require an understanding of etiquette, safety, and survival techniques. Risk recreation is a subset of outdoor recreation activities. Robb (1986:S-4) of Indiana University provided an abbreviated list of risk activities:

scuba diving	canoeing	caving
climbing	kayaking	rappelling
horseback riding	hang gliding	skiing
ropes courses	cycling	

For the purpose of this volume, each outdoor activity is classified according to the natural feature on or in which the activity is involved: land, water, and air. A section on educational activities includes nature activities and visitations to museums and to historic or prehistoric sites. The selected activities are representatives of growth, risk, high-tech, and educational activities.

Common advice and safety-survival advice is given with the activities. First aid techniques and survival methods should be updated from year to year and studied before one participates in backcountry activities. Extensive first aid and survival recommendations are not in the scope of this text. Books specializing in first aid, outdoor survival skills, and the activities specified are mentioned at the end of this chapter. A selection of related organizations, periodicals, and books are also provided.

ADVENTURES ON LAND

This section addresses hiking, backpacking, orienteering, snowshoeing, and cross-country skiing. Hiking and backpacking, addressed at length, provide a foundation for numerous other outdoor experiences.

Hiking

Trails for day hikers go through beautiful scenic areas throughout the United States. A hike may simply break up a lengthy vacation drive, lead to another recreational activity, or provide recreation in and of itself. Whatever the purpose, hiking is an outdoor activity for almost everyone. Trails are also designed for the visually and physically impaired. Other than transportation to a trailhead, very little of anything is needed for one to participate in hiking.

A hike is generally longer and more vigorous than a walk and typically occurs in a natural setting. Hiking can be done alone, with friends, or with an organized group. For safety reasons it is best not to hike alone. On the other hand, groups larger than eight or ten are not recommended (see the section on No-Trace Ethics at the end of this chapter).

One of the best cardiovascular exercises, hiking promotes fitness and strengthens muscles. It places less strain on bones and joints than

TABLE 15.1 Maximum Preferred Demand for Recreational Trips away from Home and Indices of Future Demand Growth to 2040

Resource Category and Activity	Trips in 1987 (millions)	Future Number of Trips as Percentage of 1987 Demand				
		2000	2010	2020	2030	2040
Land						
Wildlife observation and photography	69.5	116	131	146	162	174
Camping in primitive campgrounds	38.1	114	127	140	154	164
Backpacking	26.0	134	164	196	230	255
Nature study	70.8	105	113	120	131	138
Horseback riding	63.2	123	141	160	177	190
Day hiking	91.2	131	161	196	244	293
Photography	42.0	123	143	165	188	205
Visiting prehistoric sites	16.7	133	160	192	233	278
Collecting berries	19.0	113	126	143	166	192
Collecting firewood	30.3	112	124	138	157	178
Walking for pleasure	266.5	116	131	146	164	177
Running/jogging	83.7	133	163	197	234	262
Bicycle riding	114.6	125	148	173	202	222
Driving vehicles or motorcycles off-road	80.2	105	111	118	125	130
Visiting museums or info. centers	9.7	118	136	153	174	188
Attending special events	73.7	114	127	141	157	168
Visiting historic sites	73.1	122	143	169	203	241
Driving for pleasure	421.6	115	128	142	157	167
Family gatherings	74.4	119	135	152	170	182
Sightseeing	292.7	118	136	156	183	212
Picnicking	262.0	108	117	126	136	144
Camping in developed campgrounds	60.6	120	137	155	173	186
Water						
Canoeing/kayaking	39.8	113	126	140	157	169
Stream/lake/ocean swimming	238.8	105	110	117	124	129
Rafting/tubing	8.9	111	136	164	215	255
Rowing/paddling/other boating	61.8	112	124	136	150	159
Motor boating	219.5	106	111	117	123	127
Water skiing	107.5	111	121	131	141	148
Pool swimming	221.0	137	169	205	242	269
Snow and Ice						
Cross-country skiing	9.7	147	177	199	212	195
Downhill skiing	64.3	153	197	247	298	333

Source: H. K. Cordell et al. *An Analysis of the Outdoor Recreation and Wilderness Situation in the United States*: 1989–2040. (U.S. Department of Agriculture, Forest Service, Fort Collins, CO 1990), 44.

A day hiker explores remote areas while enjoying the moments of solitude and exhilaration that accompany an outdoor adventure.

Riders of All Terrain Vehicles, or ATVs, are thrilled with the excitement of the high-risk activity.

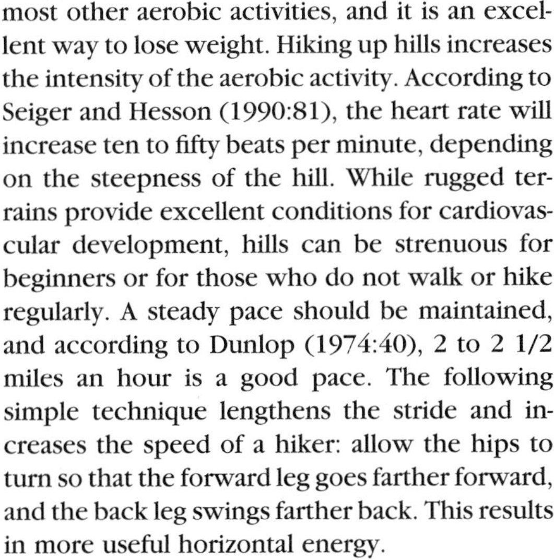

most other aerobic activities, and it is an excellent way to lose weight. Hiking up hills increases the intensity of the aerobic activity. According to Seiger and Hesson (1990:81), the heart rate will increase ten to fifty beats per minute, depending on the steepness of the hill. While rugged terrains provide excellent conditions for cardiovascular development, hills can be strenuous for beginners or for those who do not walk or hike regularly. A steady pace should be maintained, and according to Dunlop (1974:40), 2 to 2 1/2 miles an hour is a good pace. The following simple technique lengthens the stride and increases the speed of a hiker: allow the hips to turn so that the forward leg goes farther forward, and the back leg swings farther back. This results in more useful horizontal energy.

Everyone on the hike should be aware of the destination, and no one should leave the trail without asking a member of the party to wait. Whenever there is a fork or change along the trail, all members of the party should gather for directions. Off-trail hiking should be done only where permissible, for example near roads, and with topographical map and compass (see the section on Orienteering). In wilderness, with the exception of in the desert, when hiking off-trail a group should spread out width-wise rather than march single file. This avoids everyone tramping over the same ground, which creates undesirable trails. The general rule, however, is to stay on trails. This is always important in the desert, where delicate cryptogamic soil is damaged from the slightest disturbance.

Sturdy footwear that has been broken in should be worn. Lightweight hiking boots provide the best protection and traction and are advantageous for longer hikes. Socks that will not bunch or wrinkle will tend to prevent blisters. Two pairs of socks are recommended. The lighter inside pair moves with the foot and protects the heel. With only one pair of socks, the boots and the socks tend to move together and rub against the heel. Because tennis shoes absorb heat, they tend to be uncomfortable in warmer climates.

Clothing made of natural fibers suitable to existing weather conditions is recommended. Layering is helpful for day hikes. Clothing worn in warm climates should be light in color. Special precautions are necessary to protect against ultraviolet rays of the sun, including protective

TABLE 15.2 Essentials for Hiking and Backpacking

Ten Essentials:

- Compass
- Clothing (enough to survive most probable adverse conditions)
- Extra food
- Flashlight
- Fire starter (candle, heat lamp, etc.)
- First aid kit (including moleskin, tape)
- Sunglasses (goggles or clip on)
- Pocket knife
- Map (USGS topographic)
- Waterproof matches (or matches in waterproof container)

Clothing to Wear:

- Socks (either pile or wool), two pair
- Boots
- Long pants (loose fitting and preferably wool)
- Wool or pile gloves or mittens and hat
- Parka or jacket (wind and water resistant)
- Shirts and/or sweaters (have several including a wool or pile one to utilize the layer system)
- Pile cap or sun visor

Additional Items for Day Trips:

- Pack
- Canteen or poly bottle (one quart minimum)
- Emergency shelter (tube tent, space blanket)
- Insect repellent
- Ice axe or walking stick
- Sitting pad (ensolite, etc.)
- Drinking cup
- Handkerchief
- Camera and film
- Plastic bags
- Tissue and/or toilet paper
- Litter bag
- Watch
- Poncho, rain chaps, gaiters or other rain gear
- Hiking shorts
- Sun screen lotion
- Windbreaker (wind and water resistant)

Additional Equipment for Overnight Trips:

- Shelter (tent or tarp)
- Ground cloth
- Sleeping bag in waterproof stuff bag
- Sleeping pad
- Stove and fuel
- Cooking pot
- Water purifying kit
- Long underwear
- Extra flashlight battery and bulb
- Pot gripper
- Eating utensils
- Bag for hanging food
- Nylon cord
- Personal toilet items
- Biodegradable soap
- Rain cover for pack

Other Things that Are Nice to Have:

- Swimsuit
- Camp shoes
- Binoculars
- Towel
- Notebook and pencil

Source: REI, A382:rev. 4/86. (Reprinted with permission.)

lotions, hats, sunglasses, and a handkerchief around the neck. Loose pants, tucked into the boots or socks, and long-sleeved shirts provide protection in all climates and guard against brambles and brush, poison oak and poison ivy, and insects. For damp, rainy, and cool environments, Goretex cloth is breathable and provides additional protection. Gaiters, clothing made with tubes of coated nylon material attached to the bottom of the boot by a cord, protect boots and lower leggings against rain and snow.

Required equipment varies according to the length of the hike (see Table 15.2). The day hiker should generally carry at least one full canteen of water (more in the desert). A hiking stick for balance in hilly or rough terrains is desirable. The pack should be firmly padded at the shoulder straps and have a pocket large enough for a water bottle. A waistband helps to keep the pack stabilized. Prior to departure, the hiker should always leave a note at the trailhead, in the car, or with a ranger or friend to provide the intended destination and the expected time of return. Hikers should be prepared for weather, terrain, and altitude changes.

Altitude variations must be considered when planning hikes. Even the most healthy and physically fit hikers need to become acclimated. Beach hiking calls for knowledge of tide changes. Desert monsoons can lead to disaster when hiking in ravines, which are capable of transforming into running rapids with little notice.

Hiking, an excellent physical exercise, provides many diversions along the trail that occupy the mind. It reduces stress, builds self-esteem, provides for social interaction, and is inexpensive. Most hikers will say each trail leads to a unique experience.

Safety Blisters are the hiker's most common problem. Caused by improperly sized shoes, new or stiff shoes, or temperature extremes, blisters can cause incapacitation. Early signs and symptoms are hot spots or sore areas. Treatment involves changing to dry socks and readjusting the boot lacing. Moleskin or adhesive tape can be used to protect the sore area or the blister. After washing the area, the hiker can cut a piece of moleskin in the shape of a doughnut, fitting the hole around the injury. Several more doughnuts can be shaped and stacked to keep pressure off of the blister and to help prevent it from breaking. If the blister is large or appears as though it will break, it should be washed and drained. To drain a blister, insert a sterilized needle (heated with a flame) under the skin just inside the edge of the blister. The wound should be kept clean with a sterile bandage and protected with the doughnut bandage (Birkby 1990:422).

Lyme disease is a serious, tick-transmitted infection that has become increasingly common in the past several years and often occurs in stages. The signs and symptoms are not unique to Lyme disease. In the first stage they include a distinctive circular rash, fever, and head and muscle aches. The second stage may include neurological symptoms, such as muscle paralysis and loss of sensation, or arthritis. Treatment includes medical attention; antibiotics are administered. Lyme disease is curable in most cases if treated early. According to Caputo (1991:45), the small risk of acquiring the disease does not outweigh the benefits of outdoor recreation, however, caution is warranted in high-prevalence areas. Prevention includes wearing protective clothing and insect repellent containing deet on exposed skin and on clothing—especially at collars and cuffs. Careful inspection for ticks should be made immediately after an outing. Risks are also reduced by: avoiding marshy woodland areas; staying on trails in wooded areas to avoid contact with possible tick-bearing shrubs; not walking barefoot in grassy areas; and putting a tick collar on pets (Caputo 1991:45).

A hiker peers down the world famous Grand Canyon (top). Mules return from carrying visitors into the canyon (bottom). This area was first protected in 1893 as a forest preserve, then as a game preserve in 1906. In 1908 it became a national monument, and in 1919 it was set aside as a national park.

The forces of erosion have exposed an immense variety of formations which illustrate vast periods of geological history for the visitor.

Backpacking

The major difference between backpacking and hiking is that the packer can hike deep into the wilderness, carrying essentials in a backpack allowing for overnight outings. The hiker, carrying a lighter day pack, can cover more ground but must return to shelter by nightfall. The increased distance and freedom from civilization can make the burden of the heavier pack worthwhile.

Backpacking trips are usually difficult to arrange on the spur-of-the-moment. Reservations for camping are generally required for before, during, and after the trip, and it is important to order and study maps, elevations, and current weather conditions before attempting a trip in the backcountry. Beginners may prefer guided trips, which can be arranged by local outfitters, the American Forestry Association, the Wilderness Society, or the Sierra Club, for example.

The packer's hiking speed should be the same throughout the day. The weight is balanced over the feet or slightly ahead; a bent-over posture is only advisable for steep inclines. When going uphill the stride may be shortened, and when going downhill it may be lengthened. Steady, even breathing will help to keep the heart beating at an even pace. Resting is important, but for brief stops the pack should not be

Day hikers are attracted to historic sites.

removed. Instead, the waist belt is released, and the packer bends at the waist until the pack is parallel to the ground. Hands are placed on slightly bent knees to help relieve the strain on the shoulders. These stops should only last a couple of minutes so that the muscles will not stiffen as the body cools down. For longer stops the backpack is removed.

In addition to the day hiker supplies, the typical backpacker carries additional equipment (see Table 15.1). Raingear consists of a poncho or a rain jacket and pants. Rain jacket and pants are versatile and will break a cooler wind. A well-ventilated poncho will also protect the pack. Rain chaps work well with a poncho or jacket and provide ventilation. Raingear should be readily available in the pack. A cap or other protection for the head at night will help to keep the head and body warmer.

It is advisable for the backpacker to underestimate the weight that can be carried. In order to estimate properly, short trips with a pack should be made before an extensive trip is undertaken. A rule of thumb, according to Meier (1980:65), is to carry no more than one-third of the body weight when in good condition and no more than one-fourth if out of shape. The ideal weight to carry for comfort and agility is no more than one-fifth of the body weight. Generally more enjoyment is equated with less weight.

Backpacks have either external or internal frames. External frames distribute the load more evenly over the back, and the frame allows air to pass between the back and the load. Internal frames can be worn tighter to the body, making it easier to keep balanced. They are good for bushwhacking or scrambling over rock fields. Down-filled sleeping bags are light and compress easily. Small ultra-lightweight tents aid in keeping the weight down.

Backpacks should be arranged so that the weight rests on the hips and is balanced. When putting the pack on, one should tighten the shoulder straps until the pack is comfortable against the back, then the shoulders should be hunched while one fastens the waist belt. The waist belt should be cinched tightly until the weight of the pack is held directly on the hips. The shoulders simply lend stability while the hips carry the weight. Outside pockets carry items used throughout the day. Other items can be stored at the bottom of the pack or in an inside compartment. Heavier items are placed high in the pack and as close to the body as possible. This method allows for the heavier equipment to align with the center of gravity and keeps the pack from pulling off the shoulders. All equipment should be packed inside to prevent snagging trees. To protect items from moisture and to make them more accessible, they should be packed together in plastic bags according to their general use.

Safety and Survival

The importance of current first aid knowledge and an adequate first aid kit cannot be emphasized enough. According to McCloy (1990:33), every kit should contain aspirin for pain; antihistamine for respiration; valium for sedation in case of bad injury; topical medications and dressings, including moleskin; diamox tablets to help combat the headaches, nausea, and other symptoms hikers often encounter at altitudes above 11,000 feet; a snakebite kit for under 8,000 feet; and any prescription medication the hiker may require.

Packers must take care to disinfect water by one of these methods: vigorously boiling for two minutes; adding eight drops of household chlorine bleach to one gallon; adding 20 drops of iodine to one gallon; or following directions on commercial products such as halazone purifying tablets. If the water is particularly cloudy, dosages of chlorine or iodine should be doubled. Disinfecting should take place a full 30 minutes before drinking (Meier 1980:85).

Carrying the pack can be depleting on hot summer days, especially humid days. Physical exertion and exercise, work done by the muscles and cardiovascular system, generate heat. As the body heats, the heat is displaced by perspiration, increased respiration, and dissipation through the skin. Hotter conditions make it more difficult for the body to keep cool. Heat stroke and heat exhaustion are disorders that transpire when the body's capability of removing heat is surpassed by the rate at which heat is being generated.

Signs and symptoms of *heat exhaustion* include a weak, rapid pulse, headache, muscle cramps, dizziness, and general weakness. The whole body may feel cool and clammy from perspiration. Treatment includes termination of activity, moving to a cooler location, and drinking water (O'Shea 1991:30).

Heat stroke is much more serious and life-threatening. It results when the heat-regulating mechanism fails, putting the circulatory system under great strain, and medical help is needed immediately. Signs and symptoms include cessation of perspiration, dry and hot skin, and a dangerously high body temperature. The victim's face is red. Treat the victim immediately by quickly lowering body temperature with ice packs, alcohol rubs, and/or immersion in cold water (O'Shea 1991:31). Heat exhaustion and heat stroke can be avoided by drinking plenty of fluids and resting often in cool areas on hot days (see also the section on orienteering survival and winter camping safety).

Orienteering and Navigation

Nature has provided us with several means of navigation. Before the development of the compass, the North Star, the sun, the winds, moving clouds, and ocean currents served as guides. Eventually the map and compass became invaluable aides to the adventurer. Putting map and compass skills to use in order to find the correct path is called *orienteering.* Developing effective orienteering techniques requires hands-on experience. By acknowledging that nobody has a perfect "sense of direction," there is less chance of becoming lost. Whenever one is in unfamiliar surroundings, a map and compass are invaluable. Precautions must be taken when noting landmarks, and topographical maps are excellent aides.

The first steps in reading maps include learning what the various lines, symbols, and colors mean. Colors, for example, depict the work of humans, water, or the contours of hills and valleys. The shape and steepness of hillsides appear as contour lines—the closer the lines, the steeper the hill. Several forms of measurement may be offered on the scale found on the map. The *Index Circular,* a reference book that divides each state into sections or quadrangles, is useful in identifying which maps are applicable. Separate maps exist for each quadrangle, which often means that the purchase of more than one map may be necessary.

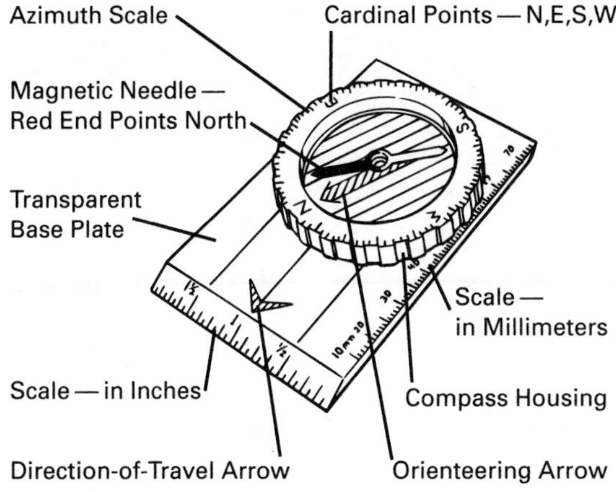

FIGURE 15.1 Orienteering compass.

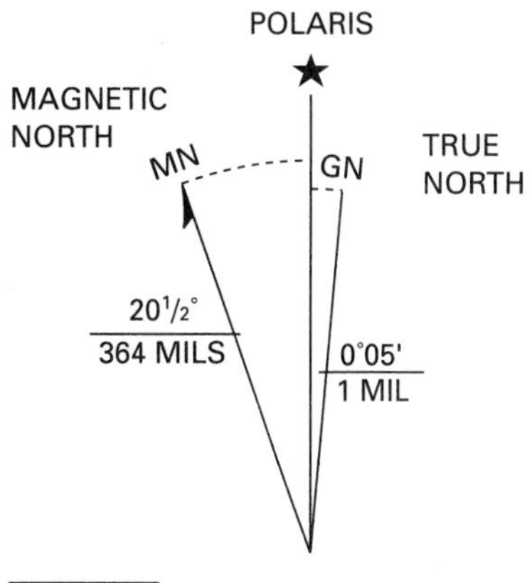

FIGURE 15.2 Declination marker.

The companion to the map is the compass. The most versatile compass for backcountry travel is the orienteering compass (Figure 15.1) with its rotating transparent plastic base plate allowing for more effortless use with a map. Care should be taken that no nearby metallic objects disturb the needle, causing a false reading. The needle points to magnetic north, not true north. To identify true north it is necessary to understand declination. *Declination* is the degree difference between magnetic and true north, shown by an offset V with a half-arrow and line which runs true north-south. This symbol, labeled "true north-south" or "magnetic north declination," is located on the bottom margin of Geological Survey quadrangle maps (see Figure 15.2). A map must be oriented by pointing the northern part of the map toward the north, and positioning it to match the terrain. By laying the compass on the map so that the arrow of the V is lined parallel to the compass needle, the map will match the terrain, and the venture can begin (Lanager 1973:238).

Survival By following the trail and carrying a map and compass, the hiker will not likely get lost. But on longer wilderness treks, observing nature is more than pleasure. Landmarks are canvassed from the front and back. There is a surprising difference in the appearance of landmarks when backtracking. Making notes mentally and on the map can save the wilderness traveler some anguish later. Nature also provides direction. For example, while the sun and moon only rise in the east and west twice a year, during the equinoxes, they do travel in a general east-west direction. Moss, on the other hand, does not always grow on the north side of a tree, as many people believe. Stars tend to rise in the east and set in the west and move toward your right when you are facing south and to the left when you are facing north. The North Star aligns with Ursa Major, the bright star in the Big Dipper.

Survival emergencies occur more often when the backcountry traveler has been pushing too hard and energy is low. Responding to an emergency with panic wastes energy, and most likely there are other travelers, campers, or rangers in the local area. Resting and waiting is ordinarily the best plan. A good night's sleep is more beneficial than taking a chance on aimless travel. Rescuers will respond to the lapsing of the planned return time and generally search during day light. They are attracted to signals which make the wilderness traveler larger, louder, and

Utilizing observation skills from a high vantage point, this hiker can benefit from orienteering skills when exploring the inhospitable desert, which requires special preparation.

more colorful than usual. ***The universal distress signal is any kind of signal repeated three times.*** For example, blasting a whistle three times signals distress. To signal aircraft use colors that contrast with the natural terrain. An X indicates distress and can be made from bright clothing. An X can be also be made in grass, sand, or snow by pulling clumps of turf, or by lining branches or stones. Flashing a mirror, tin foil, or a tin lid can be seen miles away, as will smoke signals made by lighting a collection of green grass, leaves, or evergreen boughs. Three fires set in a triangular form will alert pilots and fire wardens.

While waiting, the traveler must drink enough water to remain healthy and do everything possible to prevent the loss of moisture through perspiration. Necessary activities should be accomplished during cool hours. During the day it is important to stay in the shade, and if in the desert it is necessary to move above the desert floor. Clothing should be loose in warm weather.

Preventative measures can be taken to avoid distress situations (see Camping Safety and Survival). The backpacker should remember that storms and lightning can come on suddenly and quite unexpectedly. Once signs of lightning appear, the hiker should drop the pack, remove metal objects, descend high points, get out of water, and stay away from solitary trees and objects. Surprisingly a forest of shorter trees can be a relatively safe refuge (Breitling 1984:156–59, 188–89). A first aid kit should always be carried.

Mountain Biking

Mountain biking is one of the fastest-growing sports in the country. Upright handlebars, wide tires, and low gearing create an excellent all-purpose bike and comfortable viewing of scenic surroundings. Mountain bikes provide the cyclist with the ability to leave the pavement and enter a world of solitude and beauty.

Because mountain biking is so popular, there is pressure to restrict bikers from backcountry trails. User conflicts and threats to the environment have caused many trails to be closed to bikers. Trail access is causing mounting concern to the cyclist. To avoid trail closures, riders are advised to avoid popular hiking trails, particularly during prime time. Traveling at high speeds must also be avoided. Locking the brakes scars the surface of the trail, and bikers should never endanger others. When traveling, the cyclist should always be on the alert, watching for hikers and other cyclists. On single-track trails, the biker should stand to the side of the trail, allowing oncoming hikers or horses to pass.

Safety When selecting riding areas, primitive roads tend to be more rideable and more enjoyable than trails. During inclement weather, trails can become quite slippery due to wet leaves, rocks, and exposed roots. In areas of poor drainage, bikes can cause potholes. To avoid leaving unsightly ruts, bicyclists should carry bikes across muddy sections instead of walking or riding around the puddles, which could damage bordering vegetation. The International Mountain Bicycle Association recommends that mountain bicyclists follow the Cyclist Responsibility Code:

1. Ride on open trails only, avoiding trail closures, private land, and state and federal wilderness areas.
2. Leave no trace. Stay on trails. Do not create new ones.
3. Control the bicycle.
4. Always yield the trail.
5. Never spook animals with sudden movements or loud noise.
6. Plan ahead by preparing equipment, carrying extra supplies, and obtaining permits when needed.

Maintenance of an off-road bicycle is needed on a routine basis. The bike should be cleaned with a rag and soapy warm water; the chain should be cleaned with a chain cleaner or light solvent. After cleaning, the chain should be lubricated with a synthetic lubricant. Bearings should be repacked at least three times a year or even before every ride. A competent specialist is recommended for complicated repairs. The following inspections should be made before and after every ride:

1. Brakes and derailleur cables for frays, broken ends, and proper tension.
2. Brake pads for misalignment.
3. Nuts and bolts for looseness.

Proper clothing includes: helmet, cycling shorts or tights, gloves, sturdy shoes, wind jacket, bandanna, sunglasses, sweater, and rain gear. Essential items for backcountry riding include: two water bottles, pump, light, map, compass, tools, and first aid kit. Other items are the same as carried by a hiker, such as a whistle, candle, and extra food.

For backcountry riding, a map and compass are a necessity. Trail descriptions do not list every turn. Forest Service maps lead to trails, and firefighters' maps, which may be obtained from the U.S. Forest Service, show greater detail. Night riding when done with care and with companions may provide a new and different experience.

SNOW ACTIVITIES

Trail adventures continue after leaves have fallen. Hiking boots can be replaced with snowshoes or skis, which allow for enjoyment in a winter wonderland of crisp, fresh air. With just a few lessons and a little practice, the adventurer can travel virtually anywhere in the snow. Clean fresh snow can transform the most humble terrain into a beautiful area ideal for snowshoeing or ski touring. While traveling on snowshoes, one can move slowly enough to see and feel the presence of nature. As exercise, cross-country skiing is unexcelled. Adventures can include a brisk outing or a week-long journey into challenging backcountry. There are no crowds or lines, and equipment is simple.

Snowshoeing

Snowshoes are capable of carrying the adventurer over land that is inaccessible to skiers because of underbrush or rough terrain. While invigorating, snowshoeing is not too strenuous and offers one of the finest ways to visit the winter wilderness. First used by the North American Indians, snowshoes became a means of winter travel by hunters, trappers, loggers, and farmers. Snowshoe-clad adventurers tote their packs into the backcountry, mountaineers use them to reach alpine peaks, winter hunters depend on them, and those going ice fishing forge their way on them to remote ponds. Not only is snowshoeing excellent exercise, but the technique is easy and requires less than a day to learn.

Beginners find that they are usually not in condition for snowshoeing. The shoes are awkward to walk on, flopping and tripping the hiker, and the boots tend to come out of the bindings every few minutes, especially on rugged terrain. Ski poles can be carried for balance and for maneuvering around in tight spots. The left pole is placed in the snow ahead while the right shoe is carried forward just high enough to lift the front two-thirds of the snowshoe off the snow, dragging the tail behind. The tail pushes the shoe ahead slightly as the traveler steps down, thus allowing more momentum. A rhythmic rolling gait is established. Other skills are required, such as learning to travel on slopes, turning, and recovering from a fall. Groups travel single file, with leaders taking turns breaking the trail.

Looking like oddly shaped tennis rackets, snowshoes enable the wearer to walk over deep snow without sinking because the shoe distributes the weight over a large area. Snowshoes are at least 3 feet long and from 1 to 1 1/2 feet wide. They are traditionally made of light wooden frames that are bent into long ovals with strings of animal hide stretching over the frame. There is a wide variety of snowshoes made, with those made of white ash enjoying the best frame reputation. Plastic, metal, and aluminum frames have also entered the market. Styles vary according to the activity. Longer, wider snowshoes (Maine or Alaskan styles) will give better flotation in deeper snow and aid in carrying heavier loads. Short, narrow, and light shoes (Western or Green Mountain Bear Paw styles) provide better handling for climbing. Round-tail shoes provide greater flotation than models with pointed tails.

Footgear without heels are worn to protect the webbing. Special footwear is designed for backpackers and mountain climbers who wear lug-sole boots, gaiters, leggings, or overboots for added warmth. Shoe packs, boots with rubber bottoms up to the ankle and leather or fabric up to the mid-calf, are worn in flatter terrain. Work shoes can be worn with galoshes for short, casual hikes in moderate temperatures. An insulated boot liner may be added, along with several layers of socks. Too many socks can cut off circulation, however, and impede the body's efforts to warm the feet. Rubber boots tend to cause the feet to sweat profusely, which causes the skin to soften and blister easily. Bindings or harnesses, designed to hold a boot in place on the snowshoe, are styled for recreation, trapping, or racing. Maintenance, only necessary once a year for average use, consists of applying a coat of varnish and a preservative to the leather bindings. Snowshoes are hung during storage. The leather must be safeguarded from rodents.

Snowshoeing provides a great cardiovascular workout and is a convenient means of traversing the wild country. Most mountaineering shops will rent snowshoes.

Cross-Country Skiing

Many of the crowded parks are advocating that the outdoor adventurer take up cross-country skiing for a pristine winter nature experience. The trails are less crowded and the parks more peaceful. Cross-country, or Nordic, skiing is exhilarating and far easier to learn than Alpine, or downhill, skiing. Newly practiced in North America, it originated many centuries ago. A crude ski unearthed by archaeologists from a Swedish peat bog was estimated to be 5,000 years old (Sullivan 1980:11).

Cross-country skiing may take place on prepared or unprepared trails, parks, golf courses, and in many Alpine ski developments. Bushwhacking, skiing in deep woods and up and down hills, requires precision among trees. Wilderness schools offer excellent instruction for backcountry skiing and how to make quick-fix repairs when out in the field. They generally provide lessons in orienteering, snow camping/backpacking, and bushwhacking.

Touring on cross-country skis is simply an extension of walking. The two basic moves are the kick and the glide. The kick occurs as the skier pushes down on one ski, which causes it to grip the snow as the other ski slides or glides forward. The arms swing as if walking but they carry poles which are placed in the snow in a manner similar to snowshoeing. Poles give added power. As the knee drives ahead, the skier pushes back with the arm and pole on the same side. Other touring skills include turning, recovering from a fall, sidestepping, climbing in a herringbone pattern, moving downhill, and stopping. None of these skills is too difficult, but practice is needed for them to become natural. Lessons are available through recreational centers, schools and colleges, and at ski resorts. It is quite possible to learn the basic skills by studying an instructional manual, followed by practice.

There are three basic types of skis: touring, mountaineering, and racing, made of wood or fiberglass. Wooden skis require higher maintenance. An important decision is whether a waxable or waxless ski is desired. Depending on snow conditions, waxable skis utilize a varying hardness of wax to achieve the grip and glide effect. Because the waxable ski can be adjusted to the weather conditions, they can provide the best performance. Generally speaking the colder the weather, the harder the wax needed. Waxless skis use a synthetic base to achieve the grip and glide, and they are convenient because they function well in varying snow conditions. Working as a hinge between the foot and the ski are the boots. Comfort is the most important feature of the boot. They should flex at the same point where the toes flex. Boots are also designed for touring, mountaineering, and racing. They connect to the ski at the bindings; the heels are unattached.

Cross-country skiing offers an alternative to the typical summer exploration of crowded parks.

Clothing is layered, starting with long underwear and socks. Layering allows the wearer to shed clothing as needed. Heavy perspiration can cause a quick chill-down later. Many newer fabrics are designed for this initial layer. Cotton fabric is not recommended because it absorbs moisture and loses insulation value. The second layer should drain moisture away from the body, so wool is a good choice. Pants or knickers which do not restrict leg motion are best. Jeans are not recommended because they absorb moisture. The third layer protects against wind. This could include a wind breaker or down jacket, a wool hat, mittens, and gaiters. An extra layer can be carried in a day pack for added warmth when stopping for lunch.

Safety in the Snow For both snowshoeing and skiing adventures, a medical examination is recommended, especially if one is over age 35. Participants may choose to carry a pack with the same supplies a hiker carries. High-energy food, water or juice, and a thermos of tea or hot chocolate should be carried. Snowshoers and skiers should monitor the weather and study topographical maps long before a trip is undertaken. They should practice the same safety habits as hikers and backpackers such as observing and marking checkpoints. If lost and the weather is good, the temptation to move on should be avoided. Instead the adventurer should backtrack following his or her own tracks. If snow has filled the tracks, the route back should be reconstructed and the compass studied. Hazards of frostbite and hypothermia should be understood (see the section on winter camping).

ADVENTURES IN WHITE-WATER RIVERS

For thousands of years the earth's rivers were thoroughfares for transportation, exploration, and commerce. Log canoes, reed boats, and crude rafts traversed the rivers' currents through mountains and deserts. Modern crafts made of metal, fiberglass, and synthetic material can be smashed against river boulders with little serious damage, enabling the adventurer the thrill of moving down fast white-water currents on rivers just as different as the settings they traverse. The three most common river sport vessels, the canoe, the kayak, and the inflatable raft, are descendants of early river history. Each has its own special features and requires independent skills.

Viewing nature from the river offers the enthusiast a unique perspective of the land, its wildlife, and its rare birds. River craft can be used to explore rivers, lakes, and wilderness areas; to reach otherwise impossible terrain for backpacking; and for fishing. Most important, it is not necessary to make a life-long commitment to learn whether water crafting is enjoyable—equipment can be rented quite easily from local outfitters.

Canoeing

The modern canoe with its fine sturdy workmanship and graceful lines is a twentieth century descendent of the North American Indian birchbark canoe (see Figure 15.3). More versatile than the other river crafts, canoes can be used for many purposes. Canoes are the most popular muscle-powered boat in North America (Huser 1981:32).

Good river canoes are designed differently than lake canoes. River canoes may have higher sides and lack keels, which catch on rocks and reduce maneuverability. A shorter wider canoe is slower but more maneuverable.

While easier to master in lakes, canoeing on rivers provides challenging adventures. Navigating with a partner is an exercise in teamwork, concentration, and skill. In the slender craft paddlers fight for control of the river's force by finding safe exhilarating runs and by fighting cross currents to keep the boat from upsetting. The stern paddler (in the back of the canoe) is responsible for steering and should be experienced and the master of the "J" stroke, used to

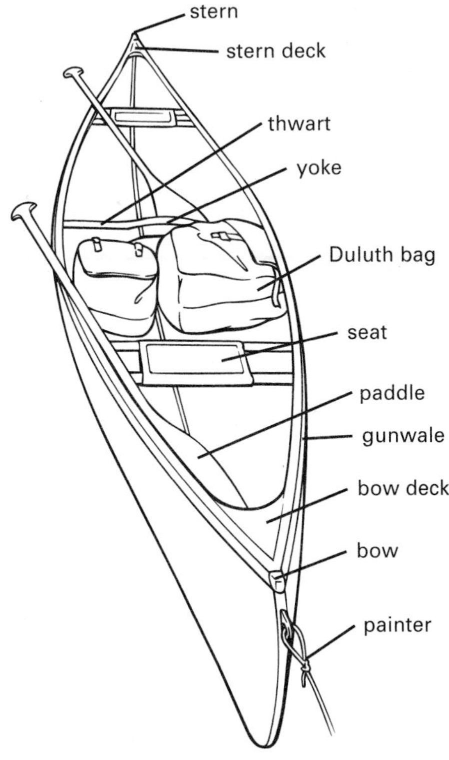

FIGURE 15.3 Diagram of the components of a typical canoe.

keep the canoe on a straight course. The bow paddler paddles on the opposite side and sets the rhythm of the stroke while looking out for rocks or snags. One can learn how to handle canoes easily by spending some time learning in tame water or by taking courses at local clubs or recreational organizations such as the YMCA and the Red Cross. Children can learn to canoe at summer camps, and local outfitters can recommend trips for beginners.

Kayaking

The kayak, traced back to the early Eskimos, was designed for hunting and fishing. Sleek modern kayaks are designed for challenging wilderness touring. They are also used for slalom, for downriver racing, and for ocean adventures. Faster than a canoe, a kayak has exceptional buoyancy that allows it to handle fiercer white water. The longer craft is faster but more difficult to turn. It lacks the same viewing opportunities provided by the canoe because of the low seating. Nor can it carry as many camping supplies. The paddler sits in a small cockpit, uses a double-bladed paddle, and is held to the vessel by foot, thigh, and knee braces. A waterproof spray skirt seals in the paddler, protecting against water spray. Both one- and two-person kayaks are available. Kayaks need to be outfitted with seats, foot braces, knee pads, thigh braces, back straps, and grab loops for both bow and stern.

The beginner experiences some uncomfortable moments. When the kayak tips, the paddler hangs upside down under the water. For this reason proper and adequate training is a necessity. Progressing from a canoe to a kayak is common; however, the skills do differ, so lessons and practice sessions are essential before rapids are approached. Control can be tricky in rapids, which seem like waves to the kayaker who sits so close to the water. Because the kayak is so agile, the paddler must be in complete control. Skill refinements come only after serious effort and practice.

Rafting

Inflatable rafts are newer vessels for wild-water river running; they are descendants of life rafts developed for World War II sea rescues. White-water rafting adventures are growing rapidly in popularity in the United States, especially in the west. Rafts are limiting because they only travel downstream, and transportation must be arranged to carry rafters up the river for another run. Ranging in style from inflatables for two to pontoons capable of holding numerous passengers and equipment, rafts can offer a variety of experiences. Exceptionally buoyant, rafts bounce off boulders and waves that demolish other boats. Made of puncture-resistant material, the raft is composed of small air chambers that link together. If one chamber is damaged, the

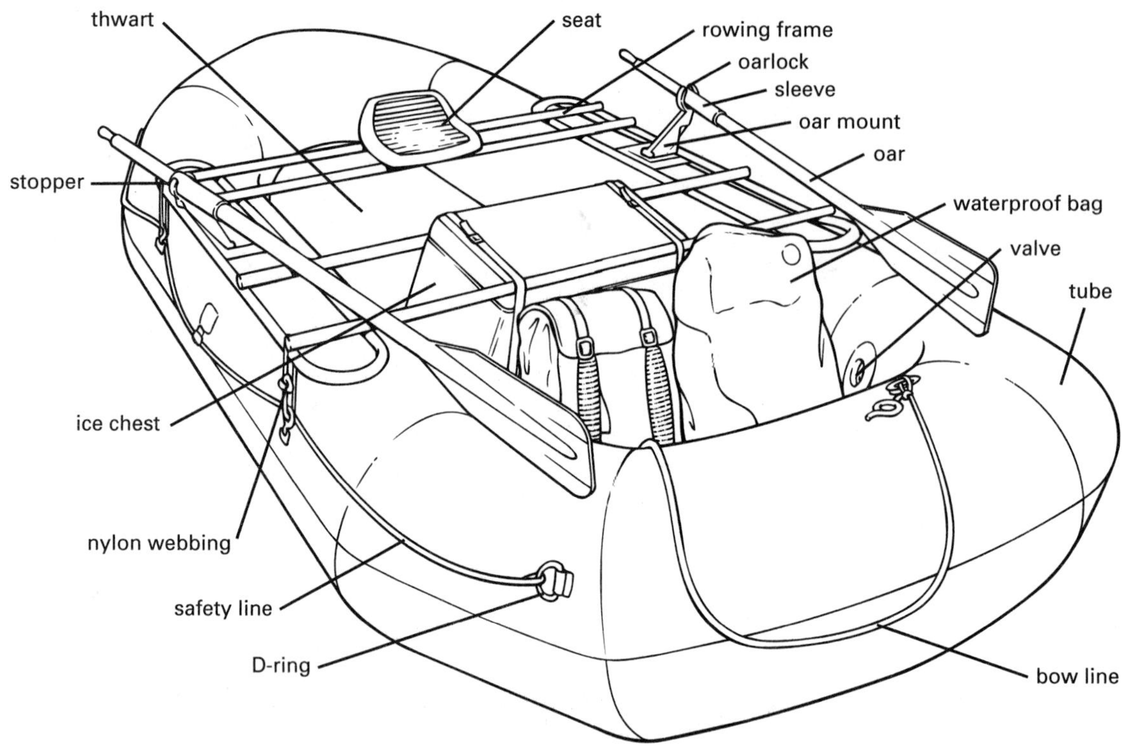

FIGURE 15.4 Diagram of the typical components of a river raft.

remaining flotation chambers retain their buoyancy. A diagram of the typical components of a river raft is shown in Figure 15.4. Rafting is probably safer and easier than other white-water activities, but if the raft flips the passenger will receive a good dunking.

Commercial raft trips provide an excellent means to experience river running. Professionals pilot the craft while passengers take a turn at the oars or shift their weight according to command. Guides often prepare meals at rest stops along the river which provides additional time for hiking, photography, swimming, and exploring. Incidentally, plastic bags are inadequate protection for cameras. Most people use army surplus ammo boxes or "pelican" style camera boxes.

Boating Equipment Boating equipment may be bought, rented, borrowed, traded, or built. Judging quality for the beginner is not complicated. Crafts should be carefully examined. According to Paulsen and Morris (1979:18), if there appears to be nothing wrong, no wild bends or obvious tears, or broken-fixed areas on the hull, it is probably good enough for the beginner. Defects are hard to hide, so if the craft floats it is probably worthwhile. Money can be saved by buying in the winter or by investing in canoe or kayak kits which are not too difficult to make.

Low-Impact Each river has different guidelines to follow for minimum-impact techniques.

The management plan for each river should be observed. On some rivers, campsites may be assigned. When a choice may be made, beach and gravel campsites cause less damage to the environment. Grassy areas can become heavily trampled, gradually losing vegetation. If it is necessary to make camp in a grassy or vegetated area, cooking should be done on rocks on the shore of the river or at the edge of the grass.

Fire pans should be carried along for fires. They contain ashes and prevent scars. Kayakers often use hub caps or oil pans. Pans are set up on rocks in order not to scorch the substrate and destroy soil microorganisms. Sand or dirt, placed in the bottom of the pan, keeps the fire from burning through. Ashes are moistened until cool and stored in an ammo can and carried out. At the next camp they can be dumped into the fire pan before starting. After being used several times they gradually are reduced to a fine dust. Smaller sticks are used for fuel, especially in the morning. They burn hot and break into smaller ashes. Larger logs burn slowly and sometimes never burn completely. Because the ground below the pan is very hot, it is watered down after a fire.

Tin cans can be burned to clean the inside, smashed, and carried out in a plastic bag. All aluminum foil and cans should be carried out and recycled. Organic garbage can be burned by scattering it in a thin layer on a fire. Once the garbage is consumed, the fire can be built up again for the next layer of garbage. Wet garbage is carried out. If no fire is available, any refuse is double bagged in plastic and then in burlap to contain spills. This includes organic refuse, which attracts flies and animals—even when buried. All refuse is then carried out. (For fire safety see the section on no-trace ethics.)

All washing is done away from the river so that no waste water drains into it. If there are several dishes, three buckets can be used. The first is filled with hot water and biodegradable soap for washing, the second is used for rinsing, and the third bucket of water with a capful of liquid bleach is used for disinfecting the dishes. The remains are disposed of by digging a hole after carefully removing sod. The hole should be away from the camp and above the high-water mark of the river. The same hole is used throughout the visit, filled in after, and the sod replaced.

Human waste should always be left above the high-water mark (see the section on no-trace ethics). Portable toilets are required on some rivers. Unless river regulations require an alternative procedure, all personal washing is done above the high-water mark. None of the waste water should run into the river or side streams, and soap is never put in rivers or side streams (University of Oregon Outdoor Program n.d.:14–17).

River Safety Successful river trips are dependent on the river runner's ability to read hazards and select routes that avoid danger. Guidebooks, U.S. Geological Survey maps, rangers, and wilderness outfitters should be consulted before a downriver adventure is attempted. The ability to swim is essential, and skillful boat handling is important but not enough. The adventurer should read extensively to learn to read water and weather. Rivers have common features such as wide V-patterns, known as tongues, which point the way downstream between rocks. V-patterns pointing upstream warn of submerged boulders, while a horizontal line indicates that a dam or vertical drop lies ahead. Dangerous water traps called suckholes form when water flows over an obstacle with force causing the flow to reverse at the obstacles' base. The currents form a hole that can trap a boat. Eddies or pools of calm water which tend to collect debris can be found in the midst of raging streams. They can provide a refuge, a place to relax and to judge the next set of rapids (David and Moran 1983:24). Even before entering the craft, efforts should be made to identify rough water, boulders, and other obstacles from shore.

River running is an exciting risk activity. Life jackets, boating helmets, and protective sport shoes should be worn. Eye glasses can be tied to the life jacket by a two-foot piece of cord or a shoelace. Rubber wet suits provide protection against hypothermia if the wearer is thrown into cold waters (see the section on winter camping). The general rule when capsized is to stay with your craft, since it should be able to support the passengers, even when it is filled with water. Ropes should be attached to the craft to allow the boater to hang on with one hand while paddling to shore with the other. Containers for boiling water, safety lines for rescues, extra flotation devices, emergency rations, first aid kits, and extra paddles should be carried. Clothing items include a wool hat, wool or synthetic sweater, wool socks, gloves, windbreaker, rain parka or paddling jacket, swimsuit, and a change of clothes for after river running. Equipment should always be checked to be sure that it is in good repair, and appropriate repair materials should be brought along. One should never boat alone. A minimum of three boats and boaters should travel together and maintain visual communication. Moreover, a trip is more comfortable with bug repellent, suntan lotion, and a hat for shore. All supplies should be placed in waterproof protectors that are strapped to the craft.

A river trip should not be attempted until the necessary skills are mastered in calm water. Rivers of higher levels are attempted only after the lower grades are mastered. Huser (1981:3) lists the International Difficulty Scale of rivers as follows:

River travel is a complete change of pace for most people.

Class I	Moving water with a few riffles and small waves. Few or no obstructions.
Class II	Easy rapids with waves up to three feet and wide, clear, obvious channels. Some maneuvering required but no scouting.
Class III	Rapids with high, irregular waves capable of swamping an open canoe. Narrow passages requiring complex maneuvers and possible scouting from shore.
Class IV	Long, difficult rapids with constricted passages that often require precise maneuvering in very turbulent waters. Scouting from shore is necessary, and rescue may be difficult. Generally not possible for open canoes.
Class V	Extremely difficult, long, violent rapids with congested routes requiring scouting from shore and precise moves. Rescue is difficult, and there is significant hazard to life. The Eskimo roll is essential for kayaks and covered canoes. Paddle rafts are at the very edge of possibility.
Class VI	Difficulties of Class V carried to the extreme of navigability. Nearly impossible and very dangerous. For teams of experts only.

Day sailing to Anacapa Island of Channel Islands National Park, comprised of five islands off the coast of southern California, is a popular activity. Nesting birds, sea lion rookeries, and unique plants are found in the area. First established as a National Monument in 1938, the area was designated as a national park in 1980.

ADVENTURES IN THE OCEAN

The ocean can invade the senses with its unique environment, its own geology, and its life forms. The ocean's mystery is intensified by its sometime serenity contrasted with its wild nature. It may be this very characteristic that induces us to explore its depths and its tidepools, and to exhilarate in its challenges.

Scuba Diving

Diving underwater dates back to the earliest of times. Eventually human lungs were aided by air-filled animal bladders, and then the development of the air compressor in the early 1800s opened the way for the modern era of underwater sea diving. By 1819 Augustus Siebe of England developed the forerunner of the modern diving outfit. In 1943 Jacques-Yves Cousteau and Emile Gagnan introduced the aqualung, which regulated air automatically in relation to the depth of the diver. By the 1960s scuba diving (that is, diving with a self-contained underwater breathing apparatus) had become the fastest growing American activity, and by the 1970s an estimated 10 percent of the population owned some type of diving gear (Fisher and Brown 1979: 297; Sullivan 1965: 1-9). Today there are 2.5 million

Waves crash over coastal rocks along the Big Sur in California.

active scuba divers in the United States, and recreational diving has become a $1 billion industry (Kraus 1990:280). Today's bright array of equipment allows the underwater adventurer to explore a unique, fascinating, and peaceful world.

Supervised lessons are essential and can be conducted in a swimming pool or in shallow water. Many enthusiasts start by snorkeling near the water's surface with mask, fins, and snorkel. Lessons for using scuba gear are available at many ocean resorts, schools and colleges, recreational centers, community organizations, and scuba clubs. After completion, certification cards are issued. Most agencies require a 28-hour course, spread over 7 to 10 weeks. Instructors should be interviewed to make certain that more than one instructor is available for the open-water dives. The ideal ratio is 2-to-1, but it is not uncommon to find a ratio of 8-to-1 (Fisher and Brown 1979:299, 301). Without appropriate attention and reassurance at this phase, many divers drop out, finding the ocean dive a traumatic experience.

Other activities may accompany diving. Artificial light, for example, can turn the blue-green atmosphere into an array of color, inviting underwater photography of tropical marine life. Some divers hunt for treasures or study ghostly remains of ship and plane wrecks. It is believed that there are hundreds of ships left for discovery. Such explorations should never be done alone. Lessons in photography, wreck diving, night diving, and spearfishing are offered through several diving shops and clubs. Considered an environmentally harmonious adventure, underwater photography has been gaining in popularity. Spearfishing with the use of scuba gear is considered unsporting by many divers. Shell and tropical fish collecting has also fallen into disfavor.

Safety and Survival The temptation to buy scuba gear should be resisted until the completion of the beginning course and after several subsequent dives. Rental gear is satisfactory when limited to a few dives a year. Caution must be applied when renting gear in some countries, however, where faulty equipment has led to unfortunate mishaps.

Before diving it is important to be in good physical health. A medical examination is highly recommended. Divers should be competent swimmers. A 1974 Los Angeles County scuba diving ordinance required that new divers demonstrate the ability to swim continuously for 200 yards without swimming aids; swim 50 feet underwater without swimming aids; swim 50 yards towing another person without swimming aids; float and/or tread water with minimal movement for 10 minutes; and tread water with legs only for 20 seconds (Fisher and Brown 1979:301).

Class instruction should include coverage of many safety measures. For example, how to react to an emergency situation such as air shortage, or what to do if another diver is stricken in the water. Divers should know the location of the nearest decompression chamber, the local rescue telephone numbers, and how to use a diver's flag and underwater distress signals. Signals are listed in the U.S. Navy *Diving Manual.* In addition, divers must always check weather conditions, and local tides and currents, and inspect their equipment. Observing the buddy system and joining a diver who knows the local waters is important in unfamiliar areas.

Many resorts, charter boats, and scuba clubs offer convenient trips with locals who are familiar with the waters. First aid kits should include seasick tablets, sodium chloride tablets, mineral oil to treat eyes, an alcohol solution to treat ears, a resuscitube, suntan lotion, and spray-on liquid bandages (Sullivan 1965:67–82).

Just as bear encounters are feared in the wilderness, shark encounters are feared in the ocean. This fear is often exaggerated because among roughly 360 shark species there are only a score that appear to attack humans. Shark aggression is not consistent, but attacks are more frequent in tropical and subtropical seas and whenever water temperatures are over 70°F. Sharks kill an average of 25 people a year. Humans kill approximately 100 million sharks a year, threatening some with extinction (LaFee 1991: D-3). Sharks may alter their normal habits and become dangerous when attracted by blood, flashing lights, colored materials, or splashing water. According to Cahill (1990), they tend to sneak up from behind, attacking a nonmoving part. He suggests carrying a broomstick with a nail in it to ward off sharks. Cousteau equipped his divers with shafts of wood or aluminum over three feet long. Small nails were placed in one end in circular formation. The nails were long enough to be felt, but not so long or sharp as to injure the shark or to aggravate an attack. Cousteau's divers also pioneered the use of cages which divers could climb into if threatened. They also operated in pairs, back-to-back, if an attack seemed probable. Some chemical repellents have received negligible success, but they continue to be investigated. Air bubbling from a diver's aqualung has deterred some sharks (Steel 1985:39–41)

Other dangerous creatures include the great barracuda and the killer whale. The great barracuda is found from the West Indies north to the Florida coast, and the killer whale is found throughout all oceans and seas of the world. Groupers swim around rocks, caverns, and old wrecks; the moray eel may lurk beneath rocks and coral; and jellyfish and sea urchins are found in the deep. The sting ray, if stepped on, will puncture the diver's foot or leg with its tail, injecting a venom that produces severe pain. Divers must always be aware and cautious, and at a minimum swim away from the danger. If dangerous predators are seen it is advisable to get out of the water. With the proper precautions scuba diving can be enjoyed for a lifetime.

The Florida Department of Natural Resources recommends the following safeguards:

1. Never dive alone.
2. Participate in appropriate training.
3. Always display a diver-down flag when in the water.
4. Be aware of other boats and diver-down flags.
5. Do not dive in narrow channels where you are a hazard to navigation.
6. Avoid direct contact with corals. Contact may kill them or cause infection or disease, and divers risk an allergic reaction.
7. Don't feed fish, as it often attracts predators such as sharks and barracuda. Certain foods eaten by humans can be unhealthy and often fatal to fish.
8. Be aware of potentially dangerous sealife.
9. A boat operator should remain on board when divers are in the water. Divers should begin the dive by proceeding upcurrent from the boat. Strong currents can carry divers far from the boat.

Windsurfing

Windsurfing or sailboarding has quickly developed into one of the world's most popular outdoor activities. A combination of sailing, surfing, water-skiing, and hang gliding, its beginnings are difficult to attribute. The ancient Polynesians and the early surfers deserve credit, but Jim Drake, an aeronautical engineer, and Hoyle Schweitzer are the recent inventors of the windsurf board. Pioneered in the United States, it was first popularized in Europe. Windsurfing is not confined to the ocean. In fact, calmer waters are recommended for beginners before progressing to wave sailing.

The board, made of plastic or fiberglass, carries a universal joint capable of swinging completely around. The universal joint carries a mast of fiberglass or aluminum to which the sail or rig is attached. A window appears in the sail which permits the windsurfer or boardsailor to see while steering with the boom. The boom tilts the sail as desired in response to the wind's direction. The skills are not difficult to master and are easy to remember. According to Mehmert (1990:C1), it takes about 12 hours of good instruction to begin to learn the activity, and a lot of spills are taken in the process. Before learning to sailboard it is important to practice raising the rig from the water, which requires both balance and strength. Two schools, Boardsailing Instructor's Group and International Windsurfer Sailing Schools, conduct classes throughout the nation.

Equipment advancements and inventions occur frequently. By 1977 footstraps were attached to boards to allow wave jumping or funboarding, which is done at high speeds with spectacular flying jumps through waves and surf. The windsurfer must learn to read the waves in order to know which one to ride and which to jump. Skilled windsurfers land smoothly after upside-down jumps and loops through the air. Tandem windsurfing is done on a board for two. In 1986 two French windsurfers crossed the Atlantic on a tandem sailboard. A board built for three is called a *tridem.* Windsurfing boards have been adapted for use on land, ice, and snow.

When buying equipment one should generally purchase a board with a reputable brand name. Due to the activity's sudden popularity, boards have been made hastily and cheaply by some manufacturers. High-quality boards have withstood the test of time, and replacement parts are easily obtainable. A top-brand craft will lose about 10 percent of its value annually, while a cheaper brand can lose as much as 75 percent of its value. Equipment is easy to maintain. Boards should be stored out of the sun, with sand removed from the universal joint immediately after use.

A wetsuit will minimize heat loss that could lead to hypothermia. Shoes with good traction are recommended. Visors help to avoid sunstroke, and a life jacket will increase survival time, particularly in cold water. Because the board is a built-in lifeboat, windsurfing has a favorable safety record (Olney 1982:28). The greatest danger is colliding with swimmers, small boats, and commercial vessels. The windsurfer should stay away from motorboats and avoid waves that are breaking on the beach. Lessons are usually available wherever windsurfers collect. Lessons often begin on land. Advanced lessons include the study of wind. Certified instructors have passed a specific course of study and testing, and are knowledgeable in first aid procedures. According to Evans (n.d.:72), the sailor must check the weather forecast before leaving; check tides and other dangers; be careful of the cold; be able to swim well or wear a buoyancy aid; check every detail of the board; learn the right-of-way rules; keep out of the way of shipping; avoid swimmers; never abandon the board; learn the International Distress Signals; not go out at night or in the fog; tell someone if out alone; learn self-help techniques before they are needed; and be able to recognize hypothermia.

ADVENTURES IN THE AIR

Humans have always envied birds' ability to fly. Outdoor enthusiasts can achieve the feeling of conquering gravity by taking part in adventures in the air. A new world awaits those who dare to soar above. Vistas sweep far below and off to the horizon, while gentle breezes beckon.

Hang Gliding

According to legend it was Daedalus, held in exile on the island of Crete, who fashioned a set of wings to suspend himself into the air. King Minos told him he would never be permitted to travel by land or sea, but the air was free, so he studied the flight of birds. After devising a set of wings for himself and his son, they flew into the air. His son Icarus flew higher and higher trying to reach the sun, until the wax holding the feathers to the framework began to melt. Disaster came when the feathers detached and Icarus fell into the sea (Olney 1976: 27–28).

Today the dream of flying can be accomplished through participation in hang gliding. There are hundreds of sites across this country where hang gliders launch from mountaintops, ski slopes, or sand dunes. Still a high-risk activity, accidents are not uncommon. The novice should under no conditions try hang gliding without the supervision of a very competent instructor. Great care is required to do the activity safely.

The pilot's body is attached to the underside of the glider's wings. The wings, looking like large triangles, are made of aluminum tubing and Dacron sailcloth. The energy for launching and landing is provided by the pilot's legs. While holding on to the control bar, the pilot runs quickly downhill into a light wind. Once airborne, speed can be increased or decreased by pulling the bar forward or backward, respectively. Riding underneath the glider, the pilot dangles from a harness and is capable of controlling the wing with the trapeze, a triangle of tubing which extends straight down under the wing structure in front of the pilot's body. By moving the body to one side, the glider will tilt and turn to the desired direction. To go up and ride an air draft the pilot pushes back. Landing judgment must be instantaneous because hesitations can be fatal. For a perfect landing, the glider is in a stall the moment the feet touch the ground. Even so the pilot must start running immediately in order to prevent the forward momentum from pulling the pilot off balance. Beginners are advised to use the standard Rogallo wing, invented by NASA scientists Francis and Gertrude Rogallo in 1951. This slow-moving wing allows for some miscalculation (Dean 1982: 59–61; Fisher and Brown 1979:354). For instance a dangerous stall, caused by tilting the wing too far, will cause the glider with the Rogallo wing to reach the ground slowly in parachute style rather than by a quick nose dive.

Most gliding lessons are associated with schools affiliated with the Hang Gliding Manufacturers' Association (HMA). This association establishes construction standards for hang gliders and guarantees that the equipment is well made. Safety gear includes high shoes to protect the ankles, knee and elbow protectors, long slacks, and a crash helmet. It only takes a day to learn the rudiments of flight. In 6 days a first mountain flight from an altitude of more than 1,000 feet can be accomplished (Doll 1990:c1). According to Jerry Bruning (Doll 1990:c1), hang gliding appeals to the person who wants to be detached and free to enjoy nature: "It's not just I-can-do anything daredevil."

Hot-Air Ballooning

Hot-air ballooning began in 1782 in France when two paper makers, Joseph and Etienne Montgolfier, launched the first hot-air balloon. They had noticed burning pieces of paper flying up the chimney and tried to float small bags over the kitchen fire. Later they constructed a much larger bag of paper and linen, filled it with smoke from burning straw, and watched it drift away. By 1783 the first balloonist was lifted from earth. Today's hot-air balloons are highly maneuverable, and more adventurers than ever are floating in the sky, creating a brightly colored scene for viewers below.

The average diameter of a balloon is 55 feet, with a height of 70 feet. The envelope or bag is made of nylon or Dacron, a very light but very strong material. Basically a balloon drifts with the wind. The pilot, however, can adjust the

The skies of La Quinta, California, are dotted with hot air balloons. The desert provides favorable wind currents for this activity.

altitude by regulating the temperature of the air within the envelope, and higher or lower altitudes may offer wind currents of different directions.

Ballooning injuries are infrequent. Fatalities are the exception. Hot-air balloon rallies are held in beautiful locations which allow spectacular views. Rallies present excellent opportunities for the beginning enthusiast to learn about piloting skills, and to be invited aboard the gondola for a ride. Volunteers are often needed, so one should not feel timid about offering services when the balloons are being prepared for inflation and launching. Preparations begin before sunrise in order to avoid dangerous air turbulence caused later in the day as the sun begins to heat wind currents in the atmosphere. Sunset flights are also popular. Formal rides can be arranged through balloon companies and tours. Usually costly, balloons can carry from 4 to 8 passengers. Commercial pilots should be FAA licensed and have many hours of flying experience. Balloons have been used for air safaris in Africa as a means to observe the animals, and risk-taking bungee jumpers have taken the leap from balloons.

Ballooning equipment is expensive, but once acquired, the only cost remaining is the propane used for an average flight of 2 hours. Lessons may be arranged through balloon touring companies, schools, or manufacturers. Training is usually completed in 10 to 14 days and includes both practical and theoretical experience. The school's safety record should be checked before lessons are begun. Balloons used for lessons and rental should be FAA certified. In most countries instructor ratings are awarded to pilots of sufficient skill and experience. Examiners are appointed by the balloon club on behalf of the national aviation authority to certify that a student has achieved a safe level of competence in practical and theoretical instruction. Ten flying hours are required in order to qualify for a license. Medical standards for ballooning are much lower than for aircraft licenses (Wirth 1980:146). Attire is casual, that is, long pants or jeans, tennis shoes, jacket or sweater. Propane burners, which heat the air inside the balloon, will keep the passenger warm in the gondola.

Parachuting

Panoramic views are enjoyed by skydivers, who claim that the experience is more like flying than falling. After World War II, many of the trained ex-paratroopers wanted to continue jumping. They organized jumping clubs for small groups of enthusiasts. Soon a jump made from a small airplane for fun was known as sport parachuting. Skydiving, which appeared later, includes a long free-fall prior to pulling the chute. Dean (1982:119) reported that skydiving was one of the fastest-growing sports in the United States, with an average of over four thousand jumps a day made for fun and adventure.

Freefall time depends on the height of the jump or the exit from the airplane to the point where the jumper's altimeter gives a reading of 2,500 feet. During this period the jumper does not use the aid of the parachute. The higher the airplane the longer the freefall opportunity. A common freefall time from 7,200 feet, for example, is 30 seconds (Fisher and Brown 1979: 356–57). Experienced jumpers, sometimes working in groups, make formations in the sky during the freefall. Group jumping is more difficult and dangerous because there is always a chance that the parachute lines could become entangled. Group skydivers must allow themselves time to move away from each other after the formation in order to open their parachutes. To end the freefall the ripcord, or cable holding the parachute pack together, is pulled, causing the parachute to release. This causes a tug to the shoulders as the jumper begins the float to the ground. Landings can be so soft that the jumper remains standing.

Advancements in equipment and techniques have made parachuting safer, although it remains a high-risk activity. One of the greatest dangers is overconfidence, which leads to carelessness. Like hang gliding, sessions must be undertaken at parachuting schools and clubs with skilled instructors and sound equipment. Parachute clubs and centers are located throughout the United States. Both may offer lessons. Centers associated with the United States Parachute Association (USPA) are likely to be a good choice, since the courses are taught by certified instructors who must follow basic safety regulations. Instructors teach everything needed for a first jump, which includes an orientation, information regarding use of equipment and the inspection of equipment, parachute packing, instruction for malfunction, and drill in emergency procedures. Skill instruction includes appropriate techniques for the jump, steering and control, landing preparation, and proper landing falls. Some lessons may include the cost of an airplane for the jump. A jumpmaster supervises student jumps from the ground and from the aircraft. First jumps are static-lined, meaning that the parachute will open automatically. A skillful beginner may begin to freefall after five or more jumps (Fisher and Brown 1979:356).

The mountains offer a variety of adventures, including cross-country and downhill skiing, hiking, rock climbing, and horseback riding. Black-eyed Susans cover the ground.

According to Benson (1979:43), people are attracted to skydiving due to the excitement and adventure, and not because they are "daredevils." Skydivers have found the adventure satisfying because it provides a feeling of accomplishment in overcoming gravity and the basic human fear of falling.

CAMPING

Overnight camping can be an adventure in itself. Whether rafting down a white-water river, snorkeling in the ocean, or hiking in the mountains, when night falls a warm meal and a place to rest offer a welcome respite from the activities of the day. With the night stars as a ceiling and the howls of the coyotes in the background, a night spent away from the comforts of home can be as refreshing and rewarding as the day's activities.

The best way to enjoy a night spent under the stars is to be prepared. The first step in setting up camp requires finding the natural advantages of a location. It is preferable to use existing sites

A motorized raft.

Adventurers can reach otherwise inaccessible sites such as this blow hole on Kuaui, Hawaii, by motorized raft.

when possible. This will save the land from new campfire and clearing scars. The camper should try to anticipate the unexpected and plan for any dangers such as high winds or floods. The following questions should be asked prior to selecting the site:

Is there an established site?

Is the site close to water?

Will the site provide shelter?

Is the land flat?

Is the area protected; could it flood?

Are there any dead trees next to the camp site?

Is the site aesthetically pleasing?

Does the site offer privacy and interesting scenery?

After site selection, each member of the party should begin different duties such as clearing a place for the tent, setting it up, starting the campfire, getting the water, and cooking.

The tent site should be located upwind from the firelay, and if possible the back of the tent should be positioned on the wind side. Facing the door toward the rising sun can make the mornings more pleasant, and it will dry the tent and gear better. Sticks and stones are cleared from the tent site, but leaves, pine needles, or humus should remain in place. They serve as a cushion and improve drainage. The tent is pitched on a waterproof ground cloth or a plastic groundsheet. This tent floor combined with a foam pad will protect the bed from moisture. On dry days a sleeping bag should be unrolled as early as possible to restore it to its original loft. On rainy days the bag should remain in its sack so that it will not absorb the moisture in the air. The dining area may be centrally located if bears are not a threat. If they are, it should be located about forty or fifty yards away and downwind from the camp.

An overnight campfire is not essential if the camp is laid out properly. (Please refer to the section on no-trace ethics for fire and sanitation procedures and safety.) The United States Department of Agriculture (1980) recommends that if campfires are needed:

- Campfires should be built away from overhanging branches, steep slopes, rotten stumps or logs, and dry grass and leaves.
- Place wood a distance from the fire, and remove litter, duff, and or other burnable materials within a 10-foot-wide circle of the campfire to avoid accidental spreading.
- Water should be handy to prevent any spread to surrounding areas.

- A good bed of coals or small fire gives off plenty of heat for cooking.
- Afterwards the campfire must be put out with water, making sure that all embers, coals, and sticks are wet. Move rocks, making certain that there are no embers underneath. The area should be stirred and water added until all material is cool enough to be touched. If no water is available, dirt should be used.

Breaking camp calls for a reverse order of tasks. The fire should be cold-out, extra firewood scattered, the tent dismantled, personal gear packed, and the area checked so that it is as clean and natural as before. After returning home the sleeping bag should be aired and any wet gear dried.

Safety and Survival The American Hiking Society's *Hiking Safety* recommends staying away from plants with three leaflets. Poison ivy and poison oak fit this description. Plants with white berries should also be avoided. Symptoms include redness, burning, and itching. This is followed by a breaking out or rash, swelling, and blisters, with possible fever. This results in itching and general discomfort. Treatment includes washing immediately and laundering clothing. The sap of poisonous plants takes about 20 minutes to bind to the skin. Scratching should be avoided, as it tends to spread the poison, increases the discomfort, and may cause secondary infection. Compresses of very hot or very cold water may be applied followed by a drying agent such as calamine lotion. A doctor should be called for severe cases.

To avoid snakes and poisonous insects, the hiker/camper should not step where it is impossible to see clearly, put hands inside holes in logs, trees, or rocks, or wander around the camp at night without a flashlight. Boots and clothing should be inspected in the morning before putting them on. There are several hundred varieties of snakes in the United States, but only four are poisonous—the coral, the rattler, the copperhead, and the cottonmouth. It is estimated that of the 7,000 people bitten per year by poisonous snakes in the United States, not more than 10 to 15 will die. Corals are found in the south, copperheads in the eastern and southern states, cottonmouth moccasins or water moccasins in swamps and various varieties of rattlers in nearly all of the fifty states (Mitchell and Meier 1983:291–94). If a rattler's buzz is heard, stop, find out where the noise came from, then retreat carefully. Normally rattlers will strike only at a moving object. Snakes seldom strike high, so leather hiking boots provide protection. The Arizona-Sonora Desert Museum and the Arizona Poison Control System recommend the following treatment: calm and reassure the victim; decrease movement of the limb; apply a light constricting band above the site (be able to insert a finger under the band and release if it becomes too tight from swelling); capture the snake if possible without risk and bring it immediately to a medical facility with the victim. The wound should not be incised and suctioned except in unusual circumstances.

In bear country the hiker/camper should watch the trail ahead and on both sides; stop and listen every 5 minutes when walking or hiking; talk or sing quietly; avoid carcasses; carry only dried or freeze-dried foods; eat in one spot and clean up any food that spills; avoid packing any smelly foods; when fires are permitted, burn any leftovers, food containers, etc.; seal food and garbage in plastic bags and suspend them at least 12 feet above the ground, 5 to 10 feet from the tree trunk, and 5 feet below the limb from which they hang (Figure 15.5); avoid areas obviously used by bears; pick a good campsite; pitch the tent at least 150 feet upwind from the cooking area; place the tent door near climbable trees; stay calm in a confrontation; retreat slowly.

If a bear approaches, move slowly downhill (the bear cannot move as quickly downhill), look for a tree, and climb as high as possible; if it is impossible to climb, play dead with your

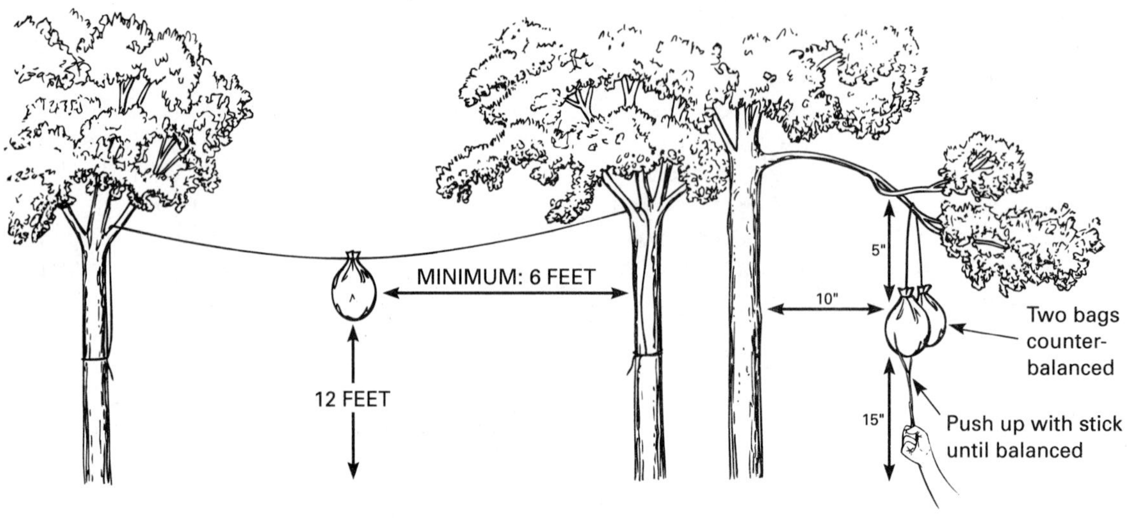

FIGURE 15.5 Diagram of a suspended food bag.

arms clasped tightly behind your neck and lying face down with your legs pressed together. If the bear rolls you around, stay curled, do not struggle or cry out (American Hiking Society). Peacock (1990:85) advises that when facing a grizzly one must not run or climb a tree. Grizzlies can move at 40 miles per hour. The best bet is to quietly stand fast and wish for luck—sometimes grizzlies will hop-charge, advancing only a few yards. If the grizzly chooses to ignore your presence or does not see you, retreat slowly.

Bears are unpredictable and there are no hard and fast rules. To tell a grizzly from a black bear, do not depend on color. Grizzlies can be any color from almost black to white. Black bears are jet black to brown to cinnamon or even blond. The grizzly's fur is grizzled and brown and has longer, silver-tipped guard hairs causing an often mixed or silver-tipped, collared appearance. Their faces are concave or dished. Grizzly bears stand 6 to 8 feet high, and their claws are enormously long. They have a humped muscle over their shoulders. Black bears have fairly straight muzzles and Roman noses. Their heads are small in proportion to their bodies. They stand 5 to 6 feet high with claws that are not as noticeable.

An old tale about how to tell a grizzly from a black bear is to "sneak up behind it, kick it, then run up a tree. If the bear knocks the tree over and eats you, it's a grizzly. If it climbs up the tree and eats you, it's a black bear," (*Backpacker* 1990:71).

WINTER CAMPING

If you have modern equipment designed for below-freezing or even subzero weather, winter can be one of the best times to visit the outdoors. One does not need to fight the crowds or the insects, but there are special challenges to camping in winter. A solid foundation in basic camping and survival techniques is essential, as well as advanced cold weather skills.

Winter campers must become familiar with cold-weather techniques, equipment, and local conditions. With night arriving earlier in the winter, camps should be set up by mid-afternoon. Cold wind should be avoided as much as possible by selecting a shielded site. Langer (1973:262–63) suggests camping among shorter younger trees, or building a snow windbreak on the weather side of the tent site. A tree can provide additional protection. Snow-laden trees should be bypassed because the snow could fall on the tent. To avoid potential avalanche conditions, locations near hills with a gradient of over 25 degrees should be avoided. Needles furnish excellent ground covering around the site and prevent the tent from freezing to the ground. If freezing does occur, the tent should be detached with boiling water to keep it from ripping. Tents should be waterproof, condensation-resistant, and sturdy in design. Hoop and dome tents are often preferred by winter campers. Snow shelters such as snow domes, snow caves, and igloos can be made and will provide greater insulation than tents. Building methods are discussed in books focused on camping and winter survival (see the list of recommended publications at the end of this chapter).

Equipment can be carried in backpacks or by pulling a toboggan. Wool clothes, hat, and a sleeping bag with a closed-cell pad underneath the bag shield against the chill. Pine needles can be collected to insulate the bed. Mummy bags with built-in hoods can add protection on cold nights. With down bags, less clothing leads to more comfort. Overdressing will cause perspiration which will make the night and early mornings even colder. Down provides the best insulation per carried pound, but it is ineffective insulation when wet. Some bags are insulated with high-tech materials and may be preferable in wet weather. Boots can be wrapped in a plastic bag and placed at the foot of the sleeping bag to keep them warm. Snowshoes or skis should be stored outside. If they warm above outside temperature, the snow will tend to stick, and the webbing on snowshoes could stretch. Snowshoes should be hung away from the reach of animals.

Even if a fire is not intended, wood, tinder, and kindling should be collected for emergencies. Fuel should be placed on plastic and kept inside the tent to help it to dry out. Fires must be carefully planned and tended. Tent heaters are a hazard; more winter camping accidents occur from asphyxiation than from freezing temperatures.

Outer clothing should be colorful to allow for more visibility. Brightly colored yarn or cord can be tied to smaller gear to avoid losing it if dropped in snow. Winter supplies should include sunglasses to protect against snow blindness, lip balm, and chewing gum. Chewing gum will stimulate facial circulation and help to protect against frostbite. A 6-inch square of 1/4-inch plywood should be carried for placement under the stove for insulation (Breitling 1984:355).

Winter campers tend to drink less than they should. It is important to drink more fluids to avoid dehydration. Hot liquids will warm the body better than hot foods. Water may be collected from streams flowing too swiftly to freeze, or by cutting through ice with a hammer and chisel. To melt snow a few cups of water should be placed at the bottom of a pot to create steam. More water results from melting chunks of ice and slab snow than from melting powdered snow. After water is collected it must be purified.

Local outfitters provide organized tours and special equipment to meet the challenges of cold weather. With advances in high-tech materials, more and more enthusiasts are expanding their camping adventures into a year-round activity. The national and state parks, in an effort to provide relief from the crowded summer months, have launched public relations campaigns encouraging winter camping.

Safety The two most common hazards are *frostbite* and *hypothermia.* Frostbite is caused by freezing temperatures. Similar to a burn, it results in local injury or death of tissue. The body parts most commonly affected by frostbite are ears, nose, hands, and feet. Signs and symptoms involve a tingling sensation, pain followed by numbness, and white or purplish appearance in more severe cases. Treatment involves removing any clothing which could cause constriction and bathing the area in lukewarm water. Hot water or heat from a fire can damage tissue, adding a burn to the frozen area (Kenney 1988:35).

When the body loses so much heat that it can no longer warm itself, hypothermia has occurred. *Hypo* means "low," and *thermia* means "heat." Untreated conditions will result in a continual drop in the body's core temperature until bodily functions cease. Signs and symptoms involve shivering, clumsiness, and mental slowness. Physical and mental deterioration will continue until the advanced stages, which include physical collapse and unconsciousness. Treatment must be immediate. For milder cases, wet clothing should be removed and replaced with warm, dry clothing. Warm liquids should be administered. In extreme cases, the victim should be kept awake. Heat should be transferred to the victim by skin-to-skin contact, the most effective way to transfer heat. Therefore, the victim should be stripped and placed in a sleeping bag with one or two other stripped persons (Kenney 1988:35). The victim should receive medical care.

EDUCATIONAL ACTIVITIES

Educational activities may include nature activities such as bird watching, rock hounding, tidepooling, plant identification, photography, sightseeing, and driving. They could also include trips to visitor centers, traditional museums, outdoor museums, and planetariums. Historic sites, battlefields, and prehistoric sites offer educational opportunities and activities.

Bird Watching

Bird watching can offer trips to wild and remote places, especially when foraging for exotic species. A *pelagic trip,* for example, is an ocean or Gulf trip far enough out to sea to find oceanic species. At the same time it is possible to identify, attract, and become fascinated by a surprising variety of birds in the backyard. As one learns to key in on details for species identification, details in general tend to become more apparent and sounds can become more distinct.

With an estimated 20 million bird watchers, finding other birders is not too difficult (Norris 1988:66). Local bird clubs or Audubon chapters schedule field trips which can be especially helpful to newcomers. These organizations can be located through telephone directories, local natural history museums, nature centers, or outdoor stores specializing in bird-feeding equipment. The National Audubon Society can advise of the nearest local Audubon chapter. Ornithology classes on the science of bird study are also available in many areas. If there appears to be no organization in the area, the activity can be self-taught. Basic abilities include looking and listening. The observer must learn to identify distinct characteristics of the bird being watched. Birds are identified by spotting certain markings, behavior, song, size, or shape. Observations can be recorded in a notebook and looked up later. Trying to observe while thumbing through a field guide is not recommended. Studying a field guide before participating in an excursion can be very helpful. When birding in a group, someone is usually able to offer an identification when simple descriptions are given. Checklists are also available to keep records of sightings. A field guide is very useful, as are two other essentials: comfortable walking shoes and binoculars.

Birds are usually found with the naked eye. Binoculars are then brought forward for a sharper closer look. One can also try *sweeping* an open area or body of water with binoculars. To find the right binoculars, according to Norris (1988:66), quality optical equipment must be matched to the particular characteristics of the individual's eyes. It is best to try several binoculars before buying. The buyer will know when the chemistry is right. In general, quality should not be sacrificed in order to save a few dollars. It could lead to frustration and difficulty later.

Standard-size binoculars are most often used, but when bird watching while hiking or biking, compact or mini binoculars may be favorable. Standard and compact binoculars are also available with a rubber coating to help withstand shock and in some cases water. The basic measure of binoculars is a formula such as 7 × 35. The first number represents the magnification. With 7 × binoculars objects appear to be seven times closer. For most beginners 6 ×, 7 ×, or 8 × are adequate. The second number indicates the objective lens diameter in millimeters. The larger the opening, the more light is collected, and the higher the ratio, the better the binoculars are for low-light use. For example, dividing the first number into the second will result in the binoculars' brightness, or *exit pupil.* The pair that is 7 × 35 has an exit pupil of 5, which is acceptable for most conditions. An 8 × 20 has an exit pupil of only 2.5, which would be dark even in bright daylight.

A good pair of binoculars should have high resolution or clarity. This is tested by focusing on an object with detail or lines. The details should be sharp near the middle and edge of the viewer's field of vision. To care for binoculars, clean them with lens tissues, not with clothes or facial tissue. More experienced birders sometimes invest in powerful lenses set up on tripods. These spotting scopes help to zero in on birds at long range. On birding trips, leaders will usually have one or two scopes.

Bird watching is a daybreak activity. Photographers find it an excellent time to photograph their surroundings. More experienced birders enjoy capturing birds on film. Hiking, backpacking, bicycling, and boating can be made more interesting with a search for various bird species.

Safety Birders must follow the same safety precautions as other adventurers, depending on the mode of transportation and length of the trip. According to Lotz (1987:249), the bird watcher on the forest trail must "Keep one eye on the treetops, the other eye on the ground." Admittedly impossible, the advice calls for watching ahead for snakes, wild animals, puddles, rocks, and other adversaries.

Rock Art Hunting

Some of the best rock art museums are found on federal lands. Canyon walls, caves, and rock faces show ancient hunting scenes, stars, wildlife, and humanlike figures which are interpreted by archaeologists as cultural, religious, or ceremonial symbols, astronomical observations, and expressions of the supernatural. When the drawing is etched onto a rock or chipped away by bone chisels and rock hammers, it is known as a *petroglyph.* Pictures on rock, known as *pictographs,* may display many colors. Pigments were formed by the Native Americans by crushing minerals. When the minerals were mixed with water, red, black, yellow, white, and blue paints could be created. These paints were applied with plant fibers or by spreading the pigment onto a rock by hand. Negative-image pictographs were created by painting around an object such as a hand (Browning 1989:37–39). Well-known examples of pictographs are found in El Morro National Monument in New Mexico and in the Virgin Island National Park. Canyonlands National Park in Utah is known for several striking polychromatic pictographs. Park interpreters lead day and overnight trips to some of the sites.

Only able hikers can locate some of the rock art found in remote desert areas. Unfortunately many of the sites are vulnerable to natural wear. Some have been destroyed by flash floods, rock exfoliation, and natural erosion. Other rock art is threatened by acid rain, invading developments, and vandalism. According to Browning (1989:37–39), until recently archaeologists refused to disclose site locations in order to prevent vandalism. But attitudes have changed among modern archaeologists, who now believe that greater public awareness of the art's frailty and historical significance are better means of preservation.

Searching for rock art can be demanding. Hiking and climbing skills are often required. There are generally no paths leading the adventurer to the art itself. Without close observation, rock art can easily be missed. Binoculars are recommended as are a good pair of hiking boots. Ancient ruins, cliffs, overhangs, and rock art should be treated with respect. Climbing on surrounding ruins to get a closer look can result in site damage and injuries. Even touching the centuries-old pigments can irreparably damage the art. Rock art delicately binds us to our distant past. Utmost care is required so that rock paintings can be enjoyed and studied by future adventurers and archaeologists. Their presence brings us closer to understanding our past.

"Leave No Trace" Ethics

The American public has demonstrated an increased interest in visiting public lands. The National Park Service has responded to the crowded conditions by providing backcountry hiking permits and a campground reservation system. The future may call for a limit to the number of visitors to some of the most popular parks. Other options include buses and a lottery system to help reduce the traffic volume going into the park. The common expression used is that people are loving the parks to death.

According to Chase (1990:55), "Leisure, wherever it occurs, should provide some sort of a fulfilling personal closure. But to experience fulfillment we need to be able to interact cognitively with the environment." Before engaging in leisure activities in the natural environment, the adventurer should establish a personal set of ethics appropriate for the environment. These ethics or values should be personally, socially, and environmentally acceptable. Participating in outdoor activities can enhance user awareness regarding the effect of leisure on the environment and create empathy for nature and for other users. Environmental change begins with individuals, who must test their ethics. According to Henderson (1990:78), "Recreation and related professions talk about recreation contributing to the quality of life . . . ," which Henderson believes infers the "human" quality of life, yet she believes that the quality of life for nonhumans must also be kept omnipresent. Some forms of recreation are more disturbing to the natural environment than others. What if some recreational choices are not contributing to the value of human and nonhuman life? To what extent may educators, philosophers, environmentalists, managers, and policymakers go to influence ethics and choices in the environment? Outdoor ethics and discussions must receive greater attention in outdoor recreation and education programs.

Adventurers visit backcountry areas for solitude and a "wilderness experience." They want to escape from crowds, noise, and the daily pressures of urban life, but many popular areas are already overcrowded. Evidence of people, horses, tents, and campfires is everywhere. Enjoying wildlands also requires a commitment to preserve them. No-trace and low-impact backcountry practices are techniques used to help reduce evidence of our presence in wild lands. According to Birkby (1990:366–67), the *no-trace ethic* is the use of methods that help to protect outdoor recreation areas and the environment around them, particularly in the backcountry when one is hiking off of established trails or cooking and sleeping where there are no developed campsites. To practice the *no-trace ethic,* two things must be remembered: first, it should be difficult for others to see you, and second, no trace of your visit should be evident after you've left. The *low-impact ethic* goes beyond no-trace by leaving areas in better shape than when they were found. This includes mending the damage left by another. The Forest Service, the National Park Service, and the

Bureau of Land Management (1989:1–13) propose that a thorough understanding of no-trace land ethics can help preserve solitude in the wildlands and provide for greater enjoyment in the backcountry. They recommend the following no-trace guidelines.

No-trace planning Planning must go into a backcountry trip if it is to be safe and fun. Gathering information can help in the planning. Government offices can provide current maps, first-hand information on trails and campsites, and anything else pertinent to the trip. In planning a trip, consider group size, when and where to go, and equipment and food selection.

Group size Small groups are ideal. Plan for traveling and camping with fewer than eight people if possible. Smaller groups are more desirable in open areas, such as deserts, meadows, and above the timber line. It is easier to plan for small groups and to keep them together. Campsites for smaller groups are easier to find, and they harmonize better with the environment.

When and where to go If high solitude is desired, backcountry trips on holidays and weekends during peak seasons should be avoided. Midweek is the best time to go for a quieter experience. A trip can be taken any time of the year, but spring and fall are an excellent consideration if you are trying to avoid crowds. Winter is potentially the best season, provided the adventurer is prepared. Popular trails and wildernesses always seem to be crowded; visitations in less popular areas can provide a more contemplative experience.

Equipment The type of equipment taken into the backcountry is important to the no-trace ethic. Bright colored clothing (some exceptions in winter), packs, and tents should be avoided—they all contribute to the crowded feeling and can be seen for long distances. Earth-tone-colored gear offers decreased visual impact in the backcountry. A lightweight backpacking stove for cooking will not scar the landscape like a campfire will. Local inquiries should be made regarding open fires, since some areas prohibit them due to fire danger or the scarcity of fuel.

Repacking food in plastic bags and containers can lighten the load and eliminate packing trash into the backcountry. Glass and aluminum packaging should be left at home; it adds extra weight and does not burn. The rule is: If you pack it in, you have to pack it out. Carry extra trash bags for camp cleaning. They also make excellent emergency rain gear. Other equipment needs are a small trowel for burying human waste and for digging no-trace fire pits if a fire is allowed.

Preparation No-trace planning includes being prepared for the trip so that others know where to find you. A good map should be obtained; a route planned; a note left with another—in case you should get lost. Minimum survival gear should be carried, including extra food, a signal mirror, a whistle, and warm clothing—even when planning a day hike. Extra water should be carried in desert areas (a minimum of two quarts per day/per person).

No-trace travel Trails are an important part of backcountry travel and are designed so that visitors can travel from one place to another with varying degrees of difficulty. They are also designed to drain off water with a minimum amount of soil erosion. When traveling, no matter by what means, efforts should be made to remain on the trails.

Switchbacks are the most abused portion of the trail system. A *switchback* is a reversal in trail direction. Many people shortcut across switchbacks, trying to save time and energy. They are only creating a new scar on the hillside which will cause soil erosion and many problems for work crews later. Please do not cut across switchbacks.

Cross-country Nonmotorized cross-country trips may be made in back-country areas. Groups should spread out when traveling in order to prevent the creation of new trails through single-file travel. For this reason motorized cross-country trips are not encouraged even where legal. Traveling through meadows and wet areas should be avoided. These fragile places will show the impact of foot or hoof prints and group travel much longer than forested and rocky areas.

Hanging ribbons or signs or blazing trees to mark a path for others to follow does not follow the no-trace ethic. The planned route should always be discussed with group members to avoid leaving an impact.

No-trace camping Choosing a campsite away from popular areas will provide for more solitude and less visibility from others. Try to camp 200 feet or more from lakes, streams, meadows, and trails. There will be less chance of damage to fragile areas. Less impact may be created by using an existing campsite rather than clearing a new one—this must be judged by the individual. Designated campsites should be used. They are designed for camping use, while minimizing damage to the land.

Location The best campsites are found on ridges or hills or near canyon walls. These areas provide natural drainage so that the camp will not flood. The campsite should be arranged around trees, rocks, and shrubs to hide it from view.

Never ditch, or build trenches around, the tent. They can start soil erosion and lasting scars will remain. The stay should be planned for as few nights as possible to avoid waste accumulation and injury to plants. One night in each campsite is best to avoid impact.

No-trace fires For a total no-trace campsite, building campfires should be avoided, with cooking done on a stove. Today's backpacking stoves are lightweight and economical to use. The camper can be assured of clean cooking even if firewood is scarce. In some heavy-use areas, fires are not permitted. In fragile environments (deserts, alpine meadows), fires leave scars for many years. Ranger stations and district offices provide information regarding fire restriction or closures.

Heavy-use areas If camping in a heavy-use area, there are probably existing campfire rings nearby which should be used to lessen the impact. These campfire areas have been left for use so that the impact is concentrated in one area.

Remote areas When camping in remote areas, campfire sites may be built. Sites should be selected away from trees and shrubs. A sandy spot or hard ground is excellent since the scar can be easily hidden. Fires should never be built next to a rock (the smoke will blacken it) or in a meadow (the fire will kill vegetation and the fire scar will remain after you leave).

With a trowel, dig up the organic layer of soil and set it aside for later use. Encircling the fire with rocks should be avoided: they will not keep a fire from spreading, the rocks may explode from intense heat, and the blackened rocks are hard to conceal.

Wood Burning small sticks is best. Only down, dead wood should be used where permitted. Cut green trees or branches should not be used and will not burn. Standing dead trees will burn but are valuable for wildlife and aesthetics; they should be left alone. Small wood will burn completely, providing good coals for cooking. The remaining white ash will be much easier to dispose of than are partially burned logs. The fire should never be left unattended.

Leaving no-trace In heavily used camping areas, fire rings are maintained and should be used. After using the fire ring, the fire should be dead-out before you pick out aluminum and other trash that did not burn in order to pack it out. A cold fire can be assured by sprinkling with water and then stirring the coals until they are cold to the touch—then it is out. The remaining ash and coals should be scattered. Ashes should be carried several hundred feet from the campsite and widely scattered for concealment and assimilation back into the soil. Burlap or a plastic cloth can be used to carry the ashes. All trash should be picked up, making the campfire area ready for the next user.

In remote areas, the same procedure should be followed. All organic material set aside earlier should be replaced. The area should be completely naturalized.

Sanitation

Sanitation practices in the backcountry require extra effort. Washing and disposal of human waste must be done carefully so as not to pollute the environment. Water sources can become polluted from the run-off of soaps, food waste, and human waste. Toilet paper and other trash also leave an unsightly impact.

Washing All washing should be done away from the camp and any water sources. A container for washing and rinsing should be used for personal grooming. Although any soap can pollute lakes and streams, causing injury to fish and other aquatic animals, biodegradable soap should be used. Water can then be poured on the ground a safe distance from any water source.

Human waste The size of the latrine will depend on group size. An individual may want to use the cat method of making a shallow hole and covering when done. A group should dig a latrine to accommodate their needs. A latrine should be dug in the top 6–8 inches of organic soil and be at least 200 feet away from camp, trails, and water sources. After each use, dirt is used to cover waste and discourage flies. If no fire restrictions are in effect, toilet paper should be burned. In order to avoid the possibility of it being exposed later by erosion, or dug up by animals it should not be buried. The latrine should be covered thoroughly with dirt, rocks, and natural material so *no trace* is left of your visit.

Trash When the trip is well planned, there should not be too much trash accumulation. Packages should be opened in such a way that they stay in one piece. Efforts should be made to pocket all trash, including cigarette butts. Pockets can be emptied into a trash bag later. Trash should never be buried; animals have a tendency to dig it up. If it was packed in full, it can be packed out empty.

Pack Animals

Many adventurers enjoy horse packing in backcountry areas. Pack stock groups must be equally conscientious about leaving no trace of their visit. Proper trip planning, selection of camp location, and containment of animals once in camp all demand special attention.

Planning The same type of planning is used for a pack stock trip as for a backpacking trip. It is important to check with local offices for trail conditions and to find out whether stock is allowed. Some areas are closed to pack animals due to overuse or fragile environments. The fewer animals taken, the less impact on the land. Keeping the group small and carrying lightweight equipment will help to reduce the number of animals needed.

Setting up camp For the horsepacker, the first rule of campsite selection is to think of the stock. The campsite should be able to accommodate the animals without any damage to the area. After riding into a potential campsite, the packer must decide whether there is enough

Horseback riding at a dude ranch is reminiscent of the days of the Old West.

feed. Consideration should also be given to the wildlife in the area. If the area is overgrazed, pack stock may remove feed otherwise needed by deer and elk during winter months. Animals should be grazed on north or east slopes, which will be snow-covered during the winter, leaving forage for wildlife on exposed south and west slopes. Stock water is another important consideration. A place downstream from camp where the stream bank can withstand hard use lowers impact.

Animal containment Hitchlines, hobbles, and pickets are all methods of containing pack animals. Hitchlines need to be erected in rocky areas and on good stout trees. Hobbles prevent horses from moving too fast, and pickets confine them to an area only as long as the rope or chain. Pickets should be moved at least twice daily to prevent overgrazing. Temporary corrals are an excellent method of containing pack animals for several days. They can be built out of natural timbers, rope, or portable electric fence.

Feed Feeding pack animals can cause a negative impact. Spreading loose hay on the ground could introduce exotic plant species to an area. Instead, processed feed should be packed in. This will also help to prevent overgrazing. National Park Service areas do not allow grazing of stock.

Breaking camp It takes extra time to naturalize an area from the impact of pack animals. Manure piles need to be scattered to aid decomposition and discourage flies, and as a courtesy to other users. Areas dug up by animal hooves will need to be filled and trampled areas made to look natural.

Historical/Archeological Sites

Many historical and archeological sites can be found throughout our national forests, national parks, and Bureau of Land Management areas. Those fortunate enough to visit these sites can enjoy and learn from the remnants of our past heritage. The adventurer can help preserve them for the next generation by not disturbing the sites in any manner. Federal law prohibits disturbing historical and archeological sites. Objects should not be disturbed or removed. Camping should not take place in or near these resources because it could inadvertently disturb valuable archeological information that can never be reclaimed.

Back Country courtesy

Courtesy toward others in the backcountry helps everyone enjoy their outdoor experience. Excessive noise, loose pets, and damaged natural surroundings create a negative atmosphere in the backcountry.

While traveling on trails campers should keep the noise level down. Radios and tape players do not belong in the backcountry. When encountering other groups, uphill hikers have the right-of-way. If encountering a cavalcade group, hikers should step off the trail on the lower side and let them pass. Noise level should be lowered and people should stand still as horses are spooked easily.

Pets should be kept under control at all times. They should not be allowed to run through any area where they can frighten people or wildlife. When visiting a national park, the visitor should check with the officials to make certain that pets are allowed in the backcountry.

Wildflowers, picturesque trees, and unusual rock formations all give backcountry areas the beauty adventurers seek. Picking flowers, hacking at trees, and chipping away at rocks detract from the primitive atmosphere.

SUMMARY

Americans' love of nature is reflected in the type, as well as the amount, of outdoor activities they partake in. Chapter 15 gives but a glimpse of these activities. Adventures on land include hiking, backpacking, orienteering and navigation, mountain biking, snowshoeing, and cross-country skiing. The equipment needed for each activity is described. Also covered are the safety rules and the steps needed to be taken to ensure maximum enjoyment of the activity.

White-water rivers of America provide ample opportunities for leisure pursuits such as canoeing, kayaking, and rafting. On the other hand the ocean is used for scuba diving and windsurfing. How to satisfactorily participate in these activities is described. In the air, Americans enjoy hang gliding, hot-air ballooning, and parachuting.

Camping is an activity that is enjoyed in both winter and summer. Maximum enjoyment is derived from adequate preparation. Winter camping techniques are described in this chapter. Educational adventures include visits to outdoor museums and park visitor centers, and scientific field trips. Despite overcrowding in wilderness areas, the recreationist can prevent adverse impact by practicing the no-trace ethic. No-trace techniques were described in detail. They help to protect the environment by leaving no sign of visitation. The low-impact ethic takes the no-trace ethic a step further by advocating leaving wilderness areas in better shape than they were found before visitation. By practicing no-trace and low-impact techniques, wilderness visitors can enjoy these beautiful and pristine environments today and tomorrow.

BIBLIOGRAPHY

A few of the many organizations and periodicals available to assist you in pursuing the activities described in this chapter are listed below. Books listed in the bibliography and other suggested readings are also recommended. Your library can assist in making a more detailed selection.

Organizations

Many organizations support outdoor opportunities.

American Alliance for Health, Physical Education, Recreation and Dance

American Camping Association

American Canoeing Association

American Youth Hostels

Appalachian Trail Conference

Appalachian Mountain Club

Council for National Cooperation

National Campers and Hikers Association

Izaak Walton League

American Aquatics Association

National Recreation and Park Association

The Sierra Club

The following organizations provide excellent resources for learning proper techniques for the activities cited.

Ballooning

Balloon Federation of America, 821 15th St. N.W., Suite 439, Washington, D.C. 20005.

Birding

National Audubon Society, 950 Third Avenue, New York, NY 10022.

Cornell Laboratory of Ornithology, 159 Sapsucker Woods Road, Ithaca, NY 14850.

Camping

American Camping Association, Inc., Bradford Woods, 5000 State Rd. 67 N., Martinsville, IN 46151-7902.

Association of Private Camps, 55 W. 42nd St., New York, NY 10036.

Christian Camping International, P.O. Box 646, Wheaton, IL 60187.

National Camping Association, 353 West 56th St., New York, NY 10019.

National Campers and Hikers Association, P.O. Box 182, 7172 Transit Road, Buffalo, NY 14221.

Canoeing, kayaking, and rafting

American Canoe Association, 4260 E. Evans Ave., Denver, CO 80222.

American Whitewater Affiliation, Box 321, Concord, NH 03301.

National Organization for River Sports, Box 6847, Colorado Springs, CO 80934.

United States Canoe Association, 606 Ross St., Middletown, OH 45042.

Cross-country skiing and snowshoeing

American Camping Association, Inc., Bradford Woods, Martinsville, IN 46151.

American Hiker, 1015 31st Street N.W., Washington, D.C. 20007.

Far West Ski Association, 812 Howard Street, San Francisco, CA 94103.

International Backpackers Association, Box 85, Lincoln Center, ME 04458.

Ski Touring Council, Inc., 342 Madison Avenue, Room 727, New York, NY 10017.

Ski Touring Council, Inc., 4437 First Avenue South, Minneapolis, MN 55409.

The National Hiking and Ski Touring Association, Box 7421, Colorado Springs, CO 80907.

The North American Telemark Organization, Box 44, Waitsfield, VT 05673.

The Sierra Club, 530 Bush St., San Francisco, CA 94108.

Hang gliding

Hang Glider Manufacturers' Association (HMA), 137 Oregon St., El Segundo, CA 90245.

United States Hang Gliding Association (USHGA), Box 66306, Los Angeles, CA 90066.

Hiking/Backpacking

American Hiker (see Cross-Country Skiing and Snowshoeing)

National Campers and Hikers Association (see Camping)

Mountain biking

International Mountain Bike Association (IMBA), P.O. Box 20007, Saratoga, CA 95080-0007.

National Mountain Bike Association (NORBA/USA), P.O. Box 1901, Chandler, AZ 85244.

Orienteering

National Outdoor Leadership School, P.O. Box AA, Lander, WY 82520.

Orienteering Service U.S.A., P.O. Box 1604, Binghamton, NY 13902.

Outward Bound, Inc., 165 West Putnam Ave., Greenwich, CT 06830.

Map Information Office, U.S. Geological Survey/General Services Building, 18th and F Street N.W., Washington, D.C. 20405. A free Topographical Map Index Circular for any state east or west of the Mississippi River can be requested.

U.S. Geological Survey, Federal Center, Denver, CO 80200.

Parachuting

The United States Parachute Association (USPA), 806 15th St. N.W., Suite 444, Washington, D.C. 20005.

Rock art

American Rock Art Research Association (ARARA), P.O. Box 1539, El Toro, CA 92630.

The National Pictographic Society, P.O. Box 94, Copperton, UT 84006.

Scuba diving

American Association of Certified Scuba Divers, Inc., 1066 Westover Road, Stanford, CT 06902.

Underwater Society of American, 1701 Lake Ave., Glenview, IL 60025.

Windsurfing

International Windsurfer Class Association, 1955 W. 190th St., Torrance, CA 90509.

U.S. Board Sailing Association (USBSA), Box 206, Oyster Bay, NY 11771.

Books

AMA Staff. *AMA Handbook of First Aid and Emergency Care.* Random House, 1990.

Barnett, Steve. *Cross-Country, Downhill and Other Nordic Mountain Skiing Techniques.* Globe Pequot, 1983.

Barrett, Norman. *Hang Gliding.* Franklin Watts Ltd., 1988.

Barrett, Norman. *Skydiving.* Franklin Watts Ltd., 1988.

Cook, J., and P. Way. *Windsurfing.* EDC, 1988.

Culliney, John and Edward Crockett. *Exploring Underwater: The Sierra Club Guide to Scuba and Snorkeling.* Sierra Club Books, 1980.

Darvill, Fred. *Mountaineering Medicine: A Wilderness Medical Guide.* Wilderness Press, 1989.

Douglas and McIntyre. *Outdoor Safety and Survival.* Salem House Pub., 1986.

Elman, Robert, and Clair Rees. *The Hiker's Bible.* Doubleday, 1982.

Evans, Jay. *The Kayaking Book.* Greene, 1983.

Evans, Jeremy. *The Complete Guide to Windsurfing.* Facts on File, ND.

Ford, P., and J. Blanchard. *Leadership and Administration of Outdoor Pursuits.* Venture, 1985.

Gould, Robert. *The Boater's Medical Companion.* Cornell Maritime, 1990.

Hart, J. *Walking Softly in the Wilderness.* Sierra Club Books, 1984.

Jones, Roger. *Windsurfing: Basic and Funboard.* Harper and Row, 1985.

Kallner, Bill, and Donna Jackson. *Kayaking Whitewater.* ICS Books, 1990.

Keech, Andy. *Skies Call.* A.C. Keech, 1981.

Ketels, Hank, and Jack McCowell. *Sports Illustrated Scuba Diving Underwater Adventuring for Everyone.* Winter Circle Books, 1988.

Kjellstrom. *Be Expert with Map and Compass. Scribners, 1976.*

Lotz, Aileen. Birding Around the World. Dodd, Mead and Co., 1987.

Martineau, LaVan. *The Rocks Begin to Speak.* KC Publications, 1976.

McNally, Rand. *Campgrounds and Trailer Parks.* Wehman, 1987.

Mead, Robert. *The Canoer's Bible.* Doubleday, 1989.

Meier, Joel. *Backpacking.* Wm. C. Brown, 1980.

Meier, Joel. *High Adventure Outdoor Pursuits.* Pub. Horizons, 1987.

Miskimins, R. W. *Guide to Floating Whitewater.* F. Amato Publications, 1987.

Nigg, J. *The Great Balloon Festival: A Season of Hot Air Balloon Meets Across North America.* Free Flight Press, 1989.

Olsen, Larry. *Outdoor Survival Skills.* Chicago Review, 1990.

Osgood, William, and Leslie Hurley. *The Snowshoe Book.* Greene, 1983.

Pasquier, Roger. *Watching Birds: An Introduction to Ornithology.* Houghton Mifflin, 1980.

Poynter, Dan. *Hang Gliding Manual with Log.* Para Pub., 1982.

Prater, Gene. *Snowshoeing.* Mountaineers, 1988.

Risk, P. *Outdoor Safety and Survival.* Wiley, 1983.

Roberts, Harry. *The Basic Essentials of Backpacking.* ICS Books, 1989.

Robinson, Jill, and A. Fox. *Scuba Diving with Disabilities.* Leisure Press, 1987.

Watters, Ron. *Ski Camping: A Guide to the Delights of Back-Country Skiing.* Great Rift, 1989.

Watters, Ron. *The Whitewater River Book: A Guide to Techniques, Equipment, Camping and Safety.* Pacific Search, 1982.

Wirth, Dick. *Ballooning.* Random House, 1984.

Periodicals

American Whitewater Journal. Hagerstown, Maryland: American Whitewater Affiliation.

Audubon. New York: National Audubon Society.

Backpacker. Boulder: CBS Magazines.

Bicycling. Emmaus, Pennsylvania: Rodale Press.

Camping Magazine. Martinsville, Indiana: American Camping Association.

Currents. Colorado Springs, Colorado: National Organization for River Sports.

Flying. New York: Diamandis Communications.

Skiing. New York: Times Mirror Magazines.

Skin Diver. Los Angeles: Petersen Pub. Co.

Sierra. San Francisco: Sierra Club.

REFERENCES

Backpacker (1990) "Our Favorite Animal Stories." *Backpacker* 18:2 (Oct.).

Benson, R. (1979) *Skydiving.* Minneapolis, MN: Lerner Publications.

Birkby, R. (1990) *The Boy Scout Handbook.* Irving, TX: Boy Scouts of America.

Breitling, J. (mng. editor) (1984) *Field Book.* Irving, TX: Boy Scouts of America.

Browning, T. (1989) "Spirits in Stone." *National Parks* 63:9–10 (Sept/Oct). Washington, D.C.: National Parks and Conservation Association.

Bureau of Land Management (1989) "Leave No Trace." in *Land Ethics.* Washington, D.C.: U.S. Government Printing Office.

Cahill, T. (1990) "Swimming with Sharks." *Reader's Digest* 137:822 (Oct.).

Caputo, G. (1991) "Lyme Disease and Hiking." *Camping Magazine* 91:3 (January).

Chase, C. (1990) "Cognition, Ethics and Direct Experience." *Journal of Physical Education, Recreation and Dance.* 61: 4 (April).

Cordell, H., L. Bergstrom, L. Hartmann, and D. English (1990) *An Analysis of the Outdoor Recreation and Wilderness Situation in the United States: 1989-2040.* U.S. Department of Agriculture Forest Service General Technical Report RM-189. Fort Collins, CO.

Cordell, K., and G. Siehl (1989) "Wildland Recreation Use." *Trends* 26:3. Alexandria, VA: National Park Service and National Parks and Recreation Association.

David, A., and T. Moran (1983) *River Thrill Sports.* Minneapolis, MN: Lerner Publications.

Dean, A. (1982) *Wind Sports.* Philadelphia, PA: Westminster Press.

Doll, P. (1990) "Sense the Invisible." *Times Advocate* (June 20). Escondido, CA: John Armstrong.

Dunlop, R. (1974) *Backpacking and Outdoor Guide.* Chicago: Rand McNally.

Evans, J. *The Complete Guide to Windsurfing.* New York: Facts on File.

Ewert, A. (1989) "Change and Diversity in Wildland Recreation: an Introduction." *Trends* 26:3. Alexandria, VA: National Park Service and National Parks and Recreation Association.

Fisher, R., and L. Brown (editors) (1979) *Fodors Outdoors America.* New York: David McKay Company.

Florida Department of Natural Resources "Reef Guide." Tallahassee, FL: Florida Department of Natural Resources.

Freysinger, V. (1990) "A Life Span Perspective on Women and Physical Education" *Journal of Physical Education, Recreation and Dance* 61:1. (Jan.).

Henderson, G. (editor) (1991) "TVA" in *The U.S. Government Manual (1990-1991).* Tanham, MD: Bernan Press.

Huser, V. (1981) *River Camping.* New York: Dial Press.

Kenney, J. (1988) "Camping in the Cold." *National Parks* 62:11-12 (Nov./Dec.). Washington, D.C.: National Parks and Conservation Association.

Kraus, R. (1990) *Recreation and Leisure in Modern Society.* Glenview, IL: Scott Foresman and Co.

LaFee, S. (1991) "The Great Shark Dive." *San Diego Union* (July 28, 1991). San Diego, CA: Copley.

Lanager, R. (1973) *The Joy of Camping.* New York: Saturday Review Press.

Lotz, A. (1987) *Birding Around the World.* New York: Dodd, Mead.

Mehmert, G. (1990) "Windsurfing." *Times Advocate.* John Armstrong Pub., Escondido.

Meier, J. (1980) *Backpacking.* Dubuque, IA: Wm. C. Brown.

McCloy, M. (1990) "Packing for Survival." *Women's Sports and Fitness* 12:5 (July/Aug.). Boulder, CO: Women's Sports and Fitness.

Mitchell, V., and J. Meier (1983) *Camp Counseling: Leadership and Programming for Organized Camp.* Philadelphia, PA: CBS College Pub.

National Geographic Society (1987) *Americans and the Outdoors.* Washington D.C.: National Geographic Society.

Norris, R. (1988) "Bird Watching." *Backpacker* 16:6 (Sept.).

Olney, R. (1976) *Hang Gliding.* New York: Putnam's Sons.

Olney, R. (1982) *Windsurfing.* New York: Walker.

O'Shea, M. (1991) "Guide to Better Fitness." *Parade Magazine* (July 7). New York: Parade Publications.

Paulsen, G., and J. Morris (1979) *Canoeing, Kayaking and Rafting.* New York: Julian Messner.

Peacock, D. (1990) "A Practical Guide to Grizzly Country." *Backpacker* 18:7 (Oct.).

President's Commission on Americans Outdoors (1986) *A Literature Review.* Washington, D.C.: U.S. Government Printing Office.

President's Commission on Americans Outdoors (1987) *Americans and the Outdoors.* Washington, D.C.: National Geographic Society.

Robb, G. (1986) "Risk Recreation and Special Populations," in *The President's Commission on American Outdoors, A Literature Review.* Washington, D.C.: U.S. Government Printing Office.

Seiger, L., and J. Hesson (1990) *Walking for Fitness.* Dubuque, IA: Wm. C. Brown.

Steel, R. (1985) *Sharks of the World.* New York: Blanford Press.

Sullivan, G. (1980) *Cross Country Skiing.* New York: Julian Messner.

Sullivan, G. (1965) *Skin and Scuba Diving.* New York: Frederick Fell.

United States Department of Agriculture (1980) "Make Campfires Safe." Pamphlet.

University of Oregon Outdoor Program *Raft Initiations Handbook.* Eugene, OR: University of Oregon.

Wirth, D. (1980) *Ballooning.* New York: Random House.

16 The Environment

*O*utdoor survival skills have been lost for the most part by urban populations. The hostile natural environment once feared by the pioneers has been developed and industrialized, eliminating the need for use of outdoor skills on a daily basis. Today, wilderness survival instincts are satisfied by outdoor enthusiasts in wilderness and nature preserves. The return to these skills by recreationists tends to stimulate sensitivity to the protection of nature and its survival. Atkinson's research (1990:47) presents several aspects of this relationship, as follows:

1. Leisure activities that focus on the appreciation of the natural (nature, walking, outdoor photography) appear to have a greater impact on one's environmental concern and one's likelihood to behave in a pro-environmental fashion when contrasted with activities that are more consumptive of energy or natural resources.
2. Recreationists may possess stronger attitudes about aspects of the environment on which their leisure activity is dependent (clean water for fishing, clean air for ballooning, etc.).
3. Pro-environmental attitudes of recreationists do not always translate into environmentally sound behavior. Some recreationists in their enthusiasm and efforts to see and experience remote or desirable public lands are guilty of damaging some of our most fragile ecosystems.

Increasingly chemicals, agriculture, and urban development place tremendous pressure on our natural resources. Because it is difficult to measure the state of the natural environment and because many environmental issues seem invisible and distant, Americans are increasingly dependent on conservation groups, public laws, the media, museums, zoos, parks, and nature centers for information regarding the condition of the natural world. Outdoor enthusiasts, however, experience nature first hand, and their recreational societies keep them abreast of environmental issues affecting their activity. As such, outdoor recreationists have a unique opportunity to share their knowledge, experiences, and interpretations with others. Outdoor leaders must understand basic concepts of environmental conservation. For not only do they also teach others to enjoy the wonders of the natural world, they also teach them how to preserve nature and to develop outdoor ethics.

According to Chase (1990:55–56), there are specific ingredients that preface interaction of people at leisure with the natural environment. These are direct experience, cognition, and ethics. *Direct experience* provides a reference point to view the effect of leisure on the natural environment and may nurture empathy for other users and an environmental conscience. This enhanced cognition through direct experience will positively influence the outdoor ethics espoused. Describing these ingredients as interdependent, Chase asserts that environmental *cognition* provides for both short-term and long-term betterment of the environment due to a strengthened knowledge base. *Ethics* produce an immediate betterment in the form of awareness of the aesthetic appeal of a natural environment that is free of debris and other traces of the user. Long-term betterment results through responsible management grounded in an ethical framework. Chase believes that these three ingredients are best learned through exposure to role models, for instance, a scout leader, coupled with experiences in the environment.

Atkinson (1990:46) divides environmentalists into two basic philosophical groups. *Reformists* believe that environmental problems can be solved through technology, increased governmental and industrial expenditures, and ceaseless public vigilance. On the other hand, *deep environmentalists* believe that an entirely new social and economic value system is needed to deal with environmental deterioration. They believe that a decrease in the consumption of the earth's resources is essential. Like the Native Americans, these environmentalists believe that society must live in harmony with all living things. Whichever philosophy is endorsed, the solutions to environmental problems will require patience and long-term commitment.

The authors have selected several environmental issues affecting outdoor recreation. Further study of these issues is needed. Future leaders will be expected to educate others and sensitize the public to problems related to the use and enjoyment of nature.

THE NATURE OF ECOSYSTEMS

All organisms share an evolutionary history and an ecological kinship. A number of interactions serve to meet environmental dependencies such as food, shelter, moisture, and respiratory gases. Kormondy (1984:1–2,159) explains that ecological relationships are manifested in physiochemical settings of nonliving, or *abiotic*, environmental substances and gradients. These groups consist of basic inorganic elements and compounds such as oxygen, water, carbon dioxide, and an array of organic compounds, the by-products of organism activity. Also included are physical factors and gradients such as moisture, winds, currents, tides, and solar radiation. *Biotic* components, or the living components, such as plants, animals, and microbes, interplay against the abiotic backdrop.

In general, Kormondy lists two major types of ecosystems: aquatic and terrestrial. Subdivisions are recognized in each. *Aquatic ecosystems* are distinguished as fresh-water, estuarine, and marine ecosystems. There are several types of *terrestrial ecosystems,* including forests, tundra, and grasslands. An ecosystem is made of animal and plant species living together in a community with physical surroundings such as land, weather, water, and sunlight. No two ecosystems are alike. *Ecologists* study structure and function of ecosystems. The term *ecology* is derived from the Greek word *oikos* meaning "house," and *ology,* meaning "to study." Ecology, simply stated, is the study of your own house.

The relationships among plants, animals, and their surroundings are so intricate that only the most obvious mysteries have been unraveled. The following cycles exhibit noteworthy relationships:

1. The Food Chain Cycle All living organisms require nourishment. Plants flourish by receiving energy from the sun and nutrients from the soil. Smaller animals consume the plants, larger animals feed on the smaller, and so on. Upon their deaths the bodies decompose and return to the soil, where plants absorb the fresh nutrients, thus completing the chain.

2. The Oxygen-Carbon Cycle Similar to the food chain cycle, the oxygen-carbon cycle generates life. Animals consume oxygen and exhale carbon dioxide. Carbon dioxide is also produced when plants and animals decay and when fuels are burned. Plants use carbon dioxide to produce oxygen. Sunlight, the source of all energy, works with the photosynthetic pigments such as green chlorophyll in plants to combine carbon from the air with water to originate sugars that plants use for food. This process, *photosynthesis,* or making something from light, allows for the production of oxygen.

3. The Water Cycle Plants and animals depend on water, which permits foods and gases to pass through the cells of plants and animals. Relying on the sun for power, water circulates through the environment in a cycle. The sun's heat evaporates water from the aquatic ecosystems. The vapors form clouds, and when the air cools or becomes filled with moisture, the vapor falls as rain, snow, sleet, or hail. Plants use the water soaked into the soil. Some water becomes part of the groundwater supply, forming springs and wells, which eventually returns to lakes and oceans where it can evaporate, continuing the cycle.

Nature Changing

Nature changes constantly. Alterations are essential for living things to thrive. For example a forest matures gradually, taking hundreds or even thousands of years to develop. In an area starting as a pond, soil washes in from hillsides and collects along the edges. Wind carries grass seeds which take root in the soil. As the grass grows and dies, it mats and decays, producing a nutrient-rich bed for larger plants. Frogs and fish find protection among the plants, and insects lay eggs on the leaves. These plants and animals eventually expire, decay, and build a more fertile soil which ultimately becomes home to bushes and small trees. As the plants decay, they form additional earth for larger trees which gradually grow into a stand or forest. The pond disappears and the forest, which has developed through the long process of succession, has a vast number of plants and animals within it. Diversity in the forest acts as a buffer against drastic change, allowing an area to adjust slowly to new conditions. For example if one tree species is destroyed another may take over. Should a solitary species exist in an area, any threat would endanger the entire forest.

Rapid natural changes can also occur from forest fires or volcanic eruptions. Destruction by forest fire allows for a continuing process of succession (more on fires later). Humans, too, have the ability to alter the earth. We may suit our needs, rather than adapting our needs to existing conditions. While not intending to harm the environment, outdoor recreationists have their impact. The steps that are taken to minimize this impact such as low-impact use and the no-trace ethic are addressed at length in Chapter 15, Outdoor Recreational Activities.

AIR POLLUTION AND OUTDOOR RECREATION

Never free from change, the earth's atmosphere varies in composition and temperature. In the last two centuries the composition of the atmosphere has undergone remarkable changes. A dramatic increase in carbon dioxide (CO_2) in the atmosphere has been caused by the burning of fossil fuels and the clearing and burning of forests for agriculture. Greater quantities of carbon dioxide are being released into the atmosphere than have been removed by photosynthesis on land or by diffusion into the oceans.

Some scientists are concerned that the growing burden of carbon dioxide will enhance a warming trend. Working as a *greenhouse,* carbon dioxide allows most solar radiation to penetrate the atmosphere, but then it traps the heat reradiated by land and bodies of water, possibly causing a warming of the planet. Scientists have recognized that the atmospheric burden of other greenhouse gases such as methane (CH_4), nitrous oxide (NO_2) and the chlorofloro-carbons (CFCs) are also escalating. According to Houghton and Woodwell (1989:37), the strongest evidence for global warming became available in 1988 when recorded temperatures were analyzed back to 1860. James E. Hansen of the National Aeronautics and Space Administration's Goddard Institute of Space Studies and his colleagues reported that the average global temperature has increased by .5 to .7 degree Celsius since that year, with the greatest increase taking place in the past decade. A correlation among the global temperature changes and the level of

Many trees are threatened by acid rain, especially near the more industrialized areas of the Midwest and the Northeast.

heat-trapping gases and carbon dioxide emissions was generated in Mauna Loa, Hawaii, by Charles D. Keeling of the Scripps Institution of Oceanography (see Figure 16.1). Global climatic warming could warm the earth, according to Houghton and Woodwell, as much as 1.5 to 4.5 degrees Celsius before the middle of the next century. The warming could cause ice sheets in the Antarctic to melt and ocean levels to rise. Wetlands, which are desirable recreation locations, could be lost. Global rainfall patterns could shift, causing arid regions to receive heavy rainfall and rich farmland to suffer droughts. Increases of carbon dioxide and other trace gases are giving rise to acid deposition, smog, and the depletion of the stratospheric ozone layer that absorbs damaging ultraviolet radiation.

Acid deposition places severe stress on many ecosystems, ultimately affecting recreational opportunities. Lakes, for example, have increased in acidity leading to reductions in fish populations, which is a concern for the angler. Forests, major outdoor recreation sites, have been damaged particularly in the northeastern states. Not conducive to outdoor activities, smog as described by Graedel and Crutzen (1989:61) is the undesirable mixture of gases formed in the lower troposphere when solar radiation acts on anthropogenic emissions to produce reactive

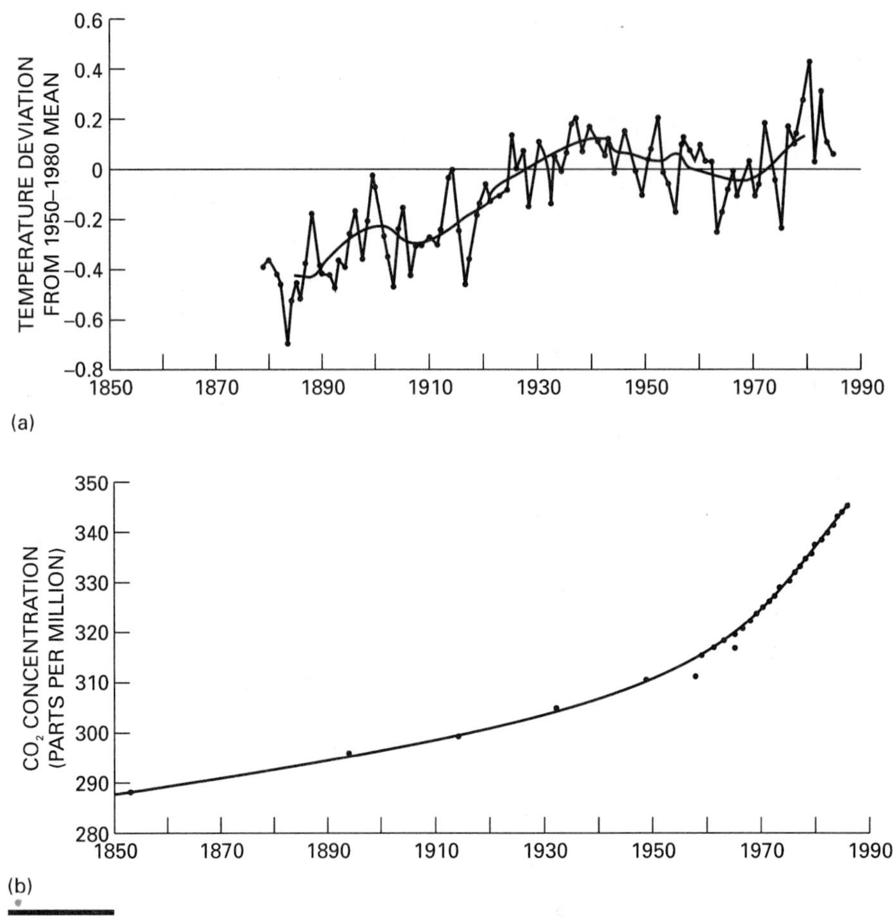

FIGURE 16.1 Correlation of global temperature change and change in gases.

gases. Severity of smog is generally assessed on the basis of ground-level ozone concentrations. *Ozone,* a by-product of combustion, especially in automobiles and jet aircraft, is the main cause of smog-induced eye irritation, impaired lung function, and damage to trees and crops. Graedel and Crutzen note that the ozone level in California and the eastern states is more than ten times higher than the natural level. In addition, ozone levels in the tropics and subtropics may climb five times higher than normal due to the periodic burning of vegetation. These increases could be particularly damaging to the vulnerable ecosystems in those regions.

Clean Air Act

The first comprehensive legislation in the United States aimed at controlling air pollution from stationary sources (such as factories or electric power stations) and mobile sources (such as automobiles and trucks) was the *Clean Air Act of 1963.* Subsequent amendments to the law established *National Ambient Air Quality Standards* for sulfur dioxide, suspended particulates (dust), carbon monoxide, nitrogen dioxide, ozone, and airborne lead. Federal emission standards were mandated for automobiles, and states were required to establish and implement industrial air pollution control programs subject to Environ-

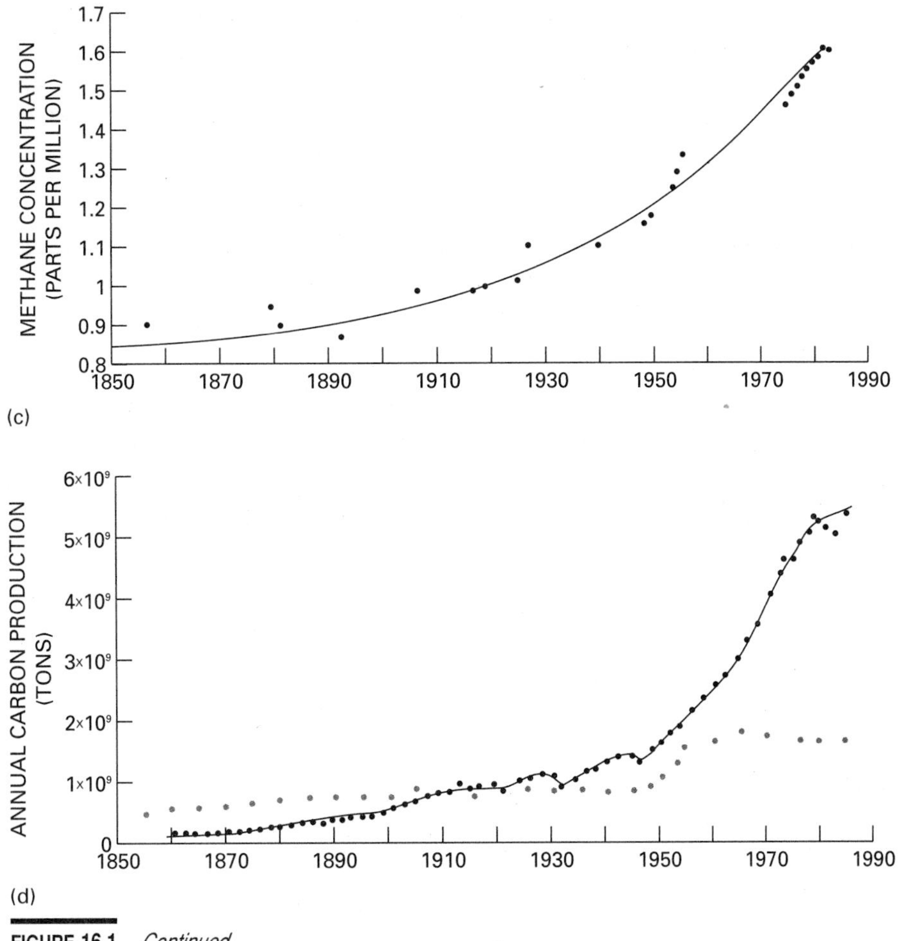

FIGURE 16.1 *Continued*

mental Protection Agency approval in order to meet the air quality standards. In 1977 an additional provision was enacted that aimed at the prevention of significant deterioration of air quality in areas, previously unpolluted, which were now threatened by new pollution sources.

On November 16, 1990, President George Bush signed the *Clean Air Act of 1990,* which he proclaimed to be the most comprehensive set of environmental laws ever enacted. The legislature established turn-of-the-century deadlines intended to force nearly every major industry to deeply cut emissions of pollutants that cause smog, acid rain, and the depletion of the earth's protective ozone layer. Also required is the production of less-polluting automobiles, cleaner fuels, and, in high-smog urban areas, eventual use of ultra-clean vehicles running on nongasoline fuels. The act requires coal-burning utility companies to halve emissions of sulfur dioxide, which causes acid rain, by the year 2000, and chemical plants and other producers of hazardous waste to reduce emissions of cancer-causing air toxins by 90 percent over the same period. Nearly one hundred cities that did not meet federal air quality standards were granted 3 to 17 years to clean up. The act represented the president's mandate that no American should be forced to leave his or her city in order to breathe clean air (National Parks and Conservation Association 1990:8).

The 1990 act was the first revision in 13 years to U.S. air pollution laws. The 748-page act represented the culmination of a long struggle between environmentalists and business. Immediately after the signing, oil companies challenged legislative interpretations. The complex legislation of the earlier Clean Air Act had been difficult to implement, but despite modifications to regulations and delays in deadlines, significant progress was made. According to Goldfarb (1989:113), carbon dioxide and carbon monoxide levels dropped by approximately 40 percent after initial enactment of the earlier act, and particulate concentrations declined by 20 percent during the 1970s. The 1990 act brings new energy to the struggle for clean air.

Air Pollution in the National Parks

Human-made air pollution from distant power plants, smelters, and automobiles is obscuring views in America's most scenic parks and wilderness areas. Air quality has been monitored by Park Service officials at dozens of national parks, monuments, and wilderness areas since an amendment was added to the Clean Air Act in 1977. Record ozone levels were reported, attesting to the fact that smog has been creeping into many of our national parks. The Associated Press (1990) reported that the number of pine trees damaged by ozone in Yosemite National Park has increased fivefold in the last 5 years. It was reported that a national park research physicist estimated that visibility is impaired in every national park as much as 80 to 90 percent of the time.

From the rim of the Grand Canyon, visitors can see 160 miles or more. However, during one day out of ten visibility is limited to 50 miles or less due to air pollution. What can be seen is blurred and/or the colors appear faded. Rock formations are indistinguishable. Dirty air from southern California, emissions from the nearby Navajo Generating Station, and airborne byproducts of a copper smelter are blamed for obscuring the view in one of America's most scenic parks and wilderness areas. Other refuges of recreation and natural beauty affected by air pollution include North Cascades National Park in Washington and the Great Smoky Mountains in Tennessee and North Carolina, where visibility can drop from 200 miles to 40 and from 40 miles to 12, respectively. Panoramic parks in the western states show startling signs of viewer distortion. Smog from the Los Angeles basin is blamed for crippling plants and muddying views at Joshua Tree National Monument, 120 miles away. The Park Service estimates that if gas emissions are allowed to continue at the current rate, summer haze will increase dramatically. Under the Clean Air Act amendments of 1977, Congress directed the Environmental Protection Agency to solve visibility problems in the parks.

AQUATIC ECOSYSTEMS AND OUTDOOR RECREATION

Aquatic ecosystems include fresh-water, estuarine, and marine systems which are distinguished on the basis of their salt content. According to Kormondy (1984:181), aquatic ecosystems compose over 70 percent of the earth's surface, making them earth's most dominant feature. Aquatic ecosystems have very diverse species.

Fresh-water Ecosystems

Fresh-water ecosystems are characterized as *lotic* or *lentic,* with running water or still water, respectively. Kormondy (1984:183) associates waterfalls with lotic ecosystems. Running fresh-water streams (springs, creeks, brooks) and rivers may vary on their course from narrow and shallow and relatively rapid to increasingly broad, deep, and slow moving. Most streams are characterized by a repeating sequence of rapids and pools (lentic ecosystems) that decrease in frequency downstream. Chemically lentic environments are rich in oxygen upstream. Downstream the water becomes more sluggish and the oxygen level tends to drop. The continual addition of nutrients en route, however, brings an increase of nutrient levels downstream. Lentic ecosystems include pools, ponds, bogs, and lakes, for example, which vary greatly in their physical, chemical, and biological characteristics.

Since the passage of the Water Quality Act of 1965 and through the administration of the Wild and Scenic Rivers System, water quality control has been monitored and has shown improvement. States are required to submit water quality standards for their interstate waters. Because water quality control is land related, through chemical pollutants, soil, bacteria, fertilizers, oil, and pesticides, the problem is complex. According to Doyle (1977:2–11), approximately 50,000 dams, built to restrain U.S. rivers, have altered and manipulated most of our major rivers, leaving few to flow purely and freely. As water use rises, rivers are pressured by an energy-hungry nation. Inevitably environmental choices will have to be made as some rivers are exploited and others are protected. Poor water quality has vastly affected recreational pursuits.

Sportfishing in Fresh Water

For years salmon have been fighting dams and other diversions built on rivers. Some dams have taken on names such as "Fish-Killer" dam because of swirling waters and backwash which disorient the salmons' delicate homing mechanisms. Predators take advantage by waiting at the bottom of the dam to feed on salmon heading upstream to spawn. A natural predator, squawfish, multiply as salmon lose ground. Many stocks of salmon are extinct, and other fish have been threatened with extinction. According to the U.S. Fish and Wildlife Service (*Sunset* 1989:96), at least two-thirds of the West's salmon have disappeared. Hatcheries have bred the wildness out of them, inhibiting genetic diversity. Anglers complain that beautiful fish have been replaced with "just another dumb fish."

Before the coming of early settlers, an estimated 10 to 16 million salmon returned to the Columbia River annually. By the early 1980s, returns had dipped to under a million. Accounting for almost 75 percent of the annual loss are nearly a dozen dams on the river and more on its tributaries. Experts agree that the only real safeguard against extinction is to restore the salmon's natural spawning grounds and stream dynamics. A passionate commitment among citizens' groups is helping to heal streams and restore fish runs. Courts have recognized the salmon's need for water as equal to human need. The Northwest Power Planning Council was established in 1980 to help coordinate conservation efforts. Fish and power were given equal priority, causing a modest salmon recovery on the Columbia. Fish ladders were built for upstream migration, and turbine intakes were screened. Deflectors were fitted on spillways, helping to speed young salmon downstream around some dams. A 1988 moratorium was called to halt dam building on 29,000 miles of stream in the Columbia Basin (*Sunset* 1989:96). More research is needed to study hatchery diseases and fish mortality; and more work remains to build fish bypasses, to reclaim spawning grounds, and to increase the number of spring spills.

Wild trout are born in a stream or lake rather than in a hatchery. They can be native or introduced. By the mid-1960s, trout habitats were also disappearing. Dams had dried some streams, and other streams were uninhabitable. Many waters were overfished. A turnaround started when anglers became concerned that wild strains of trout were disappearing. Working with state biologists, small groups of anglers helped to develop management programs that

"Go ahead if you want. I've been caught and released so much the thrill is gone for me."

protected remaining wild trout populations. Today eight states have developed wild trout programs, setting restrictions on tackle and catch limits, including *catch-and-release* programs. The popularity of these programs is illustrated in cartoon form. Few states, however, have laws to protect designated wild trout streams from poor land-use practices, and existing laws are not broad enough. Trout habitats have deteriorated due to logging, mining, agriculture, and other development. Habitat deterioration is also caused by a loss of water due to dams and diversions, and blocked access to tributary spawning beds due especially to small hydroelectric projects.

A survey conducted by the American Fisheries Society has shown a decrease for over 5 years in the number of anglers participating in fishing. According to Cone (1990:A1, A23), sportfishing license sales have dropped 24 percent since 1985. California took the lead in the decrease. Every year about 100,000 more anglers abandon the sport. Abandonment leaves California short of funds to properly protect its natural resources and wildlife. Conversely, however, midwestern and eastern states have shown an increased number of licenses sold during the same period. Experts speculate that pollution, development, drought, and general changes in life-style have caused the sport to suffer in the West. For many, a peaceful day of fishing has been replaced with more active outdoor workouts, as seen in Chapter 6. Also, divided families leave single parents with too little time or money for distant outings.

Some Californians head for other states or countries to fish. They find landscapes that are lush, rivers that run full, and water brimming with trout. According to Cone (1990:A23), they complain that in California,

1. The waters are tainted by chemicals and silt.
2. The state breeds of trout are scrawny and black.
3. Fish populations have not recovered from areas drained to supply water to farmers.
4. Too many anglers exceed limits, depleting the stock.
5. Good fisheries are too far away, and traffic is too heavy.
6. There is not enough time.
7. When they arrive there is smog.
8. There is too much congestion on trails.
9. Below-normal water levels cause trout to die.

Conservationists do not wish to strain the resources, but too few anglers means fewer funds, which causes them to fear that more of California's streams, rivers, and lakes will fall into disrepair. Preservation is possible when the public demands it. When fewer are interested in preservation, resources can suffer. According to Cone (1990:A23), 85 percent of funding for California's Department of Fish and Game comes from the sale of licenses. A shortage severely affects the ability of the department to pursue its tasks, which include safeguarding endangered species, catching poachers and polluters, stocking streams, protecting birds and marine life from oil spills, and staving off commercial development in animal habitats.

Perhaps the answer can be found at Nueltin Lake in central Canada on the border between Manitoba and the Northwest Territories, where trend-setting laws have increased the clientele. Here the "big one" must be returned—a departure from standard angling ethics, which, in the United States, allow the angler to keep all or most of the big fish caught, returning the little ones. The vast majority of anglers still follow the standard ethic, assuming that the small fish will replace the larger ones in future years. Part of the practice revolves around sportsmanship: smaller fish are easier to catch, while the larger fish is smarter and more worthy. According to Hope (1990:57, 58), however, minimum-size regulations have led to the rapid depletion of large native fish in the more popular fresh-water lakes and streams of the eastern United States. In New York state, for example, the largest brook trout ever caught was in 1908, weighing 8 pounds, 8 ounces, and the largest northern pike was caught in 1940, weighing 46 pounds, 2 ounces. Today nothing approaches these sizes. The theory that the small fish will grow to the size of the larger has not proven true. Typically smaller fish make up at least 90 percent of the population. Because they are protected, they tend to remain small or stunted due to lack of food. In addition, trophy fish have the capacity to reproduce more big fish. In many North American waterways, large fish have essentially been angled out, leaving lakes and rivers with little or no genetic potential.

As such, angling laws, according to Hope, will need to change direction if we expect to have any big fish left in 20 years. At Nueltin Lake, maximum-size restrictions are more sophisticated than minimum-size or catch-and-release laws. At Nueltin, anglers and guides may kill and eat smaller fish for their daily lunch, but no trophy fish (fish larger than 8 pounds) may be taken. To forestall any deliberate "accidental deaths" of trophy fish, anglers are told in advance that these fish become the property of lake management. They also provide a $5,000 reward to the angler who lands a world-record fish and returns it to the lake. Additional safeguards include allowing only the guides who are

The sign "Danger Keep Clear of Drain Pipe" does not keep children and waterfowl away.

trained in gentle handling to resuscitate and release the fish. ***Resuscitation*** includes sweeping the fish back and forth through the water to restore oxygen to its gills after its long struggle on the line. Anglers may not lift fish carelessly or overpose for trophy shots. Anglers may use any lure except live bait, but all multiple hooks must be removed and replaced with a barbless single hook to ensure quick and easy release. No fish may be weighed with the traditional, damaging jaw scale. Instead, the length-girth conversion system is used to calculate the weight.

Following the Nueltin Lake experiment, Manitoba became the first province or state in North America to pass a law requiring barbless hooks for all of its sportfishing. According to Hope (1990:50), one hundred of its lakes and rivers are now governed by no-trophy or one-trophy rules. Several states and provinces, including Wyoming, Montana, Minnesota, and Ontario, are now basing most of their sportfishing laws on policies specifically planned to protect big fish. On the Atlantic coast, from North Carolina to Newfoundland, maximum-size laws now regulate the taking of two imperiled species, the striped bass and the Atlantic salmon. New moral pressures can help to establish a new code so that fishing has a future in North America.

ESTUARINE ECOSYSTEMS

Estuarine ecosystems are the part of the coast over which the tide ebbs and flows. This includes the wide mouth of a river where the tide meets the current, as well as swamps and marshes where the water is brackish, that is, where fresh water and saltwater mix. *Saltwater wetlands* provide an especially valuable habitat for a variety of important coastal species. Waterfowl, shorebirds, alligators, and muskrats inhabit wetlands. Less noticeable are crab, shrimp, and juvenile stages of commercial and sport fishes. According to the Conservation Foundation (1980:49–52), the food produced in the wetlands provides an essential link to the coastal food chain by feeding the shrimp, fiddler crabs, worms, snails, and mussels, which in turn feed the larger fish, birds, and mammals higher on the coastal food chain. The wetland vegetation also removes silt, toxic chemicals, and nutrients from coastal water. If wetland vegetation were eliminated, the food supply, and thus the carrying capacity of the coastal ecosystem, would be greatly reduced. Research has demonstrated a direct positive relationship between acres of marsh and abundance of fish. In a North Carolina estuary study, the life-support capability of the estuary declined 50 percent after destruction of the associated marsh. Besides food source provision, the wetlands protect communities from sea storms by reducing the severity of coastal hazards from waves and flooding. Their vegetation stabilizes estuarine shorelines, which prevents erosion.

Decisions to convert wetland areas to real estate by filling them to create waterfront lots or dredging them to make canals or otherwise interfering with normal tidal circulation by draining, impounding, or diking are the subject of extensive controversy. Also, abundant pollution from discharges of domestic and industrial wastes may cause serious deterioration of wetland functions. Wetlands need to remain functionally intact, which means that their natural functions should not be degraded. In addition, excessive nutrient pollution may cause wetlands to breed an abundance of mosquitoes and other pests, rendering outdoor activities undesirable. The Conservation Foundation (1980:66) suggests that communities:

1. Prevent or limit disruptive activities in saltwater wetlands.
2. Control pollution of saltwater wetlands.
3. Restore former wetlands.
4. Define the boundaries of saltwater wetlands.

Wetlands include a broad range of habitats beyond estuaries. They may include bogs, prairie potholes, and swamps, for example. They provide a wide variety of recreational opportunities. Saltwater and fresh-water wetlands sustain  nearly one-third of the nation's threatened and endangered species and provide breeding grounds for millions of waterfowl and shorebirds. All wetlands are disappearing at an estimated rate of 300,000 to 450,000 acres annually (Pogatchnik 1990:A16). According to Steinhart (1990:20–21), there is no equivalent of the Wilderness Act or Wild and Scenic Rivers Act for wetlands, but there is a patchwork of laws. Still, many gains have been made at the federal level in the last 15 years. President Jimmy Carter issued an executive order in 1977 calling upon federal agencies to minimize the loss or degradation of wetlands. The 1985 Food Security Act forbade federal subsidies to farmers who plowed wetlands, and it established a program of payments for those who maintained wetlands on their farms. The 1987 Agricultural Credit Act revisions allowed the Farmers Home Administration to trade partial debt relief to borrowers in return for pledges to protect wetlands. In 1987 a National Wetlands Policy Forum, convened by the Conservation Foundation at the request of the Environmental Protection Agency, called for a national policy of no net loss of wetlands. President George Bush endorsed that policy and convened another policy group to recommend how to pursue the no-net-loss goal. Finally, court action has expanded the role of the Army Corps of Engineers to include the protection of wetlands as well as the role of permit providers. The National Audubon Society educates the public on wetland preservation and provides updates on wetland issues to members of its Audubon Activist Network.

MARINE ECOSYSTEMS

Standing on the bluffs above any ocean we see a beautiful, vast, seemingly limitless water. Oceans cover more than 70 percent of the earth's surface and contain 98.8 percent of its water. The concentration of nutrients in the ocean is low. Unlike land and fresh-water ecosystems, the sea is continuous and is in circulation via the major surface currents. Waves cause the water to oscillate back and forth. The rise and fall of the water level is caused by tides which are related to the gravitational effects of the moon and the sun.

Oceans receive enough of the world's waste to have raised public alarm concerning safety of outdoor activities such as swimming, surfing, and fishing. Shifting sands, foul water, and human-made follies present threats to coasts. Beaches offer inexpensive recreation, including tidepooling, kite flying, boogie boarding, and surfing. They have been overcrowded in the last 40 years, particularly in areas with explosive population growth. Rampant development along the Atlantic, Pacific, and Gulf coasts helped boost a population of 42 million people in 1940 to 89 million in 1980 (*Time Magazine* 1988:45–47). According to Perry (1990:11), southern California's nearly one hundred beaches are visited by more than 90 million people, more than triple the number of 20 years ago. This has led to many environmental problems. For instance, more automobiles create pollution problems from car emissions. In a 1-day volunteer beach cleanup held by the California Coastal Commission, 10 tons of trash and 52,000 cigarette butts were collected (Perry 1990:11). Most trash left on all beaches is from beachgoers who do not use trash cans. In a recent survey by the Center for Marine Conservation, plastic trash was found to be the number one source of debris on beaches from Miami to Long Beach. In 1988, incoming tides from northern New Jersey to Long Island washed up a nauseating array of waste including drug paraphernalia, medical debris, and balls of sewage 2 inches thick.

Beach homes with individual ladders mar the natural scenery and encourage cliff erosion.

Environmentalists have identified the nation's most significant marine debris problem to be so-called "offshore icebergs." Upon closer inspection these icebergs are collages of discarded cups, containers, bottles, and straws. This plastic trash is posing serious problems to wildlife. Undigestible plastic bags are confused for jellyfish and are eaten by whales, dolphins, and turtles. Gulls and other birds eat broken foam cups, eventually choking. Fish become wedged in the plastic rings used for beer and soda cans and are sliced as they grow. Sprawling "icebergs," perhaps more aptly termed "trashbergs," are caused by collections of trash flushed into oceans from storm drains, creeks, and rivers (Murphy 1990:8). Great volumes of sewage pollute beaches. Storm drains bring motor oil, garbage, pesticides, and untreated animal waste directly to beaches. Swimming near drains has

Buffer zones protect some marine sanctuaries.

resulted in skin rashes and eye and ear infections. Wastewater flow has endangered several bird species and led to warnings not to eat bottom-dwelling fish caught off ocean piers.

Problems worsen with the oil spills from offshore tankers. In February, 1990, 390,000 gallons of Alaskan crude oil leaked, fouling more than 20 miles of southern California coastline. Millions of dollars were invested in cleanup before the area was declared safe enough for reopening. It was estimated that barely one-fifth of the crude was recovered. In March 1989, 11 million gallons of crude oil gushed out into the pristine waters of scenic Prince William Sound, just below Valdez, Alaska. Eventually it passed Kenai Fjords National Park on its way farther south to pollute Katmai National Park and Kodiak Island. Pristine coastlines off Africa, Asia, Europe, and North and South America and those near the earth's poles have been sadly blighted. In addition to oil from accidents, tankers dump two million tons of oil into seas every year, mostly from flushing oily residue from empty tanks. The toll on wildlife is tragic.

Along with overcrowding and pollution, erosion has also upset the balance of the coastal ecosystem. Beaches should and do constantly change in size and shape. In many places, sand is only on the shore on a temporary basis before it begins to move. In California some of the popular beaches are kept from shrinking naturally or disappearing altogether because sand is artificially trucked in. But the disappearance of sand is not always natural. Human-made harbors and buildings block the natural flow of sand, and rivers carrying sand have been diverted or dammed. Channels with concrete bottoms devised as flood-control projects prevent the floodwaters from bringing sand to beaches. Sand that can no longer reach the oceans due to damming has caused some dams to fill up. To mitigate these adverse affects on the natural sand process, this sand is collected and transported to beaches. Bypass systems also exist which vacuum sand from harbors and pipe it onto beaches.

Coastal waters are close to reaching their capacity to absorb civilian waste. In June 1987, at least 750 dolphin died mysteriously along the Atlantic coast. Many that washed ashore had snouts, flippers, and tails pocked with blisters and craters. In the Gulf of Maine, harbor seals were rated with the highest pesticide level of any U.S. mammal on land or water. From Portland, Maine, to Morehead City, North Carolina, lobsters and crabs were found with gaping holes in their shells. Fish were reported with rotted fins and ulcerous lesions. Texas shellfish beds have many times been closed because of pollution. Seattle's Elliott Bay was contaminated by chemicals used by the electrical-equipment industry. Some bodies of water have been almost totally depleted of oxygen. A huge dead zone, 300 miles long and ten 10 miles wide, is adrift in the Gulf of Mexico (*Time Magazine* 1988: 45–47).

Rain forests can be found in Olympic National Park in Washington.

Marine scientists are only now beginning to understand the process by which coastal waters are affected by pollution. The problem may lie miles from the ocean where contaminants enter rivers. The Federal Clean Water Act of 1972 overlooked runoff pollution in setting standards for water quality. Mistakes must not be repeated. Corrective actions include beach cleanups where individuals volunteer to pick up bottles and aluminum cans. Sewage disposal is undergoing upgraded treatment in some areas. Scientists have measured a concurrent drop in the pollution level on California beaches even though sewage is dumped in greater volume. Previously unregulated storm drains are now being regulated by the State of California, and some states have required that six-pack rings be made of substances that decompose upon exposure to the ultraviolet light in sunshine.

Other positive steps toward diminishing marine pollution include legislation that places cleanup costs of oil spills on oil companies rather than on taxpayers and the Bush administration's commitment to prohibit offshore drilling in areas where environmental risks outweigh the potential energy benefits. Furthermore, on June 26, 1990, President Bush supported a plan to establish a 2,200-square-mile National Marine Sanctuary in California's Monterey Bay in California, and deposits of coral off the Florida Keys are protected from further leasing (Miller 1990:A21).

CORAL REEFS AND HUMAN ACTIVITY

Coral reefs are developed by small marine animals called *polyps.* After a polyp dies, it leaves deposits of calcium carbonate behind for other polyps to build upon. Coral reefs are the largest constructions formed by living organisms. However, when nutrient levels from sewage and fertilizers surge, polyps are overcome and eventually smothered by algae. Because of this pollution, some water quality experts believe that the coral reef along the Florida keys could become the first in the world to be killed by humans.

To protect some of the world's northernmost coral reefs, the nation's first undersea state park, Pennekamp, was created in 1960 in Florida. Boundaries were changed at a later date, placing most of the reefs within an adjacent federal preserve referred to as the Sanctuary. Alarmingly, however, in 1989 three freighters ran aground in the area within a 17-day period. This led to a proposal that all of the reefs from Biscayne National Park to Dry Tortugas be designated the Florida Keys National Marine Sanctuary to be operated by the U.S. Department of Commerce (see Chapter 7, Federal Resources). All ships were off-limits, but an initial influx of recreational boats and divers put pressure on the underwater environment. It became one of the most popular destinations in the world, with five of its most popular reefs attracting nearly 3,000 people a day (Ward 1990:123). Incompetent boat operators crashed into reefs and coral. Thousands of swimmers routinely bumped, scraped, and stood on the coral. Although unlawful in the parks, specimen collecting and spearfishing continued. Boats polluted the water with petroleum products, sewage, and litter. All of these activities weakened the coral, causing algae to begin to take over. In addition, overharvesting of algae-eating fish became another factor. Under these conditions centuries of growth can be devastated.

Besides recreational activity, nature can also intrude on the coral. Waves stirred by hurricanes can cause damage, as will fluctuations in water temperatures which may be linked to changes in the global climate. Human pollution has caused a water quality decline which also effects reef damage. Key West has the only city sewage-treatment plant in all the keys, and onshore pollution such as pesticides eventually reaches the park. Nutrient levels are raised from agricultural runoff and garbage. To save the reefs, Ward (1990:131–32) suggests immediate and drastic action as follows:

1. Reefs must be allowed time to repair.
2. A master plan should be developed to administer a plan for water quality, fishing, boating, and tourism.
3. Businesses should take on more responsibility for the preservation of the reefs.
4. Sewage systems should be established.
5. The reefs should be protected from agricultural, boating, and industrial pollutants.
6. Fishing and lobstering should be banned.

California redwoods are the tallest living things on earth.

TERRESTRIAL ECOSYSTEMS

Terrestrial ecosystems, which may be divided into forests, tundra, and grasslands, are generally distinguished, according to Kormondy (1984:159–62), on the basis of the predominant type of vegetation such as grass or trees. An interaction of temperature and rainfall is significant to the type of vegetation grown. For example, a low rainfall coupled with a low temperature or a high rainfall coupled with a higher temperature might sustain a grassland. Soil and vegetation are intimate parts of the same ecosystem.

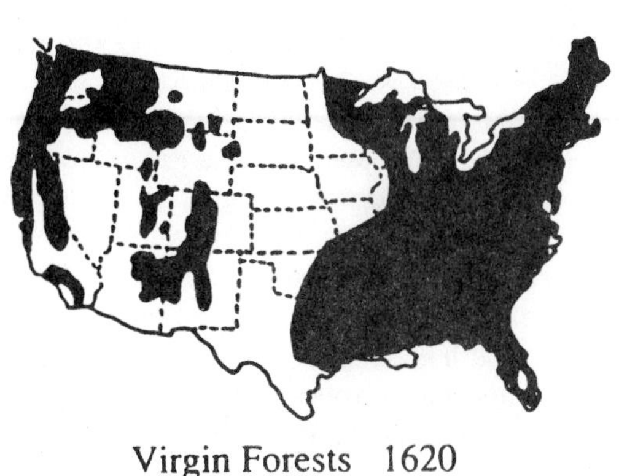
Virgin Forests 1620

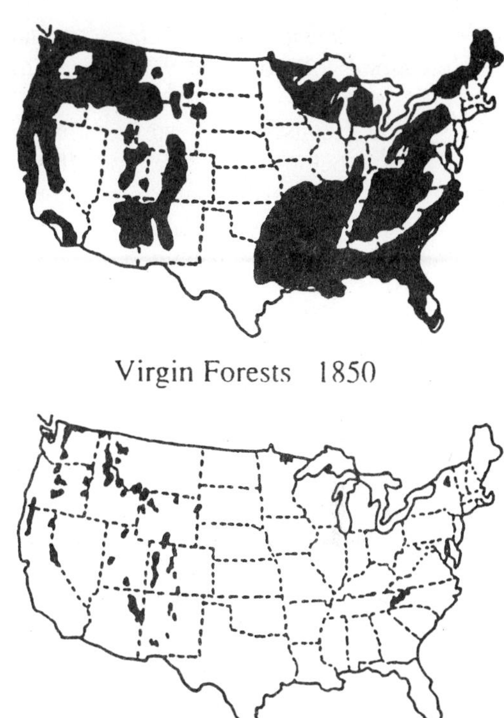
Virgin Forests 1850

Virgin Forests 1989

FIGURE 16.2 Forest decline, 1620–1989, in forty-eight states.

The Forests and Trees

Tropical forests play a vital role in regulating the global climate. Disappearance of forests is regarded by many environmental experts as the most serious global environmental problem (see Figure 16.2). They believe that carbon dioxide must be kept in balance or there could be a significant warming of the earth in the next century through the process known as the *greenhouse effect.* Major carbon dioxide emissions are created by the burning of trees and vegetation from cut forests and by the burning of fossil fuels which include coal, oil, and gasoline. Forests have the capacity to absorb huge quantities of carbon dioxide through photosynthesis. However, an increase in the use of fossil fuels with increasing deforestation increases the number of greenhouse gases which, according to the Press Democrat news service (1990:A1), have tripled over a 30-year period.

A report prepared by the World Resources Institute in collaboration with the United Nations found that forests were disappearing at a pace almost 50 percent faster than previously estimated in 1980 by the U.N. Food and Agricultural Organization (The Press Democrat 1990:A1). Finding that 1.9 billion acres of tropical forest remain, they reported that forests were disappearing at a rate of 40 to 50 million acres a year, which is attributable to harvesting by the timber industry and to demand for land for agricultural and urban development. James G. Speth, president of the World Resources Institute, made a conservative estimate that one acre of forest is being lost every second. This loss is particularly substantial because forests contain the largest and most diverse populations of plant and animal species of any habitat in the world.

Clearcutting and the Spotted Owl

Clearcutting is the practice of removing all standing timber from a given area, typically 80–120 acres. Multiple clearcuts are separated by narrow strips of timber several hundred feet in width. The consequences of clearcutting vary according to terrain, soil conditions, weather patterns, and species (Mendocino Environmental Center 1990:6). Clearcutting spoils rivers and destroys fisheries. According to Williams (1990:7), "After a clearcut it takes two or three years for the soil-supporting rootlets to rot away. Then the headwalls just fall into the rivers, sluice them out and settle into the lower reaches, sending the water braiding over or under wide, fish-proof deltas." In 1985 one such deluge of forest soil slid out from under a clearcut at the source of Gwynn Creek in Oregon's Siuslaw National Forest's Mapleton District (the district containing the best public steelhead and salmon water south of Alaska). Sliding for 4 miles, the soil crossed Pacific Coast Highway 101, where it merged with the sea. Instantly it obliterated fish habitat and abolished fish life. Afterward an attempt was made to demonstrate that creeks with landslides were not worse off than creeks without them, but ironically and unfortunately, the latter type could not even be found.

The Environmental Protection Information Center (1990:2–3) stated, "Many creatures depend on our original, uncut ancient forest. They cannot pick up and move when the old forests are cut. They cannot survive in the young forests." They list the tailed frog, the olympic salamander, the marbled murrelet, the flammulated owl, the red tree vole, and the fisher as vulnerable.

The practice of clearcutting removes all trees from the forests, but the nutrients from dead rotting trees benefit a forest. Without them the soil eventually gives out, making trees weak and spindly. Creatures such as the northern spotted owl dwell in the old and dead trees of the rain forests. The July 23, 1990, announcement that the spotted owl was listed as threatened and therefore under the protection of the federal Endangered Species Act sparked heated debate among environmentalists and the timber industry. To environmentalists the spotted owl was seen as a barometer to determine the integrity and health of the ancient forest ecosystem and the hundreds of species dependent on it for all or part of their needs. The owl became a symbol of an era before the arrival of the European settlers, when acres of primeval forest blanketed much of the continent, and natural events were the controlling fate of the forest and its creatures. The spotted owl's listing brought public attention to the 95 percent decline in these forests (Forests Forever 1990:1).

To the timber industry, the spotted owl's protection meant loss of work because acres of timber land were set aside as protected habitat by the Forest Service. Public attention turned to the owl, not to the fish in the same areas. According to Frissell of Oregon State University (Williams 1990:8), the timber industry was doing everything it could to prevent the issue of fisheries impacts from being raised. It was his opinion that they wanted "everything to hinge on the owl." "That," he said, "appears to be their agenda because there's much more public sympathy for fish and water than there is for an owl that no one's seen or heard." But, according to Williams (1990:8), "A forest unfit for spotted owls is unfit for wild salmonoid."

Positions of the timber industry include the following:

1. The logger is the endangered species.
2. Trees are a renewable resource. Redwoods, for example, grow at a phenomenal rate, sprouting from roots

and stumps in clearcut areas, and two to three trees or seedlings are planted for every one cut down.

3. Unique and truly special land has already been set aside and protected. More than one-fifth of our national forests are preserved, and an additional 50 million acres of wilderness exists outside of these national forests. Timber interests ask: how much more can justifiably be set aside?
4. Forests are an important component of the nation's economy, and Americans rely on thousands of wood products daily.

Positions of the environmentalists include the following:

1. Overharvesting will deplete the forest, leading to a continual decline in productivity and forest-related employment. Retraining for new jobs would be less demanding than losing the nation's old-growth forests forever.
2. The genetic stock from old-growth stumps and root sprouts will weaken the basic stock over time. Replacement trees are never as well adapted to their transplant environment as trees that germinate naturally, nor do they resist very well the forces of erosion unleashed by clearcutting of steep terrain. The majority of the 12-inch seedlings planted to replace a 300-foot-tall stand of old growth never make it to maturity. The practice of reforestation is too recent to have produced harvestable timber on a commercially viable scale, nor is it possible to evaluate the long-term viability of reforested timberlands. No one knows with certainty what the ultimate consequences of current forest practices will be beyond the inevitable elimination of existing all-age, ecologically balanced forests representing 10,000,000 years of biological evolution and adaptation.
3. Existing parks and wilderness areas are not nearly enough. Parks are too few, often too small, and are poorly distributed. Wilderness areas generally are mountaintop or desert areas which contain no significant forests, as a direct result of timber industry power in Congress.
4. Economic issues are outweighed by the ecological survival of life as it is known. Timberlands are inextricably connected to the fate of forests the world over and, thus, to ozone depletion, global warming, and other macroecological processes affecting all people.

Loggers have seen thousands of mill jobs disappear in the last decade, and environmentalists have seen hundreds of thousands of acres of forest in the Pacific Northwest disappear. The crisis was fueled by Japanese trade policies that allowed U.S. logs to enter Japan duty free, but that restricted the import of finished wood products. According to the *San Francisco Examiner* (1990), 47,000 acres of the 85,000 acres of Pacific timber exported in 1988 went to Japan. If the United States banned all log exports and concentrated on exporting finished wood products to Japan (without import restriction), the Japanese market, according to the report, could create 40,000 new jobs in Alaska, Oregon, Washington, and California. Many believe that we are receiving too little for our crown jewels, and legislative efforts are being made to restrict log exports.

Both the timber industry and environmentalists agree that Americans should be concerned about consumption and should explore ways to minimize the use of trees. Georgia-Pacific (1990) reported that the United States has the world's highest rate of paper use and that each American uses the equivalent of a 100-foot tree each year. Much of the paper ends in the garbage, and instead of diminishing demand, use is on the increase. Of the garbage produced by Americans each year, 42 percent is paper, with each individual using approximately 700 pounds a year.

Preservation of the World's Largest Trees

Although many giant trees have been cut, some redwoods are under the protection of Redwood National Park, which stretches for 50 miles in northern California almost to Oregon. According to the National Park Service (1981), the coast redwood towers over all other trees in the world. Giant Sequoias, the cousins of the coast redwoods, growing larger in diameter and bulk, but not in height, are protected in central California at Yosemite, Sequoia, and Kings Canyon national parks. If left to grow, Sequoias will live 500 to 700 years, only a portion of the potential age of the coast redwood, which can survive to be 2,000 years old.

In 1850, redwood "gold" lured loggers away from the depleted eastern forest. In an expanding nation, the need for wood products grew rapidly. Logging activity greatly accelerated after World War II with new machinery, chain saws, large trucks, and the bulldozer. The old-growth or "virgin" forests began to disappear with alarming speed during the 1950s and 1960s, leaving behind overcut, eroding landscapes. Sensing the need for protection of the rapidly diminishing redwood forest, concerned citizens became active in setting aside redwood lands as national, state, and local parks.

One of these was Redwood National Park, established in 1968 to preserve superlative prime coast redwood forests along the coastline and rivers of northern California. After park establishment, however, extensive logging continued on private timberlands around this narrow corridor. Large-scale logging of the unstable, highly erosive Redwood Creek watershed increased landsliding and surface erosion far above prelogging levels. Besides directly altering the landscape and causing soil compaction, loss of top-

A local lumber mill processes huge redwood trees at record pace.

soil, destruction of ground cover, elimination of shade, and massive changes to small drainages, the logging activities also produced cumulative downstream impacts. These included increased streamside landslides, elevated and wilder streambeds, greater bank erosion, higher winter stream discharge, and lower summer discharge. These physical changes of the stream system jeopardized the associated plant and animal communities, and a heightened water table directly threatened the Tall Trees Grove and other trees growing on alluvial terraces adjacent to Redwood Creek.

As a result of these problems, in March 1978, Congress expanded the existing 58,000-acre Redwood National Park by an additional 48,000 acres. Realizing that land-use practices adjoining the park can damage resources within the park, Congress made a landmark decision by establishing a 30,000-acre *Park Protection Zone* upstream in the Redwood Creek watershed. Of the 48,000 acres of new park lands, only about 9,000 acres were old-growth redwoods. Most of the area was recently logged land. As part of park expansion, Congress authorized $33 million for Redwood National Park to rehabilitate overcut forest lands, with a major emphasis on erosion control. This watershed rehabilitation program has a long-term goal of speeding the recovery of

The desert at Monument Valley Navajo Tribal Park is a fragile ecosystem that requires protection from people.

natural forest, stream systems, and life communities, while protecting park values. Rehabilitation begins with the reduction of excessive erosion and creek siltation resulting from past timber harvesting and road building, and by replanting forests and shaping their regrowth. Years will pass before evidence of logging disappears and streams are fully recovered, but in Redwood National Park lies the unique challenge and opportunity to perpetuate and restore one of nature's most majestic natural systems.

Forest Fires

For years the Forest Service and the National Park Service believed that fires should be prevented at all costs to preserve our forests. In 1945 the creation of Smokey the Bear played a vital role in the National Forest Service fire prevention campaign. By 1973 this program more than halved the number of forest fires and, according to Storer and Ling (1990:6), Smokey's message saved timber valued at over $117 million. Americans were taught that forest fires were wickedly destructive. Smokey's communique did not distinguish, however, between natural and human-made fires. Soon researchers learned that all fires are not evil. In stark contrast to the past, by the 1970s fire suppression was perceived as unnatural. Instead, natural fires were allowed to burn, except where human life and property were immediately threatened. *Let-it-burn* practices are now used in wilderness areas and wildlands. The goal is to preserve natural systems in their natural state. Allowing these fires to burn spontaneously allows for higher biological diversity. Since fires tend to jump rather than to burn cleanly over the landscape, interesting variety and diversity results.

In contrast, fires identified as originated by humans are to be promptly suppressed. Some leading unnatural causes of fire include children playing with matches, improper campfire care, cigarettes, motorcycles without spark arresters, and sparks from welding and construction equipment. True natural fire occurrences are infrequent. They are caused by lightning, for example, and are referred to as *prescribed natural fires,* meaning that they are within the limits prescribed by the fire-management plan (Romme and Despain 1989:39). Any fire, regardless of origin, with potential to damage life, property, or resources, is declared a *wildfire.* This means it is burning outside of prescribed guidelines and is to be suppressed immediately (Romme and Despain 1989:39).

A long-standing practice of foresters and wildlife managers, *prescribed burns,* is yet another type of fire. These fires are deliberately set in a particular forest area to reduce fuel loading, stimulate wildlife habitat and runoff, and control large-scale fires. Prescribed burns are particularly important to recreational areas of parks and forests where human use is high, thus creating the risk of a large unnatural fire which could cause harm to persons and property.

Fire is important and necessary to a wide range of natural ecosystems. The prairies of the Midwest, the bogs of the Southeast, the chaparral and giant Sequoias of California, and the lodgepole pines of Yellowstone all depend on periodic fires. For example, one type of lodgepole cone opens and releases its seed after exposure to heat. Other environmental conditions are created by burns: dead branches and pine needles are cleared, sunlight and nutrients allow new trees to grow and flourish, and grasses and herbs grow providing new food sources for wildlife. In the spring that follows a fire, wildflowers bloom profusely, and by summer the vegetation is well on its way to recovery.

The great fire in Yellowstone in 1988 was a result of years of fire suppressions, droughtlike conditions, high winds, and high temperatures. Controversy had mounted by late summer, when the wind-driven fires moved in on the historic Old Faithful Inn and the towns of West Yellowstone, Cooke City, and Silver Gate were threatened with incineration. Notwithstanding the efforts of some 10,000 civilian and military firefighters, nearly a million acres of the entire Yellowstone territory burned (Jeffery 1989:258). Timber and homes worth billions of dollars were destroyed. Also destroyed were wildlife habitats, wetlands, valuable watershed, and scenery (Burnett 1989: 23, 24, 25). The question arose, how can the wilderness remain wild but protected? In this case, past suppression and severe drought had made conditions worse. Early summer fires continued for weeks and weeks with small pockets still burning in November. While positive side effects existed, damages were great. Two teams of scientists and managers reevaluated fire management policies in wilderness environments. One team was appointed by the secretaries of Agriculture and the Interior and the other by the National Park Service. Some of their conclusions are as follows:

1. The use of prescribed natural fires (fires allowed to burn under predetermined conditions) is a reasonable policy but needs to be refined, strengthened, and reaffirmed.
2. Managing fire entails risks, but risks can be reduced by careful planning and preparation, reduction of hazards around high-value developments, and creation of fire breaks.
3. The ecological effects of prescribed natural fire support resource objectives in parks and wilderness, but in some cases the social and economic effects may be unacceptable. Recreation may also be affected, and outside areas may be impacted by smoke or stream sedimentation.
4. More information needs to be given out about prescribed natural burns, and the public needs to have stronger input.
5. Fire management should be improved by better training and interagency coordination of terminology and budgets.

The team appointed by the National Park Service pointed out that remaining tracts of wilderness are small in comparison to the times when fires moved freely and naturally over North America. As such it recommended that nature could not be allowed to run its course with total freedom (Romme and Despain 1989:46) Humans, not nature, then, must be designated the primary manager. In 1989 the Bush administration modified the Park Service's "let-it-burn" policy by restricting the number of natural fires that would be allowed to burn (Stammer 1990:A34).

Policy that dictates action to be taken after fire varies between the Forest Service and the National Park Service. The Forest Service responds to fires by rapidly clearing fire-killed trees and by planting new ones. The Park Service responds to wildfire as it would to any other natural forest process, that is, the remains are best left alone for scientists and park visitors to study and observe. The Forest Service and other big land management agencies must consider the production of resources such as timber on their lands, except in wilderness areas, while the national parks are managed under policies that protect and preserve all native species.

GRASSLAND

Familiar garden lawns and grassy urban parks are human-made, but the world's fast-disappearing native grassland is as natural as forests or deserts. It is estimated that before the westward movement in the nineteenth century, 75 million bison inhabited North America's expansive grasslands (Kormondy 1984:169–71). Tall grass prairies once stretched from Michigan and Ohio across large portions of the Midwest to the Dakotas and over northern Texas. Nutrients from the grasses produced a dark rich soil perfect for agriculture. Victims of their own lushness, farms, roads, industry, and development caused original grasslands to vanish from many states. The grasslands of central North America are divided into two types: the tall grass prairie toward the east, and the short grass prairie in the plains westward. The transition from tall to short grass correlates with an increased aridity, reduced rainfall, and increased evaporation. Tall grass prairie is characterized by irregular rainfall and a very rich soil.

North American prairies are thought to date back to Micene times beginning 35 million years ago. Vast areas had grass so thick and tall that pioneers on horseback feared getting lost in them. They were full of bobcats, wolves, deer, elk, rabbits, and bison. Swarms of birds hovered above in search of food. According to Duffey (1975: 8–11), grassland plants include not merely true grasses but also flowering herbaceous plants that can tolerate conditions of soil and climate that woody plants cannot. He estimates that 24 percent of the vegetation cover in the world today consists of grasslands. Even so, grasslands have in the last two centuries become today's most endangered ecosystem (Sector  1990:A1).

Conservationists are mobilizing to preserve the prairies. The National Audubon Society has proposed that 11,000 acres of bluestem grass in the Flint Hills of southern Kansas receive national monument status. Opposed are ranchers who are concerned that other grazing lands might become restricted areas. In Illinois an experimental grasslands transplant has been attempted by the state chapter of the Nature Conservancy. A one-acre swatch of virgin grassland was going to be destroyed in order to mine gravel. Conservationists enlisted the help of a commercial nursery and a construction company to help with their project. Together they dug up the prairie and its topsoil, collected 100 species of plants and 1,000 animal species, and trucked everything 6 miles away to a nature preserve. Hundreds of volunteers sodded a new hill with clumps from the old. The transplant, expected to kill some plants, may eventually be rejuvenated by seeds laced through the soil. The cooperative effort emphasizes the rarity of the once prodigious prairies, while demonstrating society's awareness of the need to preserve an endangered environment and ecosystem. Illinois, the Prairie State, was once nearly four-fifths prairie. Today only a 4-square-mile area of prairie remains (Sector 1990:A1).

An intaglio, or geoglyph, in the Mojave Desert near Blyth, California.

DESERT

For many people, deserts conjure an image of lifeless sand dunes shimmering in waves of heat. Appearing barren, deserts seem to be forsaken. Yet the clear skies, the distant horizons, and the starry nights may represent the same appeal that oceans or mountains bring to others. Although the living conditions are severe, the desert is far from uninhabited. Its plants and animals possess highly specialized abilities and mechanisms for survival. Deserts cover about 15 percent of the earth's land area (Wagner 1980:10). The plants, dispersed over otherwise bare ground, have, like the desert animals, adapted to low water levels. Cactus have shallow root systems. Some desert plants have reduced leaf size or drop their leaves in dry conditions. Others have evolved into water-storing succulents. Most desert mammals are nocturnal, burrowing during the day.

Desert Running

Because the desert is a fragile ecosystem, when abused it is damaged long-term. Recreationists traveling on dirt bikes and off-road vehicles scar the desert and kill the plants and animals. Soil compaction, caused by driving on the desert, destroys plant life. The compacted soil erodes rapidly and will not absorb water or insulate the roots against temperature extremes. The loss of plant life in turn destroys other dependent life forms. For example, scientists have reported a 90 percent drop in small-mammal populations at the start area of the Barstow-to-Las Vegas race on BLM land. The noise of approximately 1,200 motorcycles and all-terrain vehicles are extremely damaging to animal life. Desert animals have adapted to a normally quiet habitat. Some have developed an acute sense of hearing. Kangaroo rats have been found weaving in circles after the race. Their bleeding ears had burst from the noise pollution. Other animals were found crushed or buried alive in their burrows (*California* 1989:105). Tracks were seen on the cracked shells of the desert tortoises.

Giant saguaro cacti, unique to the Sonoran Desert, sometimes reach a height of 50 feet in the cactus forest of Saguaro National Monument near Tucson, Arizona.

Desert wildflowers appear for a brief week or two in April at Anza Borego State Park in California.

Petroglyphs are protected by the Antiquities Act, nevertheless, vandalism and changes in the acidity of rain continue to cause damage.

The desert tortoise, which has roamed the desert for 2 million years, was placed on the federal list of endangered species on emergency status in 1989. From 1979 to 1989 their population in the western Mojave diminished by half (*California* 1989:84). Besides dying when off-road vehicles run them over, they are used for target practice, taken home as pets, and pushed aside by developments. Ravens eat their young. Efforts to save the tortoise and the fragile desert ecosystem have been met with mixed emotions. When the Bureau of Land Management planned to shoot ravens, they were met with protests from the Humane Society. Attempts to stop the Barstow-to-Las Vegas Off-Road Vehicle Race have met with severe opposition from participants. In 1975 the race was canceled by the BLM after a study revealed extensive damage to plants and wildlife. Though bitterly opposed by environmentalists, the race was resumed in 1982. The vehicles continued to tear the Mojave every Thanksgiving weekend until 1990, when it was again cancelled for environmental reasons. Over one hundred motorcyclists demonstrated for the American right to use the nation's public lands (Warren 1990:A3).

To be sure, off-road recreation areas must be provided to minimize damage to the rest of the desert. Because the desert's aridity is a great preserver, vehicle tire tracks permanently mar not only the land but archaeological remains of past cultures. Intaglios, for example, are large desert drawings made centuries ago by Indian peoples who lived along the lower Colorado River. Today the drawings are forever scarred by these tracks.

Other federal desert properties face problems from pollution and development. Petroglyph National Monument near Albuquerque, New Mexico, was created on June 27, 1990. However, Native American petroglyphs, or rock art, dating from the Desert Archaic period, 3,000 to 5,000 years ago, will not be fully protected from

These red mangroves with massive exposed root systems fringe the waterways of the Everglades and filter material washed from the land, trapping debris and sediment. Mangrove roots provide nursery grounds to many species of fish and invertebrates, and near Key Largo, are the habitat for the endangered American crocodile.

real estate development, vandals, and trash dumpers for another decade. Acid rain presents another preservation difficulty. Saguaro (sah wah roh) National Monument near Tucson is under siege from cactus rustlers because one saguaro can be sold on the black market for upward of $1,000 (Secter 1989: A3). The delicate desert cactus grows slowly but can ultimately reach a height of 50 feet, weigh up to 12 tons, and live for 200 years. The saguaro with its long arms has been a symbol of the other 5,000 species of cactus more than any other. Serving as a home to wildlife, the tall desert monument is routinely shot by vandals with guns or bows and arrows. Acid rain and blight have also caused premature aging of the plants. Individual buyers may discourage poachers by only dealing with reputable dealers. Fines for poaching and vandalism must be increased if desert saguaro are to survive.

NOISE POLLUTION

Besides the noise pollution impacts on desert animals cited above, humans suffer from noise pollution. In the silence of the desert, all-terrain vehicles and low-flying military jets have caused violations of the peacefulness and quietude that many visitors seek in Joshua Tree National Monument, for instance. Likewise helicopters in the Grand Canyon and automobiles in Yosemite and many other recreational centers disturb the serenity. Complaints from sailors are heard about participants in motorboats and on jet skis. Cross-country skiers barely tolerate noisy snowmobiles.

According to Williams and Jacobs in their report of the President's Commission on Americans Outdoors (1986:M20), psychological annoyance depends on many factors: the extent of interference with communication, relaxation, and sleep; the settings in which the noise occurs; the importance of the activities interrupted; and the time of exposure. A standard of 70 decibels is sufficient to protect hearing loss (Weinstein 1976:229–52). However, about half of the people exposed over a period of time to noise at this level became highly dissatisfied. Considerable research has addressed community noise assessment, but the applicability of these studies to outdoor recreation has not been addressed and their use in the context of outdoor recreation resources is highly suspect. Even in community settings the degree of annoyance may be consistently underreported. Because attitudes of the perceiver affect the assessment of annoyance, noise levels are likely to be evaluated much more critically in outdoor recreation settings than in urban settings, where adaptations to noise levels have been made. Continued controversy exists between recreationists seeking a quiet afternoon, and adventurers enjoying activities dependent on motors. Each seeks his or her space and provisions must be made for both.

WILDLIFE

This section addresses edification and exotic species, wildlife habitats, and solutions and programs for wildlife such as the Endangered Species Act.

Edification and Exotic Species

Some animal species have joined humans in a population explosion. Human-made edifices (structures of especially imposing appearance) such as agricultural developments, dams, reservoirs, drainage schemes, interstate highways, and buildings have aided the evolution. Certain species that have adapted well to these structures are known by ecologists as *edification species* (Lazell 1989:19–20). Edification species have had a negative effect on general wildlife diversity. As a National Park Service research collaborator in the 1970s and 1980s, James Lazell (1989:20–21) inventoried animal species at Cape Cod, Cape Hatteras, Cape Lookout, Gulf Islands National Seashores, and Everglades National Park. He discovered that some native species were missing from their natural habitats while others had become incredibly abundant. This type of change is known as species turnover and replacement. Herring gull eggs, for example, were collected to near extinction on the New England coastal islands, but the gulls began to make a comeback in the 1950s. These victims of one generation became the beneficiaries of the next according to Lazell, when their central edifice became the sanitary landfill. The gull population grew as they fed in cities and dumps. Nesting on offshore islets, they ate the eggs and chicks of smaller species and crowded out larger ones. Biological diversity tumbled, and gull population control became mandatory. In the 1960s their nests were eradicated and greater control of landfills and fish-processing practices reduced their food base. Afterward other seabirds began nesting in greater numbers on coastal islets. How well these measures will ultimately work remains to be seen.

Other examples of edification species are: raccoons, skunks, coyotes, and eastern or Florida cottontail rabbits. Buildings offered sanctuary to the raccoon. Expanding its regional range to lakes and shores in the north where wildlife was unaccustomed to the marauders, the raccoons ate summer garbage and wintered under summer cottages. Capable of living off their fat during winter, they anxiously consumed the eggs and chicks of nesting loons in the spring. Buildings also provided shelter and fresh water to raccoons in their native coastal regions in the south. Their numbers grew to such an extent that they began to threaten the comeback of sea turtles by eating their eggs.

Other asperities occur on reservoirs, golf courses, city parks, and agricultural lands which sustain edification waterfowl. To this day, state and local governments import and release exotic (foreign) waterfowl to stock parks and preserves. The mute swan, for example, is an exotic transport from Europe which became wild, or feral, in North America. It does not migrate, and it competes with other wild species for food, depleting the resources. Its long neck allows it the opportunity to feed lower than most other migrants and breeding birds (Lazell 1989:22–23). Like the raccoon, the swan plays havoc with natural diversity.

As urbanization spreads, forest habitats are threatened by subdivisions for homes and recreational vehicle parks, which cause changes in the surrounding habitat from the presence of domesticated animals and exotic plants (Michael and Sullivan 1991:C-3). Extinction caused by invading species grows increasingly common. When alien species are introduced into systems with few natural defenses against them, those invaders may kill or crowd out native species.

Exotic stocking and artificial feeding programs must cease, and, according to Lazell (1989:23) hunting seasons should begin earlier and last longer with higher (or no) bag limits on exotics. According to Ridenour (1991:23), director of the National Park Service, it is vital that the public become educated about the obligation of the National Park Service to remove exotic species from the parks. Because national parks serve as sanctuaries for wild animals, edification species and exotics have been protected from hunters. The intent of this long-standing no-hunting policy was to allow for a natural evolution to occur. Sanctuary-aided exotics, however, have led to the displacement of natives. While some parks have programs to control exotics, many do not.

According to Knudson (1984:488–89) the national park management policy states:

> Control or eradication of noxious or exotic plant and animal species will be undertaken when they are undesirable in terms of public health, recreation use, and enjoyment, or when their presence threatens the faithful presentation of the historic scene or the perpetuation of significant scientific features, ecological communities, and native species. . . .

Carrying out the policy is a sensitive issue, especially when the Park Service is dealing with wild horses and other popular species. National parks are associated with preservation, not destruction. While it may be economical to shoot animals, objections are raised by many. Bullets found in some species may lead to lead poisoning in others who feed off of the remains. Live trapping and removal may appear to be more humane, but it is generally too expensive for the federal government. Fencing is sometimes but not always successful.

According to Poindexter (1991:90), there is perhaps no example that illustrates the problem of exotics better than the plight of the bald eagle in Montana's Glacier National Park. As many as 600 eagles used to feed on the salmon that swam upstream to spawn near a stretch of Lower McDonald Creek. As an attempt to fatten the salmon, nonnative shrimp were introduced to Glacier's waterways in 1968. Unexpectedly they competed with the larger fish for the same food source; the salmon population collapsed. Only six nesting pairs of bald eagles remain. Similarly burros, released by prospectors in the Grand Canyon, have almost completely displaced the desert bighorn sheep. Burros overuse grazing areas and natural habitat. Because park managers were charged with protecting the habitat, they ordered that the burros be shot. Public outcry led to litigation to stop the shooting. Friends of Animals, the Fund for Animals, and other humane organizations hired cowboys and helicopters to remove 565 burros at a cost of $1,000 per animal (Knudson 1984:489–90).

Domestic livestock grazing, another unnatural development, has been allowed in many national forest wilderness areas, BLM lands, and the national park system, based on long-term lease arrangements. The issue of grazing was inherited by the Bureau of Land Management, for example, when it was formed in 1946 by a merger of the General Land Office and the Grazing Service. As permits expire, grazing may gradually be phased out of federal lands due to agency emphasis on conservation, recreation, wildlife preservation, and pressure from conservation groups. This will be met with expected lobbying efforts from organizations such as the National Cattlemen's Association, which has tremendous influence on the state legislatures of the West and on Congress. It is expected that future foresters dealing with the multiple uses of land will continually be exposed to more advanced techniques of management for grazing (Knudson 1984:256, 441, 516, 526, 542).

Control of exotic species will continue to be a problem. Enforced regulations restricting the importation of exotic species is the most logical preventative measure. Removal will be necessary, however, if some parks are to meet the mandate described previously. David Wilcove, senior ecologist at the Wilderness Society, believes that in order for biodiversity to continue in parklands, "Parks should be places of minimal human intrusion. Species and natural processes should be left alone" (Poindexter 1991:90).

Wildlife Habitats

All over the world thousands of species of plants and animals are becoming extinct, vanishing forever. Extinction is viewed by some to be a natural process caused by plant and animal adaptation to changing environments. The process, however, is accelerating dramatically with the expansion of the human population. In the last three centuries, thousands of plants and animals have become extinct. Elephants are lost for ivory and butterflies to pesticides. The greatest cause of extinction related to human activity is the loss of habitat to farms, houses, and factories. Besides loss of habitat, fragmentation, overhunting, the introduction of exotic species, and pollution lead to extinction.

Norton (1987:7, 11, 191, 195) describes the anthropocentrist/nonanthropocentrist debate in species preservation. Anthropocentrists recognize value in other species only if the species is instrumental to meeting human ends or needs, thus the preservation of species are commonly pursued only as utilitarian measures. Nonanthropocentrists find that some nonhuman species have value in their own right. They argue that anthropocentrism leaves nature vulnerable to consumptive demands. Although transcendentalism provides an intellectual framework for contemporary environmentalism, Emerson (see the material on Ralph Waldo Emerson in Chapter 3) assigned no intrinsic value in nature independent of human consciousness or evaluations. Nature served as a means for humans to achieve spiritual enlightenment. Norton finds that modern environmentalists cannot adopt the transcendentalist system completely, because it provides a general structure of anthropocentric values (1982). Nonetheless a great many people are working to save species; and many species are making comebacks. For many other species the outcome is uncertain. What people do will make a difference.

SOLUTIONS AND PROGRAMS FOR WILDLIFE

The following are some solutions to the problems facing wildlife.

Endangered Species Act

The United States Endangered Species Act of 1973 became one of the most comprehensive laws ever enacted by any country to prevent the extinction of imperiled life. The act is administered by the U.S. Fish and Wildlife Service, Department of the Interior (see Chapter 7, Federal Resources). Additionally, the secretary of Commerce, acting through the National Marine Fisheries Service, has jurisdiction over most marine species. When a species is listed as threatened or endangered, it becomes protected by federal law. This alone is sometimes enough to save it from extinction and to start it back on the road to recovery.

An *endangered species,* by definition, is on the brink of extinction throughout all or a significant portion of its range. A *threatened species* is one likely to become endangered within the foreseeable future. In 1981 the U.S. Fish and Wildlife Service listed 278 native plants and animals on the U.S. List of Endangered and Threatened Wildlife and Plants, and an additional 468 foreign species were listed under the Endangered Species Act. The number is growing. Once status is official, a recovery plan identifies, describes, and schedules the actions necessary to restore the species to a more secure biological condition. Because of limited funding and the large number of listed species, recovery plans are carried out on a priority basis. Those creatures that are in the most immediate danger, whose life requirements are best known, and which are clearly unique, generally come first.

The Fish and Wildlife Service (1981:4–9) uses a variety of wildlife management techniques and approaches to aid recovery as follows:

1. **Reintroduction** Service biologists continue to develop and refine reintroduction techniques as a valuable aid in wildlife restoration. For example, eggshells of the bald eagle have thinned from pesticides. Eaglets from captive or noncontaminated wild birds are transplanted to the nests of nonproductive eagles for reintroduction in the wild.
2. **Captive Propagation** Some species are so depleted that captive propagation is

considered necessary to ensure their survival. In the case of the California condor, a recovery plan called for captive breeding to increase the population. Various animals, particularly wild birds, however, are often difficult to breed in captivity because the unnatural environment interferes with their normal mating behavior. Methods of artificial insemination and other techniques have overcome these problems. Some animal rights advocates argue that it is better for the animals to die in the wild. Captive breeding may lead to successful reintroduction to the wild, which ameliorates the concerns of some advocates.

3. Habitat Protection Recovery plans usually call for preservation of land and water needed for a species to survive. Habitats can be protected by working with private landowners, negotiating cooperative agreements with other land-managing agencies or conservation groups, and acquiring easements to ensure existing use while guarding against harmful development. When a habitat cannot be maintained any other way, it is sometimes purchased. Most of the money for land acquisition comes from the Land and Water Conservation Fund or assistance from private organizations which can move in quickly to preserve land for later repurchase by the federal government. All of this habitat then becomes part of the National Wildlife Refuge System.

4. Habitat Manipulation Changes in habitat jeopardize the survival of a species. In such cases, environmental factors can sometimes be manipulated to restore the condition necessary for a creature to exist. For example, in south central Florida certain water levels were important to the apple snail, the principal food for the endangered Everglade kite. Small dams and other control structures were built to offset the lowering of water levels for agricultural use and development.

5. Habitat Cleanup Federal restriction on contaminants which enter the food chain have been necessary. For example, DDT (see the material on Rachel Carson in Chapter 3) and other long-lived pesticides entered the food chain. Accumulating in the body of the brown pelican, they caused the production of thin eggshells which cracked during incubation. As pesticides gradually break down, the shells are slowly returning to normal, and reproductive success has increased.

Artificial Habitats

Zoos, wild animal parks, wildlife research centers, and marine mammal research centers also contribute to animal comebacks. According to Warhol and Bernirschke (1986:8), zoos, sometimes criticized for capturing and exploiting animals, have rescued some species from extinction. By introducing various species to the masses through educational programs, research and study, and concerted efforts to save species from oblivion, such organizations are expected to help to save some of the 2,000 species of vertebrate animals that are expected to need future protection. For instance, New York's Central Park Zoo has a dramatic display that alerts visitors to the fact that tropical forests, which harbor 5 to 10 million plant and animal species, are currently vanishing at the rate of 50 acres a minute. Literature is available near the display explaining how to get involved in finding solutions.

Many species that survive the present wave of extinction, according to Balog (1990:85–86), will be quasi-domesticated residents of wildlife preserves, where the ecosystems will be controlled by humans rather than by natural interaction. Others will be captives with reproduced wildernesses and with mates chosen by computer selection. Balog proclaims, "Until we become much more skilled at listening to the voices of nature in and around us, all animals—including the one called human—are in jeopardy."

Habitat Protection

Norton (1987:266–70) believes our greatest protection of biological diversity is in the preservation of various habitats or ecosystems. Wildlife should not simply be encountered in zoos and botanical gardens, but in their natural habitats. Here they draw upon resources available in the ecosystem to which they also contribute. A holistic habitat protection approach would protect the species before they reach critical stages, requiring the individual attention of a species-by-species approach. Norton asserts that through habitat protection the listing process might be phased out. In general he believes that one species should not be assumed more valuable than another. By saving habitats more species could, in the long run, be saved; and by scaling down the listing process more resources could be available to protect habitats.

Park boundaries and habitat Some animals require habitat protection in and around the national parks. For example, hunters shoot bison that wander out of Yellowstone National Park, home of the nation's last free-roaming herd. National attention was directed to the problem in January 1989 when a harsh winter drove 800 of the herd over the park's northern boundary, providing hunters the opportunity to kill 569—more than half of the celebrated northern herd. Yellowstone bison now number approximately 2,400. More than 500 of these remain on the northern range and are in danger of disappearing, according to park biologists. Critics cite this case to illustrate the arbitrary nature of national park borders which often ignore natural boundaries, such as ridgelines and watersheds, slicing through the natural boundaries of animal habitats (Kenney 1990:22).

Wetlands Protection

Worldwide, the once common amphibian, the frog, has declined through wetland destruction, acid rain and snow, pesticides, drought, and competition from exotic species. Even the relatively pristine national parks and wilderness areas are finding inexplicable simultaneous declines of frogs, which are a representative of the earliest, most primitive forms of life. Frogs were so common that when they began to disappear in the early 1970s few noticed. Habitat loss is considered the most crucial loss to this amphibian population. Many of their matchless wetland homes have been flooded or dried out by giant reclamation projects such as those that have damaged the Everglades. Clearcutting has been devastating to forest amphibians. Even where acid rain and snow levels are uncommon, such as in Sequoia and Kings Canyon national parks, acidity is flushed into ponds and lakes from melting snowbanks. In Sequoia National Park, biologists are trying to reintroduce the now-absent foothill yellow-legged frog to the lower elevations. Backcountry rangers in Canyonlands, Yosemite, and Sequoia national parks are closely watching amphibian populations. Other parks experiencing losses include Michigan's Isle Royale National Park, Colorado's Rocky Mountain National Park and Mesa Verde National Park, and California's Yosemite and Kings Canyon national parks (Milstein, 1990: 20–24).

The importance of a watershed According to Jensen (1985:307), archaeologists and historians have found that with respect to nature, civilizations pass through four stages of development. The first stage is the subduing of nature for survival. The second stage is the cooperative stage in which nature is used to produce the goods we need. The third stage involves the exploitation of nature such as overharvesting and overusing natural goods. The fourth stage involves the rehabilitation of nature after civilization has recognized the errors of the third stage.

Although Americans seem to teeter between the third and fourth stages, society has definitely begun to recognize environmental issues. There is hope that in the fourth stage new technology will be available to mend damaging environmental practices. Scientific minds and agencies are capable of meeting the problems directly, and a case in point is Florida's watershed.

The vital water system of southern Florida consists of three essential elements: the Kissimmee River, Lake Okeechobee, and the Everglades. Environmentalist Nicole Duplaix (1990:90–112) explains that each stands today at a pivotal point between viability and possible collapse. Nearly a century ago the fresh-water system of Florida nurtured an ecosystem unique to the earth. Water flowed from a chain of lakes into the Kissimmee River, which carried water through the savanna to Lake Okeechobee. Periodically the lake would overflow, moving south across the saw grass of the Everglades. This sheet of water contributed to the rain, which would constantly renew the cycle.

After the Civil War, an environmental onslaught began as efforts were made to contain the flood-prone lake. By the turn of the century a network of locks, dams, and canals were built for that purpose. Farming emerged. Topsoil dried to a powder or decomposed, releasing nutrients which traveled into the Everglades. The U.S. Army Corps of Engineers strengthened dikes and dug more channels to tame the flooding water system. Finally, plumbing projects of the 1940s changed the water wilderness forever. As the population grew, water was further diverted for human needs. In 1947 Everglades National Park opened, and later areas outside of the park were impounded as water conservation areas for flood control and wildlife preservation. During dry periods the Everglades were parched, and during the wet season they were deluged with water. Signs of malaise occurred throughout the Everglades. The 1970s brought a recognition of the need to protect the entire single water system of the park, but the damage still lingered; by the 1980s polluted Lake Okeechobee burst into blooms of blue-green algae, perhaps nature's own desperate call for help.

The last in the chain to receive water, the sensitive Everglades responded. It withered during droughts, native plants were displaced, and wildlife was lost. The park's birthright, as declared by Congress in 1947, was to have a clear and abundant water supply for the protection of its wildlife, which might otherwise become extinct. This in itself was a landmark decision because it was the first time that Congress had voted to establish a park which had the protection of wildlife in an unusual ecosystem as its primary reason for existence. Clearly if the Everglades were going to be saved, a commitment to restoration of a more natural flow of water was necessary and park boundaries had to be increased to encompass the water system.

Water managers responded to the requests for assistance by park biologists. A computer program was designed to imitate seasonal rainfall conditions. Annual water deliveries were made along the park's northern boundary for the appropriate distribution of water allotments. A levee was breached to assist the restoration of natural water flow. Successful rehabilitation of the Kissimmee was generated by engineers, and waterfowl began to return. New ordinances and laws were designed to protect Florida's water. For example: landfills had to be lined, and gas storage tanks were banned in order to prevent the contamination of groundwater. Dairy pastures had to be drained into special holding ponds so that manure nutrients would not reach Lake Okeechobee. The Florida legislature in 1987 passed the Water Improvement and Management Act, which required the state to detail plans for pollution reduction and environmental restoration. In 1989 Congress authorized through the Everglades Expansion Act an addition of 107,000 acres to Everglades National Park. At that time a federal lawsuit against the state of Florida for polluting the park was pending. In July of 1991 the state settled the suit by agreeing to acquire 37,000 acres of farm land adjacent to the park that release phosphorous. The land will serve as a natural filter to remove the contaminants from farms (Abramson 1991).

HARMONY WITH NATURE

With approximately five billion inhabitants in the world, tremendous demands are placed on the environment. We cannot afford to waste, pollute, or abuse the environment. The signs of environmental abuse are all around us. In our abundance we became careless, greedy, and wasteful, causing severe environmental stress. Our landfills are choking with the tons of garbage dumped every day. Acid rain caused by automobile and factory emissions is killing our forests and polluting our lakes. Sewage and industrial pollution are fouling rivers and oceans. Inappropriate methods of farming, mining, logging, and manufacturing are eroding land, poisoning water, and threatening wildlife.

There is hope for our planet. With restraint, technology, consideration, diligence, and understanding we are capable of slowing and perhaps even reversing much of the damage caused. The more time we spend outside, the more we seem to learn about our environment and the need to live in harmony with it. With the passage of the National Environmental Policy Act of 1969, the enhancement of harmony between people and their environment became a national policy. As a direct result the Council on Environmental Quality was established which required that all federal agencies prepare reports on the environmental impact of all major planned programs. Like the Native Americans we may learn that the earth is sacred.

The enhancement of harmony between people and their environment became a national policy with the passage of the National Environmental Policy Act of 1969. As a direct result the Council on Environmental Quality was established which required that all federal agencies prepare reports on the environmental impact of all major planned programs.

In 1854 when the United States made an offer for a large area of Indian land, Chief Seattle stressed ecological values and harmony with nature. His speech, which follows, has become one of the most powerful orations addressing the environment that has ever been made.

> How can you buy or sell the sky, the warmth of the land? The idea is strange to us.
>
> If we do not own the freshness of the air and the sparkle of the water, how can you buy them?
>
> THE EARTH IS SACRED
>
> Every part of this earth is sacred to my people. Every shining pine needle, every sandy shore, every mist in the dark woods, every clearing and humming insect is holy in the memory and experience of my people. The sap which courses through the trees carries the memories of the red man.
>
> The white man's dead forget the country of their birth when they go to walk among the stars. Our dead never forget this beautiful earth, for it is the mother of the red man.
>
> We are part of the earth and it is part of us.
>
> The perfumed flowers are our sisters; the deer, the horse, the great eagle, these are our brothers.
>
> The rocky crests, the juices in the meadow, the body heat of the pony, and man—all belong to the same family.
>
> THINGS TO REMEMBER
>
> So, when the Great Chief in Washington sends word that he wishes to buy our land, he asks much of us. The Great Chief sends word he will reserve us a place so that we can live comfortably to ourselves.
>
> He will be our father and we will be his children. So we will consider your offer to buy our land.
>
> But it will not be easy. For this land is sacred to us.
>
> This shining water that moves in the streams and rivers is not just water but the blood of our ancestors.
>
> If we sell you land, you must remember that it is sacred, and you must teach your children that it

is sacred and that each ghostly reflection in the clear water of the lakes tells of events and memories in the life of my people.

The water's murmur is the voice of my father's father.

GIVE THE RIVERS KINDNESS

The rivers are our brothers, they quench our thirst. The rivers carry our canoes, and feed our children. If we sell you our land, you must remember, and teach your children, that the rivers are our brothers, and yours, and you must henceforth give the rivers the kindness you would give any brother.

We know that the white man does not understand our ways. One portion of land is the same to him as the next, for he is a stranger who comes in the night and takes from the land whatever he needs.

The earth is not his brother, but his enemy, and when he has conquered it, he moves on.

He leaves his father's grave behind, and he does not care. He kidnaps the earth from his children, and he does not care.

His father's grave, and his children's birthright, are forgotten. He treats his mother, the earth, and his brother, the sky, as things to be bought, plundered, sold like sheep or bright beads.

His appetite will devour the earth and leave behind only a desert.

I do not know. Our ways are different from your ways.

The sight of your cities pains the eyes of the red man. But perhaps it is because the red man is a savage and does not understand.

There is no quiet place in the white man's cities. No place to hear the unfurling of leaves in spring, or the rustle of an insect's wings.

But perhaps it is because I am a savage and do not understand.

The clatter only seems to insult the ears. And what is there to life if a man cannot hear the lonely cry of the whippoorwill or the arguments of the frogs around a pond at night? I am a red man and do not understand.

The Indian prefers the soft sound of the wind darting over the face of a pond and the smell of the wind itself, cleaned by a midday rain, or scented with the piñon pine.

THE AIR SHARES ITS SPIRIT

The air is precious to the red man, for all things share the same breath—the beast, the tree, the man, they all share the same breath.

The white man does not seem to notice the air he breathes. Like a man dying for many days, he is numb to the stench.

But if we sell you our land, you must remember that the air is precious to us, that the air shares its spirit with all the life it supports. The wind that gave our grandfather his first breath also receives his last sigh.

And if we sell you our land, you must keep it apart and sacred, as a place where even the white man can go to taste the wind that is sweetened by the meadow's flowers.

TREAT THE BEASTS AS BROTHERS

So we will consider your offer to buy our land. If we decide to accept, I will make one condition: the white man must treat the beasts of this land as his brothers.

I am a savage and I do not understand any other way.

I have seen a thousand rotting buffaloes on the prairie, left by the white man who shot them from a passing train.

I am a savage and I do not understand how the smoking iron horse can be more important than the buffalo that we kill only to stay alive.

What is man without the beasts? If all the beasts were gone, man would die from a great loneliness of spirit.

For whatever happens to the beasts, soon happens to man. All things are connected.

TEACH YOUR CHILDREN

You must teach your children that the ground beneath their feet is the ashes of your grandfathers. So that they will respect the land, tell your children that the earth is rich with the lives of our kin.

Teach your children what we have taught our children, that the earth is our mother.

Whatever befalls the earth befalls the sons of the earth. If men spit upon the ground, they spit upon themselves.

This we know: The earth does not belong to man; man belongs to the earth. This we know.

All things are connected like the blood which unites one family. All things are connected.

Whatever befalls the earth befalls the sons of the earth. Man did not weave the web of life: he is merely a strand in it. Whatever he does to the web, he does to himself.

Even the white man, whose God walks and talks with him as friend to friend, cannot be exempt from the common destiny.

We may be brothers after all.

We shall see.

One thing we know, which the white man may one day discover—our God is the same God.

You may think now that you own Him as you wish to own our land; but you cannot. He is the God of man, and His compassion is equal for the red man and the white.

This earth is precious to Him, and to harm the earth is to heap contempt on its Creator.

The whites too shall pass; perhaps sooner than all other tribes. Contaminate your bed, and you will one night suffocate in you own waste.

But in your perishing you will shine brightly, fired by the strength of the God who brought you to this land and for some special purpose gave you dominion over this land and over the red man.

That destiny is a mystery to us, for we do not understand when the buffalo are all slaughtered, the wild horses are tamed, the secret corners of the forest heavy with scent of many men, and the view of the ripe hills blotted by talking wires.

Where is the thicket? Gone.

Where is the eagle? Gone.

The end of living and the beginning of survival.

If we sell you our land, love it as we have loved it. Care for it as we have cared for it. Hold in your mind the memory of the land as it is when you take it. And with all your strength, with all you mind, with all your heart, preserve it for your children and love it . . . as God loves us all.

SUMMARY

What impact do outdoor activities have on the environment? Activities selected should adhere to certain principles that protect the environment. It is evident that the two basic ecosystems, aquatic and terrestrial, are vulnerable, therefore the activities selected should adhere to a certain outdoor ethic. Human activities, including outdoor recreation, also impact air quality. Air pollution has caused havoc in national parks even with the passage of the original Clean Air Act of 1963, which was updated in 1990.

The destruction to the fresh-water aquatic system is seen in the extinction and near extinction of many fish. This led to a significant drop in the number of sport fisherpersons. It is estimated that 100,000 anglers have dropped this sport every year for the past 5 years in California alone. Proposals for preservation of rivers, lakes, and ponds have been forwarded.

Another area affected by human activities are the estuarine systems, that part of the coast over which the tide ebbs and flows. Saltwater habitats are a vital food source for many species and provide many recreational opportunities. Human activities have also adversely affected marine systems, where "trashbergs" are reducing life at an alarming rate. Coral reefs along the Florida keys could become the first in the world to be killed by humans. Fast action is needed there.

Forests and trees are disappearing at an alarming rate, the recreational values of which are gone forever. But most important is the impact of the unwise timber harvesting on the environment, which results in the loss of wildlife and creates a dangerous level of global warming. Tropical rain forests are disappearing at the rate of 40 to 50 million acres per year, or one acre per second. These old forests support established ecosystems.

Prairie lands may be the most endangered terrestrial ecosystem. A national monument in Kansas has been proposed to protect 11,000 acres of blue stem grasslands. Illinois, known as the Prairie State because it was four-fifths prairie, today has only four square miles of prairie remaining.

The desert is a fragile ecosystem that has been damaged by recreational vehicles. Steps are being taken to reduce this damage, such as the cancellation of the Barstow-to-Las Vegas

Off-Road Vehicle Race. Noise pollution from the race injured desert animals that have developed an acute sense of hearing.

The Endangered Species Act was discussed, including habitat protection and habitat manipulation. Advanced technology has resulted in a better understanding of the Everglades watershed, which provides a habitat for many species of birds. Control and regulation of the use of pesticides and fertilizers and the establishment of a buffer zone of land to protect the watershed are some of the steps taken to preserve these recreational lands.

REFERENCES

Abramson, R. (1991) "Florida Agrees to Preserve Everglades From Pollution." *Los Angeles Times.* July 12.

Associated Press (1990) "Study Finds Sharp Rise in Ozone Damage to Yosemite Pine Trees." *Los Angeles Times.* November 24.

Atkinson, G. (1990) "Outdoor Recreation's Contribution to Environmental Attitudes" *Leisure Today.* April 14–16.

Balog, J. (1990) "A Personal Vision of Vanishing Wildlife." *National Geographic.* Vol. 177, No. 4. April National Geographic Society, Washington D.C.

Burnett, H. (1989) "Report on Stressed-Out Forests." *American Forests.* March/April.

California Magazine (1989) "Vanishing California." (December).

Chase, C. (1990) "Cognition, Ethics and Direct Experience." *Journal of Physical Education, Recreation and Dance.* April, Volume 61 No. 4.

Cone, M. (1990) "Lure of Fishing Is Fading." *Los Angeles Times,* November 18.

The Conservation Foundation (1980) *Coastal Environmental Management.* Washington, D.C.: U.S. Government Printing Office.

Doyle, R. (1977) "Rivers Wild and Pure: A Priceless Legacy." *National Geographic* 152:1 (July).

Duffey, E. (1975) *Grassland Life.* Madrid, Spain: The Dunbury Press.

Duplaix, N. (1990) "Paying the Price," *National Geographic* 178:1 (July). Washington D.C.

Environmental Protection Information Center (1990) *Wildlife of the Ancient Forest.* Garberville, CA: EPIC, Inc.

Forests Forever (1990) "California Forest Facts." Ukiah, CA.

Georgia Pacific Corporation (1990) *A Natural Partnership: Georgia Pacific and the Environment.* Atlanta, GA: G.P.C.

Goldfarb, T. (1989) *Clashing Views on Controversial Environmental Issues.* The Dushkin Publishing Group, Inc., Guilford, CT.

Graedel, T., and P. Crutzen (1989) "The Changing Atmosphere." *Scientific American* 261:3 (September).

Hope, J. "Radical Fishing." *Mother Earth News* 123 (May/June).

Houghton, R., and G. Woodwell (1989) "Global Climatic Change." *Scientific American* 260:4 (April).

Jeffery, D. (1989) "Yellowstone: The Great Fires of 1988." *National Geographic* 175:2 (February).

Jensen, C. (1985) *Outdoor Recreation in America.* 4th Edition. Burgess Publishing Co., Minneapolis.

Kenney, J. (1990) "Control of the Wild." *National Parks* 65:9–10 (September/October).

Kormondy, E. (1984) *Concepts of Ecology.* Englewood Cliffs, NJ: Prentice Hall.

Knudson, D. (1984) *Outdoor Recreation.* New York: Macmillan.

Lazell, Jr., J. (1989) "Wildlife." *National Parks* 65:9–10 (September/October).

Mendocino Environmental Center (1990) *Forest Practices, the Timber Industry and the North Coast.* Ukiah, CA: M.E.C.

Michael, L., and N. Sullivan (1991) "Should Large-Lot Zoning Laws Protect Wildlife Areas?" *The San Diego Union.* July 7, C-3.

Miller, A. (1990) "Oil: Bush Bans New Drilling Off Coast of California for Remainder of Decade." *Los Angeles Times.* June 27.

Milstein, M. (1990) "Unlikely Harbingers." *National Parks* 65:7-8 (July/August).

Murphy, D. (1990) "Beaches Drowning in Refuse." *Los Angeles Times.* June 3.

National Parks and Conservation Association (1990) "Clean Air Bill on Move at Last." *National Parks* 64:5-6 (May/June).

National Park Service, U.S. Department of the Interior. (1981) *Redwood National Park, California.* Washington D.C.: U.S. Government Printing Office.

A Natural Partnership: Georgia-Pacific and the Environment. (1990) Atlanta, GA: Georgia-Pacific Corporation.

Norton, B. (1987) *Why Preserve Natural Variety?* Princeton, NJ: Princeton University Press.

Perry, C. (1990) "On the Beach." *Los Angeles Times Magazine.* June 24, LA Times Mirror Co., Los Angeles.

Pogatchnik, S. (1990) "A Former Foe, Army Corps Now Fights for Wetlands." *Los Angeles Times.* A1:16-17.

Poindexter, J. (1991) "The Fragile Balance." *Life Magazine* 14:6.

The Press Democrat (1990) "Rain Forest Loss Outstrips Estimate." Santa Rosa, CA: Press Democrat News Services. June 8.

Ridenour, J. (1991) "Building on a Legacy." *National Parks* 65:5-6 (May/June).

Romme, W., and D. Despain (1989) "The Yellowstone Fires." *Scientific American* 261:5 (November).

San Francisco Examiner (1990) "The Culprit Isn't the Owl But Japan." June 30.

Sector, B. (1989) "Saguaro Rustlers Thinning Population of a Desert King."*Los Angeles Times.* November 19.

Sector, B. (1990) "Rescuing a Shrinking Treasure." *Los Angeles Times.* July 24.

Stammer, L. (1990) "Yosemite Reflects Policy Shift." *Los Angeles Times.* August 11.

Steinhart, P. (1990) "No Net Loss." *Audubon* 92:6 (July).

Storer, B., and P. Ling (1990) "Smoke Gets in Your Eyes." *History Today.* December.

Sunset Magazine (1989) "Salmon." April: 91-97.

Time (1988) "The Dirty Seas." Vol. 132, No. 5, Pg. 44-50. August 1, Time Inc., New York.

United States Fish and Wildlife Service (1981) "Endangered Species: The Road to Recovery." Washington, D.C.: U.S. Government Printing Office.

Wagner, F. (1980) *Wildlife of the Deserts.* Harry Abrams, Inc. Publishers, New York.

Ward, F. (1990) "Florida's Coral Reefs Are Imperiled." *National Geographic* 178:1 (July).

Warhol, A. and Bernirschke, K.(1986) *Vanishing Animals.* Spinger-Verlag, New York.

Warren, J. (1990) "Bikers Kick up Dust Over Canceled Desert Run." *Los Angeles Times.* November 25.

Weinstein, N. (1976) "Human Evaluations of Environmental Noise" in *Perceiving Environmental Quality,* K. Craik and E. Zube, editors. New York: Plenum Press.

Williams, D., and G. Jacobs (1986) "Off-Site Resource Development Conflicts" in *The President's Commission on Americans Outdoors, A Literature Review.*

Williams, T. (1990) "Clearcutting Spoils Rivers, Destroys Fisheries." *Forest Voice* 2:1 (March).

Note: According to Gregory Youtz (*If We Sell You Our Land,* Tacoma, WA: Pacific Lutheran University, 1987, pp. 1-3), Chief Seattle is also referred to as Chief Sealth of the Puget Sound area. Dr. Henry Smith published his version of the speech in the Seattle *Sunday Star* in 1877, 30 years after it was made. Smith reported that the speech was given to Governor Isaac Stevens at the beginning of treaty negotiations. It is unclear exactly who took notes at the speech, but it is possible that Seattle's native tongue, Lushootseed, had to be translated into Chinook, and then into English. Smith may have reconstructed the speech over 30 years after the fact from his notes or Stevens' notes. Thus the exact words may have been lost.

Epilogue

> Climb the mountains and get their good tidings. Nature's peace will flow into you as sunshine flows into trees. The winds will blow their own freshness into you, and the storms their energy, while cares will drop off like autumn leaves.
>
> —John Muir

Nature permitted us to survive by providing plants and game, which were used for food and protection. Later, contemporary psychology convinced us that there is more to life than survival and safety. For instance, belonging is a human need, as is expression. Outdoor pursuits are ripe for fulfilling these two needs as well as many others. Part One of this volume describes the work of those who advocated that nature could help us fulfill these needs. Other pioneers put some of these ideas into action.

The psychological impetus for our pursuits of outdoor activities is tempered by socioeconomic factors that are numerous enough to make each one's experiences uniquely his or hers. Yet it is clear that enjoyment of the outdoors cuts through all social strata, underscoring outdoor activities as part of what most, if not all, humans seek.

Having reached a new height in societal offerings, American society can well afford to provide its citizens with a multitude of opportunities for outdoor pursuits. Other nations have followed suit, and it is becoming clear that the provisions of outdoor recreation areas and programs are measures of societal achievement as well as societal concern.

But the earth's natural resources are not limitless, even if some of them are renewable. Some resources have been overused and are in danger of being exhausted from our needs for survival and safety. The additional quest for recreation is adding to the problems that plague the environment. Prudent use can be achieved through wise management of outdoor recreational resources as well as through formal and informal outdoor education. Only then will the future of outdoor recreation be protected. This right is gainfully ours today and should be guaranteed to future generations.

Appendix A

State Agencies Involved in Outdoor Recreation

State	Agencies with Principal Responsibilities in Outdoor Recreation	Agencies with Limited Responsibilities in Outdoor Recreation
Alabama	Department of Conservation Division of Water Safety Division of State Parks, Monuments, and Historical Sites Division of Game and Fish Division of Seafoods Division of Outdoor Recreation	Mound State Monument Department of Highways
Alaska	Department of Natural Resources	
Arizona	Game and Fish Commission State Parks Board Outdoor Recreation Coordinating Commission	Highway Commission Economic and Planning Development Board
Arkansas	State Planning Commission Game and Fish Commission Parks, Recreation, and Travel Commission	Ozarks Regional Commission (joint federal-state agency) Geological Commission Forestry Commission Industrial Development Commission State Highway Department
California	Resources Agency Department of Parks and Recreation Division of Beaches and Parks Division of Recreation Division of Small Craft Harbors Department of Conservation Division of Forestry Department of Fish and Game Department of Water Resources	Department of Public Works Bureau of Health Education, Physical Education and Recreation State Lands Commission Water Pollution Control Department of Health

State	Agencies with Principal Responsibilities in Outdoor Recreation	Agencies with Limited Responsibilities in Outdoor Recreation
Colorado	Department of Natural Resources Division of Game, Fish and Parks	State Historical Society Department of Highways State Board of Land Commissioners
Connecticut	Park and Forest Commission Board of Fisheries and Game	State Highway Department State Department of Health Water Resources Commission State Development Commission
Delaware	Board of Game and Fish Commissioners State Park Commission	State Archives Commission State Forestry Department State Highway Department State Development Department State Board of Health Water and Air Resources Commission Soil and Water Conservation Commission
Florida	Outdoor Recreational Development Council Board of Parks and Historic Memorials Game and Fresh Water Fish Commission	Board of Forestry Board of Conservation State Road Department Development Commission Trustees of the Internal Improvement Fund Board of Archives and History
Georgia	Department of State Parks State Game and Fish Commission Jekyll Island State Park Authority	Stone Mountain Memorial Association State Highway Department Lake Lanier Islands Development Authority North Georgia Mountains Commission
Hawaii	Department of Land and Natural Resources State Parks Division Fish and Game Division Forestry Division	Marinas and Small Boat Harbors
Idaho	State Park Board Fish and Game Commission	State Forestry Department Department of Highways Department of Aeronautics State Department of Commerce and Development State Historical Society State Land Department
Illinois	Department of Conservation Division of Parks and Memorials Division of Game Division of Fisheries Division of Forestry	Department of Public Works and Buildings Department of Registration and Education Department of Public Health Illinois State Youth Commission Department of Business and Economic Development

State	Agencies with Principal Responsibilities in Outdoor Recreation	Agencies with Limited Responsibilities in Outdoor Recreation
Indiana	Department of Natural Resources Division of Fish and Game Division of Forestry Division of State Parks Division of Reservoir Management	State Highway Department Department of Recreation Great Lakes Park Training Institute State Health Department State Commission on Aging and the Aged and the Governor's Youth Council Wabash Valley Commission Department of Commerce and Public Relations Indiana Flood Control-Water Resources Commission Governor's Advisory Committee on Recreation
Iowa	State Conservation Commission Division of Administration Division of Fish and Game Division of Land and Waters	State Soil Conservation Committee Iowa Development Commission State Highway Commission Office of Planning and Programming
Kansas	State Park and Resources Authority Forestry, Fish and Game Commission Joint Council on Recreation	State Highway Commission State Recreation Consultant State Historical Society Department of Economic Development Water Resources Board
Kentucky	Department of Conservation Division of Forestry Division of Soil and Water Resources Division of Strip Mining and Reclamation Flood Control and Water Usage Board Department of Fish and Wildlife Resources Department of Parks	Department of Public Safety Department of Public Information Kentucky Highway Department State Historical Society
Louisiana	State Parks and Recreation Commission Wildlife and Fisheries Commission	Department of Highways Department of Public Works Department of Commerce and Industries State Land Office Louisiana Tourist Development Commission
Maine	Department of Inland Fisheries and Game State Park Commission Baxter State Park Authority Maine Forest Service	Atlantic Sea Run Salmon Commission Department of Sea and Shore Fisheries Water Improvement Commission Department of Economic Development State Highway Commission Department of Health and Welfare

State	Agencies with Principal Responsibilities in Outdoor Recreation	Agencies with Limited Responsibilities in Outdoor Recreation
Maryland	Board of Natural Resources Department of Forests and Parks Department of Game and Inland Fish Department of Tidewater Fisheries Department of Research and Education	Department of Geology, Mines, and Water Resources Water Pollution Control Commission State Roads Commission Department of Economic Development
Massachusetts	Department of Natural Resources Division of Fisheries Division of Water Resources Division of Forests and Parks Division of Marine Fisheries Division of Law Enforcement Metropolitan District Commission Parks Engineering Division Department of Public Works	Department of Public Health Department of Commerce Department of Correction Youth Service Board
Michigan	Department of Natural Resources Office of Administration Field Administration Division Fish and Fisheries Division Forestry Division Game Division Geological Survey Division Lands Division Parks and Recreation Division State Waterways Commission Huron-Clinton Metropolitan Authority Mackinac Island State Park Commission	Michigan Tourist Council State Highway Department Department of Health Department of Social Welfare Michigan Water Resources Commission Department of Public Instruction
Minnesota	Department of Conservation Division of Forestry Division of Game and Fish Division of Parks and Recreation Division of Enforcement and Field Service	Department of Highways Historical Society Iron Range Resources and Rehabilitation Commission Pollution Control Agency State Planning Agency Minnesota Resources Commission Minnesota-Wisconsin Boundary Area Commission Department of Economic Development
Mississippi	Mississippi Game and Fish Commission State Park Commission	Highway Department State Board of Health Mississippi Forestry Commission Pearl River Valley Water Supply District Water Resources Board Yellow Creek Watershed Authority Pearl River Industrial Commission

State	Agencies with Principal Responsibilities in Outdoor Recreation	Agencies with Limited Responsibilities in Outdoor Recreation
Missouri	State Conservation Commission State Park Board	State Highway Commission Division of Commerce and Industrial Development Bi-State Development Agency
Montana	State Fish and Game Commission State Highway Commission Park Division	Board of Land Commissioners Office of State Forester State Highway Department Board of Health State Historical Society State Water Conservation Board
Nebraska	Game and Parks Commission	Department of Health Department of Roads State Historical Society
Nevada	Department of Conservation and Natural Resources Fish and Game Commission	Department of Economic Development Department of Highways State Museum Division of Forestry
New Hampshire	Department of Resources and Economic Development Division of Parks Fish and Game Department State Advisory Commission	Natural Resources Council Water Resources Board Water Pollution Commission State Historical Commission Department of Public Works and Highways
New Jersey	Department of Conservation and Economic Development Division of Fish and Game Division of Resource Development Division of Water Policy and Supply Division of State and Regional Planning	State Department of Health Department of Highways
New Mexico	Department of Game and Fish State Park and Recreation Commission State Planning Office	State Highway Department Department of Development Department of Public Health and Welfare Museum of New Mexico Department of Education
New York	Department of Conservation Division of Lands and Forests Division of Parks Division of Saratoga Springs Reservation New York State Historic Trust Division of Fish and Game Division of Water Resources Division of Motor Boats Division of Conservation Education Lake George Park Commission Water Resources Commission	Department of Health Department of Public Works Department of Education

State	Agencies with Principal Responsibilities in Outdoor Recreation	Agencies with Limited Responsibilities in Outdoor Recreation
North Carolina	State Recreation Commission Department of Conservation and Development State Parks Division Travel and Promotion Division Wildlife Resources Commission Department of Archives and History Historical Sites Division State Planning Task Force on Recreation	Kerr Reservoir Development Commission State Highway Commission Department of Water and Air Resources Coastal Plains Regional Commission Appalachian Regional Commission Department of Conservation and Development Community Planning Division Forestry Division Seashore Commission State Board of Health
North Dakota	State Outdoor Recreation Agency State Park Service State Game and Fish Department	State Water Commission State Health Department State Historical Society State Soil Conservation Committee State Highway Department State Travel Department Economic Development Commission
Ohio	Department of Natural Resources Division of Parks and Recreation Division of Wildlife Division of Watercraft Division of Forestry and Reclamation	Department of Highways Department of Industrial and Economic Development Department of Health Department of Correction Department of Public Works Historical Society Muskingum Conservancy District
Oklahoma	Oklahoma Planning and Resources Board Wildlife Conservation Commission	State Highway Department Grand River Dam Authority
Oregon	State Highway Commission State Parks and Recreation Division State Game Commission State Committee on Natural Resources State Fish Commission State Department of Forestry	Department of Geology and Mineral Industries State Water Resources Board State Marine Board State Engineer Sanitary Authority Columbia River Gorge Commission
Pennsylvania	Department of Forests and Water State Forester Water and Power Resources Board State Fish Commission State Game Commission	Department of Commerce Department of Health Department of Internal Affairs Military Reservation Commission Department of Highways Historical and Museum Commission

State	Agencies with Principal Responsibilities in Outdoor Recreation	Agencies with Limited Responsibilities in Outdoor Recreation
Rhode Island	Department of Natural Resources	Department of Health
	Division of Parks and Recreation	State Development Council
	Division of Forestry	
	Division of Fish and Game	
	Division of Harbors and Rivers	
South Carolina	Wildlife Resources Department	Highway Department
	Forestry Commission	State Board of Health
	Department of Parks, Recreation and Tourism	Water Pollution Control Authority
		State Development Board
		State Budget and Control Board
		Public Service Authority
South Dakota	Department of Game, Fish and Parks	Commissioner of School and Public Lands
	Game Division	Department of Highways
	Fisheries Division	Department of History
	Parks Division	Water Resources Commission
	Custer State Park	State Planning Commission
Tennessee	Department of Conservation	State Planning Commission
	Division of Parks	Department of Highways
	Division of Information and Tourist Promotion	
	Game Commission	
	Fish Commission	
Texas	State Parks and Wildlife Commission	The Daughters of the Republic of Texas
		Battleship Texas Commission
		State Highway Department
Utah	Department of Natural Resources	State Road Commission
	Division of Parks and Recreation	Tourist and Publicity Council
	Division of Fish and Game	Utah National Guard
	Outdoor Recreation Assistance Agency	State Land Division
		State Historical Society
Vermont	Department of Forests and Parks	Department of Highways
	Fish and Game Department	State Health Department
	Natural Resources Interagency Committee	Water Conservation Board
	State Recreation Commission	State Development Corporation
Virginia	Department of Conservation and Economic Development	Department of Highways
	Division of Forestry	Breaks Interstate Park Commission
	Division of Parks	Water Control Board
	Commission of Game and Inland Fisheries	Department of Health
	Commission of Outdoor Recreation	Commission of Fisheries
	Interagency Committee on Recreation	Agencies Administering Historic Sites
		Historic Landmark Commission

State	Agencies with Principal Responsibilities in Outdoor Recreation	Agencies with Limited Responsibilities in Outdoor Recreation
Washington	Department of Natural Resources State Parks and Recreation Commission Department of Game Interagency Committee for Outdoor Recreation Department of Fisheries	Highway Department Department of Health Pollution Control Commission Department of Commerce and Economic Development Planning and Community Affairs Agency Department of Water Resources
West Virginia	Department of Natural Resources Division of Game and Fish Division of Forestry Division of Parks and Recreation Division of Water Resources Division of Reclamation Public Lands Corporation	State Road Commission Department of Commerce Office of Federal-State Relations

Appendix B

Organizations Involved in Outdoor Recreation

Adirondack Mountain Club
174 Glen St.
Glen Falls, NY 12801

Adirondack Trail Improvement Society
P.O. Box 565
Keene Valley, NY 12943

Advisory Council on Camps
174 Sylvan Ave.
Leonia, NJ 07605

Affiliated National Coaches Council
c/o National Association for Girls and Women in Sport
1900 Association Dr.
Reston, VA 22091

Alpine Club of Canada
P.O. Box 1026
Banff, AB, Canada
TOL OCO

American Alliance for Health, Physical Education, Recreation, and Dance
1900 Association Dr.
Reston, VA 22091

American Camping Association
5000 State Rd., 67 N.
Martinsville, IN 46151

American Canoe Association
P.O. Box 1190
Newington, VA 22122

American Forest Adventures
P.O. Box 2000
Washington, D.C. 20013

American Trails
1400 16th St. N.W., Suite 300
Washington, D.C. 20036

American Trails Foundation
c/o Ray Sherman
P.O. Box 782
Newcastle, CA 95658

Association of Girl Scout Executive Staff
4901 Briarhaven Rd.
Ft. Worth, TX 76109

Association of Jewish Sponsored Camps
130 E. 95th St.
New York, NY 10022

Boy Scouts of America
1325 Walnut Hill Ln.
P.O. Box 152079
Irving, TX 75015

Camping Women
625 W. Cornell Ave.
Fresno, CA 93705

Christian Camping International/USA
P.O. Box 646
Wheaton, IL 60189

Future Advancement of Camping
P.O. Box 8
Hatteras, NC 27943

Girl Scouts of the USA
830 Third Ave. and 51st St.
New York, NY 10022

Greater Yellowstone Coalition
13 S. Wilson
P.O. Box 1874
Bozeman, MT 59715

Greensward Foundation
104 Prospect Park W.
Brooklyn, NY 11215

International Association of Fish and Wildlife Agencies
444 N. Capitol St. N.E., Suite 534
Washington, D.C. 20001

International Erosion Control Association
Box 4904
Steamboat Springs, CO 80477

International Mountain Society
P.O. Box 3128
Boulder, CO 80307

Izaak Walton League of America
1401 Wilson Blvd., Level B
Arlington, VA 22209

Live Oak Society
c/o Mrs. Louis Pfister
3712 W. Metarie Ave. N.
Metairie, LA 70001

National Association of Conservation Districts
509 Capitol Ct. N.E.
Washington, D.C. 20002

National Association of State Outdoor Recreation Liaison Officers
P.O. Box 731
Richmond, VA 23206

National Association of State Park Directors
c/o Ney C. Landrum
126 Mill Branch Road
Tallahassee, FL 32312

National Association of State Recreation Planners
205 Butler St. S.E., Suite 1352
Atlanta, GA 30334

National Audubon Society
950 Third Ave.
New York, NY 10022

National Campers and Hikers Association
4808 Transit Rd., Building 2
Depew, NY 14043

National Camping Association
353 W. 56th St.
New York, NY 10019

National Coalition for Marine Conservation
P.O. Box 23298
Savannah, GA 31403

National Military Fish and Wildlife Association
c/o Larry D. Adams
1427 Lafayette Blvd.
Norfolk, VA 23509

National Park Foundation
P.O. Box 57473
Washington, D.C. 20037

National Parks and Conservation Association
1015 31st St. N.W.
Washington, D.C. 20007

National Recreation and Park Association
3101 Park Center Drive
Alexandria, VA 22302

National Society for Park Resources
3101 Park Center Dr.
Alexandria, VA 22302

National Wildlife Federation Corporate Conservation Council
1400 16th St. N.W.
Washington, D.C. 20036

National Wildlife Refuge Association
P.O. Box 124
Winona, MN 55987

Natural Area Council
219 Shoreham Building N.W.
Washington, D.C. 20005

Natural Areas Association
320 S. Third St.
Rockford, IL 61108

Natural Resources Council of America
1015 31st St. N.W.
Washington, D.C. 20007

The Nature Conservancy
1815 N. Lynn St.
Arlington, VA 22209

North American Family Campers Association
P.O. Box 266
Lunenburg, MA 01462

Outward Bound
384 Field Point Rd.
Greenwich, CT 06830

Seacoast Anti-Pollution League
5 Market St.
Portsmouth, NH 03801

Sierra Club
730 Polk St.
San Francisco, CA 94109

Wilderness Leadership International
Box 770
North Fork, CA 93643

The Wilderness Society
1400 I St. N.W.
Washington, D.C. 20005

Wilderness Watch
P.O. Box 782
Sturgeon Bay, WI 54235

Wild Horse Organized Assistance
P.O. Box 555
Reno, NV 89504

Wild Horses of America Registry
c/o Karen Sussman
6212 E. Sweetwater
Scottsdale, AZ 85254

Wildlife Conservation Fund of America
50 W. Broad St., Suite 1025
Columbus, OH 43215

Wildlife Disease Association
P.O. Box 886
Ames, IA 50010

Wildlife Information Center
629 Green St.
Allentown, PA 18102

Wildlife Preservation Trust International
34th St. and Girard Ave.
Philadelphia, PA 19104

Wildlife Society
5410 Grosvenor Ln.
Bethesda, MD 20814

World Commission of Environment and Development
Palais Wilson
52 Rue de Paquis
CH-1201
Geneva, Switzerland

World Environment Center
419 Park Ave. S., Suite 1403
New York, NY 10016

World Nature Association
P.O. Box 673, Woodmoor Station
Silver Spring, MD 20901

World Pheasant Association of the USA
c/o Eugene Knoder
752 Swede Gulch Rd.
Golden, CO 80401

World Women in the Environment
1250 24th St. N.W., 4th Floor
Washington, D.C. 20037

Appendix C

Federal Agencies Involved in Outdoor Recreation

DEPARTMENT OF THE ARMY

Army Corps of Engineers
Office of the Chief of Engineers
Pulaski Building, 20 Massachusetts Ave. N.W.
Washington, D.C. 20314

Divisions:

Lower Mississippi Valley: P.O. Box 80, Vicksburg, MS 39180
Missouri River: P.O. Box 103, Downtown Station, Omaha, NE 68101
New England: 424 Trapelo Rd., Waltham, MA 02154
North Atlantic: 90 Church St., New York, NY 10007
North Central: 536 S. Clark St., Chicago, IL 60605
North Pacific: P.O. Box 2870, Portland, OR 97208
Ohio River: P.O. Box 1159, Cincinnati, OH 45201
Pacific Ocean: Bldg. 230, Fort Shafter, HI, APO San Fran. 96858
South Atlantic: 510 Title Building, Atlanta, GA 30303
South Pacific: 630 Sansome St., San Francisco, CA 94111
Southwestern: 1114 Commerce St., Dallas, TX 75242

DEPARTMENT OF THE INTERIOR

Bureau of Indian Affairs
Office of the Director
1951 Constitution Avenue N.W.
Washington, D.C. 20245

Bureau of Land Management
Office of the Director
U.S. Department of the Interior
Washington, D.C. 20240

Denver Service Center (Serves AZ, CO, MT, NM, UT, WY, ID, NV):
Denver Federal Center, Building 50
Denver, CO 80225

State Directors:

AK: 701 C. St., Box 31, Anchorage, 99513
AZ: 2400 Valley Bank Center, Phoenix, 85073

CA: Federal Office Building, Rm. E-2841, 2800 Cottage Way, Sacramento, 95825
CO: 2000 Arapahoe St., Denver, 80205
ID: 398 Federal Building, 550 W. Fort St., Boise, 83724
MT: Granite Tower, 222 N. 32nd St., P.O. Box 30157, Billings, 59107
NV: Federal Building, Room 3008, 300 Booth St., Reno, 89502
NM: Federal Building, South Federal Place, Santa Fe, 87501
OR and WA: 729 N.E. Oregon St., P.O. Box 2965, Portland, 97208
UT: University Club Building, 136 E. South Temple, Salt Lake City, 84111
WY: 2515 Warren Ave., Cheyenne, 82001
Eastern States Office: 350 S. Pickett St., Alexandria, VA 22304

Bureau of Reclamation
U.S. Department of the Interior
Washington, D.C. 20240

Regional Offices:
Pacific Northwest Region: P.O. Box 043, U.S. Court House, 550 W. Fort St., Boise, ID 83724
Mid-Pacific Region: 2800 Cottage Way, Sacramento, CA 95825
Lower Colorado Region: P.O. Box 427, Boulder City, NV 89005
Upper Colorado Region: P.O. Box 11568, Salt Lake City, UT 84147
Southwest Region: 714 S. Tyler St., Amarillo, TX 79101
Upper Missouri Region: P.O. Box 2553, Billings, MT 59103
Lower Missouri Region: Building 20, Denver Federal Center, Denver, CO 80225

United States Fish and Wildlife Service
Office of the Director
U.S. Department of the Interior
Washington, D.C. 20240

Regional Offices:
Portland Region (HI, CA, ID, NV, OR, WA): 500 N.E. Multnomah St., Suite 1692, Portland, OR 97232
Southwest Region (AZ, NM, OK, TX): Federal Building, U.S. Post Office and Court House, 500 Gold Ave. S.W., Albuquerque, NM 87103
North Central Region (IL, IN, MI, MN, OH, WI): Federal Building Fort Snelling, Twin Cities, MN 55111
Southeast Region (AL, AR, FL, KY, LA, MS, NC, SC, TN): 17 Executive Park Dr., Atlanta, GA 30329
Northeast Region (CT, DE, ME, MD, NH, NJ, NY, PA, RI, VT, VA, WV): McCormack Post Office and Court House, Boston, MA 02109
Alaska Area (AK): 813 D St., Anchorage, AK 99501
Denver Region (CO, IA, KS, MO, MT, NE, ND, SD, UT, WY): 10597 Sixth St., Denver, CO 80225

National Park Service
U.S. Department of the Interior
Washington, D.C. 20240

Regional Offices:
North Atlantic Region: 15 State Street, Boston, MA 02109 (ME, NH, VT, MA, RI, CT, NY, NJ)
Mid-Atlantic Region: 143 South Third Street, Philadelphia, PA 19106 (PA, MD, WV, DE, VA)
National Capitol Region: 1100 Ohio Dr. S.W., Washington, D.C. 20242 (Metropolitan Washington, D.C., including nearby MD, VA, WV)
Rocky Mountain Region: 655 Parfet St., P.O. Box 25287, Denver, CO 80225 (MT, ND, SD, WY, UT, CO)
Western Region: 450 Golden Gate Ave., Box 36063, San Francisco, CA 94102 (AZ, CA, NV, HI)

Southwest Region: P.O. Box 728, Santa Fe, NM 87501 (AR, LA, NM, OK, TX)

Southeast Region: 75 Spring St. S.W., Atlanta, GA 30303 (AL, FL, GA, KY, MS, NC, SC, TN, Puerto Rico, Virgin Islands)

Midwest Region: 1709 Jackson St., Omaha, NE 68102 (OH, IN, MI, WI, IL, MN, IA, MO, NE, KS)

Pacific Northwest Region: 1920 Westin Building, 2001 6th Ave., Seattle, WA 98121 (AK, ID, OR, WA)

Denver Service Center: (See Rocky Mountain Region)

Harpers Ferry Center: National Park Service, Harpers Ferry, WV 25425

Alaska Region: 540 West Fifth Ave., Room 202, Anchorage, AK 99501

DEPARTMENT OF AGRICULTURE

Forest Service
U.S. Department of Agriculture
Washington, D.C. 20013

Regional Foresters:

Region 1, Northern: Federal Building, Mussoula, MT 59807

Region 2, Rocky Mountain: 11177 W. Eighth Ave., Box 25127, Lakewood, CO 80225

Region 3, Southwestern: Federal Building, 517 Gold Ave. S.W., Albuquerque, NM 87102

Region 4, Intermountain: Federal Office Building, 324 25th St., Ogden, UT 84401

Region 5, California: 630 Snasome St., San Francisco, CA 94111

Region 6, Pacific Northwest: 319 S.W. Pine St., Box 3623, Portland, OR 97208

Region 7, Southern: Suite 800, 1720 Peachtree Rd. N.W., Atlanta, GA 30309

Region 8, Eastern: Clark Building, 633 W. Wisconsin Ave., Milwaukee, WI 53203

Region 9, Alaska: Federal Office Building, Box 1628, Juneau, AK 99802

Forest and Range Experiment Stations:

Intermountain: 507 25th St., Ogden, UT 84401

North Central: Folwell Ave., St. Paul, MN 55108

Northeastern: 370 Reed Rd., Broomall, PA 19008

Pacific Northwest: 809 N.E. Sixth Ave., Portland, OR 97232

Pacific Southwest: 1960 Addison St., Box 245, Berkeley, CA 94701

Rocky Mountain: Foothills Campus, Ft. Collins, CO 80526

Southeastern: Post Office Building, Box 2570, Asheville, NC 28802

Southern: T-10210 Federal Building, 701 Loyola Ave., New Orleans, LA 70013

Institute of Tropical Forestry: University of Puerto Rico, Rio Piedras, PR 00928

INDEPENDENT AGENCY

Tennessee Valley Authority
400 West Summit Hill Drive
Knoxville, TN 37902

Appendix D

Federal Laws Related to Outdoor Recreation

Bureau of Outdoor Recreation Organic Act — 1963
P.L. 88-29 — NPS

Land and Water Conservation Fund Act — 1965
P.L. 88-578 — NPS

National Historic Preservation Fund (Title II of Land and Water Conservation Fund Act Amendments) — 1976
P.L. 94-422 — NPS

Housing and Community Development Act — 1974
P.L. 93-383 — HUD

Yellowstone National Park Act — 1897
ch. 24 — NPS

Antiquities Act — 1906
ch. 3060 — NPS

National Park Service Act — 1916
ch. 408 — NPS

Historic Sites Act — 1935
ch. 593 — NPS

National Historic Preservation Act — 1966
P.L. 89-665 — NPS

Golden Gate National Recreation Area Act — 1972
P.L. 92-589 — NPS

Migratory Bird Conservation Act — 1929
ch. 257 — FWS

Migratory Bird Hunting Stamp Act — 1934
ch. 71 — FWS

Federal Aid to Wildlife Restoration Act — 1937
ch. 899 — FWS

Fish Restoration and Management Projects Act — 1950
ch. 658 — FWS

Fish and Wildlife Act (Fish and Wildlife Service Establishment) — 1956
ch. 1036 — FWS

Refuge Recreation Act — 1962
P.L. 87-714 — FWS

National Wildlife Refuge System Administration Act (Organic Act) — 1966
P.L. 93-205 — FWS

O&C Sustained Yield Forestry Act — 1937
ch. 876 (P.L. 405 of 75th Congress) — BLM

Act	Year / Agency
Federal Property and Administrative Services Act (Surplus Property Act) (first passed 1926)	1954
ch. 263 (P.L. 387)	BLM
Federal Land Policy and Management Act (BLM Organic Act)	1976
P.L. 94-579	BLM
Forest Reserve Act (Creative Act of National Forests)	1891
ch. 561	USFS
Organic Administration Act-National Forests	1897
ch. 2	USFS
Weeks Law	1911
ch. 186	USFS
Multiple Use-Sustained Yield Act	1960
P.L. 86-517	USFS
Forest and Rangeland Renewable Resources Planning Act	1974
P.L. 93-378	USFS
National Forest Management Act	1976
P.L. 94-588	USFS
Eastern Wilderness Act	1975
P.L. 93-622	USFS
Watershed Protection and Flood Prevention Act	1954
P.L. 566	SCS
Federal Water Projects Recreation Act	1965
P.L. 89-72	COE, B. Recl.
Federal Water Pollution Control Act Amendments	1972
P.L. 92-500	
Coastal Zone Management Act	1972
P.L. 92-583	
Wilderness Act	1964
P.L. 88-577	
National Trails System Act	1968
P.L. 90-543, P.L. 98-11	1983
Wild and Scenic Rivers Act	1968
P.L. 90-542	
National Environmental Policy Act	1969
P.L. 91-190	
Environmental Education Act	1970
P.L. 91-516	
Alaska Native Claims Settlement Act	1971
P.L. 92-203	
Alaska National Interest Lands Conservation Act	1980
P.L. 96-487	
Endangered Species Act	1973
P.L. 93-205	1983
Public Lands-Local Government Funds Act or "Payment In Lieu of Taxes" Act	1976
P.L. 94-579	USFS, BLM

Credits

Part One
Opener: Photography by Jane Lammers.

Chapter 2
pp. 18, 19 (right), 20, 21, 23, 24, 25, 26 (left): Photography by Jane Lammers. **p. 18 (left):** Photography by Kathleen Cordes. **p. 26 (right)** Photography by Frank Benfante.

Chapter 4
Fig. 4.1: Ibrahim, H. "Leisure, Idleness and Ibn Khaldun." *Leisure-Studies* 7:56. London: F. E. Spon (reprinted with permission). **Fig. 4.2:** Ibrahim, H. (1979) *Leisure: A Psychological Approach,* p. 163. (Reprinted with permission from Hwong Publishing.)

Chapter 5
Fig. 5.1: *World Almanac and Book of Facts,* 1990, p. 555. Pharos Books. (Published with permission.) **pp. 70 (both), 71, 77:** Photography by Jane Lammers.

Chapter 6
Fig. 6.1: Ibrahim, H. (1991). *Leisure and Society: A Comparative Approach,* p. 37, Wm. C. Brown. (Reprinted with permission.) **Fig. 6.4:** Mr. Lynd Warren of Whittier, CA.

Part Two
Opener: Photography by Jane Lammers.

Chapter 7
Fig. 7.1, Fig. 7.8: The Wilderness Society, *A Million Square Miles.* Reprinted with permission. **Fig. 7.9:** Browning et al., *Wilderness Laws: Milestones and Management Direction in Wilderness Legislation,* 1964-1987 (Moscow, ID: University of Idaho, 1988), 103. (Reprinted with permission.) **Fig. 7.10:** The Wilderness Society, *America's Wilderness, Twenty-Five Years of Wilderness Preservation* 1964-1989 (1990), 4. (Reprinted with permission.) **Fig. 7.11:** T. Harvey et al., *The Status of Trails in National Forests, National Parks, and Bureau of Land Management Areas* (1989), 25. (Reprinted with permission.) **Figure 7.12:** U.S. Forestry Service. **pp. 128 (both), 131 (both), 132 (both), 133 (both), 136, 147 (right), 151:** Photography by Jane Lammers. **p. 130:** Photography by Kathleen Cordes. **p. 137:** Photography by Ken Box.

Chapter 8
Fig. 8.1: National Association of State Park Directors, *Annual Information Exchange* (1990). **pp. 161, 162:** Photography by Jane Lammers.

Chapter 9
Fig. 9.1: Fazio, J. "Parks and Other Recreational Resources," in H. Ibrahim and J. Shivers (eds.) *Leisure's Emergence and Expansion.* (Hwong Publishing, 1979): 208. (Reprinted with permission.)
Fig. 9.2–9.4: H. Ibrahim et al., *Effective Park and Recreation*

Boards and Commissions (Reston, VA: AAHPERD, 1987), 74-76. (Reprinted with permission.) **pp. 182, 186 (both):** Photography by Jane Lammers.

Chapter 10

p. 206: Photography by Jane Lammers.

Chapter 11

Fig. 11.1–11.3, 11.5–11.10: Mr. Lynd Warren of Whittier, CA. **Fig. 11.4:** Courtesy of Mr. Abdulah Elkhereiji. **pp. 216 (both), 218 (both), 223 (top), 235 (both), 236 (both):** Photography by Jane Lammers. **p. 223 (bottom):** Photography by Jamie Baker Addison.

Part Three

Opener: Photography by Jane Lammers

Chapter 12

p. 241: Photography by Jane Lammers.

Chapter 14

pp. 296 (both), 301 (right): Photography by Kevolyn M. White. **pp. 299, 300 (both):** Photography by Hilary Schlager. **p. 301 (left):** Photography by Jane Lammers.

Chapter 15

Fig. 15.1, 15.2: L. L. Bean, Inc. 1988. (Reprinted with permission.) **Fig. 15.3, 15.4:** V. Huser, *River Camping* (New York: The Dial Press, 1981). (Reprinted with permission.) **Fig. 15.5:** Boy Scouts of America. (Reprinted with permission.) **pp. 315 (both), 318 (both), 319, 322, 325, 330, 331, 332, 337, 348:** Photography by Jane Lammers. **pp. 336, 338 (both):** Photography by Kathleen Cordes.

Chapter 16

Fig. 16.1 (a–d): *Scientific American* (1989), 39. (Reprinted with permission.) **p. 362:** *Fly Fishing* (1984), 86. (Reprinted with permission.) **Fig. 16.2:** Mendocino Environmental Center (1989). (Reprinted with permission.) **pp. 357, 363, 365, 366, 367, 368, 372, 373, 376 (both), 377 (left), 378:** Photography by Jane Lammers. **p. 377 (right):** Photography by Kathleen Cordes.

Epilogue

p. 390: Photography by Diane Williams.

Illustrations

By Rolin Graphics: Figures 1.1, 4.1, 4.2, 5.1, 6.1, 6.2, 6.3, 6.5, 7.2, 7.3, 7.5, 7.6, 7.9, 7.10, 7.12, 9.1, 9.2, 9.3, 9.4, 9.5, 9.6, 9.7, 11.2, 13.1, 15.2, 15.3, 15.4, 15.5, 16.1.

Name Index

D

E

F

G

H

O

P

R

S

T

U

V

W

Y

Z

Subject Index

L

M

N

O

P

Q

R

S

T

U

V

W

Y

Z